PARODIES

An Anthology from Chaucer to
Beerbohm—and After

PARODIES

An Anthology from Chaucer to
Beerbohm—and After

EDITED BY

Dwight Macdonald

New introduction by

VERONICA GENG

A DA CAPO PAPERBACK

Library of Congress Cataloging in Publication Data

Main entry under title:

Parodies: an anthology from Chaucer to Beerbohm — and
 after.

  (A Da Capo Paperback)
  Reprint. Originally published: New York: Random
House, 1960.
  1. Parodies. I. Macdonald, Dwight.
PN6231.P3P37   1985   827'.008   84-29236
ISBN 0-306-80239-2 (pbk.)

Published by Da Capo Press, Inc.
A Subsidiary of Plenum Publishing Corporation
233 Spring Street, New York, N.Y. 10013

INTRODUCTION TO THE
DA CAPO EDITION

On page 233 of this edition, there is a spine-chilling description of an oyster, that most creative of mollusks, being swallowed alive and absorbed by the digestive juices of a human being — to no other end than a rarefied, super-civilized *frisson*. The theme of *Parodies* is most brutally stated here. The devouring of one creature by another. The sea — microcosm of a cruel universe in which culture is only murder going under some other name. None of which should come as any surprise to fans of Dwight Macdonald, who lived on intimate terms with such facts through the adventures of his fictional alter ego, the Florida detective Travis McGee. Although neighbors of the author's houseboat on Longboat Key, Florida often mistook him for a Yale-educated political essayist or literary critic or something of that sort, this book — originally published in 1960 (before *A Purple Place for Dying*) and at last back in print — is evidence of first-hand acquaintance with the creatures who populate the shores and estuaries of his beloved Florida: the devourers and the devoured.

ALEXANDER POPE — whose taste for fresh-caught pompano concealed a penchant for something a little more expensive — murder. . . .

T. S. ELIOT — the motel clerk who never dreamed that each time he set pen to paper, he was signing his own death warrant. . . .

STELLA GIBBONS — the girl whose striped bikini hid something explosive enough to turn a deep-sea charter party into a lethal and dangerous nightmare. . . .

i

S. J. PERELMAN—to all appearances the simple salt-air philosopher—until Travis McGee began to suspect that nobody was quite that simple. . . .

LEWIS CARROLL—the fanatic developer with a hundred ingenious scams, he drained a marshland and exposed his own deadly secret—a secret he would pay any price to hide. . . .

WILLIAM WORDSWORTH—the copper-haired corpse who seemed to float up on the beach after every hurricane. . . .

MAX BEERBOHM—"The Gator"—Never before had Travis McGee been frightened, but never before had he been pitted against a mind as monstrously formidable as his own. . . .

JANE AUSTEN—bright, petite, blonde, suntanned—she couldn't get a license to open her health spa, but she didn't *need* a license to kill. . . .

H. L. MENCKEN—the condo salesman who plied the deep waters of greed—and before he was through reeling in the biggest catch of his life, somebody or something would have a bullet in the head. . . .

RING LARDNER—just another member of the Colombia drug-smuggling underground? Or an elusive and fiendish killer? . . .

RAYMOND QUENEAU—the cynical freighter-captain who discovered it took more than charm to commit a multiple murder that spanned an ocean. . . .

CYRIL CONNOLLY—whose bait-box harbored a poisonous cargo. . . .

ROBERT BROWNING—the beach-bum Apollo with the beautiful fiancée and every reason to live—until along came murder. . . .

JAMES GOULD COZZENS — Death by smudge-pot in your own orange grove wasn't a pretty way to go, and only the buried past knew the ugly secret of why he died. Only Travis McGee knew why he *deserved* to *die — twice*. . . .

ROBERT BENCHLEY — the Vietnam vet who drifted freely between the glittering cabanas of the Fun Coast and the oil-stained walkways of a derelict marina — until one of his haunts became the deadly killing-ground for a lethal — and purposeful — murder spree. . . .

GEORGE GORDON, LORD BYRON — One of them was an impostor — or so he thought until he watched the sun set over the Bahamas and saw it come up on his own corpse . . . .

GEOFFREY CHAUCER — the one who started it, and now the only one who could stop it — if only somebody could prove he was still alive . . . .

VERONICA GENG

New York City, December 1984

To my dear sons
MICHAEL AND NICHOLAS
without whose school bills
this anthology would not have been made

ACKNOWLEDGMENTS

The editor wishes to thank the following for permission to reprint the material included in this anthology:

WILLIAM ATTWOOD—for "Alf Stringersoll's Report on Brooklyn" by William Attwood. Originally appeared in *The New Yorker*.

DANIEL BELL—for "The Parameters of Social Movement, a Formal Paradigm" by Daniel Bell.

CYRIL CONNOLLY—for "Told in Gath" by Cyril Connolly.

PETER DE VRIES—for "Requiem for a Noun" by Peter De Vries; and for "From There to Infinity" by Peter De Vries. Originally appeared in *The New Yorker*.

THE DIAL PRESS, INC.—for selection from *Gang Rule in New York* by Craig Thompson and Allen Raymond. Copyright 1940 by Craig Thompson and Allen Raymond.

DODD, MEAD & COMPANY—and MISS D. E. COLLINS and METHUEN & Co. LTD. for selection from *Collected Poems of G. K. Chesterton* by G. K. Chesterton. Copyright 1911, 1932 by Dodd, Mead & Company; —for selections from *Bed of Neuroses* by Wolcott Gibbs. "Death in the Rumble Seat," copyright 1932 by Wolcott Gibbs; "Time, Fortune, Life, Luce," copyright 1936 by Wolcott Gibbs.

DOUBLEDAY & COMPANY, INC.—and LIBRAIRIE GALLIMARD for selection from Marcel Proust's *Pleasures and Days*, edited by F. W. Dupee;— and MRS. GEORGE BAMBRIDGE and THE MACMILLAN CO. OF CANADA for selections from *Rudyard Kipling's Verse, Inclusive Edition 1885-1932*. "Service Man," copyright 1934; "Big Steamers," copyright 1911 by Rudyard Kipling.

GERALD DUCKWORTH & Co.—and the EXECUTRIX OF THE ESTATE OF MAURICE BARING for selection from *Lost Diaries* by Maurice Baring.

E. P. DUTTON & Co., INC.—and WILLIAM HEINEMANN LTD. for selections from *A Christmas Garland* by Max Beerbohm, in the Dutton Everyman Paperback edition of *And Even Now and A Christmas Garland* by Max Beerbohm.

THE ECONOMIST—for "Cwthmas Carol" from the Christmas Number, 1959, of *The Economist*.

THE EXECUTOR OF THE ESTATE OF SIR MAX BEERBOHM—for "The Sorrows of Millicent," "The Blessedness of Apple-pie Beds," "The Defossilized Plum-Pudding," and "A Vain Child" by Sir Max Beerbohm.

RUDOLPH FRIEDMANN—and NEW DIRECTIONS for "Struwwelpeter" by Rudolph Friedmann.

LIBRAIRIE GALLIMARD—for selection from *Pastiche et Mélanges* by Marcel Proust. All rights reserved;—for selection from *Exercices de Style* by Raymond Queneau. All rights reserved.

HARCOURT, BRACE AND COMPANY, INC.—and JONATHAN CAPE LIMITED for "Chard Whitlow" from *A Map of Verona and Other Poems*. Copyright, 1947, by Henry Reed.

HARPER & BROTHERS—for "Christmas Afternoon" and "Compiling an American Tragedy" from *A Benchley Round-Up* by Robert Benchley. Copyright 1921 by Harper & Brothers. Copyright 1949 by Gertrude Benchley; for "Literary Lost and Found Department" from *Love Conquers All* by Robert Benchley. Copyright 1922 by Harper & Brothers. Copyright 1950 by Gertrude D. Benchley; for "Mr. Mencken Reviews Mr. Nathan and Vice Versa" from *20,000 Leagues under the Sea* by Robert Benchley. Copyright 1928 by Harper and Brothers. Copyright, 1956, by Gertrude D. Benchley;—for "Grandfather's Old Ram" from *The Autobiography of Mark Twain,* edited by Charles Neider. © Copyright 1959 by The Mark Twain Company;—and for "Across the River and into the Grill," copyright 1944 by E. B. White, and "A Classic Waits for Me," copyright 1950 by E. B. White, from *The Second Tree from the Corner* by E. B. White. Originally published in *The New Yorker*.

WILLIAM HEINEMANN LTD.—for "The Rehearsal" and "Jason and Medea" from *Diminutive Dramas* by Maurice Baring; and "King Lear's Daughter" from *Dead Letters* by Maurice Baring.

GILBERT HIGHET—for "Homage to Ezra Pound."

FIRMAN HOUGHTON—for "She Sees Another Door Opening" by Firman Houghton. Originally appeared in *Audience;*—and for "Mr. Frost Goes South to Boston" by Firman Houghton.

THE HUDSON REVIEW—for "Squeal" by Louis Simpson. Reprinted from *The Hudson Review,* Vol. X, No. 3, Autumn 1957. Copyright 1957 by The Hudson Review, Inc.

HUMANITIES PRESS INC.—for selection by Laura Loomis in *Sources and Analogues of Chaucer's Canterbury Tales,* ed. by W. F. Bryan and G. Dempster.

PAUL JENNINGS—for "The Boy's Got Talent" by Paul Jennings. Originally appeared in *The Observer*.

ACKNOWLEDGMENTS *ix*

ALFRED A. KNOPF, INC.—and WILLIAM HEINEMANN LTD. for selection from *A Variety of Things* by Max Beerbohm. Copyright 1928 by Max Beerbohm;—and for selection from *A Mencken Chrestomathy* by H. L. Mencken. Copyright 1921, 1949 by Alfred A. Knopf, Inc.

FELICIA LAMPORT—for "By Henry James Cozened" by Felicia Lamport. © Copyright 1958 by Harper & Brothers.

LIVERIGHT PUBLISHING CORPORATION—for selection from *A Treasury of Humorous Verse* by Samuel Hoffenstein. Copyright 1946 by Liveright Publishing Corporation.

LONGMANS, GREEN & CO. LIMITED—for selection from *Cold Comfort Farm* by Stella Gibbons.

THE MACMILLAN COMPANY—for selections from *The Condemned Playground* by Cyril Connolly.

NEW DIRECTIONS—for selection from *Personae* by Ezra Pound. Copyright 1926 by Ezra Pound.

NEW REPUBLIC—for "Speaking of Books" by Donald Malcolm;—and for Eisenhower's Gettysburg Address.

THE NEW YORKER—for "By Words Obsessed" by Nathaniel Benchley. © 1958 by The New Yorker Magazine, Inc.;—and for "On the Sidewalk" by John Updike. © 1959 The New Yorker Magazine, Inc.

NONESUCH PRESS—for selection from *Swift*, edited by John Hayward.

HAROLD OBER ASSOCIATES, INC.—for "Afternoon of a Cow" by Ernest V. Trueblood (William Faulkner). © Copyright 1947 by William Faulkner. Originally appeared in *Furioso*.

OLIVER & BOYD LTD.—for selection from *Burlesque and Parody in English* by G. Kitchin.

S. J. PERELMAN—for "Who Stole My Golden Metaphor" by S. J. Perelman.

RANDOM HOUSE INC.—for selection from *The Hamlet* by William Faulkner. Copyright 1931, 1936, 1940 and renewed 1958 by William Faulkner. Copyright 1932 by The Curtis Publishing Company;—for selection from *Season in the Sun and Other Pleasures* by Wolcott Gibbs. Copyright 1941 by Wolcott Gibbs. Originally appeared in *The New Yorker*;—and THE BODLEY HEAD LTD. for selections from *Ulysses* by James Joyce. Copyright 1914, 1918 and renewed 1942, 1946 by Nora Joseph Joyce. Copyright 1934 by The Modern Library, Inc.

MAX REINHARDT LTD.—for selection from *Oddly Enough* by Paul Jennings.

BEN ROTH AGENCY—for "Breakfast with Gerard Manley Hopkins" by Anthony Brode. © Copyright Punch, London.

SAGAMORE PRESS, INC.—for selection from *The Sweeniad* by Myra Buttle.

W. B. Scott—for "Chicago Letter" and "Gaetan Fignole" by W. B. Scott. Originally appeared in *Furioso*.

Charles Scribner's Sons—for selections from *The Torrents of Spring* by Ernest Hemingway. Copyright 1926 Charles Scribner's Sons; renewal copyright 1954 Ernest Hemingway;—for "Dinner Bridge" and "I Gaspiri" from *First and Last* by Ring Lardner. Copyright 1934 Ellis A. Lardner;—and for "The Water Lilies" from *What of It?* by Ring Lardner. Copyright 1925 Charles Scribner's Sons; renewal copyright 1953 Ellis A. Lardner.

Philip Toynbee—for selection from review by Philip Toynbee of Queneau's *Exercices de Style*. Originally appeared in *The Observer*.

Kenneth Tynan—for "Just Plain Folks" by Kenneth Tynan. Originally appeared in *The Observer*.

Viking Press, Inc.—and Faber and Faber and the Society of Authors for selection from *Finnegans Wake*, copyright 1939 by James Joyce.

Edmund Wilson—for "The Omelet of A. MacLeish" by Edmund Wilson. Originally appeared in *The New Yorker*.

Ann Wolfe—for selection from *Lampoons* by Humbert Wolfe.

Preface

THIS IS AN ANTHOLOGY of parodies in English from the beginning, which I take to be Chaucer's *Tale of Sir Thopas,* up to the present. Marx's description of a commodity also applies to a parody: "a very queer thing, abounding in metaphysical subtleties and theological niceties." The genre expands or contracts, changing shape like a fish glimpsed under water, the water being one's own particular notion of the fish. My own notion is expressed, practically, in the selections that follow. For theory and history, see the Appendix at the end.

In making this anthology I have followed three rules:

(1) The authors parodied must have some currency today.

(2) The broader the worser.

(3) No parody involving fleas or seasickness is enjoyable.

I have allowed some exceptions when the parodies have seemed to me either historically important or funny. Namely: To Rule 1: the parodies of Lyly, Boyle, Philips, Corelli, Le Gallienne, and Gosse. To Rule 2: Buckingham on Dryden, Hood and Taylor on Poe, Benchley on Dickens, Flegenheimer on Stein, Kipling on Kipling. There are no exceptions to Rule 3.

A few remarks on Rules 1 and 2

(1) Parody ages faster than any other literary form, for obvious reasons. Those premature romantics, the Della Cruscans, were slaughtered by Southey, but who today would know in what cause they died? James Hogg, the Ettrick Shepherd, did well by Scott in *Wat o' the Cleuch,* but who still reads *Marmion?*

Thomas Love Peacock's *Paper-Money Lyrics* (1825) are no longer
negotiable for a different reason: some of the parodees are still
read but the economic issue is now so dead as to make the
parodies, for all their wit, incomprehensible. Similarly, the late
Monsignor Knox's *Absolute and Abitofhell* is a masterful adaptation of Dryden's *Absalom and Achitophel,* but the clerics whose
theology he attacks are now forgotten. The number of excellent
parodies which no longer "carry" is painful to contemplate; cf.,
to take only recent examples, such writers as Masefield, Maeter-
linck, W. E. Henley, Stephen Phillips, Cabell, Hergesheimer, and
Alfred Austin. Of the eighteen authors parodied in Beerbohm's
A Christmas Garland, six are now forgotten (Baring, Benson,
Gosse, Harris, Hewlett, Street), seven are in eclipse (Belloc,
Bennett, Chesterton, Galsworthy, Meredith, Moore, Wells), and
only five have enough currency to be worth parodying today
(Conrad, Hardy, Kipling, James, Shaw). The fault wasn't Beerbohm's; he included the Big Names of his time and place; it was
just an occupational hazard.

(2) The objections to breadth in parody are that it is not
sporting to hunt with a machine-gun, that jocularity is not wit,
and that the critical edge is blunted. Most of what passes for
parody is actually so broad as to be mere burlesque (see that
Appendix). Consider, for example, the opening stanzas of three
"parodies" of Tennyson's *Locksley Hall:*

(1)
Cronies, leave me in the barroom, while as yet I've cash to spend,
Leave me here and if I'm wanted, "mum's" the word to every friend.

(2)
Cousins, leave me here a little, in lawn tennis you excel;
Leave me here, you only bore me, I shall come at "luncheon bell"!

(3)
Comrades, you may pass the rosy. With permission of the chair,
I shall leave you for a little, for I'd like to take the air.

Granted that *Locksley Hall* is vulnerable, such shafts miss the
vital spot. Titles often sound a warning. Slight expectations are
raised by Carolyn Wells' parody of Sinclair Lewis, *Ptomaine*

Street, or by A. Stodart Walker's *The Moxford Book of English Verse* ("*Mocks*ford" is the point), or by A. E. Wilson's *Playwrights in Aspic,* or by the slim volume published in South Duxbury, Massachusetts, in 1949 entitled *Alice's Adventures in Atomland in the Plastic Age* (all parodies of *Alice* should be avoided) and subtitled "A Stark Fantasy by Daddy Dumps, alias Humpty-Dumpty, alias Deadeye Dick." But finer discriminations may be made. Stephen Leacock's many volumes, with titles like *Moonbeams from the Larger Lunacy,* are so broad as to be equatorial; they illustrate the tendency of parody towards philistinism. Those of Donald Ogden Stewart, Ira Wallach and Corey Ford lie more in the temperate zone, but they are only temperate, that is, mild; true parody lies farther north.

The most consistent tradition of broad parody, now over a century old, is that of *Punch.* A curious shift has taken place in the last fifty years between English and American parody. In the last century, our parodists tended toward breadth while the best of the English parodists, all non-*Punch,* were delightfully narrow: compare our H. C. Bunner, Phoebe Cary, John Kendrick Bangs, and Carolyn Wells with their C. S. Calverley, J. K. Stephen, H. D. Traill, and Shirley Brooks. (Our Bayard Taylor was an exception.) But since 1900 the roles have been reversed. *Punch* has remained broad, and British parody in general—with the major exception of Max Beerbohm—has widened, while our own parodists, centered around *The New Yorker,* have pulled in their belts. I think that with a few exceptions (Cyril Connolly, Paul Jennings, Kenneth Tynan) recent British practitioners of the art have been inferior to ours.

My own pleasure in parody is twofold.

I enjoy it as an intuitive kind of literary criticism, shorthand for what "serious" critics must write out at length. It is Method acting, since a successful parodist must live himself, imaginatively, into his parodee. It is jiujitsu, using the impetus of the opponent to defeat him, although "opponent" and "defeat" are hardly the words. Most parodies are written out of admiration rather than contempt. It is hard to make the mimetic effort unless one has enough sympathy to "identify" with the parodee. There are exceptions, as Wolcott Gibbs' profile of Henry Luce written in *Time*style, or Edmund Wilson's *The Omelet of A. MacLeish,* which ends:

> I was wired for sound as I started again down the river:
> And my colons went out on the air to the clang of a gong:
> O when shall I ring with the perilous pain and the fever?
>
> A clean and clever lad
> > who is doing
> > > his best
> > > > to get on.

But these *are* exceptions. Catherine Fanshawe's parody of Wordsworth, one of the best in a crowded field, is not. Its touch is so delicate that a casual reader might take it for the real thing:

> There is a river clear and fair,
> 'Tis neither broad nor narrow;
> It winds a little here and there—
> It winds about like any hare;
> And then it takes as straight a course
> As on the turnpike road a horse
> Or through the air an arrow.

This effect is not achieved without sympathy, or at least empathy. So, too, with the ending of J. K. Stephen's Browning:

> There's a Me Society down at Cambridge
> Where my works, *cum notis variorum,*
> Are talked about; well, I require the same bridge
> That Euclid took toll at as *Asinorum:*
>
> And as they have got through several ditties
> I thought were as stiff as a brick-built wall,
> I've composed the above, and a stiff one *it* is,
> A bridge to stop asses at, once for all.

Parody must be used with caution as literary criticism. It is, for instance, significant that in their *Rejected Addresses* the

Smiths didn't hesitate to parody Wordsworth, Byron, and Coleridge but drew the line at Samuel Rogers and Thomas Camp-
bell, two conventional versifiers untainted by either romanticism
or genius: "[They] presented so much beauty, harmony and
proportion in their writings, both as to style and sentiment, that
if we had attempted to caricature them nobody would have
recognized the likeness. . . . We were reluctantly compelled to
confine ourselves to writers whose style and habit of thought,
being more marked and peculiar, were more capable of exaggeration and distortion." As parodists, the Smiths were right,
but they failed to see that the absence of any "marked and
peculiar style" was a symptom of mediocrity rather than of
talent.

The other reason I like parody is I feel comfortable with it.
I like its bookish flavor because I like books and parody is a
kind of literary shop talk. I like its classical moderation, its
commonsensibility. And I feel at home with it because an elderly
culture like ours is suffused with parody. We are self-conscious,
we have the historical sense, we look back on the past. Our
avantgarde has done a lot of its fighting in the rear. *Ulysses* is
a museum of prose styles, *Finnegans Wake* a course in advanced
philology, *The Waste Land* echoes with quotations. Bartók and
Stravinsky are archaeologists as well as inventors, and the charm
of a work like *Four Saints in Three Acts* is the virtuosity with
which Stein and Thomson exploit everything from liturgy to
grand opera and Negro spirituals. Picasso steals everywhere—
from African sculpture, Greek vases, High and Low Renaissance, and above all from Picasso; his own fence, he disguises
the hot jewels in new settings; his parodic talent amounts to
genius. Even those professional ignoramuses, the beatniks, dig
Zen Buddhism. We are backward-looking explorers and parody
is a central expression of our times. But I had better stop before
I begin talking about the *Zeitgeist*.

Large as it is, this anthology might have been even larger.
But one has to draw the line, somewhere somehow sometime.
And since the definition of what exactly IS a parody is subjective

(though see, again, that Appendix), and since the mere brute accumulation of parodies, real or false, has become so massive as to be more in the realm of an IBM machine than of human consciousness, I have been forced to make this anthology on largely personal lines. The one parody I regret not being able to include—it proved impossible to track down the author's widow and executrix—is Hugh Kingsmill's of A. E. Housman beginning:

> What, still alive at twenty-two,
> A clean upstanding chap like you?
> Sure, if your throat 'tis hard to slit,
> Slit your girl's and swing for it.

Housman thought this the best parody of his verse, but I think Humbert Wolfe's, later on in this volume, offers some stiff competition.

DWIGHT MACDONALD

New York City, May 1960.

Contents

PART TWO: *THE NINETEENTH CENTURY*

PART THREE: *BEERBOHM—AND AFTER*

Post-Beerbohm:

PART FOUR: *SPECIALTIES*

PART ONE

The Beginnings

MEDIEVAL ROMANCES

SINCE parody is a late form in literature, it is strange that one of the best should be the work of "the father of English poetry." The explanation, of course, is that Chaucer ended a period rather than began one; he was, like Dante, a late medieval writer; hence the sophistication of *Sir Thopas*. As for its provenance and its special place in Chaucer's work, Laura H. Loomis writes in Bryan and Dempster's *Sources and Analogues of Chaucer's Canterbury Tales* (University of Chicago, 1941):

> "*Sir Thopas* has no one source. . . . Irrepressibly comic and creative, it touches lightly as a *boterflye* on a variety of romances and other poems. Though obviously a mock romance, a 'Don Quixote in little,' directed against what Thomas Tyrrwhit described as 'the palpable gross fictions and . . . the meanness of the language and versification of Chaucer's own day,' it is in no wise a parody of any one school of romances and it follows no previous patterns of parody, either social or literary. Medieval French burlesques on the *chansons de geste* or the romances of chivalry . . . differ from it entirely in style and substance. Genius is airily at play in *Thopas*. . . .
>
> "Chaucer may have read fifteen to twenty of the 113 Middle English romances that are still extant. . . . They nearly all indulge in extreme exaggerations, especially of the hero's prowess; they make excessive use of insignificant detail; they show the same bourgeois absurdities in setting forth knight-errantry. Above all, they use the same worn devices of minstrel style, the same stereotyped diction. . . . The manner even more than the matter . . . was what aroused Chaucer's derisive wit to parody."

3

Prologue to Sir Thopas

BIHOLD THE MURYE WORDES OF THE HOST TO CHAUCER

WHAN seyd was al this miracle, every man
As sobre was, that wonder was to se,
Till that our hoste Iapen tho bigan,
And than at erst he loked up-on me,
And seyde thus, "what man artow?" quod he;
"Thou lokest as thou woldest finde an hare,
For ever up-on the ground I see thee stare.

Approche neer, and loke up merily.
Now war yow, sirs, and lat this man have place;
He in the waast is shape as wel as I;
This were a popet in an arm tenbrace
For any womman, smal and fair of face.
He semeth elvish by his contenaunce,
For un-to no wight dooth he daliaunce.

Sey now somwhat, sin other folk han sayd;
Tel us a tale of mirthe, and that anoon;"—
"Hoste," quod I, "ne beth nat yvel apayd,
For other tale certes can I noon,
But of a ryme I lerned longe agoon."
"Ye, that is good," quod he; "now shul we here
Som deyntee thing, me thinketh by his chere."

Explicit

SIR THOPAS

Here biginneth Chaucers Tale of Thopas

LISTETH, lordes, in good entent,
And I wol telle verrayment
Of mirthe and of solas;

Al of a knyght was fair and gent
In bataille and in tourneyment,
   His name was sir Thopas.

Y-born he was in fer contree,
In Flaundres, al biyonde the see,
   At Popering, in the place;
His fader was a man ful free,
And lord he was of that contree,
   As it was goddes grace.

Sir Thopas wex a doghty swayn,
Whyt was his face as payndemayn,
   His lippes rede as rose;
His rode is lyk scarlet in grayn,
And I yow telle in good certayn,
   He hadde a semely nose.

His heer, his berd was lyk saffroun,
That to his girdel raughte adoun;
   His shoon of Cordewane.
Of Brugges were his hosen broun,
His robe was of ciclatoun,
   That coste many a Iane.

He coude hunte at wilde deer,
And ryde an hauking for riveer,
   With grey goshauk on honde;
Ther-to he was a good archeer,
Of wrastling was ther noon his peer,
   Ther any ram shal stonde.

Ful many a mayde, bright in bour,
They moorne for him, paramour,
   Whan hem were bet to slepe;
But he was chast and no lechour,
And sweet as is the bremble-flour
   That bereth the rede hepe.

And so bifel up-on a day,
For sothe, as I yow tell may,
   Sir Thopas wolde out ryde;
He worth upon his stede gray,
And in his honde a launcegay,
   A long swerd by his syde.

He priketh thurgh a fair forest,
Ther-inne is many a wilde best,
   Ye, bothe bukke and hare;
And, as he priketh north and est,
I telle it yow, him hadde almest
   Bitid a sory care.

Ther springen herbes grete and smale,
The lycorys and cetewale,
   And many a clowe-gilofre;
And notemuge to putte in ale,
Whether it be moyste or stale,
   Or for to leye in cofre.

The briddes singe, it is no nay,
The sparhauk and the papeiay,
   That Ioye it was to here;
The thrustelcok made eek his lay,
The wodedowve upon the spray
   She sang ful loude and clere.

Sir Thopas fil in love-longine
Al when he herde the thrustel singe,
   And priked as he were wood:
His faire stede in his prikinge
So swatte that men mighte him wringe,
   His sydes weer al blood.

Sir Thopas eek so wery was
For prikinge on the softe gras,

So fiers was his corage,
That doun he leyde him in that plas
To make his stede som solas,
And yaf him good forage.

"O seinte Marie, *benedicite!*
What eyleth this love at me
To binde me so sore?
Me dremed al this night, pardee,
An elf-queen shal my lemman be,
And slepe under my gore.

An elf-queen wol I love, y-wis,
For in this world no womman is
Worthy to be my make
In toune;
Alle othere wommen I forsake,
And to an elf-queen I me take
By dale and eek by doune!"

In-to his sadel he clamb anoon,
And priketh over style and stoon
An elf-queen for tespye,
Til he so longe had riden and goon
That he fond, in a privee woon,
The contree of Fairye
So wilde;
For in that contree was ther noon
That to him dorste ryde or goon,
Neither wyf ne childe.

Til that ther cam a greet geaunt,
His name was sir Olifaunt,
A perilous man of dede;
He seyde, "child, by Termagaunt,
But-if thou prike out of myn haunt,

Anon I slee thy stede
           With mace.
Heer is the queen of Fayërye,
With harpe and pype and simphonye
   Dwelling in this place."

The child seyde, "al-so mote I thee,
Tomorwe wol I mete thee
   Whan I have myn armoure;
And yet I hope, *par ma fay,*
That thou shalt with this launcegay
   Abyen it ful soure;
           Thy mawe
Shal I percen, if I may,
Er it be fully pryme of day,
   For heer thou shalt be slawe."

Sir Thopas drow abak ful faste;
This geaunt at him stones caste
   Out of a fel staf-slinge;
But faire escapeth child Thopas,
And al it was thurgh goddes gras,
   And thurgh his fair beringe.

Yet listeth, lordes, to my tale
Merier than the nightingale,
   For now I wol yow roune
How sir Thopas with sydes smale,
Priking over hil and dale,
   Is come agayn to toune.

His merie men comanded he
To make him bothe game and glee,
   For nedes moste he fighte
With a geaunt with hevedes three,
For paramour and Iolitee
   Of oon that shoon ful brighte.

"Do come," he seyde, "my minstrales,
And gestours, for to tellen tales
　　Anon in myn arminge;
Of romances that been royales,
Of popes and of cardinales,
　　And eek of love-lykinge."

They fette him first the swete wyn,
And mede eek in a maselyn,
　　And royal spicerye;
Of gingebreed that was ful fyn,
And lycorys, and eek comyn,
　　With sugre that is so trye.

He dide next his whyte lere
Of clooth of lake fyn and clere
　　A breech and eek a sherte;
And next his sherte an aketoun,
And over that an habergeoun
　　For percinge of his herte;

And over that a fyn hauberk,
Was al y-wroght of Iewes werk,
　　Ful strong it was of plate;
And over that his cote-armour
As whyt as is a lily-flour,
　　In which he wol debate.

His sheeld was al of gold so reed,
And ther-in was a bores heed,
　　A charbocle bisyde;
And there he swoor, on ale and breed,
How that "the geaunt shal be deed,
　　Bityde what bityde!"

His Iambeux were of quirboilly,
His swerdes shethe of yvory,

His helm of laton bright;
His sadel was of rewel-boon,
His brydel as the sonne shoon,
    Or as the mone light.

His spere was of fyn ciprees,
That bodeth werre, and no-thing pees,
    The heed ful sharpe y-grounde;
His stede was al dappel-gray,
It gooth an ambel in the way
    Ful softely and rounde
                In londe.
Lo, lordes myne, heer is a fit!
If ye wol any more of it,
    To telle it wol I fonde.

[*The Second Fit*]

Now hold your mouth, *par charitee,*
Bothe knight and lady free,
    And herkneth to my spelle;
Of bataille and of chivalry,
And of ladyes love-drury
    Anon I wol yow telle.

Men speke of romances of prys,
Of Horn child and of Ypotys,
    Of Bevis and sir Gy,
Of sir Libeux and Pleyn-damour;
But sir Thopas, he bereth the flour
    Of royal chivalry.

His gode stede al he bistrood,
And forth upon his wey he glood
    As sparkle out of the bronde;
Up-on his crest he bar a tour,

And ther-in stiked a lily-flour,
  God shilde his cors fro shonde!

And for he was a knight auntrous,
He nolde slepen in non hous,
  But liggen in his hode;
His brighte helm was his wonger,
And by him baiteth his dextrer
  Of herbes fyne and gode.

Him-self drank water of the wel,
As did the knight sir Percivel,
  So worthy under wede,
Til on a day——

Here the Host stinteth Chaucer of his Tale of Thopas

"No more of this, for goddes dignitee,"
Quod oure hoste, "for thou makest me
So wery of thy verray lewednesse
That, also wisly god my soule blesse,
Myn eres aken of thy drasty speche;
Now swiche a rym the devel I biteche!
This may wel be rym dogerel," quod he,
  "Why so?" quod I, "why wiltow lette me
More of my tale than another man,
Sin that it is the beste rym I can?"
  "By god," quod he, "for pleynly, at a word,
Thy drasty ryming is nat worth a tord;
Thou doost nought elles but despendest tyme,
Sir, at o word, thou shalt no lenger ryme.
Lat see wher thou canst tellen aught in geste,
Or telle in prose somwhat at the leste
In which ther be som mirthe or som doctryne."
  "Gladly," quod I, "by goddes swete pyne,
I wol yow telle a litel thing in prose. . . .

GEOFFREY CHAUCER

GEOFFREY CHAUCER

Imitation of Chaucer

WOMEN ben full of Ragerie,
Yet swinken not sans secresie
Thilke Moral shall ye understand,
From Schoole-boy's Tale of fayre Irelond:
Which to the Fennes hath him betake,
To filch the gray Ducke fro the Lake.
Right then, there passen by the Way
His Aunt, and eke her Daughters tway.
Ducke in his Trowses hath he hent,
Not to be spied of Ladies gent.
"But ho! our Nephew," (crieth one)
"Ho," quoth another, "Cozen John";
And stoppen, and laugh, and callen out,—
This sely Clerk full low doth lout:
They asken that, and talken this,
"Lo here is Coz, and here is Miss."
But, as he glozeth with Speeches soote,
The Ducke sore tickleth his Erse-root:
Fore-piece and buttons all-to-brest,
Forth thrust a white neck, and red crest.
"Te-he," cry'd Ladies; Clerke nought spake:
Miss star'd; and gray Ducke crieth Quake.
"O Moder, Moder" (quoth the daughter)
"Be thilke same thing Maids longen a'ter?
"Bette is to pyne on coals and chalke,
"Then trust on Mon, whose yerde can talke."

ALEXANDER POPE

A Clerk Ther Was of Cauntebrigge Also

A CLERK ther was of Cauntebrigge also,
That unto rowing haddè long y-go.
Of thinnè shidès[1] wolde he shippès makè,
And he was nat right fat, I undertakè.
And whan his ship he wrought had attè fullè,
Right gladly by the river wolde he pullè,
And eek returne as blythly as he wentè.
Him rekkèd nevere that the sonne him brentè,[2]
Ne stinted he his cours for reyn ne snowè;
ᵀt was a joyè for to seen him rowè!
Yit was him lever, in his shelves newè,
Six oldè textès,[3] clad in greenish hewè,
Of Chaucer and his oldè poesyè
Than ale, or wyn of Lepe,[4] or Malvoisyè.
And therwithal he wex a philosofre;
And peyned him to gadren gold in cofre
Of sundry folk; and al that he mighte hentè[5]
On textès and emprinting he it spentè;
And busily gan bokès to purveyè
For hem that yeve him wherwith to scoleyè.[6]
Of glossaryès took he hede and curè;[7]
And when he spyèd had, by aventurè,
A word that semèd him or strange or rarè,
To henten[8] it anon he noldè sparè,[9]
But wolde it on a shrede[10] of paper wrytè,

[1] Thin boards.
[2] Burnt.
[3] See the "six-text" edition of Chaucer.
[4] A town in Spain.
[5] Acquire.
[6] For those that gave him the means to study with.
[7] Care.
[8] Seize upon.
[9] Would not hesitate.
[10] All quotations for the "Oxford Dictionary" illustrating special uses of English words were written on pieces of paper of a particular size.

And in a cheste he dide his shredès whytè,
And preyèd every man to doon the samè;
Swich maner study was to him but gamè.
And on this wysè many a yeer he wroughtè,
Ay storing every shreed that men him broughtè,
Til, attè lastè, from the noble pressè
Of Clarendoun, at Oxenforde, I gessè,
Cam stalking forth the Gretè Dictionárie
That no man wel may pinche at[11] ne contrárie.
But for to tellen alle his queintè gerès,[12]
They wolden occupye wel seven yerès;
Therefore I passe as lightly as I may;
Ne speke I of his hatte or his array,
Ne how his berd by every wind was shakè
When as, for hete, his hat he wolde of takè.
Souning in[13] Erly English was his spechè,
"And gladly wolde he lerne, and gladly techè."

W. W. SKEAT*

JOHN LYLY

LYLY did not invent the Euphuistic style but he popularized it in his
Euphues books. Its chief characteristics are an elaborate sentence
structure based on antitheses and parallelisms (usually without worry
about making sense), plays on words, alliteration, involved images, and
highflown allusions from mythology and natural history. The style
was not hopeless—Sir Thomas More used it effectively before Lyly, as

[11] Find fault with.
[12] Curious ways.
[13] In accordance with.

* This is an occasional poem by Dr. Skeat, the nineteenth-century Chaucer-
ian scholar. The occasion is described by Walter Jerrold: "The seventy-fifth
birthday of that distinguished scholar and oarsman, the late Dr. F. J. Furni-
vall, was celebrated by the publication by the Oxford University Press of a
Festschrift." Unhappily, Dr. Skeat's contribution arrived too late for inclusion.

did Sir Thomas Browne later—but it took more talent than Lyly had to prevent it from becoming merely "elegant." In the passage below from the tavern scene in *Henry IV, Part I,* Falstaff shrewdly uses it when he plays the heavy-father King to Prince Hal's penitent son. As Victorian fathers probably sounded like Dr. Arnold of Rugby when they were lecturing their offspring, so Elizabethan fathers, one imagines, found in Euphuism just the OK combination of pomp and sententiousness.

FALSTAFF: . . . Harry, I do not only marvel where thou spendest thy time, but also how thou art accompanied: for though the camomile, the more it is trodden on the faster it grows, yet youth, the more it is wasted the sooner it wears.* That thou art my son, I have partly thy mother's word, partly my own opinion; but chiefly, a villainous trick of thine eye and a foolish hanging of thy nether lip, that doth warrant me. If then thou be son to me, here lies the point; why, being son to me, art thou so pointed at? Shall the blessed sun of heaven prove a micher and eat blackberries? a question not to be asked. Shall the son of England prove a thief and take purses? a question to be asked. There is a thing, Harry, which thou hast often heard of, and it is known to many in our land by the name of pitch: this pitch, as ancient writers do report, doth defile; so doth the company thou keepest; for, Harry, now I do not speak to thee in drink, but in tears, not in pleasure but in passion, not in words only, but in woes also. And yet there is a virtuous man whom I have often noted in thy company, but I know not his name.

PRINCE: What manner of man, an it like your majesty?

FALSTAFF: A goodly portly man, i' faith, and a corpulent; of cheerful look, a pleasing eye, and a most noble carriage; and, as I think, his age some fifty, or by'r lady, inclining to threescore; and now I remember me, his name is Falstaff: if that man should be lewdly given, he deceiveth me; for, Harry, I see virtue in his looks. If then the tree may be known by the

---

* Cf. Lyly's *Euphues:* "Though the camomile the more it is trodden and pressed down, the more it spreadeth; yet the violet the oftener it is handled and touched, the sooner it withereth and decayeth."

fruit, as the fruit by the tree, then peremptorily I speak it,
there is virtue in that Falstaff: him keep with, the rest ban-
ish . . .

WILLIAM SHAKESPEARE
(*Henry IV, Part I*, Act II, Scene 4)

CHRISTOPHER MARLOWE

THE RUGGED Pyrrhus, he whose sable arm,
Black as his purpose, did the night resemble
When he lay couched in the ominous horse,
Hath now this dread and black complexion smear'd
With heraldry more dismal; head to foot
Now is he total gules; horribly trick'd
With blood of fathers, mothers, daughters, sons,
Bak'd and impasted with the parching streets,
That lend a tyrannous and damned light
To their vile murders; roasted in wrath and fire,
And thus o'er-sized with coagulate gore,
With eyes like carbuncles, the hellish Pyrrhus
Old grandsire Priam seeks. . . .
Anon he finds him
Striking too short at Greeks; his antique sword,
Rebellious to his arm, lies where it falls,
Repugnant to command. Unequal match'd,
Pyrrhus at Priam drives, in rage strikes wide;
But with the whiff and wind of his fell sword
The unnerved father falls. Then senseless Ilium,
Seeming to feel this blow, with flaming top
Stoops to his base, and with a hideous crash
Takes prisoner Pyrrhus' ear; for lo! his sword,
Which was declining on the milky head
Of reverend Priam, seem'd i' the air to stick.

So, as a painted tyrant, Pyrrhus stood
And like a neutral to his will and matter,
Did nothing.
But, as we often see, against some storm,
A silence in the heavens, the rack stand still,
The bold winds speechless and the orb below
As hush as death, anon the dreadful thunder
Doth rend the region; so, after Pyrrhus' pause,
Aroused vengeance sets him new a-work;
And never did the Cyclops' hammers fall
On Mars's armor, forg'd for proof eterne,
With less remorse than Pyrrhus' bleeding sword
Now falls on Priam.
Out, out, thou strumpet, Fortune! All you gods,
In general synod, take away her power,
Break all the spokes and fellies from her wheel,
And bowl the round nave down the hill of heaven,
As low as to the fiends!

WILLIAM SHAKESPEARE
(*Hamlet*, Act II, Scene 2)

THOMAS NASHE

Moth: Master, will you win your love with a French brawl?
Armado: How meanest thou? brawling in French?
Moth: No, my complete master; but to jig off a tune at the
tongue's end, canary to it with your feet, humor it with turning up your eyelids, sigh a note and sing a note, sometime
through the throat, as if you swallowed love by singing love,
sometime through the nose, as if you snuffed up love by smelling love; with your hat penthouse-like o'er the shop of your
eyes; with your arms crossed on your thin belly-doublet like
a rabbit on a spit; or your hands in your pocket like a man
after the old painting; and keep not too long in one tune,
but a snip and away. These are complements, these are humors,

these betray nice wenches, that would be betrayed without
these; and make them men of note,—do you note me?—that
most are affected to these. . . . by heart you love her, because
your heart cannot come by her; in heart you love her, because
your heart is in love with her; and out of heart you love her,
being out of heart that you cannot enjoy her.

WILLIAM SHAKESPEARE
(*Love's Labour's Lost*, Act III, Scene 1)

JOHN DONNE

O! for some honest lover's ghost,
    Some kind unbodied post
    Sent from the shades below!
    I strangely long to know,
Whether the nobler chaplets wear,
Those that their mistress' scorn did bear,
    Or those that were us'd kindly.

For whatsoe'er they tell us here
    To make those sufferings dear,
    'Twill there I fear be found,
    That to the being crown'd
T' have loved alone will not suffice,
Unless we also have been wise,
    And have our loves enjoy'd.

What posture can we think him in,
    That here unlov'd again
    Departs, and 's thither gone
    Where each sits by his own?
Or how can that elysium be,
Where I my mistress still must see
    Circled in others' arms?

For there the judges all are just,
  And Sophonisba must
    Be his whom she held dear,
    Not his who lov'd her here:
The sweet Philoclea, since she died,
Lies by her Pirocles his side,
    Not by Amphialus.

Some bays, perchance, or myrtle bough,
    For difference crowns the brow
    Of those kind souls that were
    The noble martyrs here;
And if that be the only odds
(As who can tell?) ye kinder gods,
    Give me the woman here.

      SIR JOHN SUCKLING

GEORGE HERBERT
Confusion

  O HOW my mind
    Is gravell'd!
      Not a thought
  That I can find
    But's ravel'd
      All to nought.
  Short ends of threads
    And narrow shreds
      Of lists,
  Knot-snarl'd ruffs,
    Loose broken tufts
      Of twists,
Are my torn meditations' ragged clothing;
Which, wound and woven, shape a suit for nothing;

One while I think and then I am in pain
To think how to unthink that thought again.

CHRISTOPHER HERVEY

JOHN DRYDEN

THE FIRST lengthy parody in post-Chaucerian literature was *The Rehearsal* (1671), a mock-heroic play mostly by George Villiers, second Duke of Buckingham. His Lordship's target was a fashionable new kind of drama, extravagant and bombastic (one might call it cold-blooded romanticism) that had been introduced by Davenant and brought to perfection, if such be the term, by Dryden. Buckingham, wrote Malone in his *Life of Dryden,* "resolved to correct the public taste by holding [such plays] up to ridicule. In conjunction with Martin Clifford, Master of Charterhouse, Butler, Sprat and others, he wrote the celebrated farce entitled *The Rehearsal.* Some contemporary writers have stated that it took as much time as the siege of Troy and with justice express their surprise that such a combination of wits, and such a period of ten years, should have been requisite for a work which, apparently, a less numerous band could have produced without such mighty throes." With justice indeed. *The Rehearsal* is dreary stuff, either too literal or too broad. But the point is that it was done at all. The long gestation may reflect the collaborators' difficulties with the new form, and the rapture with which the burlesque was received was also probably due to its novelty. The public taste, however, was not corrected. Heroical-bombastical dramas continued to flourish as long as Dryden wrote them, which was as long as he was pressed for funds. Below are some passages from *The Rehearsal,* with the parodied passages from Dryden's plays.

Bayes: I have made, too, one of the most delicate, dainty similes
    in the whole world, I gad, if I knew but how to apply it.
Smith: Let's hear it, I pray you.
Bayes: 'Tis an allusion to love.
  So boar and sow, when any storm is nigh,
  Snuff up and smell it gathering in the sky.
  Boar beckons sow to trot in chestnut groves

And there consummate their unfinished loves.

Pensive in mud they wallow all alone,

And snort and gruntle to each other's moan.*

Bayes: Pray mark it.

Since death my earthly part will thus remove,

I'll come a humble bee to your chaste love.

With silent wings I'll follow you, dear Couz,

Or else before you in the sunbeams buzz.

And when to melancholy groves you come,

An airy ghost, you'll know me by my hum;

For sound, being air, a ghost does well become.

Smith (after a pause): Admirable!

Bayes (*reads*):

At night into your bosom will I creep

And buzz but softly if you chance to sleep;

Yet in your dreams I will pass sweeping by

And then both hum and buzz before your eye.†

* Cf. Part II, Act I, Scene 2 of Dryden's *The Conquest of Granada:*
Almah: So, two kind turtles, when a storm is nigh,
Look up and see it gathering in the sky.
Each calls his mate to shelter in the groves,
Leaving, in murmurs, their unfinished loves.
Perched on some dropping branch, they sit alone
And coo and hearken to each other's moan.
  † Cf. Act III, Scene 1 of Dryden's *Tyrannick Love:*
Berenice: My earthly part—
Which is my tyrant's right, death will remove,
I'll come all soul and spirit to your love.
With silent steps I'll follow you all day;
Or else before you in the sunbeams play.
I'll lead you thence to melancholy groves,
And there repeat the scenes of our past loves.
At night I will within your curtains peep;
With empty arms embrace you while you sleep;
In gentle dreams I often will be by,
And sweep along before your closing eye:
All dangers from your bed I will remove:
But guard it most from any future love.
And when, at last, in pity you will die,
I'll watch your birth of immortality.
Then, turtle-like, I'll to my mate repair;
And teach you your first flight in open Air.

Bayes: Now because the two Right Kings descend from above,
    I make 'em sing to the tune and style of our modern spirits.

1 King: Haste, brother king, we are sent from above.

2 King: Let us move, let us move;
        Move to remove the fate
        Of Brentford's long united state.

1 King: Tara, tara, tara, full East and by South,

2 King: We sail with thunder in our mouth,
        In scorching noonday whilst the traveller stays,
        Busy, busy, busy, busy we bustle along.
        Mounted upon warm Phoebus his rays,
        Through the heavenly throng
        Haste to those
        Who will feast us at night with a pig's pretty-toes.

1 King: And we'll fall with our pate
            In an *ollio* of hate.*

GEORGE VILLIERS, *Duke of Buckingham*

ROBERT BOYLE

THE FOLLOWING *jeu d'esprit* is the first English parody that imitates
the thought as well as the style of the victim. It will be a century
before this level is reached again, with the *Rejected Addresses*. John
Hayward, in his Nonesuch edition of Swift, gives this account:

* Cf. Act IV, Scene 1 of Dryden's *Tyrannick Love:*
Nakar: Hark, my Damilcar, we are called below.
Damilcar: Let us go, let us go!
Go to relieve the care
Of longing lovers in despair!
Nakar: Merry, merry, merry, we sail from the East
Half tippled at a rainbow feast.
Dam.: In the bright moon-shine whole winds whistle loud,
Tivy, tivy, tivy, we mount and we fly
All racking along in a downy white cloud;
And, lest our leap from the sky should prove too far,
We slide on the back of a new-falling star.
Nakar: And drop from above
In a jelly of love.

"*Meditation upon a Broomstick* is said to have been composed in 1704. . . . Swift, while chaplain to Lord Berkeley, grew weary of reading aloud to his lady extracts from 'the heavenly meditations' of her favorite author, Robert Boyle. One day he substituted 'this most solemn waggery' and under cover of a copy of Boyle's works read it, says Tom Sheridan, 'with an inflexible gravity of countenance' and 'in the same solemn tone he had used in delivering' the original. Lady Berkeley was enraptured, though not, it seems, as mortified as one would expect when the fraud was revealed. According to Sheridan, she had the good sense to laugh at herself, exclaiming: 'What a vile trick that rogue played me. But it is his way, he never balks his humor in anything.' Swift, at this time, was enjoying the happiest days of his life."

A Meditation upon a Broom-stick

THIS single Stick, which you now behold Ingloriously lying in that neglected Corner, I once knew in a Flourishing State in A Forest, it was full of Sap, full of Leaves, and full of Boughs; but now, in vain does the busie Art of Man pretend to Vye with Nature, by tying that wither'd Bundle of Twigs to its sapless Trunk; 'tis now at best but the Reverse of what it was, a Tree turn'd upside down, the Branches on the Earth, and the Root in the Air; 'tis now handled by every Dirty Wench, condemn'd to do her Drudgery, and by a Capricious kind of Fate, destin'd to make other Things Clean, and be Nasty it self: At Length, worn to the Stumps in the Service of the Maids, 'tis either thrown out of Doors, or condemn'd to its last use of kindling Fires. When I beheld this, I sigh'd, and said within my self, Surely Man is a Broom-Stick; Nature sent him into the World Strong and Lusty, in a Thriving Condition, wearing his own Hair on his Head, the proper Branches of this Reasoning Vegetable, till the Axe of Intemperance has lopt off his Green Boughs, and left him a wither'd Trunk: He then flies unto Art, and puts on a *Peruque,* valuing himself upon an Unnatural Bundle of Hairs, all cover'd with Powder that never grew on his Head; but now should this our *Broom-Stick* pretend to enter the Scene, proud of those *Birchen* Spoils it never bore, and all cover'd with Dust, tho' the Sweepings of the Finest Lady's Chamber, we should be apt to Ridicule and Despise its Vanity, Partial Judges that we are! of our own Excellencies, and other Men's Faults.

But a *Broom-stick,* perhaps you'll say, is an Emblem of a Tree standing on its Head; and pray what is Man, but a Topsy-turvy Creature, his Animal Faculties perpetually a-Cock-Horse and Rational; His Head where his Heels should be; groveling on the Earth, and yet with all his Faults, he sets up to be an universal Reformer and Corrector of Abuses, a Remover of Grievances, rakes into every Slut's Corner of Nature, bringing hidden Corruptions to the Light, and raises a mighty Dust where there was none before, sharing deeply all the while, in the very same Pollutions he pretends to sweep away: His last Days are spent in Slavery to Women, and generally the least deserving; 'till worn to the Stumps, like his Brother *Bezom,* he's either kickt out of Doors, or made use of to kindle Flames, for others to warm Themselves by.

JONATHAN SWIFT

AMBROSE PHILIPS

LIKE Dr. Boyle, Ambrose Philips (1675-1749) is remembered only because he was parodied. He wrote a great deal of pretentious verse and drama—Pope called him in *The Dunciad* "a Pindaric writer in red stockings"—but what made him perhaps the most parodied English writer before Wordsworth was a particularly fatuous style of mock-simple poetry he invented and which he used mostly in odes to noble nymphets. Humbert Humbert would have appreciated:

> Then the taper-moulded waist
> With a span of ribbon braced,
> And the swell of either breast
> And the wide, high-vaulted chest.

Or the *Ode to Miss Margaret Pulteney, Daughter of Daniel Pulteney, Esq., in the Nursery,* which begins:

Dimply damsel, sweetly smiling,
All caressing, none beguiling,
Bud of beauty, fairly blowing,
Every charm to nature owing. . . .

The lethal parody of Philips was not by Pope or Gay but by a
writer of musical farces named Henry Carey, who also wrote *Sally in
Our Alley* and may have written *God Save the King*. Very little is
known about him, despite his popularity; he may have been the
bastard of George Savile, Marquis of Halifax, and he may have committed suicide; a contemporary account states: "He led a life free
from reproach and hanged himself October 4, 1743." But even the date
is uncertain. He did write a burlesque romantic drama, *Chrononhotonthologos,* which is still amusing despite the title and the subtitle:
"the most tragical tragedy that ever was tragedized by any company
of tragedians." But his *chef d'oeuvre* was his parody of Ambrose Philips,
entitled *Namby-Pamby* (which has given us a slang term). He also
wrote a *Lilliputian Ode on Their Majesties' Accession* that begins:

New King
Bells ring;
New Queen
Blest scene. . . .

It seems to have been meant seriously, despite the similarity to Ambrose Philips.

Namby-Pamby

A PANEGYRIC ON THE NEW VERSIFICATION,

ADDRESSED TO A——— P———, ESQ.

Naughty Paughty Jack-a-Dandy,
Stole a Piece of Sugar Candy
From the Grocer's Shoppy-Shop,
And away did hoppy-hop.

ALL YE POETS of the age,
All ye witlings of the stage,
Learn your jingles to reform,

Crop your numbers and conform.
Let your little verses flow
Gently, sweetly, row by row;
Let the verse the subject fit,
Little subject, little wit.
Namby-Pamby is your guide,
Albion's joy, Hibernia's pride.
Namby-Pamby, pilly-piss,
Rhimy-pim'd on Missy Miss
Tartaretta Tartaree,
From the navel to the knee;
That her father's gracy grace
Might give him a placy place.

He no longer writes of Mammy
Andromache and her lammy,
Hanging-panging at the breast
Of a matron most distress'd.
Now the venal poet sings
Baby clouts and baby things,
Baby dolls and baby houses,
Little misses, little spouses,
Little playthings, little toys,
Little girls and little boys.
As an actor does his part,
So the nurses get by heart
Namby-Pamby's little rhimes,
Little jingle, little chimes,
To repeat to missy-miss,
Piddling ponds of pissy-piss;
Cacking-packing like a lady,
Or bye-bying in the crady.
Namby-Pamby ne'er will die
While the nurse sings lullaby.
Namby-Pamby's doubly mild,

Once a man, and twice a child;
To his hanging sleeves restor'd,
Now he foots it like a lord;
Now he pumps his little wits,
Sh . . . ing writes, and writing sh . . . ts,
All by little tiny bits.
Now methinks I hear him say,
Boys and girls, come out to play!
Moon do's shine as bright as day.

Now my Namby-Pamby's found
Sitting on the friar's ground,
Picking silver, picking gold;
Namby-Pamby's never old.
Bally-cally, they begin,
Namby-Pamby still keeps in.
Namby-Pamby is no clown.
London Bridge is broken down:
Now he courts the gay ladee,
Dancing o'er the Lady-Lee.
Now he sings of Lick-spit Lyar,
Burning in the brimstone fire;
Lyar, lyar! Lick-spit, Lick,
Turn about the candle stick!
Now he sings of Jacky Horner,
Sitting in the chimney corner,
Eating of a Christmas pye,
Putting in his thumb, O fie!
Putting in, O fie! his thumb,
Pulling out, O strange, a plum.
Now he plays at Stee-Staw-Stud,
Sticking apples in the mud;
When 'tis turn'd to Stee-Staw-Stire,
Then he sticks 'em in the mire.
Now he acts the grenadier,

Calling for a pot of beer.
Where's his money? He's forgot;
Get him gone, a drunken sot.
Now a cock-horse does he ride,
And anon on timber stride.
See and Saw, and Sacch'ry Down,
London is a gallant town!
Now he gathers riches in,
Thicker, faster, pin by pin;
Pins apiece to see his show,
Boys and girls flock row by row;
From their clothes the pins they take,
Risk a whipping for his sake;
From their cloaths the pins they pull
To fill Namby's cushion full.
So much wit at such an age
Does a genius great presage;
Second childhood gone and past,
Should he prove a man at last,
What must second manhood be
In a child so bright as he.

Guard him, ye poetic pow'rs,
Watch his minutes, watch his hours;
Let your tuneful nine inspire him.
Let poetic fury fire him;
Let the poets, one and all,
To his genius victims fall.

HENRY CAREY

JOHN MILTON

JOHN PHILIPS (1676-1709) is buried in Westminster Abbey. (His
epitaph optimistically calls him "a second Milton," but at least he is

the only parodist to have made the Poets' Corner.) He is remembered only for his Miltonic parody, *The Splendid Shilling*. It is hard for us to understand the universal delight that greeted this when it appeared in 1705. While a great improvement over *The Rehearsal*, it now seems mild enough. But one must remember the novelty of the form, and also that John Philips had had the originality to reverse the approach of Scarron and Cotton, whose travesties of Virgil had been popular in the preceding century: they had treated high matters in a low style; he treated low matters in a high style. A definite advance. The mock epic became common in the eighteenth century—Pope's *Rape of the Lock* and Swift's *Battle of the Books*, for instance—but Philips was a pioneer.

Addison called *The Splendid Shilling* "the finest burlesque piece in the English language." But Dr. Johnson was more historically minded. "To degrade the sounding words and stately construction of Milton by an application to the lowest and most trivial things gratifies the mind with a momentary triumph over that grandeur which had hitherto held it captive in admiration," he rumbled in *Lives of the Poets*. "But the merit of such performances begins and ends with the first author. He that should again adapt Milton's phrase to the gross incidents of common life, and even adapt it with more art, which would not be difficult, must yet expect a small part of the praise which Philips has obtained; he can only hope to be the repeater of the jest." A literal application of the Doctor's dictum would rule out more than one parody of an author, but his psychology was shrewd: the momentary triumph over grandeur is indeed an element in the appeal of parody.

The Splendid Shilling

HAPPY the man, who void of cares and strife,
In silken, or in leathern purse retains
A splendid shilling: he nor hears with pain
New oysters cry'd, nor sighs for chearful ale;
But with his friends, when nightly mists arise,
To Juniper's-Magpye, or Town-Hall repairs:
Where, mindful of the nymph, whose wanton eye
Transfixed his soul, and kindled amorous flames,
Chloe, or Phillis; he each circling glass

Wisheth her health, and joy, and equal love.
Mean while, he smoaks, and laughs at merry tale,
Or pun ambiguous, or conundrum quaint.
But I, whom griping penury surrounds,
And hunger, sure attendant upon want,
With scanty offals, and small acid tiff
(Wretched repast!) my meagre corps sustain:
Then solitary walk, or doze at home
In garret vile, and with a warming puff
Regale chill'd fingers; or from tube as black
As winter-chimney, or well-polish'd jet,
Exhale mundungus, ill-perfuming scent:
Not blacker tube, nor of a shorter size
Smoaks Cambro-Britain (vers'd in pedigree,
Sprung from Cadwalader and Arthur, kings
Full famous in romantick tale) when he
O'er many a craggy hill and barren cliff,
Upon a cargo of fam'd Cestrian cheese,
High over-shadowing rides, with a design
To vend his wares, or at th' Arvonian mart,
Or Maridunum, or the ancient town
Yclip'd Brechinia, or where Vaga's stream
Encircles Ariconium, fruitful soil!
Whence flow nectareous wines, that well may vie
With Massic, Setin, or renown'd Falern.

Thus, while my joyless minutes tedious flow,
With looks demure, and silent pace, a dun
Horrible monster! hated by gods and men,
To my aerial citadel ascends,
With vocal heel thrice thund'ring at my gate,
With hideous accent thrice he calls; I know
The voice ill-boding, and the solemn sound.
What shou'd I do? or whither turn? Amaz'd,
Confounded, to the dark recess I fly

Of Woodhole; strait my bristling hairs erect
Thro' sudden fear; a chilly sweat bedews
My shud'ring limbs, and (wonderful to tell!)
My tongue forgets her faculty of speech;
So horrible he seems! his faded brow
Entrench'd with many a frown, and conic beard,
And spreading band, admir'd by modern saints,
Disastrous acts forebode; in his right hand
Long scrolls of paper solemnly he waves,
With characters, and figures dire inscrib'd,
Grievous to mortal eyes; (ye gods avert
Such plagues from righteous men!) Behind him stalks
Another monster, not unlike himself,
Sullen of aspect, by the vulgar call'd
A catchpole, whose polluted hands the gods
With force incredible, and magick charms
Erst have endu'd, if he his ample palm
Should haply on ill-fated shoulder lay
Of debtor, strait his body to the touch
Obsequious, (as whilom knights were wont)
To some inchanted castle is convey'd
Where gates impregnable, and coercive chains
In durance strict detain him, till in form
Of money, Pallas sets the captive free.

Beware, ye debtors, when ye walk beware,
Be circumspect; oft with insidious ken
This caitif eyes your steps aloof, and oft
Lies perdue in a nook, or gloomy cave,
Prompt to inchant some inadvertent wretch
With his unhallow'd touch. So (poets sing)
Grimalkin to domestick vermin sworn
An everlasting foe, with watchful eye
Lies nightly brooding o'er a chinky gap
Protending her fell claws, to thoughtless mice

Sure ruin. So her disembowell'd web
Arachne in a hall, or kitchin spreads,
Obvious to vagrant flies: She secret stands
Within her woven cell; the humming prey,
Regardless of their fate, rush on the toils
Inextricable, nor will aught avail
Their arts, or arms, or shapes of lovely hue;
The wasp insidious, and the buzzing drone,
And butterfly proud of expanded wings
Distinct with gold, entangled in her snares,
Useless resistance make: With eager strides,
She tow'ring flies to her expected spoils;
Then, with envenomed jaws the vital blood
Drinks of reluctant foes, and to her cave
Their bulky carcasses triumphant drags.

So pass my days. But when nocturnal shades
This world invelop, and th' inclement air
Persuades men to repel benumming frosts
With pleasant wines, and crackling blaze of wood;
Me lonely sitting, nor the glimmering light
Of make-weight candle, nor the joyous talk
Of loving friend delights; distress'd, forlorn,
Amidst the horrors of the tedious night,
Darkling I sigh, and feed with dismal thoughts
My anxious mind; or sometimes mournful verse
Indite, and sing of groves and myrtle shades,
Or desperate lady near a purling stream
Or lover pendant on a willow-tree.
Mean while, I labour with eternal drought,
And restless with, and rave; my parched throat
Finds no relief, nor heavy eyes repose:
But if a slumber haply does invade
My weary limbs, my fancy's still awake,
Thoughtful of drink, and eager, in a dream,

Tipples imaginary pots of ale,
In vain; awake I find the settled thirst
Still gnawing, and the pleasant phantom curse.

  Thus do I live from pleasure quite debarr'd,
Nor taste the fruits that the Sun's genial rays
Mature, John-apple, nor the downy peach,
Nor walnut in rough-furrow'd coat secure,
Nor medlar-fruit, delicious in decay:
Afflictions great! yet greater still remain:
My galligaskins that have long withstood
The winter's fury, and incroaching frosts,
By time subdu'd, (what will not time subdue!)
An horrid chasm disclose, with orifice
Wide, discontinuous; at which the winds
Eurus and Auster, and the dreadful force
Of Boreas, that congeals the Cronian waves,
Tumultuous enter with dire chilling blasts,
Portending agues. Thus a well-fraught ship
Long sail'd secure, or thro' th' Aegean deep,
Or the Ionian, till cruising near
The Lilybean shore, with hideous crush
On Scylla, or Charybdis (dang'rous rocks)
She strikes rebounding, whence the shatter'd oak,
So fierce a shock unable to withstand,
Admits the sea; in at the gaping side
The crowding waves gush with impetuous rage,
Resistless, overwhelming; horrors seize
The mariners, death in their eyes appears.
They stare, they lave, they pump, they swear, they pray:
(Vain efforts!) still the battering waves rush in,
Implacable, till delug'd by the foam,
The ship sinks found'ring in the vast abyss.

                                        JOHN PHILIPS

ALEXANDER POPE

THIS AND the following on Swift are from *A Pipe of Tobacco* (1736), a slim volume of parodies of six poets—the others were Colley Cibber, James Thomson, Edward Young and the inevitable Ambrose Philips— by Isaac Hawkins Browne. They are pleasant and accurate, though with not much bite, but for some reason they were much admired and long remembered—in *Mansfield Park,* for instance, Mary Crawford asks Mrs. Grant, "Do you remember Hawkins Browne's 'Address to Tobacco' in imitation of Pope?" Perhaps this was because, as Richmond Bond points out in his *English Burlesque Poetry, 1700-1750,* "*A Pipe of Tobacco* was the initial attempt to present the style of several authors on a common subject of no elevation." (For later, and better, attempts see Variations on a Theme in Section IV of this book.) Or perhaps because Mr. Browne was highly thought of in his day. Dr. Johnson pronounced him "one of the finest wits of this country," and Pope, touchy though he was, spoke highly of the parody of his own verse which follows: "Browne is an excellent copyist, and those who take it ill of him are very much in the wrong."

Browne was well-to-do and—perhaps therefore—wrote very little. His *magnum opus* (unfinished) was a Latin poem, *De Animi Immortalitate,* of which more energetic versifiers made several English translations. He served two terms in Parliament, but, according to Johnson, never took the floor.

BLEST LEAF! whose aromatic gales dispense
To Templars modesty, to parsons sense:
So raptur'd priests, at fam'd Dodona's shrine
Drank inspiration from the steam divine.
Poison that cures, a vapour that affords
Content, more solid than the smile of lords:
Rest to the weary, to the hungry food,
The last kind refuge of the wise and good:
Inspir'd by thee, dull cits adjust the scale
Of Europe's peace, when other statesmen fail.

By thee protected, and thy sister, beer,
Poets rejoice, nor think the bailiff near.
Nor less, the critic owns thy genial aid,
While supperless he plies the piddling trade.
What tho' to love and soft delights a foe,
By ladies hated, hated by the beau,
Yet social freedom, long to courts unknown,
Fair health, fair truth, and virtue are thy own.
Come to thy poet, come with healing wings,
And let me taste thee unexcis'd by kings.

ISAAC HAWKINS BROWNE

JONATHAN SWIFT

Boy! bring an ounce of Freeman's best,
And bid the vicar be my guest:
Let all be plac'd in manner due,
A pot, wherein to spit, or spue,
And *London Journal*, and *Free Briton*,
Of use to light a pipe, or   *   *
*   *   *   *   *   *   *   *   *
*   *   *   *   *   *   *   *   *
This village, unmolested yet
By troopers, shall be my retreat:
Who cannot flatter, bribe, betray;
Who cannot write or vote for*.
Far from the vermin of the town,
Here let me rather live, my own,
Doze o'er a pipe, whose vapour bland
In sweet oblivion lulls the land;
Of all, which at Vienna passes,
As ignorant as * * Brass is:
And scorning rascals to caress,

Extol the days of good Queen Bess,
When first tobacco blest our Isle,
Then think of other queens—and smile.

Come jovial pipe, and bring along
Midnight revelry and song;
The merry catch, the madrigal,
That echoes sweet in City Hall;
The parson's pun, the smutty tale
Of country justice, o'er his ale.
I ask not what the French are doing,
Or Spain to compass ——'s ruin:
Britons, if undone, can go,
Where tobacco loves to grow.

ISAAC HAWKINS BROWNE

ROBERT SOUTHEY

AT THE END of the eighteenth century, when British intellectuals were
taking stands on the French Revolution, three friends put out a magazine of political satire, *The Anti-Jacobin.* They were: George Canning,
later to become a famous Tory statesman; John Hookham Frere, whose
Battle of the Monks and Giants had introduced the Italian burlesque
style into English poetry; and George Ellis, whose verse satire, *The
Rolliad,* fifteen years earlier, had been on the other side, attacking
George III and the Court party. *The Anti-Jacobin* printed some very
good parody. Still readable are *The Loves of the Triangles,* a lengthy
take-off of Erasmus Darwin's curious poem, *The Loves of the Plants,*
and the well-anthologized *Rogero's Song* from *The Rovers,* a burlesque
of German romantic drama by Canning and Ellis that was performed
at the Haymarket Theatre in 1811:

Whene'er with haggard eyes I view
    This dungeon that I'm rotting in,
I think of those companions true
Who studied with me at the U-

-niversity of Gottingen
-niversity of Gottingen. . . .

The four parodies of Robert Southey below represent *The Anti-Jacobin* at its most political and effective. The first is a parody of Southey's *Inscription for the Apartment in Chepstow Castle Where Henry Marten, the Regicide, Was Imprisoned Thirty Years;* Mrs. Brownrigg was a murderess notorious at the time. The fourth parodies Southey's *The Widow;* the "friend of humanity" was Mr. Tierney, M.P. for Southwark and "an assiduous member of the Society of Friends of the People." Like George Ellis, Southey later turned his liberal coat and became a Tory—also Poet Laureate, to Byron's memorable disgust. Southey omitted the poems parodied here from later editions of his work.

I

Inscription

FOR THE DOOR OF THE CELL IN NEWGATE WHERE MRS. BROWNRIGG, THE 'PRENTICE-CIDE, WAS CONFINED PREVIOUS TO HER EXECUTION.

FOR ONE long term, or e'er her trial came,
Here Brownrigg linger'd. Often have these cells
Echoed her blasphemies, as with shrill voice
She scream'd for fresh Geneva. Not to her
Did the blithe fields of Tothill, or thy street,
St. Giles, its fair varieties expand;
Till at the last, in slow-drawn cart she went
To execution. Dost thou ask her crime?
SHE WHIPP'D TWO FEMALE 'PRENTICES TO DEATH,
AND HID THEM IN THE COAL-HOLE. For her mind
Shap'd strictest plans of discipline. Sage schemes!
Such as Lycurgus taught, when at the shrine
Of the Orthyan Goddess he bade flog
The little Spartans; such as erst chastised
Our Milton, when at college. For this act

Did Brownrigg swing. Harsh laws! But time shall come
When France shall reign, and laws be all repealed!

II

The Soldiers' Friend
Dactylics

COME, little Drummer Boy, lay down your knapsack here:
I am the soldiers' friend—here are some books for you;
Nice clever books by Tom Paine the philanthropist.
Here's half-a-crown for you—here are some handbills too;
Go to the barracks and give all the soldiers some:
Tell them the sailors are all in a mutiny.

> [*Exit Drummer Boy, with Handbills and Half-Crown.*
>   —*Manet Soldiers' Friend.*]

Liberty's friends thus all learn to amalgamate,
Freedom's volcanic explosion prepares itself,
Despots shall bow to the fasces of liberty,
>   Reason, philosophy, "fiddledum diddledum,"
>   Peace and fraternity, higgledy piggledy,
>   Higgledy piggledy, "fiddledum diddledum."
>   *Et cætera, et cætera, et cætera.*

III

The Soldier's Wife

BEING THE QUINTESSENCE OF ALL THE DACTYLICS THAT EVER WERE
OR EVER WILL BE WRITTEN

WEARISOME Sonnetteer, feeble and querulous,
Painfully dragging out thy demo-cratic lays—
Moon-stricken Sonnetteer, "ah! for thy heavy chance!"

Sorely thy Dactylics lag on uneven feet:
Slow is the Syllable which thou would'st urge to speed,
Lame and o'erburden'd, and "screaming its wretchedness!"

*   *   *   *   * 1

Ne'er talk of Ears again! look at thy Spelling-book;
Dilworth and *Dyche* are both mad at thy quantities—
DACTYLICS, call'st thou 'em?—"God help thee, silly one!"

IV

The Friend of Humanity and the Knife-grinder

SAPPHICS

Friend of Humanity

"NEEDY Knife-grinder! whither are you going?
Rough is the road, your wheel is out of order—
Bleak blows the blast; your hat has got a hole in 't,
          So have your breeches!

"Weary Knife-grinder! little think the proud ones,
Who in their coaches roll along the turnpike-
-road, what hard work 'tis crying all day 'Knives and
          Scissors to grind O!'

"Tell me, Knife-grinder, how you came to grind knives?
Did some rich man tyrannically use you?
Was it the squire, or parson of the parish?
          Or the attorney?

"Was it the squire, for killing of his game? or
Covetous parson, for his tithes distraining?
Or roguish lawyer, made you lose your little
          All in a lawsuit?

1 My worthy friend, the Bellman, had promised to supply an additional stanza, but the business of assisting the lamplighter, chimney-sweeper, etc., with complimentary verses for their worthy masters and mistresses, pressing on him at this season, he was obliged to decline it. [Authors' note.]

"(Have you not read the Rights of Man, by Tom Paine?)
Drops of compassion tremble on my eyelids,
Ready to fall, as soon as you have told your
                    Pitiful story."

Knife-grinder

"Story! God bless you! I have none to tell, sir,
Only last night a-drinking at the Chequers,
This poor old hat and breeches, as you see, were
                    Torn in a scuffle.

"Constables came up for to take me into
Custody; they took me before the justice;
Justice Oldmixon put me in the parish-
                    -Stocks for a vagrant.

"I should be glad to drink your Honour's health in
A pot of beer, if you will give me sixpence;
But for my part, I never love to meddle
                    With politics, sir."

Friend of Humanity

"*I* give thee sixpence! I will see thee damn'd first—
Wretch! whom no sense of wrongs can rouse to vengeance;
Sordid, unfeeling, reprobate, degraded,
                    Spiritless outcast!"

> [*Kicks the Knife-grinder, overturns his wheel, and exit
> in a transport of Republican enthusiasm and
> universal philanthropy.*]

GEORGE CANNING AND JOHN HOOKHAM FRERE

THE SENTIMENTAL NOVEL

JANE AUSTEN wrote *Love and Freindship* (*sic*) in 1790, when she was
fifteen. "It is all the better for being juvenile in the sense of being

joyful," G. K. Chesterton writes in the preface to its first publication, in 1922. "The whole thing is full of the sort of high spirits that are always higher in private than in public; as people laugh louder in the house than in the street." It was the precocity of genius, not only because a schoolgirl wrote something we still read with pleasure but also because she was already able to define her literary personality. The sentimental novel that is parodied in *Love and Freindship* was much in vogue at the end of the eighteenth century; it has continued, with inessential modifications, to be in vogue ever since; it was written for women and largely by women. Hawthorne's publisher wrote him in 1853 that his royalties from *Mosses from an Old Manse* were $144.09 that year, tactlessly adding that this didn't mean Putnam's couldn't sell books, for Miss Susan Warner had just received $4,500 for a half-year's royalties on *The Wide, Wide World*. The author of *The Scarlet Letter* was annoyed. "America is now given over to a damned mob of scribbling women," he wrote, "and I should have no chance of success while the public taste is occupied with their trash—and should be ashamed of myself if I did succeed. What is the mystery of these innumerable editions of *The Lamplighter* [by Maria Susanna Cummins] and other books neither better nor worse—worse they could not be and better they need not be when they sell by the hundred thousand." Miss Austen would have sympathized with Mr. Hawthorne. Her own novels were Of and By but not For her own sex. In every way they were antithetical to the "woman's novel" that first became popular at the end of the eighteenth century.

I should have liked to present here some episodes from another of Jane Austen's antiromantic writings, *Northanger Abbey*, but, aside from the matter of length, the novel is satire rather than parody. The target is the Gothic novel, especially Mrs. Radcliffe's *Mysteries of Udolpho*. A perfectly nice, ordinary English girl ("No one who had ever seen Catherine Morland in her infancy would have supposed her born to be an heroine," is the magisterial first sentence) visits a country house called Northanger Abbey and there, like Don Quixote, draws all sorts of romantic and sinister (and erroneous) conclusions from data which turn out to be extremely prosaic. Unlike Don Quixote, she finally gives in:

> She remembered with what feelings she had prepared for a knowledge of Northanger. She saw that the infatuation had been created, the mischief settled, long before her quitting Bath, and it seemed as if the whole might be traced to the influence of that sort of reading which she had there indulged.

Charming as were all Mrs. Radcliffe's works, and charming even as were the works of all her imitators, it was not in them perhaps that human nature, at least in the midland counties of England was to be looked for. Of the Alps and Pyrenees, with their pine forests and their vices, they might give a faithful delineation; and Italy, Switzerland, and the South of France, might be as fruitful in horrors as they were there represented. Catherine dared not doubt beyond her own country, and even of that, if hard pressed, would have yielded the northern and western extremities. But in the central part of England there was surely some security for the existence even of a wife not beloved, in the laws of the land, and the manners of the age. Murder was not tolerated, servants were not slaves, and neither poison nor sleeping potions to be procured, like rhubarb, from every druggist. Among the Alps and Pyrenees, perhaps, there were no mixed characters. There, such as were not as spotless as an angel, might have the dispositions of a fiend. But in England it was not so; among the English, she believed, in their hearts and habits, there was a general though unequal mixture of good and bad. . . .

There were still some subjects, indeed, under which she believed they must always tremble; the mention of a chest or a cabinet, for instance, and she did not love the sight of japan in any shape; but even *she* could allow that an occasional memento of past folly, however painful, might not be without use. . . .

The anxieties of common life began soon to succeed to the alarms of romance. Her desire of hearing from Isabella grew every day greater. She was quite impatient to know how the Bath world went on, and how the Rooms were attended; and especially was she anxious to be assured of Isabella's having matched some fine netting cotton, on which she had left her intent.

Following is a section from *Love and Freindship*. Laura's further adventures, though more harrowing, add nothing essential to our knowledge of that romantic young lady who was as good at fainting as she was poor at spelling.

Letter 3rd
Laura to Marianne

As the Daughter of my most intimate friend I think you entitled to that knowledge of my unhappy story, which your Mother has so often solicited me to give you.

My Father was a native of Ireland and an inhabitant of Wales: my Mother was the natural Daughter of a Scotch Peer by an italian Opera-girl—I was born in Spain and received my Education at a Convent in France.

When I had reached my eighteenth Year I was recalled by my Parents to my paternal roof in Wales. Our mansion was situated in one of the most romantic parts of the Vale of Uske. Tho' my Charms are now considerably softened and somewhat impaired by the Misfortunes I have undergone, I was once beautiful. But lovely as I was the Graces of my Person were the least of my Perfections. Of every accomplishment accustomary to my sex, I was Mistress. When in the Convent, my progress had always exceeded my instructions, my Acquirements had been wonderfull for my age, and I had shortly surpassed my Masters.

In my Mind, every Virtue that could adorn it was centered; it was the Rendez-vous of every good Quality and of every noble sentiment.

A sensibility too tremblingly alive to every affliction of my Freinds, my Acquaintance and particularly to every affliction of my own, was my only fault, if a fault it could be called. Alas! how altered now! Tho' indeed my own Misfortunes do not make less impression on me than they ever did, yet now I never feel for those of an other. My accomplishments too, begin to fade—I can neither sing so well nor Dance so gracefully as I once did—and I have entirely forgot the *Minuet Dela Cour*.

Adeiu.
Laura.

Letter 4th

Laura to Marianne

OUR neighbourhood was small, for it consisted only of your Mother. She may probably have already told you that being left by her Parents in indigent Circumstances she had retired into Wales on eoconomical motives. There it was our freindship first commenced. Isabel was then one and twenty. Tho' pleasing both in her Person and Manners (between ourselves) she never possessed the hundredth part of my Beauty or Accomplishments. Isabel had seen the World. She had passed 2 Years at one of the first Boarding-schools in London; had spent a fortnight in Bath and had supped one night in Southampton.

"Beware my Laura (she would often say) Beware of the insipid Vanities and idle Dissipations of the Metropolis of England; Beware of the unmeaning Luxuries of Bath and of the stinking fish of Southampton."

"Alas! (exclaimed I) how am I to avoid those evils I shall never be exposed to? What probability is there of my ever tasting the Dissipations of London, the Luxuries of Bath, or the stinking Fish of Southampton? I who am doomed to waste my Days of Youth and Beauty in an humble Cottage in the Vale of Uske."

Ah! little did I then think I was ordained so soon to quit that humble Cottage for the Deceitfull Pleasures of the World.

Adeiu

Laura.

Letter 5th

Laura to Marianne

ONE Evening in December as my Father, my Mother and myself, were arranged in social converse round our Fireside, we were on a sudden, greatly astonished, by hearing a violent knocking on the outward door of our rustic Cot.

My Father started—"What noise is that," (said he.) "It sounds like a loud rapping at the door"—(replied my Mother.) "it does indeed." (cried I.) "I am of your opinion; (said my Father) it certainly does appear to proceed from some uncommon violence exerted against our unoffending door." "Yes (exclaimed I) I cannot help thinking it must be somebody who knocks for admittance."

"That is another point (replied he;) We must not pretend to determine on what motive the person may knock—tho' that someone *does* rap at the door, I am partly convinced."

Here, a 2d tremendous rap interrupted my Father in his speech, and somewhat alarmed my Mother and me.

"Had we not better go and see who it is? (said she) the servants are out." "I think we had." (replied I.) "Certainly, (added my Father) by all means." "Shall we go now?" (said my Mother,) "The sooner the better." (answered he.) "Oh! let no time be lost" (cried I.)

A third more violent Rap than ever again assaulted our ears. "I am certain there is somebody knocking at the Door." (said my Mother.) "I think there must be," (replied my Father) "I fancy the servants are returned; (said I) I think I hear Mary going to the Door." "I'm glad of it (cried my Father) for I long to know who it is."

I was right in my conjecture; for Mary instantly entering the Room, informed us that a young Gentleman and his Servant were at the door, who had lossed their way, were very cold and begged leave to warm themselves by our fire.

"Won't you admit them?" (said I.) "You have no objection, my Dear?" (said my Father.) "None in the World." (replied my Mother.)

Mary, without waiting for any further commands immediately left the room and quickly returned introducing the most beauteous and amiable Youth, I had ever beheld. The servant, she kept to herself.

My natural sensibility had already been greatly affected by the sufferings of the unfortunate stranger and no sooner did I first behold him, than I felt that on him the happiness or Misery of my future Life must depend.

Adeiu
Laura.

Letter 6th

Laura to Marianne

THE noble Youth informed us that his name was Lindsay—for particular reasons however I shall conceal it under that of Talbot. He told us that he was the son of an English Baronet, that his Mother had been many years no more and that he had a Sister of the middle size. "My Father (he continued) is a mean and mercenary wretch—it is only to such particular freinds as this Dear Party that I would thus betray his failings. Your Virtues my amiable Polydore (addressing himself to my father) yours Dear Claudia and yours my Charming Laura call on me to repose in you, my confidence." We bowed. "My Father, seduced by the false glare of Fortune and the Deluding Pomp of Title, insisted on my giving my hand to Lady Dorothea. No never exclaimed I. Lady Dorothea is lovely and Engaging; I prefer no woman to her; but know Sir, that I scorn to marry her in compliance with your Wishes. No! Never shall it be said that I obliged my Father."

We all admired the noble Manliness of his reply. He continued.

"Sir Edward was surprised; he had perhaps little expected to meet with so spirited an opposition to his will. "Where, Edward in the name of wonder (said he) did you pick up this unmeaning gibberish? You have been studying Novels I suspect." I scorned to answer: it would have been beneath my dignity. I mounted my Horse and followed by my faithful William set forwards for my Aunts."

"My Father's house is situated in Bedfordshire, my Aunts' in Middlesex, and tho' I flatter myself with being a tolerable proficient in Geography. I know not how it happened, but I found myself entering this beautiful Vale which I find is in South Wales, when I had expected to have reached my Aunts."

"After having wandered some time on the Banks of the Uske without knowing which way to go, I began to lament my cruel Destiny in the bitterest and most pathetic Manner. It was now perfectly dark, not a single star was there to direct my steps, and

I know not what might have befallen me had I not at length discerned thro' the solemn Gloom that surrounded me a distant light, which as I approached it, I discovered to be the chearfull Blaze of your fire. Impelled by the combination of Misfortunes under which I laboured, namely Fear, Cold and Hunger I hesitated not to ask admittance which at length I have gained; and now my Adorable Laura (continued he taking my Hand) when may I hope to receive that reward of all the painfull sufferings I have undergone during the course of my attachment to you, to which I have ever aspired. Oh! when will you reward me with Yourself?"

"This instant, Dear and Amiable Edward." (replied I.). We were immediately united by my Father, who tho' he had never taken orders had been bred to the Church.

Adeiu

Laura.

Letter 7th
Laura to Marianne

WE remained but a few days after our Marriage, in the Vale of Uske. After taking an affecting Farewell of my Father, my Mother and my Isabel, I accompanied Edward to his Aunts' in Middlesex. Philippa received us both with every expression of affectionate Love. My arrival was indeed a most agreable surprise to her as she had not only been totally ignorant of my Marriage with her Nephew, but had never even had the slightest idea of there being such a person in the World.

Augusta, the sister of Edward was on a visit to her when we arrived. I found her exactly what her Brother had described her to be—of the middle size. She received me with equal surprise though not with equal Cordiality, as Philippa. There was a disagreeable coldness and Forbidding Reserve in her reception of me which was equally distressing and Unexpected. None of that interesting Sensibility or amiable simpathy in her manners and

Address to me when we first met which should have distinguished our introduction to each other. Her Language was neither warm, nor affectionate, her expressions of regard were neither animated nor cordial; her arms were not opened to receive me to her Heart, tho' my own were extended to press her to mine.

A short Conversation between Augusta and her Brother, which I accidently overheard encreased my dislike to her, and convinced me that her Heart was no more formed for the soft ties of Love than for the endearing intercourse of Freindship.

"But do you think that my Father will ever be reconciled to this imprudent connection?" (said Augusta.)

"Augusta (replied the noble Youth) I thought you had a better opinion of me, than to imagine I would so abjectly degrade myself as to consider my Father's Concurrence in any of my affairs, either of Consequence or concern to me. Tell me Augusta tell me with sincerity; did you ever know me consult his inclinations or follow his Advice in the least trifling Particular since the age of fifteen?"

"Edward (replied she) you are surely too diffident in your own praise. Since you were fifteen only! My Dear Brother since you were five years old, I entirely acquit you of ever having willingly contributed to the satisfaction of your Father. But still I am not without apprehensions of your being shortly obliged to degrade yourself in your own eyes by seeking a support for your wife in the Generosity of Sir Edward."

"Never, never Augusta will I so demean myself. (said Edward). Support! What support will Laura want which she can receive from him?"

"Only those very insignificant ones of Victuals and Drink." (answered she.)

"Victuals and Drink! (replied my Husband in a most nobly contemptuous Manner) and dost thou then imagine that there is no other support for an exalted mind (such as is my Laura's) than the mean and indelicate employment of Eating and Drinking?"

"None that I know of, so efficacious." (returned Augusta).

"And did you then never feel the pleasing Pangs of Love, Augusta? (replied my Edward). Does it appear impossible to your vile and corrupted Palate, to exist on Love? Can you not conceive the Luxury of living in every distress that Poverty can inflict, with the object of your tenderest affection?"

"You are too ridiculous (said Augusta) to argue with; perhaps however you may in time be convinced that . . ."

Here I was prevented from hearing the remainder of her speech, by the appearance of a very Handsome young Woman, who was ushured into the Room at the Door of which I had been listening. On hearing her announced by the Name of "Lady Dorothea," I instantly quitted my Post and followed her into the Parlour, for I well remembered that she was the Lady, proposed as a Wife for my Edward by the Cruel and Unrelenting Baronet.

Altho' Lady Dorothea's visit was nominally to Philippa and Augusta, yet I have some reason to imagine that (acquainted with the Marriage and arrival of Edward) to see me was a principal motive to it.

I soon perceived that tho' Lovely and Elegant in her Person and tho' Easy and Polite in her Address, she was of that inferior order of Beings with regard to Delicate Feeling, tender Sentiments, and refined Sensibility, of which Augusta was one.

She staid but half an hour and neither in the Course of her Visit, confided to me any of her secret thoughts, nor requested me to confide in her, any of Mine. You will easily imagine therefore my Dear Marianne that I could not feel any ardent affection or very sincere Attachment for Lady Dorothea.

Adeiu
Laura.

Letter 8th

Laura to Marianne, in continuation

LADY DOROTHEA had not left us long before another visitor as unexpected a one as her Ladyship, was announced. It was

Sir Edward, who informed by Augusta of her Brother's marriage, came doubtless to reproach him for having dared to unite himself to me without his Knowledge. But Edward foreseeing his design, approached him with heroic fortitude as soon as he entered the Room, and addressed him in the following Manner.

"Sir Edward, I know the motive of your Journey here—You come with base Design of reproaching me for having entered into an indissolable engagement with my Laura without your Consent. But Sir, I glory in the Act—. It is my greatest boast that I have incurred the displeasure of my Father!"

So saying, he took my hand and whilst Sir Edward, Philippa, and Augusta were doubtless reflecting with admiration on his undaunted Bravery, led me from the Parlour to his Father's Carriage which yet remained at the Door and in which we were instantly conveyed from the pursuit of Sir Edward.

The Postilions had at first received orders only to take the London road; as soon as we had sufficiently reflected However, we ordered them to Drive to M——. the seat of Edward's most particular freind, which was but a few miles distant.

At M——. we arrived in a few hours; and on sending in our names were immediately admitted to Sophia, the Wife of Edward's freind. After having been deprived during the course of 3 weeks of a real freind (for such I term your Mother) imagine my transports at beholding one, most truly worthy of the Name. Sophia was rather above the middle size; most elegantly formed. A soft languor spread over her lovely features, but increased their Beauty—. It was the Charectarestic of her Mind—. She was all sensibility and Feeling. We flew into each others arms and after having exchanged vows of mutual Freindship for the rest of our Lives, instantly unfolded to each other the most inward secrets of our Hearts—. We were interrupted in the delightfull Employment by the entrance of Augustus, (Edward's friend) who was just returned from a solitary ramble.

Never did I see such an affecting Scene as was the meeting of Edward and Augustus.

"My Life! my Soul!" (exclaimed the former) "My adorable

angel!" (replied the latter) as they flew into each other's arms. It was too pathetic for the feelings of Sophia and myself—. We fainted alternately on a sofa.

Adeiu
Laura

JANE AUSTEN

PART TWO

The Nineteenth Century

GEORGE CRABBE

THIS PARODY, along with the following ones of Cobbett (*A Hampshire Farmer*) and Wordsworth (*The Baby's Debut*), appeared in *Rejected Addresses*, by James and Horace Smith, which was published in 1812 and went through many editions. The brothers Smith were amateurs—James was a lawyer, Horace a stockbroker—but they brought the art of parody, at long last, to maturity.

The occasion was the opening of the new Drury Lane Theatre, rebuilt after a fire by a committee headed by Samuel Whitbread, a public-spirited brewer whose ale is still a leading British brand. The committee offered a prize for "the best Address to be spoken upon the opening night," and they received 112 entries, mostly in verse and some by well-known writers. (The Smiths claimed that 69 "invoked the aid of that useful and much-abused bird, the Phoenix.") But the actual entries were quite overshadowed by the spurious ones concocted by the Smiths, which also included—besides the three here—parodies of Byron, Scott, Moore, Southey, Coleridge, and Dr. Johnson. The Smiths had the usual trouble of authors with an original idea who try to get into print; although they were willing to forego royalties, it looked for a time as if their Addresses would be doubly rejected. "These trifles are really not deficient in smartness," one experienced publisher condescended. "They are well, vastly well for beginners, but they will never do—never. They would not pay for advertising, and without it I should not sell fifty copies." However, they finally found a less experienced publisher, John Miller of Covent Garden, who not only put out their book but gave them half the profits. *Rejected Addresses* was an immediate success, both popular and *d'estime*. Lord Jeffrey took eighteen pages to praise it in *The Edinburgh Review*. One enterprising publisher tried to mount the bandwagon by asking the 111 unsuccessful competitors for their entries; he presented the manuscripts received in a volume entitled *Genuine Rejected Addresses*. It didn't do very well.

Even the authors parodied seem to have enjoyed the book. "To the credit of the *genus irritabile,* be it recorded that not one of them betrayed the least soreness or refused to join in the laugh," wrote the

Smiths. A month after publication, Byron wrote John Murray: "I think the *Rejected Addresses* by far the best thing of its kind since the *Rolliad*. . . . Tell the author [the first edition was anonymous] 'I forgive him were he twenty times our satirist,' and think his imitations not at all inferior to the famous ones of Hawkins Browne." His Lordship, for once, was understating.

The Theatre

Interior of a Theatre described.—Pit gradually fills.—The Check-taker.
—Pit full.—The Orchestra tuned.—One Fiddle rather dilatory.—
Is reproved—and repents.—Evolutions of a Play-bill.—Its final
Settlement on the Spikes.—The Gods taken to task—and why.—
Motley Group of Play-goers.—Holywell Street, St. Pancras.—
Emanuel Jennings binds his Son apprentice—not in London—and
why.—Episode of the Hat.

'TIS sweet to view, from half-past five to six,
Our long wax-candles, with short cotton wicks,
Touch'd by the lamplighter's Promethean art,
Start into light, and make the lighter start;
To see red Phœbus through the gallery-pane
Tinge with his beam the beams of Drury Lane;
While gradual parties fill our widen'd pit,
And gape, and gaze, and wonder, ere they sit.

At first, while vacant seats give choice and ease,
Distant or near, they settle where they please;
But when the multitude contracts the span,
And seats are rare, they settle where they can.

Now the full benches to late-comers doom
No room for standing, miscall'd *standing room.*

Hark! the check-taker moody silence breaks,
And bawling "Pit full!" gives the check he takes;
Yet onward still the gathering numbers cram,
Contending crowders shout the frequent damn,
And all is bustle, squeeze, row, jabbering, and jam.

See to their desks Apollo's sons repair—
Swift rides the rosin o'er the horse's hair!
In unison their various tones to tune,
Murmurs the hautboy, growls the hoarse bassoon;
In soft vibration sighs the whispering lute,
Tang goes the harpsichord, too-too the flute,
Brays the loud trumpet, squeaks the fiddle sharp,
Winds the French-horn, and twangs the tingling harp;
Till, like great Jove, the leader, figuring in,
Attunes to order the chaotic din.
Now all seems hush'd—but, no, one fiddle will
Give, half-ashamed, a tiny flourish still.
Foil'd in his crash, the leader of the clan
Reproves with frowns the dilatory man:
Then on his candlestick thrice taps his bow,
Nods a new signal, and away they go.

Perchance, while pit and gallery cry, "Hats off!"
And awed Consumption checks his chided cough,
Some giggling daughter of the Queen of Love
Drops, 'reft of pin, her play-bill from above:
Like Icarus, while laughing galleries clap,
Soars, ducks, and dives in air the printed scrap;
But, wiser far than he, combustion fears,
And, as it flies, eludes the chandeliers;
Till, sinking gradual, with repeated twirl,
It settles, curling, on a fiddler's curl;
Who from his powder'd pate the intruder strikes,
And, for mere malice, sticks it on the spikes.

Say, why these Babel strains from Babel tongues?
Who's that calls "Silence!" with such leathern lungs?
He who, in quest of quiet, "Silence!" hoots,
Is apt to make the hubbub he imputes.
What various swains our motley walls contain!—
Fashion from Moorfields, honour from Chick Lane;

Bankers from Paper Buildings here resort,
Bankrupts from Golden Square and Riches Court;
From the Haymarket canting rogues in grain,
Gulls from the Poultry, sots from Water Lane;
The lottery-cormorant, the auction-shark,
The full-price master, and the half-price clerk;
Boys who long linger at the gallery-door,
With pence twice five—they want but twopence more:
Till some Samaritan the twopence spares,
And sends them jumping up the gallery-stairs.

Critics we boast who ne'er their malice balk,
But talk their mind—we wish they'd mind their talk;
Big-worded bullies, who by quarrels live—
Who give the lie, and tell the lie they give;
Jews from St. Mary Axe, for jobs so wary,
That for old clothes they'd even axe St. Mary;
And bucks with pockets empty as their pate,
Lax in their gaiters, laxer in their gait;
Who oft, when we our house lock up, carouse
With tippling tipstaves in a lock-up house.

Yet here, as elsewhere, Chance can joy bestow,
Where scowling Fortune seem'd to threaten woe.

John Richard William Alexander Dwyer
Was footman to Justinian Stubbs, Esquire;
But when John Dwyer listed in the Blues,
Emanuel Jennings polish'd Stubbs's shoes.
Emanuel Jennings brought his youngest boy
Up as a corn-cutter—a safe employ;
In Holywell Street, St. Pancras, he was bred
(At number twenty-seven, it is said),
Facing the pump, and near the Granby's Head:
He would have bound him to some shop in town,
But with a premium he could not come down.

Pat was the urchin's name—a red-hair'd youth,
Fonder of purl and skittle-grounds than truth.

Silence, ye gods! to keep your tongues in awe,
The Muse shall tell an accident she saw.

Pat Jennings in the upper gallery sat,
But, leaning forward, Jennings lost his hat:
Down from the gallery the beaver flew,
And spurn'd the one to settle in the two.
How shall he act? Pay at the gallery-door
Two shillings for what cost, when new, but four?
Or till half-price, to save his shilling, wait,
And gain his hat again at half-past eight?
Now, while his fears anticipate a thief,
John Mullins whispers, "Take my handkerchief."
"Thank you," cries Pat; "but one won't make a line."
"Take mine," cried Wilson; and cried Stokes, "Take mine."
A motley cable soon Pat Jennings ties,
Where Spitalfields with real India vies.
Like Iris' bow, down darts the painted clue,
Starr'd, striped, and spotted, yellow, red, and blue,
Old calico, torn silk, and muslin new.
George Green below, with palpitating hand,
Loops the last 'kerchief to the beaver's band—
Upsoars the prize! The youth, with joy unfeign'd,
Regain'd the felt, and felt what he regain'd;
While to the applauding galleries grateful Pat
Made a low bow, and touch'd the ransom'd hat.

JAMES SMITH

WILLIAM COBBETT

A Hampshire Farmer

To the Secretary of the Managing Committee of the Drury Lane Playhouse,

Sir:

To the gewgaw fetters of rhyme (invented by the monks to enslave the people) I have a rooted objection. I have therefore written an address for your theatre in plain, homespun, yeoman's prose; in the doing whereof I hope I am swayed by nothing but an independent wish to open the eyes of this gulled people, to prevent a repetition of the dramatic bamboozling they have hitherto laboured under. If you like what I have done, and mean to make use of it, I don't want any such aristocratic reward as a piece of plate with two griffins sprawling upon it, or a dog and a jackass fighting for a ha'p'worth of gilt gingerbread, or any such Bartholomew-fair nonsense. All I ask is, that the door-keepers of your playhouse may take all the sets of my Register now on hand, and force every body who enters your doors to buy one, giving afterwards a debtor and creditor account of what they have received, post-paid, and in due course remitting me the money and unsold Registers, carriage-paid.

I am, &c.
W. C.

————Rabidâ qui concitus irâ
Implevit pariter ternis latratibus auras,
Et sparsit virides spumis albentibus agros.

OVID.

MOST THINKING PEOPLE,

WHEN persons address an audience from the stage, it is usual, either in word or gesture, to say, "Ladies and Gentlemen, your servant." If I were base enough, mean enough, paltry enough, and *brute beast* enough, to follow that fashion, I should tell two lies in a breath. In the first place, you are *not* Ladies and Gentlemen, but I hope something better, that is to say, honest men and women; and in the next place, if you were ever so much ladies, and ever so much gentlemen, I am not, *nor ever will be,* your humble servant.* You see me here, *most thinking people,* by mere chance. I have not been within the doors of a playhouse before for these ten years; nor, till that abominable custom of taking money at the doors is discontinued, will I ever sanction a theatre with my presence. The stage-door is the only gate of *freedom* in the whole edifice, and through that I made my way from Bagshaw's[1] in Brydges Street, to accost you. Look about you. Are you not all comfortable? Nay, never slink, mun; speak out, if you are dissatisfied, and tell me so before I leave town. You are now, (thanks to *Mr. Whitbread.*) got into a large, comfortable house. Not into a *gimcrack palace;* not into a *Solomon's temple;* not into a frostwork of Brobdingnag filigree; but into a plain, honest, homely, industrious, wholesome, *brown brick playhouse.* You have been struggling for independence and elbow-room these three years; and who gave it you? Who helped you out of Lilliput? Who routed you from a rat-hole, five inches by four, to perch you in a palace? Again and again I answer, *Mr. Whitbread.* You might have sweltered in that place with the Greek name[2] till doomsday, and neither *Lord Castlereagh, Mr. Canning,* no, nor the *Marquess Wellesley,* would have turned a trowel to help you out! Remember that. Never forget that. Read it to your children, and to your children's children! And now, *most thinking people,* cast your eyes over my head to what the builder (I beg his pardon, the architect) calls the *proscenium.* No motto, no slang, no popish Latin, to keep the people in the dark. No *veluti in speculum.* Nothing in the dead languages, properly so called, for they ought to die, aye and be *damned* to

---

* Editor's note: The similarity to the no-nonsense style of a later tribune of the people, George Bernard Shaw, is interesting. The rest of the footnotes to this piece are from *A Century of Parody and Imitation,* Oxford Press, edited by W. Jerrold and R. M. Leonard. This anthology, by the way, which covers the 19th century, is by far the best in the field, and I am indebted to it for many of the selections that immediately follow.

[1] Bagshaw. At that time the publisher of Cobbett's Register.

[2] The old Lyceum Theatre, pulled down by Mr. Arnold. That since destroyed by fire was erected on its site.

boot! The Covent Garden manager tried that, and a pretty business he made of it! When a man says v*eluti in speculum,* he is called a man of letters. Very well, and is not a man who cries O. P. a man of letters too? You ran your O. P. against his *veluti in speculum,* and pray which beat? I prophesied that, though I never told any body. I take it for granted, that every intelligent man, woman, and child, to whom I address myself, has stood severally and respectively in Little Russell Street, and cast their, his, her, and its eyes on the outside of this building before they paid their money to view the inside. Look at the brick-work, *English Audience!* Look at the brick-work! All plain and smooth like a quakers' meeting. None of your Egyptian pyramids, to entomb subscribers' capitals. No overgrown colonnades of stone, like an alderman's gouty legs in white cotton stockings, fit only to use as rammers for paving Tottenham Court Road. This house is neither after the model of a temple in Athens, no, nor a *temple* in *Moorfields,* but it is built to act English plays in; and, provided you have good scenery, dresses, and decorations, I daresay you wouldn't break your hearts if the outside were as plain as the pikestaff I used to carry when I was a sergeant. *Apropos,* as the French valets say, who cut their masters' throats[3]—*apropos,* a word about dresses. You must, many of you, have seen what I have read a description of, Kemble and Mrs. Siddons in Macbeth, with more gold and silver plastered on their doublets than would have kept an honest family in butcher's meat and flannel from year's end to year's end! I am informed, (now mind, I do not vouch for the fact,) but I am informed that all such extravagant idleness is to be done away with here. Lady Macbeth is to have a plain quilted petticoat, a cotton gown, and a *mob cap* (as the court parasites call it;—it will be well for them, if, one of these days, they don't wear a mob cap—I mean a *white cap,* with a *mob* to look at them); and Macbeth is to appear in an honest yeoman's drab coat, and a pair of black calamanco breeches. Not *Sal*amanca; no, nor *Talavera* neither, my most Noble Marquess; but plain, honest, black calamanco stuff breeches. This is right; this is as

---

[3] An allusion to a murder then recently committed on Barnes Terrace.

it should be. *Most thinking people,* I have heard you much abused. There is not a compound in the language but is strung fifty in a rope, like onions, by the Morning Post, and hurled in your teeth. You are called the mob; and when they have made you out to be the mob, you are called the *scum* of the people, and the *dregs* of the people. I should like to know how you can be both. Take a basin of broth—not *cheap soup, Mr. Wilberforce*—not soup for the poor, at a penny a quart, as your mixture of horses' legs, brick-dust, and old shoes, was denominated—but plain, wholesome, patriotic beef or mutton broth; take this, examine it, and you will find—mind, I don't vouch for the fact, but I am told—you will find the dregs at the bottom, and the scum at the top. I will endeavour to explain this to you: England is a large *earthenware pipkin;* John Bull is the *beef* thrown into it; taxes are the *hot water* he boils in; rotten boroughs are the *fuel* that blazes under this same pipkin; parliament is the *ladle* that stirs the hodge-podge, and sometimes——. But, hold! I don't wish to pay *Mr. Newman*[4] a second visit. I leave you better off than you have been this many a day: you have a good house over your head; you have beat the French in Spain; the harvest has turned out well; the comet keeps its distance;[5] and red slippers are hawked about in Constantinople for next to nothing; and for all this, *again and again* I tell you, you are indebted to *Mr. Whitbread! ! !*

JAMES SMITH

[4] At that time keeper of Newgate. The present superintendent is styled governor!

[5] A portentous one that made its appearance in the year 1811; in the midst of the war,

with fear of change
Perplexing nations.

ROBERT BURNS

For A' That and A' That

A NEW VERSION, RESPECTFULLY RECOMMENDED TO SUNDRY WHOM
IT CONCERNS.

MORE luck to honest poverty,
    It claims respect, and a' that;
But honest wealth's a better thing,
    We dare be rich for a' that.
        For a' that, and a' that,
            And spooney cant and a' that,
        A man may have a ten-pun note,
            And be a brick for a' that.

What though on soup and fish we dine,
    Wear evening togs and a' that,
A man may like good meat and wine,
    Nor be a knave for a' that.
        For a' that, and a' that,
            Their fustian talk and a' that,
        A gentleman, however clean,
            May have a heart for a' that.

You see yon prater called a Beales,
    Who bawls and brays and a' that,
Tho' hundreds cheer his blatant bosh,
    He's but a goose for a' that.
        For a' that, and a' that,
            His Bubblyjocks, and a' that,
        A man with twenty grains of sense,
            He looks and laughs at a' that.

A prince can make a belted knight,
    A marquis, duke, and a' that,
And if the title's earned, all right,

Old England's fond of a' that.
   For a' that, and a' that,
      Beales' balderdash, and a' that,
   A name that tells of service done
   Is worth the wear, for a' that.

Then let us pray that come it may
   And come it will for a' that,
That common sense may take the place
   Of common cant and a' that.
      For a' that, and a' that,
      Who cackles trash and a' that,
   Or be he lord, or be he low,
      The man's an ass for a' that.

SHIRLEY BROOKS

ROBERT BURNS

Rigid Body Sings

GIN a body meet a body
   Flyin' through the air,
Gin a body hit a body,
   Will it fly? and where?
Ilka impact has its measure,
   Ne'er a' ane hae I,
Yet a' the lads they measure me,
   Or, at least, they try.

Gin a body meet a body
   Altogether free,
How they travel afterwards
   We do not always see.
Ilka problem has its method

By analytics high;
For me, I ken na ane o' them,
But what the waur am I?

JAMES CLERK-MAXWELL*

LORD BYRON

Song by Mr. Cypress

THERE is a fever of the spirit,
  The brand of Cain's unresting doom,
Which in the lone dark souls that bear it
  Glows like the lamp in Tullia's tomb.
Unlike the lamp, its subtle fire
  Burns, blasts, consumes its cell, the heart.
Till, one by one, hope, joy, desire,
  Like dreams of shadowy smoke depart.

When hope, love, life itself, are only
  Dust—spectral memories—dead and cold—
The unfed fire burns bright and lonely,
  Like that undying lamp of old;
And by that drear illumination,
  Till time its clay-built home has rent,
Thought broods on feeling's desolation—
  The soul is its own monument.†

THOMAS LOVE PEACOCK

---

* The noted physicist (1831-1879). Strictly, this is a burlesque rather than
a parody, but any signs of humor in scientists should be encouraged.
  † From *Nightmare Abbey*. Byron had two styles: the Romantic Grandiose,
which made him famous and popular and which is here taken off, and the
Anti-Romantic Colloquial of *Beppo* and *Don Juan*, which he developed later
after becoming bored with the first and which J. K. Stephen parodies below.

LORD BYRON

A Grievance

DEAR MR EDITOR: I wish to say—
   If you will not be angry at my writing it—
But I've been used, since childhood's happy day,
   When I have thought of something, to inditing it:
I seldom think of things: and, by the way,
   Although this metre may not be exciting, it
Enables one to be extremely terse,
Which is not what one always is in verse.

I used to know a man,—such things befall
   The observant wayfarer through Fate's domain:
He was a man, take him for all in all,
   We shall not look upon his like again:
I know that statement's not original:
   What statement is, since Shakspere? or, since Cain,
What murder? I believe 'twas Shakspere said it, or
Perhaps it may have been your Fighting Editor.

Though why an Editor should fight, or why
   A Fighter should abase himself to edit,
Are problems far too difficult and high
   For me to solve with any sort of credit:
Some greatly more accomplished man than I
   Must tackle them: let's say then Shakspere said it:
And, if he did not, Lewis Morris may
(Or even if he did). Some other day,

When I have nothing pressing to impart,
   I should not mind dilating on this matter:
I feel its import both in head and heart,
   And always did,—especially the latter:
I could discuss it in the busy mart

Or on the lonely housetop: hold! this chatter
Diverts me from my purpose. To the point:
The time, as Hamlet said, is out of joint,

And I perhaps was born to set it right;
    A fact I greet with perfect equanimity;
I do not put it down to "cursed spite":
    I don't see any cause for cursing in it: I
Have always taken very great delight
    In such pursuits since first I read divinity:
Whoever will may write a nation's songs
As long as I'm allowed to right its wrongs.

What's Eton but a nursery of wrong-righters,
    A mighty mother of effective men,
A training-ground for amateur reciters,
    A sharpener of the sword as of the pen,
A factory of orators and fighters,
    A forcing-house of genius? Now and then,
The world at large shrinks back, abashed and beaten,
Unable to endure the glare of Eton.

I think I said I knew a man: what then?
    I don't suppose such knowledge is forbid:
We nearly all do, more or less, know men,—
    Or think we do: nor will a man get rid
Of that delusion, while he wields a pen:
    But who this man was, what, if aught, he did,
Nor why I mentioned him, I do not know:
Nor what I "wished to say" a while ago.

                                        J. K. STEPHEN

SAMUEL TAYLOR COLERIDGE

IN 1817 a London publisher brought out *The Poetic Mirror*, which
contained, or seemed to contain, poems by Wordsworth, Byron, Scott,

Coleridge, Southey, and others, including one James Hogg. The anonymous editor stated he had applied to "each of the principal living bards of Britain" for a contribution and that "the greater part of them entered into his views with more cordiality than he had reason to expect." He thanked them "for their liberal assistance, to which he is conscious that his merits have in no degree entitled him." The last statement was true, the others were not. The editor was James Hogg and he had written all the poems himself after having been unanimously rebuffed by the principal living bards; even his fellow countryman, Scott, had replied that "Every herring should hing by its ain head." The parodies were good, though mostly too long to use here. Immediately below is his Coleridge; later come two on Wordsworth.

Even for a parodist, James Hogg, the "Ettrick Shepherd," is unexpected. He was a Scotch peasant who had had only eight months of formal schooling and from the age of eight had worked as a shepherd. Up to eighteen, the only verse he had seen was the Psalms. He began to write, still in rustic isolation, at twenty-six. The next year he had a crucial experience: "The first time I heard of Robert Burns was in 1797, the year after he died," when a half-mad tramp recited *Tam O' Shanter* to him. "I wept and thought: what is to prevent me from succeeding Burns?" In fact he did write some good lyrics, but his parodies are what are most remembered; that he should have succeeded in this form, usually the province of more sophisticated writers, suggests he had a great natural talent. It also suggests the dangers of generalizing about human capabilities.

Isabelle

CAN there be a moon in heaven to-night,
That the hill and the grey cloud seem so light?
The air is whiten'd by some spell,
For there is no moon, I know it well;
On this third day, the sages say,
('Tis wonderful how well they know,)
The moon is journeying far away,
Bright somewhere in a heaven below.

It is a strange and lovely night,
A greyish pale, but not white!
Is it rain, or is it dew,

That falls so thick I see its hue?
In rays it follows, one, two, three,
Down the air so merrily,
Said Isabelle, so let it be!

Why does the Lady Isabelle
Sit in the damp and dewy dell
Counting the racks of drizzly rain,
And how often the Rail cries over again?
For she's harping, harping in the brake,
Craik, craik—Craik, craik.
Ten times nine, and thrice eleven;—
That last call was an hundred and seven.
Craik, craik—the hour is near—
Let it come, I have no fear!
Yet it is a dreadful work, I wis,
Such doings in a night like this!

Sounds the river harsh and loud?
The stream sounds harsh, but not loud.
There is a cloud that seems to hover,
By western hill the church-yard over,
What is it like?—'Tis like a whale;
'Tis like a shark with half the tail,
Not half, but third and more;
Now 'tis a wolf, and now a boar;
Its face is raised—it cometh here;
Let it come—there is no fear.
There's two for heaven, and ten for hell,
Let it come—'tis well—'tis well!
Said the Lady Isabelle.

What ails that little cut-tail'd whelp,
That it continues to yelp, yelp?
Yelp, yelp, and it turns its eye
Up to the tree and half to the sky,

Half to the sky and full to the cloud,
And still it whines and barks aloud.
Why I should dread I cannot tell;
There is a spirit; I know it well!
I see it in yon falling beam—
Is it a vision, or a dream?
It is no dream, full well I know,
I have a woful deed to do!
Hush, hush, thou little murmurer;
I tell thee hush—the dead are near!

If thou knew'st all, poor tailless whelp,
Well might'st thou tremble, growl, and yelp;
But thou know'st nothing, hast no part,
(Simple and stupid as thou art)
Save gratitude and truth of heart.
But they are coming by this way
That have been dead for a year and a day;
Without challenge, without change,
They shall have their full revenge!
They have been sent to wander in woe
In the lands of flame, and the lands of snow;
But those that are dead
Shall the green sward tread,
And those that are living
Shall soon be dead!
None to pity them, none to help!
Thou may'st quake, my cut-tail'd whelp!

There are two from the grave
That I fain would save;
Full hard is the weird
For the young and the brave!
Perchance they are rapt in vision sweet,
While the passing breezes kiss their feet;

And they are dreaming of joy and love!—
Well, let them go—there's room above.

    There are three times three, and three to these,
Count as you will, by twos or threes!
Three for the gallows, and three for the wave,
Three to roast behind the stone,
And three that shall never see the grave
Until the day and the hour are gone!
For retribution is mine alone!
The cloud is redder in its hue,
The hour is near, and vengeance due;
It cannot, and it will not fail,—
'Tis but a step to Borrowdale!
Why shouldst thou love and follow me,
Poor faithful thing? I pity thee!

    Up rose the Lady Isabelle,
I may not of her motion tell,
Yet thou may'st look upon her frame;
Look on it with a passing eye,
But think not thou upon the same,
Turn away, and ask not why;
For if thou darest look again,
Mad of heart and seared of brain,
Thou shalt never look again!

    What can ail that short-tail'd whelp?
'Tis either behind or far before,
And it hath changed its whining yelp
To a shorten'd yuff—its little core
Seems bursting with terror and dismay,
Yuff, yuff,—hear how it speeds away.
Hold thy peace, thou yemering thing,
The very night-wind's slumbering,
And thou wilt wake to woe and pain
Those that must never wake again.

Meet is its terror and its flight,
There's one on the left and two on the right!
But save the paleness of the face,
All is beauty, and all is grace!
The earth and air are tinged with blue;
There are no footsteps in the dew;
Is this to wandering spirits given,
Such stillness on the face of heaven?
The fleecy clouds that sleep above,
Are like the wing of beauteous dove,
And the leaf of the elm-tree does not move!
Yet they are coming! and they are three!
Jesu! Maria! can it be?

The Conclusion

Sleep on, fair maiden of Borrowdale!
Sleep! O sleep! and do not wake!
Dream of the dance, till the foot so pale,
And the beauteous ancle shiver and shake;
Till thou shalt press, with feeling bland,
Thine own fair breast for lover's hand.
Thy heart is light as summer breeze,
Thy heart is joyous as the day;
Man never form of angel sees,
But thou art fair as they!
So lovers ween, and so they say,
So thine shall ween for many a day!
The hour's at hand, O woe is me!
For they are coming, and they are three!

JAMES HOGG

WILLIAM WORDSWORTH

FOR OBVIOUS REASONS, Wordsworth was the most frequently parodied
serious poet in the nineteenth century; Browning was second, for the

same reasons; the score is nine to five in favor of—or rather against—Wordsworth in this anthology. It was not only that each had eccentricities of style and thought that could easily be mocked; it was also, I think, that the combination of absurdity and elevation opened especially wide the gap which the parodist exploits. Had they been either less elevated or more sensible, Wordsworth and Browning would have been spared much.

Some notes on the Wordsworth parodies printed here:

The Baby's Debut. See above, under Crabbe.

On Oxford. Keats wrote this in 1817. He sent it to a friend with a note:

> "Wordsworth sometimes, though in a fine way, gives us sentences in the style of school exercises. For instance:
>
> > 'The lake doth glitter,
> > Small birds twitter,' (etc.)
>
> Now I think this an excellent manner of giving us a very clear description of an interesting place such as Oxford is."

Fragments. Wordsworth, who didn't very much enjoy parodies of his work, did praise Miss Fanshawe's. I think he was right; she is best on his simplistic style, as Hogg on his more orotund manner. Miss Fanshawe (1765-1834) was a literary hostess and minor poet who lived in Berkeley Square and was admired by Sir Walter Scott. I have not read her *Memorials* nor even her *Literary Remains.*

Peter Bell. I give only the first eleven stanzas. The parody is a literary curiosity because it was published before the original. Reynolds had seen the manuscript and is said to have written off his parody in one day. He stated, "I do affirm I am the real Simon Pure," and added a preface signed "W.W.":

> It is now a period of one-and-twenty years since I first wrote some of the most perfect compositions (except certain pieces I have written in my later days) that ever dropped from poetical pen. . . . It has been my aim and my achievement to deduce moral thunder from buttercups, daisies, celandines, and (as a poet scarcely inferior to myself hath it) "such small deer." Out of sparrows' eggs I have hatched great truths, and with sextons' barrows have I wheeled into human hearts piles of the weightiest philosophy. . . . Of *Peter Bell* I have only thus much to say: It completes the simple system of natural narrative which I began as early as 1798.

It is written in that pure unlabored style which can only be met with among laborers. . . . In the course of the next few years I propose to write laborious lives of all the old people who enjoy sinecures in the text or are pensioned off in the notes of my poetry.

Nobody liked *Peter Bell*. Keats and Leigh Hunt were critical. Shelley dashed off a parody which runs to 153 stanzas plus a prologue; it is lively but Shelley was not a parodist; some scholars think he didn't even see the original but worked only from his friend Reynolds' parody and from Hunt's review. ("A critique on Wordsworth's *Peter Bell* reached us at Leghorn," Mrs. Shelley wrote, "which amused Shelley exceedingly and suggested the poem.") And the following year Byron in Ravenna wrote the brutal *Epilogue* printed here. (Byron did not overestimate Wordsworth. "We learn from Horace, 'Homer sometimes sleeps;'/We know without him, Wordsworth sometimes wakes," he wrote in *Don Juan*.) Wordsworth composed a rather feeble sonnet against his parodists—fittingly, it was itself an imitation of Milton's *Tetrachordon*—which begins:

> A book came forth of late called *Peter Bell;*
> Not negligent the style; the matter? good
> As aught that song records of Robin Hood. . . .

But it was difficult to defend *Peter Bell*.

A Sonnet

Two voices are there: one is of the deep;
It learns the storm-cloud's thunderous melody,
Now roars, now murmurs with the changing sea,
Now bird-like pipes, now closes soft in sleep:
And one is of an old half-witted sheep
Which bleats articulate monotony,
And indicates that two and one are three,
That grass is green, lakes damp, and mountains steep:
And, Wordsworth, both are thine: at certain times
Forth from the heart of thy melodious rhymes,
The form and pressure of high thoughts will burst:
At other times—good Lord! I'd rather be

Quite unacquainted with the ABC
Than write such hopeless rubbish as thy worst.

J. K. STEPHEN

The Baby's Debut

Thy lisping prattle and thy mincing gait,
All thy false mimic fooleries I hate;
For thou art Folly's counterfeit, and she
Who is right foolish hath the better plea:
Nature's true idiot I prefer to thee.

CUMBERLAND.

[*Spoken in the character of Nancy Lake, a girl eight
years of age, who is drawn upon the stage in a
child's chaise by Samuel Hughes, her uncle's
porter.*]

MY brother Jack was nine in May,[1]

And I was eight on New-year's-day;
So in Kate Wilson's shop
Papa (he's my papa and Jack's)
Bought me, last week, a doll of wax,
And brother Jack a top.

Jack 's in the pouts, and this it is,—
He thinks mine came to more than his;
So to my drawer he goes,
Takes out the doll, and, O, my stars!
He pokes her head between the bars,
And melts off half her nose!

[1] Jack and Nancy, as it was afterwards remarked to the Authors, are here
made to come into the world at periods not sufficiently remote. The writers
were then bachelors. One of them, unfortunately, still continues so, as he
has thus recorded in his niece's album:

"Should I seek Hymen's tie,
As a poet I die—

Quite cross, a bit of string I beg,
And tie it to his peg-top's peg,
    And bang, with might and main,
Its head against the parlour-door:
Off flies the head, and hits the floor,
    And breaks a window-pane.

This made him cry with rage and spite:
Well, let him cry, it serves him right.
    A pretty thing, forsooth!
If he's to melt, all scalding hot,
Half my doll's nose, and I am not
    To draw his peg-top's tooth!

Aunt Hannah heard the window break,
And cried, "O naughty Nancy Lake,
    Thus to distress your aunt:
No Drury Lane for you to-day!"
And while Papa said, "Pooh, she may!"
    Mamma said, "No, she sha'n't!"

Well, after many a sad reproach,
They got into a hackney coach,
    And trotted down the street.
I saw them go: one horse was blind,
The tails of both hung down behind,
    Their shoes were on their feet.

The chaise in which poor brother Bill
Used to be drawn to Pentonville

    Ye Benedicks, mourn my distresses!
      For what little fame
      Is annexed to my name
    Is derived from *Rejected Addresses*."

  The blunder, notwithstanding, remains unrectified. The reader of poetry is always dissatisfied with emendations: they sound discordantly upon the ear, like a modern song, by Bishop or Braham, introduced in *Love in a Village*.

Stood in the lumber-room:
I wiped the dust from off the top,
While Molly mopp'd it with a mop,
    And brush'd it with a broom.

My uncle's porter, Samuel Hughes,
Came in at six to black the shoes,
    (I always talk to Sam:)
So what does he, but takes, and drags
Me in the chaise along the flags,
    And leaves me where I am.

My father's walls are made of brick,
But not so tall and not so thick
    As these; and, goodness me!
My father's beams are made of wood,
But never, never half so good
    As those that now I see.

What a large floor! 'tis like a town!
The carpet, when they lay it down,
    Won't hide it, I'll be bound;
And there's a row of lamps!—my eye!
How they do blaze! I wonder why
    They keep them on the ground.

At first I caught hold of the wing,
And kept away; but Mr. Thing-
    umbob, the prompter man,
Gave with his hand my chaise a shove,
And said, "Go on, my pretty love;
    "Speak to 'em, little Nan.

"You've only got to curtsy, whisper, hold your chin up, laugh, and lisp,
    And then you're sure to take:
I've known the day when brats, not quite

Thirteen, got fifty pounds a-night;[2]
    Then why not Nancy Lake?"

But while I'm speaking, where's papa?
And where's my aunt? and where's mamma?
    Where's Jack? O, there they sit!
They smile, they nod; I'll go my ways,
And order round poor Billy's chaise,
    To join them in the pit.

And now, good gentlefolks, I go
To join mamma, and see the show;
    So, bidding you adieu,
I curtsy, like a pretty miss,
And if you'll blow to me a kiss,
    I'll blow a kiss to you.
            [Blows a kiss, and exit.]
                JAMES SMITH

On Oxford

THE Gothic looks solemn,
    The plain Doric column
Supports an old Bishop and Crosier;
    The mouldering arch,
    Shaded o'er by a larch
Stands next door to Wilson the Hosier.

    Vicè—that is, by turns,—
    O'er pale faces mourns

[2] This alludes to the young Betty mania. The writer was in the stage-box
at the height of this young gentleman's popularity. One of the other occupants offered, in a loud voice, to prove that young Betty did not understand Shakespeare. "Silence!" was the cry; but he still proceeded. "Turn him
out!" was the next ejaculation. He still vociferated, "He does not understand
Shakespeare;" and was consequently shouldered into the lobby. "I'll prove it
to you," said the critic to the door-keeper. "Prove what, sir?" "That he does.

The black tassell'd trencher and common hat;
　　The Chantry boy sings,
　　The Steeple-bell rings,
And as for the Chancellor—*dominat.*

　　There are plenty of trees,
　　And plenty of ease,
And plenty of fat deer for Parsons;
　　And when it is venison,
　　Short is the benison,—
Then each on a leg or thigh fastens.

JOHN KEATS

Fragment

THERE is a river clear and fair,
'Tis neither broad nor narrow;
It winds a little here and there—
It winds about like any hare;
And then it takes as straight a course
As on the turnpike road a horse,
　　Or through the air an arrow.

The trees that grow upon the shore,
Have grown a hundred years or more;
　　So long there is no knowing.
Old Daniel Dobson does not know
When first those trees began to grow;
But still they grew, and grew, and grew,
As if they'd nothing else to do,
　　But ever to be growing.

---

not understand Shakespeare." This was Molière's housemaid with a vengeance!
　　Young Betty may now be seen walking about town—a portly personage,
aged about forty—clad in a furred and frogged surtout; probably muttering
to himself (as he has been at college), "O mihi præteritos!" &c.

The impulses of air and sky
Have reared their stately stems so high,
    And clothed their boughs with green;
Their leaves the dews of evening quaff,—
    And when the wind blows loud and keen,
I've seen the jolly timbers laugh,
    And shake their sides with merry glee—
    Wagging their heads in mockery.

Fix'd are their feet in solid earth,
    Where winds can never blow;
But visitings of deeper birth
    Have reached their roots below.
For they have gained the river's brink,
And of the living waters drink.

There's little Will, a five years' child—
    He is my youngest boy;
To look on eyes so fair and wild,
    It is a very joy:—
He hath conversed with sun and shower,
And dwelt with every idle flower,
    As fresh and gay as them.
He loiters with the briar rose,—
The blue bells are his play-fellows,
    That dance upon their slender stem.

And I have said, my little Will,
Why should not he continue still
    A thing of Nature's rearing?
A thing beyond the world's control—
A living vegetable soul,—
    No human sorrow fearing.

It were a blessed sight to see
That child become a willow-tree,
    His brother trees among.

He'd be four times as tall as me,
  And live three times as long.

CATHERINE FANSHAWE

James Rigg

ON TUESDAY morn at half-past six o'clock,
I rose and dressed myself, and having shut
The door o' the bedroom still and leisurely,
I walk'd downstairs. When at the outer-door
I firmly grasped the key that 'ere night-fall
Had turned the lock into its wonted niche
Within the brazen implement, that shone
With no unseemly splendour,—mellow'd light,
Elicited by touch of careful-hand
On the brown lintel; and the obedient door,
As at a potent necromancer's touch,
Into the air receded suddenly,
And gave wide prospect of the sparkling lake,
Just then emerging from the snow-white mist
Like angel's veil slow-folded up to heaven.
And lo! a vision bright and beautiful
Sheds a refulgent glory o'er the sand,
The sand and gravel of my avenue!
For standing silent by the kitchen-door,
Tinged by the morning sun, and in its own
Brown natural hide most lovely, two long ears
Upstretching perpendicularly, then
With the horizon levelled—to my gaze
Superb as horn of fabled Unicorn,
Each in its own proportions grander far
Than the frontal glory of that wandering beast,
Child of the Desert! Lo! a beauteous Ass,
With paniers hanging silent at each side!

Silent as cage of bird whose song is mute,
Though silent yet not empty, fill'd with bread
The staff of life, the means by which the soul
By fate obedient to the powers of sense,
Renews its faded vigour, and keeps up
A proud communion with the eternal heavens.
Fasten'd to a ring it stood, while at its head
A boy of six years old, as angel bright,
Patted its neck and to its mouth applied
The harmless thistle that his hand had pluck'd
From the wild common, melancholy crop.

JAMES HOGG

The Flying Tailor

FURTHER EXTRACT FROM "THE RECLUSE," A POEM

IF ever chance or choice thy footsteps lead
Into that green and flowery burial-ground
That compasseth with sweet and mournful smiles
The church of Grasmere,—by the eastern gate
Enter—and underneath a stunted yew,
Some three yards distant from the gravel-walk,
On the left-hand side, thou wilt espy a grave,
With unelaborate headstone beautified,
Conspicuous 'mid the other stoneless heaps
'Neath which the children of the valley lie.
There pause—and with no common feelings read
This short inscription—"Here lies buried
The Flying Tailor, aged twenty-nine!"
    Him from his birth unto his death I knew,
And many years before he had attain'd
The fulness of his fame, I prophesied
The triumphs of that youth's agility,

And crown'd him with that name which afterwards
He nobly justified—and dying left
To fame's eternal blazon—read it here—
"The Flying Tailor!"

                          It is somewhat strange
That his mother was a cripple, and his father
Long way declined into the vale of years
When their son Hugh was born. At first the babe
Was sickly, and a smile was seen to pass
Across the midwife's cheek, when, holding up
The sickly wretch, she to the father said,
"A fine man-child!" What else could they expect?
The mother being, as I said before,
A cripple, and the father of the child
Long way declined into the vale of years.

But mark the wondrous change—ere he was put
By his mother into breeches, Nature strung
The muscular part of his economy
To an unusual strength, and he could leap
All unimpeded by his petticoats,
Over the stool on which his mother sat
When carding wool, or cleansing vegetables,
Or meek performing other household tasks.
Cunning he watch'd his opportunity,
And oft, as house-affairs did call her thence,
Overleapt Hugh, a perfect whirligig,
More than six inches o'er th' astonish'd stool.
What boots it to narrate, how at leap-frog
Over the breech'd and unbreech'd villagers
He shone conspicuous? Leap-frog do I say?
Vainly so named. What though in attitude
The Flying Tailor aped the croaking race
When issuing from the weed-entangled pool,

Tadpoles no more, they seek the new-mown fields,
A jocund people, bouncing to and fro
Amid the odorous clover—while amazed
The grasshopper sits idle on the stalk
With folded pinions and forgets to sing.
Frog-like, no doubt, in attitude he was;
But sure his bounds across the village green
Seem'd to my soul—(my soul for ever bright
With purest beams of sacred poesy)—
Like bounds of red-deer on the Highland hill,
When, close-environed by the tinchel's chain,
He lifts his branchy forehead to the sky,
Then o'er the many-headed multitude
Springs belling half in terror, half in rage,
And fleeter than the sunbeam or the wind
Speeds to his cloud-lair on the mountain-top.

No more of this—suffice it to narrate,
In his tenth year he was apprenticed
Unto a Master Tailor by a strong
And regular indenture of seven years,
Commencing from the date the parchment bore,
And ending on a certain day, that made
The term complete of seven solar years.
Oft have I heard him say, that at this time
Of life he was most wretched; for, constrain'd
To sit all day cross-legg'd upon a board,
The natural circulation of the blood
Thereby was oft impeded, and he felt
So numb'd at times, that when he strove to rise
Up from his work he could not, but fell back
Among the shreds and patches that bestrew'd
With various colours, brightening gorgeously,
The board all round him—patch of warlike red
With which he patched the regimental-suits

Of a recruiting military troop,
At that time stationed in a market town
At no great distance—eke of solemn black
Shreds of no little magnitude, with which
The parson's Sunday-coat was then repairing,
That in the new-roof'd church he might appear
With fitting dignity—and gravely fill
The sacred seat of pulpit eloquence,
Cheering with doctrinal point and words of faith
The poor man's heart, and from the shallow wit
Of atheist drying up each argument,
Or sharpening his own weapons only to turn
Their point against himself, and overthrow
His idols with the very enginery
Reared 'gainst the structure of our English Church.

Oft too, when striving all he could to finish
The stated daily task, the needle's point,
Slanting insidious from th' eluded stitch,
Hath pinched his finger, by the thimble's mail
In vain defended, and the crimson blood
Distain'd the lining of some wedding-suit;
A dismal omen! that to mind like his,
Apt to perceive in slightest circumstance
Mysterious meaning, yielded sore distress
And feverish perturbation, so that oft
He scarce could eat his dinner—nay, one night
He swore to run from his apprenticeship,
And go on board a first-rate man-of-war,
From Plymouth lately come to Liverpool,
Where, in the stir and tumult of a crew
Composed of many nations, 'mid the roar
Of wave and tempest, and the deadlier voice
Of battle, he might strive to mitigate
The fever that consumed his mighty heart.

But other doom was his. That very night
A troop of tumblers came into the village,
Tumbler, equestrian, mountebank,—on wire,
On rope, on horse, with cup and balls, intent
To please the gaping multitude, and win
The coin from labour's pocket—small perhaps
Each separate piece of money, but when join'd
Making a good round sum, destined ere long
All to be melted, (so these lawless folk
Name spending coin in loose debauchery)
Melted into ale—or haply stouter cheer,
Gin diuretic, or the liquid flame
Of baneful brandy, by the smuggler brought
From the French coast in shallop many-oar'd,
Skulking by night round headland and through bay,
Afraid of the King's cutter, or the barge
Of cruising frigate, arm'd with chosen men,
And with her sweeps across the foamy waves
Moving most beautiful with measured strokes.

It chanced that as he threw a somerset
Over three horses (each of larger size
Than our small mountain-breed) one of the troop
Put out his shoulder, and was otherwise
Considerably bruised, especially
About the loins and back. So he became
Useless unto that wandering company,
And likely to be felt a sore expense
To men just on the eve of bankruptcy,
So the master of the troop determined
To leave him in the workhouse, and proclaim'd
That if there was a man among the crowd
Willing to fill his place and able too,
Now was the time to show himself. Hugh Thwaites
Heard the proposal, as he stood apart

Striving with his own soul—and with a bound
He leapt into the circle, and agreed
To supply the place of him who had been hurt.
A shout of admiration and surprise
Then tore heaven's concave, and completely fill'd
The little field, where near a hundred people
Were standing in a circle round and fair.
Oft have I striven by meditative power,
And reason working 'mid the various forms
Of various occupations and professions,
To explain the cause of one phenomenon,
That, since the birth of science, hath remain'd
A bare enunciation, unexplain'd
By any theory, or mental light
Stream'd on it by the imaginative will,
Or spirit musing in the cloudy shrine,
The Penetralia of the immortal soul.
I now allude to that most curious fact,
That 'mid a given number, say threescore,
Of tailors, more men of agility
Will issue out, than from an equal show
From any other occupation—say
Smiths, barbers, bakers, butchers, or the like.

Let me not seem presumptuous, if I strive
This subject to illustrate; nor, while I give
My meditations to the world, will I
Conceal from it, that much I have to say
I learnt from one who knows the subject well
In theory and practice—need I name him?
The light-heel'd author of the Isle of Palms,
Illustrious more for leaping than for song.

    First, then, I would lay down this principle,
That all excessive action by the law

Of nature tends unto repose. This granted,
All action not excessive must partake
The nature of excessive action—so
That in all human beings who keep moving,
Unconscious cultivation of repose
Is going on in silence. Be it so.
Apply to men of sedentary lives
This leading principle, and we behold
That, active in their inactivity,
And unreposing in their long repose,
They are, in fact, the sole depositaries
Of all the energies by others wasted,
And come at last to teem with impulses
Of muscular motion, not to be withstood,
And either giving vent unto themselves
In numerous feats of wild agility,
Or terminating in despair and death.

Now, of all sedentary lives, none seems
So much so as the tailor's.—Weavers use
Both arms and legs, and, we may safely add,
Their bodies too, for arms and legs can't move
Without the body—as the waving branch
Of the green oak disturbs his glossy trunk.
Not so the Tailor—for he sits cross-legg'd,
Cross-legg'd for ever! save at time of meals,
In bed, or when he takes his little walk
From shop to alehouse, picking, as he goes,
Stray patch of fustian, cloth, or cassimere,
Which, as by natural instinct, he discerns,
Though soil'd with mud, and by the passing wheel
Bruised to attenuation 'gainst the stones.

Here then we pause—and need no farther go,
We have reach'd the sea-mark of our utmost sail.

Now let me trace the effect upon his mind
Of this despised profession. Deem not thou,
O rashly deem not, that his boyish days
Past at the shop-board, when the stripling bore
With bashful feeling of apprenticeship
The name of Tailor, deem not that his soul
Derived no genial influence from a life,
Which, although haply adverse in the main
To the growth of intellect, and the excursive power,
Yet in its ordinary forms possessed
A constant influence o'er his passing thoughts,
Moulded his appetences and his will,
And wrought out, by the work of sympathy,
Between his bodily and mental form,
Rare correspondence, wond'rous unity!
Perfect—complete—and fading not away.
While on his board cross-legg'd he used to sit,
Shaping of various garments, to his mind
An image rose of every character
For whom each special article was framed,
Coat, waistcoat, breeches. So at last his soul
Was like a storehouse, filled with images,
By musing hours of solitude supplied.
Nor did his ready fingers shape the cut
Of villager's uncouth habiliments
With greater readiness, than did his mind
Frame corresponding images of those
Whose corporal measurement the neat-mark'd paper
In many a mystic notch for ay retain'd.
Hence, more than any man I ever knew,
Did he possess the power intuitive
Of diving into character. A pair
Of breeches to his philosophic eye
Were not what unto other folks they seem,

Mere simple breeches, but in them he saw
The symbol of the soul—mysterious, high
Hieroglyphics! such as Egypt's Priest
Adored upon the holy Pyramid,
Vainly imagined tomb of monarchs old,
But raised by wise philosophy, that sought
By darkness to illumine, and to spread
Knowledge by dim concealment—process high
Of man's imaginative, deathless soul.
Nor, haply, in th' abasement of the life
Which stern necessity had made his own,
Did he not recognise a genial power
Of soul-ennobling fortitude. He heard
Unmoved the witling's shallow contumely,
And thus, in spite of nature, by degrees
He saw a beauty and a majesty
In this despised trade, which warrior's brow
Hath rarely circled—so that when he sat
Beneath his sky-light window, he hath cast
A gaze of triumph on the godlike sun,
And felt that orb, in all his annual round,
Beheld no happier nobler character
Than him, Hugh Thwaites, a little tailor-boy.

Thus I, with no unprofitable song,
Have, in the silence of th' umbrageous wood,
Chaunted the heroic youthful attributes
Of him the Flying Tailor. Much remains
Of highest argument, to lute or lyre
Fit to be murmur'd with impassion'd voice;
And when, by timely supper and by sleep
Refresh'd, I turn me to the welcome task,
With lofty hopes,—Reader, do thou expect
The final termination of my lay.
For, mark my words,—eternally my name

Shall last on earth, conspicuous like a star
'Mid that bright galaxy of favour'd spirits,
Who, laugh'd at constantly whene'er they publish'd,
Survived the impotent scorn of base Reviews,
Monthly or Quarterly, or that accursed
Journal, the Edinburgh Review, that lives
On tears, and sighs, and groans, and brains, and blood.

JAMES HOGG

Peter Bell: A Lyrical Ballad

I.

IT IS the thirty-first of March,
A gusty evening—half-past seven;
The moon is shining o'er the larch,
A simple shape—a cock'd-up arch,
Rising bigger than a star,
Though the stars are thick in Heaven

II.

Gentle moon! how canst thou shine
Over graves and over trees,
With as innocent a look
As my own grey eyeball sees,
When I gaze upon a brook?

III.

Od's me! how the moon doth shine:
It doth make a pretty glitter,
Playing in the waterfall;
As when Lucy Gray doth litter
Her baby-house with bugles small.

IV.

Beneath the ever blessed moon
An old man o'er an old grave stares,
You never look'd upon his fellow;
His brow is covered with grey hairs,
As though they were an umbrella.

V.

He hath a noticeable look,[1]
This old man hath—this grey old man;
He gazes at the graves, and seems,
With over waiting, over wan,
Like Susan Harvey's[2] pan of creams.

VI.

'T is Peter Bell—'t is Peter Bell,
Who never stirreth in the day;
His hand is wither'd—he is old!
On Sundays he is us'd to pray,
In winter he is very cold.[3]

VII.

I've seen him in the month of August,
At the wheatfield, hour by hour,
Picking ear,—by ear,—by ear,—
Through wind,—and rain,—and sun,—and shower,
From year,—to year,—to year,—to year.

---

[1] 'A noticeable man with large grey eyes.'—*Lyrical Ballads.*
[2] Dairy-maid to Mr. Gill.
[3] Peter Bell resembleth Harry Gill in this particular:
    "His teeth they chatter, chatter, chatter."
I should have introduced this fact in the text, but that Harry Gill would not
rhyme. I reserve this for my blank verse.

VIII.

You never saw a wiser man,
He knows his Numeration Table;
He counts the sheep of Harry Gill,[4]
Every night that he is able,
When the sheep are on the hill.

IX.

Betty Foy—*My* Betty Foy,—
Is the aunt of Peter Bell;
And credit me, as I would have you,
Simon Lee was once his nephew,
And his niece is Alice Fell.

X.

He is rurally related;
Peter Bell hath country cousins,
(He had once a worthy mother)
Bells and Peters by the dozens,
But Peter Bell he hath no brother.

XI.

Not a brother owneth he,
Peter Bell he hath no brother,
His mother had no other son,
No other son e'er call'd her mother;
Peter Bell hath brother none.*

* The remaining thirty-one verses are omitted.

JOHN HAMILTON REYNOLDS

[4] Harry Gill was the original proprietor of Barbara Lewthwaite's pet lamb;
and he also bred Betty Foy's celebrated pony, got originally out of a Nightmare, by a descendant of the great Trojan horse.

Epilogue

THERE'S something in a stupid ass:
And something in a heavy dunce;
But never since I went to school
I saw or heard so damned a fool
As William Wordsworth is for once.

And now I've seen so great a fool
As William Wordsworth is for once,
I really wish that Peter Bell
And he who wrote it were in hell,
For writing nonsense for the nonce.

I saw the "light in ninety-eight,"
Sweet Babe of one and twenty years!
And then he gave it to the nation,
And deems himself of Shakespeare's peers.
He gives the perfect works to light!
William Wordsworth—if I might advise,
Content you with the praise you get
From Sir George Beaumont, Baronet,
And with your place in the excise.

RAVENNA, March 22, 1820.

LORD BYRON

Malvolio

THOU HAST BEEN very tender to the Moon,
Malvolio! and on many a daffodil
And many a daisy hast thou yearned until
The nether jaw quivered with thy good heart.
But tell me now, Malvolio, tell me true,
Hast thou not sometimes driven from their play
The village children, when they came too near

Thy study, if hit ball rais'd shouts around,
Or if delusive trap shook off thy Muse
Pregnant with wonders for another age?
Hast thou sat still and patient (tho' sore prest
Hearthward to stoop and warm thy blue-nail'd hand)
Lest thou should frighten from a frosty fare
The speckled thrush, raising his bill aloft
To swallow the red berry on the ash
By thy white window, three short paces off?
If *this* thou hast not done, and hast done *that,*
I do exile thee from the Moon twelve whole
Calendar months, debarring thee from use
Of rose, bud blossom, odor, simile,
And furthermore I do hereby pronounce
Divorce between the nightingale and thee.

WALTER SAVAGE LANDOR

He Lived amidst th' Untrodden Ways

HE lived amidst th' untrodden ways
  To Rydal Lake that lead;
A bard whom there were none to praise,
  And very few to read.

Behind a cloud his mystic sense,
  Deep hidden, who can spy?
Bright as the night when not a star
  Is shining in the sky.

Unread his works—his "Milk White Doe"
  With dust is dark and dim;
It's still in Longman's shop, and oh!
  The difference to him!

HARTLEY COLERIDGE

JAMES FENIMORE COOPER

Muck-a-Muck

CHAPTER I

IT WAS toward the close of a bright October day. The last rays of the setting sun were reflected from one of those sylvan lakes peculiar to the Sierras of California. On the right the curling smoke of an Indian village rose between the columns of the lofty pines, while to the left the log cottage of Judge Tompkins, embowered in buckeyes, completed the enchanting picture.

Although the exterior of the cottage was humble and unpretentious, and in keeping with the wildness of the landscape, its interior gave evidence of the cultivation and refinement of its inmates. An aquarium, containing goldfishes, stood on a marble centre-table at one end of the apartment, while a magnificent grand piano occupied the other. The floor was covered with a yielding tapestry carpet, and the walls were adorned with paintings from the pencils of Van Dyke, Rubens, Tintoretto, Michael Angelo, and the productions of the more modern Turner, Kensett, Church, and Bierstadt. Although Judge Tompkins had chosen the frontiers of civilization as his home, it was impossible for him to entirely forego the habits and tastes of his former life. He was seated in a luxurious armchair, writing at a mahogany *écritoire,* while his daughter, a lovely young girl of seventeen summers, plied her crochet-needle on an ottoman beside him. A bright fire of pine logs flickered and flamed on the ample hearth.

Genevra Octavia Tompkins was Judge Tompkins' only child. Her mother had long since died on the Plains. Reared in affluence, no pains had been spared with the daughter's education. She was a graduate of one of the principal seminaries, and spoke French with a perfect Benicia accent. Peerlessly beautiful, she was dressed in a white *moire antique* robe trimmed with *tulle.* That simple rosebud, with which most heroines exclusively decorate their hair, was all she wore in her raven locks.

The Judge was the first to break the silence.

"Genevra, the logs which compose yonder fire seem to have been incautiously chosen. The sibilation produced by the sap, which exudes copiously therefrom, is not conducive to composition."

"True, father, but I thought it would be preferable to the constant crepitation which is apt to attend the combustion of more seasoned ligneous fragments."

The Judge looked admiringly at the intellectual features of the graceful girl, and half forgot the slight annoyances of the green wood in the musical accents of his daughter. He was smoothing her hair tenderly, when the shadow of a tall figure, which suddenly darkened the doorway, caused him to look up.

CHAPTER II

IT NEEDED but a glance at the new-comer to detect at once the form and features of the haughty aborigine—the untaught and untrammelled son of the forest. Over one shoulder a blanket, negligently but gracefully thrown, disclosed a bare and powerful breast, decorated with a quantity of three-cent postage-stamps which he had despoiled from an Overland Mail stage a few weeks previously. A cast-off beaver of Judge Tompkins', adorned by a simple feather, covered his erect head, from beneath which his straight locks descended. His right hand hung lightly by his side, while his left was engaged in holding on a pair of pantaloons, which the lawless grace and freedom of his lower limbs evidently could not brook.

"Why," said the Indian, in a low sweet tone,—"why does the Pale Face still follow the track of the Red Man? Why does he pursue him, even as *O-kee-chow,* the wild-cat, chases *Ka-ka,* the skunk? Why are the feet of *Sorrel-top,* the white chief, among the acorns of *Muck-a-Muck,* the mountain forest? Why," he repeated, quietly but firmly abstracting a silver spoon from the table,—"why do you seek to drive him from the wigwams of his fathers? His brothers are already gone to the happy hunting-grounds. Will the Pale Face seek him there?" And, averting his face from the Judge, he hastily slipped a silver cake-basket beneath his blanket, to conceal his emotion.

"*Muck-a-Muck* has spoken," said Genevra, softly. "Let him now listen. Are the acorns of the mountain sweeter than the esculent and nutritious bean of the Pale Face miner? Does my brother prize the edible qualities of the snail above that of the crisp and oleaginous bacon? Delicious are the grasshoppers that sport on the hillside,—are they better than the dried apples of the Pale Faces? Pleasant is the gurgle of the torrent, *Kish-Kish,* but is it better than the cluck-cluck of old Bourbon from the old stone bottle?"

"Ugh!" said the Indian,—"ugh! good. The White Rabbit is wise. Her words fall as the snow on Tootoonolo, and the rocky heart of Muck-a-Muck is hidden. What says my brother the Gray Gopher of Dutch Flat?"

"She has spoken, Muck-a-Muck," said the Judge, gazing fondly on his daughter. "It is well. Our treaty is concluded. No, thank you,—you need *not* dance the Dance of Snow Shoes, or the Moccasin Dance, the Dance of Green Corn, or the Treaty Dance. I would be alone. A strange sadness overpowers me."

"I go," said the Indian. "Tell your great chief in Washington, the Sachem Andy, that the Red Man is retiring before the footsteps of the adventurous Pioneer. Inform him, if you please, that westward the star of empire takes its way, that the chiefs of the Pi-Ute nation are for Reconstruction to a man, and that Klamath will poll a heavy Republican vote in the fall."

And folding his blanket more tightly around him, Muck-a-Muck withdrew.

CHAPTER III

GENEVRA TOMPKINS stood at the door of the log-cabin, looking after the retreating Overland Mail stage which conveyed her father to Virginia City. "He may never return again," sighed the young girl as she glanced at the frightfully rolling vehicle and wildly careering horses,—"at least, with unbroken bones. Should he meet with an accident! I mind me now a fearful legend, familiar to my childhood. Can it be that the drivers on this line are privately instructed to despatch all passengers maimed by accident, to prevent tedious litigation? No, no. But why this weight upon my heart?"

She seated herself at the piano and lightly passed her hand over the keys. Then, in a clear mezzo-soprano voice, she sang the first verse of one of the most popular Irish ballads:—

"O Arrah, my dheelish, the distant dudheen
Lies soft in the moonlight, ma bouchal vourneen:
The springing gossoons on the heather are still,
And the caubeens and colleens are heard on the hills."

But as the ravishing notes of her sweet voice died upon the air, her hands sank listlessly to her side. Music could not chase away the mysterious shadow from her heart. Again she rose. Putting on a white crape bonnet, and carefully drawing a pair of lemon-colored gloves over her taper fingers, she seized her parasol and plunged into the depths of the pine forest.

CHAPTER IV

GENEVRA had not proceeded many miles before a weariness seized upon her fragile limbs, and she would fain seat herself upon the trunk of a prostrate pine, which she previously dusted with her handkerchief. The sun was just sinking below the horizon, and the scene was one of gorgeous and sylvan beauty. "How beautiful is Nature!" murmured the innocent girl, as, reclining gracefully against the root of the tree, she gathered up her skirts and tied a handkerchief around her throat. But a low growl interrupted her meditation. Starting to her feet, her eyes met a sight which froze her blood with terror.

The only outlet to the forest was the narrow path, barely wide enough for a single person, hemmed in by trees and rocks, which she had just traversed. Down this path, in Indian file, came a monstrous grizzly, followed by a California lion, a wild-cat, and a buffalo, the rear being brought up by a wild Spanish bull. The mouths of the first three animals were distended with frightful significance; the horns of the last were lowered as ominously. As Genevra was preparing to faint, she heard a low voice behind her.

"Eternally dog-gone my skin ef this ain't the puttiest chance yet."

At the same moment, a long, shining barrel dropped lightly from behind her, and rested over her shoulder.

Genevra shuddered.

"Dern ye—don't move!"

Genevra became motionless.

The crack of a rifle rang through the woods. Three frightful yells were heard, and two sullen roars. Five animals bounded into the air and five lifeless bodies lay upon the plain. The well-aimed bullet had done its work. Entering the open throat of the grizzly, it had traversed his body only to enter the throat of the California lion, and in like manner the catamount, until it passed through into the respective foreheads of the bull and the buffalo, and finally fell flattened from the rocky hillside.

Genevra turned quickly. "My preserver!" she shrieked, and fell into the arms of Natty Bumpo, the celebrated Pike Ranger of Donner Lake.

CHAPTER V

THE MOON rose cheerfully above Donner Lake. On its placid bosom a dug-out canoe glided rapidly, containing Natty Bumpo and Genevra Tompkins.

Both were silent. The same thought possessed each, and perhaps there was sweet companionship even in the unbroken quiet. Genevra bit the handle of her parasol and blushed. Natty Bumpo took a fresh chew of tobacco. At length Genevra said, as if in half-spoken revery:—

"The soft shining of the moon and the peaceful ripple of the waves seem to say to us various things of an instructive and moral tendency."

"You may bet yer pile on that, Miss," said her companion, gravely. "It's all the preachin' and psalm-singin' I've heern since I was a boy."

"Noble being!" said Miss Tompkins to herself, glancing at the stately Pike as he bent over his paddle to conceal his emotion. "Reared in this wild seclusion, yet he has become penetrated

with visible consciousness of a Great First Cause." Then, collecting herself, she said aloud: "Methinks 't were pleasant to
glide ever thus down the stream of life, hand in hand with the
one being whom the soul claims as its affinity. But what am I
saying?"—and the delicate-minded girl hid her face in her hands.

A long silence ensued, which was at length broken by her companion.

"Ef you mean you're on the marry," he said, thoughtfully, "I
ain't in no wise partikler!"

"My husband," faltered the blushing girl; and she fell into his
arms.

In ten minutes more the loving couple had landed at Judge
Tompkins'.

CHAPTER VI

A YEAR has passed away. Natty Bumpo was returning from
Gold Hill, where he had been to purchase provisions. On his
way to Donner Lake, rumors of an Indian uprising met his ears.
"Dern their pesky skins, ef they dare to touch my Jenny," he
muttered between his clenched teeth.

It was dark when he reached the borders of the lake. Around
a glittering fire he dimly discerned dusky figures dancing. They
were in war paint. Conspicuous among them was the renowned
Muck-a-Muck. But why did the fingers of Natty Bumpo tighten
convulsively around his rifle?

The chief held in his hand long tufts of raven hair. The heart
of the pioneer sickened as he recognized the clustering curls of
Genevra. In a moment his rifle was at his shoulder, and with a
sharp "ping," Muck-a-Muck leaped into the air a corpse. To
knock out the brains of the remaining savages, tear the tresses
from the stiffening hand of Muck-a-Muck, and dash rapidly
forward to the cottage of Judge Tompkins, was the work of a
moment.

He burst open the door. Why did he stand transfixed with
open mouth and distended eyeballs? Was the sight too horrible
to be borne? On the contrary, before him, in her peerless beauty,
stood Genevra Tompkins, leaning on her father's arm.

"Ye'r not scalped, then!" gasped her lover.

"No. I have no hesitation in saying that I am not; but why this abruptness?" responded Genevra.

Bumpo could not speak, but frantically produced the silken tresses. Genevra turned her face aside.

"Why, that's her waterfall!" said the Judge.

Bumpo sank fainting to the floor.

The famous Pike chieftain never recovered from the deceit, and refused to marry Genevra, who died, twenty years afterwards, of a broken heart. Judge Tompkins lost his fortune in Wild Cat. The stage passes twice a week the deserted cottage at Donner Lake. Thus was the death of Muck-a-Muck avenged.

BRET HARTE

EDGAR ALLAN POE

The Amateur Flute

HEAR the fluter with his flute,
    Silver flute!
Oh, what a world of wailing is awakened by its toot!
    How it demi-semi quavers
      On the maddened air of night!
    And defieth all endeavors
      To escape the sound or sigh
    Of the flute, flute, flute,
    With its tootle, tootle, toot;
With reiterated tooteling of exasperating toots,
The long protracted tootelings of agonizing toots.
    Of the flute, flute, flute, flute,
      Flute, flute, flute,
And the wheezings and the spittings of its toots.
    Should he get that other flute,
      Golden flute,

Oh, what a deeper anguish will his presence institoot!
How his eyes to heaven he'll raise,
As he plays,
All the days!
How he'll stop us on our ways
With its praise!
And the people—oh, the people,
That don't live up in the steeple,
But inhabit Christian parlors
Where he visiteth and plays,
Where he plays, plays, plays
In the cruellest of ways,
And thinks we ought to listen,
And expects us to be mute,
Who would rather have the earache
Than the music of his flute,
Of his flute, flute, flute,
And the tootings of his toot,
Of the toots wherewith he tooteleth its agonizing toot,
Of the flute, flewt, fluit, floot,
Phlute, phlewt, phlewght,
And the tootle, tootle, tooting of its toot.

Anonymous

The Promissory Note

IN THE lonesome latter years
(Fatal years!)
To the dropping of my tears
Danced the mad and mystic spheres
In a rounded, reeling rune,
'Neath the moon,
To the dripping and the dropping of my tears.
Ah, my soul is swathed in gloom,
(Ulalume!)

In a dim Titanic tomb,
For my gaunt and gloomy soul
Ponders o'er the penal scroll,
O'er the parchment (not a rhyme),
Out of place,—out of time,—
I am shredded, shorn, unshifty,
    (Oh, the fifty!)
And the days have passed, the three,
    Over me!
And the debit and the credit are as one to him and me!

'T was the random runes I wrote
At the bottom of the note,
    (Wrote and freely
    Gave to Greeley)
In the middle of the night,
In the mellow, moonless night,
When the stars were out of sight,
When my pulses, like a knell,
    (Israfel!)
Danced with dim and dying fays
O'er the ruins of my days,
O'er the dimeless, timeless days,
When the fifty, drawn at thirty,
Seeming thrifty, yet the dirty
Lucre of the market, was the most that I could raise!
    Fiends controlled it,
    (Let him hold it!)
Devils held for me the inkstand and the pen;
Now the days of grace are o'er,
    (Ah, Lenore!)
I am but as other men;
What is time, time, time,
To my rare and runic rhyme,
To my random, reeling rhyme,
By the sands along the shore,

Where the tempest whispers, "Pay him!" and I answer, "Never-
more!"

BAYARD TAYLOR

Ravings

THE AUTUMN upon us was rushing,
    The Parks were deserted and lone—
    The streets were unpeopled and lone;
My foot through the sere leaves was brushing,
    That over the pathway were strown—
    By the wind in its wanderings strown.
I sighed—for my feelings were gushing
    Round Mnemosyne's porphyry throne,
Like lava liquescent lay gushing,
    And rose to the porphyry throne—
To the filigree footstool were gushing,
    That stands on the steps of that throne—
    On the stolid stone steps of that throne!

I cried—"Shall the winter-leaves fret us?"
    Oh, turn—we must turn to the fruit,
    To the freshness and force of the fruit!
To the gifts wherewith Autumn has met us—
    Her music that never grows mute
    (That maunders but never grows mute),
The tendrils the vine branches net us,
    The lily, the lettuce, the lute—
The esculent, succulent lettuce,
    And the languishing lily, and lute;—
Yes;—the lotos-like leaves of the lettuce;
    Late lily and lingering lute.

Then come—let us fly from the city!
    Let us travel in orient isles—
    In the purple of orient isles—

Oh, bear me—yes, bear me in pity
   To climes where a sun ever smiles—
   Ever smoothly and speciously smiles!
Where the swarth-browed Arabian's wild ditty
   Enhances pyramidal piles:
Where his wild, weird, and wonderful ditty
   Awakens pyramidal piles—
Yes:—his pointless perpetual ditty
   Perplexes pyramidal piles!

THOMAS HOOD, THE YOUNGER

HENRY WADSWORTH LONGFELLOW

The Metre Columbian

THIS IS the metre Columbian. The soft-flowing trochees and
   dactyls,
Blended with fragments spondaic, and here and there an iambus,
Syllables often sixteen, or more or less, as it happens,
Difficult always to scan, and depending greatly on accent,
Being a close imitation, in English, of Latin hexameters—
Fluent in sound and avoiding the stiffness of blank verse,
Having the grandeur and flow of America's mountains and rivers,
Such as no bard could achieve in a mean little island like Eng-
   land;
Oft, at the end of a line, the sentence dividing abruptly
Breaks, and in accents mellifluous, follows the thoughts of the
   author.

Anonymous

What I Think of Hiawatha

Do YOU ask me what I think of
This new song of Hiawatha,

With its legends and traditions,
And its frequent repetitions
Of hard names which make the jaw ache,
And of words most unpoetic?
I should answer, I should tell you
I esteem it wild and wayward,
Slipshod metre, scanty sense,
Honour paid to Mudjekeewis,
But no honour to the muse.

J. W. MORRIS

The Modern Hiawatha

WHEN HE killed the Mudjokivis,
 Of the skin he made him mittens,
 Made them with the fur side inside,
 Made them with the skin side outside,
 He, to get the warm side inside,
 Put the inside skin side outside;
 He, to get the cold side outside,
 Put the warm side fur side inside.
 That's why he put the fur side inside,
 Why he put the skin side outside,
 Why he turned them inside outside.

Anonymous

FREDERICK LOCKER-LAMPSON

Vers de Société

THERE, pay it, James! 'tis cheaply earned;
 My conscience! how one's cabman charges!
But never mind, so I'm returned

Safe to my native street of Clarges.
I've just an hour for one cigar
   (What style these Reinas have, and *what ash!*)
One hour to watch the evening star
   With just one Curaçao-and-potash.

Ah me! that face beneath the leaves
   And blossoms of its piquant bonnet!
Who would have thought that forty thieves
   Of years had laid their fingers on it!
Could you have managed to enchant
   At Lord's to-day old lovers simple,
Had Robber Time not played gallant,
   And spared you every youthful dimple!

That Robber bold, like courtier Claude,
   Who danced the gay coranto jesting,
By your bright beauty charmed and awed,
   Has bowed and passed you unmolesting.
No feet of many-wintered crows
   Have traced about your eyes a wrinkle;
Your sunny hair has thawed the snows
   That other heads with silver sprinkle.

I wonder if that pair of gloves
   I won of you you'll ever pay me!
I wonder if our early loves
   Were wise or foolish, cousin Amy?
I wonder if our childish tiff
   Now seems to you, like me, a blunder!
I wonder if you wonder if
   I ever wonder if you wonder.

I wonder if you'd think it bliss
   Once more to be the fashion's leader!
I wonder if the trick of this

Escapes the unsuspecting reader!
And as for him who does or can
    Delight in it, I wonder whether
He knows that almost any man
    Could reel it off by yards together!

I wonder if— What's that? a knock?
    Is that you, James? Eh? What? God bless me!
How time has flown! It's eight o'clock,
    And here's my fellow come to dress me.
Be quick, or I shall be the guest
    Whom Lady Mary never pardons;
I trust you, James, to do your best
    To save the soup at Grosvenor Gardens.

                                    H. D. TRAILL

EDWARD LEAR

The Great Panjandrum

So SHE went into the garden
to cut a cabbage-leaf
to make an apple-pie;
and at the same time
a great she-bear, coming down the street,
pops its head into the shop.
What! no soap?
            So he died,
and she very imprudently married the Barber:
and there were present
the Picninnies,
            and the Joblillies,
                and the Garyulies,
and the great Panjandrum himself,

with the little round button at top;
and they all fell to playing the game of catch-as-
     catch-can,
till the gunpowder ran out at the heels of their boots.

SAMUEL FOOTE*

CHARLES DICKENS

Christmas Afternoon

WHAT AN afternoon! Mr. Gummidge said that, in his estimation, there never had *been* such an afternoon since the
world began, a sentiment which was heartily endorsed by Mrs.
Gummidge and all the little Gummidges, not to mention the
relatives who had come over from Jersey for the day.

In the first place, there was the *ennui*. And such *ennui* as it
was! A heavy, overpowering *ennui*, such as results from a par-
ticipation in eight courses of steaming, gravied food, topping off
with salted nuts which the little old spinster Gummidge from
Oak Hill said she never knew when to stop eating—and true
enough she didn't—a dragging, devitalizing *ennui*, which left its
victims strewn about the living room in various attitudes of
prostration suggestive of those of the petrified occupants in a
newly unearthed Pompeiian dwelling; an *ennui* which carried
with it a retinue of yawns, snarls and thinly veiled insults, and
which ended in ruptures in the clan spirit serious enough to last
throughout the glad new year.

Then there were the toys! Three and a quarter dozen toys to
be divided among seven children. Surely enough, you or I might
say, to satisfy the little tots. But that would be because we didn't
know the tots. In came Baby Lester Gummidge, Lillian's boy,
dragging an electric grain-elevator which happened to be the
only toy in the entire collection that appealed to little Norman,

---

* The interesting thing about this parody is that Samuel Foote died in
1777 and that Edward Lear was born in 1812.

five-year-old son of Luther, who lived in Rahway. In came curly-
headed Effie in frantic and throaty disputation with Arthur, Jr.,
over the possession of an articulated zebra. In came Everett,
bearing a mechanical negro which would no longer dance, owing
to a previous forcible feeding by the baby of a marshmallow into
its only available aperture. In came Fonlansbee, teeth buried in
the hand of little Ormond, who bore a popular but battered
remnant of what had once been the proud false bosom of a hus-
sar's uniform. In they all came, one after another, some crying,
some snapping, some pulling, some pushing—all appealing to
their respective parents for aid in their intramural warfare.

And the cigar smoke! Mrs. Gummidge said that she didn't
mind the smoke from a good cigarette, but would they mind if
she opened the windows for just a minute in order to clear the
room of the heavy aroma of used cigars? Mr. Gummidge stoutly
maintained that they were good cigars. His brother, George Gummidge, said that he, likewise, would say that they were. At which
colloquial sally both Gummidge brothers laughed testily, thereby
breaking the laughter record for the afternoon.

Aunt Libbie, who lived with George, remarked from the dark
corner of the room that it seemed just like Sunday to her. An
amendment was offered to this statement by the cousin, who was
in the insurance business, stating that it was worse than Sunday.
Murmurings indicative of as hearty agreement with this sentiment as their lethargy would allow came from the other members of the family circle, causing Mr. Gummidge to suggest a
walk in the air to settle their dinner.

And then arose such a chorus of protestations as has seldom
been heard. It was too cloudy to walk. It was too raw. It looked
like snow. It looked like rain. Luther Gummidge said that he
must be starting along home soon, anyway, bringing forth the
acid query from Mrs. Gummidge as to whether or not he was
bored. Lillian said that she felt a cold coming on, and added
that something they had had for dinner must have been under-
cooked. And so it went, back and forth, forth and back, up and
down, and in and out, until Mr. Gummidge's suggestion of a

walk in the air was reduced to a tattered impossibility and the entire company glowed with ill-feeling.

In the meantime, we must not forget the children. No one else could. Aunt Libbie said that she didn't think there was anything like children to make a Christmas; to which Uncle Ray, the one with the Masonic fob, said, "No, thank God!" Although Christmas is supposed to be the season of good cheer, you (or I, for that matter) couldn't have told, from listening to the little ones, but what it was the children's Armageddon season, when Nature had decreed that only the fittest should survive, in order that the race might be carried on by the strongest, the most predatory and those possessing the best protective coloring. Although there were constant admonitions to Fonlansbee to "Let Ormond have that whistle now; it's his," and to Arthur, Jr., not to be selfish, but to "give the kiddie-car to Effie; she's smaller than you are," the net result was always that Fonlansbee kept the whistle and Arthur, Jr., rode in permanent, albeit disputed, possession of the kiddie-car. Oh, that we mortals should set ourselves up against the inscrutable workings of Nature!

Hallo! A great deal of commotion! That was Uncle George stumbling over the electric train which had early in the afternoon ceased to function and which had been left directly across the threshold. A great deal of crying! That was Arthur, Jr., bewailing the destruction of his already useless train, about which he had forgotten until the present moment. A great deal of recrimination! That was Arthur, Sr., and George fixing it up. And finally a great crashing! That was Baby Lester pulling over the tree on top of himself, necessitating the bringing to bear of all of Uncle Ray's knowledge of forestry to extricate him from the wreckage.

And finally Mrs. Gummidge passed the Christmas candy around. Mr. Gummidge afterward admitted that this was a tactical error on the part of his spouse. I no more believe that Mrs. Gummidge thought they wanted that Christmas candy than I believe that she thought they wanted the cold turkey which she later suggested. My opinion is that she wanted to drive them home. At any rate, that is what she succeeded in doing. Such cries as there were of "Ugh! Don't let me see another thing to eat!" and "Take it away!" Then came hurried scramblings in the coat-closet for overshoes. There were the rasping sounds made by cross parents when putting wraps on children. There were insincere exhortations to "come and see us soon" and to "get together for lunch some time." And, finally, there were slammings of doors and the silence of utter exhaustion, while Mrs. Gummidge went about picking up stray sheets of wrapping paper.

And, as Tiny Tim might say in speaking of Christmas afternoon as an institution, "God help us, every one."

ROBERT BENCHLEY

ALFRED, LORD TENNYSON

The Laureate

WHO WOULD not be
The Laureate bold,
With his butt of sherry
To keep him merry,
And nothing to do but to pocket his gold?

'T is I would be the Laureate bold!
When the days are hot, and the sun is strong,
I'd lounge in the gateway all the day long
With her Majesty's footmen in crimson and gold.
I'd care not a pin for the waiting-lord,
But I'd lie on my back on the smooth greensward
With a straw in my mouth, and an open vest,
And the cool wind blowing upon my breast,
And I'd vacantly stare at the clear blue sky,
And watch the clouds that are listless as I,
Lazily, lazily!

And I'd pick the moss and the daisies white,
And chew their stalks with a nibbling bite;
And I'd let my fancies roam abroad
In search of a hint for a birthday ode,
      Crazily, crazily!

Oh, that would be the life for me,
With plenty to get and nothing to do,
But to deck a pet poodle with ribbons of blue,
And whistle all day to the Queen's cockatoo,
      Trance-somely, trance-somely!
Then the chambermaids, that clean the rooms,
Would come to the windows and rest on their brooms,

With their saucy caps and their crispéd hair,
And they'd toss their heads in the fragrant air,
And say to each other—"Just look down there,
At the nice young man, so tidy and small,
Who is paid for writing on nothing at all,
      Handsomely, handsomely!"

They would pelt me with matches and sweet pastilles,
And crumpled-up balls of the royal bills,
Giggling and laughing, and screaming with fun,
As they'd see me start, with a leap and a run,
From the broad of my back to the points of my toes,
When a pellet of paper hit my nose,
      Teasingly, sneezingly!

Then I'd fling them bunches of garden flowers,
And hyacinths plucked from the Castle bowers;
And I'd challenge them all to come down to me,
And I'd kiss them all till they kissed me,
      Laughingly, laughingly.

Oh, would not that be a merry life,
Apart from care and apart from strife,

With the Laureate's wine, and the Laureate's pay,
And no deductions at quarter-day?
Oh, that would be the post for me!
With plenty to get and nothing to do,
But to deck a pet poodle with ribbons of blue,
And whistle a tune to the Queen's cockatoo,
And scribble of verses remarkably few,
And empty at evening a bottle or two,
          Quaffingly, quaffingly!

          'T is I would be
          The Laureate bold,
          With my butt of sherry
          To keep me merry,
     And nothing to do but to pocket my gold!

WILLIAM AYTOUN

The Higher Pantheism in a Nutshell

ONE, who is not, we see: but one, whom we see not, is;
Surely this is not that: but that is assuredly this.

What, and wherefore, and whence? for under is over and under;
If thunder could be without lightning, lightning could be without thunder.

Doubt is faith in the main: but faith, on the whole, is doubt;
We cannot believe by proof: but could we believe without?

Why, and whither, and how? for barley and rye are not clover;
Neither are straight lines curves: yet over is under and over.

Two and two may be four: but four and four are not eight;
Fate and God may be twain: but God is the same thing as fate.

Ask a man what he thinks, and get from a man what he feels;
God, once caught in the fact, shews you a fair pair of heels.

Body and spirit are twins: God only knows which is which;
The soul squats down in the flesh, like a tinker drunk in a ditch.

One and two are not one: but one and nothing is two;
Truth can hardly be false, if falsehood cannot be true.
Once the mastodon was: pterodactyls were common as cocks;
Then the mammoth was God: now is He a prize ox.

Parallels all things are: yet many of these are askew.
You are certainly I: but certainly I am not you.

Springs the rock from the plain, shoots the stream from the rock;
Cocks exist for the hen: but hens exist for the cock.

God, whom we see not, is: and God, who is not, we see;
Fiddle, we know, is diddle: and diddle, we take it, is dee.

ALGERNON CHARLES SWINBURNE

ROBERT BROWNING

Sincere Flattery of R. B.

BIRTHDAYS? yes, in a general way;
For the most if not for the best of men:
You were born (I suppose) on a certain day:
So was I: or perhaps in the night: what then?

Only this: or at least, if more,
You must know, not think it, and learn, not speak:
There is truth to be found on the unknown shore,
And many will find where few will seek.

For many are called and few are chosen,
And the few grow many as ages lapse:
But when will the many grow few: what dozen
Is fused into one by Time's hammer-taps?

A bare brown stone in a babbling brook:—
It was wanton to hurl it there, you say:
And the moss, which clung in the sheltered nook
(Yet the stream runs cooler), is washed away.

That begs the question: many a prater
Thinks such a suggestion a sound "stop thief!"
Which, may I ask, do you think the greater,
Sergeant-at-arms or a Robber Chief?

And if it were not so? still you doubt?
Ah! yours is a birthday indeed if so.
That were something to write a poem about,
If one thought a little. I only know.

P.S.

There's a Me Society down at Cambridge,
Where my works, *cum notis variorum,*
Are talked about; well, I require the same bridge
That Euclid took toll at as *Asinorum:*

And, as they have got through several ditties
I thought were as stiff as a brick-built wall,
I've composed the above, and a stiff one *it* is,
A bridge to stop asses at, once for all.

                                        J. K. STEPHEN

Angelo Orders His Dinner

I, ANGELO, obese, black-garmented,
Respectable, much in demand, well fed
With mine own larder's dainties, where, indeed,
Such cakes of myrrh or fine alyssum seed,
Thin as a mallow-leaf, embrowned o' the top.
Which, cracking, lets the ropy, trickling drop
Of sweetness touch your tongue, or potted nests
Which my recondite recipe invests

With cold conglomerate tidbits—ah, the bill!
(You say), but given it were mine to fill
My chests, the case so put were yours, we'll say
(This counter, here, your post, as mine to-day),
And you've an eye to luxuries, what harm
In smoothing down your palate with the charm
Yourself concocted? There we issue take;
And see! as thus across the rim I break
This puffy paunch of glazed embroidered cake,
So breaks, through use, the lust of watering chaps
And craveth plainness: do I so? Perhaps;
But that's my secret. Find me such a man
As Lippo yonder, built upon the plan
Of heavy storage, double-navelled, fat
From his own giblet's oils, an Ararat
Uplift o'er water, sucking rosy draughts
From Noah's vineyard,—crisp, enticing wafts
Yon kitchen now emits, which to your sense
Somewhat abate the fear of old events,
Qualms to the stomach,—I, you see, am slow
Unnecessary duties to forego,—
You understand? A venison haunch, *haut gout,*
Ducks that in Cimbrian olives mildly stew.
And sprigs of anise, might one's teeth provoke
To taste, and so we wear the complex yoke
Just as it suits,—my liking, I confess,
More to receive, and to partake no less,
Still more obese, while through thick adipose
Sensation shoots, from testing tongue to toes
Far off, dim-conscious, at the body's verge,
Where the froth-whispers of its waves emerge
On the untasting sand. Stay, now! a seat
Is bare: I, Angelo, will sit and eat.

BAYARD TAYLOR

ROBERT BROWNING

THE FOLLOWING parody of *A Grammarian's Funeral* (not a bad poem, by the way) appeared in *The Journal of Education* of May 1, 1886, with a note: "*The Academy* reports that the students of Girton College have dissolved their Browning Society and expended its remaining funds, two shillings and sixpence, upon chocolate creams." (Girton was the first women's college to be established at Cambridge.) Among Browning parodies, I think this anonymous production one of the wittiest and most restrained. A Browning parodist's grasp should exceed his reach or what's understatement for? 'Ware breadth, my masters; *videlicet:* enough's enough. Target's barn-door broad, you say? Aye, true! And so, scant 'scuse for missing *oeil de boeuf!*

A Girtonian Funeral

LET US begin and portion out these sweets,
    Sitting together.
Leave we our deep debates, our sage conceits,—
    Wherefore? and whether?
Thus with a fine that fits the work begun
    Our labours crowning,
For we, in sooth, our duty well have done
    By Robert Browning.
Have we not wrought at essay and critique,
    Scorning supine ease?
Wrestled with clauses crabbed as Bito's Greek,
    Baffling as Chinese?
Out the Inn Album's mystic heart we took,
    Lucid of soul, and
Threaded the mazes of the Ring and Book;
    Cleared up Childe Roland.
We settled Fifine's business—let her be—
    (Strangest of lasses;)
Watched by the hour some thick-veiled truth to see
    Where Pippa passes.

(Though, dare we own, secure in victors' gains,
Ample to shield us?
Red Cotton Night-cap Country for our pains
Little would yield us.)
What then to do? Our culture-feast drag out
E'en to satiety?
Oft such the fate that findeth, nothing doubt,
Such a Society.
Oh, the dull meetings! Some one yawns an *aye,*
One gapes again a *yea.*
We girls determined not to yawn, but buy
Chocolate Ménier.
Fry's creams are cheap, but Cadbury's excel,
(Quick, Maud, for none wait)
Nay, now, 'tis Ménier bears away the bell,
Sold by the ton-weight.
So, with unburdened brains and spirits light,
Blithe did we troop hence,
All our funds voted for this closing rite,—
Just two-and-two-pence.
Do—make in scorn, old Crœsus, proud and glum,
Peaked eyebrow lift eye;
Put case one stick's a halfpenny; work the sum;
Full two and fifty.
Off with the twine! who scans each smooth brown slab
Yet not supposeth
What soft, sweet, cold, pure whiteness, bound in drab,
Tooth's bite discloseth?
Are they not grand? Why (you may think it odd)
Some power alchemic
Turns, as we munch, to Zeus-assenting nod
Sneers Academic.
Till, when one cries, " 'Ware hours that fleet like clouds,
Time, deft escaper!"

We answer bold: "Leave Time to Dons and Dowds;
        (Grace, pass the paper)
Say, boots it aught to evermore affect
        Raptures high-flying?
Though *we* choose chocolate, will the world suspect
        Genius undying?"

Anonymous

From "The Puss and the Boots"

PUT CASE I circumvent and kill him: good.
Good riddance—wipes at least from book o' th' world
The ugly admiration-note-like blot—
Gives honesty more elbow-room by just
The three dimensions of one wicked knave.
But then slips in the plaguy After-voice.
"Wicked? Holloa! my friend, whither away
So fast? Who made you, Moses-like, a judge
And ruler over men to spare or slay?
A blot wiped off forsooth! Produce forthwith
Credentials of your mission to erase
The ink-spots of mankind—t' abolish ill
For being what it is, is bound to be,
Its nature being so—cut wizards off
In flower of their necromantic lives
For being wizards, when 'tis plain enough
That they have no more wrought their wizardship
Than cats their cathood." Thus the plaguy Voice,
Puzzling withal not overmuch, for thus
I turn the enemy's flank: "Meseems, my friend,
Your argument's a thought too fine of mesh,
And catches what you would not. Every mouse
Trapped i' the larder by the kitchen wench
Might reason so—but scarcely with effect.
Methinks 'twould little serve the captured thief

To plead, 'The fault's Dame Nature's, guiltless I.
Am I to blame that in the parcelling-out
Of my ingredients the Great Chemist set
Just so much here, there so much, and no more
(Since 'tis but question, after all is said,
Of mere proportion 'twixt the part that feels
And that which guides), so much proclivity
To nightly cupboard-breaking, so much lust
Of bacon-scraps, such tendency to think
Old Stilton-rind the noblest thing on earth?
Then the *per contra*—so much power to choose
The right and shun the wrong; so much of force
Of uncorrupted will to stoutly bar
The sensory inlets of the murine soul,
And, when by night the floating rare-bit fume
Lures like a siren's song, stop nostrils fast
With more than Odysseian sailor-wax:
Lastly so much of wholesome fear of trap
To keep self-abnegation sweet. Then comes
The hour of trial, when lo! the suadent scale
Sinks instant, the deterrent kicks the beam,
The heavier falls, the lighter mounts (as much
A thing of law with motives as with plums),
And I, forsooth, must die simply because
Dame Nature, having chosen so to load
The dishes, did not choose suspend for me
The gravitation of the moral world.'
How would the kitchen-wench reply? Why thus
(If given, as scullions use, to logic-fence
And keen retorsion of dilemmata
In speeches of a hundred lines or so):
'Grant your plea valid. Good. There's mine to hear.
'Twas Nature made you? well: and me, no less;
You she by forces past your own control

Made a cheese-stealer? Be it so: of me
By forces as resistless and her own
She made a mouse-killer. Thus, either plays
A rôle in no wise chosen of himself,
But takes what part the great Stage Manager
Cast him for, when the play was set afoot.
Remains we act ours—without private spite,
But still with spirit and fidelity,
As fits good actors: you I blame no whit
For nibbling cheese—simply I throw you down
Unblamed—nay, even morally assoiled,
To pussy there: blame thou not me for that.'
Or say perhaps the girl is slow of wit,
Something inapt at ethics—why, then thus.
'Enough of prating, little thief! This talk
Of "fate, free-will, foreknowledge absolute,"
Is hugely out of place! What next indeed,
If all the casuistry of the schools
Be prayed in aid by every pilfering mouse
That's caught i' th' trap? See here, my thieving friend,
Thus I resolve the problem. We prefer
To keep our cheeses for our own behoof,
And eat them with our proper jaws; and so,
Having command of mouse-traps, we will catch
Whatever mice we can, and promptly kill
Whatever mice we catch. *Entendez vous?*
Aye, and we *will,* though all the mice on earth
Pass indignation votes, obtest the faith
Of gods and men, and make the welkin ring
With world-resounding dissonance of squeak!' "

But hist! here comes my wizard! Ready then
My nerves—and talons—for the trial of strength!
A stout heart, feline cunning, and—who knows?

H. D. TRAILL

The Cock and the Bull

YOU SEE this pebble-stone? It's a thing I bought
Of a bit of a chit of a boy i' the mid o' the day—
I like to dock the smaller parts-o'-speech,
As we curtail the already cur-tail'd cur
(You catch the paronomasia, play 'po' words?),
Did, rather, i' the pre-Landseerian days.
Well, to my muttons. I purchased the concern,
And clapt it i' my poke, having given for same
By way o' chop, swop, barter or exchange—
"Chop" was my snickering dandiprat's own term—
One shilling and fourpence, current coin o' the realm.
O-n-e one and f-o-u-r four
Pence, one and fourpence—you are with me, sir?—
What hour it skills not: ten or eleven o' the clock,
One day (and what a roaring day it was
Go shop or sight-see—bar a spit o' rain!)
In February, eighteen sixty nine,
Alexandrina Victoria, Fidei
Hm—hm—how runs the jargon? being on throne.

Such, sir, are all the facts, succinctly put,
The basis or substratum—what you will—
Of the impending eighty thousand lines.
"Not much in 'em either," quoth perhaps simple Hodge.
But there's a superstructure. Wait a bit.
Mark first the rationale of the thing:
Hear logic rivel and levigate the deed.
That shilling—and for matter o' that, the pence—
I had o' course upo' me—wi' me say—
(*Mecum's* the Latin, make a note o' that)
When I popp'd pen i' stand, scratch'd ear, wip'd snout,
(Let everybody wipe his own himself)
Sniff'd—tch!—at snuffbox; tumbled up, he-heed,

Haw-haw'd (not hee-haw'd, that's another guess thing:)
Then fumbled at, and stumbled out of, door,
I shoved the timber ope wi' my omoplat;
And *in vestibulo,* i' the lobby to-wit,
(Iacobi Facciolati's rendering, sir,)
Donn'd galligaskins, antigropeloes,
And so forth; and, complete with hat and gloves,
One on and one a-dangle i' my hand,
And ombrifuge (Lord love you!), case o' rain,
I flopp'd forth, 'sbuddikins! on my own ten toes,
(I do assure you there be ten of them,)
And went clump-clumping up hill and down dale
To find myself o' the sudden i' front o' the boy.
Put case I hadn't 'em on me, could I ha' bought
This sort-o'-kind-o'-what-you-might-call toy,
This pebble-thing, o' the boy-thing? Q.E.D.
That's proven without aid from mumping Pope,
Sleek porporate or bloated Cardinal.
(Isn't it, old Fatchaps? You're in Euclid now.)
So, having the shilling—having i' fact a lot—
And pence and halfpence, ever so many o' them,
I purchased, as I think I said before,
The pebble (*lapis, lapidis, -di, -dem, -de*—
What nouns 'crease short i' the genitive, Fatchaps, eh?)
O' the boy, a bare-legg'd beggarly son of a gun,
For one-and-fourpence. Here we are again.

   Now Law steps in, bigwigg'd, voluminous-jaw'd;
Investigates and re-investigates.
Was the transaction illegal? Law shakes head.
Perpend, sir, all the bearings of the case.

   At first the coin was mine, the chattel his.
But now (by virtue of the said exchange
And barter) *vice versa* all the coin,

Per juris operationem, vests
I' the boy and his assigns till ding o' doom;
(*In sæcula sæculo-o-orum;*
I think I hear the Abate mouth out that.)
To have and hold the same to him and them. . . .
Confer some idiot on Conveyancing.
Whereas the pebble and every part thereof,
And all that appertaineth thereunto,
Quodcunque pertinet ad eam rem,
(I fancy, sir, my Latin's rather pat)
Or shall, will, may, might, can, could, would or should,
(*Subaudi cætera*—clap we to the close—
For what's the good of law in a case o' the kind)
Is mine to all intents and purposes.
This settled, I resume the thread o' the tale.

Now for a touch o' the vendor's quality.
He says a gen'lman bought a pebble of him,
(This pebble i' sooth, sir, which I hold i' my hand)—
And paid for 't, *like* a gen'lman, on the nail.
'Did I o'ercharge him a ha'penny? Devil a bit.
Fiddlepin's end! Get out, you blazing ass!
Gabble o' the goose. Don't bugaboo-baby *me!*
Go double or quits? Yah! tittup! what's the odds?'
—There's the transaction view'd i' the vendor's light.

Next ask that dumpled hag, stood snuffling by,
With her three frowsy blowsy brats o' babes,
The scum o' the kennel, cream o' the filth-heap—Faugh!
Aie, aie, aie, aie! ὀτοτοτοτοτοῖ,
('Stead which we blurt out Hoighty toighty now)—
And the baker and candlestickmaker, and Jack and Gill,
Blear'd Goody this and queasy Gaffer that.
Ask the schoolmaster. Take schoolmaster first.

He saw a gentleman purchase of a lad
A stone, and pay for it *rite,* on the square,
And carry it off *per saltum,* jauntily,
Propria quæ maribus, gentleman's property now
(Agreeably to the law explain'd above),
In proprium usum, for his private ends.
The boy he chuck'd a brown i' the air, and bit
I' the face the shilling: heaved a thumping stone
At a lean hen that ran cluck clucking by,
(And hit her, dead as nail i' post o' door,)
Then *abiit*—what's the Ciceronian phrase?—
Excessit, evasit, erupit—off slogs boy;
Off like bird, *avi similis*—(you observed
The dative? Pretty i' the Mantuan!)—Anglice,
Off in three flea skips. *Hactenus,* so far,
So good, *tam bene. Bene, satis, male*—,
Where was I with my trope 'bout one in a quag?
I did once hitch the syntax into verse:
Verbum personale, a verb personal,
Concordat—ay, "agrees," old Fatchaps—*cum*
Nominativo, with its nominative,
Genere, i' point o' gender, *numero,*
O' number, *et persona,* and person. *Ut,*
Instance: *Sol ruit,* down flops sun, *et* and,
Montes umbrantur, out flounce mountains. Pah!
Excuse me, sir, I think I'm going mad.
You see the trick on 't though, and can yourself
Continue the discourse *ad libitum.*
It takes up about eighty thousand lines,
A thing imagination boggles at;
And might, odds-bobs, sir! in judicious hands,
Extend from here to Mesopotamy.

                                        C. S. CALVERLEY

The Last Ride Together

(FROM HER POINT OF VIEW)

WHEN I had firmly answered "No,"
    And he allowed that that was so,
    I really thought I should be free
For good and all from Mr. B.,
    And that he would soberly acquiesce.
I said that it would be discreet
That for awhile we should not meet;
I promised that I would always feel
A kindly interest in his weal;
I thanked him for his amorous zeal;
    In short, I said all I could but "yes."

I said what I'm accustomed to;
I acted as I always do.
I promised he should find in me
A friend,—a sister, if that might be;
    But he was still dissatisfied.
He certainly was most polite;
He said exactly what was right,
He acted very properly,
Except indeed for this, that he
Insisted on inviting me
    To come with him for "one more last ride."

A little while in doubt I stood:
A ride, no doubt, would do me good;
I had a habit and a hat
Extremely well worth looking at;
    The weather was distinctly fine.
My horse, too, wanted exercise,
And time, when one is riding, flies;

Besides, it really seemed, you see,
The only way of ridding me
Of pertinacious Mr. B.;
  So my head I graciously incline.

I won't say much of what happened next;
I own I was extremely vexed.
Indeed I should have been aghast
If any one had seen what passed;
  But nobody need ever know
That, as I leaned forward to stir the fire,
He advanced before I could well retire;
And I suddenly felt, to my great alarm,
The grasp of a warm, unlicensed arm,
An embrace in which I found no charm;
  I was awfully glad when he let me go.

Then we began to ride; my steed
Was rather fresh, too fresh indeed,
And at first I thought of little, save
The way to escape an early grave,
  As the dust rose up on either side.
My stern companion jogged along
On a brown old cob both broad and strong.
He looked as he does when he's writing verse,
Or endeavoring not to swear and curse,
Or wondering where he has left his purse;
  Indeed it was a sombre ride.

I spoke of the weather to Mr. B.,
But he neither listened nor spoke to me.
I praised his horse, and I smiled the smile
Which was wont to move him once in a while.
  I said I was wearing his favorite flowers,
But I wasted my words on the desert air,
For he rode with a fixed and gloomy stare.

I wonder what he was thinking about.
As I don't read verse, I shan't find out.
It was something subtle and deep, no doubt,
    A theme to detain a man for hours.

Ah! there was the corner where Mr. S.
So nearly induced me to whisper "yes;"
And here it was that the next but one
Proposed on horseback, or would have done,
    Had his horse not most opportunely shied;
Which perhaps was due to the unseen flick
He received from my whip; 't was a scurvy trick,
But I never could do with that young man,—
I hope his present young woman can.
Well, I must say, never, since time began,
    Did I go for a duller or longer ride.

He never smiles and he never speaks;
He might go on like this for weeks;
He rolls a slightly frenzied eye
Towards the blue and burning sky,
    And the cob bounds on with tireless stride.
If we aren't home for lunch at two

I don't know what papa will do;
But I know full well he will say to me,
"I never approved of Mr. B.;
It's the very devil that you and he
    Ride, ride together, forever ride."

                    J. K. STEPHEN

EMILY DICKINSON

She Sees Another Door Opening

MY FORTITUDE is all awry
To sit upon this chair
And, idly lifting up my eye,
To glimpse the door ajar there.

Through that door could come what bother
In what undreamed of pelts
A cat, a dog, or God the Father,
Or—gulp—somebody else!

FIRMAN HOUGHTON

WILLIAM MORRIS

Ballad

THE AULD WIFE sat at her ivied door,
   (*Butter and eggs and a pound of cheese*)
A thing she had frequently done before;
   And her spectacles lay on her aproned knees.

The piper he piped on the hill-top high,
   (*Butter and eggs and a pound of cheese*)
Till the cow said "I die," and the goose asked "Why?"
   And the dog said nothing, but searched for fleas.

The farmer he strove through the square farmyard;
   (*Butter and eggs and a pound of cheese*)
His last brew of ale was a trifle hard—
   The connexion of which with the plot one sees.

The farmer's daughter hath frank blue eyes;
  (*Butter and eggs and a pound of cheese*)
She hears the rooks caw in the windy skies,
    As she sits at her lattice and shells her peas.

The farmer's daughter hath ripe red lips;
  (*Butter and eggs and a pound of cheese*)
If you try to approach her, away she skips
    Over tables and chairs with apparent ease.

The farmer's daughter hath soft brown hair;
  (*Butter and eggs and a pound of cheese*)
And I met with a ballad, I can't say where,
    Which wholly consisted of lines like these.

PART II.

She sat, with her hands 'neath her dimpled cheeks,
  (*Butter and eggs and a pound of cheese*)
And spake not a word. While a lady speaks
    There is hope, but she didn't even sneeze.

She sat, with her hands 'neath her crimson cheeks,
  (*Butter and eggs and a pound of cheese*)
She gave up mending her father's breeks,
    And let the cat roll in her new chemise.

She sat, with her hands 'neath her burning cheeks,
  (*Butter and eggs and a pound of cheese*)
And gazed at the piper for thirteen weeks;
    Then she followed him out o'er the misty leas.

Her sheep followed her, as their tails did them.
  (*Butter and eggs and a pound of cheese*)
And this song is considered a perfect gem,
    And as to the meaning, it's what you please.

                                C. S. CALVERLEY

Rondel

BEHOLD THE WORKS of William Morris,
  Epics, and here and there wall-papery,
  Mild, mooney, melancholy vapoury
A sort of Chaucer *minus* Horace.

Spun out like those of William Loris,
  Who wrote of amorous red-tapery,
Behold the works of William Morris,
  Epics, and here and there wall-papery!

Long ladies, knights, and earles and choris-
    ters in the most appropriate drapery,
    Samite and silk and spotless napery,
Sunflowers and apple blossoms and orris,
Behold the works of William Morris!

Anonymous

CHRISTINA ROSSETTI

Ding Dong

DING DONG, Ding dong,
    There goes the Gong,
Dick, come along,
    'Tis time for dinner.
Wash your face,
Take your place,
Where's your grace,
    You little sinner?

"Like an apple?"
  "Yes I should,
Nice, nice, nicey!
  Good, good, good!"

"Manners miss,
  Please behave,
Those who ask,
  Shan't have."

"Those who don't
  Don't want.
I'll eat it,
  You shan't."

Baby cry,
Wipe his eye.
Baby good,
Give him food.
Baby sleepy,
Go to bed.
Baby naughty,
Smack his head!

Poor little thrush,
Found dead in a bush!
When did he die?
He is rather high.
Bury him deep,
He won't keep.
Bury him well,
Or he'll smell.

What have horns?
Cows and moons.
What have crests?
Cocks and spoons.
What are nice?
Ducks and peas.
What are nasty?
Bites of fleas.

What are fast?
Tides and times.
What are slow?
Nursery Rhymes.

A. C. HILTON

DANTE GABRIEL ROSSETTI

After Dilettante Concetti

"WHY DO you wear your hair like a man,
            Sister Helen?
This week is the third since you began."
"I'm writing a ballad; be still if you can,
            Little brother.
    (*O Mother Carey, mother!*
What chickens are these between sea and heaven?)"

"But why does your figure appear so lean,
            Sister Helen?
And why do you dress in sage, sage green?"
"Children should never be heard, if seen,
            Little brother.
    (*O Mother Carey, mother!*
What fowls are a-wing in the stormy heaven!)"

"But why is your face so yellowy white,
            Sister Helen?
And why are your skirts so funnily tight?"
"Be quiet, you torment, or how can I write,
            Little brother?
    (*O Mother Carey, mother!*
How gathers thy train to the sea from the heaven!)"

"And who's Mother Carey, and what is her train,
            Sister Helen?

And why do you call her again and again?"
"You troublesome boy, why that's the refrain,
                    Little brother.
        (O Mother Carey, mother!
What work is toward in the startled heaven?)"

"And what's a refrain? What a curious word,
                    Sister Helen!
Is the ballad you're writing about a sea-bird?"
"Not at all; why should it be? Don't be absurd,
                    Little brother.
        (O Mother Carey, mother!
Try brood flies lower as lowers the heaven.)"

            (A big brother speaketh:)
"The refrain you've studied a meaning had,
                    Sister Helen!
It gave strange force to a weird ballàd,
But refrains have become a ridiculous "fad,"
                    Little brother.
        And *Mother Carey, mother,*
Has a bearing on nothing in earth or heaven.

"But the finical fashion has had its day,
                    Sister Helen.
And let's try in the style of a different lay
To bid it adieu in poetical way,
                    Little brother.
        So, Mother Carey, mother!
Collect your chickens and go to—heaven."
(A pause. Then the big brother singeth, accompanying him-
self in a plaintive wise on the triangle:)

"Look in my face. My name is Used-to-was,
I am also called Played-out and Done-to-death,
And It-will-wash-no-more. Awakeneth

Slowly, but sure awakening it has,
The common-sense of man; and I, alas!
    The ballad-burden trick, now known too well,
    Am turned to scorn, and grown contemptible—
A too transparent artifice to pass.

"What a cheap dodge I am! The cats who dart
    Tin-kettled through the streets in wild surprise
    Assail judicious ears not otherwise;
And yet no critics praise the urchin's 'art,'
Who to the wretched creature's caudal part
    Its foolish empty-jingling 'burden' ties."

H. D. TRAILL

ALGERNON CHARLES SWINBURNE

If

If LIFE were never bitter,
    And love were always sweet,
Then who would care to borrow
A moral from to-morrow—
If Thames would always glitter,
    And joy would ne'er retreat,
If life were never bitter,
    And love were always sweet?

If Care were not the waiter
    Behind a fellow's chair,
When easy-going sinners
Sit down to Richmond dinners,
And life's swift stream flows straighter—
    By Jove, it would be rare
If Care were not the waiter
    Behind a fellow's chair.

If wit were always radiant,
  And wine were always iced,
And bores were kicked out straightway
Through a convenient gateway;
Then down the years' long gradient
  'Twere sad to be enticed;
If wit were always radiant,
  And wine were always iced.

MORTIMER COLLINS

Octopus

WRITTEN AT THE CRYSTAL PALACE AQUARIUM

STRANGE BEAUTY, eight-limbed and eight-handed,
  Whence camest to dazzle our eyes?
With thy bosom bespangled and banded
  With the hues of the seas and the skies;
Is thy home European or Asian,
  O mystical monster marine?
Part molluscous and partly crustacean,
  Betwixt and between.

Wast thou born to the sound of sea-trumpets?
  Hast thou eaten and drunk to excess
Of the sponges—thy muffins and crumpets,
  Of the seaweed—thy mustard and cress?
Wast thou nurtured in caverns of coral,
  Remote from reproof or restraint?
Art thou innocent, art thou immoral,
  Sinburnian or Saint?

Lithe limbs, curling free, as a creeper
  That creeps in a desolate place,
To enrol and envelop the sleeper
  In a silent and stealthy embrace,

Cruel beak craning forward to bite us,
  Our juices to drain and to drink,
Or to whelm us in waves of Cocytus,
  Indelible ink!

O breast, that 'twere rapture to writhe on!
  O arms 'twere delicious to feel
Clinging close with the crush of the Python,
  When she maketh her murderous meal!
In thy eight-fold embraces enfolden,
  Let our empty existence escape;
Give us death that is glorious and golden,
  Crushed all out of shape!

Ah! thy red lips, lascivious and luscious,
  With death in their amorous kiss!
Cling round us, and clasp us, and crush us,
  With bitings of agonized bliss;
We are sick with the poison of pleasure,
  Dispense us the potion of pain;
Ope thy mouth to its uttermost measure
  And bite us again! *

                              A. C. HILTON

A Melton Mowbray Pork Pie

STRANGE PIE that is almost a passion,
  O passion immoral for pie!

---

* Cf. with this stanza the fourth of Swinburne's *Dolores:*
    O lips full of lust and of laughter,
      Curled snakes that are fed from my breast,
    Bite hard lest remembrance come after
      And press with new lips where you pressed.
    For my heart, too, springs up at the pressure,
      Mine eyelids, too, moisten and burn;
    Ah, feed me and fill me with pleasure,
      Ere pain come in turn.

Unknown are the ways that they fashion,
    Unknown and unseen of the eye.
The pie that is marbled and mottled,
    The pie that digests with a sigh;
For all is not Bass that is bottled
    And all is not pork that is pie.

Richard Le Gallienne

The Manlet

In stature, the Manlet was dwarfish—
    No burly big Blunderbore he:
And he wearily gazed on the crawfish
    His Wifelet had dressed for his tea.
"Now reach me, sweet Atom, my gunlet,
    And hurl the old shoelet for luck:
Let me hie to the bank of the runlet,
      And shoot thee a Duck!"

She has reached him his minikin gunlet:
    She has hurled the old shoelet for luck:
She is busily baking a bunlet,
    To welcome him home with his Duck.
On he speeds, never wasting a wordlet,
    Though thoughtlets cling, closely as wax,
To the spot where the beautiful birdlet
      So quietly quacks.

Where the Lobsterlet lurks, and the Crablet
    So slowly and sleepily crawls:
Where the Dolphin's at home, and the Dablet
    Pays long ceremonious calls:
Where the grublet is sought by the Froglet:
    Where the Frog is pursued by the Duck:
Where the Ducklet is chased by the Doglet—
      So runs the world's luck!

He has loaded with bullet and powder:
　His footfall is noiseless as air:
But the Voices grow louder and louder,
　And bellow, and bluster, and blare.
They bristle before him and after,
　They flutter above and below,
Shrill shriekings of lubberly laughter,
　　Weird wailings of woe!

They echo without him, within him:
　They thrill through his whiskers and beard:
Like a teetotum seeming to spin him,
　With sneers never hitherto sneered.
"Avengement," they cry, "on our Foelet!
　Let the Manikin weep for our wrongs!
Let us drench him, from toplet to toelet,
　　With Nursery-Songs!

"He shall muse upon 'Hey! Diddle! Diddle!'
　On the Cow that surmounted the Moon:
He shall rave of the Cat and the Fiddle,
　And the Dish that eloped with the Spoon:
And his soul shall be sad for the Spider,
　When Miss Muffet was sipping her whey,
That so tenderly sat down beside her,
　　And scared her away!

"The music of Midsummer-madness
　Shall sting him with many a bite,
Till, in rapture of rollicking sadness,
　He shall groan with a gloomy delight:
He shall swathe him, like mists of the morning,
　In platitudes luscious and limp,
Such as deck, with a deathless adorning,
　　The Song of the Shrimp!

"When the Ducklet's dark doom is decided,
  We will trundle him home in a trice:
And the banquet, so plainly provided,
  Shall round into rose-buds and rice:
In a blaze of pragmatic invention
  He shall wrestle with Fate, and shall reign:
But he has not a friend fit to mention,
      So hit him again!"

He has shot it, the delicate darling!
  And the Voices have ceased from their strife:
Not a whisper of sneering or snarling,
  As he carries it home to his wife:
Then cheerily champing the bunlet
  His spouse was so skilful to bake,
He hies him once more to the runlet,
      To fetch her the Drake!

LEWIS CARROLL

WALT WHITMAN

Sincere Flattery of W. W. (Americanus)

THE CLEAR COOL NOTE of the cuckoo which has ousted the legitimate nest-holder,

The whistle of the railway guard dispatching the train to the inevitable collision,

The maiden's monosyllabic reply to a polysyllabic proposal,

The fundamental note of the last trump, which is presumably D natural;

All of these are sounds to rejoice in, yea to let your very ribs re-echo with:

But better than all of them is the absolutely last chord of the
apparently inexhaustible pianoforte player.

J. K. STEPHEN

Camerados

EVERYWHERE, EVERYWHERE, following me;
Taking me by the buttonhole, pulling off my boots, hustling me
with the elbows;
Sitting down with me to clams and the chowder-kettle;
Plunging naked at my side into the sleek, irascible surges;
Soothing me with the strain that I neither permit nor prohibit;
Flocking this way and that, reverent, eager, orotund, irrepres-
sible;
Denser than sycamore leaves when the north-winds are scouring
Paumanok;
What can I do to restrain them? Nothing, verily nothing.
Everywhere, everywhere, crying aloud for me;
Crying, I hear; and I satisfy them out of my nature;
And he that comes at the end of the feast shall find something
over.
Whatever they want I give; though it be something else, they
shall have it.
Drunkard, leper, Tammanyite, small-pox and cholera patient,
shoddy and codfish millionaire,
And the beautiful young men, and the beautiful young women,
all the same,
Crowding, hundreds of thousands, cosmical multitudes,
Buss me and hang on my hips and lean up to my shoulders,
Everywhere listening to my yawp and glad whenever they hear it;
Everywhere saying, say it, Walt, we believe it:
Everywhere, everywhere.

BAYARD TAYLOR

A Classic Waits for Me

(WITH APOLOGIES TO WALT WHITMAN, PLUS A TRIAL
MEMBERSHIP IN THE CLASSICS CLUB)

A CLASSIC WAITS for me, it contains all, nothing is lacking,
Yet all were lacking if taste were lacking, or if the endorsement
    of the right man were lacking.
O clublife, and the pleasures of membership,
O volumes for sheer fascination unrivalled.
Into an armchair endlessly rocking,
Walter J. Black my president,
I, freely invited, cordially welcomed to membership,
My arm around John Kieran, Pearl S. Buck,
My taste in books guarded by the spirits of William Lyon Phelps,
    Hendrik Willem Van Loon,
(From your memories, sad brothers, from the fitful risings and
    callings I heard),
I to the classics devoted, brother of rough mechanics, beauty-
    parlor technicians, spot welders, radio-program directors
(It is not necessary to have a higher education to appreciate
    these books),
I, connoisseur of good reading, friend of connoisseurs of good
    reading everywhere,
I, not obligated to take any specific number of books, free to
    reject any volume, perfectly free to reject Montaigne,
    Erasmus, Milton,
I, in perfect health except for a slight cold, pressed for time,
    having only a few more years to live,
Now celebrate this opportunity.
Come, I will make the club indissoluble,
I will read the most splendid books the sun ever shone upon,
I will start divine magnetic groups,
    With the love of comrades,
        With the life-long love of distinguished committees.

I strike up for an Old Book.

Long the best-read figure in America, my dues paid, sitter in arm-
chairs everywhere, wanderer in populous cities, weeping
with Hecuba and with the late William Lyon Phelps,

Free to cancel my membership whenever I wish,

Turbulent, fleshy, sensible,

Never tiring of clublife,

Always ready to read another masterpiece provided it has the
approval of my president, Walter J. Black,

Me imperturbe, standing at ease among writers,

Rais'd by a perfect mother and now belonging to a perfect book
club,

Bearded, sunburnt, gray-neck'd, astigmatic,

Loving the masters and the masters only

(I am mad for them to be in contact with me),

My arm around Pearl S. Buck, only American woman to receive
the Nobel Prize for Literature,

I celebrate this opportunity.

And I will not read a book nor the least part of a book but has
the approval of the Committee,

For all is useless without that which you may guess at many
times and not hit, that which they hinted at,

All is useless without readability.

By God! I will accept nothing which all cannot have their
counterpart of on the same terms (89¢ for the Regular
Edition or $1.39 for the DeLuxe Edition, plus a few
cents postage).

I will make inseparable readers with their arms around each
other's necks,

By the love of classics,

By the manly love of classics.

E. B. WHITE

HENRY JAMES

IN THE PREFACE to *A Variety of Things,* Beerbohm says he wrote this "when I learned that the Order of Merit was about to be conferred on Henry James." I chose *The Guerdon* as against *The Mote in the Middle Distance,* partly because of this occasional interest, partly because *The Mote* is so well known, but chiefly because the comic situation—the Lord Chamberlain being as vague about just who Henry James *is* as his royal master—seems to me stronger. Also, though this is debatable, I think *The Guerdon* hits off the late Jamesian style better than does *The Mote.*

The Guerdon

THAT it hardly was, that it all bleakly and unbeguilingly *wasn't* for "the likes" of *him*—poor decent Stamfordham— to rap out queries about the owner of the to him unknown and unsuggestive name that had, in these days, been thrust on him with such a wealth of commendatory gesture, was precisely what now, as he took, with his prepared list of New Year *colifichets* and whatever, his way to the great gaudy palace, fairly flicked his cheek with the sense of his having never before so let himself in, as he ruefully phrased it, without letting anything, by the same token, out.

"Anything" was, after all, only another name for *the* thing. But he was to ask himself what earthly good it was, anyhow, to have kept in its confinement the furred and clawed, the bristling and now all but audibly scratching domestic pet, if he himself, defenseless Lord Chamberlain that he was, had to be figured as bearing it company inside the bag. There wasn't, he felt himself blindly protesting, room in there for the two of them; and the imminent addition of a Personage fairly caused our friend to bristle in the manner of the imagined captive that had till now symbolised well enough for him his whole dim bland ignorance of the matter in hand. Hadn't he all the time been reckoning precisely *without* that Personage—*without* the greater dimness that was to be expected of *him*—without, above all, that dreadful lesser blandness in virtue of which such Personages tend to come down on you, as it were, straight, with demands for side-lights? There wasn't a "bally" glimmer of a side-light, heaven help him, that he could throw. He hadn't the beginning of a notion—since it had been a point of pride with him, as well as of urbanity, not to ask—who the fellow, the so presumably illustrious and deserving chap in question *was*. This omission so loomed for him that he was to be conscious, as he came to the end of the great moist avenue, of a felt doubt as to whether he could, in his bemusement, now "place" anybody at all; to which condition of his may have been due the impulse that, at the reached gates of the palace, caused him to pause and all vaguely, all peeringly inquire of one of the sentries: "To whom do you beautifully belong?"

The question, however, was to answer itself, then and there, to the effect that this functionary belonged to whom *he* belonged to; and the converse of this reminder, presenting itself simultaneously to his consciousness, was to make him feel, when he was a few minutes later ushered into the Presence, that he had never so intensely, for general abjectness and sheer situational funk, belonged as now. He caught himself wondering whether, on this basis, he were even animate, so strong was his sense of being a "bit" of the furniture of the great glossy "study"—of being some oiled and ever so handy object moving smoothly on castors, or revolving, at the touch of a small red royal finger, on a pivot. It would be placed questioningly, that finger—and his prevision held him as with the long-drawn pang of nightmare—on the cryptic name. That it occurred, this name, almost at the very end of the interminable list, figured to him not as a respite but as a prolongment of the perspirational agony. So that when, at long last, that finger *was* placed, with a roll towards him of the blue, the prominent family eye of the seated reader, it was with a groan of something like relief that he faintly uttered an "Oh well, Sir, he *is,* you know—and with all submission, hang it, just *isn't* he though?—of an eminence!"

It was in the silence following this fling that there budded for him the wild, the all but unlooked-for hope that "What *sort,* my dear man, of eminence?" was a question not, possibly, going to be asked at all. It fairly burst for him and blossomed, this bud, as the royal eye rolled away from his into space. It never, till beautifully now, had struck our poor harassed friend that his master might, in some sort, be prey to those very, those inhibitive delicacies that had played, from first to last, so eminently the deuce with *him.* He was to see, a moment later, that the royal eye had poised—had, from its slow flight around the mouldings of the florid Hanoverian ceiling, positively swooped—on the fat scarlet book of reference which, fraught with a title that was a very beam of the catchy and the chatty, lay beside the blotting-pad. The royal eye rested, the royal eye even dilated, to such an extent that Stamfordham had anticipatively the sense of being commanded to turn for a few minutes his back, and of overhearing in that interval the rustle of the turned leaves.

That no such command came, that there *was* no recourse to the dreadful volume, somewhat confirmed for him his made guess that on the great grey beach of the hesitational and renunciational he was not—or wasn't all deniably not—the only pebble. For an instant, nevertheless, during which the prominent blue eye rested on a prominent blue pencil, it seemed that this guess might be, by an immense *coup de roi,* terrifically shattered. Our friend held, as for an eternity, his breath. He was to form, in later years, a theory that the name really *had* stood in peril of deletion, and that what saved it was that the good little man, as doing, under the glare shed by his predecessors, the great dynastic "job" in a land that had been under two Jameses and no less than eight Henrys, had all humbly and meltingly resolved to "let it go at that."

MAX BEERBOHM*

---

* Parody, I think, here goes about as far as it can go. "Poor decent Stamfordham" with "his whole dim bland ignorance of the matter in hand" is perfect—the cumulative adjectives not separated by commas—as is his reply to his Sovereign's terrible query: "Oh well, Sir, he *is,* you know—and with all submission, hang it, just *isn't* he though?—of an eminence!" The italics, the nuances, the pseudospontaneous rectifications, all the paraphernalia that in the later James seem to be leading us up to the final moment of illumination, and sometimes in fact do, these are all exquisitely reproduced. As

GERARD MANLEY HOPKINS

Breakfast with Gerard Manley Hopkins

"Delicious heart-of-the-corn, fresh-from-the-oven flakes are sparkled and spangled with sugar for a can't-be-resisted flavor."
                    —Legend on a packet of breakfast cereal.

SERIOUS over my cereals I broke one breakfast my fast
  With something-to-read-searching retinas retained by print on
    a packet;
Sprung rhythm sprang, and I found (the mind fact-mining at
    last)
  An influence Father-Hopkins-fathered on the copy-writing
    racket.

Parenthesis-proud, bracket-hold, happiest with hyphens
  The writers stagger intoxicated by terms, adjective-un-
    steadied—
Describing in graceless phrases fizzling like soda syphons
  All things crisp, crunchy, malted, tangy, sugared and shredded.

----

also the sequel: "It was in the silence following this fling that there budded
for him the wild, the all but unlooked-for hope that 'What *sort*, my dear
man, of eminence?' was a question not, possibly, going to be asked at all. It
fairly burst for him and blossomed, this bud, as the royal eye rolled away
from his into space." Nothing better has been done, unless it be the later
sentence: "That no such command came, that there *was* no recourse to the
dreaded volume, somewhat confirmed to him his made. guess that on the
great grey beach of the hesitational and renunciational he was not—or
wasn't all deniably not—the only pebble on the beach." The Johnsonian
Latinism of "hesitational" and "renunciational," the triple negative of
"wasn't"-"deniably"-"not," so finicky and obscure, and then the final clanging
slanging resolution ("the only pebble on the beach") is exactly right. (The
alternation of the formal and the vernacular, so characteristic of James' style,
is perfectly reproduced throughout *The Guerdon*.) And there is, finally, Stamfordham's bemused inquiry of the Busbyed pipeclayed sentry in front of
Buckingham Palace: "To whom do you beautifully belong?", in which a
single adverb strikes to the heart of James' later style. (In fact, as I have just
learned, the sentence is so Jamesian that it is to be found in James' own play,
The High Bid.)

Far too, yes, too early we are urged to be purged, to savor
   Salt, malt and phosphates in English twisted and torn,
As, sparkled and spangled with sugar for a can't-be-resisted flavor,
   Come fresh-from-the-oven flakes direct from the heart of the
     corn.

ANTHONY BRODE

RUDYARD KIPLING

A Ballad

As I WAS walkin' the jungle round, a-killin' of tigers an' time;
I seed a kind of an author man a writin' a rousin' rhyme;
'E was writin' a mile a minute an' more, an' I sez to 'im, " 'Oo are
    you?"
Sez 'e "I'm a poet—'er majesty's poet—soldier an' sailor, too!"
An 'is poem began in Ispahan an' ended in Kalamazoo,
It 'ad army in it, an' navy in it, an' jungle sprinkled through,
For 'e was a poet—'er majesty's poet—soldier an' sailor, too!

An' after, I met 'im all over the world, a doin' of things a host;
'E 'ad one foot planted in Burmah, an' one on the Gloucester
    coast;
'E's 'alf a sailor an' 'alf a whaler, 'e's captain, cook, and crew,
But most a poet—'er majesty's poet—soldier an' sailor too!
'E 's often Scot an' 'e's often not, but 'is work is never through,
For 'e laughs at blame, an' 'e writes for fame, an' a bit for
    revenoo,—
Bein' a poet—'er majesty's poet—soldier an' sailor too!

'E'll take you up to the Ar'tic zone, 'e'll take you down to the
    Nile,
'E'll give you a barrack ballad in the Tommy Atkins style,
Or 'e'll sing you a Dipsy Chantey, as the bloomin' bo'suns do,
For 'e is a poet—'er majesty's poet—soldier an' sailor too.

An' there is n't no room for others, an' there's nothin' left to do;
'E 'as sailed the main from the 'Arn to Spain, 'e 'as tramped the
    jungle through,
An' written up all there is to write—soldier an' sailor, too!

There are manners an' manners of writin', but 'is is the *proper*
    way,
An' it ain't so hard to be a bard if you'll imitate Rudyard K.;
But sea an' shore an' peace an' war, an' everything else in view—
'E 'as gobbled the lot!—'er majesty's poet—soldier an' sailor, too.
'E's not content with 'is Indian 'ome, 'e's looking for regions new,
In another year 'e'll 'ave swept 'em clear, an' what'll the rest
    of us do?
'E's crowdin' us out!—'er majesty's poet—soldier an' sailor too!

GUY WETMORE CARRYL

To R. K. (*1891*)

> As long as I dwell on some stupendous
> And tremendous (Heaven defend us!)
> Monstr'-inform'-ingens-horrendous
> Demoniaco-seraphic
> Penman's latest piece of graphic.
>
> BROWNING

Will there never come a season
Which shall rid us from the curse
Of a prose that knows no reason
And an unmelodious verse:
When the world shall cease to wonder
At the genius of an Ass,
And a boy's eccentric blunder
Shall not bring success to pass;

When mankind shall be delivered
From the clash of magazines,

And the inkstands shall be shivered
Into countless smithereens:
When there stands a muzzled stripling,
Mute, beside a muzzled bore:
When the Rudyards cease from Kipling
And the Haggards Ride no more?

J. K. STEPHEN

PART THREE

Beerbohm —and After

SOME LEAVES FROM *A Christmas Garland*

BY

MAX BEERBOHM

I N 1912 Heinemann published Max Beerbohm's *A Christmas Garland,* a set of variations on a theme which I am not alone in thinking the best single book of parodies in our language. The chief drawback to it, as of 1960, is that about half the eighteen parodees are no longer of interest. And yet even so one gets such a vivid impression of the literary personalities of, say, Maurice Hewlett (*Fond Hearts Askew*) and A. C. Benson (*Out of Harm's Way*) that one is able to reconstruct these extinct forms of life from the single parodic bone thrown to one, and perhaps to enjoy them even more than their contemporaries did. Six of the *Garland's* parodies—those on James, Kipling, Shaw, Hewlett, Chesterton and Meredith—had already appeared in Christmas issues of *The Saturday Review,* whose dramatic critic Beerbohm was from 1898 to 1910—his predecessor was Bernard Shaw. The others were written specially for the book. A single testimonial may suffice. "One night," S. N. Behrman quotes Beerbohm in his recent *New Yorker* series, "I was sitting across the table from [Henry] James. My parody of him in *A Christmas Garland* had just appeared. The lady at James' right asked for his opinion on something or other. He pointed straight at me: 'Ask that young man,' he said. 'He is in full possession of my innermost thoughts.' But James was always very gentle with me; he was very nice about that parody." Edmund Gosse, another parodee (see below), wrote Beerbohm: "Henry James has been eating his dinner here with us and . . . was full of admiration [for the *Garland*]. I told him you had a certain nervousness . . . and he desired me to let you know that no one can have read it with more wonder and delight than he. He expressed himself in superlatives. He called the book 'the most intelligent that has been produced in England for many a long day.' But he says you have destroyed the trade of writing. No one, now, can write without incurring the reproach of somewhat ineffectively imitating—*you!*"

Since it was not practical to reproduce the whole *Garland,* I have had to choose. A painful business. But I think the six selections that follow are perhaps as good as the twelve I have omitted

RUDYARD KIPLING

P.C., X, 36

Then it's collar 'im tight,
   In the name o' the Lawd!
'Ustle 'im, shake 'im till 'e's sick,
   Wot, 'e *would*, would 'e? Well,
   Then yer've got ter give 'im 'Ell,
An' it's trunch, trunch, truncheon does the trick.

POLICE STATION DITTIES.

I HAD spent Christmas Eve at the Club, listening to a grand pow-wow between certain of the choicer sons of Adam. Then Slushby had cut in. Slushby is one who writes to newspapers and is theirs obediently "HUMANITARIAN." When Slushby cuts in, men remember they have to be up early next morning.

Sharp round a corner on the way home, I collided with something firmer than the regulation pillar-box. I righted myself after the recoil and saw some stars that were very pretty indeed. Then I perceived the nature of the obstruction.

"Evening, Judlip," I said sweetly, when I had collected my hat from the gutter. "Have I broken the law, Judlip? If so, I'll go quiet."

"Time yer was in bed," grunted X, 36. "Yer Ma'll be lookin' out for yer."

This from the friend of my bosom! It hurt. Many were the night-beats I had been privileged to walk with Judlip, imbibing curious lore that made glad the civilian heart of me. Seven whole 8 x 5 inch note-books had I pitmanised to the brim with Judlip. And now to be repulsed as one of the uninitiated! It hurt horrid.

There is a thing called Dignity. Small boys sometimes stand on it. Then they have to be kicked. Then they get down, weeping. I don't stand on Dignity.

"What's wrong, Judlip?" I asked, more sweetly than ever. "Drawn a blank to-night?"

"Yuss. Drawn a blank blank blank. 'Aven't 'ad so much as a kick at a lorst dorg. Christmas Eve ain't wot it was." I felt for my note-book. "Lawd! I remembers the time when the drunks and disorderlies down this street was as thick as flies on a fly-paper. One just picked 'em orf with one's finger and thumb. A bloomin' battew, that's wot it wos."

"The night's yet young, Judlip," I insinuated, with a jerk of my thumb at the flaring windows of the "Rat and Blood Hound." At that moment the saloon-door swung open, emitting a man and woman who walked with linked arms and exceeding great care.

Judlip eyed them longingly as they tacked up the street. Then he sighed. Now, when Judlip sighs the sound is like unto that which issues from the vent of a Crosby boiler when the cog-gauges are at 260° F.

"Come, Judlip!" I said. "Possess your soul in patience. You'll soon find some one to make an example of. Meanwhile"—I threw back my head and smacked my lips—"the usual, Judlip?"

In another minute I emerged through the swing-door, bearing a furtive glass of that same "usual," and nipped down the mews where my friend was wont to await these little tokens of esteem.

"To the Majesty of the Law, Judlip!"

When he had honoured the toast, I scooted back with the glass, leaving him wiping the beads off his beard-bristles. He was in his philosophic mood when I rejoined him at the corner.

"Wot am I?" he said, as we paced along. "A bloomin' cypher. Wot's the sarjint? 'E's got the Inspector over 'im. Over above the Inspector there's the Sooprintendent. Over above 'im's the old red-tape-masticatin' Yard. Over above that there's the 'Ome Sec. Wot's 'e? A cypher, like me. Why?" Judlip looked up at the stars. "Over above 'im's We Dunno Wot. Somethin' wot issues its horders an' regulations an' divisional injunctions, inscrootable like, but p'remptory; an' we 'as ter see as 'ow they're carried out, not arskin' no questions, but each man goin' about 'is dooty."

" ' 'Is dooty,' " said I, looking up from my note-book. "Yes, I've got that."

"Life ain't a bean-feast. It's a 'arsh reality. An' them as makes it a bean-feast 'as got to be 'arshly dealt with accordin'. That's wot the Force is put 'ere for from Above. Not as 'ow we ain't fallible. We makes our mistakes. An' when we makes 'em we sticks to 'em. For the honour o' the Force. Which same is the jool Britannia wears on 'er bosom as a charm against hanarchy. That's wot the brarsted old Beaks don't understand. Yer remember Smithers of our Div.?"

I remembered Smithers—well. As fine, upstanding, square-toed, bullet-headed, clean-living a son of a gun as ever perjured himself in the box. There was nothing of the softy about Smithers. I took off my billicock to Smithers' memory.

"Sacrificed to public opinion? Yuss," said Judlip, pausing at a front door and flashing his 45 c.p. down the slot of a two-grade Yale. "Sacrificed to a parcel of screamin' old women wot ort ter 'ave gorn down on their knees an' thanked Gawd for such a protector. 'E'll be out in another 'alf year. Wot'll 'e do then, pore devil? Go a bust on 'is conduc' money an' throw in 'is lot with them same hexperts wot 'ad a 'oly terror of 'im." Then Judlip swore gently.

"What should you do, O Great One, if ever it were your duty to apprehend him?"

"Do? Why, yer blessed innocent, yer don't think I'd shirk a fair clean cop? Same time, I don't say as 'ow I wouldn't 'andle 'im tender like, for sake o' wot 'e wos. Likewise cos 'e'd be a stiff customer to tackle. Lisewise 'cos——"

He had broken off, and was peering fixedly upwards at an angle of 85° across the moonlit street. " 'Ullo!" he said in a hoarse whisper.

Striking an average between the direction of his eyes—for Judlip, when on the job, has a soul-stirring squint—I perceived some one in the act of emerging from a chimney-pot.

Judlip's voice clove the silence. "Wot are yer doin' hup there?"

The person addressed came to the edge of the parapet. I saw then that he had a hoary white beard, a red ulster with the hood up, and what looked like a sack over his shoulder. He said something or other in a voice like a concertina that has been left out in the rain.

"I dessay," answered my friend. "Just you come down, an' we'll see about that."

The old man nodded and smiled. Then—as I hope to be saved—he came floating gently down through the moonlight, with the sack over his shoulder and a young fir-tree clasped to his chest. He alighted in a friendly manner on the curb beside us.

Judlip was the first to recover himself. Out went his right arm, and the airman was slung round by the scruff of the neck, spilling his sack in the road. I made a bee-line for his shoulder-blades. Burglar or no burglar, he was the best airman out, and I was muchly desirous to know the precise nature of the apparatus under his ulster. A back-hander from Judlip's left caused me to hop quickly aside. The prisoner was squealing and whimpering. He didn't like the feel of Judlip's knuckles at his cervical vertebræ.

"Wot was yer doin' hup there?" asked Judlip tightening the grip.

"I'm S-Santa Claus, Sir. P-please, Sir, let me g-go."

"Hold him," I shouted. "He's a German!"

"It's my dooty ter caution yer that wotever yer say now may be used in hevidence against yer, yer old sinner. Pick up that there sack, an' come along o' me."

The captive snivelled something about peace on earth, good will toward men.

"Yuss," said Judlip. "That's in the Noo Testament, ain't it? The Noo Testament contains some uncommon nice readin' for old gents an' young ladies. But it ain't included in the librery o' the Force. We confine ourselves to the Old Testament—O.T., 'ot. An' 'ot you'll get it. Hup with that sack, an' quick march!"

I have seen worse attempts at a neck-wrench, but it was just not slippery enough for Judlip. And the kick that Judlip then let fly was a thing of beauty and a joy for ever.

"Frog's-march him!" I shrieked, dancing. "For the love of Heaven, frog's-march him!"

Trotting by Judlip's side to the Station, I reckoned it out that if Slushby had not been at the Club I should not have been here to see. Which shows that even Slushbys are put into this world for a purpose.

MAX BEERBOHM

JOHN GALSWORTHY

Endeavour

THE DAWN of Christmas Day found London laid out in a shroud of snow. Like a body wasted by diseases that had triumphed over it at last, London lay stark and still now, beneath a sky that was as the closed leaden shell of a coffin. It was what is called an old-fashioned Christmas.

Nothing seemed to be moving except the Thames, whose embanked waters flowed on sullenly in their eternal act of escape to the sea. All along the wan stretch of Cheyne Walk the thin trees stood exanimate, with not a breath of wind to stir the snow that pied their soot-blackened branches. Here and there on the muffled ground lay a sparrow that had been frozen in the night, its little claws sticking up heavenward. But here and there also those tinier adventurers of the London air, smuts, floated vaguely and came to rest on the snow—signs that in the seeming death of civilisation some housemaids at least survived, and some fires had been lit.

One of these fires, crackling in the grate of one of those dining-rooms which look fondly out on the river and tolerantly across to Battersea, was being watched by the critical eye of an aged canary. The cage in which this bird sat was hung in the middle of the bow-window. It contained three perches, and also a pendent hoop. The tray that was its floor had just been cleaned and sanded. In the embrasure to the right was a fresh supply of hemp-seed; in the embrasure to the left the bath-tub had just been refilled with clear water. Stuck between the bars was a

large sprig of groundsel. Yet, though all was thus in order, the
bird did not eat nor drink, nor did he bathe. With his back to
Battersea, and his head sunk deep between his little sloping
shoulders, he watched the fire. The windows had for a while
been opened, as usual, to air the room for him; and the fire had
not yet mitigated the chill. It was not his custom to bathe at so
inclement an hour; and his appetite for food and drink, less
keen than it had once been, required to be whetted by example
—he never broke his fast before his master and mistress broke
theirs. Time had been when, for sheer joy in life, he fluttered
from perch to perch, though there were none to watch him, and
even sang roulades, though there were none to hear. He would
not do these things nowadays save at the fond instigation of Mr.
and Mrs. Adrian Berridge. The housemaid who ministered to
his cage, the parlourmaid who laid the Berridges' breakfast table,
sometimes tried to incite him to perform for their own pleasure.
But the sense of caste, strong in his protuberant little bosom,
steeled him against these advances.

While the breakfast table was being laid, he heard a faint tap
against the window-pane. Turning round, he perceived on the
sill a creature like to himself, but very different—a creature who,
despite the pretensions of a red waistcoat in the worst possible
taste, belonged evidently to the ranks of the outcast and the
disinherited. In previous winters the sill had been strewn every
morning with bread-crumbs. This winter, no bread-crumbs had
been vouchsafed; and the canary, though he did not exactly
understand why this was so, was glad that so it was. He had
felt that his poor relations took advantage of the Berridges'
kindness. Two or three of them, as pensioners, might not have
been amiss. But they came in swarms, and they gobbled their
food in a disgusting fashion, not trifling coquettishly with it as
birds should. The reason for this, the canary knew, was that
they were hungry; and of that he was sorry. He hated to think
how much destitution there was in the world; and he could
not help thinking about it when samples of it were thrust under
his notice. That was the principal reason why he was glad that
the window-sill was strewn no more and seldom visited.

He would much rather not have seen this solitary applicant. The two eyes fixed on his made him feel very uncomfortable. And yet, for fear of seeming to be outfaced, he did not like to look away.

The subdued clangour of the gong, sounded for breakfast, gave him an excuse for turning suddenly round and watching the door of the room.

A few moments later there came to him a faint odour of Harris tweed, followed immediately by the short, somewhat stout figure of his master—a man whose mild, fresh, pink, round face seemed to find salvation, as it were, at the last moment, in a neatly-pointed auburn beard.

Adrian Berridge paused on the threshold, as was his wont, with closed eyes and dilated nostrils, enjoying the aroma of complex freshness which the dining-room had at this hour. Pathetically a creature of habit, he liked to savour the various scents, sweet or acrid, that went to symbolise for him the time and the place. Here were the immediate scents of dry toast, of China tea, of napery fresh from the wash, together with that vague, super-subtle scent which boiled eggs give out through their unbroken shells. And as a permanent base to these there was the scent of much-polished Chippendale, and of bees'-waxed parquet, and of Persian rugs. To-day, moreover, crowning the composition, there was the delicate pungency of the holly that topped the Queen Anne mirror and the Mantegna prints.

Coming forward into the room, Mr. Berridge greeted the canary. "Well, Amber, old fellow," he said, "a happy Christmas to you!" Affectionately he pushed the tip of a plump white finger between the bars. "Tweet!" he added.

"Tweet!" answered the bird, hopping to and fro along the perch.

"Quite an old-fashioned Christmas, Amber!" said Mr. Berridge turning to scan the weather. At sight of the robin, a little spasm of pain contracted his face. A shine of tears came to his prominent pale eyes, and he turned quickly away. Just at that moment, heralded by a slight fragrance of old lace and of that peculiar, almost unseizable odour that uncut turquoises have, Mrs. Berridge appeared.

"What is the matter, Adrian?" she asked quickly. She glanced sideways into the Queen Anne mirror, her hand fluttering, like a pale moth, to her hair, which she always wore braided in a fashion she had derived from Pollaiuolo's St. Ursula.

"Nothing, Jacynth—nothing," he answered with a lightness that carried no conviction; and he made behind his back a gesture to frighten away the robin.

"Amber isn't unwell, is he?" She came quickly to the cage. Amber executed for her a roulade of great sweetness. His voice had not perhaps the fullness for which it had been noted in earlier years; but the art with which he managed it was as exquisite as ever. It was clear to his audience that the veteran artist was hale and hearty.

But Jacynth, relieved on one point, had a misgiving on another. "This groundsel doesn't look very fresh, does it?" she murmured, withdrawing the sprig from the bars. She rang the bell, and when the servant came in answer to it, said, "Oh Jenny, will you please bring up another piece of groundsel for Master Amber? I don't think this one is quite fresh."

This formal way of naming the canary to the servants always jarred on her principles and on those of her husband. They tried to regard their servants as essentially equals of themselves, and lately had given Jenny strict orders to leave off calling them "Sir" and "Ma'am," and to call them simply "Adrian" and "Jacynth." But Jenny, after one or two efforts that ended in faint giggles, had reverted to the crude old nomenclature—as much to the relief as to the mortification of the Berridges. They did, it is true, discuss the possibility of redressing the balance by calling the parlourmaid "Miss." But, when it came to the point, their lips refused this office. And conversely their lips persisted in the social prefix to the bird's name.

Somehow that anomaly seemed to them symbolic of their lives. Both of them yearned so wistfully to live always in accordance to the nature of things. And this, they felt, ought surely to be the line of least resistance. In the immense difficulties it presented, and in their constant failures to surmount these difficulties, they often wondered whether the nature of things might not be, after all, something other than what they thought it. Again and again it seemed to be in as direct conflict with duty as with inclination; so that they were driven to wonder also whether what they conceived to be duty were not also a mirage—a marsh-light leading them on to disaster.

The fresh groundsel was brought in while Jacynth was pouring out the tea. She rose and took it to the cage; and it was then that she too saw the robin, still fluttering on the sill. With a quick instinct she knew that Adrian had seen it—knew what had brought that look to his face. She went and, bending over him, laid a hand on his shoulder. The disturbance of her touch caused the tweed to give out a tremendous volume of scent, making her feel a little dizzy.

"Adrian," she faltered, "mightn't we for once—it is Christmas Day—mightn't we, just to-day, sprinkle some bread-crumbs?"

He rose from the table, and leaned against the mantelpiece, looking down at the fire. She watched him tensely. At length, "Oh Jacynth," he groaned, "don't—don't tempt me."

"But surely, dear, surely——"

"Jacynth, don't you remember that long talk we had last winter, after the annual meeting of the Feathered Friends' League, and how we agreed that those sporadic doles could do no real good—must even degrade the birds who received them—and that we had no right to meddle in what ought to be done by collective action of the State?"

"Yes, and—oh my dear, I do still agree, with all my heart. But if the State will do nothing—nothing——"

"It won't, it daren't, go on doing nothing, unless we encourage it to do so. Don't you see, Jacynth, it is just because so many people take it on themselves to feed a few birds here and there that the State feels it can afford to shirk the responsibility?"

"All that is fearfully true. But just now— Adrian, the look in that robin's eyes——"

Berridge covered his own eyes, as though to blot out from his mind the memory of that look. But Jacynth was not silenced. She felt herself dragged on by her sense of duty to savour, and to make her husband savour, the full bitterness that the situation could yield for them both. "Adrian," she said, "a fearful thought came to me. Suppose—suppose it had been Amber!"

Even before he shuddered at the thought, he raised his finger to his lips, glancing round at the cage. It was clear that Amber had not overheard Jacynth's remark, for he threw back his head and uttered one of his blithest trills. Adrian, thus relieved, was free to shudder at the thought just suggested.

"Sometimes," murmured Jacynth, "I wonder if we, holding the views we hold, are justified in keeping Amber."

"Ah, dear, we took him in our individualistic days. We cannot repudiate him now. It wouldn't be fair. Besides, you see, he isn't here on a basis of mere charity. He's not a parasite, but an artist. He gives us of his art."

"Yes, dear, I know. But you remember our doubts about the position of artists in the community—whether the State ought to sanction them at all."

"True. But we cannot visit those doubts on our old friend yonder, can we, dear? At the same time, I admit that when— when—Jacynth: if ever anything happens to Amber, we shall perhaps not be justified in keeping another bird."

"Don't, please don't talk of such things." She moved to the window. Snow, a delicate white powder, was falling on the coverlet of snow.

Outside, on the sill, the importunate robin lay supine, his little heart beating no more behind the shabby finery of his breast, but his glazing eyes half-open as though even in death he were still questioning. Above him and all around him brooded the genius of infinity, dispassionate, inscrutable, grey.

Jacynth turned and mutely beckoned her husband to the window.

They stood there, these two, gazing silently down.

Presently Jacynth said: "Adrian, are you sure that we, you and I, for all our theories, and all our efforts, aren't futile?"

"No, dear. Sometimes I am not sure. But—there's a certain

comfort in not being sure. To die for what one knows to be true, as many saints have done—that is well. But to live, as many of us do nowadays, in service of what may, for aught we know, be only a half-truth or not true at all—this seems to me nobler still."

"Because it takes more out of us?"

"Because it takes more out of us."

Standing between the live bird and the dead, they gazed across the river, over the snow-covered wharves, over the dim, slender chimneys from which no smoke came, into the grey-black veil of the distance. And it seemed to them that the genius of infinity did not know—perhaps did not even care—whether they were futile or not, nor how much and to what purpose, if to any purpose, they must go on striving.

MAX BEERBOHM

THOMAS HARDY

A Sequelula to "The Dynasts" [1]

THE VOID is disclosed. Our own Solar System is visible, distant by some two million miles.

Enter the Ancient Spirit and Chorus of the Years, the Spirit and Chorus of the Pities, the Spirit Ironic, the Spirit Sinister, Rumours, Spirit-Messengers, and the Recording Angel.

SPIRIT OF THE PITIES.

Yonder, that swarm of things insectual
Wheeling Nowhither in Particular—
What is it?

[1] *This has been composed from a scenario thrust on me by some one else. My philosophy of life saves me from sense of responsibility for any of my writings; but I venture to hold myself specially irresponsible for this one.—* TH*M*S H*RDY.

SPIRIT OF THE YEARS.

That? Oh that is merely one
Of those innumerous congeries
Of parasites by which, since time began,
Space has been interfested.

SPIRIT SINISTER.

What a pity
We have no means of stamping out these pests!

SPIRIT IRONIC.

Nay, but I like to watch them buzzing round,
Poor little trumpery ephaeonals!

CHORUS OF THE PITIES (aerial music).

Yes, yes!
What matter a few more or less?
Here and Nowhere plus
Whence and Why makes Thus.
Let these things be.
There's room in the world for them and us.

Nothing is,
Out in the vast immensities
Where these things flit,
Irrequisite
In a minor key
To the tune of the sempiternal It

SPIRIT IRONIC.

The curious thing about them is that some
Have lesser parasites adherent to them—
Bipedular and quadrupedular
Infinitesimals. On close survey

You see these movesome. Do you not recall,
We once went in a party and beheld
All manner of absurd things happening
On one of those same—planets, don't you call them?

SPIRIT OF THE YEARS (screwing up his eyes at the
Solar System).

One of that very swarm it was, if I mistake not.
It had a parasite that called itself
Napoléon. And lately, I believe,
Another parasite has had the impudence
To publish an elaborate account
Of our (for so we deemed it) private visit.

SPIRIT SINISTER.

His name?

RECORDING ANGEL.

One moment.

(Turns over leaves.)

Hardy, Mr. Thomas,
Novelist. Author of "The Woodlanders,"
"Far from the Madding Crowd," "The Trumpet
*   Major,"*
"Tess of the D'Urbervilles," etcetera,
Etcetera. In 1895
"Jude the Obscure" was published, and a few
Hasty reviewers, having to supply
A column for the day of publication,
Filled out their space by saying that there were
Several passages that might have been
Omitted with advantage. Mr. Hardy
Saw that if that was so, well then, of course,

Obviously the only thing to do
Was to write no more novels, and forthwith
Applied himself to drama and to Us.

SPIRIT IRONIC.

Let us hear what he said about Us.

THE OTHER SPIRITS.

Let's.

RECORDING ANGEL (raising receiver of aerial telephone).

3 oh 4 double oh 5, Space. . . . Hulloa.
Is that the Superstellar Library?
I'm the Recording Angel. Kindly send me
By Spirit-Messenger a copy of
"The Dynasts" by T. Hardy. Thank you.

A pause. Enter Spirit-Messenger, with copy of "The Dynasts."

Thanks.

Exit Spirit-Messenger. The Recording Angel reads "The Dynasts" aloud.

Just as the reading draws to a close, enter the Spirit of Mr. Clement Shorter and Chorus of Subtershorters. They are visible as small grey transparencies swiftly interpenetrating the brains of the spatial Spirits.

SPIRIT OF THE PITIES.

It is a book which, once you take it up,
You cannot readily lay down.

SPIRIT SINISTER.

There is
Not a dull page in it.

SPIRIT OF THE YEARS.

A bold conception
Outcarried with that artistry for which
The author's name is guarantee. We have
No hesitation in commending to our readers
A volume which—

The Spirit of Mr. Clement Shorter and Chorus of Subtershorters are detected and expelled.

—we hasten to denounce
As giving an entirely false account
Of our impressions.

SPIRIT IRONIC.

Hear, *hear!*

SPIRIT SINISTER.

Hear, *hear!*

SPIRIT OF THE PITIES.

Hear!

SPIRIT OF THE YEARS.

Intensive vision has this Mr. Hardy,
With a dark skill in weaving word-patterns
Of subtle ideographies that mark him
A man of genius. So am not I,
But a plain Spirit, simple and forthright,
With no damned philosophical fal-lals
About me. When I visited that planet
And watched the animalculæ thereon,
I never said they were "automata"
And "jackaclocks," nor dared describe their deeds
As "Life's Impulsion by Incognizance."

It may be that those mites have no free will,
But how should I know? Nay, how Mr. Hardy?
We cannot glimpse the origin of things,
Cannot conceive a Causeless Cause, albeit
Such a Cause must have been, and must be greater
Than we whose little wits cannot conceive it.
"Incognizance"! Why deem incognizant
An infinitely higher than ourselves?
How dare define its way with us? How know
Whether it leaves us free or holds us bond?

SPIRIT OF THE PITIES.

Allow me to associate myself
With every word that's fallen from your lips.
The author of "The Dynasts" has indeed
Misused his undeniably great gifts
In striving to belittle things that are
Little enough already. I don't say
That the phrenetical behaviour
Of those aforesaid animalculæ
Did, while we watched them, seem to indicate
Possession of free-will. But, bear in mind,
We saw them in peculiar circumstances—
At war, blinded with blood and lust and fear.
Is it not likely that at other times
They are quite decent midgets, capable
Of thinking for themselves, and also acting
Discreetly on their own initiative,
Not drilled and herded, yet gregarious—
A wise yet frolicsome community?

SPIRIT IRONIC.

What are these "other times" though? I had thought
Those midgets whiled away the vacuous hours

After one war in training for the next.
And let me add that my contempt for them
Is not done justice to by Mr. Hardy.

SPIRIT SINISTER.

Nor mine. And I have reason to believe
Those midgets shone above their average
When we inspected them.

A RUMOUR (tactfully intervening).

Yet have I heard
(Though not on very good authority)
That once a year they hold a festival
And thereat all with one accord unite
In brotherly affection and good will.

SPIRIT OF THE YEARS (to Recording Angel).

Can you authenticate this Rumour?

RECORDING ANGEL.

Such festival they have, and call it "Christmas."

SPIRIT OF THE PITIES.

Then let us go and reconsider them
Next "Christmas."

SPIRIT OF THE YEARS (to Recording Angel).

When is that?

RECORDING ANGEL (consults terrene calendar).

This day three weeks.

SPIRIT OF THE YEARS.

On that day we will re-traject ourselves.
Meanwhile, 'twere well we should be posted up
In details of this feast.

SPIRIT OF THE PITIES (to Recording Angel).

Aye, tell us more.

RECORDING ANGEL.

I fancy you could best find what you need
In the Complete Works of the late Charles Dickens.
I have them here.

SPIRIT OF THE YEARS.

Read them aloud to us.

The Recording Angel reads aloud the Complete Works of
Charles Dickens.

RECORDING ANGEL (closing "Edwin Drood").

'Tis Christmas Morning.

SPIRIT OF THE YEARS.

Then must we away.

SEMICHORUS I. OF YEARS (aerial music).

'Tis time we press on to revisit
That dear little planet,
To-day of all days to be seen at
Its brightest and best.
Now holly and mistletoe girdle
Its halls and its homesteads,
And every biped is beaming
With peace and good will.

SEMICHORUS II.

With good will and why not with free will?
If clearly the former
May nest in those bosoms, then why not
The latter as well?

Let's lay down no laws to trip up on,
  Our way is in darkness,
And not but by groping unhampered
  We win to the light.

The Spirit and Chorus of the Years traject themselves,
  closely followed by the Spirit and Chorus of the Pities,
  the Spirits and Choruses Sinister and Ironic, Rumours,
  Spirit-Messengers, and the Recording Angel.
There is the sound of a rushing wind. The Solar System is
  seen for a few instants growing larger and larger—a whorl
  of dark, vastening orbs careering round the sun. All but
  one of these is lost to sight. The convex seas and con-
  tinents of our planet spring into prominence.
The Spirit of Mr. Hardy is visible as a grey transparency
  swiftly interpenetrating the brain of the Spirit of the
  Years, and urging him in a particular direction, to a particular point.
The Aerial Visitants now hover in mid-air on the outskirts
  of Casterbridge, Wessex, immediately above the County
  Gaol.

SPIRIT OF THE YEARS.

First let us watch the revelries within
This well-kept castle whose great walls connote
A home of the pre-eminently blest.

The roof of the gaol becomes transparent, and the whole
  interior is revealed, like that of a beehive under glass.
Warders are marching mechanically round the corridors of
  white stone, unlocking and clanging open the iron doors
  of the cells. Out from every door steps a convict, who
  stands at attention, his face to the wall.
At a word of command the convicts fall into gangs of
  twelve, and march down the stone stairs, out into the
  yard, where they line up against the walls.
Another word of command, and they file mechanically, but
  not more mechanically than their warders, into the
  Chapel.

SPIRIT OF THE PITIES.

Enough!

SPIRITS SINISTER AND IRONIC.

'Tis more than even we can bear.

SPIRIT OF THE PITIES.

Would we had never come!

SPIRIT OF THE YEARS.

> *Brother, 'tis well*
> *To have faced a truth however hideous,*
> *However humbling. Gladly I discipline*
> *My pride by taking back those pettish doubts*
> *Cast on the soundness of the central thought*
> *In Mr. Hardy's drama. He was right.*
> *Automata these animalculæ*
> *Are—puppets, pitiable jackaclocks.*
> *Be't as it may elsewhere, upon this planet*
> *There's no free will, only obedience*
> *To some blind, deaf, unthinking despotry*
> *That justifies the horridest pessimism.*
> *Frankly acknowledging all this, I beat*
> *A quick but not disorderly retreat.*

He re-trajects himself into Space, followed closely by his
    Chorus, and by the Spirit and Chorus of the Pities, the
    Spirits Sinister and Ironic with their Choruses, Rumours,
    Spirit Messengers, and the Recording Angel.

MAX BEERBOHM

ARNOLD BENNETT

Scruts

I

EMILY WRACKGARTH stirred the Christmas pudding till her right arm began to ache. But she did not cease for that. She stirred on till her right arm grew so numb that it might have been the right arm of some girl at the other end of Bursley. And yet something deep down in her whispered "It is *your* right arm! And you can do what you like with it!"

She did what she liked with it. Relentlessly she kept it moving till it reasserted itself as the arm of Emily Wrackgarth, prickling and tingling as with red-hot needles in every tendon from wrist to elbow. And still Emily Wrackgarth hardened her heart.

Presently she saw the spoon no longer revolving, but wavering aimlessly in the midst of the basin. Ridiculous! This must be seen to! In the down of dark hairs that connected her eyebrows there was a marked deepening of that vertical cleft which, visible at all times, warned you that here was a young woman not to be trifled with. Her brain despatched to her hand a peremptory message—which miscarried. The spoon wabbled as though held by a baby. Emily knew that she herself as a baby had been carried into this very kitchen to stir the Christmas pudding. Year after year, as she grew up, she had been allowed to stir it "for luck." And those, she reflected, were the only cookery lessons she ever got. How like Mother!

Mrs. Wrackgarth had died in the past year, of a complication of ailments.[1] Emily still wore on her left shoulder that small tag of crape which is as far as the Five Towns go in the way of mourning. Her father had died in the year previous to that, of a still more curious and enthralling complication of ailments.[2]

---

[1] See "The History of Sarah Wrackgarth," pp. 345-482.
[2] See "The History of Sarah Wrackgarth," pp. 231-344.

Jos, his son, carried on the Wrackgarth Works, and Emily kept house for Jos. She with her own hand had made this pudding. But for her this pudding would not have been. Fantastic! Utterly incredible! And yet so it was. She was grown-up. She was mistress of the house. She could make or unmake puddings at will. And yet she was Emily Wrackgarth. Which was absurd.

She would not try to explain, to reconcile. She abandoned herself to the exquisite mysteries of existence. And yet in her abandonment she kept a sharp look-out on herself, trying fiercely to make head or tail of her nature. She thought herself a fool. But the fact that she thought so was for her a proof of adult sapience. Odd! She gave herself up. And yet it was just by giving herself up that she seemed to glimpse sometimes her own inwardness. And these bleak revelations saddened her. But she savoured her sadness. It was the wine of life to her. And for her sadness she scorned herself, and in her conscious scorn she recovered her self-respect.

It is doubtful whether the people of southern England have even yet realised how much introspection there is going on all the time in the Five Towns.

Visible from the window of the Wrackgarths' parlour was that colossal statue of Commerce which rears itself aloft at the point where Oodge Lane is intersected by Blackstead Street. Commerce, executed in glossy Doultonware by some sculptor or sculptors unknown, stands pointing her thumb over her shoulder towards the chimneys of far Hanbridge. When I tell you that the circumference of that thumb is six inches, and the rest to scale, you will understand that the statue is one of the prime glories of Bursley. There were times when Emily Wrackgarth seemed to herself as vast and as lustrously impressive as it. There were other times when she seemed to herself as trivial and slavish as one of those performing fleas she had seen at the Annual Ladies' Evening Fête organised by the Bursley Mutual Burial Club. Extremist!

She was now stirring the pudding with her left hand. The ingredients had already been mingled indistinguishably in that rich, undulating mass of tawniness which proclaims perfection.

But Emily was determined to give her left hand, not less than her right, what she called "a doing." Emily was like that.

At mid-day, when her brother came home from the Works, she was still at it.

"Brought those scruts with you?" she asked, without looking up.

"That's a fact," he said, dipping his hand into the sagging pocket of his coat.

It is perhaps necessary to explain what scruts are. In the daily output of every potbank there are a certain proportion of flawed vessels. These are cast aside by the foreman, with a lordly gesture, and in due course are hammered into fragments. These fragments, which are put to various uses, are called scruts; and one of the uses they are put to is a sentimental one. The dainty and luxurious Southerner looks to find in his Christmas pudding a wedding-ring, a gold thimble, a threepenny-bit, or the like. To such fal-lals the Five Towns would say fie. A Christmas pudding in the Five Towns contains nothing but suet, flour, lemon-peel, cinnamon, brandy, almonds, raisins—and two or three scruts. There is a world of poetry, beauty, romance, in scruts—though you have to have been brought up on them to appreciate it. Scruts have passed into the proverbial philosophy of the district. "Him's a pudden with more scruts than raisins to 'm" is a criticism not infrequently heard. It implies respect, even admiration. Of Emily Wrackgarth herself people often said, in reference to her likeness to her father, "Her's a scrut o' th' owd basin."

Jos had emptied out from his pocket on to the table a good three dozen of scruts. Emily laid aside her spoon, rubbed the palms of her hands on the bib of her apron, and proceeded to finger these scruts with the air of a connoisseur, rejecting one after another. The pudding was a small one, designed merely for herself and Jos, with remainder to "the girl"; so that it could hardly accommodate more than two or three scruts. Emily knew well that one scrut is as good as another. Yet she did not want her brother to feel that anything selected by him would necessarily pass muster with her. For his benefit she ostentatiously wrinkled her nose.

"By the by," said Jos, "you remember Albert Grapp? I have asked him to step over from Hanbridge and help eat our snack on Christmas Day."

Emily gave Jos one of her looks. "You've asked that Mr. Grapp?"

"No objection, I hope? He's not a bad sort. And he's considered a bit of a ladies' man, you know."

She gathered up all the scruts and let them fall in a rattling shower on the exiguous pudding. Two or three fell wide of the basin. These she added.

"Steady on!" cried Jos. "What's that for?"

"That's for your guest," replied his sister. "And if you think you're going to palm me off on to him, or on to any other young fellow, you're a fool, Jos Wrackgarth."

The young man protested weakly, but she cut him short.

"Don't think," she said, "I don't know what you've been after, just of late. Cracking up one young sawny and then another on the chance of me marrying him! I never heard of such goings on. But here I am, and here I'll stay, as sure as my name's Emily Wrackgarth, Jos Wrackgarth!"

She was the incarnation of the adorably feminine. She was exquisitely vital. She exuded at every pore the pathos of her young undirected force. It is difficult to write calmly about her. For her, in another age, ships would have been launched and cities besieged. But brothers are a race apart, and blind. It is a fact that Jos would have been glad to see his sister "settled"— preferably in one of the other four Towns.

She took up the spoon and stirred vigorously. The scruts grated and squeaked together around the basin, while the pudding feebly wormed its way up among them.

II

Albert Grapp, ladies' man though he was, was humble of heart. Nobody knew this but himself. Not one of his fellow

clerks in Clither's Bank knew it. The general theory in Hanbridge was "Him's got a stiff opinion o' hisself." But this arose
from what was really a sign of humility in him. He made the
most of himself. He had, for instance, a way of his own in the
matter of dressing. He always wore a voluminous frockcoat,
with a pair of neatly-striped vicuna trousers, which he placed
every night under his mattress, thus preserving in perfection the
crease down the centre of each. His collar was of the highest,
secured in front with an aluminium stud, to which was attached
by a patent loop a natty bow of dove-coloured sateen. He had
two caps, one of blue serge, the other of shepherd's plaid. These
he wore on alternate days. He wore them in a way of his own—
well back from his forehead, so as not to hide his hair, and with
the peak behind. The peak made a sort of half-moon over the
back of his collar. Through a fault of his tailor, there was a
yawning gap between the back of his collar and the collar of his
coat. Whenever he shook his head, the peak of his cap had the
look of a live thing trying to investigate this abyss. Dimly aware
of the effect, Albert Grapp shook his head as seldom as possible.

On wet days he wore a mackintosh. This, as he did not yet
possess a great-coat, he wore also, but with less glory, on cold
days. He had hoped there might be rain on Christmas morning.
But there was no rain. "Like my luck," he said as he came out
of his lodgings and turned his steps to that corner of Jubilee
Avenue from which the Hanbridge-Bursley trams start every
half-hour.

Since Jos Wrackgarth had introduced him to his sister at the
Hanbridge Oddfellows' Biennial Hop, when he danced two
quadrilles with her, he had seen her but once. He had nodded
to her, Five Towns fashion, and she had nodded back at him,
but with a look that seemed to say "You needn't nod next time
you see me. I can get along well enough without your nods." A
frightening girl! And yet her brother had since told him she
seemed "a bit gone, like" on him. Impossible! He, Albert Grapp,
make an impression on the brilliant Miss Wrackgarth! Yet she
had sent him a verbal invite to spend Christmas in her own
home. And the time had come. He was on his way. Incredible

that he should arrive! The tram must surely overturn, or be struck by lightning. And yet no! He arrived safely.

The small servant who opened the door gave him another verbal message from Miss Wrackgarth. It was that he must wipe his feet "well" on the mat. In obeying this order he experienced a thrill of satisfaction he could not account for. He must have stood shuffling his boots vigorously for a full minute. This, he told himself, was life. He, Albert Grapp, was alive. And the world was full of other men, all alive; and yet, because they were not doing Miss Wrackgarth's bidding, none of them really lived. He was filled with a vague melancholy. But his melancholy pleased him.

In the parlour he found Jos awaiting him. The table was laid for three.

"So you're here, are you?" said the host, using the Five Towns formula. "Emily's in the kitchen," he added. "Happen she'll be here directly."

"I hope she's tol-lol-ish?" asked Albert.

"She is," said Jos. "But don't you go saying that to her. She doesn't care about society airs and graces. You'll make no headway if you aren't blunt."

"Oh, right you are," said Albert, with the air of a man who knew his way about.

A moment later Emily joined them, still wearing her kitchen apron. "So you're here, are you?" she said, but did not shake hands. The servant had followed her in with the tray, and the next few seconds were occupied in the disposal of the beef and trimmings.

The meal began, Emily carving. The main thought of a man less infatuated than Albert Grapp would have been "This girl can't cook. And she'll never learn to." The beef, instead of being red and brown, was pink and white. Uneatable beef! And yet he relished it more than anything he had ever tasted. This beef was her own handiwork. Thus it was because she had made it so . . . He warily refrained from complimenting her, but the idea of a second helping obsessed him.

"Happen I could do with a bit more, like," he said.

Emily hacked off the bit more and jerked it on to the plate he had held out to her.

"Thanks," he said; and then, as Emily's lip curled, and Jos gave him a warning kick under the table, he tried to look as if he had said nothing.

Only when the second course came on did he suspect that the meal was a calculated protest against his presence. This a Christmas pudding? The litter of fractured earthenware was hardly held together by the suet and raisins. All his pride of manhood—and there was plenty of pride mixed up with Albert Grapp's humility—dictated a refusal to touch that pudding. Yet he soon found himself touching it, though gingerly, with his spoon and fork.

In the matter of dealing with scruts there are two schools—the old and the new. The old school pushes its head well over its plate and drops the scrut straight from its mouth. The new school emits the scrut into the fingers of its left hand and therewith deposits it on the rim of the plate. Albert noticed that Emily was of the new school. But might she not despise as affectation in him what came natural to herself? On the other hand, if he showed himself as a prop of the old school, might she not set her face the more stringently against him? The chances were that whichever course he took would be the wrong one.

It was then that he had an inspiration—an idea of the sort that comes to a man once in his life and finds him, likely as not, unable to put it into practice. Albert was not sure he could consummate this idea of his. He had indisputably fine teeth—"a proper mouthful of grinders" in local phrase. But would they stand the strain he was going to impose on them? He could but try them. Without a sign of nervousness he raised his spoon, with one scrut in it, to his mouth. This scrut he put between two of the left-side molars, bit hard on it, and—eternity of that moment!—felt it and heard it snap in two. Emily also heard it. He was conscious that at sound of the percussion she started forward and stared at him. But he did not look at her. Calmly, systematically, with gradually diminishing crackles, he reduced that scrut to powder, and washed the powder down with a sip of beer. While he dealt with the second scrut he talked to Jos about the Borough Council's proposal to erect an electric power station on the site of the old gasworks down Hillport way. He was aware of a slight abrasion inside his left cheek. No matter. He must be more careful. There were six scruts still to be negotiated. He knew that what he was doing was a thing grandiose, unique, epical; a history-making thing; a thing that would outlive marble and the gilded monuments of princes. Yet he kept his head. He did not hurry, nor did he dawdle. Scrut by scrut, he ground slowly but he ground exceeding small. And while he did so he talked wisely and well. He passed from the power-station to a first edition of Leconte de Lisle's "Parnasse Contemporain" that he had picked up for sixpence in Liverpool, and thence to the Midland's proposal to drive a tunnel under the Knype Canal so as to link up the main-line with the Critchworth and Suddleford loop-line. Jos was too amazed to put in a word. Jos sat merely gaping—a gape that merged by imperceptible degrees into a grin. Presently he ceased to watch his guest. He sat watching his sister.

Not once did Albert himself glance in her direction. She was just a dim silhouette on the outskirts of his vision. But there she was, unmoving, and he could feel the fixture of her unseen eyes. The time was at hand when he would have to meet those eyes. Would he flinch? Was he master of himself?

The last scrut was powder. No temporising! He jerked his glass to his mouth. A moment later, holding out his plate to her, he looked Emily full in the eyes. They were Emily's eyes, but not hers alone. They were collective eyes—that was it! They were the eyes of stark, staring womanhood. Her face had been dead white, but now suddenly up from her throat, over her cheeks, through the down between her eyebrows, went a rush of colour, up over her temples, through the very parting of her hair.

"Happen," he said, without a quaver in his voice, "I'll have a bit more, like."

She flung her arms forward on the table and buried her face in them. It was a gesture wild and meek. It was the gesture foreseen and yet incredible. It was recondite, inexplicable, and yet obvious. It was the only thing to be done—and yet, by gum, she had done it.

Her brother had risen from his seat and was now at the door. "Think I'll step round to the Works," he said, "and see if they banked up that furnace aright."

NOTE.—*The author has in preparation a series of volumes dealing with the life of Albert and Emily Grapp.*

MAX BEERBOHM

H. G. WELLS

Perkins and Mankind

CHAPTER XX

I.

IT WAS the Christmas party at Heighton that was one of the turning-points in Perkins' life. The Duchess had sent him a three-page wire in the hyperbolical style of her class, conveying a vague impression that she and the Duke had arranged to commit suicide together if Perkins didn't "chuck" any previous engagement he had made. And Perkins had felt in a slipshod sort of way—for at this period he was incapable of ordered thought—he might as well be at Heighton as anywhere. . . .

The enormous house was almost full. There must have been upwards of fifty people sitting down to every meal. Many of these were members of the family. Perkins was able to recognise them by their unconvoluted ears—the well-known Grifford ear, transmitted from one generation to another. For the rest there were the usual lot from the Front Benches and the Embassies. Evesham was there, clutching at the lapels of his coat; and the Prescotts—he with his massive mask of a face, and she with her quick, hawk-like ways, talking about two things at a time; old Tommy Strickland, with his monocle and his dropped g's, telling you what he had once said to Mr. Disraeli; Boubou Seaforth and his American wife; John Pirram, ardent and elegant, spouting old French lyrics; and a score of others.

Perkins had got used to them by now. He no longer wondered what they were "up to," for he knew they were up to nothing whatever. He reflected, while he was dressing for dinner on Christmas night, how odd it was he had ever thought of Using them. He might as well have hoped to Use the Dresden shepherds and shepherdesses that grinned out in the last stages of refinement at him from the glazed cabinets in the drawing-rooms . . . Or the Labour Members themselves . . .

True there was Evesham. He had shown an exquisitely open mind about the whole thing. He had at once grasped the underlying principles, thrown out some amazingly luminous suggestions. Oh yes, Evesham was a statesman, right enough. But had even he ever really *believed* in the idea of a Provisional Government of England by the Female Foundlings?

To Perkins the whole thing had seemed so simple, so imminent —a thing that needed only a little general good-will to bring it about. And now . . . Suppose his Bill *had* passed its Second Reading, suppose it had become Law, would this poor old England be by way of functioning decently—after all? Foundlings were sometimes naughty. . . .

What was the matter with the whole human race? He remembered again those words of Scragson's that had had such a depressing effect on him at the Cambridge Union—"Look here, you know! It's all a huge nasty mess, and we're trying to swab it up with a pocket handkerchief." Well, he'd given up trying to do that. . . .

II.

During dinner his eyes wandered furtively up and down the endless ornate table, and he felt he had been, in a sort of way, right in thinking these people were the handiest instrument to prise open the national conscience with. The shining red faces of the men, the shining white necks and arms of the women, the fearless eyes, general free-and-easiness and spaciousness, the look of late hours counteracted by fresh air and exercise and the best things to eat and drink—what mightn't be made of these people, if they'd only Submit?

Perkins looked behind them, at the solemn young footmen passing and repassing, noiselessly, in blue and white liveries. *They* had Submitted. And it was just because they had been able to that they were no good.

"Damn!" said Perkins, under his breath.

III.

One of the big conifers from the park had been erected in the hall, and this, after dinner, was found to be all lighted up with electric bulbs and hung with packages in tissue paper.

The Duchess stood, a bright, feral figure, distributing these packages to the guests. Perkins' name was called out in due course and the package addressed to him was slipped into his hand. He retired with it into a corner. Inside the tissue paper was a small morocco leather case. Inside that was a set of diamond and sapphire sleeve-links—large ones.

He stood looking at them, blinking a little.

He supposed he must put them on. But something in him, some intractably tough bit of his old self, rose up protesting—frantically.

If he couldn't Use these people, at least they weren't going to Use *him!*

"No, damn it!" he said under his breath, and, thrusting the case into his pocket, slipped away unobserved.

IV.

He flung himself into a chair in his bedroom and puffed a blast of air from his lungs. . . . Yes, it had been a narrow escape. He knew that if he had put those beastly blue and white things on he would have been a lost soul. . . .

"You've got to pull yourself together, d'you hear?" he said to himself. "You've got to do a lot of clear, steady, merciless thinking—now, to-night. You've got to persuade yourself somehow that, Foundlings or no Foundlings, this regeneration of mankind business may still be set going—and by *you*."

He paced up and down the room, fuming. How recapture the generous certitudes that had one by one been slipping away from him? He found himself staring vacantly at the row of books on the little shelf by his bed. One of them seemed suddenly to detach itself—he could almost have sworn afterwards that he didn't reach out for it, but that it hopped down into his hand. . . .

"Sitting Up For The Dawn"! It was one of that sociological series by which H. G. W*lls had first touched his soul to finer issues when he was at the 'Varsity.

He opened it with tremulous fingers. Could it re-exert its old sway over him now?

The page he had opened it at was headed "General Cessation Day," and he began to read. . . .

"The re-casting of the calendar on a decimal basis seems a simple enough matter at first sight. But even here there are details that will have to be thrashed out. . . .

"Mr. Edgar Dibbs, in his able pamphlet 'Ten to the Rescue,'[1] advocates a twenty-hour day, and has drawn up an ingenious scheme for accelerating the motion of this planet by four in every twenty-four hours, so that the alternations of light and darkness shall be re-adjusted to the new reckoning. I think such re-adjustment would be indispensable (though I know there is a formidable body of opinion against me). But I am far from being convinced of the feasibility of Mr. Dibbs' scheme. I believe the twenty-four hour day has come to stay—anomalous though it certainly will seem in the ten-day week, the fifty-day month, and the thousand-day year. I should like to have incorporated Mr. Dibbs' scheme in my vision of the Dawn. But, as I have said, the scope of this vision is purely practical. . . .

"Mr. Albert Baker, in a paper[2] read before the South Brixton Hebdomadals, pleads that the first seven days of the decimal week should retain their old names, the other three to be called provisionally Huxleyday, Marxday, and Tolstoiday. But, for reasons which I have set forth elsewhere,[3] I believe that the nomenclature which I had originally suggested [4]—Aday, Bday,

[1] Published by the Young Self-Helpers' Press, Ipswich.
[2] "Are We Going Too Fast?"
[3] "A Midwife For The Millennium." H. G. W*lls.
[4] "How to Be Happy Though Yet Unborn." H. G. W*lls.

and so on to Jday—would be really the simplest way out of the difficulty. Any fanciful way of naming the days would be bad, as too sharply differentiating one day from another. What we must strive for in the Dawn is that every day shall be as nearly as possible like every other day. We must help the human units —these little pink slobbering creatures of the Future whose cradle we are rocking—to progress not in harsh jerks, but with a beautiful unconscious rhythm. . . .

"There must be nothing corresponding to our Sunday. Sunday is a canker that must be cut ruthlessly out of the social organism. At present the whole community gets 'slack' on Saturday because of the paralysis that is about to fall on it. And then 'Black Monday'!—that day when the human brain tries to re-adjust itself—tries to realise that the shutters are down, and the streets are swept, and the stove-pipe hats are back in their bandboxes. . . .

"Yet of course there must be holidays. We can no more do without holidays than without sleep. For every man there must be certain stated intervals of repose—of recreation in the original sense of the word. My views on the worthlessness of classical education are perhaps pretty well known to you, but I don't underrate the great service that my friend Professor Ezra K. Higgins has rendered by his discovery[5] that the word recreation originally signified a re-creating—i.e.,[6] a time for the nerve-tissues to renew themselves in. The problem before us is how to secure for the human units in the Dawn—these giants of whom we are but the fœtuses—the holidays necessary for their full capacity for usefulness to the State, without at the same time disorganising the whole community—and them.

"The solution is really very simple. The community will be divided into ten sections—Section A, Section B, and so on to Section J. And to every section one day of the decimal week will be assigned as a 'Cessation Day.' Thus, those people who fall under Section A will rest on Aday, those who fall under Section B will

---

[5] "Words About Words." By Ezra K. Higgins, Professor of Etymology, Abraham Z. Stubbins University, Padua, Pa., U.S.A. (2 vols.)
[6] *"Id est"*—"That is."

rest on Bday, and so on. On every day of the year one-tenth of the population will be resting, but the other nine-tenths will be at work. The joyous hum and clang of labour will never cease in the municipal workshops. . . .

"You figure the smokeless blue sky above London dotted all over with airships in which the holiday-making tenth are re-creating themselves for the labour of next week—looking down a little wistfully, perhaps, at the workshops from which they are temporarily banished. And here I scent a difficulty. So attractive a thing will labour be in the Dawn that a man will be tempted not to knock off work when his Cessation Day comes round, and will prefer to work for no wage rather than not at all. So that perhaps there will have to be a law making Cessation Day compulsory, and the Overseers will be empowered to punish infringement of this law by forbidding the culprit to work for ten days after the first offence, twenty after the second, and so on. But I don't suppose there will often be need to put this law in motion. The children of the Dawn, remember, will not be the puny self-ridden creatures that we are. They will not say, 'Is this what I want to do?' but 'Shall I, by doing this, be (*a*) harming or (*b*) benefiting—no matter in how infinitesimal a degree—the Future of the Race?'

"Sunday must go. And, as I have hinted, the progress of mankind will be steady proportionately to its own automatism. Yet I think there would be no harm in having one—just one—day in the year set aside as a day of universal rest—a day for the searching of hearts. Heaven—I mean the Future—forbid that I should be hidebound by dry-as-dust logic, in dealing with problems of flesh and blood. The sociologists of the past thought the grey matter of their own brains all-sufficing. They forgot that flesh is pink and blood is red. That is why they could not convert people. . . .

"The thousandth and last day of each year shall be a General Cessation Day. It will correspond somewhat to our present Christmas Day. But with what a difference! It will not be, as with us, a mere opportunity for relatives to make up the quarrels they have picked with each other during the past year, and to eat and drink things that will make them ill well into next year. Holly and mistletoe there will be in the Municipal Eating Rooms, but the men and women who sit down there to General Cessation High-Tea will be glowing not with a facile affection for their kith and kin, but with communal anxiety for the welfare of the great-great-grand-children of people they have never met and are never likely to meet.

"The great event of the day will be the performance of the ceremony of 'Making Way.'

"In the Dawn, death will not be the haphazard affair that it is under the present anarchic conditions. Men will not be stumbling out of the world at odd moments and for reasons over which they have no control. There will always, of course, be a percentage of deaths by misadventure. But there will be no deaths by disease. Nor, on the other hand, will people die of old age. Every child will start life knowing that (barring misadventure) he has a certain fixed period of life before him—so much and no more, but not a moment less.

"It is impossible to foretell to what average age the children of the Dawn will retain the use of all their faculties—be fully vigorous mentally and physically. We only know they will be 'going strong' at ages when we have long ceased to be any use to the State. Let us, for the sake of argument, say that on the average their faculties will have began to decay at the age of ninety—a trifle over thirty-two by the new reckoning. That, then, will be the period of life fixed for all citizens. Every man on fulfilling that period will avail himself of the Municipal Lethal Chamber. He will 'make way.' . . .

"I thought at one time that it would be best for every man to 'make way' on the actual day when he reaches the age-limit. But I see now that this would savour of private enterprise. Moreover, it would rule out that element of sentiment which, in relation to such a thing as death, we must do nothing to mar. The children and friends of a man on the brink of death would instinctively wish to gather round him. How could they accompany him to the lethal chamber, if it were an ordinary working-day, with every moment of the time mapped out for them?

"On General Cessation Day, therefore, the gates of the lethal chambers will stand open for all those who shall in the course of the past year have reached the age-limit. You figure the wide streets filled all day long with little solemn processions—solemn and yet not in the least unhappy. . . . You figure the old man walking with a firm step in the midst of his progeny, looking around him with a clear eye at this dear world which is about to lose him. He will not be thinking of himself. He will not be wishing the way to the lethal chamber was longer. He will be filled with joy at the thought that he is about to die for the good of the race—to 'make way' for the beautiful young breed of men and women who, in simple, artistic, antiseptic garments, are disporting themselves so gladly on this day of days. They pause to salute him as he passes. And presently he sees, radiant in the sunlight, the pleasant white-tiled dome of the lethal chamber. You figure him at the gate, shaking hands all round, and speaking perhaps a few well-chosen words about the Future. . . ."

v.

It was enough. The old broom hadn't lost its snap. It had swept clean the chambers of Perkins' soul—swished away the whole accumulation of nasty little cobwebs and malignant germs. Gone were the mean doubts that had formed in him, the lethargy, the cheap cynicism. Perkins was himself again.

He saw now how very stupid it was of him to have despaired just because his own particular panacea wasn't given a chance. That Provisional Government plan of his had been good, but it was only one of an infinite number of possible paths to the Dawn. He would try others—scores of others. . . .

He must get right away out of here—to-night. He must have his car brought round from the garage—now—to a side door. . . .

But first he sat down to the writing-table, and wrote quickly:

Dear Duchess,
    I regret I am called away on urgent political business. . . .
                Yours faithfully
                    J. Perkins. . .

He took the morocco leather case out of his pocket and enclosed it, with the note, in a large envelope.

Then he pressed the electric button by his bedside, almost feeling that this was a signal for the Dawn to rise without more ado. . . .

MAX BEERBOHM

EDMUND GOSSE

A Recollection

"And let us strew
Twain wreaths of holly and of yew."
WALLER.

O NE OUT of many Christmas Days abides with peculiar vividness in my memory. In setting down, however clumsily, some slight record of it, I feel that I shall be discharging a duty not only to the two disparately illustrious men who made it so very memorable, but also to all young students of English and Scandinavian literature. My use of the first person singular, delightful though that pronoun is in the works of the truly gifted, jars unspeakably on me; but reasons of space baulk my sober desire to call myself merely the present writer, or the infatuated go-between, or the cowed and imponderable young person who was in attendance.

In the third week of December, 1878, taking the opportunity of a brief and undeserved vacation, I went to Venice. On the morning after my arrival, in answer to a most kind and cordial summons, I presented myself at the Palazzo Rezzonico. Intense as was the impression he always made even in London, I think that those of us who met Robert Browning only in the stress and roar of that metropolis can hardly have gauged the fullness of his potentialities for impressing. Venice, "so weak, so quiet," as Mr. Ruskin had called her, was indeed the ideal setting for one to whom neither of those epithets could by any possibility have been deemed applicable. The steamboats that now wake the echoes of the canals had not yet been imported; but the vitality of the imported poet was in some measure a preparation for them. It did not, however, find me quite prepared for itself, and I am afraid that some minutes must have elapsed before I could, as it were, find my foot in the torrent of his geniality and high spirits and give him news of his friends in London.

He was at that time engaged in revising the proof-sheets of "Dramatic Idylls," and after luncheon, to which he very kindly bade me remain, he read aloud certain selected passages. The yellow haze of a wintry Venetian sunshine poured in through the vast windows of his *salone,* making an aureole around his silvered head. I would give much to live that hour over again. But it was vouchsafed in days before the Browning Society came and made everything so simple for us all. I am afraid that after a few minutes I sat enraptured by the sound rather than by the sense of the lines. I find, in the notes I made of the occasion, that I figured myself as plunging through some enchanted thicket on the back of an inspired bull.

That evening, as I was strolling in Piazza San Marco, my thoughts of Browning were all of a sudden scattered by the vision of a small, thick-set man seated at one of the tables in the Café Florian. This was—and my heart leapt like a young trout when I saw that it could be none other than—Henrik Ibsen. Whether joy or fear was the predominant emotion in me, I should be hard put to it to say. It had been my privilege to correspond extensively with the great Scandinavian, and to be frequently received by him, some years earlier than the date of which I write, in Rome. In that city haunted by the shades of so many Emperors and Popes I had felt comparatively at ease even in Ibsen's presence. But seated here in the homelier decay of Venice, closely buttoned in his black surcoat and crowned with his uncompromising tophat, with the lights of the Piazza flashing back wanly from his gold-rimmed spectacles, and his lips tight-shut like some steel trap into which our poor humanity had just fallen, he seemed to constitute a menace under which the boldest might well quail. Nevertheless, I took my courage in both hands, and laid it as a kind of votive offering on the little table before him.

My reward was in the surprising amiability that he then and afterwards displayed. My travelling had indeed been doubly blessed, for, whilst my subsequent afternoons were spent in Browning's presence, my evenings fell with regularity into the charge of Ibsen. One of these evenings is for me "prouder, more laurel'd than the rest" as having been the occasion when he read to me the MS. of a play which he had just completed. He was staying at the Hôtel Danieli, an edifice famous for having been, rather more than forty years previously, the socket in which the flame of an historic *grande passion* had finally sunk and guttered out with no inconsiderable accompaniment of smoke and odour. It was there, in an upper room, that I now made acquaintance with a couple very different from George Sand and Alfred de Musset, though destined to become hardly less famous than they. I refer to Torvald and Nora Helmer. My host read to me with the utmost vivacity, standing in the middle of the apartment; and I remember that in the scene where Nora Helmer dances the tarantella her creator instinctively executed a few illustrative steps.

During those days I felt very much as might a minnow swimming to and fro between Leviathan on the one hand and Behemoth on the other—a minnow tremulously pleased, but ever wistful for some means of bringing his two enormous acquaintances together. On the afternoon of December 24th I confided to Browning my aspiration. He had never heard of this brother poet and dramatist, whose fame indeed was at that time still mainly Boreal; but he cried out with the greatest heartiness, "Capital! Bring him round with you at one o'clock tomorrow for turkey and plum-pudding!"

I betook myself straight to the Hôtel Danieli, hoping against hope that Ibsen's sole answer would not be a comminatory grunt and an instant rupture of all future relations with myself. At first he was indeed resolute not to go. He had never heard of this Herr Browning. (It was one of the strengths of his strange, crustacean genius that he never had heard of anybody.) I took it on myself to say that Herr Browning would send his private gondola, propelled by his two gondoliers, to conduct Herr Ibsen to the scene of the festivity. I think it was this prospect that made him gradually unbend, for he had already acquired that taste for pomp and circumstance which was so notable a characteristic of his later years. I hastened back to the Palazzo Rezzonico before he could change his mind. I need hardly say that Browning instantly consented to send the gondola. So large and lovable was his nature that, had he owned a thousand of those conveyances, he would not have hesitated to send out the whole fleet in honour of any friend of any friend of his.

Next day, as I followed Ibsen down the Danielian water-steps into the expectant gondola, my emotion was such that I was tempted to snatch from him his neatly-furled umbrella and spread it out over his head, like the umbrella beneath which the Doges of days gone by had made their appearances in public. It was perhaps a pity that I repressed this impulse. Ibsen seemed to be already regretting that he had unbent. I could not help thinking, as we floated along the Riva Schiavoni, that he looked like some particularly ruthless member of the Council of Ten. I did, however, try faintly to attune him in some sort to the spirit of our host and of the day of the year. I adumbrated Browning's outlook on life, translating into Norwegian, I well remember, the words "God's in his Heaven, all's right with the world." In fact I cannot charge myself with not having done what I could. I can only lament that it was not enough.

When we marched into the *salone,* Browning was seated at the piano, playing (I think) a Toccata of Galuppi's. On seeing us, he brought his hands down with a great crash on the keyboard, seemed to reach us in one astonishing bound across the marble floor, and clapped Ibsen loudly on either shoulder, wishing him "the Merriest of Merry Christmases."

Ibsen, under this sudden impact, stood firm as a rock, and it flitted through my brain that here at last was solved the old problem of what would happen if an irresistible force met an immoveable mass. But it was obvious that the rock was not rejoicing in the moment of victory. I was tartly asked whether I had not explained to Herr Browning that his guest did not understand English. I hastily rectified my omission, and thenceforth our host spoke in Italian. Ibsen, though he understood that language fairly well, was averse to speaking it. Such remarks as he made in the course of the meal to which we presently sat down were made in Norwegian and translated by myself.

Browning, while he was carving the turkey, asked Ibsen whether he had visited any of the Venetian theatres. Ibsen's reply was that he never visited theatres. Browning laughed his great laugh, and cried, "That's right! We poets who write plays must give the theatres as wide a berth as possible. We aren't wanted there!" "How so?" asked Ibsen. Browning looked a little puzzled, and I had to explain that in northern Europe Herr Ibsen's plays were frequently performed. At this I seemed to see on Browning's face a slight shadow—so swift and transient a shadow as might be cast by a swallow flying across a sunlit garden. An instant, and it was gone. I was glad, however, to be able to soften my statement by adding that Herr Ibsen had in his recent plays abandoned the use of verse.

The trouble was that in Browning's company he seemed practically to have abandoned the use of prose too. When, moreover, he did speak, it was always in a sense contrary to that of our host. The Risorgimento was a theme always very near to the great heart of Browning, and on this occasion he hymned it with more than his usual animation and resource (if indeed that were possible). He descanted especially on the vast increase that had accrued to the sum of human happiness in Italy since the success of that remarkable movement. When Ibsen rapped out the conviction that what Italy needed was to be invaded and conquered once and for all by Austria, I feared that an explosion was inevitable. But hardly had my translation of the inauspicious sentiment been uttered when the plum-pudding was borne into the room, flaming on its dish. I clapped my hands wildly at sight of it, in the English fashion, and was intensely relieved when the yet more resonant applause of Robert Browning followed mine. Disaster had been averted by a crowning mercy. But I am afraid that Ibsen thought us both quite mad.

The next topic that was started, harmless though it seemed at

first, was fraught with yet graver peril. The world of scholar-
ship was at that time agitated by the recent discovery of what
might or might not prove to be a fragment of Sappho. Browning
proclaimed his unshakable belief in the authenticity of these
verses. To my surprise, Ibsen, whom I had been unprepared to
regard as a classical scholar, said positively that they had not
been written by Sappho. Browning challenged him to give a
reason. A literal translation of the reply would have been "Because no woman ever was capable of writing a fragment of
good poetry." Imagination reels at the effect this would have
had on the recipient of "Sonnets from the Portuguese." The
agonised interpreter, throwing honour to the winds, babbled
some wholly fallacious version of the words. Again the situation
had been saved; but it was of the kind that does not even in
furthest retrospect lose its power to freeze the heart and con-
strict the diaphragm.

I was fain to thank heaven when, immediately after the
termination of the meal, Ibsen rose, bowed to his host, and bade
me express his thanks for the entertainment. Out on the Grand
Canal, in the gondola which had again been placed at our disposal, his passion for "documents" that might bear on his work
was quickly manifested. He asked me whether Herr Browning
had ever married. Receiving an emphatically affirmative reply, he
inquired whether Fru Browning had been happy. Loth though
I was to cast a blight on his interest in the matter, I conveyed
to him with all possible directness the impression that Elizabeth
Barrett had assuredly been one of those wives who do *not* dance
tarantellas nor slam front-doors. He did not, to the best of my
recollection, make further mention of Browning, either then or
afterwards. Browning himself, however, thanked me warmly,
next day, for having introduced my friend to him. "A capital
fellow!" he exclaimed, and then, for a moment, seemed as though
he were about to qualify this estimate, but ended by merely
repeating, "A capital fellow!"

Ibsen remained in Venice some weeks after my return to
London. He was, it may be conjectured, bent on a specially close
study of the Bride of the Adriatic because her marriage had

been not altogether a happy one. But there appears to be no evidence whatsoever that he went again, either of his own accord, or by invitation, to the Palazzo Rezzonico.

MAX BEERBOHM

THREE TWIGS REJECTED FROM THE *Garland*

AGAIN BY

MAX BEERBOHM

IN 1926 a little book entitled *Leaves from the Garland woven by Max Beerbohm* was published in New York. "Privately printed in monotype in an edition of only 72 numbered copies and the type distributed" was the impressive if ungrammatical inscription on the flyleaf. No publisher was given, but *A Bibliography of the Works of Max Beerbohm,* by A. E. Gallatin and L. M. Oliver (Harvard University Press, 1952), states it was put out by Max Harzof of G. A. Baker & Co., a now defunct publisher, and that it is "an unauthorized first edition." It contains six parodies—of Marie Corelli, Richard Le Gallienne, H. G. Wells, Ian Maclaren (who will not be remembered for his once-popular *Beside the Bonnie Brier Bush*), Alice Meynell, and . . . Max Beerbohm.

When I first read these, in the rare book room of the New York Public Library, I noted: "NOT by Beerbohm—too crude and also too mild. The Wells is funny but marred by a flat ending. B. would never have written it." As I soon found out from the *Bibliography,* which I should have consulted first, I was wrong. They were by Beerbohm. They had appeared in the 1896 Christmas Supplement of *The Saturday Review* and also in the December 15, 1896, issue of *The Chap Book* (Chicago), showing that the young Max had already discovered the possibilities of simultaneous transatlantic publication. Yet I was also right, for they *are* below the level of the *Garland.* Nonetheless, I include below three of them and another later on, under Self-Parody. My excuse, aside from a feeling that anything recherché in the way of Beerbohm parody is worth using, is that it is interesting to see how his mastery of the form developed. Compare the 1896 Wells with the 1912. Of course Wells had changed too, but still the difference strikes one in the very titles, *The Defossilized Plum-Pudding* and *Perkins and Man-*

kind. The earlier one parodies surface mannerisms, but the later goes deeper. One might call it a political prophecy, considering the desperation of the dying Wells, thirty-five years later, when he began to suspect what his socio-scientific visions had come to.

I must add that *Leaves* is a pirated edition and that Beerbohm felt strongly about it. Mr. Harzoff of G. A. Baker & Co. made a practice of reprinting Beerbohm items and sending them out as Christmas gifts to his colleagues in the trade. Beerbohm devotes most of the Note prefacing *A Variety of Things* (Knopf, 1928) to denouncing him. *The Guerdon,* for instance, had its first authorized publication in that volume, but the enterprising Mr. Harzoff had already pirated it, from the manuscript Beerbohm had written ten years earlier and incautiously allowed to be circulated among his friends. "In 1896," he writes, "I wrote for *The Saturday Review* a set of six or seven parodies of living authors and entitled them *A Christmas Garland.* George Meredith was one of these authors, and my parody of him seemed to me worth including among some parodies that were written by me many years later and published under the same old title.* The others seemed to me crude stuff, and I would none of them."

But the parodies below of Corelli, Le Gallienne and Wells seem to *me* amusing and not rubbishy; also interesting historically, so to speak. In Mr. Harzoff's case, private vices have, with the passage of time, become public virtues, *pace* Sir Max Beerbohm.

MARIE CORELLI

The Sorrows of Millicent

A WOMAN was hastening through the frozen streets of London on the Eve of Christmas last. Over her head and all around her slender frame was stretched a threadbare shawl, tattered in places and with edges sadly frayed. Little could be seen of her face, save that it was chiselled in the delicate way so rare among our "upper" classes. She had dark, lustrous eyes, charged

---

* When he reprinted his 1896 Meredith parody in 1912, Beerbohm changed the name of the heroine from Aphasia Gibberish to Euphemia Clashthought, a revision that shows, all by itself, his increased skill.

with the awakening wonder of an earlier world, and which were fringed with long lashes. To her breast she hugged something that was very small, very still, precious exceedingly. Ever and again she sought to wrap her shawl more closely round it, lest some stray, chill snowflake should alight upon it. Closed carriages with gaudy coronets smeared over the panels dashed past and covered her with mud. Several "Mashers," who had strutted out of their clubs with cigars between their coarse lips, drawled out as she passed, "By George! there's a doosidly pwetty gal." But the woman was too inured to the insults of the world to heed them. The snow was very cold to her feet, though overhead the sky was now clear and star-spangled, and over its vast surface floated a moon of silver unalloyed.

As the woman entered the hallowed precincts of Grosvenor Square she looked up eagerly at the numbers, as one searching for a particular house. At last she came to the portico of No. 205.* Through the open door came a riot of light from numerous electric globes, and down the stone steps was unrolled a drugget, for fear the high-heeled shoes of the ladies and gentlemen should be contaminated by contact with the paving-stones. Lightly, and as to the manner born, the woman ascended the steps. The lackeys sought to bar her entrance, but one look from her eyes was enough to show them, pampered fools though they were, that she was, in the true sense of the word, a lady. The odour of rich cooking told her where the dining-room was. She entered it.

At the foot of the table sat a corpulent man with a crimson countenance—Blackheart, the great critic. At the head sat his connubial spouse, a timid, bullied-looking lady. And down each side were ranged a great company of their aristocratic guests. They were just falling to on the *entremets,* when the strange, ill-clad figure, swept into the room.

Blackheart dropped his knife and fork with an oath. " 'Ow dare you admit that—that person?" he stormed to his servants. "Turn 'er hout!"

---

* I have purposely given a false number here. The Public, however, will not be slow to guess the real one.—M. C.

"I must request you to suffer me to speak, sir," said the woman in a clear, sweet voice of exquisite refinement. *"You* know well enough who I am. It may be that you, ladies and gentlemen, do not. I am her who your host has neglected and whose being he has ignored. I have come to force him to recognize me, on this sacred night, and to recognize that which I carry in my arms, dearer than life to me! I only ask for justice!"

Here she threw back her shawl from her shoulders, and held out toward the master of the house the precious burden she had been carrying—a little, cloth-bound burden with a gold design on the front cover, and bearing the title, "The Coat of Many Colours, by Millicent Coral, 15th edition." Millicent—for she it was!—stood there before the company in an attitude of sweetest, proudest humility. It was seen, now that she had discarded her shawl, that she was clad in rich black velvet, with a point-lace *fichu* round her snow-white throat. The guests were silent in her marvellous presence. Only Blackheart—who had received a large *douceur* not to review her book and been promised a royalty of 15 per cent. on every copy not sold after the hundredth thousand †—was unmoved.

"Be hoff with you!" he shouted. But his plethoric tones were drowned in a great unanimous roar of voices from without. "Do justice to Millicent Coral!" they were crying in a chorus as of thunder. The British Public had assembled in the Square, warm and staunch of heart, and were not going to be trifled with. Through the windows came a volley of stones and other missives, crashing down among the shivered plates and glasses. The hostess and her ashen-faced guests fled screaming to an upper room. Blackheart alone remained, sheltering himself beneath the table. Millicent walked fearlessly to the window, unheeding of the stones hurtling around her, but which always glanced aside from her, and, falling at her feet, turned to coruscating gems— pearls, rubies, and other precious jewels. She held up her hand smilingly, and called upon her Public to cease, which they straightway did.

Blackheart, who feared and hated the Public as all critics do,

† A fact.—M. C.

would not come out from his shelter. But his heart was still hard as the stones he so feared.

"Not one bloomin' line will you get hout of me for your precious book," he hissed through a hole in the table-cloth.

"I have sought to move you," said Millicent calmly, "by humbling myself. My Public has threatened your life, and I have saved you. There is yet one other persuasion."

She drew from her bosom that which she had received that morning—an autograph letter from the Secretary of a Great Personage. *"His Royal Highness,"* she read aloud, *"directs me to acknowledge the receipt of your book, and to say that he anticipates reading it with much pleasure."*

There was a great silence beneath the table. The critic's soul had been shaken with terror and amazement to its utter depths. a Greater than he had spoken with no uncertain voice. Who was he (Blackheart) that he could fly in the face of the Highest Critic in the Land?

He crawled out through the legs of a chair, and held out his hands for the copy of Millicent's book.

"I do not," said the young Authoress, "give away copies for review. You must purchase it in the ordinary manner. Six shillings net."

Blackheart produced the money with a good grace, received the book from Millicent's fair hands, and sat down, blue pencil in hand, to read it for review.

And Millicent, in all her young and radiant beauty, swept into the hall, and passed through the bowing footmen to the door. And when the Public outside saw their dear one on the steps they raised a wild cheer that rent the cerulean arc of heaven; but scarce did they dare to look upon her countenance, for it was as the face of an Angel.

MAX BEERBOHM

RICHARD LE GALLIENNE

The Blessedness of Apple-Pie Beds

I T WAS Yule-Day Eve and the Poet was doing his hair. All the guests in the great, strange house where he was staying, had gone to their white beds, aweary of their revels, save some sterner males who were keeping the holy vigil of Nicotine. The Poet had been invited to help them keep it, but he had other things to do that night, let alone that the cigarettes in that house were very strong and might prevail. So he was standing before his mirror alone. One by one, he entwined the curl-papers in his hair, till they looked, he thought, just like the tiny waxen candles in the great Christmas Tree downstairs. "But I mustn't light them," he murmured. "For they are the only paper money I have." And he smiled at his own fancy.

He passed a very merry evening with the rest, although there were none there who were wise, and but one who was beautiful. This sweet exception was named Beatrice, and she was yet a school-maiden, being, indeed, not past that year which is devoted to blushing. But blushes, like blush-roses, are rather becoming. At least, the Poet thought so. And when all the presents had been given, and all the poor crackers had been pulled in twain, he had sat him down beside the damsel—or damozel, as he liked to call her—and had told her fairy-notions for much more than an hour. Nor would he suffer her to flee from him when she said he was aweary, but began to tell her another. Ere he had finished it, she said to him suddenly, "How do you manage to think of all these things, I wonder!"

"I dream them abed," he answered her. "It is always abed that I dream them. To-night I will dream many more—all for you. And I will tell you them tomorrow morning, in some cosy nook."

Beatrice dropped her eyes in thought.

"Do you know what apple-pie beds are?" she asked him presently in a kind of casual way.

"Alas! I am sadly simple," said the Poet. "You must teach me."

"I will with pleasure," she replied, with eyes all bright. "But not now."

"Ah, do!" he pleaded. "Are they at all like apple-pies? I hope they are. For apple-pies are even as little roofed-in orchards, and oh! the sweet delight to steal in through that soft roof and rob them!" And when she would not tell him what these strange beds really were, he chaffed her gently for her coyness. (That wondrous chaff that comes from lovers' lips! Were I a rich merchant, I would "make a corner" in such chaff, more valuable surely than much grain!) When he would have resumed his unfinished fairy-notion, she told him it was her bedtime and left him there whispering her name. Nor was it long afterward that he and the other grown-ups said good-night to one another.

You see, he was eager to sleep early, that he might dream many things for his Beatrice. So as soon as he had done his hair he put from him swiftly all his apparel and donned the white shroud of sleep. But lo! as he was slipping in between the sheets, his feet were strangely hindered. In vain he sought to stretch forth his limbs. "May be," he cried, "the servant who made the bed for me thought I had no body, but a soul only." With his own hands he strove to order the sheets according to his fancy, but alas! so simple was he in such tasks that he availed nothing, but rather made things worse.

A very happy idea came to him. Why need he go to bed at all? Surely he could dream his notions at that little writing-table yonder! It would be better so, for then he could write them all down as he dreamt them, with one of those great quills that had been torn from some poor dead goose's back. So he sat him down, and very soon beautiful words were quietly following one another over his hostess' note-paper. When, at eight of the clock, a maid came and knocked at his door, he was writing the last sentence of the tenth notion. How many thousands of words he had written I should not dare to say, but there were a great, great many.

The Poet looked a little wan as he entered the dining-room. Some of the guests were already gently breaking their fast. Among them was little Beatrice. Was it but his fancy, or did she blush, as he came in? He could hardly make sure, so quickly did she hide her face in her tea-cup. Ere he greeted the lady of the house, he stole softly round to the maiden's chair and whispered in her ear, "I not only dreamt ten beautiful things, but have got them in my pocket, all written down for you! I won't be long over my breakfast."

Beatrice, when he came round to her, had still been holding her tea-cup to her lips. But, as he told her his glad tidings, she dropped it with a crash, and all the tea ran out over the table-cloth—like a golden carpet spread upon white snow, the Poet thought.

MAX BEERBOHM

H. G. WELLS

The Defossilized Plum-Pudding

H AVE SOME MORE of that stuff?" asked Simpson, hoisting his club-foot onto a vacant chair, and passing his long, bony fingers down the scar that runs vertically from his forehead to his chin.

"I don't mind if I do," I answered, and he gave me another help.

I do not exactly know why I always dine with Simpson on Christmas Day. Neither of us likes the other. He thinks me a dreamer, and for some reason I never trust him, though he is undoubtedly the most brilliant Pantaeschrologist of his day, and we had been contemporaries at the F. R. Z. S. It is possible that he dislikes me, and I him, less than does anybody else. And to this may be due our annual festivity in his luxurious rooms in Gower street.

"Have some of this sherry," muttered Simpson, pushing towards me a decanter which his deformed butler had placed before him. "You'll find it middling."

I helped myself to a glass and smoothing out my shirt-front, (Simpson is one of those men who "dress,") settled myself in my chair.

"Notice anything odd about that pudding?" he asked, with a searching glance through his double-convex glasses.

"No," I said simply, "I thought it very good."

A gleam of grim pleasure came out of his face. I knew from this that the annual yarn was coming. Simpson is the most enthralling talker I ever met, but somehow I always go to sleep before he is half-way through. I did so, the year before, when he told me about "The Carnivorous Mistletoe," and the year before that, when he told me "The Secret of the Sinister Crackers," and another time, when his theme was "The Microbes in the Yule Log." It vexed him very much every time, and he pooh-poohed my excuses. I was determined it should not occur again.

"I am glad you liked the pudding," he said. "Pardon my inhospitality in not keeping your company, while you ate. Tobacco is a good preventive against indigestion. You can light up."

I did so.

"You have heard of fossilized substances?" Simpson began, in that rasping voice so familiar to his pupils at the S. V. P.

I nodded across my briar.

"Well," he continued, "it has always been a pet theory of mine that, just as a substance can, by the action of certain alkaloids operating in the course of time, become, to all purposes, metallic, so—you follow me—it can, in like manner, be restored to its previous condition. You have heard of plum-puddings being kept for twenty-one years?"

I nodded; less, I am afraid, in assent than owing to a physical cause.

"Well," I heard him saying, "the stuff that you have eaten to-night is about two hundred and fifty years old and may be much more than that, at a very moderate computation."

I started. Simpson had raised his voice rather suddenly. He took my start for surprise and continued wagging his crippled forefinger at me, "That pudding was originally a cannon-ball. It was picked up on the field of Naseby. Never mind how I came by it. It has been under treatment in my laboratory for the last ten years."

"Ten years," I muttered. "Ten . . . seems almost impossible."

"For ten years," he resumed, "I have been testing, acidizing . . . thing began to decompose under my very . . . at length . . . brown, pulpy substance, such as you might . . . sultanas . . . Now comes in the curious part of the . . ."

How long after I don't know, I was awoken by a vicious kick from Simpson's club-foot.

"You brute!" I cried, "you drugged that sherry!"

"Faugh!" he sneered, "you say that every year!"

MAX BEERBOHM

A. E. HOUSMAN

WHEN LADS have done with labor
    in Shropshire, one will cry,
"Let's go and kill a neighbor,"
    and t'other answers "Aye!"

So this one kills his cousins,
    and that one kills his dad;
and, as they hang by dozens
    at Ludlow, lad by lad,

each of them one-and-twenty,
    all of them murderers,
the hangman mutters: "Plenty
    even for Housman's verse."

HUMBERT WOLFE

WALTER DE LÁ MARE

Mr. Walter de la Mare Makes the Little Ones Dizzy

SPECKLED WITH GLINTS of star and moonshine,
The house is dark and still as stone.

And Fido sleeps in the dogwood kennel
With forelegs over his mutton bone.

Then out of the walnut wood, the squirrels
Peep, with their bushy tails upreared,
And the oak on the wood's-edge stretches his branches,
And combs with his roots his mossy beard.

Then ninnies and oafs and hook-nosed zanies,
And rabbits bred in the realm of Wales,
Dance and scream in the frosty starlight,
Swinging the squirrels by the tails.

Till out of the wood, Grandfather Nightmare
Rides in a chariot of Stilton cheese,
And eats the ninnies, the oafs and zanies,
The rabbits, the oak and the walnut trees.

SAMUEL HOFFENSTEIN

GERTRUDE STEIN

OH, OH dog biscuit. And when he is happy he doesn't get snappy. Please please to do this. Then Henry, Henry, Frankie, you didn't meet him. You didn't even meet me. The glove will fit, what I say. Oh! Kai-Yi, Kai-Yi. Sure, who cares when you are through? How do you know this? Well then, oh cocoa know, thinks he is a grandpa again. He is jumping around. No hoboe and phoboe I think he means the same thing. . . . Oh mamma I can't go on through with it. Please oh! And then he clips me. Come on. Cut that out. We don't owe a nickel. Hold it instead hold it against him. . . . How many good ones and how many bad ones? Please I had nothing with him. He was a cowboy in one of the seven days a week fights. No business no hangout no friends nothing. Just what you pick up and what you need. . . . This is a habit I get. Sometimes I give it up and sometimes I don't. . . . The sidewalk was in trouble and the bears were in trouble and I broke it up. Please put me in that room. Please keep him in control. . . . Please mother don't tear don't rip. That is something that shouldn't be spoken about. Please get me up, my friends, please look out, the shooting is a bit wild and that kind of shooting saved a man's life. . . . Please mother you pick me up now. Do you know me? No, you don't scare me. They are Englishmen and they are a type I don't know who is best they or us. Oh sir get the doll a roofing. You can play jacks and girls do that with a soft ball and play tricks with it. No no and it is no. It is confused and it says no. A boy has never wept nor dashed a thousand kim. And you hear me? . . . All right look out look out. Oh my memory is all gone. A work relief. Police. Who gets it? I don't know and I don't want to know but look out. It can be traced. He changed for the worst. Please look out. My fortunes have changed and come back and went back since that. . . . They dyed my shoes. Open those shoes. . . . Police mamma Helen mother please take me out. I will settle the indictment. Come on open the soap duckets. The chimney sweeps. Talk to the sword. Shut up you got a big mouth! Please help me get up. Henry Max come over here. French Canadian bean soup. I want to pay. Let them leave me alone.

ARTHUR FLEGENHEIMER*

* Alias "Dutch Schultz," who in the early thirties was the most powerful racketeer and bootlegger in New York City. The above are some of his dying words after he was shot, with three others of his gang, in a Newark bar on October 23, 1935. They were taken down in the city hospital by F. J. Long, stenographer of the Newark Police Department, and were later printed in *Gang Rule in New York,* by Craig Thompson and Allen Raymond (Dial Press, 1940).

THEODORE DREISER

Compiling an American Tragedy

SUGGESTIONS AS TO HOW THEODORE DREISER MIGHT WRITE
HIS NEXT HUMAN DOCUMENT AND SAVE FIVE YEARS' WORK

CHAPTER I

U P EAST DIVISION STREET, on a hot day in late July, walked two men, one five feet four, the other, the taller of the two, five feet six, the first being two inches shorter than his more elongated companion, and consequently giving the appearance to passers-by on East Division Street, or, whenever the two reached a cross street, to the passers-by on the cross street, of being at least a good two inches shorter than the taller of the little group.

Walking up East Division Street they came, in two or three minutes, to Division Street proper, which runs at right angles and a little to the left of East Division Street, but not so much to the left as Marcellus Street, or Ransome Street, for that matter. As the two continued strolling, in that fashion in which two men of their respective heights are likely to stroll, they came in succession to—

(NOTE TO PRINTER: *Attached find copy of Thurston's Street Guide. Print names of every street listed therein, beginning with East Division and up to, and including, Dawson.*)

CHAPTER II

That these two men, presented in the last chapter, would eventually stop walking up Division Street and enter a house of some sort or description, might well be anticipated by the reader, and, in fact, such was the case.

It was, indeed, the house of the shorter of the two, of the one whom we have seen in the last chapter to have been five feet four, if, indeed, he was. It was a typical dwelling, or home, of a man of the middle class in a medium-sized city such as the one in which these men found themselves living.

(NOTE TO PRINTER: *Attached find insurance inventory of household effects and architect's specifications. Reproduce in toto.*)

CHAPTER III

Reaching the living room described above, Tom Rettle, for such was the name of the shorter of the two—the one to whom the house, or home, or dwelling, belonged—was greeted by his wife, Anna, a buxom woman of perhaps thirty-four or thirty-five, certainly not *more* than thirty-five, if one were to judge by her fresh, wholesome color and the sparkle of her brownish-gray eyes, or even by her well-rounded form, her—

(*Print attached passport description of Anna Rettle.*)

"Well, hello, Anna," said Tom, pleasantly, for Tom Rettle was, as a matter of fact, a very pleasant man unless he were angered, and his blue eyes smiled in a highly agreeable manner.

"Well, hello, Tom," replied Anna, for it was indeed Anna who spoke, in a soft, well-modulated voice, too, giving the impression of being an extremely agreeable sort of a woman.

"Anna, I want you to meet a very good friend of mine, Arthur Berolston, a very good friend of mine," said Tom, politely, looking, at the same time, at both Anna and Berolston.

"I'm very happy to meet Mr. Berolston," added Anna, genially, although one could see that in her heart she wished that Tom would bring a little different type of friend home, a thing she had often spoken to him about when they were alone, as they often were.

"Dat's very good of yer ter say, Missus Rettle," replied Berolston, in modern slang, which made him sound even more uncouth than he looked, which was uncouth enough. "For de love o' Mike!"

At this indication of a rough bringing-up on the part of her husband's acquaintance, Anna Rettle winced slightly but showed no other sign of her emotions. Tom was such a kind-hearted fellow! So good! So kind-hearted! Tom was.

"What is there for supper tonight, Anna?" asked Tom, when the wincing had died down. "You know how well I like cole slaw, and have always liked it."

"I certainly do know your fondness for cole slaw, Tom," replied his wife, but with a note of regret in her voice, for she was thinking that she had no cole slaw for supper on the particular night of which we are speaking. "But you will remember that we had cole slaw last night with the cold tongue, and night before last with the baked beans and—"

(*Run attached "Fifteen Midsummer Menus for Cole Slaw Lovers."*)

CHAPTER IV

Prepared as Tom was not to have cole slaw for supper, he could not hide his disappointment. Anna had been a good wife to him.

But somehow tonight, when he had brought Arthur Berolston home to supper, his disappointment was particularly keen, for he and Arthur had been discussing cole slaw all the way up East Division Street, across Division Street and through to the southwest corner of Dawson and Margate, where Tom lived, and each had said how much he liked it.

Should he strike Anna for failing him at this juncture? He, Tom Rettle, strike his wife, Anna Rettle? And, even if he should decide to strike her, *where* should he direct the blow? Tom's mind was confused with all these questions.

(*Reprint the above paragraph twenty-five times.*)

CHAPTERS V-LXXXII INCLUSIVE

TO PRINTER: *With the above copy you will find a briefcase containing newspaper clippings giving the complete testimony of Anna Rettle, Thomas Rettle and Arthur Berolston in the case of "ANNA RETTLE VS. THOMAS RETTLE," tried in the Criminal Court of Testiman County, September 2-28, 1925. There is also a transcript of the testimony of three neighbors of the Rettles' (Herman Nordquist, Ethel Nordquist and Junior Nordquist), and of Officer Louis M. Hertzog of the Fifth Precinct. Reprint all these and, at the bottom of the last page, put "THE END."*

ROBERT BENCHLEY

H. L. MENCKEN
AND GEORGE JEAN NATHAN

Mr. Mencken Reviews Mr. Nathan and Vice Versa
(WITH APOLOGIES, IN GERMAN, TO BOTH)

The Literary Katzenjammer

ART OF THE NIGHT, by George Jean Nathan. $2.50; $10. 13½ x 6⅞.
New York: *Alfred A. Knopf.*

AMONG the more illuminating manifestations of that imbecilic ratiocination peculiar to the *mens Americana* is the belief, prevalent in some quarters of our fair land, that Mr. George Jean Nathan is a writer of importance. For preposterous rubbish this is comparable only with the more august imbecility which rates Calvin Coolidge as a great man, Offenbach as a great composer, or salted almonds as great *Vorspeise.*

That Nathan is energetic can not be denied. That he is privy to the sonorous hocus-pocus of critical jargon is a fact patent to anyone who has had the time and stomach to delve into the *Jahrbuch* issued each spring under his name by the obliging House of Knopf. Each contains current forms of prayer to O'Neill, Ziegfeld, O'Casey and other gods, together with expurgatoriana for the year's dæmons. But that these collections of *obiter dicta* furnish any more lasting contribution to the world's thought than is offered in the highfalutin rumble-bumble of Otto H. Kahn or the pish-posh incidental to the performance of the marriage service in the Church of England is an admission I am not prepared to make.

There is a current and quite preposterous impression that Nathan's hold on the intellectual booberie is a sensual one. He is supposed to titillate their nerve-centers, causing them to jump. More palpable tosh than this has not formed a part of the public superstition since the Sermon on the Mount. As a matter of fact, Nathan's appeal is spiritual. Assuming the manner of a cynical fellow, he looks sourly and with a bilious eye on the idols in the temple, but, even as he looks, he beats time to the chant of the priests and eventually, overcome with the religious razzle-dazzle, breaks into a profuse sweat, raises his arms to the heavens and performs a slow, reverent hoochie-koochie, followed by hundreds of zany converts.

To say that Nathan is a purveyor of sensory stimuli because he writes of beer-guzzling and hip-shaking is as much rubbish as to say that Aimée Semple McPherson is a purveyor of spiritual balm because she haggles with God, that a Shubert chorus man is a disciple of Karl Marx because he affects a red necktie or that Calvin Coolidge is a statesman because he wears a frock coat. If Nathan is an iconoclast, then Henry Ford makes automobiles and Otto H. Kahn has a dress-suit.

Since we find, then, that, in so far as Nathan is a force at all he is a spiritual force, he must stand back-to-back with his brother ballyhoo boys in the vineyards of the Lord and be measured. And, in competition with Rabbi Stephen S. Wise and Bishop Manning, Mr. Nathan can not hope ever to rise above the rank of drum-major's assistant. I confidently predict that in a hundred years he will be remembered solely for his cravats.

Clinical Notes
BY GEORGE JEAN NATHAN

T HE NEW MOSES.—Every now and again the critical boys, many of them still in their emotional didies themselves, get to cutting up over some new baby they have found sucking at a bulrush down by the river's bank. Here, they cry, is someone who is going to make Voltaire look like an empty seidel of Löwenbräu, Daumier like a small Emmenthaler *käse,* Brahms like an old Fedora hat and John Singer Sargent like the wet end of a Bock panetela. Such a phenomenon seems to be Professor Henry L. Mencken, who, my trusted Egyptian body-servant and spy tells me, is now being hailed as the New Hot Dickety.

Aside from the local critics, who allow themselves to be horn-swoggled with a regularity and amiability which could bring them in money if properly applied, Le Mencken seems to have a following made up of such giant intellects as believe that Cabell is better than Rachmaninoff, Sinclair Lewis better than Stravinsky, Dreiser better than Mestrović, O'Neill better than Tunney, Dreiser better than O'Neill, Lewis better than Dreiser, Cabell better than Lewis, O'Neill better than Dreiser, and Sinclair Lewis better than James Branch Cabell.

I have also reason to believe that under cross-examination they would confess to a sneaking suspicion that (1) all hack-drivers are Swedenborgians; (2) when a man asks a woman to marry him, she always thinks he is fooling and accepts him; (3) that if you cut the pages of a book with your finger it makes the book look as if the pages had been cut with someone's finger, and (4) that all hack-drivers are Swedenborgians.

From such intellectual brothels, then, are the Mencken witnesses assembled. The State rests.

Etude in E Minor.—It is occasionally my duty, as Liaison Officer for the Watch and Ward Society, to look into the state of the *res publicæ* with special reference to *sauce rémoulade*. I have been especially interested, therefore, in the pronunciamento of several of my critical colleagues in New York that the best *sauce rémoulade* is to be found at the Colony Restaurant. This I take to be piffle and recommend to my brothers in the bond that they look into the *sauce rémoulade* in the oyster-bar at Prunier's in Paris, at the Restaurant Horscher in Berlin, at Schöner's in Vienna, at Hetlig's Café in Budapest, at the Hotel zum Eisenhut in Rothenburg, at Louie's in Prague, and at the Central House in Bellows Falls, Vt.

Reprise.—It is my private opinion that Florenz Ziegfeld should receive the portfolio of Secretary of State without further shilly-shallying. As a picker of cuties, Kellogg has shown himself a dud.

ROBERT BENCHLEY

T. S. ELIOT

THIS FAMOUS PARODY was originally an entry in a *New Statesman* contest. "Most parodies of one's own work strike one as very poor," Mr. Eliot writes. "In fact one is apt to think one could parody oneself much better. (As a matter of fact some critics have said that I have done so.) But there is one which deserves the success it has had, Henry Reed's *Chard Whitlow*." Broadness is the sin of most Eliot parodies; Mr. Reed's alone seems to me to escape it. The one following, by "Myra Buttle," who is a Cambridge don, does not. I have included it because it is funny and because I thought some sample of *The Sweeniad* should be given.

Chard Whitlow

(MR. ELIOT'S SUNDAY EVENING POSTSCRIPT)

As WE GET OLDER we do not get any younger.
Seasons return, and today I am fifty-five,
And this time last year I was fifty-four,
And this time next year I shall be sixty-two.
And I cannot say I should like (to speak for myself)
To see my time over again—if you can call it time:
Fidgeting uneasily under a draughty stair,
Or counting sleepless nights in the crowded tube.

There are certain precautions—though none of them very re-
    liable—
Against the blast from bombs and the flying splinter,
But not against the blast from heaven, *vento dei venti,*
The wind within a wind unable to speak for wind;
And the frigid burnings of purgatory will not be touched
By any emollient.
                    I think you will find this put,
Better than I could ever hope to express it,
In the words of Kharma: "It is, we believe,
Idle to hope that the simple stirrup-pump

Will extinguish hell."
Oh, listeners,

And you especially who have turned off the wireless,
And sit in Stoke or Basingstoke listening appreciatively to the
    silence,
(Which is also the silence of hell) pray, not for your skins, but
    your souls.

And pray for me also under the draughty stair.
As we get older we do not get any younger.

And pray for Kharma under the holy mountain.

HENRY REED

II

Sweeney in Articulo

THE VOICE OF SWEENEY

Sunday is the dullest day, treating
Laughter as a profane sound, mixing
Worship and despair, killing
New thought with dead forms.
Weekdays give us hope, tempering
Work with reviving play, promising
A future life within this one.
Thirst overtook us, conjured up by Budweisserbrau
On a neon sign: we counted our dollar bills.
Then out into the night air, into Maloney's Bar,
And drank whiskey, and yarned by the hour.
Das Herz ist gestorben,[1] swell dame, echt Bronx.
And when we were out on bail, staying with the Dalai Lama,
My uncle, he gave me a ride on a yak,
And I was speechless. He said, Mamie,

Mamie, grasp his ears. And off we went
Beyond Yonkers, then I felt safe.
I drink most of the year and then I have a Vichy.

Where do we go from here, where do we go,
Out of the broken bottles? Pious sot!
You have no guide or clue for you know only
Puce snakes and violet mastodons, where the brain beats,
And a seltzer is no answer, a vomit no relief,
And the parched tongue no feel of water. Only
There is balm in this YMCA
(Claim now the balm inside this YMCA),
And you will see that there is more in life than
Those vigils at the doors of pubs in the morning,
Or bootings from the doors of pubs at closing-time.
I will show you fear in a pile of half-bricks.
        Wer reitet so spät
        Durch Nacht und Wind?
        Es ist der Vater mit seinem Kind.[2]
"You called me 'Baby Doll' a year ago;
You said that I was very nice to know,"
Yet when we came back late from that Wimbledon dance-hall,
Your arms limp, your hair awry, you could not
Speak, and I likewise, we were neither
Living nor dead, and we knew nothing,
Gazing blankly before us in the carriage.
"Bank Station! All change! *Heraus! Heraus!*"

(Cloax is the vilest drink, gouging
Pockets out of your giblets, mixing
Frenzy and remorse, blending
Rot-gut and white-ants.
Jalap has a use, laundering
Colons with refreshing suds, purging
The lower soul with gentle motion.)

Count Cagliostro,[3] famous impostor,
Often in gaol, nevertheless
Enjoyed a great career, adored by the ladies.
Sold them love and youth elixirs. Said he,
Take this powder, "Lymph of Aphrodite,"
("In delay there lies no plenty." [4] See!)
Made with belladonna, that lightens up your eyes,
Enhances your fascinations.
Much more than this, now listen, it gives you power
To peep into the past and future, crystalline bright.
Just a pinch, you witness the fall of ancient Troy,
Another small pinch, a deep breath, before your eyes
The Apocalypse! Just watch *me* taste.
Lo! The Four Horsemen and the Beast, as plain as the stars!
Goodbye, Marquise. If you see her Majesty the Queen,
Tell her I have the Diamond Necklace,[5]
It's hidden in my *cabinet de toilette.*

Earthly Limbo,
Chilled by the raw mist of a January day,
A crowd flowed down King's Parade, so ghostly,
Mowed down by the centuries, so ghostly.
You barely heard the gibbering and the squeaks
As each man gazed in front with staring eyes,
Flowed past Caius Insurance Offices
To where the clock in Trinity Great Court
Marked off the hours with male and female voice.
There I saw one I knew, and hailed him shouting, Muravieff-
     Amursky!
You who were with me up at Jesus,
And fought in my battalion at Thermopylae!
Your brain-box stopped an arrow, you old cadaver.
Are you Hippolytus,[6] killed by your horses' hoofs,
Revivified by Aesculapius?
"I sometimes think there never blows so red

The Rose as where some buried Caesar bled." [7]
"If Winter comes can Spring be far behind?" [8]

NARRATOR

His words are very indistinct—perhaps it's atmospherics?
He's quoting from the *Daily Telegraph*, and now there's a
    piece that sounds as if it might be Herrick's—
Ah, there he is once more, completely audible again,
Summing up his views, I think, though he seems to be in pain!

THE VOICE OF SWEENEY

This is the vacant mind,
This is the barren mind,
Empty, bereft of intellect,
Can nothing fill the yawning void?
Is there no voodoo, charm, or pious platitude
To save the world from thought?
. . . . .
But you must believe in *some*thing!
Can't you see it's only alle*gor*ical!
And what would happen to so*ci*ety?
. . . . .
*Iudica me, Deus, et discérne causam meam de gente non
    sancta: ab hómine iníquo, et dolóso érue me.*[9]
Boomalay, boomalay, boomalay, boom! [10]
L'Érèbe les eût pris pour ses coursiers funèbres,[11]

聖人因而興制不事心焉 [12]

𓏜𓈖𓋴𓃭𓂋𓎡𓋹𓊪 [13]

… ― ― ― … [14]

𓎡𓏏𓃭𓂻𓆑 [15]

"Love thy neighbour as thyself,"
"Couldn't you bring better weather with you?" and,

Above all,
"Please adjust your dress before leaving." [16]

. . . .

[1] Schiller, *Das Mädchens Klage.*
[2] Goethe, *Erlkönig.*
[3] Count Cagliostro (1743-95), Italian alchemist, whose real name was Giuseppe Balsamo. (See Note 5 below.)
[4] Shakespeare, *Sweet and Twenty.*
[5] The Affair of the Diamond Necklace (1778-86). A mysterious incident which involved Marie Antoinette. In the sensational trial which ensued, Cagliostro was acquitted.
Here Cagliostro figures as the Prophet of the Age of Unreason, which he foretold would begin in earnest in 1922.
[6] Hippolytus, son of Theseus by Hippolyta, Queen of the Amazons. He was falsely suspected of having attempted the dishonour of Theseus' second wife, Phaedra. Poseidon, at the instigation of Theseus, sent forth a bull from the water at which the horses drawing Hippolytus' chariot took fright, over-turned the chariot, and dragged Hippolytus along the ground until he was dead. Artemis, however, induced Aesculapius to restore him to life again.
Originally a Vegetation Myth, but here, for the sake of poetical consistency, Aesculapius administers arsenic instead of elixir to Hippolytus.
[7] FitzGerald, *Omar Khayyám.* "The Rose" = Pernicious Anaemia.
[8] Shelley, *Ode to the West Wind.* For "Winter" read "Spring" and vice versa.
[9] Roman Catholic *Liturgy of the Mass.* Here read in Anglican (or "Pick-wickian") sense.
[10] Vachel Lindsay, *The Congo.* Last words of St. Mumbo Jumbo.
[11] Baudelaire, *Les Chats.* Euphony only (no relevance).
[12] From *Lü Shih Ch'un Ch'iu.* "The Sage follows Nature in establishing social order, and does not invent principles out of his own head."
Since this is a rational statement in authentic Chinese it is thought to have slipped in by mistake for a quotation from Mr. Pound.
[13] From an ancient Egyptian inscription. Literally, "Thy breath of life is sweet in my nostril."
"Life" here is an occult symbol for death.
[14] The famous Morse signal of distress sent out by the *Titanic* on 14 April 1912. Here it is sent out by the inhabitants of the "Unreal City." No one answers it.
[15] "Hydor," water, short for "Ariston Men Hydor," i.e. "Take more water with it." A message in manual code from Microcephalos, the deaf-and-dumb soothsayer of Thebes, to Tiresias (who was blind anyway) on the morning after a feast. Here it signifies the Seven Types of Ambiguity.
[16] Reproduced by permission of the Westminster City Council.

MYRA BUTTLE

ARCHIBALD MACLEISH

The Omelet of A. MacLeish

I

AND the mist: and the rain in the west: and the wind steady:

There were elms in that place: and graven inflexible laws:

Men of Yale: and the shudder of Tap Day: the need for a man
  to make headway

Winning a way through the door in the window-
  less walls:

And the poems that came easy and sweet with a
  blurring of Masefield

MacLeish breaks
an egg for his
omelet.

(The same that I later denied): a young man smooth but raw

Eliot alarmed me at first: but my later abasement:

And the clean sun of France: and the freakish but beautiful
  fashion:

Striped bathhouses bright on the sand: Anabase and The Waste
  Land:

These and the Cantos of Pound: O how they
  came pat!

Nimble at other men's arts how I picked up the
  trick of it:

He puts plovers'
eggs and truffles
into his omelet.

Rode it reposed on it drifted away on it: passing

Shores that lay dim in clear air: and the cries of affliction

Suave in somniferous rhythms: there was rain there and moons:

Leaves falling: and all of a flawless and hollow felicity:

In that land there were summer and autumn and
  nighttime and noon

But all seemed alike: and the new polished
  planets by Einstein:

He slips in a
few prizes for
philosophers.

And a wind out of Valéry's graveyard but it never blew anything
  loose:

And the questions and questions
questioning
What am I? O

What shall I remember?
O my people
a pensive dismay

What have I left unsaid?
Till the hearer cried:

The omelet
becomes a
national
institution and
gets into
Fanny Farmer.

"If only MacLeish could remember if only could
say it!" . . .
And young girls came out: they were innocent
strong in the tendons
Hungry for all that was new: and hearing their
eyelids were hazy with

Hungry for all that was new: and hearing their eyelids were
hazy with

Tears and delight: and the campuses brown in November:
Hey but white shirt fronts pink faces: the prizes won:
The celluloid tower with bold intonations defended.

He experiments
with a new kind
of peppercorn.

And the mean tang of Cummings turned saltless
and sleek on the tongue:
And a Dante gone limp: and a shimmer and
musical sound

That gleamed in the void and evoked approbation and wonder

That the poet need not be a madman or even a bounder.

II

He seems likely
to lose his
investment in
his omelet.

AND at last I drew close to a land dark with
fortifications:
Men shrieking outlandish reproaches till all my
blood tingled:

It was ragged and harsh there: they hated: heart horribly quaked
in me:

Then I thought "I have staved off the pricking of many a sting:
These perchance I may placate too": I put in at that place:
I met them with scorn and good-natured agreement mingled:

Their fierce cries of "Aesthete!" and "Fascist!": and like them I
    railed at the
Bankers and builders of railroads: I said "Social Credit":
(He's a tough lad under the verse mister all the same!):

He is obliged   And the Polacks and Dagoes and Hunkies unto reopen his   doubtedly dead:
omelet and put   And behold these savage and sybarite-baiting
a little garlic in.   strangers
Had many among them like me well-mannered well-fed

Bubbling over with schoolboy heroics: their line had been chang-
    ing:
And long in that plentiful land I dwelt honored in peace:
And then schoolboys from Britain came over us flying like
    angels:

Them too I courted: and labored to roughen the sweet
To stiffen the wilt of a style that seemed lax in that land:
A starch of Greek tragedy: stark Anglo-Saxon the beat of it:

He is doomed   Stock-market talk: still my numbers as mawkishly
to go on   ran:
doctoring his   (Señora, I could go on like this forever:
omelet.

It is a strange thing to be an American):

I was wired for sound as I started again down the river:
And by colons went out on the air to the clang of a gong:
O when shall I ring with the perilous pain and the fever?

A clean and clever lad
                    who is doing
                            his best
                                to get on. . . .

                                        EDMUND WILSON

EZRA POUND

Homage to Ezra Pound

AND so depart into dark
long in limbo, hornet-stung and following battered flags
and then manufacturing various hells for his own enemies
  all stamped EZRA POUND
  (Phoebus, what a name
    to swill the speaking trump, *gloriæ futuris*)
though ole T.S.E. proclaimed his maestro
  and in *such* prose, my God
    constipated but dignified like an elderly cat
"trying his technique so that it will be ready like a well-oiled
fire engine when the moment comes to strain it to the utmost,"
ooh, my God, *splendeur Dex!*

But the *Criterion* folded
  (good old *Criterion* many a happy hour
  have I spent at the bar watching the lovelies
  shantih
   shantih?
     No, 'e shan't!)
and the Cantos went not with a bang but a fizzle
  didn't even get ther ber-luddy reviews
and the expatriate adorers all came running back to mamma's
  womb
so there was no one left to visit the shrine. . . .

We have observed, quoth Plinius, that sacrifices hitherto popular
in many provinces of the empire have now almost ceased, to the
great impoverishment of butchers, graziers, and the like. *Dabam
Romae prid. III Kal. Iul.:* that's June 1, buddy, in their dago
lingo. . . .

And there sat the well-oiled fire-engine
all ready to strain its gutmost
    eek ow ouf honk honk
unable to think, but ready to quote and paraphrase in six lan-
    guages
including Provençal . . .
    ei didl didl
    li chat e li fidl
        it took a man like Ezra to kill Provençal poetry
            for us. . . .
And he had learnt all he could
    not a hell of a lot
    στεῖραν βοῦν = sterile bulls, that was a good one, Canto I
    a significant bit of bull
    Cimbrorumque minas = Welsh coal mines, meant to be
        funny, maybe?
    pretty damn funny, anyway
    QUAINT like all his Chinese and Greeks and Romans
    they appear QUAINT to Homer Pound's boy from the
        backwoods
the Idaho poeta. . . .

And his temper was never good, you get eccentric living in
    Rapallo and loving
BEAUTY
    the emperor is at Ko
    but No
    silken strings shiver no longer, clashing of smilax, dark
    nuts on the dry bough, nuts on wet earth, nuts
it's lonesome, too, being the only one who understands
            Caius Properzius,
          'Alkaios,
        Li Pu,
       all great guys,
      an' I *know* 'em, see?

Uncle Ezry on the Acropopopoulos, the rube at the grocery stove
    gignetei colon
    :

SO?

So he took to damning his own country, living in Rapallo and
    Rome[1]
        among the blackshirted brownbottomed yellowhearted
            Heroes
        the gallant macaronis that ran from the Greeks, 3 to 1
            aera!
                              aera! !
                                          whoosh! ! !

  sure, Ezra loved 'em:
        the lover of the third-rate loving fascist Italia e l'IMPERO
            pfft
        the bogus aristocrat wanting Discipline and no Lower
            Classes

So Ezra attacked the ole USA and pluto-bolsho-Britain
        Jews, & negroes, & Roosevelt, & armament trusts, & usurers
        melodious swill-pipe for Goebbels

(Frank Sullivan says Gayda is the only newspaperman that
can write the way a Pekinese barks . . . He shd read Ezra's
XIVth Canto. . . .
        tender . . .
            like a centaur's asphodel . . .)

And so to his own hell, the last hell, the ninth hell, Antenora
    of ice
    for traitors
        teeth gnashing like the chattering of storks

GILBERT HIGHET

[1] The parody was written just after his treasonous broadcasts had begun to
hit us strongly—Author's note.

ROBERT FROST

Mr. Frost Goes South to Boston

WHEN I SEE buildings in a town together,
Stretching all around to touch the sky,
I like to know that they come down again
And so I go around the block to see,
And, sure enough, there is the downward side.
I say to myself these buildings never quite
Arrived at heaven although they went that way.
That's the way with buildings and with people.
The same applies to colts and cats and chickens
And cattle of all breeds and dogs and horses.
I think the buildings Boston has are high
Enough. I like to ride the elevator
Up to the top and then back I come again.
Now, don't get me wrong. I wouldn't want
A ticket to New York to ride up higher.
These buildings come as close to heaven now
As I myself would ever want to go.

FIRMAN HOUGHTON

ALDOUS HUXLEY

Told in Gath

"Vulgarity is the garlic in the salad of charm."

ST. BUMPUS.

IT WAS to be a long week-end, thought Giles Pentateuch apprehensively, as the menial staggered up the turret stairs with his luggage—staggered all the more consciously for the knowledge that he was under observation, just as, back in Lexham Gardens, his own tyrannical Amy would snort and groan outside the door to show how steep the back-stairs were, before entering with his simple vegetarian breakfast of stink-wort and boiled pond-weed. A long week-end; but a week-end at Groyne! And he realized, with his instinct for merciless analysis that amounted almost to torture, that in spite, yes, above all, in spite of the apprehension, because of it even, he would enjoy all the more saying afterwards, to his friend Luke Snarthes perhaps, or to little Reggie Ringworm, "Yes, I was at Groyne last week-end," or "Yes, I was there when the whole thing started, down at Groyne."

The menial had paused and was regarding him. To tip or not to tip? How many times had he not been paralysed by that problem? To tip was to give in, yes, selfishly to give in to his hatred of human contacts, to contribute half a crown as hush-money, to obtain "protection," protection from other people, so that for a little he could go on with the luxury of being Giles Pentateuch, "scatologist and eschatologist," as he dubbed himself. Whereas not to tip . . .

For a moment he hesitated. What would Luke Snarthes have done? Stayed at home, with that splayed ascetic face of his, or consulted his guru, Chandra Nandra? No—no tip! The menial slunk away. He looked round the room. It was comfortable, he had to admit; a few small Longhis round the walls, a Lupanar by Guido Guidi, and over the bed an outsize Stuprum Sabinarum, by Rubens—civilized people, his hosts, evidently.

He glanced at the books on the little table—the *Odes of Horace*, Rome 23 B.C., apparently a first edition, the *Elegancies of Meursius* (Rochester's copy), *The Piccadilly Ambulator*, *The Sufferings of Saint Rose of Lima*, *Nostradamus* (the Lérins Press), *Swedenborg*, *The Old Man's Gita*. "And cultivated," he murmured, "too." The bathroom, with its sun-lamp and Plombières apparatus, was such as might be found in any sensible therapeutic home. He went down to tea considerably refreshed by his lavage.

The butler announced that Lady Rhomboid was "serving" on the small west lawn, and he made his way over the secular turf with genuine pleasure. For Minnie Rhomboid was a remarkable woman.

"How splendid of you to come," she croaked, for she had lost her voice in the old suffragette days. "You know my daughter, Ursula Groyne."

"Only too well," laughed Giles, for they had been what his set at Balliol used to call "lovers."

"And Mrs. Amp, of course?"

"Of course!"

"And Mary Pippin?"

"Decidedly," he grimaced.

"And the men," she went on. "Giles Pentateuch—this is Luke Snarthes and Reggie Ringworm and Mr. Encolpius and Roland Narthex. Pentateuch writes—let me see?—like a boot, isn't it?" (Her voice was a husky roar.) "Yes, a boot with a mission! Oh, but I forgot"—and she laughed delightedly—"you're all writers!"

"Encantado, I'm sure!" responded Giles. "But we've all met before. I see you have the whole Almanach de Golgotha in fact," he added.

Mary Pippin, whose arm had been eaten away by termites in Tehuantepec, was pouring out with her free hand. "Orange Pekoe or *Chandu*, Giles?" she burbled in her delicious little voice. "Like a carrier pigeon's," he thought.

"*Chandu*, please." And she filled him a pipe of the consoling poppy, so that in a short while he was smoking away like all the others.

"Yes, yes," continued Mr. Encolpius, in his oily voice which rose and fell beneath the gently moving tip of his nose, "Man axalotl here below but I ask very little. Some fragments of Pamphylides, a Choctaw blood-mask, the prose of Scaliger the Elder, a painting by Fuseli, an occasional visit to the all-in wrestling, or to my meretrix; a cook who can produce a passable 'poulet à la Khmer,' a Pong vase. Simple tastes, you will agree, and it is my simple habit to indulge them!"

Giles regarded him with fascination. That nose, it was, yes, it was definitely a proboscis. . . .

"But how can you, how can you?" It was Ursula Groyne. "How *can* you when there are two million unemployed, when Russia has reintroduced anti-abortionary legislation, when Iceland has banned *Time and Tide,* when the Sedition Bill hangs over us all like a rubber truncheon?"

Mary Pippin cooed delightedly; this was intellectual life with a vengeance—definitely haybrow—only it was so difficult to know who was right. Giles, at that moment, found her infinitely desirable.

"Yes, and worse than that." It was Luke Snarthes, whose strained voice emerged from his tortured face like a cobra from the snake-charmer's basket. "Oh, decidedly, appallingly worse. The natives of Ceylon take the slender Loris and hold it over the fire till its eyes pop, to release the magic juices. Indicible things are done to geese that you may eat your runions with a sauce of *foie gras.* Caviare is ripped from the living sturgeon, karakul fur torn from the baby lamb inside its mother. The creaking plates of the live dismembered lobster scream to you from the *Homard Newburg,* the oyster winces under the lemon. How would *you* like, Mr. Encolpius, to be torn from your bed, embarrelled, prised open with a knife, seasoned with a few drips of vitriol, shall we say, and sprayed with a tabasco as strong as mustard-gas to give you flavour; then to be swallowed alive and handed over to a giant's digestive juices?"

"I shouldn't like it at all!" said Mr. Encolpius, "just as I shouldn't, for that matter, like living at the bottom of the sea and changing my sex every three years. Not that it might not"— and he twitched his nose at Mary Pippin—"have its compensations."

"S-s-s-s-s-s-s-s-s-s-s-s-s-s-s-s-s-s-s-s-s-suppose," said Reggie Ringworm, who stammered, etc., "vat ve thilly oythter is weally weady and villing to be ab-s-s-s-orbed, I mean ab-th-th-th-th-th-thorbed, by our fwend, vat vat is in f-f-f-fact exactly ve end for which it has been cweated. Vat th-then?"

"What are we to think then," snarled Snarthes savagely, "of the Person or Purpose who created creatures for such an end? Awful!" And he took out his notebook and wrote rapidly, "The end justifies the means! But the end *is* the means! And how rarely, how confoundedly rarely, can we even say the end justifies the end! Like Oxenstierna, like Ximenes, like Waldorf, we must be men of means"—he closed the book with a snap—"men of golden means."

"I know what you mean," cried Mary Pippin from her dovecot. "That if Cleopatra's nose had been half an inch longer Menelaus would never have run away with her!"

Luke's face softened, and he spread out his splayed fingers almost tenderly. "And I don't mind wagering, if we can believe Diodorus Siculus, that, the nose unaltered, she bore a remarkable likeness, Mary, to you!"

"Ah, but can we believe old Siculus?" The other nose quested speculative. "Any more than we can believe old Paterculus, old Appian, Arrian, Ossian, and Orrian? Now a Bolivar Corona or a nicely chambered glass of sparkling Douro—even a pretty tea-gown by Madame Groult, I opine"—and he bowed to Mary—"these convince me. They have a way with one. Oh, yes, a way, decidedly! And just because they have that way it is necessary for me to combine them, how often, how distressingly often, with my lamentable visits to the Ring at Blackfriars, or to my meretrix in Holland Park. Why is it that we needs must see the highest though we loathe it? That happy in my mud—my hedonistic, radio-active, but never-the-less quite genuine nostalgic *boue,* I should be reminded of the stars, of you, Miss Pippin, and of Cleopatra?" And he snuffled serio-comically, "Why can't you let Hell alone?"

A gong rang discreetly. The butler removed the pipes and Mrs. Amp and Roland Narthex, who were still in a state of kif, while the others went away to dress. Giles, who found something stimulating in Mr. Encolpius' nose, took out his notebook and wrote:

"Platitudes are eternally fresh, and even the most paradoxical are true; even when we say the days draw in we are literally right—for science has now come largely to the rescue of folk-lore; after the summer and still more after the equinoctial solstice the hours do definitely get shorter. It is this shortness of our northern day that has occasioned the luxuriance of our literature. Retractile weather—erectile poetry. No one has idealized, in our cold climate, more typically than Shakespeare and Dryden the

subtropical conditioning. But we can consider Antony and Cleopatra to have been very different from their counterparts in the
Elizabethan imagination, for on the Mediterranean they understand summer better and, with summer, sex.

"What were they really like, those prototypes of Aryan passion,
of brachycephalic amour? Were Cleopatra's breasts such as 'bore
through men's eyes' and tormented those early sensualists, Milton, Dante, Coventry Patmore, and St. John of the Cross? We
shall never know.

"Professor Pavlov has shown that when salivation has been
artificially induced in dogs by the ringing of a dinner bell, if
you fire simultaneously into them a few rounds of small shot
they exhibit an almost comical bewilderment. Human beings
have developed very little. Like dogs we are not capable of
absorbing conflicting stimuli; we cannot continue to love Cleopatra after communism and the electro-magnetic field have
played Old Harry with our romantic mythology. That characteristic modern thinker, Drage Everyman, remarks, 'Destroy the
illusion of love and you destroy love itself,' and that is exactly
what the machine age, through attempting to foster it through
cinemas and gin-palaces, deodorants and depilatories, has succeeded in doing. Glory, glory halitosis! No wonder we are happier in the present! If we think of the 'Eastern Star,' in fact, it
is as advertising something. And when we would reconstruct
those breasts of hers, again we are faced with the diversity of
modern knowledge. What were they like? To a poet twin roes,
delectable mountains; to a philanderer like Malthus festering
cancers; to a pneumatogogue simply a compound of lacticity and
heterogeneous pyrites; to a biologist a sump and a pump. Oh,
sweet are the uses, or rather the abuses, of splanchnology! No,
for details of the pathological appeal of these forgotten beauties
we must consult the poets. The ancients were aware of a good
thing when they saw it, and Horace knew, for instance, with almost scatological percipience, exactly what was what.

"There are altitudes, as well as climates, of the mind. Many
prefer the water-meadows, but some of us, like Kant and Beethoven, are at home on the heights. There we thermostatically

control the rarefied atmosphere and breathe, perforce, the appropriate mental air."

In another room Luke Snarthes was doing his exercises. Seated in the lotus position, he exhaled deeply till his stomach came against his backbone with a smart crack. After a little he relaxed and breathed carefully up one nostril and down the other and then reversed the process. He took a nail out of the calf of his leg, and after he had reinserted it, it was time to put the studs into his evening shirt. "I was there," he murmured, "when it started, down at Groyne."

When he had dressed he unlocked his despatch-case and took out a sealed tube. It was marked, "Anthrax—non-filterable virus, only to be opened by a qualified literary scientist." "Jolly little beggars," he thought, and the hard lines on his face softened. "I'll take them down to amuse Miss Pippin. She looked the kind of person who'd *understand*."

"Snuff, peotl buds, hashish, or Indian hemp, sir?" said the butler. Dinner was drawing to an end. It had been an interesting meal. For Giles and Luke (on the "regime"), grass soup and groundsel omelette, washed down with a bottle of "pulque"; for Mrs. Amp, whose huge wen, like Saint-Evremond's, made her look more than ever like some heavily wattled turkey, a chicken gumbo; for the rest Risi-bisi Mabel Dodge, bêche de mer, bear steak, and Capri pie.

"There's some *bhang* on the mantelpiece," said Minnie Rhomboid, "in poor Rhomboid's college tobacco jar."

"Delicious." It was Mr. Encolpius. "Common are to either sex artifex and opifex," he continued. "But, golly, how rare to find them contained in the same person—qualis opifex, Lady Rhomboid! I congratulate you—and this *barask*—perfection!" And he poured himself some more, while the snout wiggled delightedly.

"And you can drink that when Hungary is deliberately making a propaganda war for the recovery and re-enslavement of a hundred-thousand at last sophisticated Slovakians!" It was Ursula Groyne.

Poor Ursula, thought Giles, she carries her separate hell about with her like a snail its carapace! Not all the lost causes, all the lame dogs in the world could console her for the loss of her three husbands, and now she was condemned to the hades of promiscuity—every three or four years a new lover. Poor Ursula!

"And if you knew how the stuff was made!" The phrase was wrung from Luke Snarthes on his tortured calvary. "The apricots are trodden by the naked feet of bromidrosis-ridden Kutzo-Vlachs who have for centuries lived in conditions far below the poverty line! The very glass-blowers who spun that Venetian balloon for you are condemned to the agonies of alembic poisoning."

"Doubtless," answered Mr. Encolpius urbanely, "that is why it tastes so good. It all boils down to a question of proteins. You, my dear Ursula, are allergic to human misery; the sufferings of Slovaks and Slovenes affect you as pollen the hayfever victim, or me (no offence, Minnie) a cat in the room. To ethics, mere questions of good and evil, I am happily immune, like my cara doncella here—am I right, Mary? Let Austin have his swink to him reserved, especially when it is a swink of the Rhomboid order. Go to the slug, thou ant-herd! If you could make up to kings (you remember what Aristippus said to Diogenes, Snarthes), you would not have to live on grass!"

"B-b-b-b-b-b-b-b-b-b-b-b-b-b-b-b-but all flesh is gwath, so ve pwoblem is only sh-shelved." It was Reggie Ringworm!

"Sit down, everybody, it's time for the séance," commanded Lady Rhomboid. "We have persuaded Madame Yoni."

In darkness they took their seats, Mr. Encolpius and Giles on each side of Mary Pippin, while Snarthes elevated himself to a position of trans-Khyber ecstasy suspended between the table and the laquearia. The *bhang*-sodden bodies of Mrs. Amp and Roland Narthex they left where they were.

The darkness was abysmal, pre-lapsarian. Time flowed stanchlessly, remorselessly, from a wound inenarrable, as with catenary purpose. Madame Yoni moved restlessly, like Bethesda.

In her private dovecot Mary Pippin abandoned herself to the eery. What a thrill, to be here at Groyne, and for a séance! There had been nothing like it since she had joined the Anglican Church, to the consternation of her governess, Miss Heard, because of the deep mystical significance (as of some splendid sinner repenting on the ashes of lust) of the words, "for Ember Days." All the same, she was not quite sure if she liked Mr. Encolpius. But what was this?—another thrill, but positive, physical. With moth-like caresses something was running up and down her arm—1, 2, 3, 4, 5,—spirit fingers, perhaps: the tremulous titivation continued, the moths were relentless, inexorable, 86, 87, 88. Then on her other side, along her cheek, she felt a new set of moth antennae playing. From the chandelier above came the faintest ghostly anticipatory tinkle—someone was on the move as well, up there! 98, 99 . . . Suddenly Madame Yoni screamed—there was a crash, as of three heads bumping together, and the lights went up to reveal Pentateuch and Mr. Encolpius momentarily stunned by the Ixionic impact of the fallen Snarthes. His power had failed him.

"W-w-w-w-w-w-w—" stammered Reggie Ringworm, but he was interrupted by a shout from Luke. "My God—the anthrax!" He took from his pocket the fragments of the broken tube. "At the rate of multiplication of these bacilli"—he made a rapid calculation—"we shall all be by morning, Lady Rhomboid, dead souls." His splayed face had at last found its justification.

"Death!" said Mr. Encolpius, "the distinguished visitor! One bids good-bye, one hopes gracefully, to one's hostess, and then, why then I think one degusts the Cannabis Indica. Well, cheerio, kif-kif!" And he picked up the Brasenose jar.

Imperturbable, schizophrene, the portraits of Groynes and Rhomboids by Laurencin and the excise-man Rousseau looked down from the walls. So Miss Heard had been right, thought Mary. The wicked *do* perish. Than this there could have been no other conceivable termination to a week-end of pleasure!

> They say of old in Babylon
> That Harlequin and Pantalon
> Seized that old topiary, Truth,
> And held him by Time's Azimuth. . . .

Why had the nursery jingle recurred to her?

Luke removed a nail or two disconsolately. They would be of

little use now. He tried to reassure Minnie Rhomboid. "After all, what is anthrax? What, for that matter, are yaws, beri-beri, dengue or the Bagdad Boil, but fascinating biochemical changes in the cellular constitution of our bodies, a re-casting of their components to play their new cadaverous roles? Believe me, Lady Rhomboid," he concluded, "there are more things in heaven and earth than are dreamt of in the British Pharmacopoeia!"

Giles took out his notebook. "La Muerte, Der Tod, Thanatos," he wrote.

"Your C-c-c-Collins perhaps?" stammered Reggie.

Giles began again: "It was at Groyne, during one of Minnie Rhomboid's most succulent week-ends, that it all happened, happened because it had to happen, because it was in the very nature of Luke Snarthes and Mary Pippin that exactly such things should happen, just as it was character not destiny, character that *was* destiny, that caused Napoleon . . ." He paused and looked up. The menial was regarding him reproachfully.

CYRIL CONNOLLY

J. P. MARQUAND

The Education of Henry Apley

CHAPTER I

GRINDLE POINT was always best in the fall. If I knew how to write, I could tell how the old river went dreaming by in the sun and how the copper beeches marched down to its bank in strict and orderly procession. Sometimes in the morning, before the mist had burned away, the trees looked like silver ghosts and there were diamonds in the grass on the lawn. Time itself seemed to hang suspended in that clear, level light, so it was easy to believe that all the people who had once lived there were there still and always would be. As I've said, however, I am not a writer, and all I know is that I am part of Grindle Point. It is where I belong.

I shall never forget the day I came back to it after the war.

My father was in his study, reading the *Transcript* and eating an apple, as he always did in the later afternoon.

"Hello," he said. "Kill any Germans?"

"Eight or nine," I said. "Nothing to amount to much."

"I suppose not," he said. "Naturally you were decorated?"

"Well, yes," I said. I hadn't meant to tell anybody about the medal, because there is nothing worse than showing off. I only hoped he wouldn't mention it to the servants.

"You look older," he said. "Probably time you were thinking of getting married."

"I don't know," I said. "I've never been much good at that kind of thing."

"An awkward business," said my father. "Going off that way with a comparatively strange woman."

I could see he was embarrassed. He wanted to tell me something, but it was hard because we had never talked together very freely.

"A damned awkward business," he repeated irritably. "They ought to have told you about it at Harvard. I suppose it's customary these days to assume that a gentleman knows about these things instinctively, but sometimes he doesn't."

"Yes, sir," I said.

"All a man can do is try to play the game," he said. "It won't be easy, especially with your training, but the Apleys have always got through it somehow. With me it was always something one owed to Harvard. A matter of loyalty."

I could understand that. Harvard had made me what I was, and the least I could do in return was to make a certain amount of effort.

"I'll do my best, sir," I said.

Just the same, I wasn't happy when I got up to my old room and started unpacking my bag. Outside my window the river lay opalescent in the twilight, but for a moment I saw it as a dark and relentless torrent bearing me on into the unknowable future, and I shuddered. I didn't want to get married; I just wanted to go back to Harvard.

CHAPTER II

I was bringing George Hill's trunk up from the cellar. It was pretty heavy, and I put it down for a minute outside the library door. I didn't mean to listen, of course, but I couldn't help hearing them inside.

"We've got to be careful," said Jane. "He may be feeble-minded, but he isn't blind."

George laughed. "He went to Harvard, didn't he?" he said.

I came in and put the trunk down. My wife was sitting on George's lap. She looked tired, and I felt guilty. It was probably an imposition to ask her to entertain George, because after all he was my guest.

"Who went to Harvard?" I asked idiotically.

"Oh, my God," said Jane.

"Rutherford B. Hayes," said George. "He was the typical Harvard man—dense but energetic."

George often talked that way, probably because he had gone to school at St. Paul's in Garden City instead of the right one. Afterward, of course, he'd run sixty yards against Yale with a broken neck, and he'd made Hedgehog and the Scapula Club, but he never seemed to feel the same way about Harvard as the rest of us.

"Listen, clumsy," said Jane. "How about getting on with that trunk?"

"Well," I said, "I thought I might just sit down here with you two for a minute and have a drink. My feet hurt."

"Never mind about your feet," said Jane. "You get that trunk out in the car. George and I have to start right away if we're going to get to New York before it's dark."

"You're going to New York?" I asked. "You and George?"

"Just for the week-end," said George. "You don't mind, do you?"

"Of course not," I said, "but some people might think it was a little odd. You know how it is in Boston."

"My God," said Jane, "I think he's jealous!"

"Of old George?" That made me laugh. I knew a lot of things had changed since I was at Harvard, but of course there were a lot of other things that never changed. I hadn't quite liked George's remark about Rutherford B. Hayes, who, incidentally had only gone to the law school, but he was my best friend and I knew he was a gentleman. He might be wrong about some things, but he'd be right about the important ones, and that was what really mattered.

They came out while I was still strapping the trunk onto the car, and climbed into the front seat. George started the motor.

"Good-bye," I said. "Have a good time."

"Good-bye, darling," said Jane. "Don't forget to put the cat out."

It was like Jane to think about the cat, even when she was tired and upset. I smiled as I watched the car dropping out of sight down the drive. Things often work out a lot better than you have any business to hope they will.

WOLCOTT GIBBS

WILLIAM FAULKNER

"Requiem for a Noun, or Intruder in the Dusk"

(WHAT CAN COME OF TRYING TO READ WILLIAM FAULKNER WHILE MINDING A CHILD, OR VICE VERSA)

THE COLD BRUSSELS sprout rolled off the page of the book I was reading and lay inert and defunctive in my lap. Turning my head with a leisure at least three-fourths impotent rage, I saw him standing there holding the toy with which he had catapulted the vegetable, or rather the reverse, the toy first then the fat insolent fist clutching it and then above that the bland defiant face beneath the shock of black hair like tangible gas. It, the toy, was one of those cardboard funnels with a trigger near the point for firing a small celluloid ball. Letting the cold Brussels sprout lie there in my lap for him to absorb or anyhow apprehend rebuke from, I took a pull at a Scotch highball I had had in my hand and then set it down on the end table beside me.

"So instead of losing the shooter which would have been a mercy you had to lose the ball," I said, fixing with a stern eye what I had fathered out of all sentient and biding dust; remembering with that retroactive memory by which we count chimes seconds and even minutes after they have struck (recapitulate, even, the very grinding of the bowels of the clock before and during and after) the cunning furtive click, clicks rather, which perception should have told me then already were not the trigger plied but the icebox opened. "Even a boy of five going on six should have more respect for his father if not for food," I said, now picking the cold Brussels sprout out of my lap and setting it—not dropping it, setting it—in an ashtray; thinking how across the wax bland treachery of the kitchen linoleum were now in all likelihood distributed the remnants of string beans and cold potatoes and maybe even tapioca. "You're no son of mine."

I took up the thread of the book again or tried to: the weft of legitimate kinship that was intricate enough without the obbligato of that dark other: the sixteenths and thirty-seconds and even sixty-fourths of dishonoring cousinships brewed out of the violable blood by the ineffaceable errant lusts. Then I heard another click; a faint metallic rejoinder that this time was neither the trigger nor the icebox but the front door opened and then shut. Through the window I saw him picking his way over the season's soiled and sun-frayed vestiges of snow like shreds of rotted lace, the cheap upended toy cone in one hand and a child's cardboard suitcase in the other, toward the road.

I dropped the book and went out after him who had forgotten not only that I was in shirtsleeves but that my braces hung down over my flanks in twin festoons. "Where are you going?" I called, my voice expostulant and forlorn on the warm numb air. Then I caught it: caught it in the succinct outrage of the suitcase and the prim churning rear and marching heels as well: I had said he was no son of mine, and so he was leaving a house not only where he was not wanted but where he did not even belong.

"I see," I said in that shocked clarity with which we perceive the truth instantaneous and entire out of the very astonishment that refuses to acknowledge it. "Just as you now cannot be sure of any roof you belong more than half under, you figure there is no housetop from which you might not as well begin to shout it. Is that it?"

Something was trying to tell me something. Watching him turn off on the road—and that not only with the ostensible declaration of vagabondage but already its very assumption, attaining as though with a single footfall the very apotheosis of wandering just as with a single shutting of a door he had that of renunciation and farewell-watching him turn off on it, the road, in the direction of the Permisangs', our nearest neighbors, I thought *Wait; no; what I said was not enough for him to leave the house on; it must have been the blurted inscrutable chance confirmation of something he already knew, and was half able to assess, either out of the blown facts of boyhood or pure male divination or both.*

"What is it you know?" I said springing forward over the delicate squalor of the snow and falling in beside the boy. "Does any man come to the house to see your mother when I'm away, that you know of?" Thinking *We are mocked, first by the old mammalian snare, then, snared, by the final unilaterality of all flesh to which birth is given; not only not knowing when we may be cuckolded, but not even sure that in the veins of the very bantling we dandle does not flow the miscreant sniggering wayward blood.*

"I get it now," I said, catching in the undeviating face just as I had in the prim back and marching heels the steady articulation of disdain. "Cuckoldry is something of which the victim may be as guilty as the wrong-doers. That's what you're thinking? That by letting in this taint upon our heritage I am as accountable as she or they who have been its actual avatars. More. Though the foe may survive, the sleeping sentinel must be shot. Is that it?"

"You talk funny."

Mother-and-daughter blood conspires in the old mammalian

office. Father-and-son blood vies in the ancient phallic enmity. I caught him by the arm and we scuffled in the snow. "I will be heard," I said, holding him now as though we might be dancing, my voice intimate and furious against the furious sibilance of our feet in the snow. Thinking how revelation had had to be inherent in the very vegetable scraps to which venery was probably that instant contriving to abandon me, the cold boiled despair of whatever already featureless suburban Wednesday Thursday or Saturday supper the shot green was the remainder. "I see another thing," I panted, cursing my helplessness to curse whoever it was had given him blood and wind. Thinking *He's glad; glad to credit what is always secretly fostered and fermented out of the vats of childhood fantasy anyway (for all childhood must conceive a substitute for the father that has conceived it (finding that other inconceivable?)* ; thinking *He is walking in a nursery fairy tale to find the king his sire.* "Just as I said to you 'You're no son of mine' so now you answer back 'Neither are you any father to me.' "

The scherzo of violence ended as abruptly as it had begun. He broke away and walked on, after retrieving the toy he had dropped and adjusting his grip on the suitcase which he had not, this time faster and more urgently.

The last light was seeping out of the shabby sky, after the hemorrhage of sunset. High in the west where the fierce constellations soon would wheel, the evening star in single bombast burned and burned. The boy passed the Permisangs' without going in, then passed the Kellers'. Maybe he's heading for the McCullums', I thought, but he passed their house too. Then he, we, neared the Jelliffs'. He's got to be going there, his search will end there, I thought. Because that was the last house this side of the tracks. And because *something was trying to tell me something.*

"Were you maybe thinking of what you heard said about Mrs. Jelliff and me having relations in Spuyten Duyvil?" I said in rapid frantic speculation. "But they were talking about mutual kin—nothing else." The boy said nothing. But I had sensed it instant and complete: the boy felt that, whatever of offense his mother may or may not have given, his father had given provocation; and out of the old embattled malehood, it was the hairy ineluctable Him whose guilt and shame he was going to hold preponderant. *Because now I remembered.*

"So it's Mrs. Jelliff—Sue Jelliff—and me you have got this all mixed up with," I said, figuring he must, in that fat sly nocturnal stealth that took him creeping up and down the stairs to listen when he should have been in bed, certainly have heard his mother exclaiming to his father behind that bedroom door it had been vain to close since it was not sound-proof: "I saw you. I saw that with Sue. There may not be anything between you but you'd like there to be! Maybe there is at that!"

Now like a dentist forced to ruin sound enamel to reach decayed I had to risk telling him what he did not know to keep what he assuredly did in relative control.

"This is what happened on the night in question," I said. "It was under the mistletoe, during the Holidays, at the Jelliffs'. Wait! I will be heard out! See your father as he is, but see him in no baser light. He has his arms around his neighbor's wife. It is evening, in the heat and huddled spiced felicity of the year's end, under the mistletoe (where as well as anywhere else the thirsting and exasperated flesh might be visited by the futile pangs and jets of later lust, the omnivorous aches of fifty and forty and even thirty-five to seize what may be the last of the allotted lips). Your father seems to prolong beyond its usual moment's span that custom's usufruct. Only for an instant, but in that instant letting trickle through the fissures of appearance what your mother and probably Rudy Jelliff too saw as an earnest of a flood that would have devoured that house and one four doors away."

A moon hung over the eastern roofs like a phantasmal bladder. Somewhere an icicle crashed and splintered, fruits of the day's thaw.

"So now I've got it straight," I said. "Just as through some nameless father your mother has cuckolded me (you think), so

through one of Rudy Jelliff's five sons I have probably cuckolded him. Which would give you at least a half brother under
that roof where under ours you have none at all. So you balance
out one miscreance with another, and find your rightful kin in
our poor weft of all the teeming random bonded sentient dust."

Shifting the grip, the boy walked on past the Jelliffs'. Before
him—the tracks; and beyond that—the other side of the tracks.
And now out of whatever reserve capacity for astonished incredulity may yet have remained I prepared to face this last and
ultimate outrage. But he didn't cross. Along our own side of
the tracks ran a road which the boy turned left on. He paused
before a lighted house near the corner, a white cottage with a
shingle in the window which I knew from familiarity to read,
"Viola Pruett, Piano Lessons," and which, like a violently un-
scrambled pattern on a screen, now came to focus.

Memory adumbrates just as expectation recalls. The name on
the shingle made audible to listening recollection the last words
of the boy's mother as she'd left, which had fallen short then of
the threshold of hearing. ". . . Pruett," I remembered now.
"He's going to have supper and stay with Buzzie Pruett overnight. . . . Can take a few things with him in that little suitcase of his. If Mrs. Pruett phones about it, just say I'll take him
over when I get back," I recalled now in that chime-counting
recapitulation of retroactive memory—better than which I could
not have been expected to do. Because the eternal Who-instructs
might have got through to the whiskey-drinking husband or
might have got through to the reader immersed in that prose
vertiginous intoxicant and unique, but not to both.

"So that's it," I said. "You couldn't wait till you were taken
much less till it was time but had to sneak off by yourself, and
that not cross-lots but up the road I've told you a hundred times
to keep off even the shoulder of."

The boy had stopped and now appeared to hesitate before the
house. He turned around at last, switched the toy and the suitcase in his hands, and started back in the direction he had come.

"What are you going back for now?" I asked.

"More stuff to take in this suitcase," he said. "I was going to just sleep at the Pruetts' overnight, but now I'm going to ask them to let me stay there for good."

PETER DE VRIES

ERNEST HEMINGWAY

Death in the Rumble Seat

MOST PEOPLE don't like the pedestrian part, and it is best not to look at that if you can help it. But if you can't help seeing them, long-legged and their faces white, and then the shock and the car lifting up a little on one side, then it is best to think of it as something very unimportant but beautiful and necessary artistically. It is unimportant because the people who are pedestrians are not very important, and if they were not being *cogido* by automobiles it would just be something else. And it is beautiful and necessary because, without the possibility of somebody getting *cogido,* driving a car would be just like anything else. It would be like reading "Thanatopsis," which is neither beautiful nor necessary, but hogwash. If you drive a car, and don't like the pedestrian part, then you are one of two kinds of people. Either you haven't very much vitality and you ought to do something about it, or else you are yellow and there is nothing to be done about it at all.

If you don't know anything about driving cars you are apt to think a driver is good just because he goes fast. This may be very exciting at first, but afterwards there is a bad taste in the mouth and the feeling of dishonesty. Ann Bender, the American, drove as fast on the Merrick Road as anybody I have ever seen, but when cars came the other way she always worked out of their terrain and over in the ditch so that you never had the hard, clean feeling of danger, but only bumping up and down in the ditch, and sometimes hitting your head on the top of the car. Good drivers go fast too, but it is always down the middle of the road, so that cars coming the other way are dominated, and have to go in the ditch themselves. There are a great many ways of getting the effect of danger, such as staying in the middle of the road till the last minute and then swerving out of the pure line, but they are all tricks, and afterwards you know they were tricks, and there is nothing left but disgust.

The cook: I am a little tired of cars, sir. Do you know any stories?

I know a great many stories, but I'm not sure that they're suitable.

The cook: The hell with that.

Then I will tell you the story about God and Adam and naming the animals. You see, God was very tired after he got through making the world. He felt good about it, but he was tired so he asked Adam if he'd mind thinking up names for the animals.

"What animals?" Adam said.

"Those," God said.

"Do they have to have names?" Adam said.

"You've got a name, haven't you?" God said.

I could see—

The cook: How do *you* get into this?

Some people always write in the first person, and if you do it's very hard to write any other way, even when it doesn't altogether fit into the context. If you want to hear this story, don't keep interrupting.

The cook: O.K.

I could see that Adam thought God was crazy, but he didn't say anything. He went over to where the animals were, and after a while he came back with the list of names.

"Here you are," he said.

God read the list, and nodded.

"They're pretty good," he said. "They're all pretty good except that last one."

"That's a good name," Adam said. "What's the matter with it?"

"What do you want to call it an elephant for?" God said.

Adam looked at God.

"It looks like an elephant to me," he said.

The cook: Well?

That's all.

The cook: It is a very strange story, sir.

It is a strange world, and if a man and woman love each other, that is strange too, and what is more, it always turns out badly.

In the golden age of car-driving, which was about 1910, the sense of impending disaster, which is a very lovely thing and almost nonexistent, was kept alive in a number of ways. For one thing, there was always real glass in the windshield so that if a driver hit anything, he was very definitely and beautifully *co-gido.* The tires weren't much good either, and often they'd blow out before you'd gone ten miles. Really, the whole car was built that way. It was made not only so that it would precipitate accidents but so that when the accidents came it was honestly vulnerable, and it would fall apart, killing all the people with a passion that was very fine to watch. Then they began building the cars so that they would go much faster, but the glass and the tires were all made so that if anything happened it wasn't real danger, but only the false sense of it. You could do all kinds of things with the new cars, but it was no good because it was all planned in advance. Mickey Finn, the German, always worked very far into the other car's terrain so that the two cars always seemed to be one. Driving that way he often got the *faender,* or the clicking when two cars touch each other in passing, but because you knew that nothing was really at stake it was just an empty classicism, without any value because the insecurity was all gone and there was nothing left but a kind of mechanical agility. It is the same way when any art gets into its decadence. It is the same way about s-x—

The cook: I like it very much better when you talk about s-x, sir, and I wish you would do it more often.

I have talked a lot about s-x before, and now I thought I would talk about something else.

The cook: I think that is very unfortunate, sir, because you are at your best with s-x, but when you talk about automobiles you are just a nuisance.

WOLCOTT GIBBS

Across the Street and into the Grill

THIS IS my last and best and true and only meal, thought Mr. Perley as he descended at noon and swung east on the beat-up sidewalk of Forty-fifth Street. Just ahead of him was the girl from the reception desk. I am a little fleshed up around the crook of the elbow, thought Perley, but I commute good.

He quickened his step to overtake her and felt the pain again. What a stinking trade it is, he thought. But after what I've done to other assistant treasurers, I can't hate anybody. Sixteen deads, and I don't know how many possibles.

The girl was near enough now so he could smell her fresh receptiveness, and the lint in her hair. Her skin was light blue, like the sides of horses.

"I love you," he said, "and we are going to lunch together for the first and only time, and I love you very much."

"Hello, Mr. Perley," she said, overtaken. "Let's not think of anything."

A pair of fantails flew over from the sad old Guaranty Trust Company, their wings set for a landing. A lovely double, thought Perley, as he pulled. "Shall we go to the Hotel Biltmore, on Vanderbilt Avenue, which is merely a feeder lane for the great streets, or shall we go to Schrafft's, where my old friend Botticelli is captain of girls and where they have the mayonnaise in fiascos?"

"Let's go to Schrafft's," said the girl, low. "But first I must phone Mummy." She stepped into a public booth and dialled true and well, using her finger. Then she telephoned.

As they walked on, she smelled good. She smells good, thought Perley. But that's all right, I add good. And when we get to Schrafft's, I'll order from the menu, which I like very much indeed.

They entered the restaurant. The wind was still west, ruffling the edges of the cookies. In the elevator, Perley took the controls. "I'll run it," he said to the operator. "I checked out long ago." He stopped true at the third floor, and they stepped off into the men's grill.

"Good morning, my Assistant Treasurer," said Botticelli, coming forward with a fiasco in each hand. He nodded at the girl, who he knew was from the West Seventies and whom he desired.

"Can you drink the water here?" asked Perley. He had the fur trapper's eye and took in the room at a glance, noting that there was one empty table and three pretty waitresses.

Botticelli led the way to the table in the corner, where Perley's flanks would be covered.

"Alexanders," said Perley. "Eighty-six to one. The way Chris mixes them. Is this table all right, Daughter?"

Botticelli disappeared and returned soon, carrying the old Indian blanket.

"That's the same blanket, isn't it?" asked Perley.

"Yes. To keep the wind off," said the Captain, smiling from the backs of his eyes. "It's still west. It should bring the ducks in tomorrow, the chef thinks."

Mr. Perley and the girl from the reception desk crawled down under the table and pulled the Indian blanket over them so it was solid and good and covered them right. The girl put her hand on his wallet. It was cracked and old and held his commutation book. "We are having fun, aren't we?" she asked.

"Yes, Sister," he said.

"I have here the soft-shelled crabs, my Assistant Treasurer," said Botticelli. "And another fiasco of the 1926. This one is cold."

"Dee the soft-shelled crabs," said Perley from under the blanket. He put his arm around the receptionist good.

"Do you think we should have a green pokeweed salad?" she asked. "Or shall we not think of anything for a while?"

"We shall not think of anything for a while, and Botticelli would bring the pokeweed if there was any," said Perley. "It isn't the season." Then he spoke to the Captain. "Botticelli, do you remember when we took all the mailing envelopes from the stockroom, spit on the flaps, and then drank rubber cement till the foot soldiers arrived?"

"I remember, my Assistant Treasurer," said the Captain. It was a little joke they had.

"He used to mimeograph pretty good," said Perley to the girl. "But that was another war. Do I bore you, Mother?"

"Please keep telling me about your business experiences, but not the rough parts." She touched his hand where the knuckles were scarred and stained by so many old mimeographings. "Are both your flanks covered, my dearest?" she asked, plucking at the blanket. They felt the Alexanders in their eyeballs. Eighty-six to one.

"Schrafft's is a good place and we're having fun and I love you," Perley said. He took another swallow of the 1926, and it was a good and careful swallow. "The stockroom men were very brave," he said, "but it is a position where it is extremely difficult to stay alive. Just outside that room there is a little bare-assed highboy and it is in the way of the stuff that is being brought up. The hell with it. When you make a breakthrough, Daughter, first you clean out the baskets and the half-wits, and all the time they have the fire escapes taped. They also shell you with old production orders, many of them approved by the general manager in charge of sales. I am boring you and I will not at this time discuss the general manager in charge of sales as we are unquestionably being listened to by that waitress over there who is setting out the decoys."

"I am going to give you my piano," the girl said, "so that when you look at it you can think of me. It will be something between us."

"Call up and have them bring the piano to the restaurant," said Perley. "Another fiasco, Botticelli!"

They drank the sauce. When the piano came, it wouldn't play. The keys were stuck good. "Never mind, we'll leave it here, Cousin," said Perley.

They came out from under the blanket and Perley tipped their waitress exactly fifteen per cent minus withholding. They left the piano in the restaurant, and when they went down the elevator and out and turned in to the old, hard, beat-up pavement of Fifth Avenue and headed south toward Forty-fifth Street, where the pigeons were, the air was as clean as your grandfather's howitzer. The wind was still west.

I commute good, thought Perley, looking at his watch. And he felt the old pain of going back to Scarsdale again.

E. B. WHITE

THORNTON WILDER

*Just Plain Folks**

THE CURTAIN has just fallen on William Faulkner's *Requiem for a Nun* (Royal Court). It has been performed with imposing devoutness by Ruth Ford, Bertice Reading, Zachary Scott and John Crawford. The production (by Tony Richardson) and the settings (by Motley) have been austerely hieratic. Let us now imagine that there steps from the wings the Stage Manager of Thornton Wilder's "Our Town." Pulling on a corn-cob pipe, he speaks.

S.M.: "Well, folks, reckon that's about it. End of another day in the city of Jefferson, Yoknapatawpha County, Mississippi. Nothin' much happened. Couple of people got raped, couple more got their teeth kicked in, but way up there those faraway old stars are still doing their old cosmic criss-cross, and there ain't a thing we can do about it. It's pretty quiet now. Folk hereabouts get to bed early, those that can still walk. Down behind the morgue a few of the young people are roastin' a nigger over an open fire, but I guess every town has its night-owls, and afore long they'll be tucked up asleep like anybody else. Nothin' stirring down at the big old plantation house—you can't even hear the hummin' of that electrified barbed-wire fence, 'cause last night some drunk ran slap into it and fused the whole works. That's where Mr. Faulkner lives, and he's the fellow that thought this whole place up, kind of like God. Mr. Faulkner knows everybody round these parts like the back of his hand, 'n most everybody round these parts knows the back of Mr. Faulkner's hand. But he's not home right now, he's off on a trip round the world as Uncle Sam's culture ambassador, tellin' foreigners about how

---

* A theatre review from the London *Observer* of December 1, 1957.

we've got to love everybody, even niggers, and how integration's
bound to happen in a few thousand years anyway, so we might
just as well make haste slowly. Ain't a thing we can do about it.

(*He takes out his watch and consults it.*)

Along about now the good folk of Jefferson City usually get
around to screamin' in their sleep. Just ordinary people havin'
ordinary nightmares, the way most of us do most of the time.

(*An agonised shrieking is briefly heard.*)

Ayeah, there they go. Nothin' wrong there that an overdose of
Seconal won't fix.

(*He pockets his watch.*)

Like I say, simple folk fussin' and botherin' over simple, eternal
problems. Take this Temple Stevens, the one Mr. Faulkner's
been soundin' off about. 'Course, Mr. Faulkner don't pretend to
be a real play-writer, 'n maybe that's why he tells the whole
story backwards, 'n why he takes up so much time gabbin' about
people you never met—and what's more, ain't going to meet.
By the time he's told you what happened before you got here,
it's gettin' to be time to go home. But we were talkin' about
Temple. Ain't nothin' special about her. Got herself mixed up
in an auto accident—witnessed a killin'—got herself locked up
in a sportin' house with one of these seck-sual perverts—witnessed another killin'—got herself married up 'n bore a couple
of fine kids. Then, just's she's fixing to run off with a black-
mailer, her maid Nancy—that's the nigger dope-fiend she met
in the cathouse—takes a notion to murder her baby boy. That's
all about Temple—just a run of bad luck that could happen
to anyone. And don't come askin' me why Nancy murders the
kid. Accordin' to Mr. Faulkner, she does it to keep him from
bein' tainted by his mother's sins. Seems to me even an ignorant
nigger would know a tainted child was better'n a dead one, but
I guess I can't get under their skins the way Mr. Faulkner can.

(*He glances up at the sky.*)

Movin' along towards dawn in our town. Pretty soon folks'll
start up on that old diurnal round of sufferin' and expiatin' and
spoutin' sentences two pages long. One way or another, an awful
lot of sufferin' gets done around here. 'Specially by the black

folk—'n that's how it should be, 'cause they don't feel it like we do, 'n anyways, they've got that simple primitive faith to lean back on.

(*He consults his watch again.*)

Well, Temple's back with her husband, and in a couple of minutes they'll be hangin' Nancy. Maybe that's why darkies were born—to keep white marriages from bustin' up. Anyways, a lot of things have happened since the curtain went up to-night. Six billion gallons of water have tumbled over Niagara Falls. Three thousand boys and girls took their first puff of marijuana, 'n a puppy-dog in a flyin' coffin was sighted over Alaska. Most of you out there've been admirin' Miss Ruth Ford's play-actin', 'n a few of you've been wonderin' whether she left her pay-thos in the dressing-room or whether maybe she didn't have any to be-gin with. Out in Hollywood a big producer's been readin' Mr. Faulkner's book and figurin' whether to buy the movie rights for Miss Joan Crawford. Right enough, all over the world, it's been quite an evening. 'N now Nancy's due for the drop.

(*A thud offstage. The Stage Manager smiles philosophically.*)

Ayeah, that's it—right on time.

(*He re-pockets his watch.*)

That's the end of the play, friends. You can go out and push dope now, those of you that push dope. Down in our town there's a meetin' of the Deathwish Committee, 'n a fund-raisin' rally in aid of Holocaust Relief, 'n all over town the prettiest gals're primping themselves up for the big beauty prize—Miss Cegenation of 1957. There's always somethin' happenin'. Why —over at the schoolhouse an old-fashioned-type humanist just shot himself. *You* get a good rest, too. Good-night."

(*He exits. A sound of Bibles being thumped momentarily fills the air.*)

KENNETH TYNAN

JAMES GOULD COZZENS
By Words Obsessed

L ANCE CHAMPION gazed in solemn, half amused (or was it perhaps three-quarters?) interest—interest long since dulled by
constant use yet never quite dulled enough to let him sleep
(perchance to dream)—gazed down fondly now, no longer solemn, no longer half amused (or whatever it had been) at his
mother's cat, a cat once named Erwin but now called Grace;
a nomenclatural change brought about by a long-delayed and
too-long-overlooked (who can say how much we overlook in this
life?) (not I) examination of his (her) various characteristics;
Grace, who now rubbed half thoughtfully half anxiously against
Lance Champion's tweed-clad (but not too rough tweed) left
leg, set slightly ahead of his right leg (similarly clad) in a posture of semi-walking, as indeed he was.

From upstairs, Lance Champion's mother said: "Lance, dear,
is the cat out?"

Is the cat out? Lance Champion smiled to himself and thought
of the day at the lake when Ella had asked that same question;
poor Ella, now long since out herself—not knowing then that
she would go out before the cat (and not even for the same
reason)—Ella, loose-boned and mannish in her chamois-seated
crew pants (she had rowed bow at Wellesley, and had become
addicted—infatuated, even—to (with) having chamois next to
her skin)—Ella, who could recite the whole of "Hiawatha" or
have a child with equal ease (and interest); Ella always thought
of the cat first, even on that now too seldom remembered (a man
can't remember everything) day when Dr. Waters had slipped his
gleaming stethoscope down around his neck and had said to
Lance Champion: *Skeptophylaxis is what it appears to be.*

Recalling now, recalling by pressing his temples until he could
feel his brown, green-flecked (often red-streaked, from nights of
poring over technical manuals) eyes bulge from their spheroidally
round sockets; Lance Champion saw the scene again with startling clarity; clarity all the more startling because he was begin-

ning to black out from the pressure on his temples; he saw Dr. Waters wipe the snow from his glasses (a heavy drinker, Dr. Waters had lost his office and most of his equipment in an ill-advised mining venture, and was therefore obliged to hold his consultations out-of-doors) and start to write out a prescription.

Ashen his face, Lance Champion said: "Skeptophylaxis? Do you mean a condition in which a minute dose of substance poisonous to animals will produce immediate temporary immunity to the action of the poison?"

Dr. Waters nodded, losing his glasses.

Stunned, but not so stunned as an ox (or a cow) poleaxed by the running, hip-booted, sledgehammer swinging giant in the yellow brick local abattoir (which had been dedicated to Lance Champion Senior, The Old One, in an impressive flag-draped ceremony held in honor of his return from Law School); still and all with his senses reeling and deep gasps his breath, Lance Champion Junior said: "I take it an antiserum may be obtained from an animal. Is that correct?"

Dr. Waters said: "All too true. There are many aspects which we could discuss, and will discuss, if it suits you, but at the moment I think our first concern is for the lady, here."

Gallantly, moving as an old man but still a man with his memories, he helped Ella up from the ground, where he and Lance Champion had pinioned her for the examination, and deft-fingeredly he brushed the snow from the back of her play suit. Smiling, responding, her feet once more on the ground—the ground covered with snow but nevertheless the ground—she smiled respondingly and said: "First things come first, you know. I have to go home and feed the cat."

How like her! Lance Champion thought. How like her! And yet, looking at it from another angle, how utterly and completely unlike her! That was the thing about Ella—one thing, at least (there were others)—there were always two sides to everything about her; she had depth. And she was a woman. Everyone in town knew she was a woman, and two or three people in the adjoining town knew it, too. Lance Champion could well remember the day (afternoon, actually) not too long since but

long enough for the cicatrix to have commenced its inevitable
time-induced hardening, when Judge Mealy had called him into
his chambers—Judge Mealy, a friend and onetime wrestling companion of The Old One's, who would always see to it that Lance
Champion Junior got the best of all there was to give—and
having called Lance Champion Junior into his chambers, with
softness yet with judicial firmness had spoken: "Lance, this may
come as a shock to you, but Ella is a shoplifter. But I'm going
to have her committed this afternoon, so you don't have to
worry."

Lance Champion gazed down fondly now, no longer solemn,
no longer half amused (or whatever it had been) at his mother's
cat, who rubbed half thoughtfully half anxiously against Lance
Champion's tweed-clad left leg. Stooping, gently, yet stooping
with a purpose, Lance Champion stooped and scratched the
cat, then led her toward the door. And to his mother, Lance
Champion called:

"No, Mom, but I'll put her out."

NATHANIEL BENCHLEY

JAMES GOULD COZZENS

By Henry James Cozened

A UTHOR WINNER sat serenely contemplating his novel. His legs,
not ill-formed for his years, yet concealing the faint cyanic
marbling of incipient varicosity under grey socks of the finest
lisle, were crossed. He was settled in the fine, solidly-built, can-
nily (yet never parsimoniously, never niggardly) bargained-for
chair that had been his father's, a chair that Author Winner
himself was only beginning to think that, in the fullness of time,
hope he reasonably might that he would be able (be possessed
of the breadth and the depth) to fill. Hitching up the trousers
that had been made for his father (tailored from a fabric woven
to endure, with a hundred and sixty threads to the inch), he felt
a twinge of the sciatica that had been his father's and had come

down to him through the jeans. Author Winner was grateful for
any resemblance; his father had been a man of unusual qualities: loyal, helpful, friendly, courteous, kind, obedient, cheerful,
thrifty, brave, clean and reverent; in the simplest of terms: a
man of *dharma*.

Author Winner turned a page; his fingers, ten in number, and
remarkably, even redundantly uniform (save for the inherent,
ineluctable differences of size, shape and function), rested lightly
on the margins of pages 458 and 459, having fallen, quite without advertence, into a composition not, as a whole, lacking in
grace, yet with each of its separate parts (its distinct but not un-
connected digits) pointedly emphasizing (indeed emphatically
pointing to) one of the better phrases studding jewel-like, with
multiprismatic refractions, the four great paragraphs spread out,
deployed, splayed on the facing, the, in a sense, equal but opposite pages before him.

Author Winner said: "Not undistinguished; nor, in all candor,
inconsiderable. One might, in fact, go further: Tolstoi would,
as a sentient man, have been forced, though not without a tinge
of viridity, to cry: 'XOPOWO!' And Joyce?" Author Winner
shrugged, allowing the question to hang for a moment in the
air (that brave o'erhanging firmament!) above his head. *Re*
Joyce: could any reasonable man pretend (without hypocrisy)
to know what Joyce would have thought, or indeed what, ultimately, or for that matter, penultimately, he, in his anfractuosity
did think? The answer was pellucid: No! One could not prof-
itably go one's way *re*-Joycing.

Hearing then the sound of a key in the latch, Author Winner,
with not-unceremonius decorum, rose. Bouncing in on sturdy
feet encased in fulgent shoes of the best cordovan leather was
his wife, Clarifier, her arms, although long and well-muscled, en-
cumbered with packages. Of her burdens, relieving her (an act
he performed habitually, indeed, instinctively in all his personal
relations), Author Winner, with eloquent simplicity, said:
"Hello."

Clarifier, with a faint (leporine) vellication of her nose (a tic
Author Winner found at once repellent and subtly attractive),

removed her hat. She said: "Darling, I'll venture to guess that you, with your probing intelligence, will deduce that I've been out."

Author Winner nodded wordlessly.

Clarifier, removing her coat and turning to suspend it in the well-constructed wardrobe that had been her father's-in-law (himself defunct while this relationship was still uneventuate), revealing a nascent tendency toward steatopygia, permitted a paper to flutter from her pocket, the which Author Winner stooped (his inherent grace negating the implicit onus of the act), to retrieve.

Clarifier heartily said: "Oh, the milk bill. I had intended to give it to you, darling, before I departed from our residence at 10:08 this A.M."

Author Winner went to his desk; he was a man who liked to settle his accounts promptly, his ancestors on both sides having been early settlers.

Following him with springy steps Clarifier said: "We have, darling, a new milkman. Noting that he appeared ignorant concerning us, I invited him in for a cup of instant coffee and ventured to inform him that you, although an Author born, had only recently become a in-the-fullest-sense Winner, that I, following a chance encounter at the home of your germane cousin, Claude (the son of your mother's elder sister), and a courtship of four and a half months, became your wife in an extremely high church ceremony, and that we were now, as we had been then, childless."

Author Winner said: "What manner of man is this purveyor of milk?"

Clarifier said: "I'm glad, darling, that you asked that question; he is, as I myself discovered, a most-interesting combination. His mother was half Negro and half Jewish; his father, Catholic and Episcopalian in equal parts."

Frowning, Author Winner said: "I trust you entertained the Episcopal part only."

It was then that the storm broke: the inevitable effect of the fortuitous concatenation of air currents and pressure areas. Raging electrically, symbolically, above and on the four sides of the house, it was nevertheless able to exercise (intent upon exercising!) a subtle penetration. Author Winner and his wife, responding to a common (deep-rooted) impulse, found themselves moving toward the living-room windows, left open (no! intentionally raised some hours before against the matutinal calidity), and now admitting the (inadmissible) humectation. Together closing, then standing for a moment in the resultant closeness, they found themselves (together still!) mounting, mounting! Then a fumbling to open (the distaff distrait), superseded by Author Winner's deft dexterity; a brief interval of exploration, and then—the moment of revelation: His, and then Hers, Hers, Hers, and again and again Hers! in rapid succession, until Clarifier, sensing her husband's discomfiture, shyly said: "There was a white sale at Macy's; the Hers towels were half-price."

*　　*　　*

From the second-floor bedroom descended, in his chair once more settled, Author Winner, collecting himself in tranquility, again looked upon his work and found it good (Not by my syntax wilt thou judge me!). But was it perfect? It was this question that he had set himself sincerely to answer (One self-approving hour whole years outweighs Of stupid starers and of loud huzzas); as a Man of Reason, his impulse (itself a distillation of reason and his deeply-probing, deeply-boring knowledge of the science of probabilities that would have put the late J. M. Keynes to shame) had been: Perhaps, and perhaps not. But *if* not perfect, then, as a Man of Reason still, (that man that is not passion's slave!), *how* not? Eluding him now was the answer, if answer there were; the question itself hung (as no jury in the land could do, the verdict being, one might say, already in the "bag": *nemo me impune lacessit*) burning, suffusing the very atmosphere.

Clarifier, her healthy yet salicional voice preceding her down the stairs said: "Oh, darling, the custard has boiled over. I reproach myself with my failure to watch it more closely, but, this being Thursday, Agatha, our 'help' is 'off,' and I had, as you know, no knowledge of the domestic arts prior to our marriage seven years ago."

Author Winner wryly said: *"Quis custodiet istos* custard?" Not uncondign was her smiling gratitude as he, tightening his belt and shortening his suspenders, rose (as he invariably did to an occasion), and accompanied her to the kitchen.

Clarifier said: "There is a thing I must communicate to you, darling. Pausing for a moment in the street to pass the time of day with Rufus L. Cutler, our competent though erratic family splanchnologist, I neglected to note that I had parked under a bridge. In that brief moment I was with a parking ticket slapped."

Author Winner said: "The law, in its majestic equality, forbids the rich as well as the poor to park under bridges."

Clarifier said: "Yes, darling, but how can I get the ticket fixed? I have no desire to disburse a five-dollar fine to no purpose."

Author Winner said: "I will explain. Estoppel, whether equitable or in pais, arises upon doctrine that relevant evidence, having probative value, is prima facie admissable; relief or remedial provision of statute must be liberally construed to effectuate the objective prospectively and not retroactively; moreover, jurisdiction cannot be conferred by agreement, consent, or collusion, nor can parties be precluded from raising question by any form of laches or waiver. Is that perfectly clear, my dear?"

Clarifier gratefully said: "Oh, perfectly, darling. Could you just slip me five dollars which I require for certain minor domestic expenses?"

Of the five dollars possessed, she, with not-unaccustomed softness. Author Winner having already resumed the labors on which he had previously been engaged, tiptoed from the room. He, his mind irenic, his body composed, despite the dissipation of thought attendant on the interruption (the noble dust of Alexander stopping a bung-hole!), marshalled and polarized his not-inconsiderable faculties. Could it (veridically) be said that there was in the work before him any lacuna, omission, wantage, ullage, insufficiency? *Troppo disputare la verità fa errore:* it

could not! The conception was (in a word) magnificent: the
middle-aged man in the middle-sized town; he, in the moment of
his maximal wing-spread caught; it, by its ultimate perimeter
circumscribed; the whole including all that was truly American
(yet, in a sense, universal), all!: alcoholism, bastardy, criminality, bigamy, embezzlement, fornication—but here the compen-
dior must pause to wonder at (*admirare*) the courageous treatment accorded this subject in all its forms, aspects and manifestations (More things in heaven and earth, Kraft-Ebing, than are
dreamed of in your philosophy!). Sex, with the clinical eye,
fixed, with the lyrical pen, transfixed; the light (yet deft, pene-
trating) limning of pederasty; the pinch of scatology to titillate
the coprophilist in every critic— But why continue? The work
was indeed complete, exhaustive, plenary, consumate.

And of contemporary competition there was a blatantly
none: he had, with negligent ease, put in her painful place that
one who had dared to aspire to his primacy (though not yet his
in fact, already his in palpable incipience), transmogrifying the
base metalios with his philosopher's stone; he had successfully
challanged the nobelest master of meandering, yet avoided the
catafalknerian pall; he had even gone hand in hand with the
past master of involution all the way down the garden path!

Author Winner, having examined the question oxybleptically,
and having plucked out of this nettle (danger) the flower
(safety), was able, at last, to sink back in his chair, content. His
foundation was secure, and upon it he had builded better than
he knew.

It was then that, with a brief succusive convulsion, the chair
that had been his father's (built for sempiternity!) crumbled beneath Author Winner, disintegrating, comminuting in a flash!
He, for a moment only vacillating, then renitent, maintained
his position: spine held vertical at 96 degree angle to femur,
tibia at right angles to femur and floor. Author Winner thought:
I must be reasonable. Yet, deprived of traditional support, what
is now the reasonable thing to do? Collapse? Never; not at any
time! Rigid, rigidifying he thought: I-I-I- have the strength!

Clarifier, entering then, seeing with her exophthalmic eyes

only the obvious, rushed out to fetch a kitchen stool, which, returning, she inserted beneath the relevant part of Author Winner (Beneath him!). Could he, to descend to this shoddy, this crass, this lowly support bring himself?

Diamantine, unyielding, he said, "I am higher."

FELICIA LAMPORT

JAMES JONES

From There to Infinity

We all have a guilt-edged security.
—MOSES.

STARK romanticism" was the phrase that kept pounding through his head as he knocked on the door of Mama Paloma's, saw the slot opened and the single sloe plum that was Mama Paloma's eye scrutinizing him through the peephole. "Oh, you again," the eye grinned at him, sliding back the bolt of the door. "The girls are all pretty busy tonight but go on up." A dress of sequins that made her look like a fat mermaid with scales three-quarters instead of halfway up tightly encased the mounds of old snow that was her flesh. She glanced down at the must-be-heavy-as-lead suitcase in his hand as she closed the door. "I don't dare ast how many pages you're carting around in that by now," she grinned.

He mounted the steps with that suffocating expectation of men who are about to read their stuff, the nerves in his loins tightening like drying rawhide, the familiar knot hard in his belly. Shifting the suitcase from one hand to the other, his head swam into the densening surf of upstairs conversation, above which the tinkle of the player piano was like spray breaking all-the-time on rocks. Standing in the upper doorway, he reflected how, just as there can be damned senseless pointless want in the midst of plenty, so there can be the acutest loneliness in the midst of crowds. Fortunately, the thought passed swiftly. The whores moved, blatant as flamingos in their colored gowns, among the drinking-grinning men, and his eye ran tremulously swiftly in search of Dorine, gulpingly taking in the room for her figure moving erectly womanly through it all.

"No Princess to listen tonight," Peggy grinned toward him. "The Princess went away."

He could have slapped her. It puzzled him to find that beneath that hard, crusty exterior beat a heart of stone. What was she doing in a place like this? He turned and hurried back down the stairs.

"Come back soon, there's listeners as good as the Princess," Mama Paloma laughed jellily jollily as she let him out into the street.

With Dorine not there he couldn't bear Mama Paloma's, and he didn't know another place. Yet he had to have a woman tonight. Another woman would have to do, any woman.

Colonel Stilton's wife, he thought. Why not? She was from Boston, but there was no mistaking the look of hard insolent invitation she gave him each time she came to the Regimental Headquarters to ask if he knew where the Colonel had been since night before last. He hated Stilton's guts, or would if he, Stilton, had any. Hated that smirk and that single eyebrow always jerking sardonically skeptically up, like an anchovy that's learned to stand on end. Why not transfer out, why be a noncom under that bastard? he asked himself. I'm a noncompoop, he thought. He tried to make a joke of it but it was no good.

He knew where the Colonel lived from the time he'd taken him home stewed. He got out of the cab a block from the house. As he approached it walking, he could see Mrs. Stilton under a burning bulb on the screened terrace with her feet on a hassock, smoking a cigarette. She had on shorts and a sweater. Her slim brown legs like a pair of scissors made a clean incision in his mind. He went up the flagstone walk and rapped on the door.

"What do you want?" she said with the same insolent invitation, not stirring. He was aware of the neat, apple-hard breasts under the sweater, and of the terse, apple-hard invitation in her manner.

"I want to read this to you," he said, trying not to let his voice sound too husky.

"How much have you got in there," her voice knew all about him.

"A quarter of a million words," he said.

She came over and opened the screen door and flipped her cigarette out among the glows of the fireflies in the yard. When she turned back he caught the screen door and followed her inside. She sat down on the hassock and looked away for what seemed an eternity.

"It's a lot to ask of a woman," she said. "More than I've ever given."

He stood there shifting the suitcase to the other hand, the arm-about-to-come-out-of-its-socket ache added to that in his throat, wishing he wouldn't wish he hadn't come. She crossed her arms around her and, with that deft motion only women with their animal confidence can execute, pulled her sweater off over her head and threw it on the floor. "That's what you want, isn't it?" she said.

"You with your pair of scissors," he said. "When you can have a man who's willing to bare his soul." He gritted his teeth with impatience. "Don't you see how much we could have?"

"Come on in." She rose, and led the way inside. Nothing melts easier than ice, he thought, sad. He watched her draw the drapes across the window nook and settle herself back among the cushions. "I'm all yours," she said. "Read."

The female is a yawning chasm, he thought, glancing up from his reading at the lying listening woman. He found and read the passage explaining that, how she was the inert earth, passive potent, that waits to be beaten soft by April's fecundating rains. Rain is the male principle and there are times for it to be interminable: prosedrops into rivulets of sentences and those into streams of paragraphs, these merging into chapters flowing in turn into sectional torrents strong and hard enough to wear gullies down the flanks of mountains. After what seemed an eternity, he paused and she stirred.

"What time is it?" she sat up.

"A quarter to three."

"I never knew it could be like this," she said.

Each knew the other was thinking of Colonel Stilton.

"He never reads anything but *Quick*," she said, rolling her head away from him.

"The sonofabitch," he said, his fist involuntarily clenching as tears scalded his eyes. "Oh, the rotten sonofabitch!"

"It's no matter. Tell me about you. How did you get like this?"

Bending his head over the manuscript again he readingly told her about that part: how when he was a kid in down-state Illinois his uncle, who had wanted to be a lawyer but had never been able to finish law school because he would get roaring drunk and burn up all his textbooks, used to tell him about his dream, and about his hero, the late Justice Oliver Wendell Holmes, who in those great early days of this country was working on a manuscript which he would never let out of his sight, carrying it with him in a sack even when he went out courting or to somebody's house to dinner, setting it on the floor beside his chair. How his uncle passed this dream on to him, and how he took it with him to the big cities, where you began to feel how you had to get it all down, had to get down everything that got you down: the singing women in the cheap bars with their mouths like shrimp cocktails, the daughters-into-wives of chicken-eating digest-reading middle-class hypocrisy that you saw riding in the purring cars on Park Avenue, and nobody anywhere loving anybody they were married to. You saw that and you saw why. You had it all figured out that we in this country marry for idealistic love, and after the honeymoon there is bound to be disillusionment. That after a week or maybe a month of honest passion you woke up to find yourself trapped with the sow Respectability, which was the chicken-eating digest-reading middle-class assurance and where it lived: the house with the, oh sure, refrigerator, oil furnace and all the other automatic contraptions that snicker when they go on—the well-lighted air-conditioned mausoleum of love. She was a better listener than Fillow, a middle-aged swell who had eight hundred jazz records and who would sit in Lincoln Park in Chicago eating marsh-mallow out of a can with a spoon with gloves on. Every time he tried to read Fillow a passage, Fillow would say "Cut it out." Fillow was a negative product of bourgeois society just as Stilton with his chicken-eating digest-reading complacence was a positive one, whom his wife had and knew she had cuckolded the minute she had let the suitcase cross the threshold.

"It'll never be the same again, will it?" she said fondly softly, seeing he had paused again.

He read her some more and it was the same. Except that the thing went on so long the style would change, seeming to shift gears of itself like something living a hydramatic life of its own, so that side by side with the well-spent Hemingway patrimony and the continental cry of Wolfe would be the seachanged long tireless free-form sentences reminiscent of some but not all or maybe even much of Faulkner.

The door flew open and Stilton stood inside the room. His eyes were like two wet watermelon pips spaced close together on an otherwise almost blank plate (under the anchovies one of which had learned to stand on end).

"So," he said. The word sailed at them like a yoyo flung out horizontally by someone who can spin it that way. It sailed for what seemed an infinity and came back at him.

"So yourself," she said. "Is this how long officers' stags last?" she said.

"So he *forced his way in here,*" the Colonel cued her, at the same time talking for the benefit of a six-foot MP who hove into view behind him.

Realization went like a ball bouncing among the pegs of a pin-ball machine till it dropped into the proper slot in his mind and a bell rang and a little red flag went up reading "Leavenworth." He remembered what he'd heard. That an officer's wife is always safe because all she had to do was call out the single word rape and you were on your way to twenty years.

Why did he just stand there, almost detached? Why wasn't his anger rising from his guts into his head and setting his tongue into action? But what could you say to a chicken-eating digest-reading impediment like this anyhow, who with all the others of his kind had gelded contemporary literature and gelded it so good that an honest book that didn't mince words didn't stand a chance of getting even a smell of a best-seller list?

"This is my affair," he heard her say coolly, after what seemed a particularly long eternity.

The Colonel lighted a cigarette. "I suspected you were having one," they saw him smokingly smirk, "and since Klopstromer was seeing me home from the club I thought he might as well—" He stopped and looked down at the suitcase. "How long does he expect to *stay?*"

"I have something to say," he said, stepping forward.

"*Sir.*"

"I have something to say, sir," he said, picking up the suitcase to heft it for their benefit. "When Justice—"

"You'll get justice," the Colonel snapped as Klopstromer sprang alertly forward and bore down on him and wrested the suitcase from his grasp. "If you won't testify," the Colonel went on to his wife, "then Klopstromer at least will. That he assaulted a superior officer. It won't get him Leavenworth, but by God six months in the stockade will do him good."

"But why?" his wife protested. "You don't understand. He's a writer."

"Maybe," they saw the Colonel smirkingly smoke. The anchovy twitched and stood upright. "Maybe," he said, motioning to Klopstromer to march him out through the door to the waiting jeep, "but he needs discipline."

PETER DE VRIES

JACK KEROUAC

On the Sidewalk

I was just thinking around in my sad backyard, looking at those little drab careless starshaped clumps of crabgrass and beautiful chunks of some old bicycle crying out without words

of the American Noon and half a newspaper with an ad about
a lotion for people with dry skins and dry souls, when my
mother opened our frantic banging screendoor and shouted,
"Gogi Himmelman's here." She might have shouted the Arch-
angel Gabriel was here, or Captain Easy or Baron Charlus in
Proust's great book: Gogi Himmelman of the tattered old
greenasgrass knickers and wild teeth and the vastiest, most vorti-
cal, most insatiable wonderfilled eyes I have ever known. "Let's
go, Lee," he sang out, and I could see he looked sadder than ever,
his nose all rubbed raw by a cheap handkerchief and a dreary
Bandaid unravelling off his thumb. "I know the WAY!" That
was Gogi's inimitable unintellectual method of putting it that
he was on fire with the esoteric paradoxical Tao and there was
no holding him when he was in that mood. I said, "I'm going,
Mom," and she said, "O.K.," and when I looked back at her
hesitant in the pearly mystical UnitedStateshome light I felt
absolutely sad, thinking of all the times she had vacuumed the
same carpets.

His scooter was out front, the selfsame, the nonpareil, with
its paint scabbing off intricately and its scratchedon dirty words
and its nuts and bolts chattering with fear, and I got my tricycle
out of the garage, and he was off, his left foot kicking with that
same insuperable energy or even better. I said, "Hey wait," and
wondered if I could keep up and probably couldn't have if my
beltbuckle hadn't got involved with his rear fender. This was IT.
We scuttered down our drive and right over Mrs. Cacciatore's
rock garden with the tiny castles made out of plaster that always
made me sad when I looked at them alone. With Gogi it was
different; he just kept right on going, his foot kicking with that
delirious thirtyrevolutionsasecond frenzy, right over the top of
the biggest, a Blenheim six feet tall at the turrets; and suddenly
I saw it the way he saw it, embracing everything with his un-
fluctuating generosity, imbecile saint of our fudging age, a mad
desperado in our Twentieth Century Northern Hemisphere
Nirvana deserts.

We rattled on down through her iris bed and broke into the
wide shimmering pavement. "Contemplate those holy hydrants,"

he shouted back at me through the wind. "Get a load of those petulant operable latches; catch the magic of those pickets standing up proud and sequential like the arguments in Immanuel Kant; boom, boom, bitty-boom BOOM!" and it was true.

"What happens when we're dead?" I asked.

"The infinite never-to-be-defiled subtlety of the late Big Sid Catlett on the hushed trap drums," he continued, mad with his own dreams, imitating the whisks, "Swish, swish, swishy-swish SWOOSH!"

The sun was breaking over the tops of Mr. Linderman's privet hedge, little rows of leaves set in there delicate and justso like mints in a Howard Johnson's roadside eatery. Mitzi Leggett came out of the house, and Gogi stopped the scooter, and put his hands on her. "The virginal starchblue fabric; printed with stylized kittens and puppies," Gogi explained in his curiously beseechingly transcendent accents. "The searing incredible *innocence!* Oh! Oh! Oh!" His eyes poured water down his face like broken blisters.

"Take me along," Mitzi said openly to me, right with Gogi there and hearing every word, alive to every meaning, his nervous essence making his freckles tremble like a field of Iowa windblown nochaff barley.

"I want to," I told her, and tried to, but I couldn't, not there. I didn't have the stomach for it. She pretended to care. She was a lovely beauty. I felt my spokes snap under me; Gogi was going again, his eyes tightshut in ecstasy, his foot kicking so the hole in his shoesole showed every time, a tiny chronic rent in the iridescent miasmal veil that Intrinsic Mind tries to hide behind.

Wow! Dr. Fairweather's house came up on the left, delicious stucco like piecrust in the type of joints that attract truckers, and then the place of the beautiful Mrs. Mertz, with her *canny* deeprooted husband bringing up glorious heartbreaking tabourets and knickknacks from his workshop in the basement, a betooled woodshavingsmelling fantasy worthy of Bruegel or Hegel or a seagull. Vistas! Old Miss Hooper raced into her yard and made a grab for us, and Gogi Himmelman, the excruciating superbo, shifted to the other foot and laughed at her careworn face. Then the breathless agape green space of the Princeling mansion, with its rich calm and potted Tropic of Cancer plants. Then it was over.

Gogi and I went limp at the corner under a sign saying ELM STREET with irony because all the elms had been cut down so they wouldn't get the blight, sad stumps diminishing down the American perspective whisperingly.

"My spokes are gone," I told him.

"Friend—ahem—*zip, zip*—parting a relative concept—Bergson's invaluable marvelchoked work—tch, tch." He stood there, desperately wanting to do the right thing, yet always lacking with an indistinguishable grandeur that petty ability.

"Go," I told him. He was already halfway back, a flurrying spark, to where Mitzi waited with irrepressible womanwarmth.

Well. In landsend despair I stood there stranded. Across the asphalt that was sufficiently semifluid to receive and embalm millions of starsharp stones and bravely gay candywrappers a drugstore twinkled artificial enticement. But I was not allowed to cross the street. I stood on the gray curb thinking, They said I could cross it when I grew up, but what do they mean grown up? I'm thirty-nine now, and felt sad.

JOHN UPDIKE

ALLEN GINSBERG

Squeal

I SAW the best minds of my generation
Destroyed—Marvin
Who spat out poems; Potrzebie
Who coagulated a new bop literature in fifteen
Novels; Alvin
Who in his as yet unwritten autobiography
Gave Brooklyn an original *lex loci*.
They came from all over, from the pool room,

The bargain basement, the rod,
From Whitman, from Parkersburg, from Rimbaud
New Mexico, but mostly
They came from colleges, ejected
For drawing obscene diagrams of the Future.

They came here to L. A.,
Flexing their members, growing hair,
Planning immense unlimited poems,
More novels, more poems, more autobiographies.

It's love I'm talking about, you dirty bastards!
Love in the bushes, love in the freight car!
I saw them fornicating and being fornicated,
Saying to Hell with you!

America.
America is full of Babbitts.
America is run by money.

What was it Walt said? Go West!
But the important thing is the return ticket.
The road to publicity runs by Monterey.
I saw the best minds of my generation
Reading their poems to Vassar girls,
Being interviewed by *Mademoiselle*.
Having their publicity handled by professionals.
When can I go into an editorial office
And have my stuff published because I'm weird?
I could go on writing like this forever . . .

LOUIS SIMPSON

PART FOUR

Specialties

LEWIS CARROLL

SOME NONSENSE POEMS FROM "ALICE"
WITH THE ORIGINALS

B OTH *Alice in Wonderland* and *Through the Looking-Glass* are systematic parodies of the grown-up world from the viewpoint of a child, Alice being the norm and the grotesques she meets being exaggerations of adult behavior. Thus in the use of logic, a constant theme, Alice is common-sensible while the creatures are lunatic, technically right but actually absurd, like Sartre on the Soviet Union as a workers' state. *"Take some more tea," the March Hare said to Alice very earnestly. "I've had nothing yet," Alice replied in an offended tone, "so I can't take more." "You mean you can't take less," said the Hatter. "It's very easy to take more than nothing."*

More specifically, both books make fun of contemporary matters that are now forgotten. One need not know these references to enjoy *Alice* but it is interesting to read William Empson on the subject in *English Pastoral Poetry*. The Wool and Water chapter in *Through the Looking-Glass*, for instance, is about Oxford (the rowing, the pedantic old sheep, the elusiveness of the objects for sale); the scene in the railroad carriage is a spoof on materialism and progress (the man dressed in newspapers was drawn by Tenniel to look like Disraeli, 'the new man who gets on by self-advertisement, the newspaper-fed man who believes in progress, possibly even the rational dress of the future"); Carroll may have had Newman's *Apologia* in mind when he had the White Queen practice believing the impossible—*"When I was your age, I always did it for half an hour a day. Why sometimes I've believed as many as six impossible things before breakfast";* the Queen of Hearts, later the Red Queen, stands for sexual passion, according to Mr. Empson, who manages to be both light and reasonable in his Freudian interpretations, perhaps because he is English. In the Pool of Tears chapter he finds Darwin as well as Freud: the water is the medium through which Alice gets herself born into Wonderland; it is both the amniotic fluid and the sea from which life first came; the extinct Dodo stands for evolution; etc. One of Mr. Empson's happiest conjectures is that the talking flowers in *Looking-Glass* (they talk because they are awake and they are awake because their bed is hard and not soft "as in most gardens") make fun of Tennyson's *Maud,* a neurotic-romantic poem which would not have appealed much to Carroll:

> But the rose was awake all night for your sake,
>   Knowing your promise to me;
> The lilies and roses were all awake.
>   They sighed for the dawn and thee. . . .

> The red rose cries "She is near, she is near,"
>   And the white rose weeps "She is late,"
> The larkspur listens "I hear, I hear,"
>   And the lily whispers "I wait."

Finally, most of the "nonsense poems" in the Alice books aren't nonsense at all but burlesques of poems that were still current in the last century. One is of Wordsworth—irresistible target!—and one is of Scott, but most are of those moralizing poems that were once so profusely written for the edification of the young. (The two most famous, however, are not burlesques: *The Walrus and the Carpenter* and *Jabberwocky,* whose portmanteau words anticipated *Finnegans Wake.*)* "Children who aren't forced to learn Dr. Watts can't get the same thrill from parodies of him as the original children did," observes Mr. Empson. True. But contrariwise, adults may now get an antiquarian thrill from comparing the originals with what Carroll did to them—a thrill that may be enhanced by their strong period flavor, their *character* so to speak, foolish as they are. What Carroll did was, strictly, burlesque rather than parody; he simply injected an absurd content into the original form with no intention of literary criticism.

---

* As the scholarly Humpty Dumpty, who explains its hard words to Alice, anticipates Joyce's own attitude toward language: *"I don't know what you mean by 'glory',"* Alice said. *Humpty Dumpty smiled contemptuously. "Of course you don't—till I tell you. I mean 'there's a nice knock-down argument for you!'" "But 'glory' doesn't mean 'a nice knock-down argument,'"* Alice objected. *"When I use a word,"* Humpty Dumpty said in rather a scornful tone, *"it means just what I choose it to mean—neither more nor less." "The question is,"* said Alice, *"whether you can make words mean so many different things." "The question is,"* said Humpty Dumpty, *"which is to be master— that's all."*

When he did parody serious poets, he was not very good, tending to be either too broad (as in *Hiawatha's Photographing* and his Swinburne parody, *Atalanta in Camden Town*) or too fantastic (as in his parody of Tennyson's *The Two Voices*). But these qualities were just what he needed for the Alice Poems, since the originals were both crude and fantastic.

In the following section, each original is printed first, in italics, and Carroll's burlesque is given after it; the order is that in which the poems appear in Carroll. Those who want the full text of the originals, as well as much other fascinating information about the "Alice" books, are referred to Martin Gardner's *The Annotated Alice* (Clarkson N. Potter, $10), which appeared just as this was going to press. I must have been digging up the originals about the same time as Mr. Gardner; it is reassuring that in every case we coincide.

H ow *doth the little busy bee*
   Improve each shining hour,
And gather honey all the day
   From every opening flower!

How skillfully she builds her cell!
   How neat she spreads the wax!
And labors hard to store it well
   With the sweet food she makes.

In works of labor or of skill,
   I would be busy too;
For Satan finds some mischief still
   For idle hands to do. . . .

DR. ISAAC WATTS: *Against Idleness and Mischief*

H ow doth the little crocodile
   Improve his shining tail,
And pour the waters of the Nile
   On every golden scale!

How cheerfully he seems to grin,
How neatly spreads his claws,
And welcomes little fishes in
With gently smiling jaws!

Y ou are old, Father William," the young man cried;
"The few locks which are left you are gray;
You are hale, Father William—a hearty old man:
Now tell me the reason, I pray."

"In the days of my youth," Father William replied,
"I remembered that youth would fly fast,
And abused not my health and my vigor at first,
That I never might need them at last."

"You are old, Father William," the young man cried,
"And pleasures with youth pass away;
And yet you lament not the days that are gone:
Now tell me the reason, I pray."

"In the days of my youth," Father William replied,
"I remembered that youth could not last;
I thought of the future, whatever I did,
That I never might grieve for the past."

"You are old, Father William," the young man cried,
"And life must be hastening away;
You are cheerful and love to converse upon death:
Now tell me the reason, I pray."

"I am cheerful, young man," Father William replied;
"Let the cause thy attention engage;
In the days of my youth, I remembered my God,
And He hath not forgotten my age."

ROBERT SOUTHEY: *The Old Man's Comforts
and How He Gained Them.*

Y‍ou are old, Father William," the young man said,
  "And your hair has become very white;
And yet you incessantly stand on your head—
  Do you think, at your age, it is right?"

"In my youth," Father William replied to his son,
  "I feared it might injure the brain;
But now that I'm perfectly sure I have none,
  Why, I do it again and again."

"You are old," said the youth, "as I mentioned before,
  And have grown most uncommonly fat;
Yet you turned a back-somersault in at the door—
  Pray, what is the reason of that?"

"In my youth," said the sage, as he shook his grey locks,
  "I kept all my limbs very supple
By the use of this ointment—one shilling the box—
  Allow me to sell you a couple."

"You are old," said the youth, "and your jaws are too weak
  For anything tougher than suet;
Yet you finished the goose, with the bones and the beak—
  Pray how did you manage to do it?"

"In my youth," said his father, "I took to the law,
  And argued each case with my wife;
And the muscular strength, which it gave to my jaw,
  Has lasted the rest of my life."

"You are old," said the youth, "one would hardly suppose
  That your eye was as steady as ever;
Yet you balanced an eel on the end of your nose—
  What made you so awfully clever?"

"I have answered three questions, and that is enough,"
  Said his father; "don't give yourself airs!

Do you think I can listen all day to such stuff?
Be off, or I'll kick you downstairs!"

Speak gently; *it is better far*
To rule by love than fear;
Speak gently; let no harsh word mar
The good we may do here.

Speak gently to the little child;
Its love be sure to gain;
Teach it in accents soft and mild;
It may not long remain.

Speak gently to the young; for they
Will have enough to bear;
Pass through this life as best they may
'Tis full of anxious care. . . .

Speak gently; 'tis a little thing
Dropped in the heart's deep well;
The good, the joy that it may bring,
Eternity shall tell.

> G. W. LANGFORD: *Speak Gently*

Speak roughly to your little boy,
    And beat him when he sneezes;
He only does it to annoy,
    Because he knows it teases.

I speak severely to my boy,
    I beat him when he sneezes;
For he can thoroughly enjoy
    The pepper when he pleases!

Twinkle, twinkle, *little star*
How I wonder what you are!
Up above the world so high,
Like a diamond in the sky.

When the blazing sun is set,
And the grass with dew is wet,
Then you show your little light,
Twinkle, twinkle, all the night.

Then the traveler in the dark
Thanks you for your tiny spark,
He could not see which way to go
If you did not twinkle so.
                (*etc.*)

JANE TAYLOR: *The Star*

Twinkle, twinkle, little bat!
How I wonder what you're at!
Up above the world you fly,
Like a teatray in the sky.

Will you *walk into my parlor?" said the Spider to the Fly,*
"'*Tis the prettiest little parlor that ever you did spy;*
The way into my parlor is up a winding stair,
And I have many curious things to show when you are there."
"*Oh no, no," said the little Fly* "*to ask me is in vain;*
For who goes up your winding stair can ne'er come down
    again."

"*I'm sure you must be weary, dear, with soaring up so high;*
Will you rest upon my little bed?" said the Spider to the Fly.
"*There are pretty curtains drawn around, the sheets are fine and*
    thin;

And if you like to rest a while, I'll snugly tuck you in!"
"Oh no, no," said the little Fly, "for I've often heard it said
They never, never wake again, who sleep upon your bed!" ...

The Spider turned him round about, and went into his den
For well he knew the silly Fly would soon be back again;
So he wove a subtle web in little corner sky,
And set his table ready to dine upon the Fly.
Then he came out to his door again, and merrily did sing—
"Come hither, hither, pretty Fly, with the pearl and silver wing;
Your robes are green and purple, there's a crest upon your head;
Your eyes are like the diamond bright, but mine are dull as
*   lead."*

Alas, alas! how very soon this silly little Fly
Hearing his wily, flattering words, came slowly flitting by
With buzzing wings she hung aloft, then near and nearer
*   drew,—*
Thinking only of her brilliant eye and green and purple hue;
Thinking only of her crested head—poor foolish thing! At last,
Up jumped the cunning Spider, and fiercely held her fast,
He dragged her up his winding stair, into his dismal den
Within his little parlor—but she ne'er came out again!

And now, dear little children, who may this story read
To idle, silly, flattering words, I pray you ne'er give heed;
Unto an evil counsellor close heart, and ear, and eye,
And take a lesson from the tale of the Spider and the Fly.

MARY HOWITT: *The Spider and the Fly*

The Lobster Quadrille

WILL YOU walk a little faster?" said a whiting to a snail,
"There's a porpoise close behind us, and he's treading on my
        tail.
See how eagerly the lobsters and the turtles all advance!

They are waiting on the shingle—will you come and join the
   dance?
   Will you, won't you, will you, won't you, will you join the
      dance?
   Will you, won't you, will you, won't you, won't you join the
      dance?

"You can really have no notion how delightful it will be
When they take us up and throw us, with the lobsters, out to
   sea!"
But the snail replied "Too far, too far!" and gave a look
   askance—
Said he thanked the whiting kindly, but he would not join the
   dance.
   Would not, could not, would not, could not, would not join
      the dance.
   Would not, could not, would not, could not, could not join
      the dance.

"What matters it how far we go?" his scaly friend replied.
"There is another shore, you know, upon the other side.
The further off from England the nearer is to France—
Then turn not pale, beloved snail, but come and join the
   dance.
   Will you, won't you, will you, won't you, will you join the
      dance?
   Will you, won't you, will you, won't you, won't you join the
      dance?"

'T IS THE VOICE *of the sluggard, I heard him complain*
"You have waked me too soon, I must slumber again."
As the door on its hinges, so he on his bed,
Turns his sides and his shoulders, and his heavy head. . . .

I passed by his garden and saw the wild brier,
The thorn and the thistle, grow broader and higher;

The clothes that hang on him are turning to rags;
And his money still wastes till he starves or he begs.

I made him a visit, still hoping to find
That he took better care for improving his mind.
He told me his dreams, talked of eating and drinking;
But he scarce reads his Bible, and never loves thinking. . . .

DR. ISAAC WATTS: *The Sluggard*

'TIS THE VOICE of the Lobster; I heard him declare,
"You have baked me too brown, I must sugar my hair."
As a duck with its eyelids, so he with his nose
Trims his belt and his buttons, and turns out his toes.
When the sands are all dry, he is gay as a lark,
And will talk in contemptuous tones of the Shark:
But, when the tide rises and sharks are around,
His voice has a timid and tremulous sound.

I passed by his garden, and marked, with one eye,
How the Owl and the Panther were sharing a pie:
The Panther took pie-crust, and gravy, and meat,
While the Owl had the dish as its share of the treat.
When the pie was all finished, the Owl, as a boon,
Was kindly permitted to pocket the spoon:
While the Panther received knife and fork with a growl,
And concluded the banquet by—

BEAU—TI—FUL STAR *in heav'n so bright,*
Soft—ly falls thy sil—v'ry light,
As thou mov—est from earth a—far,
Star of the eve—ning, beauti—ful star,
Star of the eve—ning, beau—ti—ful star.

Chorus:

> *Beau—ti—ful star, ——*
> *Beau—ti—ful star, ——*
> *Star—of the eve—ning,*
> *Beau—ti—ful, beau—ti—ful star. . . .*

Shine on, oh star of love divine,
And may our soul's affections twine
Around thee as thou movest afar,
Star of the twilight, beautiful star.

JAMES M. SAYLES: *Star of the Evening*

Bᴇᴀᴜᴛɪꜰᴜʟ sᴏᴜᴘ, so rich and green,
Waiting in a hot tureen!
Who for such dainties would not stoop?
Soup of the evening, beautiful Soup!
Soup of the evening, beautiful Soup!
    Beau—ootiful Soo—oop!
    Beau—ootiful Soo—oop!
Soo—oop of the e—e—evening,
    Beautiful, beautiful Soup!

Beautiful Soup! who cares for fish,
Game, or any other dish?
Who would not give all else for two p
ennyworth only of beautiful Soup?
Pennyworth only of beautiful Soup?
    Beau—ootiful Soo—oop!
    Beau—ootiful Soo—oop!
Soo—oop of the e—e—evening
    Beautiful, beauti—FUL SOUP!

VIII

Nᴏᴡ, ᴡʜᴇᴛʜᴇʀ *it were by peculiar grace,*
A leading from above, a something given,

Yet it befell, that, in this lonely place,
When I with these untoward thoughts had striven,
Beside a pool bare to the eye of heaven
I saw a man before me unawares:
The oldest man he seemed that ever wore grey hairs.

XIII

A gentle answer did the old Man make,
In courteous speech which forth he slowly drew;
And him with further words I thus bespake,
"What occupation do you there pursue?
This is a lonesome place for one like you."
Ere he replied, a flash of mild surprise
Broke from the sable orbs of his yet vivid eyes.

XV

He told, that to these waters he had come,
To gather leeches, being old and poor:
Employment hazardous and wearisome!
And he had many hardships to endure:
From pond to pond he roamed, from moor to moor;
Housing, with God's good help, by choice or chance,
And in this way he gained an honest maintenance.

XVII

My former thoughts returned: the fear that kills;
And hope that is unwilling to be fed;
Cold, pain, and labour, and all fleshly ills;
And nightly poets in their misery dead.
Perplexed, and longing to be comforted,
My question eagerly did I renew,
"How is it that you live, and what is it you do?"

XVIII

He with a smile did then his words repeat;
And said, that, gathering leeches, far and wide
He travelled; stirring thus about his feet
The waters of the pools where they abide.
"Once I could meet with them on every side;
But they have dwindled long by slow decay;
Yet still I persevere, and find them where I may."

XIX

While he was talking thus, the lonely place,
The old Man's shape, and speech—all troubled me:
In my mind's eye I seemed to see him pace
About the heavy moors continually,
Wandering about alone and silently.
While I these thoughts within myself pursued,
He having made a pause, the same discourse renewed.

XX

And soon with this he other matter blended,
Cheerfully uttered, with demeanour kind,
But stately in the main; and when he ended,
I could have laughed myself to scorn to find
In that decrepit Man so firm a mind.
"God," said I, "be my help and stay secure;
I'll think of the Leech-gatherer on the lonely moor!"

WILLIAM WORDSWORTH: *Resolution*
and Independence

I'LL TELL thee everything I can:
   There's little to relate.
I saw an aged aged man,
   A-sitting on a gate.

"Who are you, aged man?" I said.
   "And how is it you live?"
And his answer trickled through my head,
   Like water through a sieve.

He said "I look for butterflies
   That sleep among the wheat:
I make them into mutton-pies,
   And sell them in the street.
I sell them unto men," he said,
   "Who sail on stormy seas:
And that's the way I get my bread—
   A trifle, if you please."

But I was thinking of a plan
   To dye one's whiskers green,
And always use so large a fan
   That they could not be seen.
So, having no reply to give
   To what the old man said,
   I cried "Come, tell me how you live!"
   And thumped him on the head.

His accents mild took up the tale:
   He said "I go my ways,
And when I find a mountain-rill,
   I set it in a blaze;
And thence they make a stuff they call
   Rowland's Macassar-Oil—
Yet twopence-halfpenny is all
   They give me for my toil."

But I was thinking of a way
   To feed oneself on batter,
And so go on from day to day
   Getting a little fatter.
I shook him well from side to side,

Until his face was blue:
"Come, tell me how you live," I cried,
"And what it is you do!"

He said "I hunt for haddocks' eyes
Among the heather bright,
And work them into waistcoat-buttons
In the silent night.
And these I do not sell for gold
Or coin of silvery shine,
But for a copper halfpenny,
And that will purchase nine.

"I sometimes dig for buttered rolls,
Or set limed twigs for crabs:
I sometimes search the grassy knolls
For wheels of Hansom-cabs.
And that's the way" (he gave a wink)
"By which I get my wealth—
And very gladly will I drink
Your Honour's noble health."

I heard him then, for I had just
Completed my design
To keep the Menai bridge from rust
By boiling it in wine.
I thanked him much for telling me
The way he got his wealth,
But chiefly for his wish that he
Might drink my noble health.

And now, if e'er by chance I put
My fingers into glue,
Or madly squeeze a right-hand foot
Into a left-hand shoe,
Or if I drop upon my toe
A very heavy weight,

I weep for it reminds me so
Of that old man I used to know—
Whose look was mild, whose speech was slow
Whose hair was whiter than the snow,
Whose face was very like a crow,
With eyes, like cinders, all aglow,
Who seemed distracted with his woe,
Who rocked his body to and fro.

And muttered mumblingly and low,
As if his mouth were full of dough,
Who snorted like a buffalo——
That summer evening long ago,
        A-sitting on a gate.*

T o the *Lords of Convention 'twas Claver'se who spoke,*
"Ere the King's crown shall fall, there are crowns to be broke;
So let each cavalier who loves honor and me
Come follow the bonnet of Bonnie Dundee:

> *"Come fill up my cup, come fill up my can,*
> *Come saddle your horses, and call up your men,*
> *Come open the West Port and let me gang free,*
> *And its room for the bonnets of Bonnie Dundee!"*

---

* In *English Pastoral Poetry,* Mr. Empson is very good on this burlesque. He calls *Resolution and Independence* "a genuine pastoral poem if ever there was one" and notes that from the endurance of the old leech-gatherer Wordsworth draws strength to face the pain of the world. (He might have added that, as Mr. Gardner observes in *The Annotated Alice,* the poem is a good one in spite of its absurd aspects; the mingling of the sublime and the ridiculous might almost be called one of Wordsworth's literary mannerisms.) "Dodgson was fond of saying that parody showed no lack of admiration," Mr. Empson writes, "but a certain bitterness is inherent in parody. If the meaning is not 'This poem is absurd,' it must be 'In my present mood of emotional sterility the poem will not work, or I am afraid to let it work, on *me.*' The parody here will have no truck with the dignity of the leech-gatherer . . . There may even be a reproach for Wordsworth in the lack of consideration that makes him go on asking the same question."

• • • •

"Away to the hills, to the caves, to the rocks,—
Ere I own an usurper, I'll couch with the fox;
And tremble, false Whigs in the midst of your glee,
You have not seen the last of my bonnet and me!"

[*Chorus as before*]

He waved his proud hand, and the trumpets were blown,
The kettle-drums clashed and the horsemen rode on,
Till on Ravelston's cliffs and on Clermiston's lee
Died away the wild war-notes of Bonnie Dundee.

SIR WALTER SCOTT: *Bonnie Dundee*

To THE Looking-Glass world it was Alice that said
"I've a sceptre in hand I've a crown on my head.
Let the Looking-Glass creatures, whatever they be,
Come and dine with the Red Queen, the White Queen, and me!"

Then fill up the glasses as quick as you can,
And sprinkle the table with buttons and bran:
Put cats in the coffee, and mice in the tea—
And welcome Queen Alice with thirty-times-three!

"O Looking-Glass creatures," quoth Alice, "draw near!
'Tis an honour to see me, a favour to hear:
'Tis a privilege high to have dinner and tea
Along with the Red Queen, the White Queen, and me!"

Then fill up the glasses with treacle and ink,
Or anything else that is pleasant to drink:
Mix sand with the cider, and wool with the wine—
And welcome Queen Alice with ninety-times-nine!

SOME UNRELIABLE HISTORY
BY
MAURICE BARING

IN THE STACKS of the Yale Library two years ago, looking for parodic material, I came across a fat book by Maurice Baring called *Unreliable History* (Heinemann, 1934). It was divided into "Diminutive Dramas," "Dead Letters," and "Lost Diaries." Strictly speaking, the four items below are travesties rather than parodies—see Appendix for the distinction. I have included them because they seem to me about the best of their kind.

The late Maurice Baring was one of those Edwardian writers who once glittered and now glimmer. The fourth son of the first Lord Revelstoke, linguist (his first book was written in French—a collection of parodies), war correspondent, wing commander in the R.A.F. during the First World War, dandy, critic, memoirist, poet, novelist, translator, diplomat, he is read no longer, and Beerbohm's parody in the *Garland*—that he should have been included shows his standing— is a shadow that survives after the substance has vanished. Perhaps one should try some of his dozen novels, or one of his many volumes in that old-fashioned category, belles-lettres. Meanwhile, there is *Unreliable History*.

The Rehearsal

SCENE.—*The Globe Theatre, 1595. On the stage the* AUTHOR, *the* PRODUCER, *and the* STAGE MANAGER *are standing. A rehearsal of "Macbeth" is about to begin. Waiting in the wings are the actors who are playing the* WITCHES, BANQUO, MACDUFF, *etc. They are all men.*

THE STAGE MANAGER.   We'd better begin with the last act.

THE PRODUCER.   I think we'll begin with the first act. We've never done it all through yet.

THE STAGE MANAGER.   Mr. Colman isn't here. It's no good doing the first act without Duncan.

THE PRODUCER.   Where is Mr. Colman? Did you let him know about rehearsal?

THE STAGE MANAGER. I sent a messenger to his house in Gray's Inn.

THE FIRST WITCH. Mr. Colman is playing Psyche in a masque at Kenilworth. He won't be back until the day after to-morrow.

THE PRODUCER. That settles it. We'll begin with the fifth act.

THE FIRST WITCH. Then I suppose I can go.

THE SECOND WITCH. ⎱ And I suppose we
THE THIRD WITCH.   ⎰   needn't wait.

THE STAGE MANAGER. Certainly not. We're going on to the fourth act as soon as we've done the fifth.

BANQUO. But I suppose you don't want me.

THE STAGE MANAGER. And what about your ghost entrance in Act IV? We must get the business right this time; besides, we'll do the second act if we've time. Now, Act V, Mr. Thomas and Mr. Bowles, please.

THE FIRST WITCH. Mr. Bowles can't come to-day. He told me to tell you. He's having a tooth pulled out.

THE STAGE MANAGER. Then will you read the waiting gentle-woman's part, Mr. Lyle. You can take this scrip.

[*The* FIRST WITCH *takes the scrip.*

Where is Mr. Thomas?

THE FIRST WITCH. He said he was coming.

THE STAGE MANAGER. We can't wait. I'll read his part. We'll leave out the beginning and just give Mr. Hughes his cue.

THE FIRST WITCH (*reading*). "Having no witness to confirm my speech."

THE STAGE MANAGER. Mr. Hughes.

THE FIRST WITCH. He was here a moment ago.

THE STAGE MANAGER (*louder*). Mr. Hughes.

Enter LADY MACBETH (MR. HUGHES, *a young man about* 24)

LADY MACBETH. Sorry. (*He comes on down some steps L.C.*)

THE PRODUCER. That will never do, Mr. Hughes; there's no necessity to sway as if you were intoxicated, and you mustn't look at your feet.

LADY MACBETH.   It's the steps. They're so rickety.

THE PRODUCER.   We'll begin again from "speech."

[LADY MACBETH *comes on again. He looks straight in front of him and falls heavily on to the ground.*

I said those steps were to be mended yesterday.

[*The* FIRST WITCH *is convulsed with laughter.*

LADY MACBETH.   There's nothing to laugh at.

THE PRODUCER.   Are you hurt, Mr. Hughes?

LADY MACBETH.   Not much. (*The steps are replaced by two supers.*)

THE PRODUCER.   Now from "speech."

[MR. HUGHES *comes on again.*

THE PRODUCER.   You must not hold the taper upside down.

LADY MACBETH.   How can I rub my hands and hold a taper too? What's the use of the taper?

THE PRODUCER.   You can rub the back of your hand. You needn't wash your hands in the air. That's better.

[*The dialogue between the* DOCTOR *and the* GENTLEWOMAN *proceeds until* LADY MACBETH's *cue: "hour."*

Enter the DOCTOR (MR. THOMAS). *He waits R.*

LADY MACBETH.   "Here's a damned spot."

THE STAGE MANAGER.   No, no, Mr. Hughes, "Yet here's a spot."

THE PRODUCER.   Begin again from "hands."

GENTLEWOMAN.   "It is an accustomed action with her, to seem thus washing her hands. I've known her to continue in this three-quarters of an hour."

LADY MACBETH.   "Yet here's a damned spot."

THE STAGE MANAGER.   It's not "damned" at all. That comes later.

LADY MACBETH.   It's catchy. Couldn't I say "mark" instead of "spot" in the first line?

THE DOCTOR (*coming forward*).   That would entirely spoil the effect of my "Hark!" You see "mark" rhymes with "Hark." It's impossible.

THE PRODUCER. Oh! It's you, Mr. Thomas. Will you go straight on. We'll do the whole scene over presently. Now from "hour."

LADY MACBETH. "Yes, here's a spot."

THE STAGE MANAGER. It's not "Yes," but "Yet," Mr. Hughes.

LADY MACBETH. "Yet here's a spot."

THE DOCTOR (*at the top of his voice*). "Hark!"

THE PRODUCER. Not so loud, Mr. Thomas, that would wake her up.

THE DOCTOR (*in a high falsetto*). "Har-r-rk! She spe-e-e-aks. I will . . . set . . . down."

THE PRODUCER. You needn't bleat that "speaks," Mr. Thomas, and the second part of that line is cut.

THE DOCTOR. It's not cut in my part. "Hark, she speaks."

LADY MACBETH. "Yet here's a spot."

THE STAGE MANAGER. No, Mr. Hughes; "out damned spot."

LADY MACBETH. Sorry.

THE PRODUCER. We must get that right. Now from "hour."

LADY MACBETH. "Yet here's a spot."

THE DOCTOR. "Hark! she speaks."

LADY MACBETH. "Get out, damned spot! Get out, I say! One, two, three, four: why there's plenty of time to do't. Oh! Hell! Fie, fie, my Lord! a soldier and a beard! What have we got to fear when none can call our murky power to swift account withal? You'd never have thought the old man had so much blood in him!"

THE AUTHOR. I don't think you've got those lines quite right yet, Mr. Hughes.

LADY MACBETH. What's wrong?

THE STAGE MANAGER. There's no "get." It's "one; two": and not "one, two, three, four." Then it's "Hell is murky." And there's no "plenty." And it's "a soldier and *afeared*," and not "a soldier and a *beard*."

THE AUTHOR. And after that you made two lines into rhymed verse.

MR. HUGHES. Yes, I know I did. I thought it wanted it.

THE PRODUCER. Please try to speak your lines as they are written, Mr. Hughes.

Enter MR. BURBAGE, *who plays Macbeth.*

MR. BURBAGE.   That scene doesn't go. Now don't you think Macbeth had better walk in his sleep instead of Lady Macbeth?

THE STAGE MANAGER.   That's an idea.

THE PRODUCER.   I think the whole scene might be cut. It's quite unnecessary.

LADY MACBETH.   Then I shan't come on in the whole of the fifth act. If that scene's cut I shan't play at all.

THE STAGE MANAGER.   We're thinking of transferring the scene to Macbeth. (*To the* AUTHOR.) It wouldn't need much altering. Would you mind rewriting that scene, Mr. Shakespeare? It wouldn't want much alteration. You'd have to change that line about Arabia. Instead of this "little hand," you might say: "All the perfumes of Arabia will not sweeten this horny hand." I'm not sure it isn't more effective.

THE AUTHOR.   I'm afraid it might get a laugh.

MR. BURBAGE.   Not if I play it.

THE AUTHOR.   I think it's more likely that Lady Macbeth would walk in her sleep, but——

MR. BURBAGE.   That doesn't signify. I can make a great hit in that scene.

LADY MACBETH.   If you take that scene from me, I shan't play Juliet to-night.

THE STAGE MANAGER (*aside to* PRODUCER).   We can't possibly get another Juliet.

THE PRODUCER.   On the whole, I think we must leave the scene as it is.

MR. BURBAGE.   I've got nothing to do in the last act. What's the use of my coming to rehearsal when there's nothing for me to rehearse?

THE PRODUCER.   Very well, Mr. Burbage. We'll go on to the Third Scene at once. We'll go through your scene again later, Mr. Hughes.

MR. BURBAGE.   Before we do this scene there's a point I wish to settle. In Scene V, when Seyton tells me the Queen's dead, I say: "She should have died hereafter; there would have been a time for such a word"; and then the messenger enters. I should

like a soliloquy here, about twenty or thirty lines, if possible in
rhyme, in any case ending with a tag. I should like it to be about
Lady Macbeth. Macbeth might have something touching to say
about their happy domestic life, and the early days of their marriage. He might refer to their courtship. I must have something
to make Macbeth sympathetic, otherwise the public won't stand
it. He might say his better-half had left him, and then he might
refer to her beauty. The speech might begin:

> O dearest chuck, it is unkind indeed
> To leave me in the midst of my sore need.

Or something of the kind. In any case it ought to rhyme. Could
I have that written at once, and then we could rehearse it?

THE PRODUCER. Certainly, certainly, Mr. Burbage. Will you
write it yourself, Mr. Shakespeare, or shall we get some one else
to do it?

THE AUTHOR. I'll do it myself if some one will read my part.

THE PRODUCER. Let me see; I forget what is your part.

THE STAGE MANAGER. Mr. Shakespeare is playing Seyton.
(*Aside.*) We cast him for Duncan, but he wasn't up to it.

THE PRODUCER. Mr. Kydd, will you read Mr. Shakespeare's
part?

BANQUO. Certainly.

THE PRODUCER. Please let us have that speech, Mr. Shakespeare, as quickly as possible. (*Aside.*) Don't make it too long.
Ten lines at the most.

THE AUTHOR (*aside*). Is it absolutely necessary that it should
rhyme?

THE PRODUCER (*aside*). No, of course not; that's Burbage's
fad.   *Exit the* AUTHOR *into the wings.*

MR. BURBAGE. I should like to go through the fight first.

THE PRODUCER. Very well, Mr. Burbage.

THE STAGE MANAGER. Macduff—Mr. Foote——

MACDUFF. I'm here.

MR. BURBAGE. I'll give you the cue:

"Why should I play the fool and like a Roman
  Die on my sword, while there is life, there's hope;
  The gashes are for them."

MACDUFF.   "Turn, hell-hound, turn."

MR. BURBAGE.   I don't think Macduff ought to call Macbeth
a hell-hound.

THE PRODUCER.   What do you suggest?

MR. BURBAGE.   I should suggest: "False Monarch, turn." It's
more dignified.

MACDUFF.   I would rather say "hell-hound."

THE PRODUCER.   Supposing we make it "King of Hell."

MR. BURBAGE.   I don't think that would do.

THE PRODUCER.   Then we must leave it for the present.

MACDUFF.   "Turn, hell-hound, turn."

> [*They begin to fight with wooden swords.*

THE STAGE MANAGER.   You don't begin to fight till Macduff
says "Give thee out."

MR. BURBAGE.   I think we might run those two speeches into
one, and I might say:

"Of all men I would have avoided thee,
  But come on now, although my soul is charged
  With blood of thine, I'll have no further words.
  My voice is in my sword."

Then Macduff could say:

"O bloodier villain than terms can well express."

THE PRODUCER.   We must consult the author about that.

MR. BURBAGE.   We'll do the fencing without words first.

> [*They begin to fight again.* MACDUFF *gives* MR. BURBAGE *a
> tremendous blow on the shoulder.*

MR. BURBAGE.   Oh! oh! That's my rheumatic shoulder. Please
be a little more careful, Mr. Foote. You know I've got no pad-
ding. I can't go on rehearsing now. I am very seriously hurt indeed.

MACDUFF.   I'm sure I'm very sorry. It was entirely an accident.

MR. BURBAGE.   I'm afraid I must go home. I don't feel up to it.

THE STAGE MANAGER.   I'll send for some ointment. Please be
more careful, Mr. Foote. Couldn't you possibly see your way to
take Scene III, Mr. Burbage?

MR. BURBAGE.   I know Scene III backwards. However, I'll just
run through my speech.

THE STAGE MANAGER. What? "This push will cheer me ever"?

MR. BURBAGE (*peevishly*). No, not that one. You know that's all right. That tricky speech about medicine. Give me the cue.

THE STAGE MANAGER. "That keep her from her rest."

MR. BURBAGE.   "Cure her of that:
Canst thou not minister to a sickly mind,
Pull from the memory a booted sorrow,
Rub out the troubles of the busy brain,
And with a sweet and soothing antidote
Clean the stiff bosom of that dangerous poison
Which weighs upon the heart?"
There, you see, word-perfect. What did I say?

THE STAGE MANAGER. Yes, yes, Mr. Burbage. Here's Mr. Shakespeare.

THE AUTHOR. I've written that speech. Shall I read it?

THE PRODUCER. Please.

MR. SHAKESPEARE (*reads*). "To-morrow, and to-morrow, and to-morrow,
Creeps in this petty pace from day to day,
To the last syllable of recorded time;
And all our yesterdays have lighted fools
The way to dusty death. Out, out, brief candle!
Life's but a walking shadow, a poor player
That struts and frets his hour upon the stage,
And then is heard no more; it is a tale
Told by an idiot, full of sound and fury,
Signifying nothing."

MR. BURBAGE. Well, you don't expect me to say that, I suppose. It's a third too short. There's not a single rhyme in it. It's got nothing to do with the situation, and it's an insult to the stage. "Struts and frets" indeed! I see there's nothing left for me but to throw up the part. You can get any one you please to play Macbeth. One thing is quite certain, I won't.

[*Exit* MR. BURBAGE *in a passion.*

THE STAGE MANAGER (*to the* AUTHOR). Now you've done it.

THE AUTHOR (*to the* PRODUCER). You said it needn't rhyme.

THE PRODUCER. It's Macduff. It was all your fault, Mr. Foote.

LADY MACBETH.   Am I to wear a fair wig or a dark wig?

THE PRODUCER.   Oh! I don't know.

THE AUTHOR.   Dark, if you please. People are always saying I'm making portraits. So, if you're dark, nobody can say I meant the character for the Queen or for Mistress Mary Fytton.

THE STAGE MANAGER.   It's no good going on now. It's all up —it's all up.

CURTAIN.

Jason and Medea

SCENE.—*A room in the house of* JASON, *looking on to garden, at Corinth. Discovered:* JASON *and* GLAUCE.

JASON.   I think you really had better go. She may be in any minute now.

GLAUCE.   Very well; but you promise to tell her to-day?

JASON.   I swear.

GLAUCE.   It's all very well, but you said that yesterday.

JASON.   Yes, and I would have told her yesterday, only I was interrupted——

GLAUCE.   I know; the only thing I say is, you must tell her to-day and do it nicely, because I shouldn't like poor little Medea to be hurt.

JASON.   No, of course not. Good-bye.

GLAUCE.   Good-bye. Then to-morrow at eleven, at the Creon Institute.

JASON.   Very well, at eleven.

GLAUCE.   And then we might—no.

JASON.   What?

GLAUCE.   Nothing. I was only thinking we might have some food at the "Golden Fleece," *downstairs.*

JASON.   The whole of Corinth would see us.

GLAUCE.   There is never a soul downstairs, and I don't see now that it much matters.

JASON.   It's a pity to make oneself conspicuous; your father——

GLAUCE.   You know best, but I should have thought——

JASON.   That's Medea coming through the garden.

GLAUCE.   To-morrow, at eleven.

JASON.   Yes—yes—to-morrow. (GLAUCE *goes out L.*)

Enter MEDEA *from the garden*

MEDEA.   I can't get any one for dinner to-morrow night. We want somebody amusing.

JASON (*wearily*).   Would Orpheus do?

MEDEA.   We've got too many heroes as it is. And then, if Orpheus comes, we shall be obliged to ask him to play.

JASON.   What about Castor and Pollux?

MEDEA.   Heroes again—and I think it's a mistake to ask brothers together.

JASON.   Heracles is staying at Corinth.

MEDEA.   He would do beautifully.

JASON.   I'm not sure he would do. He doesn't get on with Admetus.

MEDEA.   Why not? Admetus ought to be very grateful.

JASON.   For bringing back his wife from the grave?

MEDEA.   Yes, of course.

JASON.   Of course. (JASON *looks pensive.*)

MEDEA.   Then we shall want another woman.

JASON.   How would Ariadne do?

MEDEA.   What are you thinking of? Theseus is coming.

JASON.   I thought all that had entirely blown over.

MEDEA.   We want an unmarried woman, if possible.

JASON.   I don't know any one.

MEDEA.   Do you think we could get King Creon's daughter by herself? She's so pretty. I mean Glauce.

JASON (*blushing scarlet*).   I don't think—er—no—you see—we can't very well.

MEDEA.   Why not?

JASON.   She's a girl.

MEDEA.   She goes everywhere. She doesn't count as a girl.

JASON.   Then we should have to ask King Creon.

MEDEA.   No, Alcestis will bring her. That will do beautifully. I'll send a message at once.

JASON.   For the sake of the gods, do nothing of the kind.

MEDEA.   But she'll do beautifully.

JASON.   You don't understand. You see, King Creon has—he's —well, I don't quite know how to say it.

MEDEA.   What *do* you mean?

JASON.   Well, it's very awkward. The fact is, King Creon has approached me politically—about something——

MEDEA.   What has that got to do with asking Glauce?

JASON.   No, nothing, of course, except that we should have to ask him.

MEDEA.   I've already told you that it's unnecessary.

JASON (*firmly*).   I shouldn't dream of asking her without her father, and we can't ask him.

MEDEA.   Why not?

JASON.   Oh, because he never does dine out.

MEDEA.   I'm sure he would come here.

JASON.   It's impossible. You see, to tell you the truth—I've been meaning to tell you this for some time, only I've never had the opportunity—the King is rather severe about you.

MEDEA.   Severe! How?

JASON.   Well, you see, he's old-fashioned, and he doesn't consider our marriage is a marriage.

MEDEA.   We were married in the temple of Aphrodite. What more does he want?

JASON.   He doesn't consider that a girl's marriage is valid when it is made without the consent of her parents; and your poor dear father, you know, was most unreasonable.

MEDEA.   Papa being silly has got nothing to do with it. When a man and a woman are married in a temple, with the proper rites, they are man and wife. Nothing can ever alter the fact.

JASON.   Yes, but it's not only that. Creon goes much farther than that. He made me certain revelations concerning some family business which, I must say, surprised me immensely.

MEDEA.   What family business?

JASON.   Well, it appears that soon after I started for Clochis my father entered into secret negotiations with King Creon, and signed an offensive and defensive alliance with him, with the object of safeguarding himself against Pelias. The word-alliance remained secret. But at a State banquet Creon laid great stress on the friendship between himself and the Æolidæ, and brought in the words "friendly understanding" several times. Now in the treaty, which was drawn up and published, to mask the alliance, there were several secret clauses. One of them concerned the Sardine Fisheries in the Isthmus of Corinth, and the other—well —er, my marriage.

MEDEA. Your marriage.

JASON. Yes, it is extraordinary, isn't it? It appears that during my absence, and without my being consulted in any way whatsoever, I was formally married, by proxy, of course, to Creon's daughter Glauce—who was at that time a mere child. It was further settled that as soon as she was grown up, the marriage should be announced and the King should publicly adopt me as his heir.

MEDEA. No wonder he was annoyed at your having married me.

JASON. Well, you see, he isn't annoyed at that, because he says our marriage wasn't valid.

MEDEA. Not in the eyes of the law, perhaps; but I am sure Aphrodite would not only be pained, but extremely angry if we cancelled vows which were made in her temple.

JASON. No, that's just it. It appears he consulted all the oracles and the priestesses, and the Pythonesses, and they all say that our marriage is not only illegal, but positively criminal, and that my lawful wife, both in the eyes of man and of the gods, is Glauce.

MEDEA. And my children?

JASON. Well, about the children, opinion was slightly divided; but they inclined to think that, if I adopted them, they would be considered legitimate.

MEDEA. Legitimate! I should hope so. But what did you say to Creon? I suppose you told him you were very sorry, but that it couldn't be helped. (*She laughs.*) Poor Glauce! It's a shame to make a girl so ridiculous.

JASON. I don't think you quite realise how seriously Creon regards the matter.

MEDEA. I don't care an obol what he thinks. What I want to be told is how you told him what you think.

JASON. Of course, I said that I felt highly flattered.

MEDEA.   But that you were married already.

JASON.   No, it was no use saying that, because—as I've already said twice—he does not think our marriage counts.

MEDEA.   Then what did you say?

JASON.   Oh, I said I would lay the matter before you, and trust to your great good sense.

MEDEA.   Do you mean to say that you did not give him to understand that the whole thing was altogether mad, absurd, and utterly preposterous?

JASON.   How could I? After all, he is the King; and, moreover, he is backed up by all the legal and hieratic authorities. I could do nothing. I was quite helpless, quite defenceless. I simply had to incline myself before his higher authority.

MEDEA.   Oh, I see; you accepted, in fact.

[*She reflects a moment.*

JASON.   I didn't exactly accept. But what else could I do?

MEDEA.   No, of course, it's quite simple. You said that our marriage didn't count; you would be delighted to marry Glauce.

JASON.   I didn't use the world "delighted."

MEDEA.   "Highly honoured," perhaps?

JASON.   Something like that.

MEDEA.   So you are engaged to be married? (*Without any irony in her voice*) Well, I congratulate you.

JASON.   Not engaged. You see, the King——

MEDEA. (*cheerfully*).   I know. You mean you are married to Glauce theoretically, and now you are going to make the marriage a reality.

JASON (*intensely relieved at there not being a scene*).   How clearly you put things!

MEDEA.   I'm delighted for your sake. She's a charming girl, and I am sure she will make you very happy.

JASON.   But, Medea, what about you? You quite understand that I am ready to give up the whole thing unless you are quite sure you don't mind?

MEDEA.   My dear Jason, why should I mind? My only wish is that you should be happy.

JASON.   I'm afraid that's impossible. I need hardly say I am not in the least in love with Glauce.

MEDEA.   Of course not. But what about my children?

JASON.   Ah, there's the difficulty. The King says they will have to remain with me. But you will be able to come and see them whenever you like.

MEDEA.   Oh, I see.

JASON.   The King is very particular about children being brought up by their father. He thinks women make them into mollycoddles.

MEDEA.   Yes, of course. I suppose, since the marriage ceremony has already been performed, you won't have to go through it again.

JASON.   It's unnecessary; but I'm sorry to say the King wishes it.

MEDEA.   Then I suppose it will be soon. I shall leave Corinth as soon as my things can be packed.

JASON.   The King wants the ceremony to be this week; but you mustn't inconvenience yourself in any way.

MEDEA. (*smiling*).   No, I won't. Good-bye for the moment. I am going out to buy Glauce a present.   [*She goes out.*

JASON *walks up to a flower-pot and takes a lily from it. He speaks into the lily:* Is that oooo Corinth Wall? Darling, is that you? Yes, it's all over. She's taken it wonderfully. No. Yes, certainly ask her to stay later. Creon Institute to-morrow at eleven. Good-bye, darling.

CURTAIN.

King Lear's Daughter

LETTER FROM GONERIL, DAUGHTER OF KING LEAR,
TO HER SISTER REGAN

I have writ my sister.
King Lear, Act I, Scene iv.

THE PALACE, *November.*

DEAREST REGAN,

I am sending you this letter by Oswald. We have been having the most trying time lately with Papa, and it ended to-day in one of those scenes which are so painful to people like you and me, who *hate* scenes. I am writing now to tell you all about it, so that you may be prepared. This is what has happened.

When Papa came here he brought a hundred knights with him, which is a great deal more than we could put up, and some of them had to live in the village. The first thing that happened was that they quarrelled with our people and refused to take orders from them, and whenever one told any one to do anything it was either—if it was one of Papa's men—"not his place to do it"; or if it was one of our men, they said that Papa's people made work impossible. For instance, only the day before yesterday I found that blue vase which you brought back from Dover for me on my last birthday broken to bits. Of course I made a fuss, and Oswald declared that one of Papa's knights had knocked it over in a drunken brawl. I complained to Papa, who flew into a passion and said that his knights, and in fact all his retainers, were the most peaceful and courteous people in the world, and that it was my fault, as I was not treating him or them with the respect which they deserved. He even said that I was lacking in filial duty. I was determined to keep my temper, so I said nothing.

The day after this the chief steward and the housekeeper and both my maids came to me and said that they wished to give notice. I asked them why. They said they couldn't possibly live in a house where there were such "goings-on." I asked them what they meant. They refused to say, but they hinted that Papa's men were behaving not only in an insolent but in a positively outrageous manner to them. The steward said that Papa's knights were never sober, that they had entirely demoralized the household, and that life was simply not worth living in the house; it was *impossible* to get anything done, and they couldn't sleep at night for the noise.

I went to Papa and talked to him about it quite quietly, but no sooner had I mentioned the subject than he lost all self-control, and began to abuse me. I kept my temper as long as I could, but of course one is only human, and after I had borne his revilings for some time, which were monstrously unfair and untrue, I at last turned and said something about people of his age being trying. Upon which he said that I was mocking him in his old age, that I was a monster of ingratitude—and he began to cry. I cannot tell you how painful all this was to me. I did everything I could to soothe him and quiet him, but the truth is, ever since Papa has been here he has lost control of his wits. He suffers from the oddest kind of delusions. He thinks that for some reason he is being treated like a beggar; and although he has a hundred knights—a hundred, mind you! (a great deal more than we have)—in the house, who do nothing but eat and drink all day long, he says he is not being treated like a King! I do hate unfairness.

When he gave up the crown he said he was tired of affairs, and meant to have a long rest; but from the very moment that he handed over the management of affairs to us he never stopped interfering, and was cross if he was not consulted about everything, and if his advice was not taken.

And what is still worse: ever since his last illness he has lost not only his memory but his control over language, so that often when he wants to say one thing he says just the opposite, and sometimes when he wishes to say some quite simple thing he uses *bad* language quite unconsciously. Of course we are used to this, and *we* don't mind, but I must say it is very awkward when strangers are here. For instance, the other day before quite a lot of people, quite unconsciously, he called me a dreadful name. Everybody was uncomfortable and tried not to laugh, but some people could not contain themselves. This sort of thing is constantly happening. So you will understand that Papa needs perpetual looking after and management. At the same time, the moment one suggests the slightest thing to him he boils over with rage.

But perhaps the most annoying thing which happened lately, or, at least, the thing which happens to annoy me most, is Papa's Fool. You know, darling, that I have always hated that kind of humour. He comes in just as one is sitting down to dinner, and beats one on the head with a hard, empty bladder, and sings utterly idiotic songs, which make me feel inclined to cry. The other day, when we had a lot of people here, just as we were sitting down in the banqueting-hall, Papa's Fool pulled my chair from behind me so that I fell sharply down on the floor. Papa shook with laughter, and said: "Well done, little Fool," and all the courtiers who were there, out of pure snobbishness, of course, laughed too. I call this not only very humiliating for me, but undignified in an old man and a king; of course Albany refused to interfere. Like all men and all husbands, he is an arrant coward.

However, the crisis came yesterday. I had got a bad headache, and was lying down in my room, when Papa came in from the hunt and sent Oswald to me, saying that he wished to speak to me. I said that I wasn't well, and that I was lying down—which was perfectly true—but that I would be down to dinner. When Oswald went to give my message Papa beat him, and one of his men threw him about the room and really hurt him, so that he has now got a large bruise on his forehead and a sprained ankle.

This was the climax. All our knights came to Albany and myself, and said that they would not stay with us a moment longer unless Papa exercised some sort of control over his men. I did not know what to do, but I knew the situation would have to be cleared up sooner or later. So I went to Papa and told him frankly that the situation was intolerable; that he must send away some of his people, and choose for the remainder men fitting to his age. The words were scarcely out of my mouth than he called me the most terrible names, ordered his horses to be saddled, and said that he would shake the dust from his feet and not stay a moment longer in this house. Albany tried to calm him, and begged him to stay, but he would not listen to a word, and said he would go and live with you.

So I am sending this by Oswald, that you may get it before Papa arrives and know how the matter stands. All I did was to suggest he should send away fifty of his men. Even fifty is a great deal, and puts us to any amount of inconvenience, and is a source of waste and extravagance—two things which I cannot bear. I am perfectly certain you will not be able to put up with his hundred knights any more than I was. And I beg you, my dearest Regan, to do your best to make Papa listen to sense. No one is fonder of him than I am. I think it would have been difficult to find a more dutiful daughter than I have always been. But there

is a limit to all things, and one cannot have one's whole household turned into a pandemonium, and one's whole life into a
series of wrangles, complaints, and brawls, simply because Papa
in his old age is losing the control of his faculties. At the same
time, I own that although I kept my temper for a long time,
when it finally gave way I was perhaps a little sharp. I am not a
saint, nor an angel, nor a lamb, but I do hate unfairness and
injustice. It makes my blood boil. But I hope that you, with your
angelic nature and your tact and your gentleness, will put everything right and make poor Papa listen to reason.

Let me hear at once what happens.

Your loving

GONERIL.

P.S.—Another thing Papa does which is most exasperating is
to quote Cordelia to one every moment. He keeps on saying: "If
only Cordelia were here," or "How unlike Cordelia!" And you
will remember, darling, that when Cordelia was here Papa could
not endure the sight of her. Her irritating trick of mumbling
and never speaking up used to get terribly on his nerves. Of
course, I thought he was even rather unfair on her, trying as she
is. We had a letter from the French Court yesterday, saying that
she is driving the poor King of France almost mad.

P.P.S.—It is wretched weather. The poor little ponies on the
heath will have to be brought in.

From the Diary of Mary, Mrs. John Milton (née Powell)

Aldersgate Street, July 1, 1643.—Housekeeping not quite such
fun as I thought it would be. John is very particular. He cannot
eat mutton, or any kind of hashed meat. He compares the cooking here unfavourably with that of Italy. He says the boys in the
school are very naughty and that, during the Latin lesson this
morning, one boy, called Jones minor, put a pin on his chair,
just before he sat down on it. I couldn't help laughing; and this
made John cross. He is thinking of writing a poem about King
Arthur *(sic)* and the burnt cakes.

July 6.—John has begun his poem. He makes it up during meals, which makes him forget to eat, and makes the meal very gloomy; he writes it down afterwards. He read me a long piece of it last night; but as it is in Latin I did not understand very much of it.

July 7.—John and I quarrelled. It was about Jones minor. John announced the news of a reported rebel success during the boys' Greek lesson, and told the boys to give three cheers for the rebel army, which, of course, they all did, as they would never dare to disobey, except one brave *hero,* I call him, called Jones minor (the son of a tinker, bless him!), who called out as loud as he could: "Long live King Charles and death to all traitors!" John told him to repeat what he had said, and he did, and John caned him. I think this was very wrong on John's part, because, of course, the rebels *are* traitors. I took the part of the boy, and this made John angry. Then I said: "Of course, if all loyalists are so wicked, why did you marry me? My father is loyal and I am heart and soul for the King and the Church." John said that women's politics didn't count; but that the young must be taught discipline; that he was tolerant of all *sincere* opinion, however much he disagreed with it; but that the boy had merely wished to be insolent, by flying in the face of public opinion and the will of the school, which was the will of the *people,* and therefore the will of God, merely to gain a cheap notoriety. I said that probably all the boys felt the same, but didn't dare say so, as they knew that he, John, was on the other side. John said there are only seven "malignants" in the school. He said the boys were very angry with Jones minor and kicked him. I said they were a set of cowards. John said did I mean he was a coward, and quoted Greek. I said I didn't understand Greek. and didn't want to. "That comes from your false education," said John; "your parents deserve the severest blame." I said that if he said anything against my parents, I would leave the house, and that my father knew Latin as well as he did. John said I was exaggerating. I said that I had often heard Papa say that John's *Latin* verses were poor. John said when his epick on King Alfred and the Lady of the Lake would be published, we should see who knew how to write Latin. I said: "Who?" John said I was flighty and ignorant. I said I might be ignorant, but at least I wasn't a rebel. John said I was too young to understand these things, and that, considering my bringing up, I was right to hold the opinions I did. When I was older I would see that they were false. Then I cried.

July 8.—We made up our quarrel. John was ashamed of himself, and very dear, and said he regretted that he had used such vehement language. I forgave him at once.

July 9.—We had some friends to dinner. Before we sat down, John said: "We will not mention politicks, as we might not all agree and that would mar the harmony of the symposium." But towards the end of dinner, I drank the King's health, quite unwittingly and from force of habit, forgetting——

This made John angry and led to a discussion, some of our guests taking the King's part and others saying that he was quite wrong. The men became very excited, and a young student, called Wyatt, whom John had invited because he is very musical and cultivated, threw a glass of wine in the face of Mr. Lely, the wine-merchant, who is a violent rebel, and this broke up the party. John said that all "malignants" were the same; and that they none of them had any manners; that they were a set of roystering, nose-slitting, dissolute debauchees. When I thought of my dear father, and my dear brothers, this made me very angry; but I thought it best to say nothing at the time, as John was already annoyed and excited.

July 10.—John says he can't make up his mind whether to write his epick poem in Latin or in Hebrew. I asked him whether he couldn't write it in English. He told me not to be irrelevant. The city is very dreary. John disapproves of places of public amusement. He is at the school all day; and in the evening he is busy thinking over his poem. Being married is not such fun as I thought it would be, and John is quite different from what he was when he courted me in the country. Sometimes I don't think he notices that I am there at all. I wish I were in the country.

July 11.—John was in good temper to-day, because a scholar came here yesterday who said he wrote Italian very well. He asked me for my advice about his epick poem—which I thought was the best subject for an epick, King Arthur and the Cakes or the story of Adam and Eve. This made me feel inclined to laugh very much. Fancy writing a poem on the story of Adam and ·Eve! Everybody knows it! But I didn't laugh out loud, so as not to hurt his feelings, and I said "Adam and Eve," because I felt, somehow, that he wanted me to say that. He was so pleased, and said that I had an extraordinarily good judgment, when I chose. We had some cowslip wine for dinner which I brought from the country with me. John drank my health in Latin, which was a great favour, as he never says grace in Latin, because he says it's Popish.

July 14.—John is thinking of not writing an epick poem after all, at least not yet, but a history of the world instead. He says it has never been properly written yet.

July 15.—John has settled to translating the Bible into Latin verse. I am afraid I annoyed him; because when he told me this, I said I had always heard Papa say that the Bible was written in Latin. He said I oughtn't to talk about things which I didn't understand.

July 28.—I am altogether put about. There are two Irish boys in the school; one is called Kelley and comes from the North, and the other is called O'Sullivan and comes from the South. They had a quarrel about politicks and O'Sullivan called Kelley a rebel, a heretick, a traitor to his country, a renegade, a coward and a bastard; and Kelley said that O'Sullivan was an idolator and a foreigner, and ended up by saying he hoped he would go and meet the Pope.

"Do you mean to insult the Pope before me?" said O'Sullivan.

"Yes," said Kelley, "to hell with your Pope."

I could hear and see all this from my window, as the boys were talking in the yard.

Kelley then shouted, "To hell with the Pope!" as loud as he could three times, and O'Sullivan turned quite white with rage, but he only laughed and said quite slowly:

"Your father turned traitor for money, just like Judas." Then the boys flew at each other and began to fight; and at that moment John, who was thinking over his epick poem in the dining-room, rushed out and stopped them. Then he sent for both the boys and asked them what it was all about, but they both refused to say a word. Then John sent for the whole school, and said that unless some boy told him exactly what had happened, he would stop all half-holidays for a month. So Pyke, a boy who had been there, told the whole story. John caned both O'Sullivan and Kelley for using strong language.

In the evening Mr. Pye came to dinner, from Oxford. He teaches the Oxford boys physic or Greek philosophy; I forget which. But no sooner had we sat down to dinner than he began to abuse the rebels, and John, who was already cross, said that he did not suppose Mr. Pye meant to defend the King. Mr. Pye said he had always supposed that that was a duty every true-born Englishman took for granted; and John became very angry. I never heard anybody use such dreadful language. He said the King was a double-faced, lying monkey, full of Popish anticks, a wolf disguised as a jackass, a son of Belial, a double-tongued, double-faced, clay-footed, scarlet Ahithophel, and Mr. Pye was so shocked that he got up and went away. I said that people who insulted the King were rebels, however clever they might be, and that it was dreadful to use such language; and when I thought of his beating those two little boys this morning for using not half such strong language it made me quite mad. John said that I was illogical. I said I wouldn't hear any more bad language; and I ran upstairs and locked myself in my room.

August 1, *Oxfordshire.*—I have come home. I couldn't bear it. John was too unjust. Whenever I think of those two Irish boys and of John's language at dinner, my blood boils. Went out riding this morning with the boys. Papa says the war news is better, and that the rebels will soon be brought to heel.

FRAGMENT OF A GREEK TRAGEDY

BY A. E. HOUSMAN

CHORUS: O suitably-attired-in-leather-boots
Head of a traveler, wherefore seeking whom
Whence by what way how purposed art thou come

To this well-nightingaled vicinity?
My object in inquiring is to know.
But if you happen to be deaf and dumb
And do not understand a word I say,
Then wave your hand, to signify as much.

ALC: I journeyed hither a Boetian road.

CHORUS: Sailing on horseback, or with feet for oars?

ALC: Plying with speed my partnership of legs.

CHORUS: Beneath a shining or a rainy Zeus?

ALC: Mud's sister, not himself, adorns my shoes.

CHORUS: To learn your name would not displease me much.

ALC: Not all that men desire do they obtain.

CHORUS: Might I then hear at what your presence shoots?

ALC: A shepherd's questioned mouth informed me that—

CHORUS: What? for I know not yet what you will say.

ALC: Nor will you ever, if you interrupt.

CHORUS: Proceed, and I will hold my speechless tongue.

ALC: This house was Eriphyla's, no one's else.

CHORUS: Nor did he shame his throat with shameful lies.

ALC: May I then enter, passing through the door?

CHORUS: Go chase into the house a lucky foot.

And, O my son, be, on the one hand, good,
And do not, on the other hand, be bad;
For that is very much the safest plan.

ALC: I go into the house with heels and speed.

CHORUS

Strophe

In speculation
I would not willingly acquire a name
    For ill-digested thought;
    But after pondering much
To this conclusion I at last have come:
    Life is uncertain.
    This truth I have written deep

In my reflective midriff
   On tablets not of wax,
Nor with a pen did I inscribe it there,
For many reasons: *Life,* I say, *is not*
   A stranger to uncertainty.
Not from the flight of omen-yelling fowls
   This fact did I discover,
Nor did the Delphine tripod bark it out,
   Nor yet Dodona.
Its native ingenuity sufficed
   My self-taught diaphragm.

   Antistrophe

Why should I mention
The Inachean daughter, loved of Zeus?
   Her whom of old the gods,
   More provident than kind,
Provided with four hoofs, two horns, one tail,
   A gift not asked for,
   And sent her forth to learn
   The unfamiliar science
   Of how to chew the cud.
She therefore, all about the Argive fields,
Went cropping pale green grass and nettle-tops,
   Nor did they disagree with her.
But yet, howe'er nutritious, such repasts
   I do not hanker after:
Never may Cypris for her seat select
   My dappled liver!
Why should I mention Io? Why indeed?
   I have no notion why.

   Epode

But now does my boding heart,
Unhired, unaccompanied, sing

A strain not meet for the dance.
Yea even the palace appears
To my yoke of circular eyes
(The right, nor omit I the left)
Like a slaughterhouse, so to speak,
Garnished with woolly deaths
And many shipwrecks of cows.
I therefore in a Cissian strain lament;
  And to the rapid
  Loud, linen-tattering thumps upon my chest
  Resounds in concert
The battering of my unlucky head.

ERI (*within*): O, I am smitten with a hatchet's jaw;
And that in deed and not in word alone.

CHORUS: I thought I heard a sound within the house
Unlike the voice of one that jumps for joy.

ERI: He splits my skull, not in a friendly way,
Once more: he purposes to kill me dead

CHORUS: I would not be reputed rash, but yet
I doubt if all be gay within the house.

ERI: O! O! another stroke! that makes the third.
He stabs me to the heart against my wish.

CHORUS: If that be so, thy state of health is poor;
But thine arithmetic is quite correct.*

---

* This was originally printed in 1893 in *The Bromsgrovian*. It has often been reprinted—in *The University College Gazette* (1897), *The Cornhill* (1901), etc. up to *The Yale Review* (1928) and the New York *Herald Tribune* (1936)—but I think it can stand another. The horrors of classical translation, mitigated of late years by the noble work of Dudley Fitts, Robert Fitzgerald and Richmond Lattimore, have never been so brutally expressed. The opening words gave Nicholas Blake, who is really C. Day Lewis, the title and the idea for a good detective story: *Head of a Traveller*.

VARIATIONS ON A THEME

I. Salad

BY MORTIMER COLLINS

After Swinburne

O COOL in the summer is salad,
  And warm in the winter is love;
And a poet shall sing you a ballad
  Delicious thereon and thereof.

A singer am I, if no sinner,
  My Muse has a marvellous wing,
And I willingly worship at dinner
    The Sirens of Spring.

Take endive . . . like love it is bitter;
  Take beet . . . for like love it is red;
Crisp leaf of the lettuce shall glitter,
  And cress from the rivulet's bed;
Anchovies foam-born, like the Lady
  Whose beauty has maddened this bard;
And olives, from groves that are shady;
    And eggs—boil 'em hard.

After Browning

WAITRESS, with eyes so marvellous black
  And the blackest possible lustrous gay tress,
This is the month of the Zodiac
  When I want a pretty deft-handed waitress.
Bring a china-bowl, you merry young soul;
  Bring anything green, from worsted to celery;
Bring pure olive-oil, from Italy's soil . . .
  Then your china-bowl we'll well array.

When the time arrives chip choicest chives,
  And administer quietly chili and capsicum . . .
(Young girls do not quite know what's what
  Till as a Poet into their laps I come).
Then a lobster fresh as fresh can be
  (When it screams in the pot I feel a murderer);
After which I fancy we
  Shall want a few bottles of Heidsieck or Roederer.

After Tennyson

KING ARTHUR, growing very tired indeed
Of wild Tintagel, now that Lancelot
Had gone to Jersey or to Jericho,
And there was nobody to make a rhyme,
And Cornish girls were christened Jennifer,
And the Round Table had grown rickety,
Said unto Merlin (who had been asleep
For a few centuries in Broceliande,
But woke, and had a bath, and felt refreshed):
"What shall I do to pull myself together?"
Quoth Merlin, "Salad is the very thing,
And you can get it at the 'Cheshire Cheese.'"
King Arthur went there: *verily,* I believe
That he has dined there every day since then.
Have you not marked the portly gentleman
In his cool corner, with his plate of greens?
The great knight Lancelot prefers the "Cock,"
Where port is excellent (in pints), and waiters
Are portlier than kings, and steaks are tender,
And poets have been known to meditate . . .
Ox-fed orating ominous octastichs.

II. *The Poets at Tea*

BY BARRY PAIN

1.—(*Macaulay, who made it*)

POUR, VARLET, pour the water,
　The water steaming hot!
　A spoonful for each man of us,
　Another for the pot!
We shall not drink from amber,
　Nor Capuan slave shall mix
For us the snows of Athos
　With port at thirty-six;
Whiter than snow the crystals,
　Grown sweet 'neath tropic fires,
More rich the herbs of China's field,
The pasture-lands more fragrance yield;
For ever let Britannia wield
　The tea-pot of her sires!

2.—(*Tennyson, who took it hot*)

I think that I am drawing to an end:
For on a sudden came a gasp for breath,
And stretching of the hands, and blinded eyes,
And a great darkness falling on my soul.
O Hallelujah! . . . Kindly pass the milk.

3.—(*Swinburne, who let it get cold*)

As the sin that was sweet in the sinning
　Is foul in the ending thereof,
As the heat of the summer's beginning
　Is past in the winter of love:
O purity, painful and pleading!
　O coldness, ineffably gray!
Oh, hear us, our handmaid unheeding,
　And take it away!

4.— (*Cowper, who thoroughly enjoyed it*)

The cosy fire is bright and gay,
The merry kettle boils away
        And hums a cheerful song.
I sing the saucer and the cup;
Pray, Mary, fill the tea-pot up,
        And do not make it strong.

5.— (*Browning, who treated it allegorically*)

Tut! Bah! We take as another case—
    Pass the bills on the pills on the window-sill; notice the capsule
(A sick man's fancy, no doubt, but I place
    Reliance on trade-marks, Sir)—so perhaps you'll
Excuse the digression—this cup which I hold
    Light-poised— Bah, it's spilt in the bed!—well, let's on go—
Hold Bohea and sugar, Sir; if you were told
    The sugar was salt, would the Bohea be Congo?

6.— (*Wordsworth, who gave it away*)

"Come, little cottage girl, you seem
    To want my cup of tea;
And will you take a little cream?
    Now tell the truth to me."

She had a rustic, woodland grin,
    Her cheek was soft as silk,
And she replied, "Sir, please put in
    A little drop of milk."

"Why, what put milk into your head?
    'T is cream my cows supply;"
And five times to the child I said,
    "Why, pig-head, tell me, why?"

"You call me pig-head," she replied;
    "My proper name is Ruth.

I called that milk"—she blushed with pride—
"You bade me speak the truth."

7.— (*Poe, who got excited over it*)

Here's a mellow cup of tea, golden tea!
What a world of rapturous thought its fragrance brings to me!
  Oh, from out the silver cells
  How it wells!
  How it smells!
Keeping tune, tune, tune
To the tintinnabulation of the spoon.
And the kettle on the fire
Boils its spout off with desir
With a desperate desire
And a crystalline endeavour
Now, now to sit, or never,
On the top of the pale-faced moon,
But he always came home to tea, tea, tea, tea, tea,
    Tea to the n—th.

8.—(*Rossetti, who took six cups of it*)

  The lilies lie in my lady's bower
  (O weary mother, drive the cows to roost),
  They faintly droop for a little hour;
  My lady's head droops like a flower.
  She took the porcelain in her hand
  (O weary mother, drive the cows to roost),
  She poured; I drank at her command;
  Drank deep, and now—you understand!
  (O weary mother, drive the cows to roost.)

9.— (*Burns, who liked it adulterated*)

  Weel, gin ye speir, I'm no inclined,
  Whusky or tay—to state my mind,
    Fore ane or ither;

For, gin I tak the first, I'm fou,
And gin the next, I'm dull as you,
    Mix a' thegither.

10.— (*Walt Whitman, who didn't stay more than a minute*)

One cup for my self-hood,
Many for you. Allons, camerados, we will drink together,
O hand-in-hand! That tea-spoon, please, when you've done with it.
What butter-colour'd hair you've got. I don't want to be personal.
All right, then, you needn't. You're a stale-cadaver.
Eighteen-pence if the bottles are returned.
Allons, from all bat-eyed formula.

III. Variations of an Air

COMPOSED ON HAVING TO APPEAR IN A PAGEANT
AS OLD KING COLE
BY G. K. CHESTERTON

OLD KING COLE was a merry old soul,
And a merry old soul was he;
He called for his pipe,
He called for his bowl,
And he called for his fiddlers three.

After Lord Tennyson

Cole, that unwearied prince of Colchester,
Growing more gay with age and with long days
Deeper in laughter and desire of life,
As that Virginian climber on our walls
Flames scarlet with the fading of the year;
Called for his wassail and that other weed
Virginian also, from the western woods
Where English Raleigh checked the boast of Spain,

And lighting joy with joy, and piling up
Pleasure as crown for pleasure, bade men bring
Those three, the minstrels whose emblazoned coats
Shone with the oyster-shells of Colchester;
And these three played, and playing grew more fain
Of mirth and music; till the heathen came,
And the King slept beside the northern sea.

After W. B. Yeats

Of an old King in a story
    From the grey sea-folk I have heard,
Whose heart was no more broken
    Than the wings of a bird.

As soon as the moon was silver
    And the thin stars began,
He took his pipe and his tankard,
    Like an old peasant man.

And three tall shadows were with him
    And came at his command;
And played before him for ever
    The fiddles of fairyland.

And he died in the young summer
    Of the world's desire;
Before our hearts were broken
    Like sticks in a fire.

After Robert Browning

Who smoke-snorts toasts o' My Lady Nicotine,
Kicks stuffing out of Pussyfoot, bids his trio
Stick up their Stradivarii (that's the plural)
Or near enough, my fatheads; *nimium*
Vincina Cremonæ; that's a bit too near).
Is there some stockfish fails to understand?

Catch hold o' the notion, bellow and blurt back "Cole"?
Must I bawl lessons from a horn-book, howl,
Cat-call the cat-gut "fiddles"? Fiddlesticks!

After Walt Whitman

Me clairvoyant,
Me conscious of you, old camarado,
Needing no telescope, lorgnette, field-glass, opera-glass, myopic
    pince-nez,
Me piercing two thousand years with eye naked and not ashamed;
The crown cannot hide you from me;
Musty old feudal-heraldic trappings cannot hide you from me,
I perceive that you drink.
(I am drinking with you. I am as drunk as you are.)
I see you are inhaling tobacco, puffing, smoking, spitting
(I do not object to your spitting),
You prophetic of American largeness,
You anticipating the broad masculine manners of these States:
I see in you also there are movements, tremors, tears, desire for
    the melodious,
I salute your three violinists, endlessly making vibrations,
Rigid, relentless, capable of going on for ever;
They play my accompaniment; but I shall take no notice of any
    accompaniment;
I myself am a complete orchestra.
So long.

After Swinburne

In the time of old sin without sadness
    And golden with wastage of gold
Like the gods that grow old in their gladness
    Was the king that was glad, growing old;
And with sound of loud lyres from his palace
    The voice of his oracles spoke,
And the lips that were red from his chalice

Were splendid with smoke.
When the weed was as flame for a token
  And the wine was as blood for a sign;
And upheld in his hands and unbroken
  The fountains of fire and of wine.
And a song without speech, without singer,
  Stung the soul of a thousand in three
As the flesh of the earth has to sting her,
  The soul of the sea.

IV. That English Weather
BY VARIOUS HANDS

1. After Browning

Home Truths from Abroad

I.

"Oн! to be in England
  Now that April's there,
  And whoever wakes in England
  Sees some morning" in despair;
There's a horrible fog i' the heart o' the town,
And the greasy pavement is damp and brown;
While the rain-drop falls from the laden bough,
  In England—now!

II.

"And after April when May follows,"
  How foolish seem the returning swallows.
  Hark! how the east wind sweeps along the street,
  And how we give one universal sneeze!
  The hapless lambs at thought of mint-sauce bleat,
  And ducks are conscious of the coming peas.

Lest you should think the Spring is really present,
A biting frost will come to make things pleasant,
And though the reckless flowers begin to blow,
They'd better far have nestled down below;
An English spring sets men and women frowning,
Despite the rhapsodies of Robert Browning.

Punch, 1883.

2. *After Charles Kingsley*

Another Ode to the North-East Wind

HANG THEE, vile North Easter;
  Other things may be
Very bad to bear with,
  Nothing equals thee.
Grim and grey North Easter,
  From each Essex-bog,
From the Plaistow marshes,
  Rolling London fog—
"Tired we are of Summer"
  Kingsley may declare,
I give the assertion
  Contradiction bare,
I, in bed, this morning
  Felt thee, as I lay:
"There's a vile North Easter
  Out of doors to-day!"
Set the dust clouds blowing
  Till each face they strike,
With the blacks is growing
  Chimney-sweeper like.
Fill our rooms with smoke gusts
  From the chimney-pipe.
Fill our eyes with water,
  That defies the wipe.

Through the draughty passage
  Whistle loud and high,
Making doors and windows
  Rattle, flap and fly;
Mark, that vile North Easter
  Roaring up the vent,
Nipping soul and body,
  Breeding discontent!
Squall, my noisy children;
  Smoke, my parlour grate;
Scold, my shrewish partner;
  I accept my fate.
All is quite in tune with
  This North Eastern Blast;
Who can look for comfort
  Till this wind be past?
If all goes contrary,
  Who can feel surprise,
With this Rude North Easter
  In his teeth and eyes?
It blows much too often.
  Nine days out of ten,
Yet we boast our climate,
  Like true English men!
In their soft South Easters
  Could I bask at ease,
I'd let France and Naples
  Bully as they please,
But while this North Easter
  In one's teeth is hurled,
Liberty seems worth just
  Nothing in the world.
Come, as came our fathers
  Heralded by thee,
Blasting, blighting, burning

Out of Normandy.
Come and flay and skin us,
And dry up our blood—
All to have a Kingsley
Swear it does him good!

Anonymous

3. After a Medieval Song

Ancient Music

WINTER IS icummen in,
Lhude sing Goddamm,
Raineth drop and staineth slop,
And how the wind doth ramm!
Sing: Goddamm.
Skiddeth bus and sloppeth us,
An ague hath my ham.
Freezeth river, turneth liver,
Damn you, sing: Goddamm.
Goddamm, Goddamm, 'tis why I am, Goddamm,
So 'gainst the winter's balm.
Sing goddamm, damm, sing Goddamm,
Sing goddamm, sing goddamm, DAMM.

EZRA POUND

REVIEWS OF UNWRITTEN BOOKS

BY

"BARON CORVO" AND/OR SHOLTO DOUGLAS

IN 1903 the *Monthly Review* of London published nine Reviews of
Unwritten Books. They had originally been written by a young,
obscure and penniless tutor named Sholto Douglas who had sent, a
year or two before, an admiring letter to a middle-aged, obscure and
penniless writer named Frederick Rolfe about a book the latter had

published called *In His Own Image*. The story of their brief friendship is told in Chapter XI of A. J. A. Symons' *The Quest for Corvo*. Corvo became a re-write man and literary agent for some of young Douglas' manuscripts, among them the following two. (Some of the others were: *IV. Leonardo da Vinci's "Notes on Modern Engineering," VIII. Herodotus' "History of England,"* and *IX. Plato's "Dialogue on the Music of Wagner."*) At first Douglas was enthusiastic: "You have transformed my rubbish into literature with your wondrous Attick talent," he wrote Corvo. Later—after a quarrel about Corvo's alterations in a translation of Meleager by Douglas in which the latter was probably in the right—Douglas was less enthusiastic. But, as he wrote Symons, Corvo had at least made the Unwritten Reviews saleable: "He damaged them, in my estimation, but I admit he sold them to the *Monthly Review* when I had failed to sell them at all. And he took no money for them; I got it all." Mr. Symons thinks "the *Reviews* remain unworthy of revival, though there are interesting phrases in them, as in everything Rolfe touched." I disagree, to the extent of two of them, with cuts.

I

Machiavelli's Despatches from the South African Campaign

SO MANY BOOKS have been written about the Great Boer War that a reviewer, who seeks to interest his readers in yet another work upon the same subject, is bound to offer some attraction of a novel and peculiar kind, which may lead an undesiring world to consider a rather tabid affair from an unexpected point of view. Here, the excuse seems to be valid. The publication of Machiavelli's "Boer and Briton" was the sensation of last season. Sky-signs and sandwich-boards cannot have failed to impress the title at least upon all who have eyes to see; and the controversy which raged around the work in all the newspapers hardly can have faded from the memory. This book purported to be the despatches which Messer Niccolo Machiavelli, as the official representative of the Signory of Fiorenza on the staff of the Commander-in-Chief in South Africa, sent home to his Government. But as soon as "Boer and Briton" began to be asked for at the libraries, a mysterious paragraph, it may be remembered, appeared in our columns, denying that these were the original and authentic despatches of Machiavelli; and we added that, in due time, proof of the validity of this astounding allegation would be forthcoming. Instantly, every one who could manipulate a pen performed his function. Stationers put up their prices, and compositors worked overtime. Newspaper rooms at clubs and free libraries were besieged. At the Universities, the Unions seethed with bursars, bedels, bachelors, baronets, benedictines, bores, and all kinds of dry-bobs, bounding to the writing-rooms to express opinions on irrelevant subjects to long-suffering editors. The *Daily News* said that "Boer and Briton" was "the writing on the wall." The *Pall Mall Gazette* split four infinitives to show that it was the work of Dr. Leyds. Certainly it was virulently Anglophobic. The *Clerkenwell News* published a statement from "A Constant Reader" to the effect that Mr. Henry Harland had said to him that the despatches really were Mr. Laurence Housman's, adding, "and there are others." Messrs. Gay and Bird naturally came out incontinent with a cryptogram proving that Machiavelli also was the author of the Kabbala and the Second Book of Chronicles; and Mr. J. Holt Schooling furnished the monthlies with statistics of a number of Taal words which he had found in "Boer and Briton." After nine days, the wonder lost its charm. The citizens of Macdonaldville, Pe., roasted a negro lad alive. The products of the Education Act of 1870 rushed to peruse in the columns of the *Worldly Christian* special telegraphic bulletins of the progress of his contortuplications at the stake; and "Boer and Briton" lapsed into the twopenny box.

Now comes the publication of the present volume, which we have no hesitation in calling quite conclusive. This book, we learn from the preface, does contain the "others." Machiavelli has lived up to his name; and these are the actual despatches which he indited from South Africa. He tells us that, when he returned to Fiorenza to arrange about the publication of his book, the Signory were between the horns of a dilemma. The feeling of the Continent was Anglophobic. It would hardly do (financially) for Fiorenza to pose as Anglophile; and Their Magnificencies of the Signory feared lest Machiavelli's despatches should cause unpleasantness. That astute politician immediately offered to render them fit for publication. He proposed to put them into such a form as would be consonant with the European Concert, and, at the same time, would make them serve as a valuable advertisement for the real despatches against the time for their subsequent publication. In short, Machiavelli has machiavellianly played upon the twentieth century precisely the same trick as that which he played upon the sixteenth in the matter of the *colpo di stato* of Senigaglia. In both cases the despatches, which he originally sent to the Signory from the seat of war, were as veridical as he knew how to make them. In both cases he was induced, on returning to Fiorenza, to publish (shall we call it?) a revised version, in the interests of (let us say) the book-trade. Subsequently, when the Little Florentines and Little Englanders respectively were simply bursting with unctuous rectitude, and the attention of the library public was excited, he gave, and he gives, to the world the genuine article on which he naturally prefers to base his reputation as historian. We do not see that he could have done otherwise, considering the name he bears. With these premises we address ourselves to an appreciation of his book.

So far, no serious treatise on the Great Boer War has been brought before the public written by a man who died before the outbreak of hostilities. This in itself is sufficient to make Machiavelli's work extremely interesting. One is always glad to know how our mere mundane matters strike those down there. And further, the writer's military experiences during the previous campaign in the Romagna, and his knowledge of Italian affairs during his own critical lifetime, should make his judgment on political and military subjects worthy of our careful attention. These despatches, written from the front, practically form a complete history of the rebellion. Their value to us, however, does not lie so much in the accurate narrative of facts, but rather in the novel point of view from which the facts are observed and criticised. Even people who were neither Englishmen nor

Boers got excited about this conflict, and discussed it with personal interest, taking one side or the other. Now a really impartial historian ought to take both sides—this is so very much better than taking neither side. Here, then, is the explanation of the strange fact that contemporary historians are seldom successful. They may know the facts, but they cannot estimate their value. They cannot get far enough away to distinguish the molehills from the mountains. Probably, before the South African campaign, no historian ever was in a position to write, as an eye-witness, an account of affairs which took place four hundred years after his own demise. The interval is sufficient to adjust the historic perspective; and, if Machiavelli were so placed, his position surely was unique.

*   *   *   *

The whole episode of Mafeking fills Machiavelli with scorn and indignation. To begin with, the Boers never ought to have besieged it. It would have been of little value to them if they had secured it. The English, on the other hand, recognising this, ought to have made no attempt to relieve it. Its fall could in no wise have damaged their position. Machiavelli has no sympathy with the sentimental excitement which pervaded England over Mafeking; and the soul of the artistic Florentine passionately declaims against the wholesale desecration of peacock's plumes which ensued. This leads him into a long digression on the power of sentiment in modern warfare. He vituperates us for confusing issues. The object of the belligerent is to damage the enemy. He ought to do so in every possible way. He ought not to fight as a gentleman, but merely as a man. Ultimately, you cannot fight a man without hurting him. If you must fight, hit hard and be done with it, says Machiavelli. Of course he does not forget the argument upon which so much of the sentimental outcry in England purported to be based, namely, that after the war England desired to turn the Transvaal and the Orange Free State into prosperous and contented British Colonies. He asks the rather pertinent question: Was this an excuse or a reason? In both cases it was unsatisfactory. In both cases it was ridiculous. Logically, England could best make the republics into contented and prosperous Colonies by annihilating the Dutch element in the population. Practically, she could best do it by killing the largest possible number of them, and taking their effects for her trouble. Of course it is out of the question that we should accept Machiavelli's reasoning here. It is also impossible to contravene it on his own grounds. We can do no more than make the statement that we look at the matter from a different point of view, and disagree with him. To sweep the concentration camps into the sea (to use a Boer idiom) would have been repugnant to every Englishman. In practice, we also may believe, it would have been repugnant to Machiavelli. He was not the man to live down to his ideals. Then, too, we had no Duke of Valentinois in command of our forces.

*   *   *   *

Machiavelli has gained a reputation, among those who have not read his books, which damns him as a type of wily rascal. Of course that reputation is totally undeserved. Like most prominent people whom the world condemns, he is not half as bad as many reputable men whose obscurity hides their faults. He is honest; he is not hypocritical. If only he were less logical, one could agree with him more often.

II

Tacitus's "Scripturæ de Populis Consociatis Americæ Septentrionalis"

THERE are many ways of writing history. There is the artless and chronological method, in which the writer merely states a lot of facts which he has gleaned from other people's writings. Sometimes he proves some of them to be true. His chief desire is to be accurate. And therefore he is never artistic. Then there is the second-intentional method, in which the writer never says all that he means; and always implies more than he says. This method is used chiefly by contemporaneous historians. It was used to perfection by Julius Cæsar. It is an artistic method; and demands the fullest attention of the reader. There is also the poetic method, in which the writer uses his subject as an inspiration to his verse. Here we have quite parted from mere truthfulness. Shakespeare, of course, has made this mode entirely his own. Even Æschylus in his *Persæ* failed to reach Shakespeare's level. A variant of this mode was used by Carlyle in his *French Revolution,* which resembles Shakespearean history in its sumptuous deflections from accuracy. Undoubtedly to Carlyle history was merely a prop on which to display his phrases. But there is yet another way of writing history, the satiric method. Tacitus was the inventor of the method; and he has had no successors. He indeed epitomises the styles of all historians. His arrangement apes the simple chronological methods of to-day: his phrases seem to point to the influence of Carlyle: his multitudinous breadth of view is quite Shakespearean; and his motive bears a resemblance to that which inspired the *Bellum Gallicum.* He always writes with a purpose. For instance, he wrote the *Annals,* not to give an account of things which happened at Rome during the early Principate, but to support his theory that government by one man was the wrong thing for Rome. Incidentally he had to abuse Tiberius, or rather to select facts which would lead one to suppose that he was abusing Tiberius. There is no doubt at all but that, in private life, Tacitus and Tiberius were two men who would have got on together splendidly. With regard to his *Scripturæ de Populis Consociatis Americæ Septentrionalis* the case is very different. We possess an idiotically accurate knowledge of the history of North America. Consequently we can read Tacitus's account of the American Democracy with the clear remembrance that he is selecting and arranging his facts to prove his point. If we had only Tacitus to read, we should no doubt have an entirely different notion of the prominent men in America from Washington to Roosevelt.

Just as Tacitus wrote his *Annals* with a purpose, so he wrote his *Scriptures* with a purpose, to prove that modern democracy is a sham because it is socialistic to the core when it ought to be individualistic. He conclusively proves that the apparent "liberty" of the American citizen is a fraud; and that, far from being free, he is tied and bound by the tyrannous chains of the demos-brute and the opulent caucus which tends the brute. It would be a simple matter for a man of Tacitus's ability to turn round and write an anti-Scripture to show that this theory is erroneous, just as it would be easy to point out the overwhelming advantages which the Roman world gained in the first century from autocratic rule.

An analysis of the first five books of the *Scriptures* reveals a curious result. The first book deals with the War of Independence and the career of Washington. The second entreats of the long period from the death of Washington to the election of Lincoln: it is chiefly concerned with the constitutional troubles which led to the Civil War. The third book is entirely taken up with the campaigns of this war. The fourth discusses the negro question, taking us back to early times, through the war, and down to our own day. And the final book is occupied by a masterly review of the industrial decadence of the last thirty years, culminating in the marriage of the Duke of Marlborough, and the accession of Mr. Pierpont Morgan. Now this is clearly a disproportionate arrangement from a chronological point of view. The second book covers far too long a period. This indicates that Tacitus selected his facts with distinct intention; and was quite indifferent about the accurate completion of his work. Any' critic who supposes that some intervening books have been lost is exactly in the same position as one who supposes that we do not possess in their entirety the *Annals* and the *Histories*.

* * * *

But it is the last book which is of the most absorbing interest to those of us who have not yet visited America. In it Tacitus mercilessly dissects, by the scalpel of implication, the character of the modern American. He does not vituperate the people. He shows that their awful plight is only the final outcome of the policy of Washington which cut them off from the blessings now enjoyed by loyal Canada. He discusses with scientific care that crude and almost barbarous retrogression, which makes it so hard for us to realise that these strange people are—as they really and truly are—descendants of the men of the Middle Ages, of the men from whom we ourselves are descended. Their extraordinary uniformity of appearance and manner, their unnatural yearnings after pick-me-ups and the wrong ideals, their senseless velocity which makes them seem like poor trapped creatures rushing madly "around" to escape their inevitable and half-realised doom, their suicidal attempts at salvation by Trusts or by marriage—these are the reasons why Tacitus has branded Washington to the infamy of all who read the *Scriptures*. It is like the final act of a great tragedy, this fifth book; and the curtain artistically falls just before the climax.

But . . . oh yes, certainly, Tacitus must be read with great caution by those who desire accuracy.

TIME . . . FORTUNE . . . LIFE . . . LUCE

BY

WOLCOTT GIBBS

IN THE NOVEMBER 28, 1936, *New Yorker* Wolcott Gibbs published a parodic "profile" of Henry Luce that is said to have made Luce so furious he meditated some terrible journalistic revenge, such as a "take-out" piece in *Time* about Harold Ross. At about the same time as Gibbs did his celebrated profile—the next spring, to be exact—I published in *The Nation* a series on the Luce magazines in which I drew on my six years' experience on *Fortune* to make some critical observations. Gibbs' critique has stood up better than mine has. I think the reason is that I concentrated on the content of the Luce-papers while he dealt with the form. My predictions that Time, Inc., would evolve in a pro-fascist direction were falsified within a year or two, but Wolcott Gibbs' creative distortion of *Time*style and his exposure of the inner spirit of the Lucepapers is still relevant. Also his piece is much funnier.

S AD-EYED last month was nimble, middle-sized *Life*-President Clair Maxwell as he told newshawks of the sale of the fifty-three-year-old gagmag to *Time.* For celebrated name alone, price: $85,000.

Said he: *"Life* . . . introduced to the world the drawings . . . of such men as Charles Dana Gibson, the verses of . . . James Whitcomb Riley and Oliver Herford, such writers as John Kendrick Bangs. . . . Beginning next month the magazine *Life* will embark on a new venture entirely unrelated to the old."

How unrelated to the world of the Gibson Girl is this new venture might have been gathered at the time from a prospectus issued by enormous, Apollo-faced C. D. Jackson, of Time, Inc.

"Life," wrote he, "will show us the Man-of-the-Week . . . his body clothed and, if possible, nude." It will expose "the loves, scandals, and personal affairs of the plain and fancy citizen . . . and write around them a light, good-tempered 'colyumnist' review of these once-private lives."

29,000 die-hard subscribers to *Life,*[1] long accustomed to he-she jokes, many ignorant of King of England's once-private life (*Time,* July 25 *et seq.*), will be comforted for the balance of their subscription periods by familiar, innocent jocosities of *Judge.* First issue of new publication went out last week to 250,000 readers, carried advertisements suggesting an annual revenue of $1,500,000, pictured Russian peasants in the nude, the love life of the Black Widow spider, referred inevitably to Mrs. Ernest Simpson.

Behind this latest, most incomprehensible Timenterprise looms, as usual, ambitious, gimlet-eyed, Baby Tycoon Henry Robinson Luce, co-founder of *Time,* promulgator of *Fortune,* potent in associated radio & cinema ventures.

"High-Buttoned . . . Brilliant"

Headman Luce was born in Teng-chowfu, China, on April 3, 1898, the son of Henry Winters & Elizabeth Middleton Luce, Presbyterian missionaries. Very unlike the novels of Pearl Buck

---

[1] Peak of *Life* circulation (1921): 250,000.

were his early days. Under brows too beetling for a baby, young
Luce grew up inside the compound, played with his two sisters,
lisped first Chinese, dreamed much of the Occident. At 14, weary
of poverty, already respecting wealth & power, he sailed alone
for England, entered school at St. Albans. Restless again, he came
to the United States, enrolled at Hotchkiss, met up & coming
young Brooklynite Briton Hadden. Both even then were troubled
with an itch to harass the public. Intoned Luce years later: "We
reached the conclusion that most people were not well informed
& that something should be done. . . ."

First publication to inform fellowman was *Hotchkiss Weekly
Record;* next *Yale Daily News,* which they turned into a tabloid;
fought to double hours of military training, fought alumni who
wished to change tune of Yale song from *Die Wacht am Rhein.*
Traditionally unshaven, wearing high-buttoned Brooks jackets,
soft white collars, cordovan shoes, no garters, Luce & Hadden
were Big Men on a campus then depleted of other, older Big
Men by the war. Luce, pale, intense, nervous, was Skull & Bones,
Alpha Delta Phi, Phi Beta Kappa, member of the Student Council, editor of the *News;* wrote sad poems, read the *New Republic,*
studied political philosophy. As successful, less earnest, more
convivial, Hadden collected china dogs, made jokes.[2] In 1920 the
senior class voted Hadden Most Likely to Succeed, Luce Most
Brilliant. Most Brilliant he, Luce sloped off to Christ Church,
Oxford, there to study European conditions, take field trips into
the churning Balkans.

Best Advice: Don't

Twenty months after commencement, in the city room of
Paperkiller Frank Munsey's *Baltimore News,* met again Luce,
Hadden. Newshawks by day, at night they wrangled over policies
of the magazine they had been planning since Hotchkiss. Boasted
the final prospectus: *"Time* will be free from cheap sensational-
ism . . . windy bias."

In May, 1922, began the long struggle to raise money to start
Time. Skeptical at the outset proved Newton D. Baker, Nicholas

[2] Once, watching Luce going past, laden with cares & responsibilities,
Hadden chuckled, upspoke: "Look out, Harry. You'll drop the college."

Murray Butler, Herbert Bayard Swope, William Lyon Phelps. Pooh-poohed *Review of Reviews* Owner Charles Lanier: "My best advice . . . don't do it." From studious, pint-sized Henry Seidel Canby, later editor of Lamont-backed *Saturday Review of Literature,* came only encouraging voice in this threnody.

Undismayed Luce & Hadden took the first of many offices in an old brownstone house at 9 East 17th Street, furnished it with a filing cabinet, four second-hand desks, a big brass bowl for cigarette stubs, sought backers.[3]

JPMorganapoleon H. P. Davison, Yale classmate of Luce, Hadden, great & good friend of both, in June contributed $4,000. Next to succumb: Mrs. David S. Ingalls, sister of Classmate William Hale Harkness; amount, $10,000. From Brother Bill, $5,000. Biggest early angel, Mrs. William Hale Harkness, mother of Brother Bill & Mrs. Ingalls, invested $20,000. Other original

---

[3] In return for $50 cash, original investors were given two shares 6% Preferred Stock with a par value of $25, one share Class A Common Stock without par value. 3,440 Preferred, 1,720 Class A Common were so sold.

170 shares of Class A Common, 8,000 shares of Class B Common, also without par value, not entitled to dividends until Preferred Shares had been retired, were issued to Briton Hadden, Henry R. Luce, who gave one-third to associates, divided remainder equally.

In 1925, authorized capital of Time, Inc., was increased to 19,000 shares; of which 8,000 were Preferred, 3,000 Class A; as before, 8,000 Class B.

In June, 1930 (if you are still following this), the Preferred Stock was retired in full & dividends were initiated for both Common Stocks. Corporation at this time had 2,400 shares Class A, 7,900 Class B outstanding.

By the spring of 1931 *Time* had begun to march, shares were nominally quoted at $1,000. Best financial minds advised splitting stock on basis of twenty shares for one. Outstanding after clever maneuver: 206,400 shares Common.

In 1933, outlook still gorgeous, each share of stock was reclassified into 1/10th share of $6.50 Dividend Cumulative Convertible Preferred Stock ($6.50 div. cum. con. pfd. stk.) and one share of New Common Stock. New div. cum. con. pfd. stk. was convertible into a share and a half of New Common Stock, then selling around $40 a share, now quoted at over $200.

Present number of shares outstanding, 238,000; paper value of shares, $47,000,000; conservative estimate of Luce holding, 102,300 shares; paper value, $20,460,000; conservative estimate of Luce income from *Time* stock (shares earned $9.74 in 1935, paid so far in 1936, $6.50; anticipated dividend for full year, $8), $818,400; reported Luce income from other investments, $100,000; reported Luce bagatelle as editor of Time, Inc., $45,000; reported total Lucemolument, $963,400.

Boy!

stockholders: Robert A. Chambers, Ward Cheney, F. Trubee Davison, E. Roland Harriman, Dwight W. Morrow, Harvey S. Firestone, Jr., Seymour H. Knox, William V. Griffin. By November Luce & Hadden had raised $86,000, decided to go to work on fellowman.

"Snaggle-Toothed . . . Pig-Faced"

Puny in spite of these preparations, prosy in spite of the contributions of Yale poets Archibald MacLeish & John Farrar, was the first issue of *Time* on March 3, 1923. Magazine went to 9,000 subscribers; readers learned that Uncle Joe Cannon had retired at 86, that there was a famine in Russia, that Thornton Wilder friend Tunney had defeated Greb.

Yet to suggest itself as a rational method of communication, of infuriating readers into buying the magazine, was strange inverted Timestyle. It was months before Hadden's impish contempt for his readers,[4] his impatience with the English language, crystallized into gibberish. By the end of the first year, however, Timeditors were calling people able, potent, nimble; "Tycoon," most successful Timepithet, had been coined by Editor Laird Shields Goldsborough; so fascinated Hadden with "beady-eyed" that for months nobody was anything else. Timeworthy were deemed such designations as "Tom-tom" Heflin, "Body-lover" Macfadden.

"Great word! Great word!" would crow Hadden, coming upon "snaggle-toothed," "pig-faced." Appearing already were such maddening coagulations as "cinemaddict," "radiorator." Appearing also were first gratuitous invasions of privacy. Always mentioned as William Randolph Hearst's "great & good friend" was Cinemactress Marion Davies, stressed was the bastardy of Ramsay MacDonald, the "cozy hospitality" of Mae West. Backward ran sentences until reeled the mind.

By March, 1924, the circulation had doubled, has risen since then 40,000 a year, reaches now the gratifying peak of 640,000, is still growing. From four meagre pages in first issue, *Time*

---

[4] Still framed at *Time* is Hadden's scrawled dictum: "Let Subscriber Goodkind mend his ways!"

advertising has now come to eclipse that in *Satevepost*. Published *Time* in first six months of 1936, 1,590 pages; *Satevepost*, 1,480.

No Slugabed, He . . .

Strongly contrasted from the outset of their venture were Hadden, Luce. Hadden, handsome, black-haired, eccentric, irritated his partner by playing baseball with the office boys, by making jokes, by lack of respect for autocratic business. Conformist Luce disapproved of heavy drinking, played hard, sensible game of tennis, said once: "I have no use for a man who lies in bed after nine o'clock in the morning," walked to work every morning, reproved a writer who asked for a desk for lack of "log-cabin spirit."

In 1925, when *Time* moved its offices to Cleveland, bored, rebellious was Editor Hadden; Luce, busy & social, lunched with local bigwigs, addressed Chamber of Commerce, subscribed to Symphony Orchestra, had neat house in the suburbs. Dismayed was Luce when Hadden met him on return from Europe with premature plans to move the magazine back to New York. In 1929, dying of a streptococcus infection, Hadden still opposed certain details of success-formula of *Fortune*, new, beloved Lucenterprise.

Oats, Hogs, Cheese . . .

In January, 1930, first issue of *Fortune* was mailed to 30,000 subscribers, cost as now $1 a copy, contained articles on branch banking, hogs, glass-blowing, how to live in Chicago on $25,000 a year. Latest issue (Nov., 1936) went to 130,000 subscribers, contained articles on bacon, tires, the New Deal, weighed as much as a good-sized flounder.[5]

Although in 1935 *Fortune* made a net profit of $500,000, vaguely dissatisfied was Editor Luce. Anxious to find & express "the technological significance of industry," he has been handicapped by the fact that his writers are often hostile to Big Business, prone to insert sneers, slithering insults. In an article on

---

[5] Two pounds, nine ounces.

344 PARODIES: *An Anthology*

Bernard Baruch, the banker was described as calling resident Hoover "old cheese-face." Protested Tycoon Baruch that he had said no such thing. Shotup of this was that Luce, embarrassed, printed a retraction; now often removes too-vivid phrasing from writers' copy.

¶ Typical perhaps of Luce methods is *Fortune* system of getting material. Writers in first draft put down wild gossip, any figures that occur to them. This is sent to victim, who indignantly corrects the errors, inadvertently supplies facts he might otherwise have withheld.

¶ *March of Time* in approximately its present form was first broadcast on March 6, 1931, paid the Columbia System for privilege, dropped from the air in February, 1932, with Luce attacking radio's "blatant claim to be a medium of education." Said he: "Should *Time* or any other business feel obliged to be the philanthropist of the air; to continue to pay for radio advertising it doesn't want in order to provide radio with something worthwhile?" So popular, so valuable to the studio was *March of Time* that it was restored in September of the same year, with Columbia donating its time & facilities. Since then *March of Time* has been sponsored by Remington-Rand typewriter company, by Wrigley's gum, by its own cinema *March of Time*, has made 400 broadcasts.[6] Apparently reconciled to philanthropy is Luce, because time for latest version will be bought & paid for by his organization.

¶ No active connection now has Luce with the moving-picture edition of *March of Time*, which was first shown on February 1, 1935, appears thirteen times a year in over 6,000 theatres, has so far failed to make money, to repay $900,000 investment. Even less connection has he with *Time's* only other unprofitable venture. Fifty-year-old *Architectural Forum*, acquired in 1932, loses still between $30,000 and $50,000 a year, circulates to 31,000.

¶ *Letters*, five-cent fortnightly collection of *Time's* correspondence with its indefatigable readers, was started in 1931, goes to 30,000, makes a little money.

---

[6] By some devious necromancy, statisticians have calculated that *March of Time* ranks just behind *Amos & Andy* as most popular of all radio programs; reaches between 8,000,000 and 9,000,000 newshungry addicts.

¶ For a time, Luce was on Board of Directors of Paramount Pictures. Hoped to learn something of cinema, heard nothing discussed but banking, resigned sadly.

Fascinating Facts . . . Dreamy Figures . . .

Net profits of Time, Inc., for the past nine years:

1927	3,860
1928	125,787
1929	325,412
1930	818,936
1931	847,447
1932	613,727[7]
1933	1,009,628
1934	1,773,094
1935	$2,249,823[8]

In 1935 gross revenue of *Time-Fortune* was $8,621,170, of which the newsmagazine brought in approximately $6,000,000. Outside investments netted $562,295. For rent, salaries, production & distribution, other expenses went $6,594,076. Other deductions: $41,397. Allowance for federal income tax: $298,169.

Time's books, according to Chicago Statisticians Gerwig & Gerwig, show total assets of $6,755,451. Liabilities, $3,101,584. These figures, conventionally allowing $1 for name, prestige of *Time,* come far from reflecting actual prosperity of Luce, his enterprises. Sitting pretty are the boys.

Luce . . . Marches On!

Transmogrified by this success are the offices, personnel of *Time-Fortune.* Last reliable report: *Time,* 308 employees; *Fortune,* 103; Cinemarch, 58; Radiomarch, 10; *Architectural Forum,* 40; *Life,* 47. In New York; total, 566. In Chicago, mailing, editorial, mechanical employees, 216. Grand total Timemployees on God's earth, 782. Average weekly recompense for informing fellowman, $45.67802.

[7] Hmm.
[8] Exceeded only by Curtis Publishing Co. (*Satevepost*): $5,329,900; Crowell Publishing Co. (*Collier's*): $2,399,600.

From first single office, Timen have come to bulge to bursting six floors of spiked, shiny Chrysler Building, occupy 150 rooms, eat daily, many at famed Cloud Club, over 1,000 eggs, 500 cups of coffee, much bicarbonate of soda. Other offices: Cinemarch, 10th Avenue at 54th Street; Radiomarch, Columbia Broadcasting Building.

Ornamented with Yale, Harvard, Princeton diplomas, stuffed fish, terrestrial globes are offices of Luce & other headmen; bleak, uncarpeted the writer's dingy lair.

¶ Heir apparent to mantle of Luce is dapper, tennis-playing, $35,000-a-year Roy Larsen, nimble in Radio- & Cinemarch, vice-president & second largest stockholder in Time, Inc. Stock income: $120,000.

¶ Looming behind him is burly, able, tumbledown Yaleman Ralph McAllister Ingersoll, former Fortuneditor, now general manager of all Timenterprises, descendant of 400-famed Ward McAllister. Littered his desk with pills, unguents, Kleenex, Socialite Ingersoll is *Time's* No. 1 hypochondriac, introduced ant palaces for study & emulation of employees, writes copious memoranda about filing systems, other trivia, seldom misses a Yale football game. His salary: $30,000; income from stock: $40,000.

¶ Early in life Timeditor John Stuart Martin lost his left arm in an accident. Unhandicapped he, resentful of sympathy, Martin played par golf at Princeton, is a crack shot with a rifle or shotgun, holds a telephone with no hands, using shoulder & chin, chews paperclips. First cousin of Cofounder Hadden, joined in second marriage to daughter of Cunard Tycoon Sir Ashley Sparks, Timartin is managing editor of newsmagazine, has been nimble in Cinemarch, other Timenterprises, makes $25,000 a year salary, gets from stock $60,000.

¶ $20,000 salary, $20,000 from stock gets shyest, least-known of all Timeditors, Harvardman John S. Billings, Jr., now under Luce in charge of revamped *Life,* once Washington correspondent for the Brooklyn *Eagle,* once National Affairs Editor for *Time.* Yclept "most important man in shop" by Colleague Martin, Billings, brother of famed muralist Henry Billings, is naïve, solemn, absent-minded, once printed same story twice, wanted to print, as news, story of van Gogh's self-mutilation,

drives to office in car with liveried chauffeur, likes Jones Beach.
¶ Fortuneditor Eric Hodgins is thin-haired, orbicular, no Big
Three graduate. Formerly on *Redbook,* boy & girl informing
Youth's Companion, Hodgins inherited Pill-Swallower Ingersoll's
editorial job two years ago when latter was called to greater glory,
higher usefulness, still writes much of content of magazine, is
paid $15,000; from stock only $8,000.
¶ Doomed to strict anonymity are *Time-Fortune* staff writers,
but generally known in spite of this are former *Times* Bookritic
John Chamberlain, Meistersinger Archibald MacLeish. Both out
of sympathy with domineering business, both irked by stylistic
restrictions, thorns to Luce as well as jewels they. Reward for
lack of fame: Chamberlain, $10,000; MacLeish, $15,000; each,
two months' vacation.

Brisk beyond belief are carryings-on these days in Luce's
chromium tower. *Time,* marching on more militantly than ever,
is a shambles on Sundays & Mondays, when week's news is tele-
typed to Chicago printing plant; *Fortune,* energetic, dignified, its
offices smelling comfortably of cookies, is ever astir with such
stupefying projects as sending the entire staff to Japan; new
whoopsheet *Life* so deep in organization that staff breakfasts are
held to choose from 6,000 submitted photographs the Nude of
the Week; so harried perpetually all editors that even interoffice
memoranda are couched in familiar Timestyle,[9] that an ap-
pointment to lunch with Editor Luce must be made three weeks
in advance.

Caught up also in the whirlwind of progress are *Time,*
Fortune's 19 maiden checkers. Bryn Mawr, Wellesley, Vassar
graduates they, each is assigned to a staff writer, checks every
word he writes, works hard & late, is barred by magazine's anti-
feminine policy from editorial advancement.

Cold, Baggy, Temperate . . .

At work today, Luce is efficient, humorless, revered by colleagues; arrives always at 9:15, leaves at 6, carrying armfuls of
work, talks jerkily, carefully, avoiding visitor's eye; stutters in

[9] Sample Luce memorandum: "Let *Time's* editors next week put thought
on the Japanese beetle. H. R. L."

conversation, never in speechmaking. In early days kept standing at Luce desk like butlers were writers while he praised or blamed; now most business is done by time-saving memoranda called "Luce's bulls." Prone he to wave aside pleasantries, social preliminaries, to get at once to the matter in hand. Once to interviewer who said, "I hope I'm not disturbing you," snapped Luce, "Well, you are." To ladies full of gentle misinformation he is brusque, contradictory, hostile; says that his only hobby is "conversing with somebody who knows something," argues still that "names make news," that he would not hesitate to print a scandal involving his best friend.

Because of his Chinese birth, constantly besieged is Luce by visiting Orientals; he is polite, forbearing, seethes secretly. Lunch, usually in a private room at the Cloud Club, is eaten quickly, little attention paid to the food, much to business. He drinks not at all at midday, sparingly at all times, takes sometimes champagne at dinner, an occasional cocktail at parties. Embarrassed perhaps by reputation for unusual abstemiousness, he confesses proudly that he smokes too much.

Serious, ambitious Yale standards are still reflected in much of his conduct; in indiscriminate admiration for bustling success, in strong regard for conventional morality, in honest passion for accuracy; physically, in conservative, baggy clothes, white shirts with buttoned-down collars, solid-color ties. A budding joiner, in New York, Luce belongs to the Yale, Coffee House, Racquet & Tennis, Union, & Cloud Clubs; owns a box at the Metropolitan; is listed in *Who's Who* & *Social Register*.

Colder, more certain, more dignified than in the early days of the magazine, his prose style has grown less ebullient, resembles pontifical *Fortune* rather than chattering *Time*. Before some important body he makes now at least one speech a year, partly as a form of self-discipline, partly because he feels that his position as head of a national institution demands it. His interests wider, he likes to travel, meet & observe the Great. Five or six times in Europe, he has observed many Great & Near Great. Of a twenty-minute conversation with King Edward, then Prince of Wales, says only "Very interesting." Returning from such trips, he always provides staff members with 10 & 12-page memoranda carefully explaining conditions.

Orated recently of conditions in this country: "Without the aristocratic principle no society can endure. . . . What slowly deadened our aristocratic sense was the expanding frontier, but more the expanding machine. . . . But the aristocratic principle persisted in the United States in our fetish of comparative success. . . . We got a plutocracy without any common sense of dignity and obligation. Money became more and more the only mark of success, but still we insisted that the rich man was no better than the poor man—and the rich man accepted the verdict. And so let me make it plain, the triumph of the mass mind is nowhere more apparent than in the frustration of the upper classes." Also remarked in conversation: "Trouble is—great antisocial development—is the automobile trailer. Greatest failure of this country is that it hasn't provided good homes for its people. Trailer shows that."

Milestones

Good-naturedly amused by Luce tycoon ambitions was Lila Hotz, of Chicago, whom he married there on Dec. 22, 1923. In 1935, the father of two boys, Luce was divorced by her in Reno on Oct. 5. Married in Old Greenwich, Conn., without attendants, on Nov. 23, 1935, were Luce, Novelist-Playwright Clare Boothe Brokaw, described once by Anglo-aesthete Cecil Beaton as "most drenchingly beautiful," former wife of elderly Pantycoon George Tuttle Brokaw.

Two days before ceremony, "Abide with Me," by new, beautiful Mrs. Luce, was produced at the Ritz Theatre. Play dealt with young woman married to sadistic drunkard, was unfavorably reviewed by all newspaper critics.[10]

[10] Of it said Richard Watts, blue-shirted, moon-faced *Tribune* dramappraiser:

"One almost forgave 'Abide with Me' its faults when its lovely playwright, who must have been crouched in the wings for a sprinter's start as the final curtain mercifully descended, heard a cry of 'author,' which was not audible in my vicinity, and arrived onstage to accept the audience's applause just as the actors, who had a head-start on her, were properly lined up and smoothed out to receive their customary adulation."

In a quandary was Bridegroom Luce when *Time's* own critic submitted a review suggesting play had some merit. Said he: "Show isn't that good. . . . Go back. . . . Write what you thought." Seven times, however, struggled the writer before achieving an acceptable compromise between criticism, tact.

A Million Rooms, a Thousand Baths . . .

Long accustomed to being entertained, entertaining, is Mrs. Luce, intimate of Mr. & Mrs. A. Coster Schermerhorn, Bernard M. Baruch, Jock Whitney, glistening stage & literary stars. Many were invited last summer to 30-acre estate in Stamford to play tennis, croquet, swim; many more will be when Mrs. Luce has finished her new play, "The Women," [11] when *Life's* problems, budding policies have been settled by Luce.

Many, too, will come to 7,000-acre, $100,000 Luce plantation, near Charleston, S. C.; will sleep there in four streamlined, pre-fabricated guest cottages. Given to first Mrs. Luce in divorce settlement, along with $500,000 in cash & securities, was French Manoir at Gladstone, N. J., where Luce once planned to raise Black Angus cows, to become gentleman farmer.

Described too modestly by him to Newyorkereporter as "small-est apartment in River House," [12] Luce duplex at 435 East 52nd Street contains 15 rooms, 5 baths, a lavatory; was leased furnished from Mrs. Bodrero Macy for $7,300 annually, contains many valuable French, English, Italian antiques, looks north and east on the river. In décor, Mrs. Luce prefers the modern; evasive is Luce. Says he: "Just like things convenient & sensible." Says also: "Whatever furniture or houses we buy in the future will be my wife's buying, not mine."

Whither, Whither?

Accused by many of Fascist leanings, of soaring journalistic ambition, much & conflicting is the evidence on Luce political faith, future plans. By tradition a Tory, in 1928 he voted for Alfred E. Smith, in 1932 for Herbert Hoover, this year for Al-

---

[11] Among backers are sad, ramshackle George S. Kaufman, high-domed fur-bearing Moss Hart.

[12] Smallest apartment in River House has six rooms, one bath.

fred M. Landon. Long at outs with William Randolph Hearst, it was rumored that a visit last spring to California included a truce with ruthless, shifting publisher. Close friend for years of Thomas Lamont, Henry P. Davison, the late Dwight Morrow, it has been hinted that an official connection with the House of Morgan in the future is not impossible. Vehemently denies this Luce, denies any personal political ambition, admits only that he would like eventually to own a daily newspaper in New York.

Most persistent, most fantastic rumor, however, declares that Yaleman Luce already has a wistful eye on the White House. Reported this recently Chicago's *Ringmaster,* added: "A legally-minded friend . . . told him that his Chinese birth made him ineligible. Luce dashed to another lawyer to check. Relief! He was born of American parents and properly registered at the Consulate."

Whatever the facts in that matter, indicative of Luce consciousness of budding greatness, of responsibility to whole nation, was his report to *Time's* Board of Directors on March 19, 1936. Declaimed he: "The expansion of your company has brought it to a point beyond which it will cease to be even a big Small Business and become a small Big Business. . . . The problem of public relations also arises. *Time,* the Weekly Newsmagazine, has been, and still is, its own adequate apologist. Ditto, *Fortune.* But with a motion-picture journal, a nightly radio broadcast, and with four magazines, the public interpretation of your company's alleged viewpoint of viewpoints must be taken with great seriousness." Certainly to be taken with seriousness is Luce at thirty-eight, his fellowman already informed up to his ears, the shadow of his enterprises long across the land, his future plans impossible to imagine, staggering to contemplate. Where it all will end, knows God!

LITERARY LIFE
ON THE *TIMES*: I

ONE OF OUR few cultural institutions that has survived unchanged for generations (unfortunately) is the "Queries and Answers" department of the *New York Times Book Review*. Benchley wrote the parody below almost forty years ago. It is still to the point. "J.M. writes: [we read in the May 29, 1960 issue] 'I would appreciate knowing the source of the following lines which I believe to be a poem that was popular during the First World War: "Somewhere in France, no matter where, / That they are there, the soldiers in their khaki brown, / The angels in heaven and God look down . . ."' "

Literary Lost & Found Department

"OLD BLACK TILLIE"

H. G.L.—When I was a little girl, my nurse used to recite a poem something like the following (as near as I can remember). I wonder if anyone can give me the missing lines?

> "*Old Black Tillie lived in the dell,*
> *Heigh-ho with a rum-tum-tum!*
> *Something, something, something like a lot of hell,*
> *Heigh-ho with a rum-tum-tum!*
> *She wasn't very something and she wasn't very fat*
> *But—*"

"VICTOR HUGO'S DEATH"

M.K.C.—Is it true that Victor Hugo did not die but is still living in a little shack in Colorado?

"I'M SORRY THAT I SPELT THE WORD"

J.R.A.—Can anyone help me out by furnishing the last three words to the following stanza which I learned in school and of which I have forgotten the last three words, thereby driving myself crazy?

" 'I'm sorry that I spelt the word,
    I hate to go above you,
    Because—' the brown eyes lower fell,
    'Because, you see, — — —.' "

"GOD'S IN HIS HEAVEN"

J.A.E.—Where did Mark Twain write the following?

"God's in his heaven:
    All's right with the world."

"SHE DWELT BESIDE"

N.K.Y.—Can someone locate this for me and tell the author?

"She dwelt among untrodden ways,
    Beside the springs of Dove,
    To me she gave sweet Charity,
    But greater far is Love."

"THE GOLDEN WEDDING"

K.L.F.—Who wrote the following and what does it mean?

"Oh, de golden wedding,
    Oh, de golden wedding,
    Oh, de golden wedding,
    De golden, golden wedding!"

Answers

"WHEN GRANDMA WAS A GIRL"

LUTHER F. NEAM, Flushing, L. I.—The poem asked for by "E.J.K." was recited at a Free Soil riot in Ashburg, Kansas, in July, 1850. It was entitled, "And That's the Way They Did It When Grandma Was a Girl," and was written by Bishop Leander B. Rizzard. The last line runs:

"And that's the way they did it, when Grandma was a girl."

Others who answered this query were: Lillian W. East, of Albany; Martin B. Frosch, New York City, and Henry Cabot Lodge, Nahant.

"LET US THEN BE UP AND DOING"

ROGER F. NILKETTE, Presto, N. J.—Replying to the query in your last issue concerning the origin of the lines:

> *"Let us then be up and doing,*
> *With a heart for any fate.*
> *Still achieving, still pursuing,*
> *Learn to labor and to wait."*

I remember hearing these lines read at a gathering in the Second Baptist Church of Presto, N. J., when I was a young man, by the Reverend Harley N. Ankle. It was said at the time among his parishioners that he himself wrote them and on being questioned on the matter he did not deny it, simply smiling and saying, "I'm glad if you liked them." They were henceforth known in Presto as "Dr. Ankle's verse" and were set to music and sung at his funeral.

"THE DECEMBER BRIDE, OR OLD ROBIN"

CHARLES B. RENNIT, Boston, N. H.—The whole poem wanted by "H.J.O." is as follows, and appeared in *Hostetter's Annual* in 1843.

1

> "'Twas in the bleak December that I took her for my bride;
> How well do I remember how she fluttered by my side;
> My Nellie dear, it was not long before you up and died,
> And they buried her at eight-thirty in the morning.

2

> "Oh, do not tell me of the charms of maidens far and near,
> Their charming ways and manners I do not care to hear,
> For Lucy dear was to me so very, very dear,
> And they buried her at eight-thirty in the morning.

3

"Then it's merrily, merrily, merrily, whoa!
To the old gray church they come and go,
Some to be married and some to be buried,
And old Robin has gone for the mail."

ROBERT BENCHLEY

LITERARY LIFE
ON THE *TIMES:* II

ANOTHER VENERABLE if not always venerated institution in *The New York Times Book Review* is J. Donald Adams' column, "Speaking of Books," which has been fighting a losing battle against innovation for (it seems) several generations. Mr. Adams' style, verbose and otiose, seems to have been learned from the paper's news columns.

Speaking of Books

THE READER may recall that for the past three weeks this column has been devoted to a discussion of the difficulty of saying everything there is to say about any given topic in the limits of space imposed by its position in *The New York Times Book Review.* Much remains to be said about this interesting subject. However, my thoughts have been diverted from this interesting channel by an interesting query that has come to me from a reader.

"How is it," this reader inquires, "that the snobbish critics who rave themselves hoarse over D. H. Lawrence have conspired to ignore the stinging rebuttal of all he represents in Jehanne D'Orliac's sequel to *Lady Chatterley's Lover?*"

I confess I do not know how to answer. This too-little-known work of Miss D'Orliac, published in 1935 by Robert M. McBride & Co., does contain, it seems to me, a wealth of wisdom for those of us who live in this bedeviled but exciting century. Yet the critics have been unanimous in ignoring *Lady Chatterley's Second Husband.* Why? This is an interesting question.

Perhaps it is partly because Miss D'Orliac does not share

Lawrence's repulsive obsession with S-x. Instead, with a delicacy worthy of L. Manning Vines, she explores Constance's relationship to the gamekeeper *after* the birth of their illegitimate child. "He has only to break off his childish games and ask us: 'What is God?' " Miss D'Orliac observes. "The simplest of his questions shatters the best established systems of philosophy."

Yet Miss D'Orliac, thank heaven, is no prude of the Henry James variety. She faces squarely up to the issue of S-x, realizing that it is, after all, only a n-tural f-nction. "Constance had desired, and she had gone to meet her desire. . . . Not with courage, but with heedlessness, that heedlessness which she got from her father, the dilettante artist, and from the chronic confusion of her mother, the member of the Fabian Society fuddled with Socialistic illuminism."

Yet this frank sensuality is always subordinate to her central purpose—exposing the shallowness of Lawrence's thought. She brings all her talent to bear on this matter, skillfully contrasting the moral confusion of Constance with the firm grasp of principle displayed by her sister. "Hilda, too, had got a divorce, but it was to marry a man richer than the one she had left. Like her sister, she felt the need of a change. Unlike her sister, however, she did not want to make less of herself, rather to make more of herself, to increase herself. . . . Hilda went up; Constance went down."

It is indeed difficult to understand how a work of such merit could have been ignored for so many years. It is a situation for which the critics must take a large share of the responsibility, since it is their duty to lead the public to important and wholesome books. After all, before a novel can be enjoyed completely, it must be read.

So stated, this is, or seems to me, an obvious truth, and I emphasize it only because it is frequently forgotten. So much criticism today ignores the fact that before we can appreciate an author's prose style, or his skill in characterization, we must first read his work. This appears to me almost self-evident. Unless we read what an author has written, how are we to judge, or even understand, his place in the world of letters?

This is an interesting question and one which brings me round again to what I said in the beginning about its being difficult, or even impossible, to say within the limits of space imposed upon me by the length of this column everything I would like to say about any given topic. I have raised questions I would like to touch upon, space permitting, in next Sunday's column.

DONALD MALCOLM

ALF STRINGERSOLL'S REPORT ON BROOKLYN

Although *PM,* the daily newspaper that Ralph Ingersoll published during the war years is by now happily forgotten, the following parody seems to me amusing enough in its own right to be worth reviving. And for those ancients who still remember *PM*, it does give the precise tone of the newspaper Mr. Ingersoll, after many years as first managing editor of *The New Yorker* and then editor of *Fortune,* and a top-echelon executive in the Luce organization, unexpectedly began to put out with the help of assorted left-liberals, mostly of the Stalinoid persuasion. *PM* created a new style in journalism, in which the writer took the reader through the whole travail of researching the article, spelling it out in words of one syllable—for were they not both Common Men together?—and keeping absolutely nothing up his sleeve. The style didn't take, perhaps because there *was* nothing up its sleeve, or in its head. The closest any one ever came to defining *PM*'s editorial line, by the way, was a once-celebrated dictum by Mr. Ingersoll: "*PM* is against people who push other people around."

(Alf Stringersoll, editor of AM, has just returned from Brooklyn, where he spent the last three days and nights covering the borough. His trip took him from Borough Hall to the Heights, thence to Greenpoint, Bensonhurst, New Utrecht, and Flatbush. He came home through Prospect Park and via Grand Army Plaza. Today he starts a series of articles written exclusively for AM, telling what he saw, heard, and felt in those 72 hours. AM is stapled and takes no advertising.)

BY ALF STRINGERSOLL

I HAVE just come back from Brooklyn. For the past three days I have travelled the length and breadth of the borough, talking, listening, eating, sleeping, laughing. I travelled by subway, taxicab, surface car, and on foot. I talked with subway guards, taxicab-drivers, streetcar conductors, and traffic cops.

Now I am writing at breakneck speed trying to put down what I saw and heard and felt in those 72 hours. In my first piece I am going to try to knit my stuff together and make sense out of it. In my subsequent pieces I am going to take it all apart and in my last piece I am going to fit all the pieces together again, like a mosaic.

I am writing as fast as I can and I have a secretary who is picking up the pieces as fast as I knock them out.

The biggest news I bring back from Brooklyn is this:

Brooklyn is not lying down. It hasn't all the answers yet, but it's working them out.

The man in the street is not standing still. He is going places.

Ralph Ingersoll, with whom I had an audience just before I left, is not a chain smoker.

I got my first glimpse of Brooklyn from Manhattan Bridge. It was dusk, and my pretty blonde interpreter and I were riding in a Sunshine cab. I lit a cigaret. Then I said:

"Why are there so many red lights ahead?"

The red lights were strung out along what seemed to be a main thoroughfare. They looked like a string of ruby beads.

She said:

"Those are traffic lights. Watch them closely and they will turn green."

I looked at them intently. For a minute. Maybe more.

Suddenly the lights turned green.

I asked the driver to stop the cab. He did and we got out. First I got out. Then my pretty blonde interpreter got out.

We were in Brooklyn.

I paid the driver. As I did so, I could not help noticing his face. His eyes were bright and intelligent. His teeth were straight and white. I said to myself: Here is a dignified human being. I wondered: What makes him tick?

I put the change back in my pocket. I noticed that the coins were similar to those back home. They are called kerns, however.

We set out on foot towards Borough Hall. But first I wanted

to talk to a man in the street. I did not care to talk with the big shots, the bosses and the politicians. I wanted to find out what the little guys were doing, thinking, drinking, saying, writing. I wanted to tell about it in AM, because AM is interested in little fellows.

Finally we found a little guy by a newsstand. The papers he sold were printed in English. I watched him. My guess was that he was four feet eleven. A little guy. My pretty blonde interpreter guessed too, but I was closer.

He said he was four feet ten.

Then I asked my interpreter to ask him what he thought about what is going on in the world.

She said he said wait until next year. She said he meant the Dodgers.

I told him that where I came from we had two ball teams and that some people were for one team and some for the other.

He said that did not make sense to him, because if you are not for the home team then you are against it and should be kicked out. He said that in Brooklyn there is only one team and that is the Dodgers.

I was jotting all this down because I did not want to miss anything, so I did not hear my interpreter when she told me what he said. I asked her to tell him did he mind if she repeated what he said.

She said he said she shouldn't.

I thought she said "couldn't," so I asked him what he did for a living.

He said that in the summer he pushed a wheel chair on the boardwalk at Coney Island.

I said to my interpreter, "Let's go." AM is against people who push other people around.

We went to a hotel room, because I wanted to add up the score and get my first impressions of Brooklyn into focus. I knew I had a story and did not want to let it evaporate before I went to bed. But I knew, too, that it wouldn't be a complete story until I had talked with Ralph Ingersoll, the newest newspaper editor in Brooklyn. If I could get to him, then I *would* have a story.

It developed that I was to spend three days in Brooklyn before I got my break. I had almost given up hope and was standing in the Grand Army Plaza station waiting for the express that was to take me back home when someone tapped me on the shoulder. I turned around. It was a young man. Clear-eyed. American-looking. My guess was that he was 22 years old. My interpreter did not bother to guess.

"Mr. Ingersoll will see you now," he said.

He led me upstairs to the street, then we turned left and walked about a block. My heart was pounding hard. I tried to light a cigaret but the match burnt my fingers and I had to drop it. Suddenly we stopped in front of a cafeteria.

"You may go in now," said the young man.

Inside was a long counter. Lining the counter were stools. On the farthest stool sat Ingersoll. He seemed to be talking to the attendant behind the counter, but I could not be sure.

As I approached he motioned me to the adjacent stool. I felt that he sensed my excitement and was trying to put me at my ease.

For at least five minutes I could think of nothing to say. I kept repeating over and over again, "Now you are going to get your story. Now you are going to be able to tell people about Ralph Ingersoll."

Finally he smiled and told me to relax and stop babbling. Instantly I was at my ease and we began to talk.

When Ralph Ingersoll smiles, the corners of his mouth seem to stretch towards his cheeks and his eyes crinkle up. When he stops smiling, his mouth and eyes resume their normal shape.

I said I found the weather in Brooklyn rather warm for this time of year. I asked him was it unusually warm for Brooklyn.

Ingersoll hesitated a moment. I could see that he was weighing his words. Then he said that although it was warmer than it generally was, such weather was not unusual at this time of year.

I had no difficulty in understanding Ingersoll when he spoke. He looks at you frankly and sincerely, and forms his words with his tongue and lips.

Then I told him that I was planning to return home by subway and asked his advice on trains. I said that I did not wish to wind up at New Lots Ave., as I had been there before.

Ingersoll smiled and lit a well-known brand of cigaret. (AM takes no advertising.) Then he dropped some lumps of sugar into his coffee. I think he used two lumps but I am not certain. There were fourteen lumps in the bowl when I arrived and only eleven when I left, but the attendant may have taken one. I will check on this later.

"I don't think you will have much trouble," he said finally, "and I hope you have a pleasant journey."

I gathered that he wished to draw the interview to a close. I thanked him for his kindness and we shook hands. Then I said good-by.

"Good-by," he said. "I enjoyed talking with you."

I thanked him again and then I walked out.

On the way back to the subway station I remembered one thing about the man that I knew people back home would want to know. Before I went to Brooklyn a lot of people told me to watch Ingersoll smoke. They said he was a chain smoker.

That is not so. I sat with Ralph Ingersoll for ten minutes. During that time he smoked two cigarets. *But he did not light one from the other.* I noticed that he carefully mashed out his first cigaret before extracting another from his pack. In other words, *there was a lapse of approximately thirty seconds between his cigarets.* I have seen chain smokers, and that is not the way they smoke.

TOMORROW: *A Day on the Gowanus Canal.*

—WILLIAM ATTWOOD

W. B. SCOTT

THE FOLLOWING two parodies originally appeared in the Summer, 1949, and Winter, 1950, numbers of *Furioso*. This Little Magazine, which came out from 1946 to 1953, was distinguished for humor and irreverence; it was published first at Yale and later at Carleton College in Minnesota; Reed Whittemore, its guiding spirit, has lately revived it as *The Carleton Miscellany*. One of *Furioso's* happiest discoveries was the parodic talent of Walter B. Scott, who teaches English at Northwestern University. His *Chicago Letter,* immediately below, is a cry from the heart against the more precious and insider-oriented snobberies of our Little Magazines; I think he must have had some of *Partisan Review's* foreign correspondents in mind. As for Mr. Scott's other contribution, those who have suffered from an even more precious and cliqueist quality in certain memoirs of certain recent French writers will have no trouble identifying the originals of M. Fignole and his Journal.

Chicago Letter

April, 1949

> *"Voyage infortuné! Rivage malheureux,*
> *Falloit-il approcher de tes bords dangereux?"*
> —Racine

AGONY, a sense of plight; a sense of agony, plight—such, one soon perceives, are the attributes of the Chicago of our time. But I shall have more to say about them later in this letter.

I travelled by the Erie, as one must, I think, do, now and then. The trip is longer, to be sure, on its ancient twisting right-of-way than on other roads. But there one escapes the *"lumpen-aristokratie"* (in Roscoe Chutney's phrase) of the Century or the Broadway, and it is only from the Erie, of course, that one may catch those extraordinary night glimpses of Youngstown and Akron.

I had not planned to do much reading on the train, but recalling how trying the journey could be (in certain weathers) between Hankins and Horseheads, I had as a precaution bought the latest *Peristalsis* at a kiosk in the Jersey City station. It was thus, at lunch (in the diner) that I happened upon Hjalmar Ekdal's essay, "Kafka's Ulcer"—a subject I had outlined to Hjalmar at Ocean Grove in the late summer of 1945. Had he quite *realized* it, though, in Cézanne's sense? I could not, at the moment, be entirely certain.

Some hours later, settled in my berth (there is something to be said for the old standard sleeper, after all), and glancing through the rest of the magazine (which [as it happened] I had no clear intention of reading then), I discovered Mildred's Belgrade Letter, Sam's Naples Letter, Boris's Pskov Letter, Fred's Capetown Letter, Deirdre's Quito Letter, Jaroslav's Paris Letter, and Harry's Prague Letter. These were precisely the people I had looked forward most to seeing in Chicago, and it was small comfort to be told (on my arrival) of the fate already suffered by several of them—Boris and Harry shot by Stalinists (on a trumped-up charge of cosmopolitan rootlessness), Mildred hanged by Titoists in the woods north of Slunj, Sam abducted by the resurgent Maffia, Deirdre raped, robbed, and butchered by Clerical-Trotskyists. How explain these horrors? Those who remained in Chicago shrugged their shoulders in anxious silence at my question. What was in store for others, who had just left or were about to leave—Erma and Roscoe Chutney, already on their way to Shiraz; the Ekdals, who were departing the day after my arrival?

"It doesn't much matter where I go," Hjalmar told me. "Hatred and envy are my shadows. I had thought of the Yukon, God knows why, but Gina's already promised two Aleppo Letters to *Peristalsis,* so I suppose we might as well go there. Is it true that they still use the old water torture in Aleppo? One might (at least) have that to look forward to."

I could not tell him: I have not been in Aleppo since I was eight or nine. All the same, I knew that Hjalmar was suffering. Kafka's ulcer had, in some sense, become *his* ulcer. Or, was the world his ulcer? Does our proper pleasure in Kafka lie (after all) in this mutual *anagnorisis* of symptoms—in what I have ventured elsewhere[1] to describe as "an act of critical nosology"?

I had not yet become aware of Hjalmar's torment when Jens Kobold met me at Dearborn Station—where the grimy Victorian interior has been entirely remodelled (I do not allude, of course, to the trainshed, but to the waiting-rooms, ticket-counters, and so on) in what may best be called a sort of middle- upper-brow notion of "modern" *décor.* As for Jens, he seemed during the first few seconds much as ever—monolithic, *rébarbatif,* with that quality of tempered urgency which Roscoe Chutney has so profoundly pictured in *The Critical Stud-Book.* But as we drove

---

[1] "Criticism as Diagnosis." *Peristalsis,* Winter-Summer, 1943.

through the rotting streets of the Loop and the Near North Side, I detected something new: he appeared discrete, shattered. His only reply to my questions was to spit from the taxi window and mumble an evasive phrase about riots in the Bosnian quarter. I could not imagine what he meant: there is always rioting in Chicago's Bosnian quarter, and Jens had always boasted his entire indifference to *la question Bosnienne*. For the moment I said no more, and contemplated the buildings and the hoardings. On one of these latter, an enormous photo-mural (of Truman Capote [I think] balanced perilously in ballet costume on a high wire) had already been savagely ripped by the lake wind. But worse was to come.

At Jens's studio pretty much all that was left of the *premier rang* of Chicago's *avant garde* was spiritlessly waiting for us: the Ekdals, appalled by the amount of packing still to be done and by the strawberry rash which Gina's ringworm shots had produced; Bernard Mosher, apprehensively drunk; Geoge Barnwell, Máire Ní Laoghaire, Jeremy Irk (unshakeably gloomy, despite the putative success of his new play—of which more later).

The party was, of course, a desperate failure: I find it a torture to record my own corrosive memories of it. The lovely Máire no longer stretched on the floor with Jeremy to say wise dreadful things about Dostoevsky; now she sat hunched and nearly silent on the Grand Rapids divan which is so familiar and amusing a shape in Jens's pictures of the '30's. As for the others—but why persist on this level of discourse? I sensed that much was missing—but what? Recently I had read somewhere that French intellectuals are gayer, less elegiac than their opposite numbers in America. I had not dreamed, however, that American intellectuals are so little gay, so formidably elegiac. What was the nexus?

In the course of that long, disenchanted first day in Chicago I discovered that Jens had given up easel painting, and that he now, in his phrase, "soils" pages torn at random from the *Tribune,* at which he flings wildly-punctured cans of ten-cent-store oil paint. The results are, of course, often magnificent—Máire Ní Laoghaire has written superbly of Jens's *jetage*—but all the same they hint (possibly) at something not far removed from uncertainty—an uncertainty even more apparent in the work of those imitators of his who have attempted the same sort of thing with the *Sun-Times* or *Herald-American*. I cannot avoid being enormously impressed by many of these new pictures of Jens's, yet I find it not easy to conceive what is central to their strategy. Jens himself, who once talked and wrote so copiously about the nature of life and painting, labels them—almost hatefully—as "Tribunemalerei," and appears contemptuous of the opinions of Máire, with whom (I am told) he is no longer living.

It was Bernard Mosher who first found precise words for what I had sensed of menace and despair in Chicago. "Call it what you will," he said as we walked along Van Buren street after seeing the Ekdals off, "it is, in my phrase, 'a sense of plight.'" At this point he left me abruptly (we had reached the corner of Van Buren and Wells), and I turned north in the shadow of the "L" for my first stroll in the doomed city.

A casual visitor might not at first glance suspect the tragic tension which torments Chicago's intellectuals and artists. Trifles are taken for wonders: under the administration of Mayor Kennelly political corruption has ceased, and what the philistine press calls "vice" has been driven out (I have yet to meet a police reporter who truly apprehends the nature of original sin). Lake Michigan seems, on the surface, unchanged. The same dingy pigeons swarm for peanuts on the "L" platforms of the Loop, and the shabby skyscrapers blot out the afternoon sun. The new streetcars already look old (as everything new looks old in Chicago). Towards the end of the day they are filled, in monotonous ritual fashion, with anthropoid businessmen frowning heavily over the *Daily News,* and bored high-school girls carelessly swinging their eternal battered copies of *The Brothers Karamazov.* On Sundays humorless bourgeois families go picnicking in the fogs along the Drainage Canal, or watch the passionless "play" of the White Sox or the Cubs (also gripped by plight—of [I suspect] a rather different order).

Little by little, as the leaden hours slog by in this joyless metropolis, one clutches at further tokens of the truth of Bernard Mosher's *aperçu.* I do not (of course) propose to burden this letter with statistics, but where are the great Chicago essays of the mid-1940's? [2] Who, for example, writes about Melville now? Three years ago the mean annual production in Cook County of Melville books and articles was 274; today it is scarcely fifteen. Three years ago we were finding new hope in George Barnwell's "Melville's Whale and M. de Charlus," Hjalmar Ekdal's "Melville's Tumor," Bernard Mosher's "Barnwell, Ekdal, and the Melville World." Nowadays one encounters, at best—and it is simply not good enough—some Northwestern University pedant's cynical and barren, "Smile When You Call Me Ishmael." Und weiter nichts.

Other facts suggest the city's agony. A fortnight after my arrival I read in the *Cicero Quarterly* (which last week ceased publication) of the dissolution of the Goose Island Sartre Club, whose president, with ironic ambivalence, rather than commit suicide had taken a job as check-out boy in a supermarket. Early today, as I started to compose this letter, Jeremy Irk phoned to tell me that the Rogers Park *Cercle Rimbaud* is down to nine members, eight of whom do not speak to each other. Yet, with all this endemic apathy, one learns of eruptions of violence as well (I do not here allude to the Bosnian riots, of course). In the dim alleys of the South Side, I am told, "goon squads" from the Aristotle A.C. sally out after nightfall to sack hostile bookshops, or worse. Such things are, to be sure, a kind of action, although I cannot say what hope one is to take from it.

It is along South State and North Clark streets that one is most sharply conscious of the pervasive sense of plight. Here, as in the past, one discovers the youth of the *avant garde,* but now much altered—frustrated painters, *poètes par trop manqués,* defeated composers, disappointed novelists, exhausted sculptors, beaten playwrights, embittered critics, bilious critics of critics, all of them shivering in the cold spring rain, but too tired, indolent, indifferent to seek the relative warmth of the bars. I do not propose to intrude upon my readers that improbable figure of American myth, the philosophical bartender, but I did chance

---

[2] One recalls, above all, perhaps, Irk and Chutney, "The Heresy of Fallacy" (*Peristalsis,* Winter-Summer, 1945); Chutney and Irk, "The Fallacy of Heresy" (*Peristalsis,* Winter-Summer, 1946).

upon one old man—he had known Kierkegaard at Trondhjem, as it happened—who put the case for me about as clearly as anyone else had done. I was watching him construct North Clark street's favorite drink, a double *pousse-café*, and as he worked at it with his precise artist's fingers, he nodded through the door towards the crowds outside.

"These kids got the sense of plight so bad they ain't even writing or talking about it, nor trying to reduce it somehow to canvas or stone," he said. "You take as recent as six, eight months ago they'd r'ar up and snap at each other like they was Stanley Edgar Kazin. You know how I mean—'Jake that dope he don't really unnerstand the nature of Myth,' 'Mike, all the psychoanalysis he ever read, *if* he ever read it, is Joseph Jastrow,' 'Moe combines ignorance wit brashness to an amazing degree,' 'Joe's got about as much innerest in the *text* of a poem—by which I mean *what* a poem *is*—as a Van Buren street pigeon has in clean feathers.' In there pitching. This joint used to sound like it was, you might say, collective criticism by symposium going on all the time. But what do they do now? Just set out there in the rain on the *terrasse* and mope. I ain't even heard Hemingway sneered at in rising two months. You looking for the sense of plight, boy, you come to the right town!"

If plight has come close to silencing the artists and critics, it has (for all practical purposes) obliterated the philosophers and political theorists. A few, I gather, have entered general semantics, a few have killed themselves or each other. As for still others—

> "*Tout fuit; et sans s'armer d'un courage inutile,*
> *Dans le temple voisin chacun cherche un asile*"

in Racine's sense of the phrase. Only yesterday the Cafe Désespoir et du Terminus closed its doors. The Hiedegger Bar and Grill has (I hear) taken to watering its *pousse-cafés*. Where is an answer to be found?

It is clearly not to be found in the Chicago theatre. In the commodity houses of the Loop one is faced (inevitably) with pure *Kitsch*—ill-made well-made plays, well-made ill-made plays, tepidly performed before drowsy lower-middle-brow audiences which wake into sudden anxious laughter at bathroom jokes, then sink back into the somnolence of the damned.

The best theatre in Chicago was available (I use "was" here in its sense of past tense of "to be") very distant from the Loop, in an abandoned warehouse on the Far Northwest Side, where one climbed four flights of condemned wooden stairs to a makeshift hall under a decaying roof. The second-hand seats in the orchestra, gnawed incessantly by rats, were scantily occupied by bewildered bourgeois couples and drunken slummers from the Gold Coast. The rickety balcony was packed with sullen students, who showed little interest in what was going on, little sign of the passion for theatre which may once have possessed them.

Máire Ní Laoghaire took me one night to see Jean-Jean Baroque act Jeremy Irk's *Les Voyeurs de Rogers Park,* in Irk's own extraordinary translation. This is (in some respects) a puzzling play, and until I have read the script, I shall not venture to pronounce a final judgment on it. "Mordant, plangent, repellent," (in Máire Ní Laoghaire's phrase) it is at once strikingly astringent, yet rather like warm marshmallows. There are eight acts (five of them, of course, in verse) of which the first three, played in a blackout, are almost hauntingly rhetorical. But more than any other play I have seen in years (in London, Paris, New York, Rome, Moscow, Stambouli, Narvik, that is), Irk's drama comes to close grips with certain deeply-imbedded constituents of the American myth—particularly various suburban *rites de passage* reminiscent—at first hearing, in any event—of those which Rudge observed in Lower Borneo. I am persuaded, however, that Irk's parallel between Salmon P. Chase and the Corn God may be at once too tenuous and too obvious.

But I shall not attempt to summarize the play here—the fourth and seventh acts are to appear in the Winter-Summer *Peristalsis* —because I wish to comment rather on the amazing art of Baroque. An ugly little man, with a whiskey baritone which engaged one like a wood rasp (I have heard that he had been [at one time] a bouncer in the Pump Room), he was able to transmute himself into an entire world of characters, none of them conventional and all of them complex. In the course of the action he was by turns (one could almost swear simultaneously, and this may, indeed, have been in large measure the *clef* of his achievement) an existentialist high-school junior, a "bop" xylophonist, a sentimental police sergeant, a sort of philosophy professor, a myopic anthropologist, Raskolnikov's ghost, and the oldest sadist in Rogers Park. Baroque made impressively little use of his body: "He seems," Máire Ní Laoghaire told me, "somehow to do it all with his skin." Did Baroque betray the sense of plight? There was no time for me to ascertain an answer to this question.

It may, very possibly, have been a greater tragedy for the Chicago stage, and for our decomposing culture in general, than we yet realize, when (two days after my visit, as it happened) the theatre suddenly caved in, and Baroque (with his entire company), three bourgeois couples, a sodden débutante and her elderly lover, innumerable rats, and the balconyful of students were plunged four flights into a flooded basement. All of them were crushed to death, or drowned. I cannot (it seems to me) escape the conviction that this incident was a further token of the city's fate—perhaps (though, of course, by no means certainly) more momentous than most.

Jeremy Irk, staggered as he was by this occurrence, has not yet been able to complete his poem about it. But I was fortunate enough to inspect several fragments of the work in progress before they (together with Bernard Mosher's discussion of them) were shipped off to Buffalo, and I am privileged to announce that Irk's work is quite *indicible*. I had, of course, hoped to persuade Jeremy to allow their publication with this letter, but he refused with the tired, broken smile which he had learned so well from Jens Kobold's portrait of him.

"It's too late," he said, although I had pointed out to him that publication of his fragments might be one means of leading the city out of its plight.

"Too late . . . too late," he continued. (These words cling to one like lint in the Chicago of the mid-twentieth century.) "It is too late for too many things. Too late for Máire's film on

Bernard Mosher. Too late for Gina's ballet, though the slippers have already been ordered. Too late for Erma Chutney's novel about our common predicament. It is too late for Roscoe Chutney's study of Hjalmar as critic, and for Hjalmar's monograph on Jens's lithographs. It is too late for George Barnwell to take issue with Roscoe. It is too late for Jens's note, with sketches, on Gina's choreography. It is, of course, much too late for Bernard's book on Máire. Like an arthritic juggler, one feels no longer able to keep the balls in the air. It is just too late."

I shall, perhaps, let these words of Jeremy's stand in this letter as a kind of epiphany, in the various senses of the word.

*   *   *

> *"On dit qu'un prompt départ vous éloigne de nous, Seigneur."*
>
> —RACINE

Tonight I propose to quit this crumbling city. I have just observed in the *Official Railway Guide* that the International Limited on the Grand Trunk leaves for Halifax at 8 p.m. But my copy of the *Guide* is dated November, 1944, and belongs, thus, one suspects, to another world. The time may be wrong. Perhaps this train has been cancelled. Perhaps the timetable of the Grand Trunk has achieved (at last) a fresh and more telling synthesis. Yet, if not this train, then another.

I shall not tell Máire, who has expressed a desire (which it would not [all things considered] be improper to call insistent) to go with me when I go. It might be rather amusing to show her the bleak old city on its crags, to introduce her to the *avant garde* of Nova Scotia. But I cannot risk carrying any part of Chicago with me: I take it that my Halifax Letter must concern itself with Halifax *as* Halifax.

Perhaps there too I shall encounter a sense of plight. Perhaps it is not limited to Chicago or to Halifax. One wonders about these things as one packs, looking out of one's window at the slaty April sky of Chicago, at the lethargic gulls sagging listlessly towards the bruise-colored lake. One wonders. But one cannot, of course, be quite sure.

W. B. SCOTT

Gaëtan Fignole: Pages de Journal

I. *Introduction*

THE DISPATCH was laconic, the names not unpredictably askew. A newspaper somewhere—in Pittsburgh, or in Omaha—ran it under the head, YAWL IN SQUALL—DIES. It read: "FREJUS, France, July 25—Gaston [*sic*] *Fegnoule* [*sic*], French author and writer, drowned early today when his yawl the Alphonsine II foundered in a sudden squall off this port. The body was recovered towards evening, somewhat damaged by sharks."

One doubts whether many readers of the two or three American papers which bothered to publish the "item" really stopped to wonder who this "Gaston Fegnoule" might be: after all, the country was obsessed at the time with, possibly, Rita Hayworth. It was a hot summer too, and then, the races were tight in both major leagues. As for Gaëtan Fignole himself, he would have been less surprised than indulgent at the stupendous indifference which greeted his passing.

For indeed, taking one consideration with another, few contemporary authors have enjoyed so striking an obscurity as Gaëtan Fignole, although few have at the same time summed up more richly the varied elements of that tradition which has made France securely French. He was, to be sure, not a prolific writer as these things go in a country where the artist is still loved and respected and honored and made much of [1] rather than shunned, alienated, relegated to signing autographs for clubwomen in department-store book sections: his pre-post-humous publications included a scant four novels, none of them conspicuously cyclical; eight rather casual plays; two small volumes of critical essays; an inconclusive sheaf of verses; a collection of maxims jotted down during a voyage to Marrakesh

---

[1] Someone, Professor Peyre or Professor Fowlie, or someone, has pointed out that "the recent death in Paris of Paul Valéry, in July 1945, became an event of national significance."

in 1919; a few dozen almost slapdash *comptes-rendus;* translations of three cantos from a minor Bulgarian epic[2]; and the customary esthetic of the cinema. Of these works only one—the short novel Rongée (*A Woman Gnawed*)—has appeared in translation on this side of the Atlantic, where it attracted restrained enthusiasm in the limited circle of readers who care for that sort of writing.

Fignole lived by choice in a decidedly unfashionable quarter of Paris, not easily accessible to the trifling body of admirers who turned up now and then to pay him homage; on rare occasions he was to be seen at the Café Bled, usually at the cracked table in the murky corner. Of the very few published accounts of his appearance and manner, the most dependable may after all be Edouard Lorenzo's:

> Fignole is rather brown-haired, if anything, with pale blueish eyes which appear to reject the light. Dressed invariably in an ancient mustard-colored tweed jacket and unpressed grey flannel trousers, and never without a pipe which he is forever lighting and letting go out and lighting again and letting go out again, he suggests rather some British younger son who has gone in for breeding pigs, or perhaps an American professor—of English, or philosophy—than the unknown yet all the same illustrious Frenchman of letters that in fact he is. It is in his handling of the pipe especially that he recalls the American professor, as he chews it in grave and silent detachment until "the moment of truth" [3] arrives when, thrusting its stem like a dagger under the noses of the chatterers, he finally cuts the metaphysical knot in which everyone else is all tied up.[4]

Over the years Fignole was at one time or another a symbolist, a fourierist, a dadaist, an existentialist, a neo-existentialist, a

[2] Fignole learned Bulgarian while still a student at the Lycée Landru in Toulouse ("the Harvard of Toulouse"), at a time when the study of that language had not yet become fashionable. In later years he sometimes wryly remarked, "If I had known it would be a bandwagon, I would never have jumped on it."

[3] A term derived, one imagines, from the tragic ritual of the bullfight.

[4] Edouard Lorenzo, in a paper first read over transatlantic telephone to the Great Lakes local, Modern Language Association of America, at their annual Balzac's Birthday picnic (Petoskey, 1934).

jusquauboutist, a royalist, a surrealist, a jemenfoutist, an anarchist, and a legumist, and while not notably devout he had for
more than thirty years never failed to attend Easter Mass,
usually two or three pews behind François Mauriac. He was in
his quiet and rather snobbish way the friend and confidant of
most of the great names of his time in France, although we may
I think take with a grain of salt Professor Ratchet's overbold
assertion that he was Proust's model for Zosime de Perpignan.[5]

It was as a *lycéen*, or perhaps earlier, that Fignole began to
keep the diary in which for the rest of his life (and in the style to
which Edouard Lorenzo has referred as "tellement quotidien!")
he was to record his day-by-day activities, his conversations with
various personages, and his reflections on the arts and the world.
From time to time over a period of forty or fifty years brief excerpts from this diary have appeared in French reviews, but
Fignole with firm modesty refused to allow the publication during
his lifetime of the entire *journal*. "*C'est un rien*" ("It is a
nothing") or "*Ça sera pour la postérité*" ("That will be for
posterity") was his invariable response to publishers who urged
him to what they described as a patriotic duty. "*Qu'un français
ne veut pas faire publier son journal, voilà une infamie!*" ("That
a Frenchman does not wish to have his diary published, that is an
infamy!") a certain distinguished *éditeur* once angrily exclaimed.
But Fignole was not to be shaken, and beyond an occasional duel
from which he invariably emerged the victor, he paid little
attention to insults or innuendoes, other than occasionally (in
this or that novel or play or *compte rendu*) to portray his critics
in rather grotesque attitudes.

---

[5] W. W. Ratchet, *A Glance at Wordsworth with Some Divagations on
Proust*, 483. The passage in Proust may be worth citing here: "It was in the
course of that same night through which I stood silent and shivering, knee-
deep in an icy puddle, listening to the voices in the garage—a night from the
consequences of which I was to suffer for many years to come—that I became aware, as one becomes aware of these things at such moments and
under such circumstances, that the other voice in the garage, the voice which
was not Odette's, was not the voice of Swann, but another voice which I
would not for several years, and then only by chance and in the course of
a masked ball to which I had been reluctantly invited by Madame de
Verdurin, recognize as the harsh, imperious, yet somewhat fruity voice of
Zosime de Perpignan."

Since his death, however, extensive passages from Fignole's diary have been appearing in *Les Temps Horveux,* and quite recently has come the announcement that the complete work will soon be issued in sixteen large quarto volumes. One awaits impatiently this intricate record of French literary life, from Zénaïde Fleuriot (who was among other things Fignole's godmother) to the quite youthful Ambroise Tocard, whose poems one critic[6] has called "the warped faces of a clamorous tomorrow."

We are greatly privileged to be able to reproduce here, through the generous permission of M. Claude Fignole, brother and literary executor of the writer, a few *pages de journal* which may be of special interest to American readers. The contribution of French critics over the past century and a quarter or century and a half to a sounder understanding by Americans of their own literature is, of course, at this late date incontestable: we cannot overlook or forget Baudelaire on Poe, Jean Giono on Melville, the elder Marius Broussaille on Fitz-Greene Halleck, the younger Dumas on the Connecticut Wits, Zola on Emily Dickinson, Gide and Sartre on Faulkner, Henri-Marie Frip on Clyde Fitch, Bernard Fay on Franklin, Asmodée Cagoule on the Southern School, and others.[7] Fignole's place in this company is not an entirely spectacular one, nor would he have wished it to be: his knowledge of English was in some respects limited, and his indifference to it considerable. But the observations embedded in the following pages, scattered and casual as they may be, remind us once more and with particular force of the justice of Harrison Fenwick's observation: "A Frenchman is at every moment of his life a critic, in one sense or another, so to speak." [8]

[6] J. Lyndon Dasher, in *Unacceptable Essays.*

[7] To this list might be added, for example, André Levinson's description of Thornton Wilder, recently quoted in *The Saturday Review of Literature,* as "that rare avis, someone writing in English and who possesses the Latin sense of form."

[8] This remark of Fenwick's was first overheard by the author of these notes in the club car of the Advance Commodore Vanderbilt; again during an intermission of *La Tosca* in Saint Louis; and yet again in the tourist lounge of the S.S. Standish J. O'Grady during a moonlight cruise on the Bay of Fundy. It is here printed for the first time, with the kind permission of Dr. Fenwick.

We regret exceedingly that considerations of space forbid our reproducing all the excerpts in the original, for the benefit of those readers who prefer to get at the language of Bossuet and Céline directly, rather than through the (at best) fogging and distorting medium of a translation. But we are happy to be able to print in French as well as in English at least the first of the entries with which we are here concerned.

II. *Pages de Journal*

21 Mai, Paris. Levé trop tard. Déjeuné à la maison. Décidé que, somme toute, n'aime pas les buîtres frites. Trouvé une molaire qui branle. Sale temps. Alphonsine[9] a téléphoné, son mari a évidemment escamoté la caisse encore une fois. Quel salaud! Mais heureusement il y a toujours l'assurance contre les vols. Relu Polyeucte. *Un pneu[matique] de Gide, qui me demande l'emprunt de mon smoking. Passé l'après-midi tout seul au Jardin des Plantes. Les singes, ressemblent-ils plus aux hommes que les hommes aux singes? Question assez singulière et que l'on ne saurait résoudre comme ça! Trouvé abandonné sur un banc du J. des P. un livre, que j'ai rapporté. Soirée chez Montherlant, qui a raconté quelques histoires sur les taureaux. Avant de me coucher relu* Le Neveu de Rameau. *Observé vers une heure du matin que la molaire branle toujours.*

May 21, Paris. Got up too late. Lunch at home. Decided that, all in all, do not like fried oysters. Found a loose molar. Dirty weather. Alphonsine[9] telephoned, her husband has evidently made off with the cash box again. What a rotter! But fortunately there is always the theft insurance. Re-read *Polyeucte.* A special delivery from Gide, who asks for the loan of my dinner jacket. Spent the afternoon alone at the Jardin des Plantes [a kind of zoo in Paris]. Do monkeys resemble men more than men do monkeys? Quite a singular question and which one could not

---

[9] Alphonsine Ploc was Fignole's mistress during the final decade and more of his life. The allusion here is to the small poultry business in which she and her husband, Auguste Ploc, had been set up by the writer. The irresponsible conduct of Auguste Ploc, frequently mentioned in the diary, was a constant source of torment and embarrassment and anguish and annoyance to Fignole.

376 Parodies: *An Anthology*

resolve like *that!* Found abandoned on a bench at the J. des P.
a book, which I brought home with me. The evening at Montherlant's, who told various stories about bulls. Before going to bed
re-read *Le Neveu de Rameau*. Noticed toward one a.m. that the
molar is still loose.

May 29, Paris. Up early. Bored. No word before noon from
Alphonsine, who yesterday received an abusive telegram from
A[uguste] P[loc] in Marseilles. Rainy all day and my cough is
worse. Hasty note from Gide, who has taken the dinner jacket
to Avignon. The molar still loose. Looked idly into the book I
found on the bench at the Jardin des Plantes. *"Nevada"* [10] by
Zane-Grey. In English I would think. Possibly American (noted
word "California"). Read one or two passages. Vast and brutal
landscapes. Possibly the subject for a *compte-rendu* is to be
found here. Alphonsine came to tea, much agitated. Re-read La
Fontaine's fables to her, but to no avail.

June 8, Paris. Telegram from Gide in Morocco, where he
thoughtlessly took the dinner jacket. Threatening letter from
Auguste. Lunch with the Archbishop, who spoke disapprovingly
of my ideas for a book on the monkeys at the Jardin des Plantes.
Re-read *La Princesse de Clèves*. What perfection! No change
in the looseness of the molar. Dinner with Mauriac, who did not
quite agree or disagree with the Archbishop. Alphonsine has disappeared [*Alphonsine disparue*] but think she has gone to
the country to bargain for guinea hens, for which the market is
looking up. This evening glanced again at the *"Nevada"* of

---

[10] Zane Grey's *"Nevada"* was first published in 1929 or sooner. It is the
story of Jim Lacy, known to his dearest friends, the brother and sister Ben
and Hettie Ide, by the nickname "Nevada," although Lacy is a Texan.
Ashamed of his violent past as one of the notorious gunmen of the early
West, and fearful lest his friends discover it, "Nevada" flees them and becomes a cowboy in Arizona. The Ide family, for reasons of their mother's
health, leave California for Arizona, where they buy a ranch and suffer
from the depredations of rustlers. Jim Lacy (under that name) cultivates the
rustlers and becomes known as one of them, but only in order to destroy
them. Near the end of the novel he kills the leading rustler, who has been a
sinister threat to the Ides, and only then is it revealed to the Ides that the
notorious Jim Lacy and their old friend "Nevada" are the same person. The
work ends with "Nevada" gazing at the sunset glow upon the rapt face of
Hettie Ide.

Zane-Grey, and found myself inescapably seized by it. Who is this Z-G? A man? A woman? An American, in any event [*en tous cas*], I am sure by now. Telephoned Sartre, perhaps he would know, but he is out of town and his butler refuses to say where. All the same, what vigor! what pervasive brutality! Evidently the new world has some things to say about death! Wonder if *Les Temps Morveux* would take an article? Has Z-G written other works? [11] Haunted by this question and by the molar fell asleep while re-reading *Britannicus.*

June 11, Nice. Arrived Nice this morning with Alphonsine, who insists that I help her arrange the release from jail of A.P. Midi enormously lovely! Auguste surly and insolent on our visit to the jail. Gide answered by wire from Suez that he has never heard of Z-G; fear he suspects my question was simply to cover anxiety about the dinner jacket. Still haunted by the Zane-Grey, which I brought with me on the train. Thoughts of it intruded incessantly upon my re-reading of Pascal. One suspects that in this strange work the American character has found a shatteringly precise statement. Ah, these savage puritans! Fear I shall not sleep well tonight, the molar quiet, but Z-G plagues me and Alphonsine has the sniffles.

June 17, Nice. Still at Nice. Encountered Cocteau on the beach this morning, we discussed Zane-Grey whom he too had not read or heard of. A.P. still in jail, but Alphonsine has not given up hope. Read in *Eclaireur du Soir* that Gide is journeying to the headwaters of the Nile! Obsessed by this strange American work of Zane-Grey, so monstrous in its fashion, so frightening! Have these people souls as we understand souls in our old Europe? Have not been able to complete my re-reading of *Les Lettres Persanes.* In Z-G's fable of cowboys and criminals what horrors are not apparent! One recalls, somehow, Aeschylus, at any rate nothing French [*rien de français*]. Must remember that Cocteau told me "nevada" means in Spanish "snowy." Thus one senses the frigid purity to which the new world pretends! But what splendors of style, though one hardly knows whether

[11] Other works by Zane Grey are *Riders of the Purple Sage, Heritage of the Desert,* and *Ken Ward in the Jungle.*

to call it prose. Dreamed last night that the monkeys of the J. des Plantes had somehow changed places with the curious figures of Z-G. My nightmare woke Alphonsine, who sobbed until morning. Molar seemed less loose today.

June 27, Paris. Alphonsine and Auguste once more together at the poultry shop and order finally restored! [*tout est rentré enfin dans l'ordre!*] Our good French order [*notre bon ordre français*] of which there is little trace in Zane-Grey. But what a devil of a job getting Auguste out of that jail in Nice; fortunately the police superintendent was, like me, a godson of Zénaïde Fleuriot. The molar turned slightly in its socket about noon. After lunch to the Café Bled for a few hours, where I overheard several young Americans who seemed to be chattering about the problem of evil and the tragic sense of life. Ventured to ask their opinion of Zane-Grey, but perhaps their English was not clear to me, or my French to them. But what a country is theirs, all the same! evidently it is true that there [*là-bas*] one despises and ignores the man of letters!

July 3, Paris. Wakened by telephone call from Alphonsine, who told me joyously that yesterday's receipts had exceeded all previous ones! How happy I was for her and for all of us who have engaged ourselves in this poultry business. While lunching wrote Gide as follows:

Cher collègue,

Forgive, I beg of you, dear and much esteemed colleague, my writing to you about matters of the utmost unimportance, when you are at this very moment, perhaps, contemplating in an ecstasy which it would be a sacrilege to venture to imagine, the superb panoramas of the Blue Nile. I hasten to reassure you, admired master, as I am confident that you will hasten to be reassured, that my letter is not on account of the dinner jacket, which is yours to wear as long as you like. I shall not need it in any event before the reception at the Elysée on the 9th of October. It is sufficient honor and reward for me that you, free to choose any dinner jacket in Paris, have chosen to choose mine!

I regret very much that you do not know the American writer, Zane-Grey, whom I mentioned in my unfortunate telegram of some weeks past. One talks often in Paris of the formidable literature which the America of these days produces and of its effects on the young [*les jeunes*], and I have too long neglected it, I confess. But I am desolated to discover that no one, *no one!* is familiar with the work of this extraordinary genius who, masking his deepest thoughts with crude images of the "Far-West," exposes a surpassing awareness of the hopeless and despairing violence of the new world, its feverish concern with sexual purity and its almost sexual concern with sudden death! The hero "Nevada" (of whom the true name is Jimm Lacy) I see as someone much resembling an American Orestes, haunted by an anglo-saxon sense of guilt which drives him at once away from and ineluctably towards the young lady, so ominously chaste, his ideal beauty, and who is named Hettie Ide.

And imagine [*figure-toi*] a work in which the hero and his friend refer to each other with casual callousness as "old panther"! [12]

I had hoped, my old one, that you might lead me to other works of this writer of whom, apparently, no one has heard. But I am happy to be able to introduce you to this volume, so sinister, even menacing [*menaçant*], and which suggests in its own fashion the gulf between this Europe and that America.

Again, I beg of you, give yourself no concern about the dinner jacket; if I should like to have it back, it is rather for reasons of tradition (my father wore it as assistant mayor of Toulouse!) than on account of the cost. I would write at greater length but am bothered by a loose molar which makes composition difficult. Alphonsine is of the happiest, and would, I know, insist on being remembered to you. The poultry business is flourishing, there are regular orders now from three embassies! and the profits exceed all expectations. Our old France will find a way out, eh? [*Notre vielle France se débrouillera, hein?*]

Ever thine, Ga-Ga [*Toujours à toi, Ga-Ga*] [13]

July 19, Paris. At last have finished the *"Nevada"* of Zane-Grey! What an experience, almost an ordeal! One recalls Dante! But

[12] Fignole's occasional uncertainty with English betrays him here: evidently he is referring to the frequent use in *"Nevada"* of "pard" or "old pard" (in the sense of "pal" or "chum"). The older sense of "pard" ("leopard," "panther") was almost certainly not intended by Zane Grey, but Fignole may not have had access to Harrap's large English-French dictionary, in which botn senses are given.

[13] "Ga-Ga" (from "Gaëtan," presumably) was Fignole's nickname among his friends.

this happy ending, so profoundly cynical, so striking a comment
on the gelid ideal of the puritan! What influence it will have
on my own future work I cannot say now. Perhaps I shall ask
Camus to predict this influence in an article, perhaps I shall
predict it myself in the interview which I have promised
M. Edouard Lorenzo. Attempted at lunch to re-read *Bérénice,* but
Racine savorless [*sans saveur*] and very 17th-century after Z-G.
Auguste has once more made off with the cash! A violent scene
with the theft insurance people; I was shaken for hours afterwards! It is their sort of scepticism and lack of faith which may
wreck us all! Alphonsine crushed again. Sartre still out of town.
Mauriac abruptly changed the subject when I mentioned Z-G
at lunch yesterday. How melancholy I feel! The molar has flared
up again. Have decided to escape it all for a few days' sailing.

July 22, Toulouse. Once more in my own country! [*dans mon
pays à moi!*] But in Paris a heartrending departure from Alphonsine, who wished me to go with her to Antwerp where Auguste
is now in jail. Told her of my arrangements to revisit Toulouse,
to go sailing, but she accused me of denying the fact that I
exist, of fearing to engage myself, to involve my destiny with
the destiny of all men. Haunted on the train by these words of
hers! Can I be yielding thus to the influence of "Nevada," who
also attempted to run away from his existence? What fate awaits
me as I sail from Toulouse to Fréjus? Took water and seabiscuit
aboard Alphonsine II this afternoon. Weigh anchor tomorrow
dawn. Brought with me two books: the *"Nevada"* of Zane-
Grey and the *Oresteia* of Aeschylus, works so remote from each
other in time and place, one Greek, one American (of which the
Greeks would have had no idea!), one ancient, one modern.
Yet who is to say that they are entirely different? Deposited
my will with a notary of Toulouse. Have left dinner jacket to
Gide, a quarter-share of the poultry profits to Athalie.[14]

July 24, on board Alphonsine II. Weather clear, with slight
quartering wind. How peaceful is the immensity of sea and sky,
how immense their peace! Tied the tiller down all morning to

[14] Fignole's wife.

busy myself with the diary and with thoughts of this dear Zane-Grey [*ce cher Zane-Grey*]. That dratted molar [*cette foutue molaire*] lost overboard during the night: must one see this as an omen? Thought of Alphonsine alone in Antwerp. Mild sunstroke about noon. Towards dusk found a lamprey in the scuppers, and with the addition of candle-drippings and barnacles achieved a magnificent *bouillabaisse* over the spirit lamp. One is not French for nothing! [*On n'est pas français pour des prunes!*][15] Superb sunset! Reading Aeschylus and Zane-Grey alternately as the light failed. Curious dream last night: a new arrangement of counters in the poultry shop. Must write Alphonsine.

July 25, on board Alphonsine II. Landfall shortly past sunrise. Will there be word at Fréjus from Alphonsine? from Sartre? from Gide? from Mauriac? from Montherlant? from Camus? from Cocteau? One cannot say. During night a book took shape in my mind, Zane-Greyish, perhaps, but, of course, French to the bottom [*Zane-Greyesque, peut-être, mais, bien entendu, français au fond.*] Wonder whether it would be quite wise, after all, to tell Sartre about Z-G before I have finished my own novel? Possibly not. A slight rash from the lamprey, but this was to be expected. Wind freshening. Could "Nevada" have found in his Arizona views of sea and sky so magnificent as these? One is led to reflect on the nature of space. Must tell Picasso. Dull throbbing in the empty molar socket. Fréjus now off the port bow. My article (to be published before the novel) will begin somewhat as follows: (title) *Ce qu'on trouve chez Zane-Grey: réflexions sur l'Amérique de nos jours, ou le roman "convulsif."* [*What is found in Zane Grey: reflections on the America of our time, or the "convulsive" novel.*] (first paragraph) In reading Zane-Grey, an American author less well known among us [*chez nous*] than he deserves to be, one is to begin with forced to consider. . . .

[This is the final entry in Fignole's diary. Following the last words printed here, the handwriting becomes indistinguishable,

---

[15] According to a widespread Toulouse legend, Fignole's grandfather was the inventor of *sauce fignolade*.

degenerates into meaningless squiggles. One can only assume that Fignole "went down writing," as it were, stubbornly intent, in the very teeth of the squall which destroyed him, on completing the sentence in which at this, the ultimate moment of his life, he had become involved. The inexpensive notebook in which he kept his *journal* was still grasped tightly in one hand when his shark-mauled body was retrieved, a pencil stamped "A. Ploc & Cie., Volailles de Marque" in the other.[16] His interlinear edition of the *Oresteia* turned up, badly waterlogged, in the foundered hulk of the yawl. But there was no trace of *"Nevada."* One supposes that it sank slowly to the bottom of the sea, or that it was washed ashore, perhaps, in some deserted cove or sparcely-settled inlet of that ancient rocky coast, there to be found by a simple sailor or peasant or fisherman to whom its underlinings, its marginal comments, its very language would be quite meaningless!]

CYRIL CONNOLLY

THE FIRST of the following two pieces from Cyril Connolly's *The Condemned Playground* is included because it is amusing. It was written in 1940 when military commentators were still listened to seriously. The second is not amusing. Published in 1938, *Year Nine* is a curious anticipation of Orwell's *1984*. There is the future anti-utopia along Communist lines, the doublethink and newspeak, the victim's sincere conviction of the benevolence of his torturers. In fact, in some ways, I prefer this earlier, capsule version of *1984*. The torture, for instance, that Orwell lingers over to the point of sado-masochistic obsession here gets its satiric value and no more: "Our justice is swift; our trials are fair; hardly was the preliminary bone-breaking over than my case came up. . . . My silly old legs were no use to me now and I was allowed the privilege of wheeling myself in on a kind of invalid's chair."

[16] These facts were mentioned with great tact and eloquence by Asmodée Cagoule in the funeral oration which he pronounced before the relatively tiny crowd which followed Fignole's coffin to its last resting-place in the old cemetery of the family parish of Sainte Agrippine at Toulouse. Fignole's death occurred soon enough for this oration to find a place in Cagoule's recently-published *Oraisons Funèbres Diverses* (*Sundry Funeral Orations*), under the title *"A la revoyure, brave Fignole"* (Farewell, worthy Fignole").

Orwell probably read *Year Nine;* it would be interesting to know if he was influenced by it.

What Will He Do Next?

BY REAR-COLONEL CONNOLLY

A S FAR BACK as 1873 I was advocating a small highly mecha-
nized striking force to be employed in "expanding torrent"
tactics, i.e. "deep infiltration." The War Office paid no attention. Clausewitz did. "Dear Captain Connolly," he wrote,
"I have read *The Lesson of Omdurman* with interest, and
was most impressed by your definition of Peace." [Peace, I
had written, is a morbid condition, due to a surplus of civilians,
which war seeks to remedy.] In my *Lesson of Norway* (April
1940), *Lesson of the Bulge* (May 1940), and *Lesson of Britain* (in
preparation), as well as in this series of fifteen articles, I have
consistently advocated the same principles. "A defensive force,"
I wrote in 1884, "should be in a certain ratio to an offensive
force, depending on (*a*) the size of the offensive force, (*b*) its
striking power." For that force to become an offensive-defensive
force the ratio will have to be considerably higher. How can I
explain this to the non-military mind? I think it can best be expressed by a formula. Invasion = The incidence of men and
material on hostile or unfriendly territory where that incidence is
of sufficient impact to do permanent or semi-permanent damage
to military objectives. Thus incidence of material without man-
power (air-raids) or of man-power without material (parachut-
ists) do not in themselves constitute invasion. Will, in this sense,
an invasion be forthcoming? Certain it is that some such step has
been contemplated. We can, in fact, state the problem as
follows:

(1) Will Hitler invade us?

(2) Will that invasion be successful?

(3) If not, will some counter-move be made in the Mediterranean or the Far East?

(4) Or will both (1) and (3) or some variation of them be
attempted?

To all these questions we may answer, categorically, yes and no. What we can be certain of is that the attack, when it does come, will attempt to take us by surprise, either in the time chosen, or the place, or the means, and that in any eventuality I shall be ready with my article. A study of the map will reveal that the situation, if not grave, is at least critical. Nevertheless it must constantly be pounded out to the lay mind that (1) for every tactical danger there is a strategical *quid pro quo*. (2) 'Retreat is an advance in a reverse direction.'[1] As I understand the position, and taking into account what we know of Hitler's previous moves and what may be termed his psycho-strategical make-up, there will be an element of bluff. Thus either the main attack is on these islands (England, Ireland, Iceland, etc.) or elsewhere— it is no good, if it is elsewhere, keeping all our forces at home, it is no good sending them elsewhere if it is here.

Which of these alternatives will be adopted? Which will be, if adopted, feints? The answer is that, since a feint will hardly follow the main attack, *the first offensive* in point of time will be a feint and destined, if here, to prevent our troops being sent elsewhere; if elsewhere, to get them away from here. Should the offensives open simultaneously, a further elucidation, in a new series of articles, will be necessary. What can be told now by those of us whose training enables us to dominate military events is that, should Hitler invade us at a moment when thick fog, high tides, and bright moonlight are in conjunction (and these moments only occur once in three weeks), he would meet with very serious difficulties, which only the possession of new "secret weapons" would enable him to surmount. Such weapons as he is known to possess, an undetectable new gas which puts us all to sleep for a fortnight, after which we wake up raving mad, an artificial fog of enormous dimensions, a channel tunnel, a fleet of *stationary* planes, and a key to the Great Pyramid, are sufficient to produce total annihilation, but that would hardly amount to annexation in a military sense. As a fellow strategist remarks in his book, printed as long ago as 1939:

[1] Fabius Cunctator, *Manual.*

"The war was born under strange stars . . . it will end suddenly: and the manner of its ending will prove for all time the vanity of human anticipations. . . . It will be a very short war or last for longer than the three years visualized by politicians. . . . It started with the invasion of Poland, and it will finish with the invasion of some other country after a decisive sea-action. The frontier of no country in Europe can be regarded as safe." (R. H. Naylor, *What the Stars Foretell for 1940*, Hutchinson, 3s. 6d.)

Meanwhile there are three questions, arising out of invasion, which I am constantly asked, and which I will now reply to:

1. *How to stop a tank.*

Most of you who have had no experience of stopping tanks will have had some of shooting elephants. A tank is simply an armoured elephant. In every group of tanks there is a leading tank, whose signals are obeyed by the others; if the leading tank is trapped, the others will "come quietly." The best elephant trap was a large pit over which branches were laid. For a tank trap it is only necessary to remove the paving stones outside your house (borrow a wheelbarrow from the man next door) and dig a pit some forty feet wide by twenty deep. Place a sheet of wire netting over the road, cover it with cardboard or brown paper, and a top dressing of asphalt. Your trap is made. If you are lucky enough to live near a blast-furnace, borrow some sheets of eleven-inch steel, solder them with a blower's lamp, and lean them up supported by a prop over the water-hole; when the tank comes down to drink, pull the prop away, or, if you are very close, insert a knitting-needle into the tank's most vulnerable spot, the back-ratchet. But remember, nothing will really stop a tank except another tank going in the opposite direction, and these should be left to the competent military authority.

2. *What further safety measures do you advise?*

The greatest danger to the military in war-time is the civilian, because he is not subject to military discipline; a moving civilian is even more dangerous—he is anarchy in two places at once. I therefore advocate a permanent day-time curfew and night-time lock-up for civilians, with an internal passport system for those whose deployment is essential. The internal passport would include reports on the civilian from his school, university, employer, and bank manager, and the visa to move about would be granted, if at all, by a military policeman.

' 3. What will He do next? For that I must refer you to my subsequent article: *Pros and Cons of Invasion.*

CYRIL CONNOLLY

Year Nine

AUGUR'S PRISON—YEAR IX. I have been treated with great kindness, with a consideration utterly out of keeping with the gravity of my offence, yet typical of the high conception of justice implicit in our state. Justice in sentence, celerity in execution in the words of Our Leader. Excuse my fatal impediment. I call attention to it, as eagerly as in Tintoretto's plague hospital they point to bleeding bubos on the legs and shoulders. Let me tell you how it all happened. With a friend, a young woman, I arranged to spend last Leaderday evening. We met under the clock outside the Youngleaderboys building. Having some minutes to spare before the Commonmeal and because it was raining slightly, we took shelter in the glorious Artshouse. There were the ineffable misterpasses of our glorious culture, the pastermieces of titalitorian tra, the magnificent Leadersequence, the superstatues of Comradeship, Blatherhood, and Botherly Love, the 73 Martyrs of the Defence of the Bourse, the Leader as a simple special constable. There they were, so familiar that my sinful feet were doubly to be blamed for straying—for they strayed not only beyond the radius of divine beauty but beyond the sphere of ever-loving Authority, creeping with their putrid freight down the stairs to the forgotten basement. There, breeding filth in the filth that gravitates around it, glows the stagnant rottenness called Degenerate Art, though only perfect Leadercourtesy could bestow the term Art on such Degeneration! There are the vile pustules of the rotting Demos,

on canvases his sores have hideously excoriated. Still Lives—as if
life could be ever still! Plates of food, bowls of fruit; under the
old regime the last deplorable nightdreams and imaginations of
starving millions, the prurient lucubrations of the unsterilized—
bathing coves of womblike obscenity, phallic church towers and
monoliths, lighthouses and pyramids, trees even painted singly
in their stark suggestiveness, instead of in the official groups;
all hideous and perverted symbols of an age of private love,
ignorant of the harmony of our Commonmeals, and the State administration of Sheepthinkers Groupbegettingday. There were
illicit couples, depicted in *articulo amoris,* women who had
never heard of the three K's, whose so-called clothes were
gaudy dishrags, whose mouths were painted offal. Engrossed
in disgust and mental anguish I thoughtlessly began to mark on
my official catalogue the names of the most detestable fartists.
This was partly to hold them up to ridicule at Commonmeals,
partly to use in articles which would refute the pseudocriticism
of our enemies, but above all unconsciously—a tic expressive
of my odious habit, for *I only chose names that were easily or
interestingly reversible.* That is my only justification. Nacnud
Tnarg; Sutsugua Nhoj; Ossacip. Repip. The filthy anti-Fascists
who dared to oppose our glorious fishynazists! Hurriedly we
made for the clean outdoors, the welcoming statues of the
great upstairs, and outside where the supreme spectae streams
on the filament—the neon Leaderface. In my haste I dropped my
catalog by the turnstyle. The rest of the evening passed as usual.
We attended Commonmeal in seats 7111037 and 7111038 respectively, and after the digestive drill and the documentaries went
to our dormitories. The young woman on departing blew me a
kiss and I called out merrily yet admonishingly: "None of that
stuff, 7111038, otherwise we shall never be allowed to produce a
little 7111037-8. ♂ on Groupbegettingday."

During the next week nothing happened. But some four days
after that, having occasion to telephone the young woman, and
while speaking to her in a spirit of party badinage, I was
astounded to hear a playful repartee of mine answered by a
male eructation. "Was that you?" I said—but no answer
came. On picking up the receiver again to ask the janitor for

ten minutes' extra light, I heard—above the ringing noise—
for he had not yet answered—an impatient yawn. These two
noises made an enormous impression, for I realized that I was
an object of attention (although unwelcome attention) to a
member of a class far above my own, a superior with the broad
chest and masculine virility of a Stoop Trauma!

The next morning my paper bore the dreaded headline,
"Who are the Censors Looking for?" At the office we were
lined up at 10.10 and some officials from the censor's department, in their camouflaged uniforms, carrying the white-hot
Tongs, symbol of Truth, the Thumbcaps of Enquiry, and the
Head on the Dish, emblem of Justice, passed down the line.
As the hot breath of the tongs approached, many of us confessed
involuntarily to grave peccadilloes. A man on my left screamed
that he had stayed too long in the lavatory. But the glorious
department disdained force. We were each given three photographs to consider, and told to arrange them in order of aesthetic merit. The first was a reproduction of a steel helmet,
the second of a sack of potatoes, the third of some couples with
their arms round their necks in an attitude of illicit sexual group-
activity. I arranged them in that order. One of the inspectors
looked for a long time at me. We were then asked to write down
the names of any infamous poets or painters we could remember
from the old regime. "Badshaw, Deadwells, Staleworthy, Bald-
pole," I wrote. Then, in an emotion, a veritable paroxysm
stronger than me, with the eyes of the examiner upon me, my
hands bearing the pen downwards as ineluctably as the State di-
viner bears down on his twig, I added: "Toilet, Red Neps." And
once more: "Nacnud Tnarg, Sutsugua Nhoj, Ossacip. *Jewlysses.
Winagains Fake.*" The censors this time did not look at me, but
passing down the line made an ever more and more perfunctory
examination, towards the end simply gathering the papers from
the willing outstretched hands of the workers and carelessly tearing them up. They then swept out of the room, escorted by the
foreman, the political and industrial commissars of our office, and
Mr. Abject, the Ownerslave. We were instructed to continue our
duties. As the envelopes came by on the belt I seized them with
trembling hand, and vainly tried to perform my task as if nothing

had happened. It was my business to lick the top flap of the envelope, whose bottom flap would then be licked by my neighbour,
the one beyond him sticking the flaps together—for all sponges
and rollers were needed for munitions. At the same time I used
my free hand to inscribe on the corner of the envelope my contribution to the address (for all envelopes were addressed to the
censor's headquarters) the letters S.W.3. Alas how many illegible
S.W.3's that morning betrayed my trepidation, and when I
came to licking the outer flap my tongue was either so parched
by terror as to be unable to wet the corner at all, or so drowned
in nervous salivation as to spread small bubbles of spittle over the
whole surface, causing the flap to curl upwards and producing
in my near neighbours many a sign of their indignant impatience
and true party horror of bad work. Shortly before leaderbreak
the commissars, followed by Mr. Abject, returned down the line.
My companions on the belt, now feeling that I manifested emotional abnormality, were doing everything to attract attention
to me by causing me to fail in my work, kicking me on the
ankles as they received my envelopes, and one of them, seizing a
ruler, made a vicious jab upwards with it as I was adding S.W.3,
causing acute agony to my public parts. As the commissars
came near me they began to joke, smiling across at my neighbours and grunting: "As long as you can spit, man, the State
will have a use for you," and "Don't try and find out where the
gum you lick comes from, my boyo." Friendly condescensions
which seemed designed to render more pregnant and miserable
the silence with which they came to me. At last, with a terrible
downward look, the commissar paused before me. The smile had
faded from his face, his eyes flashed lightning, his mouth was
thin as a backsight, his nose was a hairtrigger. Mr. Abject looked
at me with profound commiseration till he received a nudge
from the other commissar, and said in a loud voice: "This is your
man." I was marched out between them while the serried ranks
of my old beltmates sang the Leaderchorus and cried: "Show
mercy to us by showing no mercy to him, the dog and the
traitor." Outside the newsboys were screaming: "Long live the
Censor. Gumlicking wrecker discovered."
   Our justice is swift: our trials are fair: hardly was the pre-

liminary bone-breaking over than my case came up. I was tried by the secret censor's tribunal in a pitchdark circular room. My silly old legs were no use to me now and I was allowed the privilege of wheeling myself in on a kind of invalid's chair. In the darkness I could just see the aperture high up in the wall from whence I should be cross-examined, for it is part of our new justice that no prejudicial view is obtained of the personal forces at work between accused and accuser. The charge was read out and I was asked if I had anything to say. I explained the circumstances as I have related them to you, and made my defence. Since an early initiation accident I have never been considered sound of mind, hence my trick of reversing words—quite automatically and without the intention of seeking hidden and antinomian meanings, hence my subordinate position in the Spitshop. My action, I repeated, was purely involuntary. The voice of my chief witness-accuser-judge replied from the orifice:

"Involuntary! But don't you see, that makes it so much worse! For what we voluntarily do, voluntarily we may undo, but what we do not of our own free will, we lack the will to revoke. What sort of a person are you, whose feet carry you helplessly to the forbidden basement? Yet not forbidden, for that basement is an open trap. Poor flies walk down it as down the gummy sides of a pitcher plant; a metronome marks the time they spend there, a radioactive plate interprets the pulsations which those works inspire, a pulsemeter projects them on a luminous screen which is perpetually under observation in the censor's office. It was at once known that you were there and what you felt there. But instead of being followed to your Blokery in the normal way you eluded your pursuers by dropping your catalogue. They decided it was their duty to carry it immediately to the cipher department and thus allowed you to escape. Your crime is fivefold:

" 'That you of your own impulse visited the basement of degenerate art and were aesthetically stimulated thereby.'

" 'That you attempted to convince a young woman, 7111038, of the merit of the daubs you found there, thereby being guilty of treason—for Our Leader is a painter too, and thereby being guilty of the far worse sin of inciting to treason a member of the non-rational (and therefore not responsible for her actions) sex.'

" 'That you made notes on the daubs in question with a view to perverting your fellow-workers.'

" 'That you caused deliberate inconvenience to the board of censors, attempting to throw them off your trail, thus making improper use of them.'

" 'That you did not confess before your offence was notified, or even at the time of your examination.'

"The penalty, as you know, for all these crimes is death. But there has interceded on your behalf the young woman whose denunciation helped us to find you. To reward her we have commuted your crime to that of coprophagy—for that is what your bestial appreciation of the faeces of so-called democratic art amounts to. Your plea of involuntary compulsion forces me to proclaim the full sentence. For with such a subconscious libido there must surely be a cancerous ego! I therefore proclaim that you will be cut open by a qualified surgeon in the presence of the State Augur. You will be able to observe the operation, and if the Augur decides the entrails are favourable they will be put back. If not, not. You may congratulate yourself on being of more use to your leader in your end than your beginning. For on this augury an important decision on foreign policy will be taken. Annexation or Annihilation? Be worthy of your responsibility. Should the worst befall, you will be sent to the gumfactory, and part of you may even form the flap of an envelope which your successor on the belt, Miss 7111038, may lick! You lucky dog."

Yes, I have been treated with great kindness.

PAUL JENNINGS

FOR YEARS Paul Jennings has been contributing to the London *Observer* a humorous column called "Oddly Enough," which is looked for by certain readers the way F. P. A.'s "The Conning Tower" was looked for by certain readers thirty years ago. The first item below is from the issue of February 9, 1958. *Report on Resistentialism* is from a book called, oddly enough, *Oddly Enough* (Max Reinhardt, London, 1950). Like our own S. J. Perelman, Paul Jennings has what might be called a diffused parodic sense, that is, he parodies not so much individual authors as general styles of thinking and language.

The Boy's Got Talent

GENTLEMAN (31), wide knowledge ancient history, especially ancient Egypt, comparative religion, rationalism, very experienced public orator and lecturer, author of daring thesis on the origin of world civilisation, artist, fluent Spanish, many years commercial experience, seeks position where this unusual combination of talents could be used.—*The Times* PERSONAL COLUMN, Feb. 3.

W ELL, it's pure imagination of course, but the picture I have is this: When Lucas Pickering's young wife bore him their only child in 1927 there was plenty of head-shaking among their neighbours in the little grey weaving town of Bragdyke. Some of them resented the slight fair-haired girl whom this tall, solitary, deep-eyed man, apparently a confirmed bachelor at fifty-one, had unexpectedly brought back as his bride from a rationalist congress in London. Others, discovering that Elsie Pickering was not a London hussy but a quiet, shy girl ("Aye, a gradely lass to be wed to thon old atheist"), pitied her.

Most of the townspeople were used to the sight of Pickering on his stand outside the Corn Exchange every Saturday night, rain or fine, declaiming passionately from Herbert Spencer, Bradshaw or Ingersoll to a few curious bystanders or giggling adolescents. He was respected as a solid craftsman (after many years as a ring-doubler and two-end winder he was now overlooker in the cheese-winding department), and Lucas Pickering's credit was as good as the next man's. But undoubtedly he did not fit into the cheerful Bragdyke life of pub and club and the annual performance of *The Messiah*. "Happen it'll be a lonely life for the child" was the verdict.

In some ways this was true. But Herbert Renan Pickering, who grew up a slight though healthy boy, was adored by his father. Together the two would go for long walks on the moors. Gazing down at the town, from which the sound of church bells floated up, Lucas would exclaim "Eh, the daft fools, there they go, worshipping their gaseous vertebrate. That's what Haeckel called their God, lad, the gaseous vetebrate—but thou aren't listening."

"Oh yes, dad, I am," said Herbert, looking up with a start from his sketch-book. For it was clear the boy was an artist. A rich local lady (and church worker), Miss Thwaitethwaite of the Manor House, swallowing her dislike of Pickering, told him "that boy's got talent." With her generous help Herbert became an art student.

The exciting turmoil of post-war London was a fertilising influence on the dreamy eighteen-year-old from Bragdyke. He was particularly influenced by the History of Art classes given by kindly old Professor Tonkins, and spent many hours in the Egyptian Room at the British Museum, in a trance before the glories of this hieratic art. On holidays in Bragdyke he would try to explain to his father. "Well, dad, it depends what you mean by religion. Now when Amenhotep IV founded his religion of the sun . . ." But he loyally accompanied Lucas to rationalist meetings in the dales, himself becoming a very experienced public orator.

Suddenly there was tragedy. Lucas caught a chill at an open-air meeting and was dead within a week. Herbert abandoned his art studies and went into commerce to help his mother. He got a job with Jarkins, Clanger and Pobjoy, Importers and Exporters, hoping to be sent to their Cairo branch. But because of Middle Eastern politics he found himself a trainee in the Buenos Aires office of J.C.P. He tried hard, learning fluent Spanish, studying Company Law. But his heart was not in it, and one day his boss, Mr. McCluskey, a tough old South America hand who spent all his leisure drinking whisky in the English Club and had no time for artists, came unexpectedly into the office and found Herbert writing in a large exercise book. "Well, Mr. McCluskey, it's a kind of thesis on the origins of world civilisation. I . . ." The result was a blistering letter to Head Office, and, eventually, this advertisement.

Meanwhile, in the dark, rich, oak-panelled City offices of Wilbye, Morley and Bateson, Sherry Importers, Travers Morley, Old Etonian head of the firm, is saying angrily: "Can't we keep a manager on our *fonda* for six months? Here's a letter from that young puppy Henderson. He's resigned and goin' to be a *Jesuit,* if you please. Carter, before him, went off to learn bullfightin'. Can't understand why these young fellers get bowled over by Spain nowadays. I was there meself, turn of the century—enjoyed it, larked with the gels after the fiesta an' all that—but none of this rot about *hispanidad* and dignity. We want a chap immune to all that, philosophy of his own, able to talk to the Marquis— he's a dotty old scholar, mummies an' that in his castle, but our vineyards *are* on his land; a chap able to harangue the *obreros* in their own lingo if there's any trouble—but, above all, im- mune to all this Spanish-civilisation stuff—yes, Simpson, what is it?''

Well, you know what Simpson, the head clerk, is excitedly bringing in.

PAUL JENNINGS

Report on Resistentialism

IT IS the peculiar genius of the French to express their phil- osophical thought in aphorisms, sayings hard and tight as diamonds, each one the crystal centre of a whole con- stellation of ideas. Thus, the entire scheme of seventeenth- century intellectual rationalism may be said to branch out from that single, pregnant saying of Descartes, *cogito ergo sum*— I think, therefore I am. Resistentialism, the philosophy which has swept present-day France, runs true to this aphoristic form. Go into any of the little cafés or *horlogeries* on Paris' Left Bank (make sure the Seine is flowing *away* from you, otherwise you'll be on the Right Bank, where *no* one is *ever* seen) and sooner or later you will hear someone say, *"Les choses sont contre nous."*

"Things are against us." This is the nearest English transla- tion I can find for the basic concept of Resistentialism, the grim but enthralling philosophy now identified with be- spectacled, betrousered, two-eyed Pierre-Marie Ventre. In trans- ferring the dynamic of philosophy from man to a world of hostile Things, Ventre has achieved a major revolution of thought, to which he himself gave the name "Resistentialism." Things (*res*) resist (*résister*) man (*homme,* understood). Ventre makes a complete break with traditional philosophic method. Except for his German precursors, Freidegg and Heidansiecker, all previous thinkers from the Eleatics to Marx have allowed at least some legitimacy to human thought and effort. Some, like Hegel or Berkeley, go so far as to make man's thought the supreme reality. In the Resistentialist cosmology, that is now the intellectual rage of Paris, Ventre offers us a grand vision of the Universe as One Thing—the Ultimate Thing (*Dernière Chose*). And it is against us.

Two world wars have led to a general dissatisfaction with the traditional Western approach to cosmology, that of scientific domination. In Ventre's view, the World-Thing, to which he sometimes refers impartially as the Thing-World, opposes man's partial *stealing,* as it were, of consciousness—of his dividing it into the separate "minds" with which human history has made increasingly fatal attempts to create a separate world of men. Man's increase in this illusory domination over Things has been matched, *pari passu,* by the increasing hostility (and greater force) of the Things arrayed against him. Medieval man, for instance, had only a few actual Things to worry about—the lack of satisfactory illumination at night, the primitive hole in the roof blowing the smoke back and letting the rain in, and one or two other small Things like that. Modern, domesticated Western man has far more opportunities for battle-losing against Things —can-openers, collar-studs, chests of drawers, open manholes, shoelaces. . . .

Now that Ventre has done it for us, it is easy to see that the reaction against nineteenth-century idealism begun by Martin Freidegg and Martin Heidansiecker was bound eventually to coalesce with the findings of modern physics in a philosophical synthesis for our time. Since much stress has been laid on the "scientific" basis of Resistentialism, it will not be out of place here, before passing on to a more detailed outline of Ventre's thought, to give a brief account of those recent developments in physical science which have so blurred the line that separates it from metaphysics. It is an account which will surprise those whose acquaintance with Ventre is limited to reading reviews of his plays and who, therefore, are apt to think that Resistentialism is largely a matter of sitting inside a wet sack and moaning.

A convenient point of departure is provided by the famous Clark-Trimble experiments of 1935. Clark-Trimble was not primarily a physicist, and his great discovery of the Graduated Hostility of Things was made almost accidentally. During some research into the relation between periods of the day and human bad temper, Clark-Trimble, a leading Cambridge psychologist, came to the conclusion that low human dynamics in the early morning could not sufficiently explain the apparent hostility of Things at the breakfast table—the way honey gets between the fingers, the unfoldability of newspapers, etc. In the experiments which finally confirmed him in this view, and which he demonstrated before the Royal Society in London, Clark-Trimble arranged four hundred pieces of carpet in ascending degrees of quality, from coarse matting to priceless Chinese silk. Pieces of toast and marmalade, graded, weighed and measured, were then dropped on each piece of carpet, and the marmalade-downwards incidence was statistically analyzed. The toast fell right-side-up every time on the cheap carpet, except when the cheap carpet was screened from the rest (in which case the toast didn't know that Clark-Trimble had other and better carpets), and it fell marmalade-downwards every time on the Chinese silk. Most remarkable of all, the marmalade-downwards incidence for the intermediate grades was found to vary *exactly* with the quality of carpet.

The success of these experiments naturally switched Clark-Trimble's attention to further research on *resistentia,* a fact which was directly responsible for the tragic and sudden end to his career when he trod on a garden rake at the Cambridge School of Agronomy. In the meantime, Noys and Crangenbacker had been doing some notable work in America. Noys carried out literally thousands of experiments, in which subjects of all ages and sexes, sitting in chairs of every conceivable kind, dropped various kinds of pencils. In only three cases did the pencil come to rest within easy reach. Crangenbacker's work in the social-industrial field, on the relation of human willpower to specific problems such as whether a train or subway will stop with the door opposite you on a crowded platform, or whether there will be a mail box anywhere on your side of the street, was attracting much attention.

Resistentialism, a sombre, post-atomic philosophy of pagan, despairing nobility, advocates complete withdrawal from Things. Now that Ventre has done the thinking for us it is easy to see how the soil was being prepared for Resistentialism in the purely speculative field by the thought of Martin Freidegg (1839-1904) and Martin Heidansiecker (1850-1910), both well-known anti-idealists and anti-intellectualists. It is in the latter's *Werke* (Works) published at Tübingen in 1894, that the word *Resistentialismus* first appears, although it has not the definite meaning assigned to it by Ventre. It is now possible to trace a clear line of development to Ventre from Goethe, who said, with prophetic insight into the hostility of one Thing, at least, "Three times has an apple proved fatal. First to the human race, in the fall of Adam; secondly to Troy, through the gift of Paris; and last of all, to science through the fall of Newton's apple" (*Werke XVI, 17*). Later we find Heidansiecker's concept of *Dingenhass,* the hatred of Things. But in the confused terminology of this tortured German mystic we are never sure whether it is the Things who hate us, or we who hate the Things.

To the disillusioned youth of post-war France there was an immediate appeal in Ventre's relentlessly logical concept of man's destiny as a *néant,* or No-Thing, and it was the aesthetic expression of this that gave Resistentialism such great popular currency outside the philosophical textbooks. Ventre himself is an extraordinarily powerful dramatist; his first play, *Puits Clos,* concerns three old men who walk round ceaselessly at the bottom of a well. There are also some bricks in the well. These symbolise Things, and all the old men hate the bricks as much as they do each other. The play is full of their pitiful attempts to throw the bricks out of the top of the well, but they can, of course, never throw high enough, and the bricks always fall back on them. *Puits Clos* has only recently been taken off at the little Théatre Jambon to make room for another Resistentialist piece by Blanco del Huevo, called *Comment Sont Les Choses?*

Del Huevo is an ardent young disciple of Ventre, and in this play, which is also running in London under the title *The Things That Are Caesar,* he makes a very bold step forward in the application of Resistentialist imagery to the theatre. He has made Things the characters, and reduced the human beings to what are known in Resistentialist language as *poussés.* The nearest English translation that suggests itself for this philosophical term is "pushed-arounds."

The chief "characters" in *Comment Sont Les Choses?* are thus a piano and a medicine cabinet; attached to the piano is *Poussé* Number One—no human beings are given actual names, because names are one of the devices by which man has for so long blinded himself to his fundamental inability to mark himself out from the Universe (*Dernière Chose*). *Poussé* Number One is determined to play the piano, and the piano is determined to resist him. For the first twenty minutes of Act I, he plays a Beethoven sonata up to a certain bar, which always defeats him. He stops, and plays this bar over a hundred times, very slowly. He gets it right. He begins the sonata again and when he gets to this bar he makes the very same mistake. He pours petrol on the piano and is just about to set it on fire when he hears a huge crash from the bathroom, also visible to the audience on the other side of a stage partition.

All this time the medicine cabinet has been resisting the attempts of *Poussé* Number Two to fix it on the wall, and it has now fallen into the bath. *Poussé* Number One who is in love, naturally, with *Poussé* Number Two's wife, *Poussée,* mimes his derision at the woeful lack of manhood of one who cannot even dominate Things to the extent of fixing a medicine cabinet. While he does so, the piano, with the tragic irony of a Greek chorus, speaks of *Poussé* Number One's own *hubris* and insolence in imagining that he can master the piano. *Poussé* Number Two is too busy to retaliate, as he is sweeping up the mess of camphorated oil, essence of peppermint, hair cream, calomine lotion, and broken glass towards the plug end of the bath, meaning to swill them out with hot water. He is desperately anxious to get this done before *Poussée* arrives home. She comes, however, while he is still trying ignominiously to get the bits of glass off one

sticky hand with the other sticky hand, the glass then sticking to
the other sticky hand and having to be got off with the first sticky
hand (a good example of *choses co-rélatives* in the Resistentialist
sense). *Poussée* expresses her scorn and asks her husband, all in
mime, why he can't play the piano like *Poussé* Number One
(who has persuaded her that he can). Eventually she goes out
with *Poussé* Number One, and *Poussé* Number Two, exhausted
by his labours at the bath, falls into it and into a deep coma.

Act II is extremely unconventional, and although some critics
have hailed it as a great attempt to break down the modern
separation between players and audience it seems to me to be the
weakest part of the play, the nearest to a mere philosophical
treatise. The curtain simply goes up on a Resistentialist exhibi-
tion, and the audience are invited to walk round. While they are
examining the exhibits, which contain not only Resistentialist
paintings but also what Ventre as well as Del Huevo calls *objets
de vie* (chests of drawers, toothpaste caps, collar buttons, etc.),
the stage manager comes on in his shirt sleeves and reads the
chapter on sex from Ventre's *Résistentialisme*. Ventre takes a
tragic view of sex, concerned as it is with the body, by which the
World-thing obtains its mastery over human territory. In so far as
man is not merely a body he is only a pseudo-Thing (*pseudo-
chose*), a logical "monster." Ventre sees woman, with her capacity
for reproduction indefinitely prolonging this state of affairs, as
the chief cause of humanity's present dilemma of Thing-separa-
tion and therefore Thing-warfare. Love between humans, i.e.
between Man (Not-woman) and Woman (Not-man), perpetuates
bodies as Things, because a man, in being a Not-woman, shows
the capacity of all things for being only *one* Thing (it is all much
clearer in the French, of course). Just as a man is a Not-woman,
he is also a Not-sideboard, a Not-airplane. But this is as far
as man can go in Thing-ness, and if it were not for women we
could all die and be merged comfortably in the Universe or
Ultimate Thing.

In Act III, the action, if one can call it that, is resumed.
When the curtain goes up *Poussé* Number Two is discovered
still lying in the bath. The tragedy of man's futile struggle
against the power of Things begins to draw towards its fatal

climax as we hear a conversation between the piano and the medicine cabinet in which the piano suggests an exchange of their respective *Poussés*. The piano, realising that *Poussée* doesn't know anything about music anyway and will probably accept *Poussé* Number One's word that he can play, queering the pitch for Things, with this ambivalent concept of love, wishes to lure Number Two on instead. (In Ventre's system, Things are quite capable of emanations and influences by reason of their affinity with man's Thing-body or Not-other.) Accordingly, when *Poussé* Number Two wakes up in the bath he feels a compulsive desire to play the piano, forgetting that his fingers are still sticky—and of course it is not his piano anyway. The piano, biding its time, lets him play quite well. (In Resistentialist jargon, which unashamedly borrows from the terminology of Gonk and others when necessary, the resistance of the I-Thing is infinite and that of the Thou-Thing is zero—it is always *my* bootlaces that break —and of course *Poussé* Number Two thinks he is playing *Poussé* Number One's piano.) Number Two only leaves the instrument when he hears the others coming back. He goes to the bathroom and listens through the partition with a knowing smile as *Poussé* Number One begins to play for *Poussée*. Naturally, *his* fingers stick to the keys the piano being an I-Thing for him, or so he thinks. This makes *Poussé* Number Two feel so good that he actually manages to fix the medicine cabinet. *Poussée,* returning to him disillusioned from the pseudo-pianist, flings herself into his arms, but it is too late. He has cut an artery on a piece of the broken glass sticking out of the medicine cabinet. In despair she rushes back to the music room, where *Poussé* Number One has just lit a cigarette to console himself and think out the next move. ("As if that mattered," says the piano scornfully.) As she comes in there is a great explosion. *Poussé* Number One has forgotten the petrol he had poured on the piano in Act I.

The drama is not the only art to have been revivified in France (and therefore everywhere) by Resistentialism. This remorseless modern philosophy has been reflected in the work of all the important younger composers and painters in Paris. Resistentialist music, based on acceptance of the tragic Thing-ness, and therefore limitation, of musical instruments, makes use of a new scale based on the Absolute Mathematical Reluctance of each instrument. The A.M.R. of the violin, for instance, is the critical speed beyond which it is impossible to play it because of the strings' melting. The new scale is conceived, says Dufay, as "a geometric rather than a tonic progression. Each note is seen as a point on the circumference of a circle of which the centre is the A.M.R. The circle must then be conceived as *inside-out*." Dufay has expressed in mathematical terms that cosmic dissatisfaction of the artist with the physical medium in which he is forced to work. Kodak, approaching the problem from a different angle, has taken more positive steps to limit the "cosmic offence-power" of the conventional scale by *reducing* the number of notes available. His first concerto, for solo tympanum and thirty conductors, is an extension of the argument put forward some years ago, in remarkable anticipation of Resistentialism, by Ernest Newman, music critic of the London *Sunday Times,* who said that the highest musical pleasure was to be derived much more from score-reading than from actual performance. Kodak is now believed to be working on a piece for conductors only.

I have left Resistentialism in painting to the end because it is over the quarrel between Ventre and Agfa, at one time his chief adherent among the artists, that the little cafés and bistros of the Quartier Latin are seething to-day. When Agfa first came under Ventre's influence he accepted the latter's detachment, not so much Franciscan as Olympic, from Things. His method was to sit for hours in front of a canvas brooding over disasters, partic-ularly earthquakes, in which Things are hostile in the biggest and most obvious way. Sometimes he would discover that the can-vas had been covered during his abstraction, sometimes not. At any rate, Agfa enjoyed a *succès fou* as a painter of earthquakes and recently he has shown himself impatient of the thorough-going *néantisme* (no-thingery) of Ventre, who insists relentlessly that to conform completely to the pure Resistentialist ideal a picture should not only have no paint but should be without canvas and without frame, since, as he irrefutably points out, these Things are all Things (*ces choses sont toutes des choses.*)

The defection of Agfa and of other "moderates" among the Resistentialists has been brought to a head by the formation, under a thinker named Qwertyuiop, of a neo-Resistentialist group. The enthusiasm with which medieval students brawled in the streets of Paris over the Categories of Being has lost none of its keenness to-day, and the recent pitched battle between Ventristes and followers of Qwertyuiop outside the Café aux Fines Herbes, by now famous as Ventre's headquarters, has, if nothing else, demonstrated that Paris still maintains her position as the world's intellectual centre. It is rather difficult to state the terms of the problem without using some of the Resistentialists' phraseology, so I hope I may be pardoned for briefly introducing it.

Briefly, the issue is between Ventre, the pessimist, and Qwertyuiop, the optimist. Ventre, in elaborating on his central aphorism, *les choses sont contre nous,* distinguishes carefully between what he calls *chose-en-soi,* the Thing in itself, and *chose-pour-soi,* the Thing *for* itself. *Chose-en-soi* is his phrase for Things existing in their own right, sublimely and tragically independent of man. In so far as Ventre's pregnant terminology can be related to traditional Western categories, *chose-en-soi* stands for the Aristotelian outlook, which tends to ascribe a certain measure of reality to Things without reference to any objective Form in any mind, human or divine. There are even closer parallels with the later, medieval philosophy of Nominalism, which says, roughly, that there are as many Things as we can find names for; Ventre has an interesting passage about what he calls inversion (*inversion*) in which he exploits to the full the contrast between the multiplicity of actions which Things can perform against us—from a slightly overhanging tray falling off a table when the removal of one lump of sugar over-balances it, to the atomic bomb—and the paucity of our vocabulary of names on such occasions.

The third great concept of Ventre is *le néant* (the No-Thing). Man is ultimately, as I have said, a No-Thing, a metaphysical monster doomed to battle, with increasing non-success, against real Things. Resistentialism, with what Ventre's followers admire as stark, pagan courage, bids man abandon his hopeless struggle.

Into the dignified tragic, Olympian detachment of Ventre's "primitive" Resistentialism the swarthy, flamboyant Qwertyuiop has made a startling, meteoric irruption. Denounced scornfully by the Ventristes as a plagiarist. Qwertyuiop was, indeed, at one time a pupil of Ventre. He also asserts the hostility of Things to man—but he sees grounds for hope in the concept of *chose-pour-soi* (the Thing for itself) with which it is at least possible to enter into relationship. But he is more a dramatist than a philosopher, and what enrages the Ventristes is the bouncing optimism of his plays and also the curious symbolic figure of the *géant* is a kind of Resistentialist version of Nietzsche's superman, a buskined, moustachioed figure who intervenes, often with great comic effect, just when the characters in the play are about to jump down a well (the well is, of course, a frequent Resistentialist symbol—cf. Ventre's own *Puits Clos*).

The Ventristes point out acidly that in the first edition of *Résistentialisme* the word *géant* appears throughout as a misprint for *néant*. Friction between the two groups was brought to a head by Qwertyuiop's new play *Messieurs, Les Choses Sont Terribles* (loosely, *Gentlemen, Things are Terrible*). On the first night at the Théatre des Somnambules, the Ventristes in the gallery created an uproar and had to be expelled when, at the end of the second act, the inevitable *géant* had stepped in to prevent three torturings, seven betrayals, and two suicides. The battle was renewed later with brickbats and bottles when Qwertyuiop and his followers interrupted one of Ventre's *choseries*, or Thing-talks, at the Café aux Fines Herbes. Five of the moderates and two Ventristes were arrested by the gendarmerie and later released on bail. All Paris is speculating on the outcome of the trial, at which many important literary figures are expected to give evidence.

It is, however, not in the law courts that the influence of Resistentialism on our time will be decided. It is in the little *charcuteries* and *épiceries* of the Left Bank. It is in the stimulating mental climate of Paris that the artists and dramatists will decide for themselves whether there is any future for art in the refined philosophical atmosphere to which Ventre's remorseless logic would have them penetrate. Although Qwertyuiop has succeeded in attracting many of Ventre's more lukewarm followers among the arts, who had begun to rebel against the

Master's uncompromising insistence on pictures without paint and music without instruments, without any Things at all, there seems no doubt that Ventre is the greater thinker, and it is an open question whether he will achieve his object of persuading the world to adandon Things without the indispensable help of the artistic confraternity in moulding public opinion.

There is no doubt, either, that Ventre's thought strikes a deep chord in everyone during these sombre, post-atomic times. Ventre has, I think, liberated the vast flood of creative hatred which makes modern civilization possible. My body, says Ventre, is *chose-en-soi* for me, a Thing which I cannot control, a Thing which uses me. But it is *chose-pour-soi* for the Other. I am thus a Hostile Thing to the Other, and so is he to me. At the same time it follows (or it does in the French) that I am a No-Thing to the world. But I cannot be united or merged with the World-Thing because my Thing-Body, or Not-other gives me an illicit and tragically deceptive claim on existence and "happiness." I am thus tragically committed to extending the area of my always illusory control over the Thing-body—and as the "mind" associated with my Thing-body is merely the storing up of recollected struggles with Things, it follows that I cannot know the Other except as one of the weapons with which the World-Thing has increased its area of hostile action.

Resistentialism thus formalizes hatred both in the cosmological and in the psychological sphere. It is becoming generally realized that the complex apparatus of our modern life—the hurried meals, the dashing for trains, the constant meeting of people who are seen only as "functions"—the barman, the wife, etc.—could not operate if our behaviour were truly dictated by the old, reactionary categories of human love and reason. This is where Ventre's true greatness lies. He has transformed, indeed reversed the traditional mechanism of thought, steered it away from the old dogmatic assumption that we could use Things, and cleared the decks for the evolution of the Thing-process without futile human opposition. Ventre's work brings us a great deal nearer to the realization of the Resistentialist goal summed up in the words, "Every Thing out of Control."

PRIMITIVISM: ENGLISH

FROM *Cold Comfort Farm*
BY STELLA GIBBONS

THE AUTHORS to whom *Cold Comfort Farm* is indebted—Mary Webb, John Cowper Powys, Sheila Kaye-Smith, Thomas Hardy—are variously talented but they have two things in common. Their novels suggest that urban life is trivial compared to the dumb, deep, stark life of The Soil, and the dumber and starker the better. (Pastorals used to make country life gayer than it is, but of late cheerfulness has become suspect.) And they were all, with the partial exception of Hardy, rather "literary." There was therefore in 1932, when *Cold Comfort Farm* first appeared, a parodic vacuum that Miss Gibbons filled with success.

The chapter given here is the third. The first two are in the British understated mode, a combination of Daisy Ashford and Evelyn Waugh. The heroine is Flora Poste, suddenly orphaned at twenty. ("The death of her parents did not cause Flora much grief, for she had barely known them.") She is left with a hundred pounds a year and "every art and grace save that of earning her own living." Against the advice of her rich friend, Mrs. Smiling (who is mildly interested in attracting and frustrating young lovers and passionately interested in her search for the perfect brassière), Flora, a realistic young woman, decides not to try to earn her living but rather to go live with one of her four extant relatives. She writes diplomatic letters to three of them: "That addressed to the aunt at Worthing was offensively jolly, yet tempered by a certain inarticulate Public School grief for her bereavement. The one to the bachelor uncle in Scotland was sweetly girlish and just a wee bit arch; it hinted she was only a poor little orphan. She wrote to the cousin in South Kensington a distant, dignified epistle, grieved yet businesslike." To the fourth, some distant and unknown relatives in Sussex who live at a place oddly called Cold Comfort Farm, she writes simply "a straightforward letter explaining her position" since she cannot decide how to appeal to them. Mrs. Smiling expresses a hope that none of them will answer, especially "those people in Sussex" because their name, Starkadder, is "*too* ageing and off-putting." Flora agrees the name is "certainly not propitious" and adds that if any of her third cousins at the farm are named Seth or Reuben she will definitely not go "because highly sexed young men living on farms are always called Seth or Reuben and it would be such a nuisance." However, the three other relatives all offer accommodations that for various reasons Flora and her friend think unsuitable, and there is left only "the last letter written upon cheap lined paper in a bold but illiterate hand":

Dear Niece:

So you are after your rights at last. . . . Child, my man once did your father a great wrong. If you will come to us I will do my best to atone, but you must never ask me what for. My lips are sealed. We are not like other folk, maybe, but there have always been Starkadders at Cold Comfort and we will do our best to welcome Robert Poste's child. Child, child, if you come to this doomed house, what is to save you? Perhaps you may be able to help us when our hour comes.

Yr. affec. Aunt,

J. Starkadder

Intrigued by the reference to "rights" ("Oh, do you think she means some money? Or perhaps a little house? I should like that even better.") Flora decides on Cold Comfort Farm ("Suppose I go down on Tuesday, after lunch?"). Now go on with the story

CHAPTER 3

DAWN crept over the Downs like a sinister white animal, followed by the snarling cries of a wind eating its way between the black boughs of the thorns. The wind was the furious voice of this sluggish animal light that was baring the dormers and mullions and scullions of Cold Comfort Farm.

The farm was crouched on a bleak hill-side, whence its fields, fanged with flints, dropped steeply to the village of Howling a mile away. Its stables and out-houses were built in the shape of a rough octangle surrounding the farmhouse itself, which was built in the shape of a rough triangle. The left point of the triangle abutted on the farthest point of the octangle, which was formed by the cowsheds, which lay parallel with the big barn. The out-houses were built of rough-cast stone, with thatched roofs, while the farm itself was partly built of local flint, set in cement, and partly of some stone brought at great trouble and enormous expense from Perthshire.

The farmhouse was a long, low building, two-storied in parts. Other parts of it were three-storied. Edward the Sixth had originally owned it in the form of a shed in which he housed his swineherds, but he had grown tired of it, and had it rebuilt in Sussex clay. Then he pulled it down. Elizabeth had rebuilt it, with a good many chimneys in one way and another. The Charleses had let it alone; but William and Mary had pulled it down again, and George the First had rebuilt it. George the Second, however, burned it down. George the Third added another wing. George the Fourth pulled it down again.

By the time England began to develop that magnificent blossoming of trade and imperial expansion which fell to her lot under Victoria, there was not much of the original building left, save the tradition that it had always been there. It crouched, like a beast about to spring, under the bulk of Mock-uncle Hill. Like ghosts embedded in brick and stone, the architectural variations of each period through which it had passed were mute history. It was known locally as "The King's Whim."

The front door of the farm faced a perfectly inaccessible ploughed field at the back of the house; it had been the whim of Red Raleigh Starkadder, in 1835, to have it so; and so the family always used to come in by the back door, which abutted on the general yard facing the cowsheds. A long corridor ran half-way through the house on the second story and then stopped. One could not get into the attics at all. It was all very awkward.

. . . Growing with the viscous light that was invading the sky, there came the solemn, tortured-snake voice of the sea, two miles away, falling in sharp folds upon the mirror-expanses of the beach.

Under the ominous bowl of the sky a man was ploughing the sloping field immediately below the farm, where the flints shone bone-sharp and white in the growing light. The ice-cascade of the wind leaped over him, as he guided the plough over the flinty runnels. Now and again he called roughly to his team:

"Upidee, Travail! Ho, there, Arsenic! Jug-jug!" But for the most part he worked in silence, and silent were his team. The light showed no more of his face than a grey expanse of flesh, expressionless as the land he ploughed, from which looked out two sluggish eyes.

Every now and again, when he came to the corner of the field and was forced to tilt the scranlet of his plough almost on to its axle to make the turn, he glanced up at the farm where it squatted on the gaunt shoulder of the hill, and something like a possessive gleam shone in his dull eyes. But he only turned his team again, watching the crooked passage of the scranlet through the yeasty earth, and muttered: "Hola, Arsenic! Belay there, Travail!" while the bitter light waned into full day.

Because of the peculiar formation of the out-houses surrounding the farm, the light was always longer in reaching the yard than the rest of the house. Long after the sunlight was shining through the cobwebs on the uppermost windows of the old house the yard was in damp blue shadow.

It was in shadow now, but sharp gleams sprang from the ranged milk-buckets along the ford-piece outside the cowshed.

Leaving the house by the back-door, you came up sharply against a stone wall running right across the yard, and turning abruptly, at right angles, just before it reached the shed where the bull was housed, and running down to the gate leading out into the ragged garden where mallows, dog's-body, and wild turnip were running riot. The bull's shed abutted upon the right corner of the dairy, which faced the cowsheds. The cowsheds faced the house, but the back-door faced the bull's shed. From here a long-roofed barn extended the whole length of the octangle until it reached the front door of the house. Here it took a quick turn, and ended. The dairy was awkwardly placed; it had been a thorn in the side of old Fig Starkadder, the last owner of the farm, who had died three years ago. The dairy overlooked the front door, in face of the extreme point of its triangle which formed the ancient buildings of the farmhouse.

From the dairy a wall extended which formed the right-hand boundary of the octangle, joining the bull's shed and the pig-pens at the extreme end of the right point of the triangle. A staircase, put in to make it more difficult, ran parallel with the octangle, half-way round the yard, against the wall which led down to the garden gate.

The spurt and regular ping! of milk against metal came from the reeking interior of the sheds. The bucket was pressed between Adam Lambsbreath's knees, and his head was pressed deep into the flank of Feckless, the big Jersey. His gnarled hands mechanically stroked the teat, while a low crooning, mindless as the Down wind itself, came from his lips.

He was asleep. He had been awake all night, wandering in thought over the indifferent bare shoulders of the Downs after his wild bird, his little flower . . .

Elfine. The name, unspoken but sharply musical as a glittering bead shaken from a fountain's tossing necklace, hovered audibly in the rancid air of the shed.

The beasts stood with heads lowered dejectedly against the wooden hoot-pieces of their stalls. Graceless, Pointless, Feckless, and Aimless awaited their turn to be milked. Sometimes Aimless ran her dry tongue, with a rasping sound sharp as a file through silk, awkwardly across the bony flank of Feckless, which was still moist with the rain that had fallen upon it through the roof during the night, or Pointless turned her large dull eyes sideways as she swung her head upwards to tear down a mouthful of cobwebs from the wooden runnet above her head. A lowering, moist, steamy light, almost like that which gleams below the eyelids of a man in fever, filled the cowshed.

Suddenly a tortured bellow, a blaring welter of sound that shattered the quiescence of the morning, tore its way across the yard, and died away in a croak that was almost a sob. It was Big Business, the bull, wakening to another day, in the clammy darkness of his cell.

The sound woke Adam. He lifted his head from the flank of Feckless and looked around him in bewilderment for a moment; then slowly his eyes, which looked small and wet and lifeless in his primitive face, lost their terror as he realized that he was in the cowshed, that it was half-past six on a winter morning, and that his gnarled fingers were about the task which they had performed at this hour and in this place for the past eighty years and more.

He stood up, sighing, and crossed over to Pointless, who was eating Graceless's tail. Adam, who was linked to all dumb brutes by a chain forged in soil and sweat, took it out of her mouth and put into it, instead, his neckerchief—the last he had. She mumbled it, while he milked her, but stealthily spat it out so soon as he passed on to Aimless, and concealed it under the reeking straw with her hoof. She did not want to hurt the old man's feelings by declining to eat his gift. There was a close bond: a slow, deep, primitive, silent down-dragging link between Adam and all living beasts; they knew each other's simple needs. They lay close to the earth, and something of earth's old fierce simplicities had seeped into their beings.

Suddenly a shadow fell athwart the wooden stanchions of the door. It was no more than a darkening of the pallid paws of the day which were now embracing the shed, but all the cows instinctively stiffened, and Adam's eyes, as he stood up to face the new-comer, were again piteously full of twisted fear.

"Adam," uttered the woman who stood in the doorway, "how many pails of milk will there be this morning?"

"I dunnamany," responded Adam, cringingly; " 'tes hard to tell. If so be as our Pointless has got over her indigestion, maybe 'twill be four. If so be as she hain't, maybe three."

Judith Starkadder made an impatient movement. Her large hands had a quality which made them seem to sketch vast horizons with their slightest gesture. She looked a woman without boundaries as she stood wrapped in a crimson shawl to protect her bitter, magnificent shoulders from the splintery cold of the early air. She seemed fitted for any stage, however enormous.

"Well, get as many buckets as you can," she said, lifelessly, half-turning away. "Mrs. Starkadder questioned me about the milk yesterday. She has been comparing our output with that from other farms in the district, and she says we are five-six-teenths of a bucket below what our rate should be, considering how many cows we have."

A strange film passed over Adam's eyes, giving him the lifeless primeval look that a lizard has, basking in the swooning Southern heat. But he said nothing.

"And another thing," continued Judith, "you will probably have to drive down into Beershorn to-night to meet a train. Robert Poste's child is coming to stay with us for a while. I expect to hear some time this morning what time she is arriving. I will tell you later about it."

Adam shrank back against the gangrened flank of Pointless. "Mun I?" he asked, piteously. "Mun I, Miss Judith? Oh, dunna send me. How can I look into her liddle flower-face, and me knowin' what I know? Oh, Miss Judith, I beg of 'ee not to send me. Besides," he added, more practically, " 'tes close on sixty-five years since I put hands to a pair of reins, and I might upset the maidy."

Judith, who had slowly turned from him while he was speaking, was now half-way across the yard. She turned her head to reply to him with a slow, graceful movement. Her deep voice clanged like a bell in the frosty air:

"No, you must go, Adam. You must forget what you know—as we all must, while she is here. As for the driving, you had best harness Viper to the trap, and drive down into Howling and back six times this afternoon, to get your hand in again."

"Could not Master Seth go instead o' me?"

Emotion shook the frozen grief of her face. She said low and sharp:

"You remember what happened when he went to meet the new kitchenmaid . . . No. You must go."

Adam's eyes, like blind pools of water in his primitive face, suddenly grew cunning. He turned back to Aimless and resumed his mechanical stroking of the teat, saying in a sing-song rhythm:

"Ay, then I'll go, Miss Judith. I dunnamany times I've thought as how this day might come . . . And now I mun go to bring Robert Poste's child back to Cold Comfort. Aye, 'tes strange. The seed to the flower, the flower to the fruit, the fruit to the belly. Aye, so 'twill go."

Judith had crossed the muck and rabble of the yard, and now entered the house by the back door.

In the large kitchen, which occupied most of the middle of the house, a sullen fire burned, the smoke of which wavered up the blackened walls and over the deal table, darkened by age and dirt, which was roughly set for a meal. A snood full of coarse porridge hung over the fire, and standing with one arm resting upon the high mantel, looking moodily down into the

412 PARODIES: *An Anthology*

heaving contents of the snood, was a tall young man whose riding-boots were splashed with mud to the thigh, and whose coarse linen shirt was open to his waist. The firelight lit up his diaphragm muscles as they heaved slowly in rough rhythm with the porridge.

He looked up as Judith entered, and gave a short, defiant laugh, but said nothing. Judith crossed slowly over until she stood by his side. She was as tall as he. They stood in silence, she staring at him, and he down into the secret crevasses of the porridge.

"Well, mother mine," he said at last, "here I am, you see. I said I would be in time for breakfast, and I have kept my word."

His voice had a low, throaty, animal quality, a sneering warmth that wound a velvet ribbon of sexuality over the outward coarseness of the man.

Judith's breath came in long shudders. She thrust her arms deeper into her shawl. The porridge gave an ominous leering heave; it might almost have been endowed with life, so uncannily did its movements keep pace with the human passions that throbbed above it.

"Cur," said Judith, levelly, at last. "Coward! Liar! Libertine! Who were you with last night? Moll at the mill or Violet at the vicarage? Or Ivy, perhaps, at the ironmongery? Seth—my son . . ." Her deep, dry voice quivered, but she whipped it back, and her next words flew out at him like a lash.

"Do you want to break my heart?"

"Yes," said Seth, with an elemental simplicity.

The porridge boiled over.

Judith knelt, and hastily and absently ladled it off the floor back into the snood, biting back her tears. While she was thus engaged, there was a confused blur of voices and boots in the yard outside. The men were coming in to breakfast.

The meal for the men was set on a long trestle at the farther end of the kitchen, as far away from the fire as possible. They came into the room in awkward little clumps, eleven of them. Five were distant cousins of the Starkadders, and two others were half-brothers of Amos, Judith's husband. This left only four men who were not in some way connected with the family; so it will readily be understood that the general feeling among the farm-hands was not exactly one of hilarity. Mark Dolour, one of the four, had been heard to remark: "Happen it had been another kind o' eleven, us might ha' had a cricket team, wi' me for umpire. As ut is, 'twould be more befittin' if we was to hire oursen out for carryin' coffins at sixpence a mile."

The five half-cousins and the two half-brothers came over to the table, for they took their meals with the family. Amos liked to have his kith about him, though, of course, he never said so or cheered up when they were.

A strong family likeness wavered in and out of the fierce, earth-reddened faces of the seven, like a capricious light. Micah Starkadder, mightiest of the cousins, was a ruined giant of a man, paralysed in one knee and wrist. His nephew, Urk, was a little, red, hard-bitten man with foxy ears. Urk's brother, Ezra, was of the same physical type, but horsy where Urk was foxy. Caraway, a silent man, wind-shaven and lean, with long wandering fingers, had some of Seth's animal grace, and this had been passed on to his son, Harkaway, a young, silent, nervous man given to bursts of fury about very little, when you came to sift matters.

Amos's half-brothers, Luke and Mark, were thickly built and high-featured; gross, silent men with an eye to the bed and the board.

When all were seated two shadows darkened the sharp, cold light pouring in through the door. They were no more than a growing imminence of humanity, but the porridge boiled over again.

Amos Starkadder and his eldest son, Reuben, came into the kitchen.

Amos, who was even larger and more of a wreck than Micah, silently put his pruning-snoot and reaping-hook in a corner by the fender, while Reuben put the scranlet with which he had been ploughing down beside them.

The two men took their places in silence, and after Amos had muttered a long and fervent grace, the meal was eaten in silence. Seth sat moodily tying and untying a green scarf round the magnificent throat he had inherited from Judith; he did not touch his porridge, and Judith only made a pretence of eating hers, playing with her spoon, patting the porridge up and down and idly building castles with the burnt bits. Her eyes burned under their penthouses, sometimes straying towards Seth as he sat sprawling in the lusty pride of casual manhood, with a good many buttons and tapes undone. Then those same eyes, dark as prisoned king-cobras, would slide round until they rested upon the bitter white head and raddled red neck of Amos, her husband, and then, like praying mantises, they would retreat between their lids. Secrecy pouted her full mouth.

Suddenly Amos, looking up from his food, asked abruptly: "Where's Elfine?"

"She is not up yet. I did not wake her. She hinders more than she helps o' mornings," replied Judith.

Amos grunted.

" 'Tes a godless habit to lie abed of a working day, and the reeking red pits of the Lord's eternal wrathy fires lie in wait for them as do so. Aye"—his blue blazing eyes swivelled round and rested upon Seth, who was stealthily looking at a packet of Parisian art pictures under the table—"aye, and for those who break the seventh commandment, too. And for those"—the eye rested on Reuben, who was hopefully studying his parent's apoplectic countenance—"for those as waits for dead men's shoes."

"Nay, Amos, lad—" remonstrated Micah, heavily.

"Hold your peace," thundered Amos; and Micah, though a fierce tremor rushed through his mighty form, held it.

When the meal was done the hands trooped out to get on with the day's work of harvesting the swedes. This harvest was now in full swing; it took a long time and was very difficult to do. The Starkadders, too, rose and went out into the thin rain which had begun to fall. They were engaged in digging a well beside the dairy; it had been started a year ago, but it was taking a long time to do because things kept on going wrong. Once—a terrible day, when Nature seemed to hold her breath, and release it again in a furious gale of wind—Harkaway had fallen into it. Once Urk had pushed Caraway down it. Still, it was nearly finished; and everybody felt that it would not be long now.

In the middle of the morning a wire came from London announcing that the expected visitor would arrive by the six o'clock train.

Judith received it alone. Long after she had read it she stood motionless, the rain driving through the open door against her crimson shawl. Then slowly, with dragging steps, she mounted the staircase which led to the upper part of the house. Over her shoulder she said to old Adam, who had come into the room to do the washing up:

"Robert Poste's child will be here by the six o'clock train at Beershorn. You must leave to meet it at five. I am going up to tell Mrs. Starkadder that she is coming to-day."

Adam did not reply, and Seth, sitting by the fire, was growing tired of looking at his postcards, which were a three-year-old gift from the vicar's son, with whom he occasionally went poaching. He knew them all by now. Meriam, the hired girl, would not be in until after dinner. When she came, she would avoid his eyes, and tremble and weep.

He laughed insolently, triumphantly. Undoing another button of his shirt he lounged out across the yard to the shed where Big Business, the bull, was imprisoned in darkness.

Laughing softly, Seth struck the door of the shed.

And so though answering the deep call of male to male, the bull uttered a loud, tortured bellow that rose undefeated through the dead sky that brooded over the farm.

Seth undid yet another button, and lounged away.

Adam Lambsbreath, alone in the kitchen, stood looking down unseeingly at the dirtied plates, which it was his task to wash, for the hired girl, Meriam, would not be here until after dinner, and when she came she would be all but useless. Her hour was near at hand, as all Howling knew. Was it not February, and the earth a-teem with newing life? A grin twisted Adam's writhen lips. He gathered up the plates one by one and carried them to the pump, which stood in a corner of the kitchen, above a stone sink. Her hour was nigh. And when April like an over-lustful lover leaped upon the lush flanks of the Downs there would be yet another child in the wretched hut down at Nettle Flitch Field, where Meriam housed the fruits of her shame.

"Aye, dog's-fennel or beard's-crow, by their fruits they shall be betrayed," muttered Adam, shooting a stream of cold water over the coagulated plates. "Come cloud, come sun, 'tes ay so."

While he was listlessly dabbing at the crusted edges of the porridge-plates with a thorn twig, a soft step descended the stairs outside the door which closed off the staircase from the kitchen. Someone paused on the threshold.

The step was light as thistledown. If Adam had not had the rush of the running water in his ears too loudly for him to be able to hear any other noise, he might have thought this delicate, hesitant step was the beating of his own blood.

But, suddenly, something like a kingfisher streaked across the kitchen, in a glimmer of green skirts and flying gold hair and the chime of a laugh was followed a second later by the slam of the gate leading through the starveling garden out on to the Downs.

Adam flung round violently on hearing the sound, dropping his thorn twig and breaking two plates.

"Elfine . . . my little bird," he whispered, starting towards the open door.

A brittle silence mocked his whisper; through it wound the rank odours of rattan and barn.

"My pharisee . . . my cowdling . . ." he whispered, piteously. His eyes had again that look as of waste grey pools, sightless primeval wastes reflecting the wan evening sky in some lonely marsh, as they wandered about the kitchen.

His hands fell slackly against his sides, and he dropped another plate. It broke.

He sighed, and began to move slowly towards the open door, his task forgotten. His eyes were fixed upon the cowshed.

"Aye, the beasts . . ." he muttered, dully; "the dumb beasts never fail a man. They know. Aye, I'd 'a' done better to cowdle our Feckless in my bosom than liddle Elfine. Aye, wild as a marsh-tigget in May, 'tes. And a will never listen to a word from annyone. Well, so t'must be. Sour or sweet, by barn or bye, so 'twill go. Ah, but if he"—the blind grey pools grew suddenly terrible, as though a storm were blowing in across the marsh from the Atlantic wastes—"if he but harms a hair o' her liddle goldy head I'll *kill* um."

So muttering, he crossed the yard and entered the cow-shed, where he untied the beasts from their hoot-pieces and drove them across the yard, down the muddy rutted lane that led to Nettle Flitch Field. He was enmeshed in his grief. He did not notice that Graceless's leg had come off and that she was managing as best she could with three.

Left alone, the kitchen fire went out.

PRIMITIVISM: AMERICAN

FROM *Torrents of Spring*
BY ERNEST HEMINGWAY

Torrents of Spring was Hemingway's second book, following *In Our Time* (1924) and immediately preceding, in 1926, *The Sun Also Rises*. It parodies the more earthy—used here to mean in relation to "earth" what "arty" means in relation to "art"—aspects of Sherwood Anderson's writing.

The question is why did Hemingway write it? Parody seems hardly his line. The simplest explanation is that he wanted to break his contract with Horace Liveright, who had published *In Our Time* and who had an option on his next book, and go over to Scribner's, a more important house which also had the gifted Maxwell Perkins as its editor. Since Anderson was then Liveright's most famous author, the firm would be unlikely to publish a parody of him. And in fact Liveright did turn down *Torrents* and Hemingway did go to Scribner's. Also, as he knew, both Liveright and Scribner's were eager to get *The Sun Also Rises;* that he wrote *Torrents* in seven days, between the first and the final drafts of *The Sun,* looks suspicious. The evidence is only circumstantial; Hemingway has denied he had any such idea in mind. But even if he did—he has always been a most practical writer—one may see deeper impulses at work.

The young and unknown Hemingway first met Anderson in Chicago in 1920; he admired the celebrated author of *Winesburg, Ohio* (on which, as he told Scott Fitzgerald later, he modeled some of his first stories). Anderson, after all, Had It Made. But Hemingway had misgivings even then, which he was too shy or too shrewd to express: he disliked Anderson's bohemianism and his pose of being a naïve, almost an automatic, writer, which Hemingway took seriously and which offended his professional concept of writing. Furthermore, Anderson was generous with help; he used his influence to get some of Hemingway's early work published and, when Hemingway went abroad for the first time the following year, he gave him letters of introduction to various people, including Ezra Pound and Gertrude Stein, who became his next tutors. By 1926 Hemingway had gone, or thought he had, far beyond Anderson, who may have appeared to him then as a Freudian father he had to kill in order to make his own place in the world of letters. This at least is a less materialistic explanation of *Torrents of Spring*. There may have also been a bit of matricide; Gertrude Stein's prose is sideswiped in *Torrents*. (Ventriloquially speaking through Alice B. Toklas, Stein later wrote: "He [Hemingway] had been formed by them [Stein and Anderson].")

Anderson was hurt by *Torrents*. He reacted moderately—"Absorption in his ideas may have affected his capacity for friendship"—though he did permit himself a dig: "It might have been humorous had Max Beerbohm condensed it to twelve pages." But the dig was unjustified. *Torrents of Spring* is accurate and cruel parody, all the more so since Hemingway understood Anderson's literary affectations precisely because they were his own. He was able to render the *faux-naïf* style so well only because it was as natural to him as to Sherwood Anderson; it was just a matter of a different placement of the plus and minus emotional signs, and I think it is arguable that Anderson placed them at least as well as Hemingway did.

CHAPTER ONE

YOGI JOHNSON stood looking out of the window of a big pump-factory in Michigan. Spring would soon be here. Could it be that what this writing fellow Hutchinson had said, "If winter comes can spring be far behind?" would be true again this year? Yogi Johnson wondered. Near Yogi at the next window but one stood Scripps O'Neil, a tall, lean man with a tall, lean face. Both stood and looked out at the empty yard of the pump-factory. Snow covered the crated pumps that would soon be shipped away. Once the spring should come and the snow melt, workmen from the factory would break out the pumps from piles where they were snowed in and haul them down to the G. R. & I.

Station, where they would be loaded on flat-cars and shipped away. Yogi Johnson looked out of the window at the snowed-in pumps, and his breath made little fairy tracings on the cold window-pane. Yogi Johnson thought of Paris. Perhaps it was the little fairy tracings that reminded him of the gay city where he had once spent two weeks. Two weeks that were to have been the happiest weeks of his life. That was all behind him now. That and everything else.

Scripps O'Neil had two wives. As he looked out of the window, standing tall and lean and resilient with his own tenuous hardness, he thought of both of them. One lived in Mancelona and the other lived in Petoskey. He had not seen the wife who lived in Mancelona since last spring. He looked out at the snow-covered pump-yards and thought what spring would mean. With his wife in Mancelona Scripps often got drunk. When he was drunk he and his wife were happy. They would go down together to the railway station and walk out along the tracks, and then sit together and drink and watch the trains go by. They would sit under a pine tree on a little hill that overlooked the railway and drink. Sometimes they drank all night. Sometimes they drank for a week at a time. It did them good. It made Scripps strong.

Scripps had a daughter whom he playfully called Lousy O'Neil. Her real name was Lucy O'Neil. One night, after Scripps and his old woman had been out drinking on the railroad line for three or four days, he lost his wife. He didn't know where she was. When he came to himself everything was dark. He walked along the railroad track toward town. The ties were stiff and hard under his feet. He tried walking on the rails. He couldn't do it. He had the dope on that all right. He went back to walking along the ties. It was a long way into town. Finally he came to where he could see the lights of the switch-yard. He cut away from the tracks and passed the Mancelona High School. It was a yellow-brick building. There was nothing rococo about it, like the buildings he had seen in Paris. No, he had never been in Paris. That was not he. That was his friend Yogi Johnson.

Yogi Johnson looked out of the window. Soon it would be time to shut the pump-factory for the night. He opened the window carefully, just a crack. Just a crack, but that was enough. Outside in the yard the snow had begun to melt. A warm breeze was blowing. A chinook wind the pump fellows called it. The warm chinook wind came in through the window into the pump-factory. All the workmen laid down their tools. Many of them were Indians.

The foreman was a short, iron-jawed man. He had once made a trip as far as Duluth. Duluth was far across the blue waters of the lake in the hills of Minnesota. A wonderful thing had happened to him there.

The foreman put his finger in his mouth to moisten it and held it up in the air. He felt the warm breeze on his finger. He shook his head ruefully and smiled at the men, a little grimly perhaps.

"Well, it's a regular chinook, boys," he said.

Silently for the most part, the workmen hung up their tools. The half-completed pumps were put away in their racks. The workmen filed, some of them talking, others silent, a few muttering, to the washroom to wash up.

Outside through the window came the sound of an Indian warwhoop.

CHAPTER TWO

SCRIPPS O'NEIL stood outside the Mancelona High School looking up at the lighted windows. It was dark and the snow was falling. It had been falling ever since Scripps could remember. A passer-by stopped and stared at Scripps. After all, what was this man to him? He went on.

Scripps stood in the snow and stared up at the lighted windows of the High School. Inside there people were learning things. Far into the night they worked, the boys vying with the girls in their search for knowledge, this urge for the learning of things that was sweeping America. His girl, little Lousy, a girl that had cost him a cool seventy-five dollars in doctors' bills, was in there learning. Scripps was proud. It was too late for him to learn, but there, day after day and night after night, Lousy was learning. She had the stuff in her, that girl.

Scripps went on up to his house. It was not a big house, but it wasn't size that mattered to Scripps's old woman.

"Scripps," she often said when they were drinking together, "I don't want a palace. All I want is a place to keep the wind out." Scripps had taken her at her word. Now, as he walked in the late evening through the snow and saw the lights of his own home, he felt glad that he had taken her at her word. It was better this way than if he were coming home to a palace. He, Scripps, was not the sort of chap that wanted a palace.

He opened the door of his house and went in. Something kept going through his head. He tried to get it out, but it was no good. What was it that poet chap his friend Harry Parker had met once in Detroit had written? Harry used to recite it: "Through pleasures and palaces though I may roam. When you something something something there's no place like home." He could not remember the words. Not all of them. He had written a simple tune to it and taught Lucy to sing it. That was when they first were married. Scripps might have been a composer, one of these chaps that write the stuff the Chicago Symphony Orchestra plays, if he had had a chance to go on. He would get Lucy to sing that song to-night. He would never drink again. Drinking robbed him of his ear for music. Times when he was drunk the sound of the whistles of the trains at night pulling up the Boyne Falls grade seemed more lovely than anything this chap Stravinsky had ever written. Drinking had done that. It was wrong. He would get away to Paris. Like this chap Albert Spalding that played the violin.

Scripps opened the door. He went in. "Lucy," he called, "it is I, Scripps." He would never drink again. No more nights out on the railroad. Perhaps Lucy needed a new fur coat. Perhaps, after all, she had wanted a palace instead of this place. You never knew how you were treating a woman. Perhaps, after all, this place was not keeping out the wind. Fantastic. He lit a match. "Lucy!" he called, and there was a note of dumb terror in his mouth. His friend Walt Simmons had heard just such a cry from a stallion that had once been run over by a passing autobus in the Place Vendôme in Paris. In Paris there were no geldings. All the horses were stallions. They did not breed mares. Not since the war. The war changed all that.

"Lucy!" he called, and again "Lucy!" There was no answer. The house was empty. Through the snow-filled air, as he stood there alone in his tall leanness, in his own deserted house, there came to Scripps's ears the distant sound of an Indian war-whoop.

CHAPTER THREE

SCRIPPS left Mancelona. He was through with that place. What had a town like that to give him? There was nothing to it. You worked all your life and then a thing like that happened. The savings of years wiped out. Everything gone. He started to Chicago to get a job. Chicago was the place. Look at its geographical situation, right at the end of Lake Michigan. Chicago would do big things. Any fool could see that. He would buy land in what is now the Loop, the big shopping and manufacturing district. He would buy the land at a low price and then hang onto it. Let them try and get it away from him. He knew a thing or two now.

Alone, bareheaded, the snow blowing in his hair, he walked down the G. R. & I. railway tracks. It was the coldest night he had ever known. He picked up a dead bird that had frozen and fallen onto the railroad tracks and put it inside his shirt to warm it. The bird nestled close to his warm body and pecked at his chest gratefully.

"Poor little chap," Scripps said. "You feel the cold too."

Tears came into his eyes.

"Drat that wind," Scripps said and once again faced into the blowing snow. The wind was blowing straight down from Lake Superior. The telegraph wires above Scripps's head sang in the wind. Through the dark, Scripps saw a great yellow eye coming toward him. The giant locomotive came nearer through the snow-storm. Scripps stepped to one side of the track to let it go by. What is it that old writing fellow Shakespeare says: "Might makes right"? Scripps thought of that quotation as the train went past him in the snowing darkness. First the engine passed.

He saw the fireman bending to fling great shovelfuls of coal into
the open furnace door. The engineer wore goggles. His face was
lit up by the light from the open door of the engine. He was
the engineer. It was he who had his hand on the throttle. Scripps
thought of the Chicago anarchists who, when they were hanged,
said: "Though you throttle us to-day, still you cannot something
something our souls." There was a monument where they were
buried in Waldheim Cemetery, right beside the Forest Park
Amusement Park, in Chicago. His father used to take Scripps out
there on Sundays. The monument was all black and there was a
black angel. That was when Scripps had been a little boy. He
used often to ask his father: "Father, why if we come to look at
the anarchists on Sunday why can't we ride on the shoot the
chutes?" He had never been satisfied with his father's answer.
He had been a little boy in knee pants then. His father had been
a great composer. His mother was an Italian woman from the
north of Italy. They are strange people, these North Italians.

Scripps stood beside the track, and the long black segments of
the train clicked by him in the snow. All the cars were Pullmans.
The blinds were down. Light came in thin slits from the bottom
of the dark windows as the cars went by. The train did not roar
by as it might have if it had been going in the other direction,
because it was climbing the Boyne Falls grade. It went slower
than if it had been going down. Still it went too fast for Scripps
to hitch on. He thought how he had been an expert at hitching
on grocery wagons when he was a young boy in knee pants.

The long black train of Pullman cars passed Scripps as he
stood beside the tracks. Who were in those cars? Were they
Americans, piling up money while they slept? Were they mothers?
Were they fathers? Were there lovers among them? Or were they
Europeans, members of a worn-out civilization world-weary from
the war? Scripps wondered.

The last car passed him and the train went on up the track.
Scripps watched the red light at its stern disappearing into the
blackness through which the snowflakes now came softly. The
bird fluttered inside his shirt. Scripps started along the ties. He
wanted to get to Chicago that night, if possible, to start work
in the morning. The bird fluttered again. It was not so feeble

now. Scripps put his hand on it to still its little bird flutterings. The bird was calmed. Scripps strode on up the track.

After all, he did not need to go as far as Chicago. There were other places. What if that critic fellow Henry Mencken had called Chicago the Literary Capital of America? There was Grand Rapids. Once in Grand Rapids, he could start in in the furniture business. Fortunes had been made that way. Grand Rapids furniture was famous wherever young couples walked in the evening to talk of home-making. He remembered a sign he had seen in Chicago as a little boy. His mother had pointed it out to him as together they walked barefoot through what now is probably the Loop, begging from door to door. His mother loved the bright flashing of the electric lights in the sign.

"They are like San Miniato in my native Florence," she told Scripps. "Look at them, my son," she said, "for some day your music will be played there by the Firenze Symphony Orchestra."

Scripps had often watched the sign for hours while his mother slept wrapped in an old shawl on what is now probably the Blackstone Hotel. The sign had made a great impression on him.

LET HARTMAN FEATHER YOUR NEST

it had said. It flashed in many different colors. First a pure, dazzling white. That was what Scripps loved best. Then it flashed a lovely green. Then it flashed red. One night as he lay crouched against his mother's body warmth and watched the sign flash, a policeman came up. "You'll have to move along," he said.

Ah, yes, there was big money to be made in the furniture business if you knew how to go about it. He, Scripps, knew all the wrinkles of that game. In his own mind it was settled. He would stop at Grand Rapids. The little bird fluttered, happily now.

"Ah, what a beautiful gilded cage I'll build for you, my pretty one," Scripps said exultantly. The little bird pecked him confidently. Scripps strode on in the storm. The snow was beginning to drift across the track. Borne on the wind, there came to Scripps's ears the sound of a far-off Indian war-whoop.

*   *   *   *   *

CHAPTER SEVEN

THAT NIGHT, after his first day in the pump-factory, the first day in what was or were to become an endless succession of days of dull piston-collaring, Scripps went again to the beanery to eat. All day he had kept his bird concealed. Something told him that the pump-factory was not the place to bring his bird out in. During the day the bird had several times made him uncomfortable, but he had adjusted his clothes to it and even cut a little slit the bird could poke his beak out through in search of fresh air. Now the day's work was over. It was finished. Scripps on his way to the beanery. Scripps happy that he was working with his hands. Scripps thinking of the old pump-makers. Scripps going to the society of the friendly waitress. Who was that waitress, anyway? What was it had happened to her in Paris? He must find out more about this Paris. Yogi Johnson had been there. He would quiz Yogi. Get him to talk. Draw him out. Make him tell what he knew. He knew a trick or two about that.

Watching the sunset out over the Petoskey Harbor, the lake now frozen and great blocks of ice jutting up over the breakwater, Scripps strode down the streets of Petoskey to the beanery. He would have liked to ask Yogi Johnson to eat with him, but he didn't dare. Not yet. That would come later. All in good time. No need to rush matters with a man like Yogi. Who was Yogi, anyway? Had he really been in the war? What had the war meant to him? Was he really the first man to enlist from Cadillac? Where was Cadillac anyway? Time would tell.

Scripps O'Neil opened the door and went into the beanery. The elderly waitress got up from the chair where she had been reading the overseas edition of *The Manchester Guardian,* and put the paper and her steel-rimmed spectacles on top of the cash register.

"Good evening," she said simply. "It's good to have *you* back."

Something stirred inside Scripps O'Neil. A feeling that he could not define came within him.

"I've been working all day long"—he looked at the waitress—"for *you,*" he added.

"How lovely!" she said. And then smiled shyly. "And I have been working all day long—for *you*."

Tears came into Scripps's eyes. Something stirred inside him again. He reached forward to take the elderly waitress's hand, and with quiet dignity she laid it within his own. "You are my woman," he said. Tears came into her eyes, too.

"You are my man," she said.

"Once again I say: you are my woman." Scripps pronounced the words solemnly. Something had broken inside him again. He felt he could not keep from crying.

"Let this be our wedding ceremony," the elderly waitress said. Scripps pressed her hand. "You are my woman," he said simply.

"You are my man and more than my man." She looked into his eyes. "You are all of America to me."

"Let us go," Scripps said.

"Have you your bird?" asked the waitress, laying aside her apron and folding the copy of *The Manchester Guardian Weekly*. "I'll bring *The Guardian*, if you don't mind," she said, wrapping the paper in her apron. "It's a new paper and I've not read it yet."

"I'm very fond of *The Guardian*," Scripps said. "My family have taken it ever since I can remember. My father was a great admirer of Gladstone."

"My father went to Eton with Gladstone," the elderly waitress said. "And now I am ready."

She had donned a coat and stood ready, her apron, her steel-rimmed spectacles in their worn black morocco case, her copy of *The Manchester Guardian* held in her hand.

"Have you no hat?" asked Scripps.

"No."

"Then I will buy you one," Scripps said tenderly.

"It will be your wedding gift," the elderly waitress said. Again there were tears shone in her eyes.

"And now let us go," Scripps said.

The elderly waitress came out from behind the counter, and together, hand in hand, they strode out into the night.

Inside the beanery the black cook pushed up the wicket and looked through from the kitchen. "Dey've gone off," he chuckled.

"Gone off into de night. Well, well, well." He closed the wicket
softly. Even he was a little impressed.

SOME EXCURSIONS INTO THE VERNACULAR

THE FOLLOWING nine items are burlesques or imitations rather than
parodies, but I thought it might be interesting, and amusing, to
show how writers have dealt with spoken language over several
centuries.

SIR JOHN SUCKLING

A Ballad

UPON A WEDDING

I TELL thee, Dick, where I have been;
Where I the rarest things have seen,
    O, things without compare!
Such sights again cannot be found
In any place on English ground,
    Be it at wake or fair.

At Charing Cross, hard by the way
Where we (thou know'st) do sell our hay,
    There is a house with stairs;
And there did I see coming down
Such folk as are not in our town,
    Vorty at least, in pairs.

Amongst the rest, one pest'lent fine
(His beard no bigger though than thine)
    Walkt on before the rest:
Our landlord looks like nothing to him:
The King (God bless him!), 'twould undo him,
    Should he go still so drest.

At Course-a-Park, without all doubt,
He should have first been taken out
    By all the maids i' th' town:
Though lusty Roger there had been,
Or little George upon the Green,
    Or Vincent of the Crown.

But wot you what? the youth was going
To make an end of all his wooing;
    The parson for him staid:
Yet by his leave (for all his haste)
He did not so much wish all past
    (Perchance) as did the maid.

The maid—and thereby hangs a tale;
For such a maid no Whitson-ale
    Could ever yet produce:
No grape, that's kindly ripe, could be
So round, so plump, so soft as she,
    Nor half so full of juice.

Her finger was so small, the ring
Would not stay on, which they did bring;
    It was too wide a peck:
And to say truth (for out it must)
It lookt like the great collar (just)
    About our young colt's neck.

Her feet beneath her petticoat,
Like little mice, stole in and out,
    As if they fear'd the light:
But O, she dances such a way!
No sun upon an Easter-day
    Is half so fine a sight.

He would have kist her once or twice;
But she would not, she was so nice,
    She would not do 't in sight:

And then she lookt as who should say,
'I will do what I list to-day,
    And you shall do 't at night.'

Her cheeks so rare a white was on,
No daisy makes comparison
    (Who sees them is undone);
For streaks of red were mingled there,
Such as are on a Katherne pear
    (The side that's next the sun).

Her lips were red; and one was thin,
Compar'd to that was next her chin
    (Some bee had stung it newly):
But, Dick, her eyes so guard her face,
I durst no more upon them gaze
    Than on the sun in July.

Her mouth so small, when she does speak,
Thou 'dst swear her teeth her words did break
    That they might passage get;
But she so handled still the matter,
They came as good as ours, or better,
    And are not spent a whit.

If wishing should be any sin,
The parson himself had guilty been
    (She lookt that day so purely);
And, did the youth so oft the feat
At night, as some did in conceit,
    It would have spoil'd him surely.

Just in the nick the cook knockt thrice,
And all the waiters in a trice
    His summons did obey:
Each serving-man, with dish in hand,
Marcht boldly up, like our train'd band,
    Presented, and away.

When all the meat was on the table,
What man of knife or teeth was able
    To stay to be intreated?
And this the very reason was—
Before the parson could say grace,
    The company was seated.

The bus'ness of the kitchen's great,
For it is fit that man should eat;
    Nor was it there deni'd—
Passion o' me, how I run on!
There's that that would be thought upon
    (I trow) besides the bride.

Now hats fly off, and youths carouse,
Healths first go round, and then the house:
    The bride's came thick and thick;
And, when 'twas nam'd another's health,
Perhaps he made it hers by stealth;
    (And who could help it, Dick?)

O'th'sudden up they rise and dance;
Then sit again and sigh, and glance;
    Then dance again and kiss:
Thus several ways the time did pass,
Whilst ev'ry woman wished her place,
    And every man wished his.

By this time all were stol'n aside
To counsel and undress the bride;
    But that he must not know:
But yet 'twas thought he guess'd her mind,
And did not mean to stay behind
    Above an hour or so.

When in he came, Dick, there she lay
Like new-fall'n snow melting away
    ('Twas time, I trow, to part):

Kisses were now the only stay,
Which soon she gave, as who would say,
   God b' w' ye, with all my heart.

But, just as Heav'ns would have, to cross it,
In came the bridemaids with the posset:
   The bridegroom eat in spite;
For, had he left the women to 't,
It would have cost two hours to do 't,
   Which were too much that night.

At length the candle's out; and now
All that they had not done they do:
   What that is, who can tell?
But I believe it was no more
Than thou and I have done before
   With Bridget and with Nell.

JONATHAN SWIFT

To their Excellencies the Lords Justices of Ireland

THE HUMBLE PETITION OF FRANCES HARRIS

Who must Starve, and Die a Maid if it miscarries.

ANNO 1700

Humbly Sheweth.

THAT I WENT to warm my self in Lady *Betty's* Chamber, because
   I was cold,
And I had in a Purse, seven Pound, four Shillings and six Pence,
   besides Farthings, in Money, and Gold;
So because I had been buying things for my *Lady* last Night,
I was resolved to tell my Money, to see if it was right:

Now you must know, because my Trunk has a very bad Lock,
Therefore all the Money, I have, which, *God* knows, is a very
    small Stock,
I keep in my Pocket ty'd about my Middle, next my Smock.
So when I went to put up my Purse, as *God* would have it, my
    Smock was unript,
And, instead of putting it into my Pocket, down it slipt:
Then the Bell rung, and I went down to put my *Lady* to Bed.
And, *God* knows, I thought my Money was as safe as my Maiden-
    head.
So when I came up again, I found my Pocket feel very light,
But when I search'd, and miss'd my Purse, *Lord!* I thought I
    should have sunk outright:
Lord! Madam, says *Mary,* how d'ye do? Indeed, says I, never
    worse;
But pray, *Mary,* can you tell what I have done with my Purse!
Lord help me, said *Mary,* I never stirr'd out of this Place!
Nay, said I, I had it in Lady *Betty's* Chamber, that's a plain
    Case.
So *Mary* got me to Bed, and cover'd me up warm;
However, she stole away my Garters, that I might do my self
    no Harm:
So I tumbl'd and toss'd all Night, as you may very well think,
But hardly ever set my Eyes together, or slept a Wink.
So I was a-dream'd, methought, that we went and search'd the
    Folks round,
And in a Corner of Mrs. *Dukes's* Box, ty'd in a Rag, the Money
    was found.
So next Morning we told *Whittle,* and he fell a Swearing;
Then my Dame *Wadgar* came, and she, you know, is thick of
    Hearing;
Dame, said I, as loud as I could bawl, Do you know what a Loss I
    have had?
Nay, said she, my Lord **Collway's* Folks are all very sad,

   * *Gallway.*

For my Lord **Dromedary* comes a *Tuesday* without fail;
Pugh! said I, but that's not the Business that I ail.
Says *Cary,* says he, I have been a Servant this Five and Twenty
    Years, come Spring,
And in all the Places I Liv'd, I never heard of such a Thing.
Yes, says the *Steward,* I remember when I was at my Lady *Shrews-*
    bury's,
Such a Thing as this happen'd, just about the time of *Goos-*
    berries.
So I went to the Party suspected, and I found her full of Grief;
(Now you must know, of all Things in the World, I hate a
    Thief.)
However I was resolv'd to bring the Discourse slily about,
Mrs. *Dukes,* said I, here's an ugly Accident has happen'd out;
'Tis not that I value the Money three Skips of a Louse;
But the Thing I stand upon, is the Credit of the House;
'Tis true, seven Pounds, four Shillings and six Pence, makes a
    great Hole in my Wages.
Besides, as they say, Service is no Inheritance in these Ages.
Now, Mrs. *Dukes,* you know, and every Body understands,
That tho' 'tis hard to judge, yet Money can't go without Hands.
The *Devil* take me, said she, (blessing her self,) if ever I saw't!
So she roar'd like a *Bedlam,* as tho' I had call'd her all to naught;
So you know, what could I say to her any more,
I e'en left her, and came away as wise as I was before.
Well: But then they would have had me gone to the Cunning
    Man;
No, said I, 'tis the same Thing, the *Chaplain* will be here anon.
So the *Chaplain* came in; now the Servants say, he is my Sweet-
    heart,
Because he's always in my Chamber, and I always take his Part;
So, as the *Devil* would have it, before I was aware, out I
    blunder'd,
Parson, said I, can you cast a *Nativity,* when a Body's plunder'd?

    * *Drogheda.*

(Now you must know, he hates to be call'd *Parson,* like the
    Devil.)
Truly, says he, Mrs. *Nab,* it might become you to be more civil:
If your Money be gone, as a Learned *Divine* says, d'ye see,
You are no *Text* for my Handling, so take that from me:
I was never taken for a *Conjurer* before, I'd have you to know.
Lord, said I, don't be angry, I'm sure I never thought you so;
You know, I honour the Cloth, I design to be a *Parson's* Wife,
I never took one in *Your Coat* for a *Conjurer* in all my Life.
With that, he twisted his Girdle at me like a Rope, as who should
    say,
Now you may go hang your self for me, and so went away.
Well; I thought I should have swoon'd; *Lord,* said I, what shall
    I do?
I have lost my *Money,* and shall lose my *True-Love* too.
Then my *Lord* call'd me; *Harry,* said my *Lord,* don't cry,
I'll give something towards thy Loss; and says my *Lady,* so will I.
Oh! but, said I, what if after all my Chaplain won't *come to?*
For that, he said, (an't please your *Excellencies*) I must petition
    You.
The Premises tenderly consider'd, I desire your *Excellencies*
    Protection,
And that I may have a Share in next *Sunday's* Collection:
And over and above, that I may have your *Excellencies* Letter,
With an Order for the *Chaplain* aforesaid: or instead of Him,
    a Better:
And then your poor *Petitioner,* both Night and Day,
Or the *Chaplain,* (for 'tis his *Trade*) as in Duty bound, shall
    ever *Pray.*

MARK TWAIN

Grandfather's Old Ram

MARK TWAIN wrote three superb humorous stories in the vernacular:
this one, the Jumping Frog, and Jim Baker's Blue-Jay Story. I have

used this one because the other two are better known. In all three, the vernacular goes below the surface level of grammar and usage— which are precisely rendered, for that matter—right into the way the narrator *thinks*. (Most "dialect stories" are dreary because the language doesn't fit the thought, which is that of the author, not of the supposed speaker.) The text below is the one Twain used in his public readings, not the written one that appears in *Roughing It*. He explains the difference (and also shows his awareness that in dialect stories psychology is as important as orthography—or rather malography) in his *Autobiography:*

One of the readings which I used was a part of an extravagant chapter in dialect from *Roughing It* which I entitled "His Grand-father's Old Ram." After I had memorized it, it began to undergo changes on the platform and it continued to edit and revise itself night after night until, by and by, from dreading to begin on it before an audience I came to like it and enjoy it. I never knew how considerable the changes had been when I finished the season's work; I never knew until ten or eleven years later, when I took up that book in a parlor in New York one night to read that chapter to a dozen friends of the two sexes who had asked for it. It *wouldn't read*—that is, it wouldn't read aloud. I struggled along with it for five minutes and then gave it up and said I should have to tell the tale as best I might from memory. It turned out that my memory was equal to the emergency; it reproduced the platform form of the story pretty faithfully after that interval of years. I still remember that form of it, I think, and I wish to recite it here, so that the reader may compare it with the story as told in *Roughing It,* if he pleases, and note how different the spoken version is from the written and printed version.

The idea of the tale is to exhibit certain bad effects of a good memory: the sort of memory which is too good, which remembers everything and forgets nothing, which has no sense of proportion and can't tell an important event from an unimportant one but preserves them all, states them all, and thus retards the progress of a narrative, at the same time making a tangled, inextricable confusion of it and intolerably wearisome to the listener. The historian of "His Grandfather's Old Ram" had that kind of a memory. He often tried to communicate that history to his comrades, the other surface miners, but he could never complete it because his memory defeated his every attempt to march a straight course; it

persistently threw remembered details in his way that had nothing
to do with the tale; these unrelated details would interest him and
sidetrack him; if he came across a name or a family or any other
thing that had nothing to do with his tale he would diverge from
his course to tell about the person who owned that name or explain
all about that family—with the result that as he plodded on he
always got further and further from his grandfather's memorable
adventure with the ram, and finally went to sleep before he got
to the end of the story, and so did his comrades. Once he did
manage to approach so nearly to the end, apparently, that the boys
were filled with an eager hope; they believed that at last they were
going to find out all about the grandfather's adventure and what it
was that had happened.

WELL, AS I was a-sayin', he bought that old ram from a
feller up in Siskiyou County and fetched him home and
turned him loose in the medder, and next morning he went
down to have a look at him, and accident'ly dropped a ten-cent
piece in the grass and stooped down—so—and was a-fumblin'
around in the grass to git it, and the ram he was a-standin' up
the slope taking notice; but my grandfather wasn't taking notice,
because he had his back to the ram and was int'rested about the
dime. Well, there he was, as I was a-sayin', down at the foot of
the slope a-bendin' over—so—fumblin' in the grass, and the ram
he was up there at the top of the slope, and Smith—Smith was
a-standin' there—no, not jest there, a little further way—fifteen
foot perhaps—well, my grandfather was a-stoopin' way down—
so—and the ram was up there observing, you know, and Smith
he . . . (musing) . . . the ram he bent his head down, so . . .
Smith of Calaveras . . . no, no it couldn't ben Smith of Calaveras—I remember now that he—b'George it was Smith of Tulare
County—course it was, I remember it now perfectly plain.

"Well, Smith he stood just there, and my grandfather he stood
just here, you know, and he was a-bendin' down just so, fumblin'
in the grass, and when the old ram see him in that attitude he
took it fur an invitation—and here he come! down the slope
thirty mile an hour and his eye full of business. You see my
grandfather's back being to him, and him stooping down like
that, of course he—why sho! it *warn't* Smith of Tulare at all, it

was Smith of Sacramento—my goodness, how did I ever come to get them Smiths mixed like that—why, Smith of Tulare was jest a nobody, but Smith of Sacramento—why the Smiths of Sacramento come of the best Southern blood in the United States; there warn't ever any better blood south of the line than the Sacramento Smiths. Why look here, one of them married a Whitaker! I reckon that gives you an idea of the kind of society the Sacramento Smiths could 'sociate around in; there ain't no better blood than that Whitaker blood; I reckon anybody'll tell you that.

"Look at Mariar Whitaker—there was a girl for you! Little? Why yes, she was little, but what of that? Look at the heart of her—had a heart like a bullock—just as good and sweet and lovely and generous as the day is long; if she had a thing and you wanted it, you could have it—have it and welcome; why Mariar Whitaker couldn't have a thing and another person need it and not get it—get it and welcome. She had a glass eye, and she used to lend it to Flora Ann Baxter that hadn't any, to receive company with; well, she was pretty large, and it didn't fit; it was a number seven, and she was excavated for a fourteen, and so that eye wouldn't lay still; every time she winked it would turn over. It was a beautiful eye and set her off admirable, because it was a lovely pale blue on the front side—the side you look out of—and it was gilded on the back side; didn't match the other eye, which was one of them browny-yellery eyes and tranquil and quiet, you know, the way that kind of eyes are; but that warn't any matter—they worked together all right and plenty picturesque. When Flora Ann winked, that blue and gilt eye would whirl over, and the other one stand still, and as soon as she begun to get excited that hand-made eye would give a whirl and then go on a-whirlin' and a-whirlin' faster and faster, and a-flashin' first blue and then yaller and then blue and then yaller, and when it got to whizzing and flashing like that, the oldest man in the world couldn't keep up with the expression on that side of her face. Flora Ann Baxter married a Hogadorn. I reckon that lets you understand what kind of blood she was— old Maryland Eastern Shore blood; not a better family in the United States than the Hogadorns.

"Sally—that's Sally Hogadorn—Sally married a missionary, and they went off carrying the good news to the cannibals out in one of them way-off islands round the world in the middle of the ocean somers, and they et her; et him too, which was irregular; it warn't the custom to eat the missionary, but only the family, and when they see what they had done they was dreadful sorry about it, and when the relations sent down there to fetch away the things they said so—said so right out—said they was sorry, and 'pologized, and said it shouldn't happen again; said 'twas an accident.

"Accident! now that's foolishness; there ain't no such thing as an accident; there ain't nothing happens in the world but what's ordered just so by a wiser Power than us, and it's always fur a good purpose; we don't know what the good purpose was, some-times—and it was the same with the families that was short a missionary and his wife. But that ain't no matter, and it ain't any of our business; all that concerns us is that it was a special providence and it had a good intention. No, sir, there ain't no such thing as an accident. Whenever a thing happens that you think is an accident you make up your mind it ain't no accident at all—it's a special providence.

"You look at my Uncle Lem—what do you say to that? That's all I ask you—you just look at my Uncle Lem and talk to me about accidents! It was like this: one day my Uncle Lem and his dog was downtown, and he was a-leanin' up against a scaffolding —sick, or drunk, or somethin'—and there was an Irishman with a hod of bricks up the ladder along about the third story, and his foot slipped and down he come, bricks and all, and hit a stranger fair and square and knocked the everlasting aspirations out of him; he was ready for the coroner in two minutes. Now then people said it was an accident.

"Accident! there warn't no accident about it; 'twas a special providence, and had a mysterious, noble intention back of it. The idea was to save that Irishman. If the stranger hadn't been there that Irishman would have been killed. The people said 'special providence—sho! the dog was there—why didn't the Irishman fall on the dog? Why warn't the dog app'inted?' Fer a mighty good reason—the dog would'a' seen him a-coming; you can't depend on no dog to carry out a special providence. You couldn't hit a dog with an Irishman because—lemme see, what was that dog's name . . . (musing) . . . oh, yes, Jasper—and a mighty good dog too; he wa'n't no common dog, he wa'n't no mongrel; he was a composite. A composite dog is a dog that's made up of all the valuable qualities that's in the dog breed— kind of a syndicate; and a mongrel is made up of the riffraff that's left over. That Jasper was one of the most wonderful dogs you ever see. Uncle Lem got him of the Wheelers. I reckon you've heard of the Wheelers; ain't no better blood south of the line than the Wheelers.

"Well, one day Wheeler was a-meditating and dreaming around in the carpet factory and the machinery made a snatch at him and first you know he was a-meandering all over that factory, from the garret to the cellar, and everywhere, at such another gait as—why you couldn't even see him; you could only hear him whiz when he went by. Well, you know a person can't go through an experience like that and arrive back home the way he was when he went. No, Wheeler got wove up into thirty-nine yards of best three-ply carpeting. The widder was sorry, she was uncommon sorry, and loved him and done the best she could fur him in the circumstances, which was unusual. She took the whole piece—thirty-nine yards—and she wanted to give him proper and honorable burial, but she couldn't bear to roll him up; she took and spread him out full length, and said she wouldn't have it any other way. She wanted to buy a tunnel for him but there wasn't any tunnel for sale, so she boxed him in a beautiful box and stood it on the hill on a pedestal twenty-one foot high, and so it was monument and grave together, and economical—sixty foot high—you could see it from everywhere—and she painted on it 'To the loving memory of thirty-nine yards best three-ply carpeting containing the mortal remainders of Millington G. Wheeler go thou and do likewise.' " *

* Mark Twain adds, in the *Autobiography:* "At this point the historian's voice began to wobble and his eyelids to droop with weariness and he fell asleep; and so from that day to this we are still in ignorance; we don't know whether the old grandfather ever got the ten-cent piece out of the grass; we haven't any idea what it was that happened or whether anything happened at all."

JAMES JOYCE

Museum Tour

T HIS THE WAY to the museyroom. Mind your hats goan in!
Now yiz are in the Willingdone Museyroom. This is a Prooshious gunn. This is a ffrinch. Tip. This is the flag of the Prooshious, the Cap and Soracer. This is the bullet that byng the flag of the Prooshious. This is the ffrinch that fire on the Bull that bang the flag of the Prooshious. Saloos the Crossgunn! Up with your pike and fork! Tip. (Bullsfoot! Fine!) This is the triplewon hat of Lipoleum. Tip. Lipoleumhat. This is the Willingdone on his same white harse, the Cokenhape. This is the big Sraughter Willingdone, grand and magentic in his goldtin spurs and his ironed dux and his quarterbrass woodyshoes and his magnate's gharters and his bangkok's best and goliar's goloshes and his pulluponeasyan wartrews. This is his big wide harse. Tip. This is the three lipoleum boyne grouching down in the living detch. This is an inimyskilling inglis, this is a scotcher grey, this is a davy, stooping. This is the bog lipoleum mordering the lipoleum beg. A Gallawghurs argaumunt. This is the petty lipoleum boy that was nayther bag nor bug. Assaye, assaye! Touchole Fitz Tuomush. Dirty MacDyke. And Hairy O'Hurry. All of them arminus-varminus. This is Delian alps. This is Mont Tivel, this is Mont Tipsey, this is the Grand Mons Injun. This is the crimealine of the alps hooping to sheltershock the three lipoleums. This is the jinnies with their legahorns feinting to read in their handmade's book of stralegy while making their war undisides the Willingdone. The jinnies is a cooin her hand and the jinnies is a ravin her hair and the Willingdone git the band up. This is big Willingdone mormorial tallowscoop Wounderworker obscides on the flanks of the jinnies. Sexcaliber hrosspower. Tip. This is me Belchum sneaking his phillippy out of his most Awful Grimmest Sunshat Cromwelly. Looted. This is the jinnies' hastings dispatch for to irrigate the Willingdone. Dispatch in thin red lines cross the shortfront of me Belchum. Yaw, yaw, yaw! Leaper Orthor. Fear siecken! Fieldgaze thy tiny frow. Hugacting. Nap. That was the tictacs of the jinnies for to fontannoy the

Willingdone. Shee, shee, shee! The jinnies is jillous agincourting
all the lopoleums. And the lipoleums is gonn boycottoncrezy onto
the one Willingdone. And the Willingdone git the band up. This
is bode Belchum, bonnet to busby, breaking his secred word with
a ball up his ear to the Willingdone. This is the Willingdone's
hurold dispitchback. Dispitch desployed on the regions rare of
me Belchum. Salamangra! Ayi, ayi, ayi! Cherry jinnies. Figtree-
you! Damn fairy ann, Voutre. Willingdone. That was the first
joke of Willingdone, tic for tac. Hee, hee, hee! This is me Belchum in his twelvemile cowchooks, weet, tweet and stampforth
foremost, footing the camp for the jinnies. Drink a sip, dranka-
sup, for he's as sooner buy a guinness than he'd stale store stout.
This is Rooshious balls. This is a ttrinch. This is mistletropes.
This is Canon Futter with the popynose. After his hundred days'
indulgence. This is the blessed. Tarra's widdars! This is jinnies
in the bonny bawn blooches. This is lipoleums in the rowdy
howses. This is the Willingdone, by the splinters of Cork, order
fire. Tonnerre! (Bullsear! Play!) This is camelry, this is floodens,
this is the solphereens in action, this is their mobbily, this is
panickburns. Almeidagad! Arthiz too loose! This is Willingdone
cry. Brum! Brum! Cumbrum! This is jinnies cry. Underwetter!
Goat strip Finnlambs! This is jinnies rinning away to their ouster-
lists dowan a bunkersheels. With a nip nippy nip and a trip
trippy trip so airy. For their heart's right there. Tip. This is me
Belchum's tinkyou tankyou silvoor plate for citchin the crapes in
the cool of his canister. Poor the pay! This is the bissmark of the
marathon merry of the jinnies they left behind them. This is the
Willingdone branlish his same marmorial tallowscoop Sophy-
Key-Po for his royal divorsion on the rinnaway jinnies. Gam-
bariste della porca! Dalaveras fimmieras! This is the pettiest
of the lipoleums, Toffeethief, that spy on the Willingdone from
his big white harse, the Capeinhope. Stonewall Willingdone is
an old maxy montrumeny. Lipoleums is nice hung bushellors.
This is hiena hinnessy laughing alout at the Willingdone.
This is lipsyg dooley krieging the funk from the hinnessy. This
is the hinndoo Shimar Shin between the dooley boy and the
hinnessy. Tip. This is the wixy old Willingdone picket up the
half of the threefoiled hat of lipoleums fromoud of the bluddle

filth. This is the hinndoo waxing ranjymad for a bombshoob. This is the Willingdone hanking the half of the hat of lipoleums up the tail on the buckside of his big white harse. Tip. That was the last joke of Willingdone. Hit, hit, hit! This is the same white harse of the Willingdone, Culpenhelp, waggling his tailoscrupp with the half of a hat of lipoleums to insoult on the hinndoo seeboy. Hney, hney, hney! (Bullsrag! Foul!) This is the seeboy, madrashattaras, upjump and pumpim, cry to the Willingdone: Ap Pukkaru! Pukka Yurap! This is the Willingdone, bornstable ghentleman, tinders his maxbotch to the cursigan Shimar Shin. Basucker youstead! This is the dooforim seeboy blow the whole of the half of the hat of lipoleums off of the top of the tail on the back of his big wide harse. Tip (Bullseye! Game!) How Copenhagen ended. This way the museyroom. Mind your boots goan out.

Phew!

(From *Finnegans Wake*)

H. L. MENCKEN

The Declaration of Independence in American

WHEN THINGS get so balled up that the people of a country got to cut loose from some other country, and go it on their own hook, without asking no permission from nobody, excepting maybe God Almighty, then they ought to let everybody know why they done it, so that everybody can see they are not trying to put nothing over on nobody.

All we got to say on this proposition is this: first, me and you is as good as anybody else, and maybe a damn sight better; second, nobody ain't got no right to take away none of our rights; third, every man has got a right to live, to come and go as he pleases, and to have a good time whichever way he likes, so long as he don't interfere with nobody else. That any government that don't give a man them rights ain't worth a damn; also, people ought to choose the kind of government they want themselves, and nobody else ought to have no say in the matter.

That whenever any government don't do this, then the people have got a right to give it the bum's rush and put in one that will take care of their interests. Of course, that don't mean having a revolution every day like them South American yellow-bellies, or every time some jobholder goes to work and does something he ain't got no business to do. It is better to stand a little graft, etc., than to have revolutions all the time, like them coons, and any man that wasn't a anarchist or one of them I.W.W.'s would say the same. But when things get so bad that a man ain't hardly got no rights at all no more, but you might almost call him a slave, then everybody ought to get together and throw the grafters out, and put in new ones who won't carry on so high and steal so much, and then watch them. This is the proposition the people of these Colonies is up against, and they have got tired of it, and won't stand it no more. The administration of the present King, George III, has been rotten from the start, and when anybody kicked about it he always tried to get away with it by strong-arm work. Here is some of the rough stuff he has pulled:

He vetoed bills in the Legislature that everybody was in favor of, and hardly nobody was against.

He wouldn't allow no law to be passed without it was first put up to him, and then he stuck it in his pocket and let on he forgot about it, and didn't pay no attention to no kicks.

When people went to work and gone to him and asked him to put through a law about this or that, he give them their choice: either they had to shut down the Legislature and let him pass it all by himself, or they couldn't have it at all.

He made the Legislature meet at one-horse tank-towns, so that hardly nobody could get there and most of the leaders would stay home and let him go to work and do things like he wanted.

He give the Legislature the air, and sent the members home every time they stood up to him and give him a call-down or bawled him out.

When a Legislature was busted up he wouldn't allow no new one to be elected, so that there wasn't nobody left to run things, but anybody could walk in and do whatever they pleased.

He tried to scare people outen moving into these States, and made it so hard for a wop or one of these here kikes to get his papers that he would rather stay home and not try it, and then, when he come in, he wouldn't let him have no land, and so he either went home again or never come.

He monkeyed with the courts, and didn't hire enough judges to do the work, and so a person had to wait so long for his case to come up that he got sick of waiting, and went home, and so never got what was coming to him.

He got the judges under his thumb by turning them out when they done anything he didn't like, or by holding up their salaries, so that they had to knuckle down or not get no money.

He made a lot of new jobs, and give them to loafers that nobody knowed nothing about, and the poor people had to pay the bill, whether they could or not.

Without no war going on, he kept an army loafing around the country, no matter how much people kicked about it.

He let the army run things to suit theirself and never paid no attention whatsoever to nobody which didn't wear no uniform.

He let grafters run loose, from God knows where, and give them the say in everything, and let them put over such things as the following:

Making poor people board and lodge a lot of soldiers they ain't got no use for, and don't want to see loafing around.

When the soldiers kill a man, framing it up so that they would get off.

Interfering with business.

Making us pay taxes without asking us whether we thought the things we had to pay taxes for was something that was worth paying taxes for or not.

When a man was arrested and asked for a jury trial, not letting him have no jury trial.

Chasing men out of the country, without being guilty of nothing, and trying them somewheres else for what they done here.

In countries that border on us, he put in bum governments, and then tried to spread them out, so that by and by they would take in this country too, or make our own government as bum as they was.

He never paid no attention whatever to the Constitution, but he went to work and repealed laws that everybody was satisfied with and hardly nobody was against, and tried to fix the government so that he could do whatever he pleased.

He busted up the Legislatures and let on he could do all the work better by himself.

Now he washes his hands of us and even goes to work and declares war on us, so we don't owe him nothing, and whatever authority he ever had he ain't got no more.

He has burned down towns, shot down people like dogs, and raised hell against us out on the ocean.

He hired whole regiments of Dutch, etc., to fight us, and told them they could have anything they wanted if they could take it away from us, and sicked these Dutch, etc., on us.

He grabbed our own people when he found them in ships on the ocean, and shoved guns into their hands, and made them fight against us, no matter how much they didn't want to.

He stirred up the Indians, and give them arms and ammunition, and told them to go to it, and they have killed men, women and children, and don't care which.

Every time he has went to work and pulled any of these things, we have went to work and put in a kick, but every time we have went to work and put in a kick he has went to work and did it again. When a man keeps on handing out such rough stuff all the time, all you can say is that he ain't got no class and ain't fitten to have no authority over people who have got any rights, and he ought to be kicked out.

When we complained to the English we didn't get no more satisfaction. Almost every day we give them plenty of warning that the politicians over there was doing things to us that they didn't have no right to do. We kept on reminding them who we was, and what we was doing here, and how we come to come here. We asked them to get us a square deal, and told them that if this thing kept on we'd have to do something about it and maybe they wouldn't like it. But the more we talked, the more they didn't pay no attention to us. Therefore, if they ain't for us they must be agin us, and we are ready to give them the fight of their lives, or to shake hands when it is over.

Therefore be it resolved, That we, the representatives of the people of the United States of America, in Congress assembled, hereby declare as follows: That the United States, which was the United Colonies in former times, is now a free country, and ought to be; that we have throwed out the English King and don't want to have nothing to do with him no more, and are not taking no more English orders no more; and that, being as we are now a free country, we can do anything that free countries can do, especially declare war, make peace, sign treaties, go into business, etc. And we swear on the Bible on this proposition, one and all, and agree to stick to it no matter what happens, whether we win or we lose, and whether we get away with it or get the worst of it, no matter whether we lose all our property by it or even get hung for it.*

* When this was reprinted in *A Mencken Chrestomathy*, the author added the following note:

"From THE AMERICAN LANGUAGE, THIRD EDITION, 1923, pp. 398-402. First printed, as Essay in American, in the Baltimore *Evening Sun*, Nov. 7, 1921. Reprinted in THE AMERICAN LANGUAGE, SECOND EDITION, 1921, pp. 388-92. From the preface thereof: 'It must be obvious that more than one section of the original is now quite unintelligible to the average American of the sort using the Common Speech. What would he make, for example, of such a sentence as this one: "He has called together bodies at places unusual, uncomfortable, and distant from the depository of their public records, for the sole purpose of fatiguing them into compliance with his measures"? Or of this: "He has refused for a long time, after such dissolutions, to cause others to be elected, whereby the legislative powers, incapable of annihilation, have returned to the people at large for their exercise." Such Johnsonian periods are quite beyond his comprehension, and no doubt the fact is at least partly to blame for the neglect upon which the Declaration has fallen in recent years. When, during the Wilson-Palmer saturnalia of oppressions [1918-20], specialists in liberty began protesting that the Declaration plainly gave the people the right to alter the government under which they lived and even to abolish it altogether, they encountered the utmost incredulity. On more than one occasion, in fact, such an exegete was tarred and feathered by shocked members of the American Legion, even after the Declaration had been read to them. What ailed them was simply that they could not understand its Eighteenth Century English.' This jocosity was denounced as seditious by various patriotic Americans, and in England it was accepted gravely and deplored sadly as a specimen of current Standard American."

OLIVER JENSEN

The Gettysburg Address in Eisenhowese

SEVERAL YEARS AGO Oliver Jensen, now editor of *American Heritage*, composed the following after being exposed to too many White House press conferences. It was circulated in carbon first, then mimeograph, Doris Fleeson printed it in her column, and *The New Republic* of June 17, 1957, also gave a version. Neither attributed it to Jensen; it had become a bit of anonymous folklore. The version below is the original as given me by Jensen, with two or three variations in which *The New Republic's* version seemed to me to have added a turn of the screw.

I HAVEN'T CHECKED these figures but 87 years ago, I think it was, a number of individuals organized a governmental set-up here in this country, I believe it covered certain Eastern areas, with this idea they were following up based on a sort of national independence arrangement and the program that every individual is just as good as every other individual. Well, now, of course, we are dealing with this big difference of opinion, civil disturbance you might say, although I don't like to appear to take sides or name any individuals, and the point is naturally to check up, by actual experience in the field, to see whether any governmental set-up with a basis like the one I was mentioning has any validity and find out whether that dedication by those early individuals will pay off in lasting values and things of that kind.

Well, here we are, at the scene where one of these disturbances between different sides got going. We want to pay our tribute to those loved ones, those departed individuals who made the supreme sacrifice here on the basis of their opinions about how this thing ought to be handled. And I would say this. It is absolutely in order to do this.

But if you look at the over-all picture of this, we can't pay any tribute—we can't sanctify this area, you might say—we can't hallow according to whatever individual creeds or faiths or sort of religious outlooks are involved like I said about this particular area. It was those individuals themselves, including the enlisted men, very brave individuals, who have given this religious character to the area. The way I see it, the rest of the world will not remember any statements issued here but it will never forget how these men put their shoulders to the wheel and carried this idea down the fairway.

Now frankly, our job, the living individuals' job here, is to pick up the burden and sink the putt they made these big efforts here for. It is our job to get on with the assignment—and from these deceased fine individuals to take extra inspiration, you could call it, for the same theories about the set-up for which they made such a big contribution. We have to make up our minds right here and now, as I see it, that they didn't put out all that blood, perspiration and—well—that they didn't just make a dry run here, and that all of us here, under God, that is, the God of our choice, shall beef up this idea about freedom and liberty and those kind of arrangements, and that government of all individuals, by all individuals and for the individuals, shall not pass out of the world-picture.

DWIGHT DAVID EISENHOWER

The West Point Address

ON JUNE 5, 1960, just in time to be included here, President Eisenhower gave a talk which makes a nice pendant to Oliver Jensen's parody above. The occasion was a Republican campaign dinner and the doubly reassuring atmosphere, military and political, seems to have dissolved utterly the President's grammatical inhibitions, never too strong at best. Stumbling and slipping on syntactical banana peels, saving himself by a desperate grab at "I want to say this" only to trip over a dangling participle and execute a pratfall worthy of Sliding Billy Watson, doggedly toiling through thickets of subordinate clauses without emerging into a sentence, the President eisenhowered the language to a fare-thee-well. Anyway that is the way I see it, my impression of this matter we are discussing, and I want to say this quite frankly that this is not in any way shape or matter a partisan view of this manner. In fact you might call it, and whatever abilities he may or may not have in other walks of action, I think the most accurate term for this view is bipartisan.

M RS. ST. GEORGE, Senator Keating, and my friends:
It is indeed, difficult, in the circumstances in which I find myself, to discover words that seem applicable to this situation. . . .

Now tonight we meet at a time of bewilderment, I don't like this term or the using of the term that we are living always in crisis. We are not. There is no nation in this world that dares at this moment to attack the United States, and they know it.

But we wonder what is the outcome of every decent, proper gesture we make to those that live in the other camp. They live in a closed society, secrecy of intent—which we try to penetrate, and in my opinion properly, but we are certain of this: Our problem is not only keeping ourselves strong, and by strong I don't mean merely militarily, I mean spiritually, intellectually, scientifically, economically and militarily; and then, we must make certain that all of those people who live with us, in the hope that those concepts of human dignity and freedom and liberty are going to prevail in the world, will stand always by our side in the determination that freedom and liberty will eventually triumph over tyranny. . . .

Now I am talking about matters, for this moment, that are not partisan. They are bipartisan. But I want to say this: It is a tremendous satisfaction to me to know that the Republican party believes in the kind of things that I have tried so haltingly to express to you.

My colleagues here in Government, Senator Keating, and your guest of honor, Mrs. St. George, have in every single vote that has anything to do with these important world questions, stood exactly in the ranks exactly like any soldier would when asked by his commander to do so.

So I want to say to you a very simple word—and I promised my classmates I would only be five minutes, and I think I have used ten minutes already, but I just want to ask you to do this: Look at the records of your Republican representatives in Congress. Do they represent what you understand to be firm, sound middle-of-the-road government that refuses to make government a centralized Government capable of governing your lives in every single item, refuses to accede to the doctrine of collectivity or centralization, or is it the kind of philosophy that says, "We want to live in liberty, in freedom"? . . . .*

Because I tell you, this kind of policy, internally and externally, is the thing that will keep America strong, safe and sure—for you and every single person that comes behind you.

This is what I hope to do myself, so far as it is proper and the people who will meet within a few short weeks to take over the direction of campaigns—I am ready to do my part.

And I tell you this, it will be an honor to be associated with such people as you are, as you do your part.

Thank you, and good night.

Postscript on Gamaliese

I had intended to insert at this point, as another example of political vernacular, some pages from the Inaugural Address of the only other President whose English was as defective as Eisenhower's, namely Warren Gamaliel Harding. But I finally decided against it simply because reading it even as parody was impossible; the mind wandered, the eye became glassy. Perhaps a few fragments will give the idea:

"MY COUNTRYMEN, when one surveys the world about him after the great storm [Mr. Harding begins] noting the marks of destruction and yet rejoicing in the ruggedness of the things which withstood it, if he is an American he breathes the clarified atmosphere with a strange mixture of regret and new hope. . . . Standing in this presence, mindful of the solemnity of this occasion, feeling the emotions which no one may know until he senses the great weight of responsibility for himself, I must utter my belief in the divine inspiration of the founding fathers. Surely there must have been God's intent in the making

---

* As a bipartisan, I must point out that, although the syntax seems to put the Republican Party on record against freedom and liberty, the speaker almost certainly intended to say the opposite. He just got lost in one of those thickets.

of this new world republic. Ours is an organic law which had but one ambiguity [slavery—D.M.] and we saw that effaced in a baptism of sacrifice and blood, with union maintained, the nation supreme and its concord inspiring. . . .

"The success of our popular government rests wholly upon the correct interpretation of the deliberate, intelligent, dependable popular will of America. In deliberate questioning of a suggested change of national policy where internationality was to supersede nationality we turned to a referendum of the American people. There was ample discussion, and there is a public mandate in manifest understanding. [He refers to the fight about entering the League of Nations; I don't understand the last five words.—D.M.]. . . .

"The business world reflects the disturbance of war's reaction. Herein flows the life blood of material existence. . . . We must seek the readjustment with care and courage. Our people must give and take. Prices must reflect the receding fever of war activities. Perhaps we never shall know the old level of wages again because war inevitably readjusts compensations and the necessaries of life will show their inseparable relationship, but we must strive for normalcy to reach stability. [I read this rather gnomic sentence, in which the President launched that great neologism, "normalcy," as meaning that wages will now be lower than their wartime levels. One recalls Mencken's description of Harding's prose style as suggestive of a hippopotamus struggling to free itself from a slough of molasses.]. . . . No altered system will work a miracle. Any wild experiment will only add to the confusion. Our best assurance lies in efficient administration of our proven system. . . .

"Service is the supreme commitment of life. I would rejoice to acclaim the era of the golden rule and crown it with the autocracy of service. [Something wrong here.—D.M.] I pledge an administration wherein all the agencies of government are called to serve and ever promote an understanding of government purely as an expression of the popular will. [Teapot Dome was two years away.—D.M.]. . . .

"I have taken the solemn oath of office on that passage of holy writ wherein it is asked: 'What doth the Lord require of thee but to do justly and to love mercy and walk humbly with thy God?' This I plight to God and country."

Amateurs of political prose may find the complete text on pages 103 to 114 of *The Illustrious Life and Work of Warren G. Harding: From Farm to White House,* written and published in 1923 after Harding's death, by Thomas H. Russell, A.M., LL.D., author of *Life and Work of Theodore Roosevelt* and Editor-in-Chief of the International Business Library, with an Introduction by the Hon. Medill McCormick, U. S. Senator from Illinois. The volume is dedicated "To the young people of America, to whom the life of Warren Gamaliel Harding furnishes a high ideal of American citizenship and an inspiration for striving after and attaining the true success that is based on service." It is Copiously Illustrated with Photographs in Half-Tone.

THE AVANTGARDE VERNACULAR

Who Stole My Golden Metaphor? by S. J. PERELMAN

I HAD A SUIT over my arm and was heading west down Eighth Street, debating whether to take it to one of those 24-hour dry-cleaning establishments or a Same-Day Cleaner or even a place that might return it before I left it, when I ran smack into Vernon Equinox in front of the Waffle Shop. Fair weather or foul, Vernon can usually be found along there between Mac-Dougal Street and Sixth Avenue, scanning the bargain Jung in the corner bookshop or disparaging the fake Negro primitive masks at the stationery store. His gaunt, greenish-white face, edged in the whiskers once characteristic of fisherfolk and stage Irishmen and now favored by Existentialist poets, his dungarees flecked with paint, and his huaraches and massive turquoise rings clearly stamp Vernon as a practitioner of the arts, though which one is doubtful. The fact is that he favors them all impartially. He writes an occasional diatribe for magazines called *Neurotica* and *Ichor,* paints violent canvases portraying one's sensations under mescaline, dabbles in wire sculpture, and composes music for abstract films as yet unphotographed. He derives his sustenance, if any, from a minuscule shop on Christopher Street, where he designs and fashions copper sconces and jewelry, but since the place is open only from six-thirty in the evening until eight, its revenue is nominal. It has been whispered, late at night in Alex's Borsch Bowl, that Vernon holds a Black Mass now and again in his shop. How he can get a naked woman and a goat into that tiny store, though—let alone himself—is a puzzle.

Anyway, there he was outside the Waffle, staring at the three rows of Dolly Madison ice-cream cones slowly revolving in the window before a background of prisms, and his contempt was magnificent to behold. It was a pretty unnerving display, actually; the ice cream was so obviously pink-tinted cotton and the cones themselves made of the plywood used in orange crates that you instinctively shuddered at the oral damage they could inflict. As he turned away from the window with an almost audible snarl, Vernon caught sight of me.

"Look there," he said furiously, pointing at the multiple rosy reflections shimmering in the glass. "That's what you're up against. Is it any wonder Modigliani died at thirty-three?" I stood transfixed, seeking to fathom the connection between Dolly Madison and the ill-starred Italian Painter, but Vernon had already hurdled his rhetorical question. "I give up! I throw in the towel!" he proclaimed. "You spend your whole life trying to imprison a moment of beauty, and they go for borax like that. Gad!"

"When did you get back?" I asked placatingly. There was nothing in his appearance to indicate that he had been away at all, or even exposed to direct sunlight for the past six months; still, it seemed a reasonably safe gambit.

"End of January," he said with a morose backward look at the window.

"Er—how did you like Haiti?" I asked. That too was a wild stab, but I dimly remembered being waylaid outside the Bamboo Forest in an icy wind and told of up-country voodoo rites.

"Haiti?" Vernon repeated, with such withering scorn that two passers-by veered toward the curb. "That tourist drop? Nobody goes there any more. I was in Oaxaca. Not Oaxaca proper, mind you," he corrected, anxious to scotch the impression that he frequented resorts, "a tiny village about sixty miles north, San Juan Doloroso. Completely unspoiled—Elspeth and I lived there for three pesos a day."

"Oh, yes," I said fluently. "Henry Miller mentions it in *Tropic of Capricorn*." From the quick look Vernon gave me, I knew I had planted the seeds of a sleepless night. "Well, old boy," I inquired, giving his shoulder an encouraging clap, "what are you up to these days? When are we going to see a show of those nereids made out of pipe-cleaners?"

"I'm through with that dilettante stuff," said Vernon. "I've been designing some nonobjective puppets. It's a combination of dance and mime. Schoenberg wants to do the music."

"I'd let him," I recommended. "It sounds exciting. Tip me off before the recital, won't you?"

"There isn't going to be any," he said. "The puppets are suspended in zones of light and the music comes over. That is, its superimposed. We're trying to establish a mood."

"Very definitely," I agreed. "I'm sure it'll work out. Well, good luck, and—"

"I'd have finished it months ago if Truman Capote hadn't sabotaged me," Vernon went on irascibly. "The aggravation I suffered from that episode—well, never mind. Why burden you?"

Arrested by the bitterness in his tone, I turned back. "What do you mean?" I asked. "What did he do?"

"Come in here and I'll show you," said Vernon, propelling me into a coffeepot a few doors away. After extensive byplay with the counterman involving the preparation of a muffin, obviously calculated to heighten the suspense, he drew a clipping from his wallet. "Did you read this interview with Capote by Harvey Breit? It came out in the *Times Book Review* around a year ago."

"Why, yes," I said vaguely, scanning the text. "It was rather tiptoe, but then, most of the publicity about him is. I didn't notice anything special."

"Nothing except that the little creep helped himself to my whole style," said Vernon with rancor. "Things I said at different parties. It's the most barefaced—"

"Wait a minute," I interrupted. "Those are blunt words, neighbor. You sure of your facts?"

"Ha *ha!*" Vernon emitted a savage cackle. "I just happen to have about two hundred witnesses, that's all! People who were there! Look at this, for instance." He ran his forefinger down a column. "Breit asked Capote to describe himself, and what do you think he said? 'I'm about as tall as a shotgun—and just as noisy. I think I have rather heated eyes.'"

"He's rumored to have ball-and-claw feet too, like a Queen Anne dresser," I returned, "but why should *you* get worked up?"

"Because it's a straight paraphrase of a thumbnail sketch I gave of myself," said Vernon tigerishly. "You know Robin Nankivel, the ceramist—the girl who does the caricatures in porcelain? Well, it was in her studio, next to the Cherry Lane Theater. I remember the whole thing plainly. They were all milling around Capote, making a big fuss. He was wearing a chameleon silk vest and blue tennis sneakers; I could draw you a picture of him. Arpad Fustian, the rug-chandler, and Polly Entrail and I were over in a corner, discussing how we visualized ourselves, and I said I was about as tall as an Osage bow and just as relentless. Right then I happened to look over, and there was Capote looking at me."

"I guess his eyes *are* really heated, though," I said. "The only time I ever saw him, in the balcony of Loew's Valencia, they glowed in the dark like a carnation."

"At first," continued Vernon, too full of his grievance to encompass anything outside it, "I didn't associate this puling little simile of his with my remark. But after I read on further, where he analyzes his voice and features for Breit, I nearly dropped dead. My entire idiom! The same unique, highly individual way I express myself! Here it is—the end of the paragraph. 'Let's see,' he (Capote) said. 'I have a very sassy voice. I like my nose but you can't see it because I wear these thick glasses. If you looked at my face from both sides, you'd see they were completely different. (Mr. Capote demonstrated.) It's sort of a changeling face.'"

I studied the photograph imbedded in the letterpress. "A changeling," I said, thinking out loud, "is a child supposed to have been secretly substituted for another by elves. Does he mean he's not really Truman Capote?"

"Of course he is," said Vernon irritably, "but read the rest—"

"Hold on," I said. "We may have uncovered something pretty peculiar here. This party admits in so many words that he's not legit. How do we know that he hasn't done away with the real Capote—dissolved him in corrosive sublimate or buried him under a floor someplace—and is impersonating him? He's certainly talking funny."

"God damn it, let me finish, will you?" Vernon implored. "It's this last part where he copied my stuff bodily. Listen: 'Do you want to know the real reason why I push my hair down on my forehead? Because I have two cowlicks. If I didn't push my hair forward it would make me look as though I had two feathery horns.' "

"Great Scott!" I exclaimed, a light suddenly dawning. "Don't you see who's talking? It's not Capote at all—it's *Pan*. The feathery horns, the ball-and-claw feet—it all ties together!"

"He can be the Grand Mufti of Jerusalem for all I care," snapped Vernon. "All I know is that I was having brunch at Lee Chumley's one Sunday with Karen Nudnic, the choreographer, and she was wearing a bang. I said she looked like one of those impish little satyrs of Aubrey Beardsley's, and that just for kicks she ought to do up her hair in points to accentuate it. Well, I don't have to tell you who was in the next booth with his ear flapping. Of course, I never thought anything of it at the time."

"It's open and shut," I said. "The jury wouldn't even leave the box."

"Ah, why sue a guy like that?" he replied disgustedly. "So I'd expose him publicly and get six cents in damages. Would that recompense me for my humiliation?"

I tried not to appear obtuse, but the odds were against me. "I don't quite understand how he hurt you," I said. "Did any of your friends spot this—er—similarity between Capote's dialogue and your own?"

"No-o-o, not until I wised them up," admitted Vernon.

"Well, did they avoid you subsequently, or did you lose any customers as a result of it?"

"*What?*" he shouted. "You think that twirp could make the

slightest difference in my life? You must have a lousy opinion
of my—"

"Hey, you in the back!" sang out the counterman. "Pipe down!
This ain't Webster Hall!"

"No, and it's not Voisin's either!" Vernon snarled. "The coffee
here's pure slop. Who are you paying off down at the Board of
Health?"

As the two of them, spitting like tomcats, converged from opposite ends of the bar and joyfully began exchanging abuse, I
recovered my suit and squirmed out into Eighth Street. The
Dolly Madison cones were still revolving turgidly in the Waffle
Shop, and a light spring rain fell on the just and the unjust
alike. All at once, the fatuity of dry-cleaning a garment that
would only become soiled again overcame me. How much more
sensible to put the money into some sound cultural investment,
such as a copy of *Other Voices, Other Rooms,* for instance,
thereby enriching both its talented author and one's own psyche.
I instantly directed my steps toward the corner bookshop, but as
luck would have it, halfway there I ran into a young bard I know
named T. S. Heliogabalus. The story that kid told me!

SELF-PARODIES: *CONSCIOUS*

COLERIDGE ON COLERIDGE

On a Ruined House in a Romantic Country

AND THIS reft house is that the which ne built,
Lamented Jack! And here his malt he pil'd,
Cautious in vain! These rats that squeak so wild,
Squeak, not unconscious of their father's guilt.
Did ye not see her gleaming thro' the glade?
Belike, 'twas she, the maiden all forlorn.
What though she milk no cow with crumpled horn,
Yet *aye* she haunts the dale where *erst* she stray'd;
And *aye* beside her stalks her amorous knight!

Still on his thighs their wonted brogues are worn,
And thro' those brogues, still tatter'd and betorn,
His hindward charms gleam an unearthly white;
As when thro' broken clouds at night's high noon
Peeps in fair fragments forth the full-orb'd harvest-moon! *

SWINBURNE ON SWINBURNE

Nephelidia

FROM THE depth of the dreamy decline of the dawn through a
    notable nimbus of nebulous noonshine,
    Pallid and pink as the palm of the flag-flower that flickers with
        fear of the flies as they float,
Are they looks of our lovers that lustrously lean from a marvel
    of mystic miraculous moonshine,
    These that we feel in the blood of our blushes that thicken
        and threaten with throbs through the throat?
Thicken and thrill as a theatre thronged at appeal of an actor's
    appalled agitation,
    Fainter with fear of the fires of the future than pale with the
        promise of pride in the past;

---

* This is one of three *Sonnets Attempted in the Manner of Contemporary
Writers* which Coleridge published in the *Monthly Magazine* in 1797 under
the pen name "Nehemiah Higginbottom." He later described them as
"written in ridicule of my own poems and Charles Lloyd's and Lamb's, exposing that affection of unaffectedness, of jumping and misplaced accents in
commonplace epithets, flat lines forced into poetry by italics (signifying how
well and mouthishly the author would read them) puny pathos, etc. . . .
The third [the one given above] of which the phrases were borrowed entirely from my own poems, concentrates on the indiscriminate use of
elaborate and swelling language and imagery. . . . So general at that time
and so decided was the opinion concerning the characteristic vices of my
style that a celebrated physician . . . speaking of me in other respects with
his usual kindness to a gentleman who was about to meet me at a dinner-
party, could not resist giving him a hint not to mention *The House That
Jack Built* in my presence, for that I was sore as a boil about that sonnet,
he not knowing that I was myself the author of it."

Flushed with the famishing fullness of fever that reddens with
   radiance of rathe recreation,
   Gaunt as the ghastliest of glimpses that gleam through the
   gloom of the gloaming when ghosts go aghast?
Nay, for the nick of the tick of the time is a tremulous touch on
   the temples of terror,
   Strained as the sinews yet strenuous with strife of the dead
   who is dumb as the dust-heaps of death:
Surely no soul is it, sweet as the spasm of erotic emotional exquisite error,
   Bathed in the balms of beatified bliss, beatific itself by beati-
   tude's breath.
Surely no spirit or sense of a soul that was soft to the spirit and
   soul of our senses
   Sweetens the stress of suspiring suspicion that sobs in the sem-
   blance and sound of a sigh;
Only this oracle opens Olympian, in mystical moods and tri-
   angular tenses—
   'Life is the lust of a lamp for the light that is dark till the
   dawn of the day when we die.'
Mild is the mirk and monotonous music of memory, melodiously
   mute as it may be,
   While the hope in the heart of a hero is bruised by the breach
   of men's rapiers, resigned to the rod;
Made meek as a mother whose bosom-beats bound with the
   bliss-bringing bulk of a balm-breathing baby,
   As they grope through the graveyard of creeds, under skies
   growing green at a groan for the grimness of God.
Blank is the book of his bounty beholden of old, and its binding
   is blacker than bluer:
   Out of blue into black is the scheme of the skies, and their
   dews are the wine of the bloodshed of things;
Till the darkling desire of delight shall be free as a fawn that is
   freed from the fangs that pursue her,

Till the heart-beats of hell shall be hushed by a hymn from
the hunt that has harried the kennel of kings.*

BEERBOHM ON BEERBOHM

A Vain Child

H OW VERY DELIGHTFUL Struwwelpeter is! For all its crude
translation and cheap aspect, it has indeed the sentiment of
style, and it reveals, with surer delicacy than does any other
record, the spirit of a German Christmas Day. Over the first
page presides an angel with bunt wings, such as were fashionable
in the Empress Augusta's period. There stand, on her either
side, studded with tapers and erect among pink clouds, two
patulous Christmas trees, from beneath whose shade two smaller
angels sprinkle toys for good children. A delightful group! Hoffman guides me, as Mephisto, Faust, through all the nurseries of
that childish world. He shows me those undersized, sharp-
featured, bright-tunicked children, mocking the blackamoor
along the flowered pathway, or fidgeting at a table, or refusing
soup. At his word, a door springs open for the furial inrush of
that tailor who does ever dock miscreant thumbs, and Harriet,
also, *avidis circumdata flammis,* comes flying from her great
folly. Struwwelpeter himself does not please me. His tangled
density of chevelure and meek exposure of interminable nails,
his ill-made tunic and green gaiters, make altogether a quite
repellent picture. More pleasing to seek those gracious pages

---

* *Nephelidia* is from a little book Swinburne published in 1880: *The
Heptalogia, or the Seven Against Sense; A Cap with Seven Bells.* Both in
its wit and its copiousness the title resembles the parodies—there is, for
example, a remarkably inventive and amusing one of Lord Lytton's verse
but it goes on for twenty-one pages. Swinburne's facility is slightly appalling:
Tennyson printed *Despair: A Dramatic Monologue* in *The Nineteenth
Century* for November, 1881, and *The Fortnightly Review* a month later
printed Swinburne's long parody, *Disgust;* it was with him a form of book
reviewing! I must add that *Nephelidia,* although it has been admired by such
nice judges as Louis Kronenberger, seems to me rather self-sparing; Swinburne only mocks his mechanical alliteration, but there was much else to
be criticized.

traversed by Johnny's history! The landscape there is nothing but a lamp-post and some cobble-stones; the boy *Très dégagé*, his chin aloft, his combed hair fugient in the breeze, one scarlet boot advanced, the fingers of one hand outstretched, under his arm a book of bright scarlet. These or those, it may be of my readers do not remember the story of his strange immersion, and for their sake I will rehearse it, briefly. Johnny was ever wont to ignore the pavement, the grass of his treading; curious, rather of the flight of birds or of the clouds' ordering, περιφρονῶν τὸν ἥλιον. Once from the river that was their home, three little fishes saw him and marvelled at his mein, nor were they surprised, but frightened only when he fell among them. Long on the surface of the water lay he, finless and immobile, till he was retrieved by "two strong men," was set by their hands upon the dyke. And, as he stood there, a poor cascade of water, the three fishes swam to the water's surface, mocking him, for lo! the scarlet book that was his treasure had been swept far from him and lost in further waters.

It is now quite fifteen years since my nurse read to me this tragedy, but time has not made it less poignant. At school, at Oxford, often, often, did I wonder what was written in Johnny's scarlet book, who were his saviours, whether 'twas indeed transcendent whimsy that merged him in the sudden waters, or whether, in the language of our rural police he had anything on his mind? Last spring, though, I chanced to stay for a few days in Frankfort, Hoffman's city. Here, I thought, I might pierce the mysteries of that old disaster. As I passed through the streets, I seemed to recognize Johnny's mature features over every grey beard. I made inquiries. None knew Johnny. In my distracted wandering, I did, at length, find the dyke, the cobble-stone, the lamp-post, just as Hoffman had drawn them, but, though I had the river dragged for many hours, the remnant of no scarlet book rose to the surface. I left Frankfort in some annoyance. Wearied with research, I slept soundly in the train, and, in a dream, sleep gave me, found the secret of my vain quest. In a dream, I saw myself strutting, even as Johnny had strutted, a creature of high and insolent carriage, bearing beneath my arm a scarlet book, labelled "The Works of Max Beerbohm." No heed was I giving to the realities of life around me, as I strutted on. Before my feet lay a river that was the river of Journalism, and from the surface of its water three inkstained fishes were gaping at me. In a tragic instant, I had fallen among them. I awoke shivering.

Yes! Hoffman's tale had been an allegory, a subtle prophecy of my own estate. Need one clinch the parallel; I was, of yore, a haughty and remote artist, careless how little I earned in writing perfect things, writing but quarterly. Now, in the delusion that editors, loving the pauper, will fill his pockets, I write for a weekly paper, and call myself "We." But the stress of anonymity overwhelms me. I belong to the Beerbohm period. I have tumbled into the dark waters of current journalism, and am glad to sign my name,

MAX BEERBOHM

FAULKNER ON FAULKNER

Afternoon of a Cow
BY ERNEST V. TRUEBLOOD*

MR. FAULKNER and I were sitting under the mulberry with the afternoon's first julep while he informed me what to write on the morrow, when Oliver appeared suddenly around the corner of the smokehouse, running and with his eyes looking quite large and white. "Mr. Bill!" he cried. "Day done sot fire to de pasture!"

"——" cried Mr. Faulkner, with that promptitude which quite often marks his actions, "—— those boys to ——!" springing up and referring to his own son, Malcolm, and to his brother's son, James, and to the cook's son, Rover or Grover. Grover his name is, though both Malcolm and James (they and Grover are of an age and have, indeed, grown up not only contemporaneously but almost inextricably) have insisted upon calling him Rover since they could speak, so that now all the household, including the child's own mother and naturally the child itself, call him

---

* Mr. Faulkner's ghost writer.

Rover too, with the exception of myself, whose practice and belief it has never been to call any creature, man, woman, child or beast, out of its rightful name—just as I permit no one to call me out of mine, though I am aware that behind my back both Malcolm and James (and doubtless Rover or Grover) refer to me as Ernest be Toogood—a crass and low form of so-called wit or humor to which children, these two in particular—are only too prone. I have attempted on more than one occasion (this was years ago; I have long since ceased) to explain to them that my position in the household is in no sense menial, since I have been writing Mr. Faulkner's novels and short stories for years. But I long ago became convinced (and even reconciled) that neither of them knew or cared about the meaning of the term.

I do not think that I anticipate myself in saying that we did not know where the three boys would now be. We would not be expected to know, beyond a general feeling or conviction that they would by now be concealed in the loft of the barn or stable —this from previous experience, though experience had never before included or comprised arson. Nor do I feel that I further violate the formal rules or order, unity and emphasis by saying that we would never for one moment have conceived them to be where later evidence indicated that they now were. But more on this subject anon: we were not thinking of the boys now; as Mr. Faulkner himself might have observed, someone should have been thinking about them ten or fifteen minutes ago; that now it was too late. No, our concern was to reach the pasture, though not with any hope of saving the hay which had been Mr. Faulkner's pride and even hope—a fine, though small, plantation of this grain or forage fenced lightly away from the pasture proper and the certain inroads of the three stocks whose pleasance the pasture was, which had been intended as an alternative or balancing factor in the winter's victualing of the three beasts. We had no hope of saving this, since the month was September following a dry summer, and we knew that this as well as the remainder of the pasture would burn with almost the instantaneous celerity of gunpowder or celluloid. That is, I had no hope of it and doubtless Oliver had no hope of it. I do not know what Mr. Faulkner's emotion was, since it appears (or so

I have read and heard) a fundamental human trait to decline to recognize misfortune with regard to some object which man either desires or already possesses and holds dear, until it has run him down and then over like a Juggernaut itself. I do not know if this emotion would function in the presence of a field of hay, since I have neither owned nor desired to own one. No, it was not the hay which we were concerned about. It was the three animals, the two horses and the cow, in particular the cow, who, less gifted or equipped for speed than the horses, might be overtaken by the flames and perhaps asphyxiated, or at least so badly scorched as to be rendered temporarily unfit for her natural function; and that the two horses might bolt in terror, and to their detriment, into the further fence of barbed wire or might even turn and rush back into the actual flames, as is one of the more intelligent characteristics of this so-called servant and friend of man.

So, led by Mr. Faulkner and not even waiting to go around to the arched passage, we burst through the hedge itself and, led by Mr. Faulkner who moved at a really astonishing pace for a man of what might be called almost violently sedentary habit by nature, we ran across the yard and through Mrs. Faulkner's flower beds and then through her rose garden, although I will say that both Oliver and myself made some effort to avoid the plants; and on across the adjacent vegetable garden, where even Mr. Faulkner could accomplish no harm since at this season of the year it was innocent of edible matter; and on to the panel pasture fence over which Mr. Faulkner hurled himself with that same agility and speed and palpable disregard of limb which was actually amazing—not only because of his natural lethargic humor, which I have already indicated, but because of that shape and figure which ordinarily accompanies it (or at least does so in Mr. Faulkner's case)—and were enveloped immediately in smoke.

But it was at once evident by its odor that this came, not from the hay which must have stood intact even if not green and then vanished in holocaust doubtless during the few seconds while Oliver was crying his news, but, from the cedar grove at the pasture's foot. Nevertheless, odor or not, its pall covered the entire visible scene, although ahead of us we could see the creeping line of conflagration beyond which the three unfortunate beasts now huddled or rushed in terror of their lives. Or so we thought until, still led by Mr. Faulkner and hastening now across a stygian and desolate floor which almost at once became quite unpleasant to the soles of the feet and promised to become more so, something monstrous and wild of shape rushed out of the smoke. It was the larger horse, Stonewall—a congenitally vicious brute which no one durst approach save Mr. Faulkner and Oliver, and not even Oliver durst mount (though why either Oliver or Mr. Faulkner should want to is forever beyond me) which rushed down upon us with the evident intent of taking advantage of this opportunity to destroy its owner and attendant both, with myself included for lagniappe or perhaps for pure hatred of the entire human race. It evidently altered its mind, however, swerving and vanishing again into smoke. Mr. Faulkner and Oliver had paused and given it but a glance. "I reckin dey all right," Oliver said. "But where you reckin Beulah at?"

"On the other side of that——fire, backing up in front of it and bellowing," replied Mr. Faulkner. He was correct, because almost at once we began to hear the poor creature's lugubrious lamenting. I have often remarked now how both Mr. Faulkner and Oliver apparently possess some curious rapport with horned and hooved beasts and even dogs, which I cheerfully admit that I do not possess myself and do not even understand. That is, I cannot understand it in Mr. Faulkner. With Oliver, of course, cattle of all kinds might be said to be his avocation, and his dallying (that is the exact word; I have watched him more than once, motionless and apparently pensive and really almost pilgrim-like, with the handle of the mower or hoe or rake for support) with lawn mower and garden tools his sideline or hobby. But Mr. Faulkner, a member in good standing of the ancient and gentle profession of letters! But then neither can I understand why he should wish to ride a horse, and the notion has occurred to me that Mr. Faulkner acquired his rapport gradually and perhaps over a long period of time from contact of his posterior with the animal he bestrode.

We hastened on toward the sound of the doomed creature's

bellowing. I thought that it came from the flames perhaps and
was the final plaint of her agony—a dumb brute's indictment
of heaven itself—but Oliver said not, that it came from beyond
the fire. Now there occurred in it a most peculiar alteration. It
was not an increase in terror, which scarcely could have been
possible. I can describe it best by saying that she now sounded
as if she had descended abruptly into the earth. This we found
to be true. I believe however that this time order requires, and
the element of suspense and surprise which the Greeks themselves have authorized will permit, that the story progress in the
sequence of events as they occurred to the narrator, even though
the accomplishment of the actual event recalled to the narrator
the fact or circumstance with which he was already familiar and
of which the reader should have been previously made acquainted. So I shall proceed.

Imagine us, then, hastening (even if the abysmal terror in the
voice of the hapless beast had not been inventive enough, we had
another: on the morrow, when I raised one of the shoes which
I had worn on this momentous afternoon, the entire sole crumbled into a substance resembling nothing so much as that which
might have been scraped from the ink-wells of childhood's
school days at the beginning of the fall term) across that stygian
plain, our eyes and lungs smarting with that smoke along whose
further edge the border of fire crept. Again a wild and monstrous shape materialized in violent motion before us, again
apparently with the avowed and frantic aim of running us down.
For a horrid moment I believed it to be the horse, Stonewall,
returned because after passing us for some distance (persons do
this; possibly it might likewise occur in an animal, its finer
native senses dulled with smoke and terror), remembering having seen myself or recognized me, and had now returned to
destroy me alone. I had never liked the horse. It was an emotion
even stronger than mere fear; it was that horrified disgust which
I imagine one must feel toward a python and doubtless even
the horse's subhuman sensibilities had felt and had come to
reciprocate. I was mistaken, however. It was the other horse, the
smaller one which Malcolm and James rode, apparently with

enjoyment, as though in miniature of the besotted perversion of their father and uncle—an indiscriminate, round-bodied creature, as gentle as the larger one was vicious, with a drooping sad upper lip and an inarticulate and bemused (though to me still sly and untrustworthy) gaze; it, too, swerved past us and also vanished just before we reached the line of flame which was neither as large nor as fearful as it had looked, though the smoke was thicker, and seemed to be filled with the now loud terrified voice of the cow. In fact, the poor creature's voice seemed now to be everywhere: in the air above us and in the earth beneath. With Mr. Faulkner still in the lead we sprang over it, whereupon Mr. Faulkner immediately vanished. Still in the act of running, he simply vanished out of the smoke before the eyes of Oliver and myself as though he too had dropped into the earth.

This is what he had also done. With the voice of Mr. Faulkner and the loud terror of the cow coming out of the earth at our feet and the creeping line of the conflagration just behind us, I now realized what had happened and so solved Mr. Faulkner's disappearance as well as the previous alteration in the voice of the cow. I now realized that, confused by the smoke and the incandescent sensation about the soles of the feet, I had become disoriented and had failed to be aware that all the while we had been approaching a gully or ravine of whose presence I was quite aware, having looked down into it more than once while strolling in the afternoons while Mr. Faulkner would be riding the large horse, and upon whose brink or verge Oliver and I now stood and into which Mr. Faulkner and the cow had, in turn and in the reverse order, fallen.

"Are you hurt, Mr. Faulkner?" I cried. I shall not attempt to reproduce Mr. Faulkner's reply, other than to indicate that it was couched in that pure ancient classic Saxon which the best of our literature sanctions and authorizes and which, due to the exigencies of Mr. Faulkner's style and subject matter, I often employ but which I myself never use although Mr. Faulkner even in his private life is quite addicted to it and which, when he employs it, indicates what might be called a state of the most robust, even though not at all calm, wellbeing. So I knew that he was not hurt. "What shall we now do?" I inquired of Oliver.

"We better get down in dat hole too," Oliver replied. "Ain't you feel dat fire right behime us?" I had forgot about the fire in my concern over Mr. Faulkner, but upon glancing behind me I felt instinctively that Oliver was right. So we scrambled or fell down the steep sandy declivity, to the bottom of the ravine where Mr. Faulkner, still speaking, stood and where the cow was now safely ensconced though still in a state of complete hysteria, from which point or sanctuary we watched the conflagration pass over, the flames crumbling and flickering and dying away along the brink of the ravine. Then Mr. Faulkner spoke:

"Go catch Dan, and bring the big rope from the storehouse."

"Do you mean me?" said I. Mr. Faulkner did not reply, so he and I stood beside the cow who did not yet seem to realize that the danger was past or perhaps whose more occult brute intellect knew that the actual suffering and outrage and despair had yet to occur—and watched Oliver climb or scramble back up the declivity. He was gone for some time, although after a while he returned, leading the smaller and tractable horse who was adorned with a section of harness, and carrying the rope; whereupon commenced the arduous business of extricating the cow. One end of the rope was attached to her horns, she still objecting violently; the other end was attached to the horse. "What shall I do?" I inquired.

"Push," said Mr. Faulkner.

"Where shall I push?" I asked.

"I don't give a ——," said Mr. Faulkner. "Just push."

But it appeared that it could not be done. The creature resisted, perhaps to the pull of the rope or perhaps to Oliver's encouraging shouts and cries from the brink overhead or possibly to the motive power supplied by Mr. Faulkner (he was directly behind, almost beneath her, his shoulder against her buttocks or loins and swearing steadily now) and myself. She made a gallant effort, scrambled quite half way up the declivity, lost her footing and slid back. Once more we tried and failed, and then again. And then a most regrettable accident occurred. This third time the rope either slipped or parted, and Mr. Faulkner and the cow were hurled violently to the foot of the precipice with Mr. Faulkner underneath.

Later—that evening, to be exact—I recalled how, at the moment while we watched Oliver scramble out of the ravine, I seem to have received, as though by telepathy, from the poor creature (a female mind; the lone female among three men) not only her terror but the subject of it: that she knew by woman's sacred instinct that the future held for her that which is to a female far worse than any fear of bodily injury or suffering: one of those invasions of female privacy where, helpless victim of her own physical body, she seems to see herself as object of some malignant power for irony and outrage; and this none the less bitter for the fact that those who are to witness it, gentlemen though they be, will never be able to forget it but will walk the earth with the remembrance of it so long as she lives;—yes, even the more bitter for the fact that they who are to witness it are gentlemen, people of her own class. Remember how the poor spent terrified creature had for an entire afternoon been the anguished and blind victim of a circumstance which it could not comprehend, had been sported with by an element which it instinctively feared, and had now been hurled recently and violently down a precipice whose crest it doubtless now believed it would never see again.—I have been told by soldiers (I served in France, in the Y.M.C.A.) how, upon entering battle, there often sets up within them, prematurely as it were, a certain impulse or desire which brings on a result quite logical and quite natural, the fulfillment of which is incontestible and of course irrevocable.—In a word, Mr. Faulkner underneath received the full discharge of the poor creature's afternoon of anguish and despair.

It has been my fortune or misfortune to lead what is—or might be—called a quiet, even though not retired, life; and I have even preferred to acquire my experience from reading what had happened to others or what other men believe or think might have logically happened to creatures of their invention or even in inventing what Mr. Faulkner conceives might have happened to certain and sundry creatures who compose his novels and stories. Nevertheless, I would imagine that a man is never too old nor too secure to suffer what might be called experiences of initial and bizarre originality, though of course not always outrage, following which his reaction would be quite almost invariably out of character. Or rather, following which his reaction would reveal that actual character which for years he may have successfully concealed from the public, his intimates, and his wife and family; perhaps even from himself. I would take it to be one of these which Mr. Faulkner had just suffered.

Anyway, his actions during the subsequent few minutes were most peculiar for him. The cow—poor female alone among three men—struggled up almost at once and stood, hysterically still though no longer violent, trembling rather with a kind of aghast abasement not yet become despair. But for a time Mr. Faulkner, prone on the earth, did not stir at all. Then he rose. He said, "Wait," which naturally we should do until he gave further orders or instructions. Then—the poor cow and myself, and Oliver looking down from the crest beside the horse—we watched Mr. Faulkner walk quietly a few paces down the ravine and sit down, his elbows on his knees and his chin supported between his hands. It was not the sitting down which was peculiar. Mr. Faulkner did this often—steadily perhaps is a better word—if not in the house, then (in summer) well down in a large chair on the veranda just outside the library window where I would be working, his feet on the railing, reading a detective magazine; in winter in the kitchen, his stocking feet inside the oven to the stove. It was the attitude in which he now sat. As I have indicated, there was a quality almost violent about Mr. Faulkner's sedentation; it would be immobile without at all being lethargic, if I may put it so. He now sat in the attitude of M. Rodin's *Penseur* increased to his tenth geometric power say, since le penseur's principal bewilderment appears to be at what has bemused him, while Mr. Faulkner can have had no doubt. We watched him quietly—myself, and the poor cow who now stood with her head lowered and not even trembling in utter and now hopeless female shame; Oliver and the horse on the brink above. I remarked then that Oliver no longer had smoke for his background. The immediate conflagration was now over, though the cedar grove would doubtless smoulder until the equinox.

Then Mr. Faulkner rose. He returned quietly and he spoke as quietly (or even more so) to Oliver as I have ever heard him: "Drop the rope, Jack." Oliver removed his end of the rope from the horse and dropped it, and Mr. Faulkner took it up and turned and led the cow down the ravine. For a moment I watched him with an amazement of which Oliver doubtless partook; in the next moment doubtless Oliver and I would have looked at one another in that same astonishment. But we did not; we moved; doubtless we moved at the same moment. Oliver did not even bother to descend into the ravine. He just went around it while I hastened on and overtook Mr. Faulkner and the cow; indeed, the three of us were actually soldiers recovered from the amnesia of battle, the battle with the flames for the life of the cow. It has been often remarked and even insisted upon in literature (novels have been built upon it, though none of them are Mr. Faulkner's) how, when faced with catastrophe, man does everything but the simple one. But from the fund of my own experience, though it does consist almost entirely of that afternoon, it is my belief that it is in the face of danger and disaster that he does the simple thing. It is merely simply wrong.

We moved down the ravine to where it turned at right angles and entered the woods which descended to its level. With Mr. Faulkner and the cow in the lead we turned up through the woods and came presently to the black desolation of the pasture in the fence to which Oliver, waiting, had already contrived a gap or orifice through which we passed. Then with Mr. Faulkner again in the lead and with Oliver, leading the horse and the cow, and myself side by side, we retraced across that desolate plain the course of our recent desperate race to offer succor, though bearing somewhat to the left in order to approach the stable—or barnlot. We had almost reached the late hay plantation when, without warning, we found ourselves faced by three apparitions. They were not ten paces away when we saw them and I believe that neither Mr. Faulkner nor Oliver recognized them at all, though I did. In fact, I had an instantaneous and curious sense, not that I had anticipated this moment so much as that I had been waiting for it over a period which might be computed in years.

Imagine yourself, if you will, set suddenly down in a world in complete ocular or chromatic reversal. Imagine yourself faced with three small ghosts, not of white but of purest and unrelieved black. The mind, the intelligence, simply refuses to believe that they should have taken refuge from their recent crime or misdemeanor in the hay plantation before it took fire, and lived. Yet there they were. Apparently they had neither brows, lashes nor hair; and clothing epidermis and all, they were of one identical sable, and the only way in which Rover or Grover could be distinguished from the other two was by Malcolm's and James' blue eyes. They stood looking at us in complete immobility until Mr. Faulkner said, again with that chastened gentleness and quietude which, granted my theory that the soul, plunged without warning into some unforeseen and outrageous catastrophe, comes out in its true colors, has been Mr. Faulkner's true and hidden character all these years: "Go to the house."

They turned and vanished immediately, since it had been only by the eyeballs that we had distinguished them from the stygian surface of the earth at all. They may have preceded us or we may have passed them. I do not know. At least, we did not see them again, because presently we quitted the sable plain which had witnessed our Gethsemane, and presently entered the barnlot where Mr. Faulkner turned and took the halter of the horse while Oliver led the cow into its private and detached domicile, from which there came presently the sound of chewing as, freed now of anguish and shame she ruminated, maiden meditant and—I hope—once more fancy free.

Mr. Faulkner stood in the door of the stable (within which, by and by, I could hear the larger and vicious horse, Stonewall, already at his food, stamp now and then or strike the board wall with his hoof as though even in the act of eating it could not forbear making sounds of threat and derision toward the very man whose food nourished it) and removed his clothing.

Then, in full sight of the house and of whoever might care or not care to see, he lathered himself with saddle soap and then stood at the watering trough while Oliver doused or flushed him down with pail after pail of water. "Never mind the clothes just now," he said to Oliver. "Get me a drink."

"Make it two," said I; I felt that the occasion justified, even though it may not have warranted, that temporary aberration into the vernacular of the fleeting moment. So presently, Mr. Faulkner now wearing a light summer horse blanket belonging to Stonewall, we sat again beneath the mulberry with the second julep of the afternoon.

"Well, Mr. Faulkner," said I after a time, "shall we continue?"

"Continue what?" said Mr. Faulkner.

"Your suggestions for tomorrow," said I. Mr. Faulkner said nothing at all. He just drank, with that static violence which was his familiar character, and so I knew that he was himself once more and that the real Mr. Faulkner which had appeared momentarily to Oliver and myself in the pasture had already retreated to that inaccessible bourne from which only the cow, Beulah, had ever evoked it, and that doubtless we would never see it again. So after a time I said, "Then, with your permission, tomorrow I shall venture into fact and employ the material which we ourselves have this afternoon created."

"Do so," Mr. Faulkner said—shortly, I thought.

"Only," I continued, "I shall insist upon my prerogative and right to tell this one in my own diction and style, and not yours."

"By ——!" said Mr. Faulkner. "You better had." *

* The above is from the Summer, 1947, issue of *Furioso*, whose editors reprinted it, with the author's—that is Mr. Faulkner's—permission from an Algerian magazine called *Fontaine*. How it got *there*, they don't say. *Afternoon of a Cow* seems to have been mainly inspired by an episode described in pages 174-181 of *The Hamlet* (Modern Library Paperback edition). A few quotations may suggest the mood which Mr. Faulkner's personal ghost writer has transposed from high drama into low farce—or should one say from unconscious to conscious comedy?

"The smoke lay like a wall before him; beyond it he could hear the steady terrified bellowing of the cow. He ran into the smoke and toward the voice. The earth was now hot to his feet . . . the horse appeared, materialized furiously out of the smoke, monstrous and distorted, . . . The

SELF-PARODIES: *UNCONSCIOUS*

BY AN UNCONSCIOUS SELF-PARODY I mean a poem or a passage in which
the author is both characteristic and unintentionally absurd. I regret it
has not been possible to include any Carlyle because, when I came to
look through that fulgurating prose again after a happy lapse of
thirty years since I had to read it in Freshman English at Yale, I discovered it was *all* self-parody. I should also have liked to include a few
pages from certain living writers—such as Hemingway's *Across the
River and into the Trees,* MacLeish's radio plays, and Kerouac's *On the
Road*—but this was impossible for obvious reasons.

RICHARD CRASHAW

AND NOW where're he strayes,
Among the Galilean mountaines,
Or more unwellcome wayes,
He's followed by two faithfull fountaines;
Two walking baths; two weeping motions;
Portable and compendious oceans.

(from *Saint Mary Magdalene*)

---

air was filled with furious wings and four crescent-glints of shod hooves as,
still screaming, the horse vanished beyond the ravine's lip, sucking first the
cow and then himself after it as though by the violent vacuum of its passing.
. . . He made no sound as the three of them plunged down the crumbling
sheer . . . where he, lying beneath the struggling and bellowing cow, received the violent relaxing of her fear-constricted bowels. . . . She scrambled
to her feet, . . . When he moved toward her, she whirled and ran at the
crumbling sheer of the slope, scrambling furiously at the vain and shifting
sand as though in a blind paroxysm of shame, to escape not him alone but
the very scene of the outragement of privacy where she had been sprung
suddenly upon and without warning from the dark and betrayed and out-
raged by her own treacherous biological inheritance, he following again,
speaking to her, trying to tell her how this violent violation of her maiden's
delicacy is no shame, since such is the very iron imperishable warp of the
fabric of love. But she would not hear . . . at last he steps down into the
water . . . and touches her. She does not even stop drinking; his hand has
lain on her flank for a second or two before she lifts her dripping muzzle
and looks back at him, once more maiden meditant, shame-free."

ABRAHAM COWLEY

Coy Nature (which remain'd, though aged grown,
A beauteous virgin still, enjoy'd by none,
    Nor seen unveil'd by any one),
When Harvey's violent passion she did see,
    Began to tremble and to flee,
Took sanctuary, like Daphne, in a tree:
There Daphne's lover stopt, and thought it much
    The very leaves of her to touch,
But Harvey, our Apollo, stopt not so,
Into the bark and root he after her did go.* . . .
What should she do? through all the moving wood
Of lives endow'd with sense she took her flight;
Harvey pursues, and keeps her still in sight.
But as the deer long-hunted takes a flood,
She leapt at last into the winding streams of blood;
Of man's Meander all the purple reaches made,
    Till at the heart she stay'd,
    Where, turning head, and at a bay,
Thus, by well-purgèd ears, was she o'erheard to say:
"Here sure shall I be safe," said she;
"None will be able sure to see
    This my retreat, but only He
    Who made both it and me.
The heart of man, what art can e'er reveal?
    A wall impervious between
    Divides the very parts within,
And doth the heart of man ev'n from itself conceal."
    She spoke, but ere she was aware,
    Harvey was with her there. . . .

Before the liver understood
The noble scarlet dye of blood,

---

* It should perhaps be explained that the poet is here celebrating Harvey's
discovery of the circulation of the blood.

Before one drop was by it made,
Or brought into it, to set up the trade;
Before the untaught heart began to beat
The tuneful march to vital heat,
From all the souls that living buildings rear,
Whether implied for earth, or sea, or air,
Whether it in the womb or egg be wrought,
A strict account to him is hourly brought,
How the great fabric does proceed,
What time and what materials it does need.
He so exactly does the work survey
As if he hir'd the workers by the day.

(from *Ode upon Dr. Harvey*)

SAMUEL JOHNSON

Lucubrations on Glass

WHO, WHEN he saw the first sand or ashes by a casual intenseness of heat melted into metalline form, rugged with excrescences and clouded with impurities, would have imagined that in this formless lump lay concealed so many conveniences of life as would in time constitute a great part of the happiness of the world? Yet by some such fortuitous liquefaction was mankind taught to procure a body, at once in a high degree solid and transparent, which might admit the light of the sun and exclude the violence of the wind.

(from *The Rambler*)

EDWARD GIBBON

I HESITATE, from the apprehension of ridicule, when I approach the delicate subject of my early love. By this word I do not mean the polite attention of the gallantry, without hope or design, which has originated from the spirit of chivalry, and is interwoven with the texture of French manners. I do not confine myself to the grosser appetite which our pride may affect to disdain, because it has been implanted by Nature in the whole animal creation, "Amor omnibus idem." The discovery of a sixth sense, the first consciousness of manhood, is a very interesting moment of our lives; but it less properly belongs to the memoirs of an individual, than to the natural history of the species. I understand by this passion the union of desire, friendship, and tenderness, which is inflamed by a single female, which prefers her to the rest of her sex, and which seeks her possession as the supreme or the sole happiness of our being. I need not blush at recollecting the object of my choice; and though my love was disappointed of success, I am rather proud that I was once capable of feeling such a pure and exalted sentiment. The personal attractions of Mademoiselle Susanne Curchod were embellished by the virtues and talents of the mind. Her fortune was humble, but her family was respectable: her mother, a native of France, had preferred her religion to her country; the profession of her father did not extinguish the moderation and philosophy of his temper, and he lived content with a small salary and laborious duty in the obscure lot of Minister of Crassy, in the mountains that separate the pays de Vaud from the County of Burgundy. In the solitude of a sequestered village he bestowed a liberal, and even learned, education on his only daughter; she surpassed his hopes by her proficiency in the sciences and languages; and in her short visits to some relations at Lausanne, the wit and beauty and erudition of Mademoiselle Curchod were the theme of universal applause. The report of such a prodigy awakened by (*sic*) curiosity; I saw and loved. I found her learned without pedantry, lively in conversation, pure in sentiment, and elegant in manners; and the first sudden emotion was fortified by the habits and knowledge of a more familiar acquaintance. She permitted me to make her two or three visits at her father's house: I passed some happy days in the mountains of Burgundy; and her parents honourably encouraged a connection which might raise their daughter above want and dependence. In a calm retirement the gay vanity of youth no longer fluttered in her bosom; she listened to the voice of truth and passion, and I might presume to hope that I had made some impression on a virtuous heart. At Crassy and Lausanne I indulged my dream of felicity; but, on my return to England, I soon discovered that my father would not hear of this strange alliance, and that, without his consent, I was myself destitute and helpless. After a painful struggle I yielded to my fate; the remedies of absence and time were at length effectual, and my love subsided in friendship and esteem.* The minister of Crassy soon afterwards died; his stipend died with him: his daughter retired to Geneva, where, by teaching young ladies, she earned a hard subsistence for herself and her mother; but in her lowest distress she maintained a spotless reputation and a dignified behaviour. The Dutchess of Grafton (now Lady Ossory) has often told me that she had nearly engaged Mademoiselle Curchod as a Governess, and her declining a life of servitude was most probably blamed by the wisdom of her shortsighted friends. A rich banker of Paris, a citizen of Geneva, had the good-fortune and good sense to discover and possess this inestimable treasure; and in the capital of taste and luxury she resisted the temptations of wealth, as she had sustained the hardships of indigence. The Genius of her husband has exalted him to the most conspicuous station in Europe: in every change of prosperity and disgrace he has reclined on the bosom of a faithful friend; and Mademoiselle Curchod is now the wife of Mr. Necker the Minister, and perhaps the legislator, of the French Monarchy.

(from Memoir B of the *Autobiography*)

GEORGE CRABBE

SOMETHING one day occurr'd about a bill
That was not drawn with true mercantile skill,

---

* The famous "I sighed as a lover, I obeyed as a son."—a one-sentence parody of all Gibbon—occurs at this point in another of the versions of the *Autobiography*, but I think the whole passage is more Gibbonesquely rendered here. The late Spike Kennedy, a classmate of mine at Yale, used to quote another and even better Gibbon bonbon but I've been unable to find it. He claimed that Gibbon described his first view of Chartres: "I darted a look of contempt at the stately monument of superstition." But this may be apocryphal.

And I was ask'd and authorised to go
To seek the firm of Clutterbuck and Co.;
Their hour was past—but when I urg'd the case,
There was a youth who named a second place,
Where, on occasions of important kind,
I might the man of occupation find,
In his retirement, where he found repose
From the vexations that in Business rose.

The house was good, but not so pure and clean
As I had houses of retirement seen;
Yet men, I knew, of meditation deep,
Love not their maidens should their studies sweep
His room I saw, and must acknowledge, there
Were not the signs of cleanliness or care:
A female servant, void of female grace,
Loose in attire, proceeded to the place;
She stared intrusive on my slender frame,
And boldly ask'd my business and my name.

I gave them both; and, left to be amused,
Well as I might, the parlour I perused. . . .

(from *Tales of the Hall*)

LORD BYRON

The Tear

WHEN Friendship or Love our sympathies move,
    When Truth in a glance should appear,
The lips may beguile with a dimple or smile,
    But the test of affection's a Tear. . . .

The man doom'd to sail with the blast of the gale,
    Through billows Atlantic to steer,

As he bends o'er the wave which may soon be his grave,
  The green sparkles bright with a Tear.

The soldier braves death for a fanciful wreath
  In Glory's romantic career;
But he raises the foe when in battle laid low,
  And bathes every wound with a Tear.

If with high-bounding pride he return to his bride,
  Renouncing the gore-crimson'd spear,
All his toils are repaid when, embracing the maid,
  From her eyelid he kisses the Tear. . . .

Ye friends of my heart, ere from you I depart,
  This hope to my breast is most near:
If again we shall meet in this rural retreat,
  May we meet, as we part, with a Tear.

When my soul wings her flight to the regions of night,
  And my corse shall recline on its bier,
As ye pass by the tomb where my ashes consume,
  Oh! moisten their dust with a Tear.

May no marble bestow the splendour of woe,
  Which the children of vanity rear;
No fiction of fame shall blazon my name;
  All I ask—all I wish—is a Tear.

                    (from *Hours of Idleness*)

EDGAR ALLAN POE

Eulalie

          I DWELT alone
          In a world of moan,
       And my soul was a stagnant tide,
Till the fair and gentle Eulalie became my blushing bride—

Till the yellow-haired young Eulalie became my smiling bride.

> Ah less—less bright
> The stars of the night
> Than the eyes of the radiant girl!
> And never a flake
> That the vapour can make
> With the moon-tints of purple and pearl,
Can vie with the modest Eulalie's most unregarded curl—
Can compare with the bright-eyed Eulalie's most humble and
    careless curl.

> Now Doubt—now Pain
> Come never again,
> For her soul gives me sigh for sigh,
> And all the day long
> Shines bright and strong
> Astartè within the sky,
While ever to her dear Eulalie upturns her matron eye—
While ever to her young Eulalie upturns her violet eye.

PERCY BYSSHE SHELLEY

Time

UNFATHOMABLE Sea! whose waves are years,
    Ocean of Time, whose waters of deep woe
Are brackish with the salt of human tears!
    Thou shoreless flood, which in thy ebb and flow
Claspest the limits of mortality!
And sick of prey, yet howling on for more,
Vomitest they wrecks on its inhospitable shore;
Treacherous in calm, and terrible in storm,
        Who shall put forth on thee,
        Unfathomable Sea?

*A Little Wordsworth Anthology**

OH! what's the matter? what's the matter?
What is't that ails young Harry Gill?
That evermore his teeth they chatter,
Chatter, chatter, chatter still!
Of waistcoats Harry has no lack,
Good duffle grey, and flannel fine;
He has a blanket on his back,
And coats enough to smother nine.

In March, December, and in July,
'Tis all the same with Harry Gill;
The neighbours tell, and tell you truly,
His teeth they chatter, chatter still.
At night, at morning, and at noon,
'Tis all the same with Harry Gill;
Beneath the sun, beneath the moon,
His teeth they chatter, chatter still.

(Goody Blake and Harry Gill)

——HAST thou then survived——
Mild offspring of infirm humanity,
Meek infant! among all forlornest things
The most forlorn—one life of that bright star,
The second glory of the Heavens?—Thou hast.

(Address to my Infant Daughter)

AND thus continuing, she said,
"I had a son, who many a day
Sailed on the sea; but he is dead;

---

* I am indebted for this—as for the gems from Crashaw, Cowley, Crabbe, Byron, and Poe in this section—to that curious work by D. B. Wyndham Lewis and Charles Lee: *The Stuffed Owl, An Anthology of Bad Verse* (J. M. Dent, London, 1930-1948). It should be on every library shelf alongside Hugh Kingsmill's *An Anthology of Invective and Abuse*.

In Denmark he was cast away;
And I have travelled far as Hull to see
What clothes he might have left, or other property."

(*The Sailor's Mother*
[Original Version])

THE beetle loves his unpretending track,
The snail the house he carries on his back;
The far-fetched worm with pleasure would disown
The bed we give him, though of softest down.

(*Liberty*)

HIGH on a mountain's highest ridge,
Where oft the stormy winter gale
Cuts like a scythe, while through the clouds
It sweeps from vale to vale;
Not five yards from the mountain path,
This Thorn you on your left espy;
And to the left, three yards beyond,
You see a little muddy pond,
Though but of compass small, and bare
To thirsty suns and parching air.
I've measured it from side to side;
'Tis three feet long, and two feet wide. . . .

Nay, rack your brain—'tis all in vain,
I'll tell you every thing I know;
But to the Thorn, and to the pond
Which is a little step beyond,
I wish that you would go:
Perhaps, when you are at the place,
You something of her tale may trace.

I'll give you the best help I can:
Before you up the mountain go,
Up to the dreary mountain-top,

I'll tell you all I know.
'Tis now some two-and-twenty years
Since she (her name is Martha Ray)
Gave, with a maiden's true good will,
Her company to Stephen Hill;
And she was blithe and gay,
And she was happy, happy still
Whene'er she thought of Stephen Hill

And they had fixed the wedding day,
The morning that must wed them both;
But Stephen to another Maid
Had sworn another oath;
And with this other Maid, to church
Unthinking Stephen went—
Poor Martha! on that woeful day
A cruel, cruel fire, they say,
Into her bones was sent:
It dried her body like a cinder,
And almost turned her brain to tinder.

(*The Thorn* [Original Version])

The Stuffed Owl

[*This is taken from the account given by Miss Jewsbury of the
pleasure she derived, when long confined to her bed by sickness,
from the inanimate object on which this Sonnet turns.—W. W.*]

WHILE Anna's peers and early playmates tread,
In freedom, mountain-turf and river's marge;
Or float with music in the festal barge;
Rein the proud steed, or through the dance are led;
Her doom it is to press a weary bed—
Till oft her guardian Angel, to some charge
More urgent called, will stretch his wings at large,
And friends too rarely prop the languid head.

Yet, helped by Genius—untired Comforter,
The presence even of a stuffed Owl for her
Can cheat the time; sending her fancy out
To ivied castles and to moonlight skies,
Though he can neither stir a plume, nor shout;
Nor veil, with restless film, his staring eyes.

ROBERT BROWNING

AND SO I somehow-nohow played
The whole o' the pretty piece; and then . . . whatever weighed
My eyes down, furled the film about my wits? suppose
The morning-bath—the sweet monotony of those
Three keys, flat, flat, and flat, never a sharp at all—
Or else the brain's fatigue, forced even here to fall
Into the same old track, and recognize the shift
From old to new and back to old again, and—swift
Or slow, no matter—still the certainty of change,
Conviction we shall find the false, where'er we range,
In art no less than nature: or what if wrist were numb,
And overtense the muscle, abductor of the thumb,
Taxed by those tenths' and twelfths' unconscionable stretch?
Howe'er it came to pass, I soon was far to fetch—
Gone off in company with Music!

(from *Fifine at the Fair,* stanza XCIII)

THOMAS BABINGTON MACAULAY

IN THE MEANTIME the government of Charles had suffered a
succession of humiliating disasters. The extravagance of the
Court had dissipated all the means which Parliament had supplied for the purpose of carrying on offensive hostilities. It was
determined to wage only a defensive war; and even for defensive

war the vast resources of England, managed by triflers and public robbers, were found insufficient. The Dutch insulted the British coasts, sailed up the Thames, took Sheerness, and carried their ravages to Chatham. The blaze of the ships burning in the river was seen at London: it was rumoured that a foreign army had landed at Gravesend; and military men seriously proposed to abandon the Tower. To such a depth of infamy had a bad administration reduced that proud and victorious country, which a few years before had dictated its pleasure to Mazarine, to the States General, and to the Vatican. Humbled by the events of the war, and dreading the just anger of Parliament, the English Ministry hastened to huddle up a peace with France and Holland at Breda.

But a new scene was about to open. It had already been for some time apparent to discerning observers, that England and Holland were threatened by a common danger, much more formidable than any which they had reason to apprehend from each other. The old enemy of their independence and of their religion was no longer to be dreaded. The sceptre had passed away from Spain. That mighty empire, on which the sun never set, which had crushed the liberties of Italy and Germany, which had occupied Paris with its armies, and covered the British seas with its sails, was at the mercy of every spoiler; and Europe observed with dismay the rapid growth of a new and more formidable power. Men looked to Spain and saw only weakness disguised and increased by pride, dominions of vast bulk and little strength, tempting, unwieldy, and defenceless, an empty treasury, a sullen and torpid nation, a child on the throne, factions in the council, ministers who served only themselves, and soldiers who were terrible only to their countrymen. Men looked to France, and saw a large and compact territory, a rich soil, a central situation, a bold, alert, and ingenious people, large revenues, numerous and well-disciplined troops, an active and ambitious prince, in the flower of his age, surrounded by gen-erals of unrivalled skill.

(from *Sir William Temple*)

CHARLES DICKENS

The Death of Little Nell

"SHE IS SLEEPING soundly," he said; "but no wonder. Angel hands have strewn the ground deep with snow, that the lightest footsteps may be lighter yet; and the very birds are dead, that they may not wake her. She used to feed them, sir. Though never so cold and hungry, the timid things would fly from us. They never flew from her!"

Again he stopped to listen, and scarcely drawing breath, listened for a long, long time. That fancy past, he opened an old chest, took out some clothes as fondly as if they had been living things, and began to smooth and brush them with his hand.

"Why dost thou lie so idle there, dear Nell," he murmured, "when there are bright red berries out of doors waiting for thee to pluck them! Why dost thou lie so idle there, when thy little friends come creeping to the door, crying 'where is Nell— sweet Nell?'—and sob, and weep, because they do not see thee! She was always gentle with children. The wildest would do her bidding—she had a tender way with them, indeed she had!"

Kit had no power to speak. His eyes were filled with tears.

"Her little homely dress,—her favourite!" cried the old man, pressing it to his breast, and patting it with his shrivelled hand. "She will miss it when she wakes. They have hid it here in sport, but she shall have it—she shall have it. I would not vex my darling, for the wild world's riches. See here—these shoes—how worn they are—she kept them to remind her of our last long journey. You see where the little feet went bare upon the ground. They told me, afterwards, that the stones had cut and bruised them. *She* never told me that. No, no, God bless her! and, I have remembered since, she walked behind me, sir, that I might not see how lame she was—but yet she had my hand in hers, and seemed to lead me still."

He pressed them to his lips, and having carefully put them back again, went on communing with himself—looking wistfully from time to time towards the chamber he had lately visited.

"She was not wont to be a lie-abed; but she was well then. We must have patience. When she is well again, she will rise early, as she used to do, and ramble abroad in the healthy morning time. I often tried to track the way she had gone, but her small footstep left no print upon the dewy ground, to guide me. Who is that? Shut the door. Quick!—Have we not enough to do to drive away that marble cold, and keep her warm!"

The door was indeed opened, for the entrance of Mr. Garland and his friend, accompanied by two other persons. These were the schoolmaster, and the bachelor. The former held a light in his hand. He had, it seemed, but gone to his own cottage to replenish the exhausted lamp, at the moment when Kit came up and found the old man alone.

[*Several pages are here omitted.*]

By little and little, the old man had drawn back towards the inner chamber, while these words were spoken. He pointed there, as he replied, with trembling lips,

"You plot among you to wean my heart from her. You never will do that—never while I have life. I have no relative or friend but her—I never had—I never will have. She is all in all to me. It is too late to part us now."

Waving them off with his hand, and calling softly to her as he went, he stole into the room. They who were left behind, drew close together, and after a few whispered words—not unbroken by emotion, or easily uttered—followed him. They moved so gently, that their footsteps made no noise; but there were sobs from among the group, and sounds of grief and mourning.

For she was dead. There, upon her little bed, she lay at rest. The solemn stillness was no marvel now.

She was dead. No sleep so beautiful and calm, so free from trace of pain, so fair to look upon. She seemed a creature fresh from the hand of God, and waiting for the breath of life; not one who had lived and suffered death.

Her couch was dressed with here and there some winter berries and green leaves, gathered in a spot she had been used to favour. "When I die, put near me something that has loved the light, and had the sky above it always." Those were her words.

She was dead. Dear, gentle, patient, noble Nell was dead. Her little bird—a poor slight thing the pressure of a finger would have crushed—was stirring nimbly in its cage; and the strong heart of its child mistress was mute and motionless for ever.

Where were the traces of her early cares, her sufferings, and fatigues? All gone. Sorrow was dead indeed in her, but peace and perfect happiness were born; imaged in her tranquil beauty and profound repose.

And still her former self lay there, unaltered in this change. Yes. The old fireside had smiled upon that same sweet face; it had passed, like a dream, through haunts of misery and care; at the door of the poor schoolmaster on the summer evening, before the furnace fire upon the cold wet night, at the still bedside of the dying boy, there had been the same mild lovely look. So shall we know the angels in their majesty, after death.

(from *The Old Curiosity Shop,* Chapter 72)

WALT WHITMAN

Others May Praise What They Like

OTHERS MAY PRAISE what they like;
But I, from the banks of the running Missouri, praise nothing in
    art or aught else,
Till it has well inhaled the atmosphere of this river, also the
    western prairie-scent,
And exudes it again.

RUDYARD KIPLING

"The Service Man"

(BOER WAR, 1899)

"TOMMY" you was when it began,
    But now that it is o'er

You shall be called The Service Man
　'Enceforward, evermore.
Batt'ry, brigade, flank, centre, van,
　Defaulter, Army-corps—
From first to last, The Service Man
　'Enceforward, evermore.

From 'Alifax to 'Industan,
　From York to Singapore—
'Orse, foot an' guns, The Service Man
　'Enceforward, evermore!

Big Steamers

(1914-1918)

"OH WHERE are you going to, all you Big Steamers,
　With England's own coal, up and down the salt seas?"
"We are going to fetch you your bread and your butter,
　Your beef, pork and mutton, eggs, apples and cheese."

"And where will you fetch it from, all you Big Steamers,
　And where shall I write you when you are away?"
"We fetch it from Melbourne, Quebec and Vancouver—
　Address us at Hobart, Hong-Kong, and Bombay."

"But if anything happened to all you Big Steamers,
　And suppose you were wrecked up and down the salt sea?"
"Then you'd have no coffee or bacon for breakfast,
　And you'd have no muffins or toast for your tea."

"Then I'll pray for fine weather for all you Big Steamers,
　For little blue billows and breezes so soft."
"Oh billows and breezes don't bother Big Steamers,
　For we're iron below and steel-rigging aloft."

"Then I'll build a new lighthouse for all you Big Steamers,
  With plenty wise pilots to pilot you through."
"Oh the Channel's as bright as a ballroom already,
  And pilots are thicker than pilchards at Looe."

"Then what can I do for you, all you Big Steamers,
  Oh what can I do for your comfort and good?"
"Send out your big warships to watch your big waters,
  That no one may stop us from bringing you food."

"For the bread that you eat and the biscuits you nibble,
  The sweets that you suck and the joints that you carve,
They are brought to you daily by all us Big Steamers—
  And if any one hinders our coming you'll starve!"

When 'omer Smote 'is Bloomin' Lyre

WHEN 'OMER SMOTE 'is bloomin' lyre,
  He'd 'eard men sing by land an' sea;
An' what 'e thought he might require,
  'E went an' took—the same as me!

The market-girls an' fishermen,
  The shepherds an' the sailors too,
They 'eard old songs turn up again,
  But kep' it quiet—same as you!

They knew 'e stole; 'e knew they knowed.
  They didn't tell nor make a fuss,
But winked at 'Omer down the road,
  An' 'e winked back—the same as us!

SCIENTIFICATION (I)

TWO YEARS AGO Daniel Bell, Professor of Sociology at Columbia and author of *The End of Ideology,* spent a year at the expense of the Ford Foundation in its sociological Shangri-La in California, the Center for Advanced Study in the Behavioral Sciences. One product was the following Paradigm, concocted in a moment of disaffection. Some of the reactions were disturbing. "I sent it off to two sociological friends," he writes, "who I thought would appreciate it, and one sent me back a serious letter about some of the categories, while the other, not knowing whether it was a spoof or not, wrote: 'You are too good a sociologist not to have created something which itself is quite useful.' And a third asked me for a copy of my 'earlier scheme' (see footnote 1)."

The Parameters of Social Movements: A Formal Paradigm[1]

BY DANIEL BELL

T HE PURPOSE of this scheme is to present a taxonomic dichotomization which would allow for unilinear comparisons. In this fashion we could hope to distinguish the relevant variables which determine the functional specificities of social movements. Any classificatory scheme is, essentially, an answer to some implicit other scheme. In this instance, it is an attempt to answer the various hylozoic theories which deny that social categories can be separable.[2]

Social movements can be divided primarily into two *types*. These we shall call:

I. *Homologous,* i.e., similar in structure, though different in aim; e.g., the Catholic Church and the Communist Party

II. *Metonymous,* i.e., similar in aim, though structure may differ; e.g., the Socialist Party and the Communist Party.

Each of the two can be further dichotomized as antonyms. While we would hope, through further refinement to make each moiety exactly complementary, at this stage of social theory, we can only make rough approximations.

[1] This is a revision of an earlier scheme, presented in 1945 under the title of "The Configurative Patterning of Social Movements."
[2] For a contrary view, see Leo Strauss, "Natural Rights and History."

I. *Homologous Movements*
(Organizational types)
  1.1. *Structural Variables*

    1.1.a. monocotyledonous
      (one seed) e.g., Ju-
      daism: the Jahweh
      God)
    1.1.b. dicotyledonous (two
      seeds) (e.g., Eastern
      religions:
      Astarte-Adonis
      Ishtar-Tammuz)

II. *Metonymous Movements*
(Ideological types)
  1.1. *Goal Definitions*
    (Teleological structure)
    1.1.a. transcendental

    1.1.b. eschatological

1.2. *Matrix Variables*
  1.2.a. ultramontane (law-
    ful change)
  1.2.b. anti-nomian (unlaw-
    ful change)

1.2. *Matrix of Change*
  1.2.a. quietistic (homeo-
    static)
  1.2.b. chiliastic (thermo-
    dynamic)
    1.2.b.1. sec-tarian
      (bureaucrat)
    1.2.b.2. lacrima-tarian
      (enthusiast)

1.3. *Process Variables*
  1.3.a. syncretistic
    (co-mingling of
    equal value)
  1.3.b. diastrophic (un-
    equal changes result-
    ing in bunched
    movement)

1.3. *Modes of Change*
  1.3.a. immanent
    (continuum)

  1.3.b. kairos (diastasis)

SCIENTIFICATION (II)

THE FOLLOWING psychoanalytic interpretation of *Struwwelpeter* appeared in *New Directions 14*, which I reviewed in 1954. I was then
puzzled by Dr. Friedmann's piece. Was it a parody? Indeed, was there

an actual Dr. Friedmann? I have recently written him and the answers are no and yes. (My letter explained I wanted to use his piece in an anthology of parodies.)

Dr. Friedmann, who lives in England, states: "The article was written as a serious analytical-literary contribution. . . . All my work is serious, although sometimes I use an aphoristic style to hammer home something that some writers take pages and pages to explain because their repressions never allow succinctness, or even formulation. . . . You may certainly use the article." [The reader might like to compare Dr. Friedmann's treatment of *Struwwelpeter* with Max Beerbohm's given earlier (under Self-Parodies); *Struwwelpeter* is also the subject of another parody, even more to the point here: Monsignor Ronald Knox's *Jottings from a Psycho-Analyst's Notebook* in his *Essays in Satire* (1930).]

I don't say there is nothing "in" the analysis below. On the contrary, there is too much. *Struwwelpeter* is clearly a sick book, full of sadism and, for all I know, castration, masturbation, and all the other exciting themes Dr. Friedmann descries in it. The trouble is that his rhetoric constantly hurries him on to catastrophe, like a spirited but untrained mount. Thus, the casual remark in the first sentence about the Christmas presents: ". . . for the little girl a doll and a cot, and, of course, the missing penis in the shape of an umbrella and a teapot." I object to "of course." It also makes one dizzy to come across such Biblical exegeses, thrown in as asides and assumed to be self-evident, as the reference to "Christ's constant aggression against his own mother deriving from the fact that his unconscious did not believe her to be a virgin." This exaggeration of the Freudian style is what qualifies the article for inclusion here. And yet that idea about Christ—it *is* interesting . . .

Struwwelpeter

BY DR. RUDOLPH FRIEDMANN

AUTHOR'S NOTE: *Dr. Heinrich Hoffman, the creator of Struwwelpeter (Shock-headed Peter or Slovenly Peter), was born on June 13, 1809 in Frankfurt-am-Main and studied medicine at Heidelberg, Halle and Paris; then became teacher of anatomy at the Senckenberg Foundation in Frankfurt. From 1851-89 he was house surgeon at the State Asylum, the building of which he first instituted. He died September 20, 1894 in Frankfurt. On the medical side he published Observations and Experiences on Men-*

tal Disturbances in connection with Epilepsy (1859). Dr. Hoffman was best known for his illustrated children's books; *Struwwelpeter*, first published in 1845, went into many editions and
was translated into almost all European languages. *Similar
books followed, like King Nutcracker, In Heaven and on Earth,
Bastian the Lazybones* (written under the pseudonym "Poly-
karpus Gastfenger"); a satire called *Spar Salthole* (*Badeort
Salzloch*, 1861), then a *Breviary of Marriage* (*Leipzig*, 1853);
Humoristic Studies (1847)—in these studies there is included a
comedy called *The Late-comers to the Moon* (*Mondzügler*).
He also published in 1858 *The Booklet of All Souls*, a humoristic
cemetery anthology (*Friedhofsanthologie*). But *Struwwelpeter is
the imago among his books*.

THE TITLE PAGE of *Struwwelpeter* shows two Christmas angels
dropping gifts from heaven to earth—for the little girl a doll
and a cot, and, of course, the missing penis in the shape of an
umbrella and a teapot; for the boy a smiling angel hopes he
will come to some harm with a sword and a bayonet. In the
lower center picture a child is eating and to the right there is
a superb abstract study of a mother's back consisting of bonnet,
pointed red shawl and crinoline, leading a child through a street
of cobblestones and gothic spires. We turn over and encounter
Struwwelpeter—Shock-headed Peter—and he really is a shock.
He stands on a dais which has a design of open scissors let into
its front. He contains in his own person all the elements
running through the other characters in the book. He is a
castrated child, grown fat as a result of glandular disturbance
caused by the castration. His hair is a luminous halo of un-
combed black and yellow out of which a frightened feminine face
tries to gaze with schizoid severity and direction to compensate
for the lost and holy genital eye which alone can see in the
vagina of life and the coffin of death. There are stories that the
penis still moves in the first few days sojourn in the cemetery and
that bell-like drops of blood drip from the bud. The mop of
hair also serves as a veil behind which the face may hide to
avoid injury and the expression flies into some special introversion. To make up for the genital loss his outstretched hands

possess five fingernails uncut and grown into five long sadistic claws sharp like erect tails. And yet the claws are no longer really cruel, there is only a façade of cruelty. The whole growing pyknic obesity of the figure gives the nails a self-crucifying and drooping look; just as the hair at its ends curls again inwards and downwards onto the breast of introversion. There are no life-lines or heart-lines in these outstretched hands, only stigmata forming little folds of death. The whole figure, dating from 1845, as one is moved by its mute message to unveil it, is a tragic commentary on the impending fate of the German nation.

Struwwelpeter himself is followed by a regression in time to the period of his phallic flowering as Cruel Frederick. The top illustration shows Frederick, with body erect, shouting. Shouting is a symbolical form of sexual aggression in which the voice is used as a substitute for the penis. In this picture the thin whip-lash howl of the boy is directed against the nurse (the mother-imago in the form of the nurse) and has to do with the recognition that by giving birth to the son the mother has shown herself to be an animal. In this connection one is reminded of Christ's constant aggression against his own mother deriving from the fact that his unconscious did not believe her to be a virgin. Brandishing a chair over his head Frederick overturns a cage and kills the two birds which were in it; a small bird (the innocent tender white penis) and a large bird, its neck already heavily suffused with the sticky blood of masturbation. He tears the wings off flies (my genital hopes cannot soar; therefore yours shall not), kills the kitten with a brick and, in the farthest right-hand corner of the picture, as a frantic child far smaller than she, proceeds to whip his Mary (the mother of Christ). The son's hatred for the mother arises because she is a castrated being who has not got a penis to take off and give to him so that he may have a spare one handy after the father has done his work. (Cf. "Woman, I know thee not," with its frank expression of unconcern for the mother with whom the son has not had sexual intercourse and whose body He has thus not been able to explore to learn if it conceals a penis.) Frederick then proceeds to whip his dog Tray (amidst a wonderful setting of mountainous hills and gothic church spire) and ultimately is put to bed after the roused dog has bitten his leg.

There follows the story of Harriet and the matches; Harriet lights a match and her doll, which she has dropped, rushes out of the bottom corner of the illustration with flying petticoats. Harriet's apron-strings catch fire and the chorus of two crying cats, looking like two rats (the double penis she would not wait for, preferring the flame-like love which is as death to the young girl) send a stream of water to fertilize her two little scarlet shoes which is all that is left of her.

The Inky Boys (to begin with quite white) breathe out racial hatred for Black-a-moor symbolizing the exotic sinfulness of African and Asiatic potency. But the punishing father and still living German super-ego, Agrippa, lived close by, "so tall he almost touched the sky";

> "He had a mighty inkstand, too,
> In which a great goose-feather grew."

(Cf. The long thin, almost imperceptible, black hair growing out of the middle of the palm of the left hand of masturbators.)* Agrippa drops the three horrors into the inkstand so that they emerge blacker than Black-a-moor. The three are thrown back into the black well of the mother's womb to be reminded of their origin. "Inter urinas et faeces nascimur."

There follows a curious interlude, "The Story of the Man that went out Shooting." A man out hunting, falls asleep in the warm smiling sun and has his gun stolen by the hare he is hunting. The man dreams and sees the hare pointing the gun at his anus. Through the magic of the drawing he seems to be facing

---

* Editor's Note: When I reached this point on rereading this piece, certain doubts as to either Dr. Friedmann's sanity or mine became inescapable. I began to wonder if the author means there *is* such a "long, thin, almost imperceptible black hair" on masturbators' palms, or if he is referring to an erroneous folk belief. The style suggests the former and this suspicion swelled monstrously—one can imagine what Dr. Friedmann would do with *that* image—as I read on and on . . . and on. We live in a very strange intellectual world these days. And why the *left* hand? No, my dear doctor, please don't explain.

both front and back simultaneously as he flees. And just as he reaches the safety of the mother through falling down a well, the hare fires and misses him. Struwwelpeter flirts with homo-sexuality but wakes up in time to save his virginity.

In "The Story of Little Suck-a-Thumb" the analyst in Hoff-man breaks through, with the fire of the first and last word, the veil of nineteenth-century repression. The first illustration is framed by the heads of two fathers; the motif of pointed beard and two eyes intertwined is repeated in the abstract pattern of a Cross inside a beard down both sides of the picture in which Conrad is being warned not to suck his thumb (not to mastur-bate) while his mother is out, as:

> "The great tall tailor always comes
> To little boys who suck their thumbs;
> And ere they dream what he's about,
> He takes his great sharp scissors out,
> And cuts their thumbs clean off—and then,
> You know, they never grow again."

The moment Mamma has turned her back Conrad's thumb is in his mouth (the child is sexually stimulated by the prohibition coming from the mother), and at the top of the second picture the frowning father surveys him from the wall. In rushes "the great, long, red-legged scissor-man" and cuts off both thumbs with snip-snap slashes amidst a pool of blood. And in the final illustration the father beams down with deep ripe pleasure at castrated Conrad. This story, in its illumination of the nuances of life, is as great a contribution to world literature as is Goethe's *Faust*. To Schiller's maxim that "Hunger and Love make the world go round," can be added "and Castration stops it."

The first illustration of "The Story of Augustus who would not have any Soup" shows a boy in whom the pyknic disposition is only sustained by food; in the four subsequent illustrations (even including the end which is schizoid through and through in its heartless realistic irony) the innate dynamism towards nothingness of Northern schizoid tendencies is revealed in all its melting pathos. This schizophrenia contains a very real dyna-

mism both of body and mind; in contrast to the degenerate European schizophrenia of today with its well-developed rigidity
of movement and thought with consequent tomb-like facial
expression which has become a substitute for the grandeur of
the schizoid imago. However, "The Story of Augustus" is essentially the story of the boy who is so sickened by his own
masturbatory excretions that he cannot bear the sight of soup.
Through excessive masturbation he becomes thinner and thinner
until—on the fifth day—he dies. The final illustration shows a
tureen marked "soup" lying against a Cross. The correctness of
Hoffman's viewpoint is borne out by the fact that analysis is
more and more returning to the folk-viewpoint that excessive
masturbation leads to early death. This is especially the case
among biologically degenerate men whose bony tissue is gradually wasted away.

The masturbatory theme is continued with "The Story of
Fidgety Philip," who rocks himself to and fro until he topples
over onto the floor and pulls the tablecloth and the contents of
the table down upon himself so that he is covered in white sauce!
In the final illustration a pendant bird hangs prophetically
amongst knives and a broken bottle.

"The Story of Johnny Head-In-Air" shows Johnny so busy
masturbating that he becomes blind, cannot see where he is
going, collides with an aggressive dog (the father), and falls over
the river embankment which is lighted by a curious lamppost.
In the next illustration the boy lies face downward, half
drowned, in the water and only the base of the lamppost is
visible, the top being snapped off by the angle of the drawing.
He is then hooked out by two strong men.

The final "Story of Flying Robert" ends this essentially tragic
book. Robert leaves his home, in spite of all commands to stay
indoors on windy days, opens his red umbrella and is at once
borne away on the wind into the Unknown. It consists of three
pictures ("3"—the number which is lucky because it contains in
its ancient Hebrew hieroglyphic form the shape of the penis).
Robert has masturbated so copiously and become so light that as
soon as he raises his umbrella he is swept off the face of the earth.
He lacks all ballast because his parents have cut off his genitals

and made giblet soup of them. The death of the child is the birth of the parents. Although flying free, Robert was sucked along the avenue leading up to the opening of death and his dead head banged against the sky. "It is very hot and afterwards very lonely." His head is presented to death and the ashes of the past are thrown over him to acclimatize the ashes of the future. As Robert is borne aloft on the phantasy wings of his last erection there is no more movement on earth, only a packed swaying in a drawn circle.

Struwwelpeter recognizes and gives expression to the sexuality and criminality of the child; in the case of the little girl, the wish to set fire to her genitals; in the case of the boy, masturbation inspired by cruelty to animals and to the mother together with the self-realization that castration is the only cure for him. In consequence the nineteenth-century child was healthily repressed. Woe betide those who weaken the super-ego amongst primitives (and the child is a degenerate primitive). Only after castration does the son feel ready to receive the father's blessing. Arising out of the tendency to substitute analysis for repression in our dealings with the intellectually unripe, the tremendous growth of contemporary aggression is best exemplified by reference to a phrase from the court of linguistics; in a former age to "do" someone meant to cheat them financially; now it means to injure their genital organs with a razor.

The best in *Struwwelpeter* represents the psychology of distance made into human art through a nearness to the natural. And it is essentially modern in its outlook because it reveals the child's need for sexual expression; indeed the child who does not experience sexuality now may find that it will lose its virginity to the atom bomb and not to man. Struwwelpeter is like a boil or a nipple bursting with milk; he represents the expression of a repression and his swollen larger-than-life appearance is a symbolic representation of the painful, blocked orgasm and the phantasy of pregnancy in childhood.

The book is closed and the cover faces us. The schizoid talons and the shadows of the feet overcome the pyknic obesity of the figure, and the eyes searching the woman-reader separate the animal in her from the imago. But Struwwelpeter is not concerned with life; the finding of the warm instinctive animal side of the woman does not heal him or stimulate him creatively; on the contrary he whips and destroys her. Whereas originally, at least, his aggression sprang from interest in life, today Struw-welpeter cannot visualize life and has no interest in it; he is a shot and reeling monument to the whiteness of the way where good and bad youth treads carefully to death.

L'AFFAIRE LEMOINE

PAR

MARCEL PROUST

ALTHOUGH THIS ANTHOLOGY is limited to parodies in the Anglo-American language, this and the Queneau material that immediately follows seemed to me of such interest as to make it worth breaking the rule. I was also tempted to put in some of the famous *A la Manière de . . .* books of parodies (the first two are by Paul Reboux and Charles Muller, the last two by Reboux alone), but this would have been breaking the rule too much.

The parodies by Proust of Balzac, Michelet and Flaubert below are from a little book, *Pastiches et Mélanges,* he published in 1919, the same year as *A l'Ombre des Jeunes Filles en Fleurs* appeared (and won him the Prix Goncourt, his first important recognition). The parody section of *Pastiches et Mélanges* contains nine versions, in various writer's styles, of L'Affaire Lemoine. The footnote to the first, that below on Balzac, gives the theme on which Proust played his variations.

Parody was a kind of therapy for Proust. In his essay, *About Flaubert's Style,* he writes:

> While I am on the subject of Flaubert's "spell," let me say that the best advice I can give to my fellow writers is that they would be well advised to indulge in the cleansing, exorcising pastime of parody. When we come to the end of a book, we find that not only do we want to go on living with its characters, with Madame de Beauséant, with Frédéric Moreau, etc., but that our own inner voice, which has grown accustomed, through the long hours of perusal, to follow the Balzacian or Flaubertian rhythm, insists on

talking just like those authors. The one means of escape from the
toils lies in letting the influence have its way for a while, in keeping one's foot on the pedal and permitting the resonance to continue: in other words, in embarking upon a deliberate act of parody,
with the object, once we have got the stuff out of our system, of
becoming ourselves again instead of spending the rest of our working lives producing *unconscious* parodies.

The rest of the essay (now available in an Anchor book, *Pleasures and
Days*, edited by F. W. Dupee) gives evidence of Proust's remarkable
sensitivity to style—he has a full page on the Flaubertian "and."

L'AFFAIRE LEMOINE*

I

Dans un Roman de Balzac

DANS UN DES derniers mois de l'année 1907, à un de ces "routs"
de la marquise d'Espard où se pressait alors l'élite de
l'aristocratie parisienne (la plus élégante de l'Europe, au dire
de M. de Talleyrand, ce Roger Bacon de la nature sociale, qui
fut évêque et prince de Bénévent), de Marsay et Rastignac, le
comte Félix de Vandenesse, les ducs de Rhétoré et de Grandlieu,
le comte Adam Laginski, Mᵉ Octave de Camps, lord Dudley,
faisaient cercle autour de Mme la princesse de Cadignan, sans
exciter pourtant la jalousie de la marquise. N'est-ce pas en effet
une des grandeurs de la maîtresse de maison—cette carmélite de

* On a peut-être oublié, depuis dix ans, que Lemoine ayant faussement
prétendu avoir découvert le secret de la fabrication du diamant et ayant
reçu, de ce chef, plus d'un million du président de la De Beers, Sir Julius
Werner, fut ensuite, sur la plainte de celui-ci, condamné le 6 juillet 1909 à
six ans de prison. Cette insignifiante affaire de police correctionnelle, mais
qui passionnait alors l'opinion, fut choisie un soir par moi, tout à fait au
hasard, comme thème unique de morceaux, où j'essayerais d'imiter la manière
d'un certain nombre d'écrivains. Bien qu'en donnant sur des pastiches la
moindre explication on risque d'en diminuer l'effet, je rappelle pour éviter
de froisser de légitimes amours-propres, que c'est l'écrivain pastiché qui est
censé parler, non seulement selon son esprit, mais dans le langage de son
temps. A celui de Saint-Simon par exemple, les mots bonhomme, bonne
femme n'ont nullement le sens familier et protecteur d'aujourd'hui. Dans ses
Mémoires, Saint-Simon dit couramment le bonhomme Chaulnes pour le duc
de Chaulnes qu'il respectait infiniment, et pareillement de beaucoup d'autres.

la réussite mondaine—qu'elle doit immoler sa coquetterie, son orgueil, son amour même, à la nécessité de se faire un salon dont ses rivales seront parfois le plus piquant ornement? N'est-elle pas en cela l'égale de la sainte? Ne mérite-t-elle pas sa part, si chèrement acquise, du paradis social? La marquise—une demoiselle de Blamont-Chauvry, alliée des Navarreins, des Lenoncourt, des Chaulieu—tendait à chaque nouvel arrivant cette main que Desplein, le plus grand savant de notre époque, sans en excepter Claude Bernard, et qui avait été élève de Lavater, déclarait là plus profondément calculée qu'il lui eût été donné d'examiner. Tout à coup la porte s'ouvrit devant l'illustre romancier Daniel d'Arthez. Un physicien du monde moral qui aurait à la fois le gênie de Lavoisier et de Bichat—le créateur de la chimie organique—serait seul capable d'isoler les éléments qui composent la sonorité spéciale du pas des hommes supérieurs. En entendant résonner celui de d'Arthez vous eussiez frémi. Seul pouvait ainsi marcher un sublime génie ou un grand criminel. Le génie n'est-il pas d'ailleurs une sorte de crime contre la routine du passé que notre temps punit plus sévèrement que le crime même, puisque les savants meurent à l'hôpital qui est plus triste que le bagne.

Athénaïs ne se sentait pas de joie en voyant revenir chez elle l'amant qu'elle espérait bien enlever à sa meilleure amie. Aussi pressa-t-elle la main de la princesse en gardant le calme impénétrable que possèdent les femmes de la haute société au moment même où elles vous enfoncent un poignard dans le cœur.

—Je suis heureuse pour vous, ma chère, que M. d'Arthez soit venu, dit-elle à Mme de Cadignan, d'autant plus qu'il aura une surprise complète, il ne savait pas que vous seriez ici.

—Il croyait sans doute y rencontrer M. de Rubempré dont il admire le talent, répondit Diane avec une moue câline qui cachait la plus mordante des railleries, car on savait que Mme d'Espard ne pardonnait pas à Lucien de l'avoir abandonnée.

—Oh! mon ange, répondit la marquise avec une aisance surprenante, nous ne pouvons retenir ces gens-là, Lucien subira le sort du petit d'Esgrignon, ajouta-t-elle en confondant les personnes présentes par l'infamie de ces paroles dont chacune était un trait accablant pour la princesse. (Voir le *Cabinet des Antiques*.)

—Vous parlez de M. de Rubempré, dit la vicomtesse de Beauséant qui n'avait pas reparu dans le monde depuis la mort de M. de Nueil et qui, par une habitude particulière aux personnes qui ont longtemps vécu en province, se faisait une fête d'étonner des Parisiens avec une nouvelle qu'elle venait d'apprendre. Vous savez qu'il est fiancé à Clotilde de Grandlieu.

Chacun fit signe à la vicomtesse de se taire, ce mariage étant encore ignoré de Mme de Sérizy, qu'il allait jeter dans le désespoir.

—On me l'a affirmé, mais cela peut être faux, reprit la vicomtesse qui, sans comprendre exactement en quoi elle avait fait une gaucherie, regretta d'avoir été aussi démonstrative.

Ce que vous dites ne me surprend pas, ajouta-t-elle, car j'étais étonnée que Clotilde se fut éprise de quelqu'un d'aussi peu séduisant.

—Mais au contraire, personne n'est de votre avis, Claire, s'écria la princesse en montrant la comtesse de Sérizy qui écoutait.

Ces paroles furent d'autant moins saisies par la vicomtesse qu'elle ignorait entièrement la liaison de Mme de Sérizy avec Lucien.

—Pas séduisant, essaya-t-elle de corriger, pas séduisant . . . du moins pour une jeune fille!

—Imaginez-vous, s'écria d'Arthez avant même, d'avoir remis son manteau à Paddy, le célèbre tigre de feu Beaudenord (voir les *Secrets de la princesse de Cadignan*), qui se tenait devant lui avec l'immobilité spéciale à la domesticité du Faubourg Saint-Germain, oui, imaginez-vous, répéta le grand homme avec cet enthousiasme des penseurs qui paraît ridicule au milieu de la profonde dissimulation du grand monde.

—Qu'y a-t-il? que devons-nous nous imaginer, demanda ironiquement de Marsay en jetant à Félix de Vandenesse et au prince Galathione ce regard à double entente, véritable privilège de ceux qui avaient longtemps vécu dans l'intimité de MADAME.

—*Tuchurs pô!* renchérit le baron de Nucingen avec l'affreuse vulgarité des parvenus qui croient, à l'aide des plus grossières rubriques, se donner du genre et singer les Maxime de Trailles ou les de Marsay; *et fous afez du quir; fous esde le frai brodecdir tes baufres, à la Jambre.*

(Le célèbre financier avait d'ailleurs des raisons particulières d'en vouloir à d'Arthez qui ne l'avait pas suffisamment soutenu, quand l'ancien amant d'Esther avait cherché en vain à faire admettre sa femme, née Goriot, chez Diane de Maufrigneuse).

—*Fite, fite, mennesir, la ponhire zera gomblète bir mi si vi mi druffez tigne ti savre ke vaudille himachinei?*

—Rien, répondit avec à-propos d'Arthez, je m'adresse à la marquise.

Cela fut dit d'un ton si perfidement épigrammatique que Paul Morand, un de nos plus impertinents secrétaires d'ambassade, murmura:—Il est plus fort que nous! Le baron, se sentant joué, avait froid dans le dos. Mme Firmiani suait dans ses pantoufles, un des chefs-d'œuvre de l'industrie polonaise. D'Arthez fit semblant de ne pas s'être aperçu de la comédie qui venait de se jouer, telle que la vie de Paris peut seule en offrir d'aussi profonde (ce que explique pourquoi la province a toujours donné si peu de grands hommes d'Etat à la France) et sans s'arrêter à la belle Négre-pelisse, se tournant vers Mme de Sérizy avec cet effrayant sang-froid qui peut triompher des plus grands obstacles (en est-il pour les belles âmes de comparables à ceux du cœur?):

—On vient, madame, de découvrir le secret de la fabrication du diamant.

—*Cesde iffire esd eine crant dressor,* s'écria le baron ébloui.

—Mais j'aurais cru qu'on en avait toujours fabriqué, répondit naïvement Léontine.

Mme de Cadignan, en femme de goût, se garda bien de dire un mot, là où des bourgeoises se fussent lancées dans une conversation où elles eussent niaisement étalé leurs connaissances en chimis. Mais Mme de Sérizy n'avait pas achevé cette phrase qui dévoilait une incroyable ignorance, que Diane, en enveloppant la comtesse tout entière, eut un regard sublime. Seul Raphaël eût peut-être été capable de le peindre. Et certes, s'il y eût réussi, il eût donné un pendant à sa célèbre *Fornarina,* la plus saillante de ses toiles, la seule qui le place au-dessus d'André del Sarto dans l'estime des connaisseurs.

Pour comprendre le drame qui va suivre, et auquel la scène que nous venons de raconter peut servir d'introduction, quelques mots d'explication sont nécessaires. A la fin de l'année 1905, une affreuse tension régna dans les rapports de la France et de l'Allemagne. Soit que Guillaume II comptât effectivement déclarer la guerre à la France, soit qu'il eût voulu seulement le laisser croire afin de rompre notre alliance avec l'Angleterre, l'ambassadeur d'Allemagne reçut l'ordre d'annoncer au gouvernement français qu'il allait présenter ses lettres de rappel. Les rois de la finance jouèrent alors à la baisse sur la nouvelle d'une mobilisation prochaine. Des sommes considérables furent perdues à la Bourse. Pendant toute une journée on vendit des titres de rente que le banquier Nucingen, secrètement averti par son ami le ministre de Marsay de la démission du chancelier Delcassé, qu'on ne sut à Paris que vers quatre heures, racheta à un prix dérisoire et qu'il a gardées depuis.

Il n'est pas jusqu'à Raoul Nathan qui ne crut à la guerre, bien que l'amant de Florine, depuis que du Tillet, dont il avait voulu séduire la belle-sœur (voir *une Fille d'Eve*), lui avait fait faire un puff à la Bourse, soutint dans son journal la paix à tout prix.

La France ne fut alors sauvée d'une guerre désastreuse que par l'intervention, restée longtemps inconnue des historiens, du maréchal de Montcornet, l'homme le plus fort de son siècle après Napoléon. Encore Napoléon n'a-t-il pu mettre à exécution son projet de descente en Angleterre, la grande pensée de son règne. Napoléon, Montcornet, n'y a-t-il pas entre ces deux noms comme une sorte de ressemblance mystérieuse? Je me garderais bien d'affirmer qu'ils ne sont pas rattachés l'un à l'autre par quelque lien occulte. Peut-être notre temps, après avoir douté de toutes les grandes choses sans essayer de les comprendre, sera-t-il forcé de revenir à l'harmonie préétablie de Leibniz. Bien plus, l'homme qui était alors à la tête de la plus colossale affaire de diamants de l'Angleterre s'appelait Werner, Julius Werner, Werner! ce nom ne vous semble-t-il pas évoquer bizarrement le moyen âge? Rien qu'à l'entendre, ne voyez-vous pas déjà le docteur Faust, penché sur ses creusets, avec ou sans Marguerite? N'implique-t-il pas l'idée de la pierre philosophale? Werner! Julius! Werner! Changez deux lettres et vous avez Werther. *Werther* est de Gœthe.

Julius Werner se servit de Lemoine, un de ces hommes extraordinaires qui, s'ils sont guidés par un destin favorable, s'appellent Geoffroy Saint-Hilaire, Cuvier, Ivan le Terrible, Pierre le Grand, Charlemagne, Berthollet, Spalanzani, Volta. Changez les circonstances et ils finiront comme le maréchal d'Ancre, Balthazar Cleas, Pugatchef, Le Tasse, la comtesse de la Motte ou Vautrin. En France, le brevet que le gouvernement octroie aux inventeurs n'a aucune valeur par lui-même. C'est là qu'il faut chercher la cause qui paralyse, chez nous, toute grande entreprise industrielle. Avant la Révolution, les Séchard, ces géants de l'imprimerie, se servaient encore à Angoulême des presses à bois, et les frères Cointet hésitaient à acheter le second brevet d'imprimeur. (Voir les *Illusions perdues*.) Certes peu de personnes comprirent la réponse que Lemoine fit aux gendarmes venus pour l'arrêter.—Quoi? L'Europe m'abandonnerait-elle? s'écria le faux inventeur avec une terreur profonde. Le mot colporté le soir dans les salons du ministre Rastignac y passa inaperçu.

—Cet homme serait-il devenu for? dit le comte de Granville étonné.

L'ancien clerc de l'avoué Bordin devait précisément prendre la parole dans cette affaire au nom du ministère public, ayant retrouvé depuis peu, par le mariage de sa seconde fille avec le banquier du Tillet, la faveur que lui avait fait perdre auprès du nouveau gouvernement son alliance avec les Vandenesse, etc.

II

L'Affaire Lemoine par Gustave Flaubert

LA CHALEUR devenait étouffante, une cloche tinta, des tourterelles s'envolèrent, et, les fenêtres ayant été fermées sur l'ordre du président, une odeur de poussière se répandit. Il était vieux, avec un visage de pitre, une robe trop étroite pour sa corpulence, des prétentions è l'esprit; et ses favoris égaux, qu'un reste de tabac salissait, donnaient à toute sa personne quelque chose de décoratif et de vulgaire. Comme la suspension d'audience se prolongeait, des intimités s'ébauchèrent; pour entrer en conversation, les malins se plaignaient à haute voix du manque d'air, et, quelqu'un ayant dit reconnaître le ministre de l'intérieur dans un monsieur qui sortait, un réactionnaire soupira: "Pauvre France!" En tirant de sa poche une orange, un nègre s'acquit de la considération, et, par amour de la popularité, en offrit les quartiers à ses voisins, en s'excusant, sur un journal: d'abord à un ecclésiastique, qui affirma "n'en avoir jamais mangé d'aussi bonne; c'est un excellent fruit, rafraîchissant"; mais une douairière prit un air offensé, défendit à ses filles de rien accepter "de quelqu'un qu'elles ne connaissaient pas," pendant que d'autres personnes, ne sachant pas si le journal arriverait jusqu'à elles, cherchaient une contenance: plusieurs tirèrent leur montre, une dame enleva son chapeau. Un perroquet le surmontait. Deux jeunes gens s'en étonnèrent, auraient voulu savoir s'il avait été placé là comme souvenir ou peut-être par goût excentrique. Déjà les farceurs commençaient à s'interpeller d'un banc à l'autre, et les femmes, regardant leurs maris, s'étouffaient de rire dans un mouchoir, quand un silence s'établit, le président parut s'absorber pour dormir, l'avocat de Werner prononçait sa plaidoirie. Il avait débuté sur un ton d'emphase, parla deux heures, semblait dyspeptique, et chaque fois qu'il disait "Monsieur le Président" s'effondrait dans une révérence si profonde qu'on aurait dit une jeune fille devant un roi, un diacre quittant l'autel. Il fut terrible pour Lemoine, mais l'élégance des formules atténuait l'âpreté du réquisitoire. Et ses périodes se succédaient sans interruption, comme les eaux d'une cascade, comme un ruban qu'on déroule. Par moment, la monotonie de son discours était telle qu'il ne se distinguait plus du silence, comme une cloche dont la vibration persiste, comme un écho qui s'affaiblit. Pour finir, il attesta les portraits des présidents Grévy et Carnot, placés au-dessus du tribunal; et chacun, ayant levé la tête, constata que la moisissure les avait gagnés dans cette salle officielle et malpropre qui exhibait nos gloires et sentait le renfermé. Une large baie la divisait par le milieu, des bancs s'y alignaient jusqu'au pied du tribunal; elle avait de la poussière sur le parquet des araignées aux angles du plafond, un rat dans chaque trou, et on était oblige de l'aérer souvent a cause du voisinage du calorifère, parfois d'une odeur plus nauséabonde. L'avocat de Lemoine répliquant, fut bref. Mais il avait un accent méridional, faisait appel aux passions généreuses, ôtait à tout moment son lorgnon. En l'écoutant, Nathalie ressentait ce trouble où conduit l'éloquence; une douceur l'envahit et son cœur s'étant soulevé, la batiste de son corsage palpitait, comme une herbe au bord d'une fontaine prête à sourdre, comme le plumage d'un pigeon qui va s'envoler. Enfin le président fit un signe, un murmure s'éleva, deux parapluies tombèrent: on allait entendre à nouveau l'accusé. Tout de suite les gestes de colère des assistants le désignèrent; pourquoi n'avait-il pas dit vrai, fabriqué du diamant, divulgué son invention? Tous, et jusqu'au plus pauvre, auraient su—c'était certain—en direr des millions. Même ils les voyaient devant eux, dans la violence du regret où l'on croit posséder ce qu'on pleure. Et beaucoup se livrèrent une fois encore à la douceur des rêves qu'ils avaient formés, quand ils avaient entrevu la fortune, sur la nouvelle de la découverte, avant d'avoir dépisté l'escroc.

Pour les uns, c'était l'abandon de leurs affaires, un hôtel avenue du Bois, de l'influence à l'Académie; et même un yacht qui les aurait menés l'été dans des pays froids, pas au Pôle pourtant, qui est curieux, mais la nourriture y sent l'huile, le jour de vingt-quatre heures doit être gênant pour dormir, et puis comment se garer des ours blancs?

A certains, les millions ne suffisaient pas; tout de suite ils les auraient joués à la Bourse; et, achetant les valeurs au plus bas cours la veille du jour où elles remonteraient—un ami les aurait renseignés—verraient centupler leur capital en quelques heures. Riches alors comme Carnegie, ils se garderaient de donner dans l'utopie humanitaire. (D'ailleurs, à quoi bon? Un milliard partagé entre tous les Franças n'en enrichirait pas un seul, on l'a calculé.) Mais laissant le luxe aux vaniteux, ils rechercheraient seulement le confort et l'influence, se feraient nommé président de la République, ambassadeur à Constantinople, auraient dans leur chambre un capitonnage de liège qui amortît le bruit des voisins. Ils n'entreraient pas au Jockey-Club, jugeant l'aristocratie à sa valeur. Un titre du pape les attirait davantage. Peut-être pourrait-on l'avoir sans payer. Mais alors à quoi bon tant de millions? Bref, ils grossiraient le denier de saint Pierre tout en blâmant l'institution. Que peut bien faire le pape de cinq millions de dentelles, tant de curés de campagne meurent de faim?

Mais quelques-uns, en songeant que la richesse aurait pu venir à eux, se sentaient prêts à défaillir; car ils l'auraient mise aux pieds d'une femme dont ils avaient été dédaignés jusqu'ici, et qui leur aurait enfin livré le secret de son baiser et la douceur de son corps. Ils se voyaient avec elle, à la campagne, jusqu'à la fin de leurs jours, dans une maison tout en bois blanc, sur le bord triste d'un grand fleuve. Ils auraient connu le cri du pétrel, la venue des brouillards, l'oscillation des navires, le développement des nuées, et seraient restés des heures avec son corps sur leurs genoux, à regarder monter la marée et s'entre-choquer les amarres, de leur terrasse, dans un fauteuil d'osier, sous une tente rayée de bleu, entre des boules de métal. Et ils finissaient par ne plus voir que deux grappes de fleurs violettes, descendant jusqu'à l'eau rapide qu'elles touchent presque, dans la lumière crue d'un après-midi sans soleil, le long d'un mur rougeâtre qui s'effritait. A ceux-là, l'excès de leur détresse ôtait la force de maudire l'accusé; mais tous le détestaient, jugeant qu'il les avait frustrés de la débauche, des honneurs, de la célébrité, du génie; parfois de chimères plus indéfinissables, de ce que chacun recélait de profond et de doux, depuis son enfance, dans la niaiserie particulière de son rêve.

VI

L'Affaire Lemoine par Michelet

L E DIAMANT, lui, se peut extraire à d'étranges profondeurs (1.300 mètres). Pour en ramener la pierre fort brillante, qui seule peut soutenir le feu d'un regard de femme (en Afghanistan, diamant se dit "œil de flamme"), sans fin faudra-t-il descendre au royaume sombre. Que de fois Orphée s'égarera avant de ramener au jour Eurydice! Nul découragement pourtant. Si le cœur faiblit, la pierre est là qui, de sa flamme fort distincte, semble dire: "Courage, encore un coup de pioche, je suis à toi." Du reste une hésitation, et c'est la mort. Le salut n'est que dans

la vitesse. Touchant dilemme. A le résoudre, bien des vies
s'épuisèrent au moyen âge. Plus durement se posa-t-il au commencement du vingtième siècle (décembre 1907-janvier 1908). Je
raconterai quelque jour cette magnifique affaire Lemoine dont
aucun contemporain n'a soupçonné la grandeur, je montrerai ce
petit homme, aux mains débiles, aux yeux brûlés par la terrible
recherche, juif probablement (M. Drumont l'a affirmé non sans
vraisemblance; aujourd'hui encore les Lemoustiers—contraction
de Monastère—ne sont pas rares en Dauphiné terre d'élection
d'Israël pendant tout le moyen âge), menant pendant trois mois
toute la politique de l'Europe, courbant l'orgueilleuse Angleterre
à consentir un traité de commerce ruineux pour elle, pour sauver
ses mines menacées, ses compagnies en discrédit. Que nous qui
livrions l'homme, sans hésiter elle le payerait au poids de sa chair.
La liberté provisoire, la plus grande conquête des temps mod-
ernes (Sayous, Batbie), trois fois fut refusée. L'Allemand fort
déductivement devant son pot de bière, voyant chaque jour les
cours de la De Beers baisser, reprenait courage (revision du
procès Harden, loi polonaise, refus de répondre au Reichstag).
Touchante immolation du juif au long des âges! "Tu me calom-
nies, obstinément m'accuses de trahison contre toute vraisemblance, sur terre, sur mer (affaire Dreyfus, affaire Ullmo); eh
bien! je te donne mon or (voir le grand développement des
banques juives à la fin du xxie siècle), et plus que l'or, ce qu'au
poids de l'or tu ne pourrais pas toujours acheter: le diamant."—
Grave leçon; fort tristement la méditais-je souvent durant cet
hiver de 1908 où la nature même, abdiquant toute violence, se
faisait perfide. Jamais on ne vit moins de grands froids, mais un
brouillard qu'à midi même le soleil ne parvenait pas à percer.
D'ailleurs, une température fort douce,—d'autant plus meur-
trière. Beaucoup de morts—plus que dans les dix années précé-
dentes—et, dès janvier, des violettes sous la neige. L'esprit fort
troublé de cette affaire Lemoine, qui très justement m'apparut
tout de suite comme un épisode de la grande lutte de la richesse
contre la science, chaque jour j'allais au Louvre où d'instinct le
peuple, plus souvent que devant la *Joconde* du Vinci, s'arrête
aux diamants de la Couronne. Plus d'une fois j'eus peine à en
approcher. Faut-il le dire, cette étude m'attirait, je ne l'aimais

pas. Le secret de ceci? Je n'y sentais pas la vie. Toujours ce fut ma force, ma faiblesse aussi, ce besoin de la vie. Au point culminant du règne de Louis XIV, quand l'absolutisme semble avoir tué toute liberté en France, durant deux longues années—plus d'un siècle— (1680-1789), d'étranges maux de tête me faisaient croire chaque jour que j'allais être obligé d'interrompre mon histoire. Je ne retrouvai vraiment mes forces qu'au serment du Jeu de Paume (20 juin 1789). Pareillement me sentais-je troublé devant cet étrange règne de la cristallisation qu'est le monde de la pierre. Ici plus rien de la flexibilité de la fleur qui au plus ardu de mes recherches botaniques, fort timidement—d'autant mieux —ne cessa jamais de me rendre courage: "Aie confiance, ne crains rien, tu es toujours dans la vie, dans l'histoire."

EXERCICES DE STYLE
PAR
RAYMOND QUENEAU

QUENEAU's *Exercices,* from which the following extracts are taken, are variations on a theme. The theme is stated in its least distorted form in the first one, *Notations,* although since the whole point of these stylistic setting-up exercises is that an event is changed by the way it is reported, even *Notations* is simply *a* form, since *the* form doesn't exist any more than *the* event does.

As for who Queneau is, cf. the beginning of Philip Toynbee's review (London *Observer,* January 18, 1959) of an English translation of the book. It is a parody of a parody:

> *Raymond Queneau is a distinguished former surrealist who has seemed in the past to be as unexportable as Henri Michaux or Alfred Jarry.*
>
> *
>
> *Ex-surrealist Queneau, idol of Paris coteries, never made the grade over here.*
>
> *
>
> *Monsieur Queneau, Parisian as a* coq au vin *or the Gare de Montparnasse, is one of those delicious* petits vins *whose bouquets so frequently elude the coarse palates of the British.*

Queneau is a bloody frog, and if you're the type who goes for their back legs you might be able to stomach him.

*

Queneau, Raymond. Nationality, French. Status, Distinguished. Known literary background, Surrealist. English experience of, Negligible.

*

I came into the Flore. It was hot in there. Raymond was bunched over a table, and he didn't look so good.
"Jo," he said, "I used to be a surrealist."
"Fine!" I said.
"I was good," he said, "in those days."
"You're still good," I told him.
"They don't know it in England." he said.
"Look!" I said. "Limey's! Let's have a Vermouth Cassis. Let's have a whole lot of Vermouth Cassis."

*

I *Know*
Queneau.
But do you know Queneau?
No!

*

Mondray Eauquen is a guisheddistin merfor listsurrea. . . .

Notations

Dᴀɴs ɪ'S, à une heure d'affluence. Un type dans les vingt-six ans, chapeau mou avec cordon remplaçant le ruban, cou trop long comme si on lui avait tiré dessus. Les gens descendent. Le type en question s'irrite contre un voisin. Il lui reproche de le bousculer chaque fois qu'il passe quelqu'un. Ton pleurnichard qui se veut méchant. Comme il voit une place libre, se précipite dessus.

Deux heures plus tard, je le rencontre Cour de Rome, devant la gare Saint-Lazare. Il est avec un camarade qui lui dit: "tu devrais faire mettre un bouton supplémentaire à ton pardessus." Il lui montre où (à l'échancrure) et pourquoi.

Métaphoriquement

A U CENTRE DU JOUR, jeté dans le tas des sardines voyageuses d'un coléoptère à grosse carapace blanche, un poulet au grand cou déplumé harangua soudain l'une, paisible, d'entre elles et son langage se déploya dans les airs, humide d'une protestation. Puis attiré par un vide, l'oisillon s'y précipita.

Dans un morne désert urbain, je le revis le jour même se faisant moucher l'arrogance pour un quelconque bouton.

Rétrograde

T U DEVRAIS AJOUTER un bouton à ton pardessus, lui dit son ami. Je le recontrai au milieu de la Cour de Rome, après l'avoir quitté se précipitant avec avidité vers une place assise. Il venait de protester contre la poussée d'un autre voyageur, qui, disait-il le bousculait, chaque fois qu'il descendait quelqu'un. Ce jeune homme décharné était porteur d'un chapeau ridicule. Cela se passa sur la plate-forme d'un S complet ce midi-là.

Surprises

C E QUE nous étions serrés sur cette plate-forme d'autobus! Et ce que ce garçon pouvait avoir l'air bête et ridicule! Et que fait-il? Ne le voilà-t-il pas qui se met à vouloir se quereller avec un bonhomme qui—prétendait-il! ce damoiseau!—le bousculait! Et ensuite il ne trouve rien de mieux à faire que d'aller vite occuper une place laissée libre! Au lieu de la laisser à une dame!

Deux heures après, devinez qui je rencontre devant la gare Saint-Lazare? Le même godelureau! En train de se faire donner des conseils vestimentaires! Par un camarade!

Le Côté Subjectif

J E N'ÉTAIS pas mécontent de ma vêture, ce jourd'hui. J'inaugurai un nouveau chapeau, assez coquin, et un pardessus dont je pensai grand bien. Rencontré X devant la gare Saint-Lazare qui essaye de gâcher mon plaisir en essayant de me démontrer que ce pardessus est trop échancré et que j'y devrais rajouter un bouton supplémentaire. Il n'a tout de même pas osé s'attaquer à mon couvre-chef.

Un peu auparavant, rembarré de belle façon une sorte de goujat qui faisait exprès de me brutaliser chaque fois qu'il passait du monde, à la descente ou à la montée. Cela se passait dans un de ces immondes autobi qui s'emplissent de populus précisément aux heures où je dois consentir à les utiliser.

Animisme

U̲N CHAPEAU mou, brun, fendu, les bords baissés, la forme entourée d'une tresse de galon, un chapeau se tenait parmi les autres, tressautant seulement des inégalités du sol transmises par les roues du véhicule automobile qui le transportait, lui le chapeau. A chaque arrêt, les allées et venues des voyageurs lui donnaient des mouvements latéraux parfois assez prononcés, ce que finit par le fâcher, lui le chapeau. Il exprima son ire par l'intermédiaire d'une voix humaine à lun rattachée par une masse de chair structuralement disposée autour d'une quasi-sphère osseuse perforée de quelques trous qui se trouvait sous lui, lui le chapeau. Puis il alla soudain s'asseoir, lui le chapeau.

Une ou deux heures plus tard je le revis se déplaçant à quelque un mètre soixante-six au-dessus du sol et de long en large devant la gare Saint-Lazare, lui le chapeau. Un ami lui conseillait de faire ajouter un bouton supplémentaire à son pardessus . . . un bouton supplémentaire . . . à son pardessus . . . lui dire ça . . . à lui . . . lui le chapeau . . .

Homeoptotes

U̲N JOUR de canicule sur un véhicule où je circule, gesticule un funambule au bulbe minuscule, à la mandibule en virgule et au capitule ridicule. Un somnambule l'accule et l'annule, l'autre articule: "crapule," mais dissimule ses scrupules, recule, capitule et va poser ailleurs son cul.

Une hule aprule, devant la gule Saint-Lazule je l'aperçule qui discule à propos de boutules, de boutules de pardessule.

Lettre Officielle

J AI L'HONNEUR de vous informer des faits suivants dont j'ai pu être le témoin aussi impartial qu'horrifié.

Ce jour même, aux environs de midi, je me trouvais sur la plate-forme d'un autobus qui remontait la rue de Courcelles en direction de la place Champerret, Ledit autobus était complet, plus que complet même, oserai-je dire, car le receveur avait pris en surcharge plusieurs impétrants, sans raison valable et mû par une bonté d'âme exagérée qui le faisait passer outre aux règlements et qui, par suite, frisait l'indulgence. A chaque arrêt, les allées et venues des voyageurs descendants et montants ne manquaient pas de provoquer une certaine bousculade qui incita l'un de ces voyageurs à protester, mais non sans timidité. Je dois dire qu'il alla s'asseoir dès que la chose fut possible.

J'ajouterai à ce bref récit cet addendum: j'eus l'occasion d'apercevoir ce voyageur quelque temps après en compagnie d'un personnage que je n'ai pu identifier. La conversation qu'ils échangeaient avec animation semblait avoir trait à des questions de nature esthétique.

Étant donné ces conditions, je vous prie de vouloir bien, Monsieur, m'indiquer les conséquences que je dois tirer de ces faits et l'attitude qu'ensuite il vous semblera bon que je prenne dans la conduite de ma vie subséquente.

Dans l'attente de votre réponse, je vous assure, Monsieur, de ma parfaite considération empressée au moins.

Apocopes

J E MON dans un auto plein de voya. Je remar un jeu hom dont le cou é sembla à ce de la gira et qui por un cha a un ga tres. Il se mit en colè con un au voya, lui repro de lui mar sur les pi cha fois qu'il mon ou descen du mon. Puis il al s'as car u pla é li.

Retour ri gau, je l'aper qui mar en long et en lar a un a qui lui don des con d'élégan en lui mon le pre bou de son pardes.

Syncopes

JE MTAI ds aubus plein dvyageurs. Je rarquai un jhomme au coublebleluirafe et au chapaltrés. Il se mit en colcautre vyageur car il lui rechait de lui marpier. Puis il ocpa une pce denue lbre.

En fant le mêmin en sinverse, je l'açus à Courome qui prait une lon d'égance àjet d'un bton.

Alors

ALORS L'AUTOBUS est arrivé. Alors j'ai monté dedans. Alors j'ai vu un citoyen qui m'a saisi l'œil. Alors j'ai vu son long cou et j'ai vu la tresse qu'il y avait autour de son chapeau. Alors il s'est mis à pester contre son voisin qui lui marchait alors sur les pieds. Alors, il est allé s'asseoir.

Alors, plus tard, je l'ai revu Cour de Rome. Alors il était avec un copain. Alors il lui disait, le copain: tu devrais faire mettre un autre bouton à ton pardessus. Alors.

Noble

A L'HEURE OÙ COMMENCENT à se gercer les doigts roses de l'aurore, je montai tel un dard rapide dans un autobus à la puissante stature et aux yeux de vache de la ligne. S au trajet sinueux. Je remarquai, avec la précision et l'acuité de l'Indien sur le sentier de la guerre, la présence d'un jeune homme dont le col était plus long que celui de la girafe au pied rapide, et dont le chapeau de feutre fou fendu s'ornait d'une tresse, tel le héros d'un exercice de style. La funeste Discorde aux seins de suie vint de sa bouche empestée par un néant de dentifrice, la Discorde, dis-je, vint souffler son virus malin entre ce jeune homme au col de girafe et à la tresse autour du chapeau, et un voyageur à la mine indécise et farineuse. Celui-là s'adressa en ces termes à celui-ci: "Dites-donc vous, on dirait que vous le faites exprès de me marcher sur les pieds!" Ayant dit ces mots, le jeune homme au col de girafe et à la tresse autour du chapeau s'alla vite asseoir.

Plus tard, dans la Cour de Rome aux majestueuses proportions, j'aperçus de nouveau le jeune homme au cou de girafe et à la tresse autour du chapeau, accompagné d'un camarade arbitre des élégances qui proférait cette critique que je pus entendre de mon oreille agile, critique adressée au vêtement le plus extérieur du jeune homme au col de girafe et à la tresse autour du chapeau: "Tu devrais en diminuer l'échancrure par l'addition ou l'exhaussement d'un bouton à la périphérie circulaire."

Comédie

ACTE PREMIER

Scène I

(*Sur la plate-forme arrière d'un autobus S, un jour, vers midi.*)
LE RECEVEUR.—La monnaie, s'iou plaît.
(*Des voyageurs lui passent la monnaie.*)

Scène II

(*L'autobus s'arrête.*)
LE RECEVEUR.—Laissons descendre. Priorités?
Une priorité! C'est complet. Drelin, drelin, drelin.

ACTE SECOND

Scène I

(*Même décor.*)
PREMIER VOYAGEUR (*jeune, long cou, une tresse autour du chapeau*).—On dirait, monsieur, que vous le faites exprès de me marcher sur les pieds chaque fois qu'il passe des gens.
SECOND VOYAGEUR (*hausse les épaules*).

Scène II

(*Un troisième voyageur descend.*)
PREMIER VOYAGEUR (*s'adressant au public*): Chouette! une place libre! J'y cours. (*Il se précipite dessus et l'occupe.*)

ACTE TROISIÈME

Scène I

(*La Cour de Rome.*)
UN JEUNE ÉLÉGANT (*au premier voyageur, maintenant piéton*).
—L'échancrure de ton pardessus est trop large. Tu devrais la
fermer un peu en faisant remonter le bouton du haut.

Scène II

(*A bord d'un autobus S passant devant la Cour de Rome.*)
QUATRIÈME VOYAGEUR.—Tiens, le type qui se trouvait tout à
l'heure avec moi dans l'autobus et qui s'engueulait avec un bonhomme. Curieuse rencontre. J'en ferai une comédie en trois actes
et en prose.

Maladroit

JE N'AI PAS l'habitude d'écrire. Je ne sais pas. J'aimerais bien
écrire une tragédie ou un sonnet ou une ode, mais il y a les
règles. Ça me gêne. C'est pas fait pour les amateurs. Tout ça
c'est déjà bien mal écrit. Enfin. En tout cas, j'ai vu aujourd'hui
quelque chose que je voudrais bien coucher par écrit. Coucher
par écrit ne me paraît pas bien fameux. Ça doit être une de ces
expressions toutes faites qui rebutent les lecteurs qui lisent pour
les éditeurs qui recherchent l'originalité qui leur paraît nécessaire
dans les manuscrits que les éditeurs publient lorsqu'ils ont été
lus par les lecteurs que rebutent les expressions toutes faites dans
le genre de "coucher par écrit" qui est pourtant ce que je
voudrais faire de quelque chose que j'ai vu aujourd'hui bien que
je ne sois qu'un amateur que gênent les règles de la tragédie du
sonnet ou de l'ode car je n'ai pas l'habitude d'écrire. Merde, je
ne sais pas comment j'ai fait mais me voilà revenu tout au
début. Je ne vais jamais en sortir. Tant pis. Prenons le taureau
par les cornes. Encore une platitude. Et puis ce gars-là n'avait
rien d'un taureau. Tiens, elle n'est pas mauvaise celle-là. Si
j'écrivais: prenons le godelureau par la tresse de son chapeau de
feutre mou emmanché d'un long cou, peut-être bien que ce serait

original. Peut-être bien que ça me ferait connaître des messieurs de l'Académie française, du Flore et de la rue Sébastien-Bottin. Pourquoi ne ferais-je pas de progrès après tout. C'est en écrivant qu'on devient écriveron. Elle est forte celle-là. Tout de même faut de la mesure. Le type sur la plate-forme de l'autobus, il en manquait quand il s'est mis à engueuler son voisin sous prétexte que ce dernier lui marchait sur les pieds chaque fois qu'il se tassait pour laisser monter ou descendre des voyageurs. D'autant plus qu'après avoir protesté comme cela, il est allé vite s'asseoir dès qu'il a vu une place libre à l'intérieur comme s'il craignait les coups. Tiens j'ai déjà raconté la moitié de mon histoire. Je me demande comment j'ai fait. C'est tout de même agréable d'écrire. Mais il reste le plus difficile. Le plus calé. La transition. D'autant plus qu'il n'y a pas de transition. Je préfère m'arrêter.

Sonnet

GLABRE DE LA VAISSELLE et tressé du bonnet,
Un paltoquet chétif au cou mélancolique
Et long se préparait, quotidienne colique,
A prendre un autobus le plus souvent complet.

L'un vint, c'était un dix ou bien peut-être un S.
La plate-forme, hochet adjoint au véhicule,
Trimballait une foule en son sein minuscule
Où des richards pervers allumaient des londrès.
Le jeune girafeau, cité première strophe,
Grimpé sur cette planche entreprend un péquin
Lequel, proclame-t-il, voulait sa catastrophe,

Pour sortir du pétrin bigle une place assise
Et s'y met. Le temps passe. Au retour un faquin
A propos d'un bouton examinait sa mise.

Télégraphique

BUS BONDE STOP JNHOMME LONG COU CHAPEAU CERCLE TRESSE
APOSTROPHE VOYAGEUR INCONNU SANS PRETEXTE VALABLE STOP

QUESTION DOIGTS PIEDS FROISSES CONTACT TALON PRETENDU VOLON-
TAIRE STOP JNHOMME ABANDONNE DISCUSSION POUR PLACE LIBRE STOP
QUATORZE HEURES PLACE ROME. JNHOMME ECOUTE CONSEILS VESTI-
MENTAIRES CAMARADE STOP DEPLACER BOUTON STOP SIGNE ARCTURUS.

Féminin

QUELLE BANDE D'EMPOTÉS! Aujourd'hui vers midi (ce qu'il faisait chaud, heureusement que je m'étais mis de l'odorono sous les bras, sans ça ma petite robe d'été en cretonne de ma petite couturière qui me fait des prix, elle était fichue) du côté du Parc Monceaux (c'est mieux que le Luxembourg où j'envoie mon fils, quelle idée d'avoir la pelade à son âge), l'autobus passe, il était plein, mais j'ai vampé le receveur et je suis montée. Naturellement le tas d'abrutis qui avait des numéros a protesté, mais pfuitt! l'autobus était loin. Et moi dedans. C'était surcomplet. Ce que j'étais serrée, et pas un homme assis à l'intérieur qui m'aurait cédé sa place. Quels goujats! A côté de moi, il y avait un homme assez élégant (c'est très chic une tresse autour d'un feutre mou au lieu de ruban, *Adam* a dû parler de cette nouvelle mode), malheureusement il avait le cou trop long pour mon goût. J'ai des amies qui prétendent que lorsqu'un homme a une partie du corps plus grande que la normale (par exemple un nez trop grand) ça indique aussi des capacités marquées dans un autre domaine. Mais je n'en crois rien. En tout cas, ce monsieur très bien se trémoussait tout le temps et je me demandais ce qu'il attendait pour m'adresser la parole ou me mettre la main quelque part. C'est un timide, me disais-je. Je n'avais pas tout à fait tort. Car le voilà qui se met à interpeller un autre bonhomme qui avait une sale tête d'ailleurs et qui faisait exprès de lui marcher sur les pieds. Si j'avais été ce jeune homme, je lui aurais cassé la figure, mais au lieu de cela il est allé vite s'asseoir dès qu'il a vu une place libre et il n'a d'ailleurs pas songé un seul instant à me l'offrir. Ce qu'il ne faut pas voir, tout de même, au pays de la galanterie.

Un peu plus tard, comme je passais devant la gare Saint-Lazare (cette fois j'étais assise), je l'ai aperçu qui discutait avec un ami (un assez joli garçon, ma foi) à propos de l'échancrure de son pardessus (une drôle d'idée de mettre un manteau par une chaleur pareille, mais ça fait toujours habillé). Je l'ai regardé, mais l'imbécile il ne m'a même pas reconnue.

Interjections

Psst! HEU! ah! oh! hum! ah! ouf! eh! tiens! oh! peuh! pouah! ouïe! ou! aïe! eh! hein! heu! pfuitt! Tiens! eh! peuh! oh! heu! bon!

THE OXEN OF THE SUN
BY JAMES JOYCE

LIKE *Tristram Shandy, Ulysses* is to some extent a parodic novel. Parody keeps cropping up throughout. There are the prurient-romantic letters exchanged between Bloom and his female correspondents in the beginning, the burlesque of journalism in the "Cave of the Winds" episode, the parody of the cheap sentimental novel—interesting to compare it with Jane Austen's *Love and Freindship*—that opens the "Nausicaa" episode:

> The Summer evening had begun to fold the world in its mysterious embrace. Far away in the west the sun was setting and the last glow of all too fleeting day lingered lovingly on sea and strand, on the proud promontory of dear old Howth guarding as ever the waters of the bay, on the weedgrown rocks along Sandymount shore and, last but not least, on the quiet church whence there streamed forth at times upon the stillness the voice of prayer to her who is in her pure radiance a beacon ever to the stormtossed heart of man, Mary, star of the sea. . . .
>
> No prince charming is her beau ideal to lay a rare and wondrous love at her feet but rather a manly man with a strong quiet face who had not found his ideal, perhaps his hair slightly flecked with grey, and who would understand, take her in his sheltering arms, strain her to him in all the strength of his deep passionate nature and comfort her with a long long kiss. It would be like heaven. For such a one she yearns this balmy summer eve. With all the heart of her she longs to be his only, his affianced bride for riches for poor, in sickness in health, till death us two part, from this to this day forward.

Four of the five episodes that make up the last half of *Ulysses* are full of parody. The "Oxen of the Sun" is all parody; "Circe"—the Nighttown phantasmagoria—keeps breaking out into journalese, novel-ese, and officialese; "Ithaca" is seventy pages of catechism parodying legal-scientific method; and "Penelope," Molly Bloom's final soliloquy, is the greatest Excursion into the Vernacular in our language. "Ithaca" immediately precedes "Penelope," a brilliant juxtaposition of extremes. We go directly from this kind of speech:

> What action did Bloom make on their arrival at their destination?
> At the housesteps of the 4th of the equidifferent uneven numbers, number 7 Eccles street, he inserted his hand mechanically into the back pocket of his trousers to obtain his latchkey.
> Was it there?
> It was in the corresponding pocket of the trousers which he had worn on the day but one preceding.
> Why was he doubly irritated?
> Because he had forgotten and because he remembered that he had reminded himself twice not to forget.

to this kind:

> Yes because he never did a thing like that before as ask to get his breakfast in bed with a couple of eggs since the *City Arms* hotel when he used to be pretending to be laid up with a sick voice doing his highness to made himself interesting to that old faggot Mrs. Riordan that he thought he had a great leg of and she never left us a farthing all for masses for herself and her soul greatest miser ever was actually afraid to lay out 4d for her methylated spirit telling me all her . . .

In the "Oxen of the Sun" episode, Stephen, Bloom, and other characters are assembled in Dr. Andrew J. Horne's National Maternity Hospital. They are drinking while they wait for Mrs. Purefoy to have her baby. The progress of the birth is rendered in parodies of the progress of English prose—ontogeny recapitulates phylogeny, or rather in this case the other way round—beginning with primitive incantation and ending (as they become drunker) in a general deliquescence of language. As Frank Budgen puts it in *James Joyce and the Making of Ulysses*, they "rush from Horne's house to Burke's pub, in no style at all, slang of half-drunken human utterance—pidgin English, nigger English, Cockney, Irish, Scots, Welsh, Bowery slang and broken doggerel."

Immediately before this collapse into mongrelized incoherence, we have the parody of Thomas Carlyle, who racked and tortured our sweet English tongue as mercilessly as any pidgin-speaking South Sea islander; that he was considered a literary giant (instead of the inventor of *Time*style) shows a decline in standards; using Carlyle's frenetic, bastardized style as the transition to the death of English in the gutter was one of Joyce's happiest inspirations. All through the "Oxen of the Sun" episode, and especially in the last few pages, *Finnegans Wake* is struggling to be born, along with Mrs. Purefoy's baby.

The selections from "Oxen of the Sun" that follow, and identification of the authors imitated, were made by myself with some help from Stuart Gilbert's *James Joyce's "Ulysses"* and from Richard Ellmann of Northwestern University, who also suggested the "Museum Tour" from *Finnegans Wake*.

Primitive

DESHIL HOLLES EAMUS. Deshil Holles Eamus. Deshil Holles Eamus.

Send us, bright one, light one, Horhorn, quickening and wombfruit. Send us, bright one, light one, Horhorn, quickening and wombfruit. Send us, bright one, light one, Horhorn, quickening and wombfruit.

Hoopsa, boyaboy, hoopsa! Hoopsa, boyaboy, hoopsa! Hoopsa, boyaboy, hoopsa.

Anglo-Saxon

OF THAT house A. Horne is lord. Seventy beds keeps he there teeming mothers are wont that they lie for to thole and bring forth bairns hale so God's angel to Mary quoth. Watchers twey there walk, white sisters in ward sleepless. Smarts they still sickness soothing: in twelve moons thrice an hundred. Truest bed thanes they twain are, for Horne holding wariest ward.

In ward wary the watcher hearing come that man mildhearted eft rising with swire ywimpled to him her gate wide undid. Lo, levin leaping lightens in eyeblink Ireland's westward welkin! Full she dread that God the Wreaker all mankind would fordo with water for his evil sins. Christ's rood made she on breastbone and him drew that he would rathe infare under her thatch. That man her will wotting worthful went in Horne's house.

Loth to irk in Horne's hall hat holding the seeker stood. On her stow he ere was living with dear wife and lovesome daughter that then over land and seafloor nine years had long outwandered. Once her in townhithe meeting he to her bow had not doffed. Her to forgive now he craved with good ground of her allowed that that of him swiftseen face, hers, so young then had looked. Light swift her eyes kindled, bloom of blushes his word winning.

Sir John Mandeville

A ND WHILES they spake the door of the castle was opened and there nighed them a mickle noise as of many that sat there at meat. And there came against the place as they stood a young learning knight yclept Dixon. And the traveller Leopold was couth to him sithen it had happed that they had had ado each with other in the house of misericord where this learning knight lay by cause the traveller Leopold came there to be healed for he was sore wounded in his breast by a spear wherewith a horrible and dreadful dragon was smitten him for which he did do make a salve of volatile salt and chrism as much as he might suffice. And he said now that he should go into that castle for to make merry with them that were there. And the traveller Leopold said that he should go otherwhither for he was a man of cautels and a subtle. Also the lady was of his avis and reproved the learning knight though she trowed well that the traveller had said thing that was false for his subtility. But the learning knight would not hear say nay nor do her mandement ne have him in aught contrarious to his list and he said how it was a marvellous castle. And the traveller Leopold went into the castle for to rest him for a space being sore of limb after many marches environing in divers lands and sometimes venery.

And in the castle was set a board that was of the birchwood of Finlandy and it was upheld by four dwarfmen of that country but they durst not move more for enchantment. And on this

board were frightful swords and knives that are made in a great
cavern by swinking demons out of white flames that they fix in
the horns of buffaloes and stags that there abound marvellously.
And there were vessels that are wrought by magic of Mahound
out of seasand and the air by a warlock with his breath that he
blares into them like to bubbles. And full fair cheer and rich was
on the board that no wight could devise a fuller ne richer. And
there was a vat of silver that was moved by craft to open in the
which lay strange fishes withouten heads though misbelieving
men nie that this be possible thing without they see it natheless
they are so. And these fishes lie in an oily water brought there
from Portugal land because of the fatness that therein is like to
the juices of the olive press. And also it was marvel to see in that
castle how by magic they make a compost out of fecund wheat
kidneys out of Chaldee that by aid of certain angry spirits that
they do into it swells up wondrously like to a vast mountain.
And they teach the serpents there to entwine themselves up on
long sticks out of the ground and of the scales of these serpents
they brew out of brewage like to mead.

Sir Thomas Browne; King James Bible

THEREAT MIRTH grew in them the more and they rehearsed to
him his curious rite of wedlock for the disrobing and de-
flowering of spouses, as the priests use in Madagascar island, she
to be in guise of white and saffron her groom in white and grain,
with burning of nard and tapers, on a bridebed while clerks sung
kyries and the anthem *Ut novetur sexus omnis corporis mys-
terium* till she was there unmaided. He gave them then a much
admirable hymen minim by those delicate poets Master John
Fletcher and Master Francis Beaumont that is in their *Maid's
Tragedy* that was writ for a like twining of lovers: *To bed, to
bed,* was the burden of it to be played with accompanable con-
cent upon the virginals. An exquisite dulcet epithalame of most
mollificative suadency for juveniles amatory whom the odorifer-
ous flambeaus of the paranymphs have escorted to the quad-
rupedal proscenium of connubial communion. Well met they
were, said Master Dixon, joyed, but, harkee, young sir, better

were they named Beau Mount and Lecher for, by my troth, of
such a mingling much might come. Young Stephen said indeed
to his best remembrance they had but the one doxy between
them and she of the stews to make shift with in delights amorous
for life ran very high in those days and the custom of the country
approved with it. Greater love than this, he said, no man hath
that a man lay down his wife for his friend. Go thou and do
likewise. Thus, or words to that effect, saith Zarathustra, sometime regius professor of French letters to the university of Oxtail
nor breathed there ever that man to whom mankind was more
beholden. Bring a stranger within thy tower it will go hard but
thou wilt have the secondbest bed. *Orate, fratres, pro memetipso.*
And all the people shall say, Amen. Remember, Erin, thy generations and thy days of old, how thou settedst little by me and by
my word and broughtest in a stranger to my gates to commit
fornication in my sight and to wax fat and kick like Jeshurum.
Therefore hast thou sinned against the light and hast made me,
thy lord, to be the slave of servants. Return, return, Clan Milly:
forget me not, O Milesian. Why hast thou done this abomination
before me that thou didst spurn me for a merchant of jalaps and
didst deny me to the Roman and the Indian of dark speech with
whom thy daughters did lie luxuriously? Look forth now, my
people, upon the land of behest, even from Horeb and from
Nebo and from Pisgah and from the Horns of Hatten unto a
land flowing with milk and money. But thou hast suckled me
with a bitter milk: my moon and my sun thou hast quenched
for ever. And thou hast left me alone for ever in the dark ways
of my bitterness: and with a kiss of ashes hast thou kissed my
mouth. This tenebrosity of the interior, he proceeded to say,
hath not been illumined by the wit of the septuagint nor so
much as mentioned for the Orient from on high which brake
hell's gates visited a darkness that was foraneous. Assuefaction
minorates atrocities (as Tully saith of his darling Stoics) and
Hamlet his father showeth the prince no blister of combustion.
The adiaphane in the noon of life is an Egypt's plague which in
the nights of prenativity and postmortemity is their most proper
ubi and *quomodo*. And as the ends and ultimates of all things
accord in some mean and measure with their inceptions and

originals, that same multiplicit concordance which leads forth growth from birth accomplishing by a retrogressive metamorphosis that minishing and ablation towards the final which is agreeable unto nature so is it with our subsolar being. The aged sisters draw us into life: we wail, batten, sport, clip, clasp, sunder, dwindle, die: over us dead they bend. First saved from water of old Nile, among bulrushes, a bed of fasciated wattles: at last the cavity of a mountain, an occulted sepulchre amid the conclamation of the hillcat and the ossifrage. And as no man knows the ubicity of his tumulus nor to what processes we shall thereby be ushered nor whether to Tophet or to Edenville in the like way is all hidden when we would backward see from what region of remoteness the whatness of our whoness hath fetched his whenceness.

John Bunyan

B UT WAS young Boasthard's fear vanquished by Calmer's words? No, for he had in his bosom a spike named Bitterness which could not by words be done away. And was he then neither calm like the one nor godly like the other? He was neither as much as he would have liked to be either. But could he not have endeavoured to have found again as in his youth the bottle Holiness that then he lived withal? Indeed not for Grace was not there to find that bottle. Heard he then in that clap the voice of the god Bringforth or, what Calmer said, a hubbub of Phenomenon? Heard? Why, he could not but hear unless he had plugged up the tube Understanding (which he had not done). For through that tube he saw that he was in the land of Phenomenon where he must for a certain one day die as he was like the rest too a passing show. And would he not accept to die like the rest and pass away? By no means would he and make more shows according as men do with wives which Phenomenon has commanded them to do by the book Law. Then wotted he nought of that other land which is called Believe-on-Me, that is the land of promise which behoves to the king Delightful and shall be for ever where there is no death and no birth neither wiving nor mothering at which all shall come as many as believe on it? Yes,

Pious had told him of that land and Chaste had pointed him to the way but the reason was that in the way he fell in with a certain whore of an eyepleasing exterior whose name, she said, is Bird-in-the-Hand and she beguiled him wrongways from the true path by her flatteries that she said to him, as Ho, you pretty man, turn aside hither and I will show you a brave place, and she lay at him so flatteringly that she had him in her grot which is named Two-in-the-Bush or, by some learned, Carnal Concupiscence.

This was it what all that company that sat there at commons in Manse of Mothers the most lusted after and if they met with this whore Bird-in-the-Hand (which was within all foul plagues, monsters and a wicked devil) they would strain the last but they would make at her and know her. For regarding Believe-on-Me they said it was nought else but notion and they could conceive no thought of it for, first, Two-in-the-Bush whither she ticed them was the very goodliest grot and in it were four pillows on which were four tickets with these words printed on them, Pickaback and Topsyturvy and Shameface and Cheek by Jowl and, second, for that foul plague Allpox and the monsters they cared not for them, for Preservative had given them a stout shield of oxengut and, third, that they might take no hurt neither from Offspring that was that wicked devil by virtue of this same shield which was named Killchild. So were they all in their blind fancy, Mr. Cavil and Mr. Sometimes Godly, Mr. Ape Swillale, Mr. False Franklin, Mr. Dainty Dixon, Young Boasthard and Mr. Cautious Calmer. Wherein, O wretched company were ye all deceived for that was the voice of the god that was in a very grievous rage that he would presently lift his arm and spill their souls for their abuses and their spillings done by them contrariwise to his word which forth to bring brenningly biddeth.

Pepys' Diary

S O THURSDAY sixteenth June Patk. Dignam laid in clay of an apoplexy and after hard drought, please God, rained, a bargeman coming in by water a fifty mile or thereabout with turf saying the seed won't sprout, fields athirst, very sadcoloured and stunk mightily, the quags and tofts too. Hard to breathe and all the young quicks clean consumed without sprinkle this long while back as no man remembered to be without. The rosy buds all gone brown and spread out blobs and on the hills nought but dry flag and faggots that would catch at first fire. All the world saying, for aught they knew, the big wind of last February a year that did havoc the land so pitifully a small thing beside this barrenness. But by and by, as said, this evening after sundown, the wind sitting in the west, biggish swollen clouds to be seen as the night increased and the weatherwise poring up at them and some sheet lightnings at first and after, past ten of the clock, one great stroke with a long thunder and in a brace of shakes all scamper pellmell within door for the smoking shower, the men making shelter for their straws with a clout or kerchief, womenfolk skipping off with kirtles catched up soon as the pour came. In Ely place, Baggot street, Duke's lawn, thence through Merrion green up to Holles street, a swash of water running that was before bonedry and not one chair or coach or fiacre seen about but no more crack after that first. Over against the Rt. Hon. Mr. Justice Fitzgibbon's door (that is to sit with Mr. Healy the lawyer upon the college lands) Mal. Mulligan a gentleman's gentleman that had but come from Mr. Moore's the writer's (that was a papish but is now, folk say, a good Williamite) chanced against Alec. Bannon in a cut bob (which are now in with dance cloaks of Kendal green) that was new got to town from Mullingar with the stage where his coz and Mal M's brother will stay a month yet till Saint Swithin and asks what in the earth he does there, he bound home and he to Andrew Horne's being stayed for to crush a cup of wine, so he said, but would tell him of a skittish heifer, big of her age and beef to the heel and all this while poured with rain and so both together or to Horne's.

Addison and Steele

OUR WORTHY acquaintance, Mr. Malachi Mulligan, now appeared in the doorway as the students were finishing their apologue accompanied with a friend whom he had just rencountered, a young gentleman, his name Alec Bannon, who had late come to town, it being his intention to buy a colour or a cornetcy in the fencibles and list for the wars. Mr. Mulligan was civil enough to express some relish of it all the more as it jumped with a project of his own for the cure of the very evil that had been touched on. Whereat he handed round to the company a set of pasteboard cards which he had had printed that day at Mr. Quinnell's bearing a legend printed in fair italics: *Mr. Malachi Mulligan, Fertiliser and Incubator, Lambay Island*. His project, as he went on to expound, was to withdraw from the round of idle pleasures such as form the chief business of sir Fopling Popinjay and sir Milksop Quidnunc in town and to devote himself to the noblest task for which our bodily organism has been framed. Well, let us hear of it, good my friend, said Mr. Dixon. I make no doubt it smacks of wenching. Come, be seated, both. 'Tis as cheap sitting as standing. Mr. Mulligan accepted of the invitation and, expatiating on his design, told his hearers that he had been led into this thought by a consideration of the causes of sterility, both the inhibitory and the prohibitory, whether the inhibition in its turn were due to conjugal vexations or to a parsimony of the balance as well as whether the prohibition proceeded from defects congenital or from proclivities acquired. It grieved him plaguily, he said, to see the nuptial couch defrauded of its dearest pledges: and to reflect upon so many agreeable females with rich jointures, a prey for the vilest bonzes, who hide their flambeau under a bushel in an uncongenial cloister or lose their womanly bloom in the embraces of some unaccountable muskin when they might multiply the inlets of happiness, sacrificing the inestimable jewel of their sex when a hundred pretty fellows were at hand to caress, this, he assured them, made his heart weep. To curb this inconvenient (which he concluded due to a suppression of latent heat), having advised with certain counsellors of worth and inspected into this matter, he had resolved to purchase in fee simple for ever the freehold of Lambay island from its holder, lord Talbot de Malahide, a Tory gentleman of not much in favour with our ascendancy party. He proposed to set up there a national fertilising farm to be named *Omphalos* with an obelisk

hewn and erected after the fashion of Egypt and to offer his
dutiful yeoman services for the fecundation of any female of
what grade of life soever who should there direct to him with
the desire of fulfilling the functions of her natural. Money was
no object, he said, nor would he take a penny for his pains. The
poorest kitchenwench no less than the opulent lady of fashion,
if so be their constructions and their tempers were warm persuad-
ers for their petitions, would find in him their man. For his
nutriment he shewed how he would feed himself exclusively
upon a diet of savoury tubercles and fish and coneys there, the
flesh of these latter prolific rodents being highly recommended
for his purpose, both broiled and stewed with a blade of mace
and a pod or two of capsicum chillies. After this homily which
he delivered with much warmth of asseveration Mr. Mulligan
in a trice put off from his hat a kerchief with which he had
shielded it. They both, it seems, had been overtaken by the rain
and for all their mending their pace had taken water, as might
be observed by Mr. Mulligan's smallclothes of a hodden grey
which was now somewhat piebald. His project meanwhile was
very favourably entertained by his auditors and won hearty
eulogies from all though Mr. Dixon of Mary's excepted to it,
asking with a finicking air did he purpose also to carry coals to
Newcastle. Mr. Mulligan however made court to the scholarly by
an apt quotation from the classics which as it dwelt upon his
memory seemed to him a sound and tasteful support of his con-
tention: *Talis ac tanta depravatio hujus seculi, O quirites, ut
matres familiarum nostræ lascivas cujuslibet semiviri libici titilla-
tiones testibus ponderosis atque excelsis erectionibus centurionum
Romanorum magnopere anteponunt* while for those of ruder wit
he drove home his point by analogies of the animal kingdom
more suitable to their stomach, the buck and doe of the forest
glade, the farmyard drake and duck.

Laurence Sterne

HERE THE LISTENER who was none other than the Scotch student, a little fume of a fellow, blond as tow, congratulated
in the liveliest fashion with the young gentleman and, interrupt-

ing the narrative at a salient point, having desired his visavis with
a polite beck to have the obligingness to pass him a flagon of cordial waters at the same time by a questioning poise of the head
(a whole century of polite breeding had not achieved so nice a
gesture) to which was united an equivalent but contrary balance
of the head asked the narrator as plainly as was ever done in
words if he might treat him with a cup of it. *Mais bien sûr,* noble
stranger, said he cheerily, *et mille compliments.* That you may
and very opportunely. There wanted nothing but this cup to
crown my felicity. But, gracious heaven, was I left with but a
crust in my wallet and a cupful of water from the well, my God,
I would accept of them and find it in my heart to kneel down
upon the ground and give thanks to the powers above for the
happiness vouchsafed me by the Giver of good things. With
these words he approached the goblet to his lips, took a com-
placent draught of the cordial, slicked his hair and, opening his
bosom, out popped a locket that hung from a silk riband that
very picture which he had cherished ever since her hand had
wrote therein. Gazing upon those features with a world of tenderness, Ah, Monsieur, he said, had you but beheld her as I did
with these eyes at that affecting instant with her dainty tucker
and her new coquette cap (a gift for her feast day as she told me)
in such an artless disorder, of so melting a tenderness, 'pon my
conscience, even you, Monsieur, had been impelled by generous
nature to deliver yourself wholly into the hands of such an
enemy or to quit the field for ever. I declare, I was never so
touched in all my life. God I thank thee as the Author of my
days! Thrice happy will he be whom so amiable a creature will
bless with her favours. . . . But indeed, sir, I wander from the
point. How mingled and imperfect are all our sublunary joys!
Maledicity! Would to God that foresight had remembered me to
take my cloak along! I could weep to think of it. Then, though it
had poured seven showers we were neither of us a penny the
worse. But beshrew me, he cried, clapping hand to his forehead,
tomorrow will be a new day and, thousand thunders, I know of
a *marchand de capotes,* Monsieur Poyntz, from whom I can have
for a *livre* as snug a cloak of the French fashion as ever kept a
lady from wetting. Tut, tut! cries Le Fécondateur, tripping in,

my friend Monsieur Moore, that most accomplished traveller (I
have just cracked a half bottle *avec lui* in a circle of the best
wits of the town), is my authority that in Cape Horn, *ventre
biche,* they have a rain that will wet through any, even the
stoutest cloak. A drenching of that violence, he tells me, *sans
blague,* has sent more than one luckless fellow in good earnest
posthaste to another world. Pooh! A *livre!* cries Monsieur Lynch.
The clumsy things are dear at a sou. One umbrella, were it no
bigger than a fairy mushroom, is worth ten such stopgaps. No
woman of any wit would wear one. My dear Kitty told me today
that she would dance in a deluge before ever she would starve
in such an ark of salvation for, as she reminded me (blushing
piquantly and whispering in my ear though there was none to
snap her words but giddy butterflies), dame Nature, by the divine
blessing, has implanted it in our heart and it has become a
household word that *il y a a deux choses* for which the innocence
of our original garb, in other circumstances a breach of the
proprieties, is the fittest, nay the only, garment. The first, said
she (and here my pretty philosopher, as I handed her to her
tilbury, to fix my attention, gently tipped with her tongue the
outer chamber of my ear), the first is a bath . . . but at this
point a bell tinkling in the hall cut short a discourse which
promised so bravely for the enrichment of our store of knowledge.

Charles Lamb

WHAT is the age of the soul of man? As she hath the virtue
of the chameleon to change her hue at every new approach,
to be gay with the merry and mournful with the downcast, so too
is her age changeable as her mood. No longer is Leopold, as he
sits there, ruminating, chewing the cud of reminiscence, that
staid agent of publicity and holder of a modest substance in the
funds. He is young Leopold, as in a retrospective arrangement, a
mirror within a mirror (hy, presto!), he beholdeth himself.
That young figure of then is seen, precociously manly, walking
on a nipping morning from the old house in Clambrassil street
to the high school, his booksatchel on him bandolierwise, and
in it a goodly hunk of wheaten loaf, a mother's thought. Or it is

the same figure, a year or so gone over, in his first hard hat (ah, that was a day!), already on the road, a fullfledged traveller for the family firm, equipped with an orderbook, a scented handkerchief (not for show only), his case of bright trinketware (alas, a thing now of the past!), and a quiverful of compliant smiles for this or that halfwon housewife reckoning it out upon her fingertips or for a budding virgin shyly acknowledging (but the heart? tell me!) his studied baisemoins. The scent, the smile but more than these, the dark eyes and oleaginous address brought home at duskfall many a commission to the head of the firm seated with Jacob's pipe after like labours in the paternal ingle (a meal of noodles, you may be sure, is aheating), reading through round horned spectacles some paper from the Europe of a month before. But hey, presto, the mirror is breathed on and the young knighterrant recedes, shrivels, to a tiny speck within the mist. Now he is himself paternal and these about him might be his sons. Who can say? The wise father knows his own child. He thinks of a drizzling night in Hatch street, hard by the bonded stores there, the first. Together (she is a poor waif, a child of shame, yours and mine and of all for a bare shilling and her luckpenny), together they hear the heavy tread of the watch as two raincaped shadows pass the new royal university. Bridie! Bridie Kelly! He will never forget the name, ever remember the night, first night, the bridenight. They are entwined in nethermost darkness, the willer with the willed, and in an instant ⟨fiat!⟩ light shall flood the world. Did heart leap to heart? Nay, fair reader. In a breath 'twas done but—hold! Back! It must not be! In terror the poor girl flees away through the murk. She is the bride of darkness, a daughter of night. She dare not bear the sunnygolden babe of day. No, Leopold! Name and memory solace thee not. That youthful illusion of thy strength was taken from thee and in vain. No son of thy loins is by thee. There is none now to be for Leopold, what Leopold was for Rudolph.

Thomas de Quincey

T HE VOICES blend and fuse in clouded silence: silence that is the infinite of space: and swiftly, silently the soul is wafted over regions of cycles of cycles of generations that have lived. A region where grey twilight ever descends, never falls on wide sagegreen pasturefields, shedding her dusk, scattering a perennial dew of stars. She follows her mother with ungainly steps, a mare leading her fillyfoal. Twilight phantoms are they yet moulded in prophetic grace of structure, slim shapely haunches, a supple tendonous neck, the meek apprehensive skull. They fade, sad phantoms: all is gone. Agendath is a waste land, a home of screechowls and the sandblind upupa. Netaim, the golden, is no more. And on the highway of the clouds they come, muttering thunder of rebellion, the ghosts of beasts. Huuh! Hark! Huuh! Parallax stalks behind and goads them, the lancinating lightnings of whose brow are scorpions. Elk and yak, the bulls of Bashan and of Babylon, mammoth and mastodon, they come trooping to the sunken sea, *Lacus Mortis*. Ominous, revengeful zodiacal host! They moan, passing upon the clouds, horned and capricorned, the trumpeted with the tusked, the lionmaned the giantantlered, snouter and crawler, rodent, ruminant and pachyderm, all their moving moaning multitude, murderers of the sun.

Onward to the dead sea they tramp to drink, unslaked and with horrible gulpings, the salt somnolent inexhaustible flood. And the equine portent grows again, magnified in the deserted heavens, nay to heaven's own magnitude till it looms, vast, over the house of Virgo. And, lo, wonder of metempsychosis, it is she, the everlasting bride, harbinger of the daystar, the bride, ever virgin. It is she, Martha, thou lost one, Millicent, the young, the dear, the radiant. How serene does she now arise, a queen among the Pleiades, in the penultimate antelucan hour, shod in sandals of bright gold, coifed with a veil of what do you call it gossamer! It floats, it flows about her starborn flesh and loose it streams emerald, sapphire, mauve and heliotrope, sustained on currents of cold interstellar wind, winding, coiling, simply swirling, writhing in the skies a mysterious writing till after a myriad metamorphoses of symbol, it blazes, Alpha, a ruby and triangled sign upon the forehead of Taurus.

Thomas Babington Macaulay

T HE DEBATE which ensued was in its scope and progress an epitome of the course of life. Neither place nor council was lacking in dignity. The debaters were the keenest in the land, the theme they were engaged on the loftiest and most vital. The high hall of Horne's house had never beheld an assembly so representative and so varied nor had the old rafters of that establishment ever listened to a language so encyclopaedic. A gallant scene in truth it made. Crotthers was there at the foot of the table in his striking Highland garb, his face glowing from the briny airs of the Mull of Galloway. There too, opposite to him was Lynch, whose countenance bore already the stigmata of early depravity and premature wisdom. Next the Scotchman was the place assigned to Costello, the eccentric, while at his side was seated in stolid repose the squat form of Madden. The chair of the resident indeed stood vacant before the hearth but on either flank of it the figure of Bannon in explorer's kit of tweed shorts and salted cowhide brogues contrasted sharply with the primrose elegance and townbred manners of Malachi Roland St. John Mulligan. Lastly at the head of the board was the young poet who found a refuge from his labours of pedagogy and metaphysical inquisition in the convivial atmosphere of Socratic discussion, while to right and left of him were accommodated the flippant prognosticator, fresh from the hippodrome, and that vigilant wanderer, soiled by the dust of travel and combat and stained by the mire of an indelible dishonour, but from whose steadfast and constant heart no lure or peril or threat or degradation could ever efface the image of that voluptuous loveliness which the inspired pencil of Lafayette has limned for ages yet to come.

Thomas Huxley

I T HAD better be stated here and now at the outset that the perverted transcendentalism to which Mr. S. Dedalus' (Div. Scep.) contentions would appear to prove him pretty badly addicted runs directly counter to accepted scientific methods.

Science, it cannot be too often repeated, deals with tangible phenomena. The man of science like the man in the street has to face hardheaded facts that cannot be blinked and explain them as best he can. There may be, it is true, some questions which science cannot answer—at present—such as the first problem submitted by Mr. L. Bloom (Pubb. Canv.) regarding the future determination of sex. Must we accept the view of Empedocles of Trinacria that the right ovary (the postmenstrual period, assert others) is responsible for the birth of males or are the too long neglected spermatozoa or nemasperms the differentiating factors or is it, as most embryologists incline to opine, such as Culpepper, Spallanzani, Blumenbach, Lusk, Hertwig, Leopold and Valenti, a mixture of both? This would be tantamount to a co-operation (one of nature's favorite devices) between the *nisus formativus* of the nemasperm on the one hand and on the other a happily chosen position, *succubitus felix,* of the passive element. The other problem raised by the same inquirer is scarcely less vital: infant mortality. It is interesting because, as he pertinently remarks, we are all born in the same way but we all die in different ways. . . . Mr. J. Crotthers (Disc. Bacc.) attributes some of these demises to abdominal trauma in the case of women workers subjected to heavy labours in the workshop and to marital discipline in the home but by far the vast majority to neglect, private or official, culminating in the exposure of newborn infants, the practice of criminal abortion or in the atrocious crime of infanticide. Although the former (we are thinking of neglect) is undoubtedly only too true the case he cites of nurses forgetting to count the sponges in the peritoneal cavity is too rare to be normative. In fact when one comes to look into it the wonder is that so many pregnancies and deliveries go off so well as they do, all things considered and in spite of our human shortcomings which often balk nature in her intentions. An ingenious suggestion is that thrown out by Mr. V. Lynch (Bacc. Arith.) that both natality and mortality, as well as all other phenomena of evolution, tidal movements, lunar phases, blood temperatures, diseases in general, everything, in fine, in nature's vast workshop from the extinction of some remote sun to the blossoming of one of the countless flowers which beautify our public parks is subject to a law of numeration as yet unascertained. Still the plain straightforward question why a child of normally healthy parents and seemingly a healthy child and properly looked after succumbs unaccountably in early childhood (though other children of the same marriage do not) must certainly, in the poet's words, give us pause. Nature, we may rest assured, has her own good and cogent reasons for whatever she does and in all probability such deaths are due to some law of anticipation by which organisms in which morbous germs have taken up their residence (modern science has conclusively shown that only the plasmic substance can be said to be immortal) tend to disappear at an increasingly earlier stage of development, an arrangement, which, though productive of pain to some of our feelings (notably the maternal) is nevertheless, some of us think, in the long run beneficial to the race in general in securing thereby the survival of the fittest.

Charles Dickens

MEANWHILE the skill and patience of the physician had brought about a happy *accouchement*. It had been a weary weary while both for patient and doctor. All that surgical skill could do was done and the brave woman had manfully helped. She had. She had fought the good fight and now she was very very happy. Those who have passed on, who have gone before, are happy too as they gaze down and smile upon the touching scene. Reverently look at her as she reclines there with the motherlight in her eyes, that longing hunger for baby fingers (a pretty sight it is to see), in the first bloom of her new motherhood, breathing a silent prayer of thanksgiving to One above, the Universal Husband. And as her loving eyes behold her babe she wishes only one blessing more, to have her dear Doady there with her to share her joy, to lay in his arms that mite of God's clay, the fruit of their lawful embraces. He is older now (you and I may whisper it) and a trifle stooped in the shoulders yet in the whirligig of years a grave dignity has come to the conscientious second accountant of the Ulster bank, College Green branch. O'Doady, loved one of old, faithful lifemate now it may never be again, that faroff time of the roses! With the old shake of her pretty head she recalls those days. God, how beautiful now across the mist of years! But their children are grouped in her imagination about the bedside, hers and his, Charley, Mary Alice, Frederick Albert (if he had lived), Mamy, Budgy (Victoria Frances), Tom, Violet Constance Louisa, darling little Bobsy (called after our famous hero of the South African war, lord Bobs of Waterford and Candahar) and now this last pledge of their union, a Purefoy if ever there was one, with the true Purefoy nose. Young hopeful will be christened Mortimer Edward after the influential third cousin of Mr Purefoy in the Treasury Remembrancer's office, Dublin Castle. And so time wags on: but father Cronion has dealt lightly here. No, let no sigh break from that bosom, dear gentle Mina. And Doady, knock the ashes from your pipe, the seasoned brier you still fancy when the curfew rings for you (may it be the distant day!) and dout the light whereby you read in the Sacred Book for the oil too has run low and so with a tranquil heart to bed, to rest. He knows and will call in His own good time. You too have fought the good fight and played loyally your man's part. Sir, to you my hand. Well done, thou good and faithful servant!

Thomas Carlyle

Burke's! Outflings my lord Stephen, giving the cry, and a tag and bobtail of all them after, cockerel, jackanapes, welsher, pill-doctor, punctual Bloom at heels with a universal grabbing at headgear, ashplants, bilbos, Panama hats and scabbards, Zermatt alpenstocks and what not. A dedale of lusty youth, noble every student there. Nurse Callan taken aback in the hallway cannot stay them nor smiling surgeon coming downstairs with news of placentation ended, a full pound if a milligramme. They hark him on. The door! It is open? Ha! They are out tumultuously, off for a minute's race, all bravely legging it, Burke's of Denzille and Holles their ulterior goal. Dixon follows, giving them sharp language but raps out an oath, he too, and on. Bloom stays with nurse a thought to send a kind word to happy mother and nurseling up there. Doctor Diet and Doctor Quiet.

Looks she too not other now? Ward of watching in Horne's house has told its tale in that washedout pallor. Them all being gone, a glance of motherwit helping he whispers close in going: Madam, when comes the storkbird for thee?

The air without is impregnated with raindew moisture, life essence celestial, glistering on Dublin stone there under starshiny *cœlum*. God's air the Allfather's air, scintillant circumambient cessile air. Breathe it deep into thee. By heaven, Theodore Purefoy, thou hast done a doughty deed and no botch! Thou art, I vow, the remarkablest progenitor barring none in this chaffering allincluding most farraginous chronicle. Astounding! In her lay a Godframed Godgiven preformed possibility which thou hast fructified with thy modicum of man's work. Cleave to her! Serve! Toil on, labour like a very bandog and let scholarment and all Malthusiasts go hang. Thou art all their daddies, Theodore. Art drooping under thy load, bemoiled with butcher's bills at home and ingots (not thine!) in the countinghouse? Head up! For every newbegotten thou shalt gather thy homer of ripe wheat. See, thy fleece is drenched. Dost envy Darby Dullman there with his Joan? A canting jay and a rheumeyed curdog is all their progeny. Pshaw, I tell thee! He is a mule, a dead gasteropod, without vim or stamina, not worth a cracked kreutzer. Copulation without population! No, say I! Herod's slaughter of the innocents were the truer name. Vegetables, forsooth, and sterile cohabitation! Give her beefsteaks, red, raw, bleeding! She is a hoary pandemonium of ills, enlarged glands, mumps, quinsy, bunions, hayfever, bedsores, ringworm, floating kidney, Derbyshire neck, warts, bilious attacks, gallstones, cold feet, varicose veins. A truce to threnes and trentals and jeremies and all such congenital defunctive music. Twenty years of it, regret them not. With thee it was not as with many that will and would and wait and never do. Thou sawest thy America, thy lifetask, and didst charge to cover like the transpontine bison. How saith Zarathusthra? *Deine Kuh Truebsal melkest Du. Nun trinkst Du die suesse Milch des Euters.* See! It displodes for thee in abundance. Drink, man, an udderful! Mother's milk, Purefoy, the milk of human kin, milk too of those burgeoning stars overhead, tutilant in thin rainvapour, punch milk, such as those rioters will quaff in their guzzlingden, milk of madness, the honeymilk of Canaan's land. Thy cow's dug was tough, what? Ay, but her milk is hot and sweet and fattening. No dollop this but thick rich bonnyclaber. To her, old patriarch! Pap! *Per deam Partulam et Pertundam nunc est bibendum!*

The End

GOLLY, whatten tunket's yon guy in the mackintosh? Dusty Rhodes. Peep at his wearables. By mighty? What's he got? Jubilee mutton. Bovril, by James. Wants it real bad. D'ye ken bare socks? Seedy cuss in the Richmond? Rawthere! Thought he had a deposit of lead in his penis. Trumpery insanity. Bartle the Bread we calls him. That, sir, was once a prosperous cit. Man all tattered and torn that married a maiden all forlorn. Slung her hook, she did. Here see lost love. Walking Mackintosh of lonely canyon. Tuck and turn in. Schedule time. Nix for the hornies. Pardon? See him today at a runefal? Chum o yourn passed in his checks? Ludamassy! Pore picanninies! Thou'll no be telling me thot, Pold veg! Did ums blubble bigsplash crytears cos frien Padney was took off in black bag? Of all de darkies Massa Pat was verra best. I never see the like since I was born. *Tiens, tiens,* but it is well sad, that, my faith, yes. O get, rev on a gradient one in nine. Live axle drives are souped. Lay you two to one Jenatzy licks him ruddy well hollow. Jappies? High angle fire, inyah! Sunk by war specials. Be worse for him, says he, nor any Rooshian. Time all. There's eleven of them. Get ye gone Forward, woozy wobblers! Night. Night. May Allah, the Excellent One, your soul this night ever tremendously conserve.

Your attention! We're nae the fou. The Leith police dismisseth us. The least tholice. Ware hawks for the chap puking. Unwell in his abominable regions. Yooka. Night. Mona, my thrue love. Yook. Mona, my own love. Ook.

Hark! Shut your obstropolos. Pflaap! Pflaap! Blaze on. There she goes. Brigade! Bout ship. Mount street way. Cut up. Pflaap! Tally ho. You not come? Run, skelter, race. Pflaaaap!

Lynch! Hey? Sign on long o me. Denzille lane this way. Change here for Bawdyhouse. We two, she said, will seek the kips where shady Mary is. Righto, any old time. *Laetabuntur in cubilibus suis.* You coming long? Whisper, who the sooty hell's the johnny in the black duds? Hush! Sinned against the light and even now that day is at hand when he shall come to judge the world by fire. Pflaap! *Ut implerentur scripturæ.* Strike up a ballad. Then outspake medical Dick to his comrade medical Davy. Christicle, who's this excrement yellow gospeller on the Merion hall? Elijah is coming. Washed in the Blood of the Lamb. Come on, you winefizzling ginsizzling booseguzzling existences! Come on, you doggone, bullnecked, beetlebrowed, hogjowled, peanutbrained, weaseleyed fourflushers, false alarms and excess baggage! Come on, you triple extract of infamy! Alexander J. Christ Dowie, that's yanked to glory most half this planet from 'Frisco Beach to Vladivostok. The Deity aint no nickel dime bumshow. I put it to you that he's on the square and a corking fine business proposition. He's the grandest thing yet and don't you forget it. Shout salvation in king Jesus. You'll need to rise precious early, you sinner there, if you want to diddle the Almighty God. Pflaaaap! Not half. He's got a coughmixture with a punch in it for you, my friend, in his backpocket. Just you try it on.

THREE PLAYS
BY
RING LARDNER

WHETHER RING LARDNER'S NONSENSE plays belong in a parody anthology is doubtful. They might just possibly be called psychological parodies. Edmund Wilson compared them with Dada: "Their non sequiturs and practical jokes seem the product of similar situations: in France the collapse of Europe and the intellectual chaos that accompanied it; in America what is perhaps another aspect of a general crisis: the bewildering confusion of the modern city and the enfeeblement of the faculty of attention. It relieves some anxiety to laugh at pointlessness." Specifically, they seem to be directed at expressionism, grand opera, the Moscow Art Théatre, and Eugene O'Neill. But, as with Dada, there is also a strong element of nonsense for nonsense's sake.

I Gaspiri (*The Upholsterers*) was first published in Ben Hecht's *The Chicago Literary Times* and then in *The Transatlantic Review* (Paris) in 1924, with a note by the editor calling it to the attention of André Breton and suggesting it was doing what the surrealists were doing, only better. *Dinner Bridge* was written for a Dutch Treat show in 1927; the cast included Will Irwin, Robert Benchley, Percy Hammond, Rea Irvin, George S. Kaufman and Robert Sherwood. Edmund Wilson published it in *The New Republic*, of which he was then literary editor.

I am indebted for the above data to Donald Elder's biography of Lardner (Doubleday, 1956). Also for a description of the special quality of the plays: "The truth is that people don't listen to what other people say, and so they make irrelevant answers; they are always trying to tell something that nobody wants to hear, so they interrupt desperately and repeat; they tell labored and pointless stories, half-remembered and misunderstood jokes, trying to recall what was funny about them; their minds wander and they can't keep on one subject for long." Or, in Wilson's terminology, a general "enfeeblement of the faculty of attention."

Dinner Bridge

CHARACTERS

CROWLEY, *the foreman*

AMOROSI, *an Italian laborer*

TAYLOR, *a Negro laborer*

CHAMALES, *a Greek laborer*

HANSEN, *a Scandinavian laborer*

LLANUZA, *a Mexican laborer*

THE INQUISITIVE WAITER

THE DUMB WAITER

PROGRAM NOTE

THIS PLAYLET is an adaptation from the Wallachian of Willie Stevens. For a great many years, Long Islanders and Manhattanites have been wondering why the Fifty-ninth Street Bridge was always torn up at one or more points. Mr. Stevens heard the following legend: that Alexander Woollcott, chief engineer in charge of the construction of the bridge, was something of a practical joker; that on the day preceding the completion of the bridge, he was invited to dinner by his wife's brother; that he bought a loaded cigar to give his brother-in-law after the meal, and that the cigar dropped out of his pocket and rolled under the unfinished surface planking. Ever since, gangs of men have been ripping up the surface of the bridge in search of the cigar, but an article the shape of a cigar is apt to roll in any and all directions. This is what has made it so difficult to find the lost article, and the (so far) vain search is the theme of Mr. Stevens' playlet.—*Adapter.*

SCENE: *An area under repair on the Fifty-ninth Street Bridge. Part of the surface has been torn up, and, at the curtain's rise, three of the men are tearing up the rest of it with picks. Shovels, axes, and other tools are scattered around the scene. Two men are fussing with a concrete mixer. Crowley is bossing the job. Crowley and the laborers are dressed in dirty working clothes. In the foreground is a flat-topped truck or wagon. The two waiters, dressed in waiters' jackets, dickies, etc., enter the scene, one of them carrying a tray with cocktails and the other a tray with caviar, etc. The laborers cease their work and consume these appetizers. The noon whistle blows. The waiters bring in a white table cloth and spread it over the truck or wagon. They also distribute six place cards and six chairs, or camp stools, around the truck, but the "table" is left bare of eating implements.*

FIRST WAITER, *to* CROWLEY: Dinner is served.

(CROWLEY *and the laborers move toward the table.*)

TAYLOR, *to* AMOROSI: I believe I am to take you in.

(AMOROSI *gives* TAYLOR *his arm and* TAYLOR *escorts him to the table. The laborers all pick up the place cards to find out where they are to sit.*)

CROWLEY, *to* AMOROSI: Here is your place, Mr. Amorosi. And Taylor is right beside you.

(*Note to producer: Inasmuch as* TAYLOR *and* AMOROSI *do most of the talking, they ought to face the audience. In spite of their nationalities, the laborers are to talk in correct Crowninshield dinner English, except that occasionally, say every fourth or fifth speech, whoever is talking suddenly bursts into dialect, either his own or Jewish or Chinese or what you will.*

All find their places and sit down. The two waiters now re-enter, each carrying one dinner pail. One serves CROWLEY *and the other serves* AMOROSI. *The serving is done by the waiter's removing the cover of the pail and holding it in front of the diner. The latter looks into the pail and takes out some viand with his fingers. First he takes out, say, a sandwich. The waiter then replaces the cover on the pail and exits with it. All the laborers are served in this manner, two at a time, from their own dinner pails. As soon as one of them has completed the sandwich course, the waiter brings him the pail again and he helps himself to a piece of pie or an apple or orange. But the contents of all the pails should be different, according to the diner's taste. The serving goes on all through the scene, toward the end of which everyone is served with coffee from the cups on top of the pails.*)

CROWLEY (*to* AMOROSI): Well, Mr. Amorosi, welcome to the Fifty-ninth Street Bridge.

AMOROSI: Thank you, I really feel as if this was where I belonged.

HANSEN (*politely*): How is that?

AMOROSI: On account of my father. He was among the pioneer Fifty-ninth Street Bridge destroyers. He had the sobriquet of Giacomo "Rip-Up-the-Bridge" Amorosi.

TAYLOR (*sotto voce, aside to* HANSEN): This fellow seems to be quite a card!

LLANUZA: I wonder if you could tell me the approximate date when your father worked here.

AMOROSI: Why, yes. The bridge was completed on the fifth day of August, 1909. So that would make it the sixth day of August, 1909, when father started ripping it up.

TAYLOR (*aside to* HANSEN, *in marked Negro dialect*): I repeats my assertation that this baby is quite a card!

AMOROSI (*in Jewish dialect*): But I guess it must be a lot more fun nowadays, with so much motor traffic to pester.

TAYLOR: And all the funerals. I sure does have fun with the funerals.

CROWLEY (*in Irish brogue*): Taylor has a great time with the funerals.

HANSEN, CHAMALES, *and* LLANUZA (*in unison*): Taylor has a great time with the funerals.

AMOROSI (*to* TAYLOR): How do you do it?

TAYLOR (*in dialect*): Well, you see, I'm flagman for this outfit. When I get out and wave my flag, whatever is coming, it's got to stop. When I see a funeral coming, I let the hearse go by and stop the rest of the parade. Then when I see another funeral coming, I stop their hearse and let the rest of *their* procession go on. I keep doing this all morning to different funerals and by the time they get to Forest Hills, the wrong set of mourners is following the wrong hearse. It generally always winds up with the friends and relatives of the late Mr. Cohen attending the final obsequies of Mrs. Levinsky.

CROWLEY, HANSEN, CHAMALES, *and* LLANUZA (*in unison*): Taylor has a great time with the funerals.

AMOROSI: I'm a *trumpet* medium myself.

TAYLOR (*aside to* HANSEN): This boy will turn out to be quite a card!

LLANUZA: Why do you always have to keep repairing it?

CROWLEY: What do you mean, what's the matter?

LLANUZA: Why do they always have to keep repairing it?

AMOROSI: Perhaps Mr. Crowley has the repairian rights.

TAYLOR (*guffawing and slapping* HANSEN *or* CHAMALES *on the back*): What did I tell you?

LLANUZA (*in dialect*): But down in Mexico, where I come from, they don't keep repairing the same bridge.

AMOROSI (*to* LLANUZA): If you'll pardon a newcomer. Mr. —, I don't believe I got your name.

LLANUZA: Llanuza.

AMOROSI: If you'll pardon a newcomer, Mr. Keeler, I want to say that if the United States isn't good enough for you, I'd be glad to start a subscription to send you back to where you came from.

LLANUZA: I was beginning to like you, Mr. Amorosi.

AMOROSI: You get that right out of your mind, Mr. Barrows. I'm married; been married twice. My first wife died.

HANSEN: How long were you married to her?

AMOROSI: Right up to the time she died.

CHAMALES (*interrupting*): Mr. Amorosi, you said you had been married twice.

AMOROSI: Yes, sir. My second wife is a Swiss girl.

HANSEN: Is she here with you?

AMOROSI: No, she's in Switzerland, in jail. She turned out to be a murderer.

CROWLEY: When it's a woman, you call her a murderess.

TAYLOR: And when it's a Swiss woman, you call her a Swiss-ess.

(*One of the waiters is now engaged in serving* AMOROSI *with his dinner pail.*)

WAITER, *to* AMOROSI: Whom did she murder?

(WAITER *exits hurriedly without seeming to care to hear the answer.*)

AMOROSI (*after looking wonderingly at the disappearing* WAITER): What's the matter with *him?*

TAYLOR: He's been that way for years—a born questioner but he hates answers.

CROWLEY: Just the same, the rest of us would like to know whom your wife murdered.

TAYLOR, HANSEN, CHAMALES, *and* LLANUZA (*to* CROWLEY): Speak for yourself. We don't want to know.

CROWLEY: Remember, boys, I'm foreman of this outfit. (*Aside to* AMOROSI.) Who was it?

AMOROSI: (*Whispers name in his ear.*)

CROWLEY: I don't believe I knew him.

AMOROSI: Neither did my wife.

CROWLEY: Why did she kill him?

AMOROSI: Well, you see, over in Italy and Switzerland, it's different from, say, Chicago. When they find a man murdered over in those places, they generally try to learn who it is and put his name in the papers. So my wife was curious about this fellow's identity and she figured that the easiest way to get the information was to pop him.

TAYLOR: I'm a *trumpet* medium myself.

(WAITER *enters and serves one of the laborers from his dinner pail.*)

WAITER: How long is she in for?

(WAITER *exits hurriedly without waiting for the answer.* AMOROSI *again looks after him wonderingly.*)

HANSEN (*to* AMOROSI): Did you quarrel much?

AMOROSI: Only when we were together.

TAYLOR: I was a newspaper man once myself.

LLANUZA (*skeptically*): You! What paper did you work on?

TAYLOR: It was a tabloid—The Porno-graphic.

(WAITER *enters to serve somebody.*)

WAITER, *to* TAYLOR: Newspaper men must have lots of interesting experiences. (*Exits without waiting for a response.*)

AMOROSI: I suppose you've all heard this story—

THE OTHER LABORERS (*in unison*): Is it a golf story?

AMOROSI: No.

THE OTHERS (*resignedly*): Tell it.

AMOROSI (*in dialect*): It seems there was a woman went into a photographer's and asked the photographer if he took pictures of children.

(WAITER *enters to serve somebody.*)

WAITER: How does it end? (WAITER *exits hurriedly.*)

AMOROSI: She asked the photographer if he took pictures of children. "Why, yes, madam," replied the photographer—

TAYLOR: He called her "madam."

AMOROSI: The photographer told her yes, that he did take pictures of children. "And how much do you charge?" inquired the madam, and the photographer replied, "Three dollars a dozen." "Well," said the woman, "I guess I'll have to come back later. I've only got eleven."

(*The other laborers act just as if no story had been told.*)

LLANUZA: Down in Mexico, where I come from, they don't keep repairing the same bridge.

TAYLOR (*to* HANSEN): Can you imitate birds?

HANSEN: *No.*

TAYLOR, *to* CHAMALES: Can you imitate birds?

CHAMALES: No.

TAYLOR: Can anybody here imitate birds?

THE OTHER LABORERS (*in unison*): No.

TAYLOR: *I* can do it. Long before I got a job on this bridge, while I was helping tear up the crosstown streets, I used to entertain the boys all day, imitating birds.

AMOROSI: What kind of birds can you imitate?

TAYLOR: All kinds.

AMOROSI: Well, what do you say we play some other game?

CROWLEY (*rising*): Gentlemen, we are drawing near to the end of this dinner and I feel we should not leave the table until some one has spoken a few words of welcome to our newcomer, Mr. Amorosi. Myself, I am not much of a talker. (*Pauses for a denial.*)

TAYLOR: You said a full quart.

CROWLEY: Therefore, I will call on the man who is second to me in length of service on the Fifty-ninth Street Bridge, Mr. Harvey Taylor. (*Sits down.*)

TAYLOR (*rising amid a dead silence*): Mr. Foreman, Mr. Amorosi, and gentlemen: Welcoming Mr. Amorosi to our little group recalls vividly to my mind an experience of my own on the levee at New Orleans before Prohibition. (*He bursts suddenly into Negro dialect, mingled with Jewish.*) In those days my job was to load and unload those great big bales of cotton and my old mammy used to always be there at the dock to take me in her lap and croon me to sleep.

(WAITER *enters, serves somebody with coffee.*)

WAITER: What was the experience you was going to tell? (*Exits hurriedly.*)

TAYLOR: It was in those days that I studied bird life and learned to imitate the different bird calls. (*Before they can stop him, he gives a bird call.*) The finch. (*The others pay no attention. He gives another call.*) A Dowager. (TAYLOR *is pushed forcibly into his seat.*)

AMOROSI (*rising to respond*): Mr. Foreman and gentlemen: I judge from Mr. Taylor's performance that the practice of imitating birds is quite popular in America. Over where I come from, we often engage in the pastime of mimicking public buildings. For example (*he gives a cry*). The American Express Company's office at Rome. (*He gives another cry.*) The Vatican. (*He gives another cry.*) Hotel McAlpin. (*A whistle blows, denoting that the dinner hour is over.*)

CROWLEY (*rising*): Shall we join the ladies?

(*All rise and resume the work of tearing up the bridge. The waiters enter to remove the table cloth and chairs.*)

WAITER (*the more talkative one*): How many Mack trucks would you guess had crossed this bridge in the last half hour? (*He exits without waiting for a reply.*)

CURTAIN

Clemo Uti—"The Water Lilies"

CHARACTERS

PADRE, *a Priest.*
SETHSO ⎱
GETHSO ⎰ *both twins.*
WAYSHATTEN, *a shepherd's boy.*
TWO CAPITALISTS.[1]
WAMA TAMMISCH, *her daughter.*
KLEMA, *a janitor's third daughter.*
KEVELA, *their mother, afterwards their aunt.*

[TRANSLATOR'S NOTE: *This show was written as if people were there to see it.*]

ACT I

The Outskirts of a Parchesi Board. People are wondering what has become of the discs. They quit wondering and sit up and sing the following song.

CHORUS:
      What has become of the discs?
      What has become of the discs?
      We took them at our own risks,
      But what has become of the discs?

(WAMA *enters from an exclusive waffle parlor. She exits as if she had had waffles.*)

---

[1] NOTE: The two Capitalists don't appear in this show.

ACTS II & III

(*These two acts were thrown out because nothing seemed to happen.*)

ACT IV

A silo. Two RATS *have got in there by mistake. One of them seems diseased. The other looks at him. They go out. Both* RATS *come in again and wait for a laugh. They don't get it, and go out.* WAMA *enters from an off-stage barn. She is made up to represent the Homecoming of Casanova. She has a fainting spell. She goes out.*

KEVELA: Where was you born?
PADRE: In Adrian, Michigan.
KEVELA: Yes, but I thought I was confessing to you.
(*The Padre goes out on an old-fashioned high-wheel bicycle. He acts as if he had never ridden many of them. He falls off and is brought back. He is in pretty bad shape.*)

ACT V

A COUPLE OF SALESMEN *enter. They are trying to sell Portable Houses. The rest of the cast don't want Portable Houses.*

REST OF THE CAST: We don't want Portable Houses.
(*The* SALESMEN *become hysterical and walk off-stage left.*)
KEVELA: What a man!
WAYSHATTEN (*the Shepherd's Boy*): Why wasn't you out there his morning to help me look after my sheep?
CHORUS OF ASSISTANT SHEPHERDS:
     Why did you lay there asleep
     When you should of looked after his sheep?
     Why did you send telegrams
     When you should of looked after his lambs?
     Why did you sleep there, so old,
     When you should of looked after his fold?
SETHSO: Who is our father?
GETHSO: What of it? We're twins, ain't we?
WAMA: Hush, clemo uti (*the Water Lilies*).

(*Two queels enter, overcome with water lilies. They both make fools of themselves. They don't seem to have any self-control. They quiver. They want to play the show over again, but it looks useless.*)

SHADES

I Gaspiri

(*The Upholsterers*)

A DRAMA IN THREE ACTS

Adapted from the Bukovinan of Casper Redmonda

CHARACTERS

IAN OBRI, *a blotter salesman.*
JOHAN WASPER, *his wife.*
GRETA, *their daughter.*
HERBERT SWOPE, *a nonentity.*
FFENA, *their daughter, later their wife.*
EGSO, *a pencil guster.*
TONO, *a typical wastebasket.*

ACT I

A public street in a bathroom. A man named Tupper has evidently just taken a bath. A man named Brindle is now taking a bath. A man named Newburn comes out of the faucet which has been left running. He exits through the exhaust. Two strangers to each other meet on the bath mat.

FIRST STRANGER: Where was you born?
SECOND STRANGER: Out of wedlock.
FIRST STRANGER: That's a mighty pretty country around there.
SECOND STRANGER: Are you married?
FIRST STRANGER: I don't know. There's a woman living with me, but I can't place her.
(*Three outsiders named Klein go across the stage three times.*

They think they are in a public library. A woman's cough is heard off-stage left.)

A NEW CHARACTER: Who is that cough?

TWO MOORS: That is my cousin. She died a little while ago in a haphazard way.

A GREEK: And what a woman she was!

(*The curtain is lowered for seven days to denote the lapse of a week.*)

ACT III

The Lincoln Highway. Two bearded glue lifters are seated at one side of the road.

(TRANSLATOR'S NOTE: *The principal industry in Phlace is hoarding hay. Peasants sit alongside of a road on which hay wagons are likely to pass. When a hay wagon does pass, the hay hoarders leap from their points of vantage and help themselves to a wisp of hay. On an average a hay hoarder accumulates a ton of hay every four years. This is called Mah Jong.*)

FIRST GLUE LIFTER: Well, my man, how goes it?

SECOND GLUE LIFTER: (*Sings "My Man," to show how it goes.*)

(*Eight realtors cross the stage in a friendly way. They are out of place.*)

CURTAIN

OUR PARODIES are ended. These our authors,
As we foretold you, were all Spirits, and
Are melted into air, into thin air.
And, like the baseless fabric of these verses,
The Critic's puff, the Trade's advertisement,
The Patron's promise, and the World's applause,—
Yea, all the hopes of poets,—shall dissolve,
And, like this unsubstantial fable fated,
Leave not a groat behind!

HORACE TWISS

APPENDIX

SOME NOTES ON PARODY

THE FIRST QUESTION is: What *is* parody? The dictionaries are not helpful. Dr. Johnson defines parody as "a kind of writing in which the words of an author or his thoughts are taken and by a slight change adapted to some new purpose," which is imprecise and incomplete. The Oxford dictionary comes closer: "a composition . . . in which characteristic turns of an author . . . are imitated in such a way as to make them appear ridiculous, especially by applying them to ludicrously inappropriate subjects." This at least brings in humor. But it does not distinguish parody from its poor relations, *travesty* ("a grotesque or debased imitation or likeness") and *burlesque* ("aims at exciting laughter by caricature of the manner or spirit of serious works, or by ludicrous treatment of their subjects"). Such definitions tend to run together, which is just what a definition shouldn't do, since *definire* means "to set limits." I therefore propose the following hierarchy:

TRAVESTY (literally "changing clothes," as in "transvestite") is the most primitive form. It raises laughs, from the belly rather than the head, by putting high, classic characters into prosaic situations, with a corresponding stepping-down of the language. Achilles becomes a football hero, Penelope a suburban housewife, Helen a beauty queen. Scarron did it in the seventeenth century with his enormously popular *Virgile Travesti,* John Erskine in the twentieth with his *The Private Life of Helen of Troy.* Boileau was severe on Scarron:

> Au mépris du bon sens, le burlesque effronté
>
> Trompa les yeux d'abord, plut par sa nouveauté. . . .
>
> Cette contagion infecta les provinces,
>
> Du clerc et du bourgeois passa jusques aux princes.

It hardly bears thinking what his reaction would have been to Erskine's book. Or to the contemporary imitation of Scarron by the English poetaster, Charles Cotton, which begins:

> I sing the man (read it who list)
>
> A Trojan true as ever pist,
>
> Who from Troy-town by wind and weather
>
> To Italy (and God knows whither)

557

Was pack'd and rack'd and lost and tost
And bounced from pillar unto post.

BURLESQUE (from Italian *burla*, "ridicule") is a more advanced form since it at least imitates the style of the original. It differs from parody in that the writer is concerned with the original not in itself but merely as a device for topical humor. Hawthorne's charming *The Celestial Railway*, for example, is not a parody of Bunyan but a satire on materialistic progress that is hung on the peg of *Pilgrim's Progress*. The instinct for filling a familiar form with a new content is old as history. The *Iliad* was burlesqued a few generations after it was composed. Sacred themes were popular in the Middle Ages, such as the Drunkards' Mass (*Missa de Potatoribus*), which began:

Va. Introibo ad altare Bachi.
R.   Ad eum qui letificat cor homins.
     Confiteor reo Bacho omnepotanti, et reo vino coloris rubei, et omnibus ciphis eius, et vobis potatoribus, me nimis gulose potasse per nimiam nauseam rei Bachi dei mei potatione, sternutatione, ocitatione maxima, mea crupa, mea maxima crupa. . . . Potemus.

Twenty-five years ago, when the eleven-year-old Gloria Vanderbilt was the subject of a famous custody suit between her mother and her aunt, the court's decision awarding her to the aunt except for week ends was summarized by an anonymous newspaper wit:

Rockabye baby
Up on a writ,
Monday to Friday, mother's unfit.
As the week ends, she rises in virtue;
Saturday, Sunday,
Mother won't hurt you.

And last year, the London *Economist* printed a political carol:

On the tenth day of Cwthmas,* the Com-
    monwealth brought to me

Ten Sovereign Nations
Nine Governors General
Eight Federations

* Contraction of "Commonwealthmas."

Seven Disputed Areas
Six Trust Territories
Five Old Realms
Four Present or Prospective Republics
Three High Commission Territories
Two Ghana-Guinea Fowl

One Sterling Area
One Dollar Dominion
One Sun That Never Sets
One Maltese Cross
One Marylebone Cricket Club
One Trans-Arctic Expedition

And a Mother Country up a Gum Tree.

Finally and at last, PARODY, from the Greek *parodia* ("a beside- or against-song"), concentrates on the style and thought of the original.* If burlesque is pouring new wine into old bottles, parody is making a new wine that tastes like the old but has a slightly lethal effect. At its best, it is a form of literary criticism. The beginning of Max Beerbohm's parody of a Shaw preface may give the general idea:

A STRAIGHT TALK

When a public man lays his hand on his heart and declares that his conduct needs no apology, the audience hastens to put up its umbrellas against the particularly severe downpour of apologies in store for it. I won't give the customary warning. My conduct shrieks aloud for apology, and you are in for a thorough drenching.

Flatly, I stole this play. The one valid excuse for the theft would be mental starvation. That excuse I shan't plead. I could have made a dozen better plays than this out of my own head. You don't suppose Shakespeare was so vacant in the upper storey that there was nothing for it but to rummage through cinquecento romances, Towneley mysteries, and suchlike insanitary rubbishheaps in order that he might fish out enough scraps for his artistic fangs to fasten on. Depend on it, there were plenty of decent original notions

---

* Parody belongs to the family of para-words: parasite, parapsychology, paratyphoid, paranoia (against mind), paradox (against received opinion), paraphrase, paranymph (bridesmaid). It is not related to Paraguay, although that country is beside and against Uruguay.

seething behind yon marble brow. Why didn't our William use *them?* He was too lazy. And so am I.

Shaw's polemical style is unerringly reproduced—the short, punchy sentences; the familiarity ("yon marble brow . . . our William"), the Anglo-Saxon vigor, the calculated irreverences ("and suchlike insanitary rubbishheaps"). But Beerbohm goes deeper, into the peculiar combination in Shaw of arrogance and self-depreciation, of aggressiveness and mateyness, so that the audience is at once bullied and flattered; shocking ideas are asserted but as if they were a matter of course between sensible people. Beerbohm's exposé of this strategy is true parody.

PARODY is conservative and classical. (I use these terms as Irving Babbitt did in *Rousseau and Romanticism.*) In *Burlesque and Parody in English* (Edinburgh, 1931), the only general survey of this subject, George Kitchin describes parody as "the reaction of centrally-minded persons to the vagaries of the modes," adding: "For the last three centuries, it has been inveterately social and anti-romantic. Politically it has been the watchdog of national interests, socially of respectability, and, in the world of letters, of established forms." Exaggeration, the vice and the virtue of romanticism, is the meat that parody feeds on. The extremes can be either of simplicity or of ornateness. The two most effectively parodied nineteenth-century English poets were the very simple Wordsworth and the very complex Browning. The most parodied American poet is Whitman—Poe was burlesqued rather than parodied —who combined the simple and the ornate in a peculiarly irritating, and individual, way. A whole volume of Whitman parodies was published in 1923, edited by H. S. Saunders, which shows that the parodists were at work as early as 1857. The level is high, which I take to be a tribute to Whitman. One curiosity is a 1909 parody by Pound which begins:

> Lo, behold, I eat watermelons. When I eat
>   watermelons the world eats watermelons through me.
> When the world eats watermelons,
> I partake of the world's watermelons.

It would seem Pound was not a parodist.

The offensive against oversimplicity stretches from Henry Carey's *Namby-Pamby* to Ernest Hemingway's novella parodying Sherwood Anderson, *Torrents of Spring* (1926) and the later parodies of Hemingway himself by Wolcott Gibbs and E. B. White. Dr. Johnson, a most central-minded critic, was mightily offended by the new simple style, so different from the Augustan rhetoric he himself employed, which Percy, of the *Reliques,* and others were smuggling in disguised as old ballads. His impromptu is well known:

> I put my hat upon my head
> And walk'd into the Strand,
> And there I met another man
> Whose hat was in his hand.*

* Boswell gives us a glimpse of Johnson as parodist:
"He observed that a gentleman of eminence in literature had got into a bad style of poetry of late. 'He puts (said he) a very common thing into a strange dress till he does not know it himself and thinks other people do not know it.' BOSWELL: 'That is owing to his being so much versant in old English poetry.' JOHNSON: 'What is that to the purpose, Sir? If I say a man is drunk and you tell me it is owing to his taking much drink, the matter is not mended. No, Sir, he has taken to an old mode. For example, he'd write thus:
> Hermit hoar, in solemn cell,
> Wearing out life's evening gray . . .
Gray evening is common enough but *evening gray* he'd think fine. Stay, we'll make out the stanza:
> Hermit hoar, in solemn cell,
> Wearing out life's evening gray:
> Smite thy bosom, sage, and tell
> What is bliss? and which the way?
BOSWELL: 'But why smite his bosom, Sir?' JOHNSON: 'Why to show he was in earnest.' (smiling) He at an after period added the following stanza:
> Thus I spoke and speaking sighed,
> Scarce repress'd the starting tear,
> When the smiling sage replied:
> 'Come, my lad, and drink some beer.' "

Johnson's parody was an adumbration of the simple style developed by Wordsworth and Coleridge out of the old ballads. In the Preface to the *Lyrical Ballads* Wordsworth objected, with justice, that simplicity is not *per se* absurd and that Johnson's "I put my hat upon my head" might be turned against good as well as against affected poetry. True, yet why has Blake never been successfully parodied although his style is even simpler than Wordsworth's? Perhaps his naïveté was authentic in a way that Wordsworth, for all his genius, couldn't attain.

The parodic campaign against the romantic-ornate stretches all the way from the Duke of Buckingham's play, *The Rehearsal,* in 1671 to William Faulkner's self-parody, *Afternoon of a Cow.* The persistence of plays parodying the grand style is striking: *The Rehearsal* in the seventeenth century; Carey's *Chrononhotonthologos*, Fielding's *Tom Thumb* and Sheridan's *The Critic* in the eighteenth; the Canning-Frere parody of German romantic drama, *The Rovers,* and Aytoun's *Firmilian, or the Student of Badajoz, a Spasmodic Tragedy* in the nineteenth; and Beerbohm's *Savonarola* (which has interesting similarities to *Firmilian*) and the mock-Shakespearean play in Nigel Dennis' *Cards of Identity* in the twentieth.

PARODY SEEMS not to have appealed to the ancient Hebrews or the early Christians; at least there is no trace of it in either the Old or the New Testament. The Egyptians were also immune—*The Book of the Dead* was more their kind of thing. But the Greeks, an invincibly secular and rational people, were addicts. "The rhapsodists who strolled from town to town to chant the poems of Homer," Isaac D'Israeli writes in *Curiosities of Literature,* "were immediately followed by another set of strollers—buffoons who made the audiences merry by the burlesque turn which they gave to the solemn strains." The most famous of these Homeric burlesques was the *Batrachomyomachia,* or *Battle of the Frogs and Mice,* which describes in elevated style the quaint arms and heroic exploits of the tiny warriors. But the literary form which gave us the word was the *parodia* of the Athenian drama, contained in the satyr play which followed the tragedies and was performed by the same actors wearing grotesque costumes. The only surviving examples are the *Cyclops* of Euripides and *The Searching Satyrs,* attributed to Sophocles, but the most celebrated was the *Gigantomachia,* which delighted the Athenians even though they had just received news of the catastrophic fate of the Syracusan expedition. It was Aristophanes, however, who first took the giant step from burlesque to true parody, with his satirical imitations of Aeschylus, Euripides and Socrates in such comedies as *The Frogs, The Birds* and *The Acharnians.* Parody is a late form, for obvious reasons; the difference between the mild fun of the *Batrachomyomachia,* which consists merely of treating frogs and mice as if they were Homeric heroes, and Aristophanes' criticism of the philosophy as well as the manner of Euripides and Socrates is the difference between an early and a late period.

The same evolution took place in English literature. Chaucer's *Sir Thopas* is an apparent exception, but only apparent. Although Chaucer is the father of English literature, there was a long break in the succession, the break between the Middle Ages and the Renaissance; like Dante, he comes at the end, not the beginning, of a culture. His wit is urbane, his mastery of form effortless, and he is even able to see himself humorously, a "late" characteristic.* It will be four centuries before the parodic level of *Sir Thopas* is reached again. Parody requires a high degree of self-consciousness and the Elizabethans were too busy creating a new renaissance literature to go in for it. There was a good deal of satire and burlesque, as in the many "Replies" to poems, such as Raleigh's to Marlowe's "Come live with me and be my love." And Ben Jonson often came close to parody in his plays, with his satirical imitations of literary affectations.† But the only true parodies I have found are by Shakespeare, whose genius was such that he, un-historically, mastered even this form.

The eighteenth century, so rich in satire and literary *jeux d'esprit* should have been a great age of parody. Writers were by then con-scious of themselves and of their past; they were technically accom-plished; and they were not creating a new literature. But somehow it wasn't, perhaps because neither of the two conditions were present which stimulate parody: an outworn but still powerful tradition (*Sir Thopas*) or an avantgarde whose innovations are felt to be absurd (the many parodies, in the next century, of Wordsworth, Browning and Whitman). There were a few gleams and flashes, but satire or burlesque was the dominant mode: mock epics like Pope's *Dunciad* and *Rape of the Lock;* Gay's *Beggars' Opera,* which travestied the grand operatic style; Swift's *The Battle of the Books, A Tale of a Tub, A Modest Proposal*—indeed see Swift *passim.* There was a strong parodic element in the century's two most popular works, *Gulliver's Travels* and *Robinson Crusoe,* both of which got their effect from imitating the

---

* In the closing dialogue of *Sir Thopas,* the host complains that Chaucer's rhyming is "nat worth a tord" and demands something more substantial "in which ther be som mirthe or som doctryne." The accomplished pro-fessional is not at all put out: "Gladly . . . I wol yow telle a litel thing in prose," he replies.

† In *Volpone* there's a parody of a genre that came into being three centuries later, the singing commercial:

> You that would last long, list to my song,
> Make no more coil but buy of this oill.
> Would you be ever fair and young?
> Stout of teeth and strong of tongue?
> Tart of palate? quick of ear?
> Sharp of sight? of nostril clear?
> Moist of hand and light of foot?
> Or I will come nearer to 't—
> Would you live free from all diseases?
> Do the act your mistress pleases,
> Yet fright all aches from your bones?
> Here's a med'cine for the nones.

well-established genre of travelers' tales. But of definite parody, there was surprisingly little. One might say there was a great deal of talent but nothing much to parody. From Addison to Johnson, an Augustan status quo reigned unchallenged. The old literary tradition was feeble —the Elizabethan-Jacobean élan had either been channelled into classical form since Milton or else etiolated into rhetoric in the plays of Dryden and Davenant. And innovation was almost nonexistent. Henry Fielding did produce two book-length parodies, too long for inclusion here, in his *Tom Thumb the Great,* which mocked the Drydenesque drama ("The greatest perfection of the language of a tragedy," he wrote in the Foreword, "is that it is not to be understood") and in his take-off of the bourgeois-sentimental style of Richardson's *Pamela* in the perfectly titled *Shamela.* He also started out to parody Richardson in *Joseph Andrews* but his novelistic talent took over and the parody was lost sight of. The century seems to have been too self-confident to feel the need for parody.

The eighteenth-century stasis was broken up politically by the French Revolution and esthetically by the rise of romanticism. In *The Anti-Jacobin*—a Little Magazine founded in 1797 by George Canning, later a Tory political leader, and two friends—and in the Smith brothers' *Rejected Addresses* (1812), the first full-scale parodic offenses were mounted.

> The 18th century sees the English State and Society welded into a seemingly unbreakable whole [Kitchin writes] . . . That immersion in classical learning and wit to which we have referred was taking place at the great schools and colleges. The English gentleman was being moulded. When the Revolution shook Europe and the Napoleonic wars devastated it, England stood fast and her effort on the field was matched by the wit of her satirists. . . . In the Victorian age there was no cataclysm, and the splendid race of satirists who had likewise been bred on the classics turned their shafts against eccentricity and underbreeding in letters. . . . Poetical manners, not political, were the inspiration of our great age of parody which we take to be the age of Calverley and Swinburne and J. K. Stephen. No age and no country can show anything approaching the combined sparkle and finish of the mid-Victorian parodists.

One could now add the Edwardian Beerbohm and the Hooverian-Rooseveltian *New Yorker* school, but certainly it was a, if not the, great age. The best of the Victorian parodists—Calverley, Carroll, Hilton, Stephen, Traill—were "bred on the classics" and closely connected with Oxford or Cambridge. My favorite is James Kenneth Stephen. Calverley is more generally admired and his work is indeed formidable, but I find Stephen the more spontaneous and amusing.

It was not masters like Stephen and Calverley, however, that made the Victorian age unique, however, but the fact that parody and burlesque were so widespread. Never before or since has there been such a popular appetite for the genre. The nineteenth century marked the transition between the old elite culture and the new mass culture; on the one hand, the audience had enormously expanded with the increase in literacy; on the other, the newcomers were still close enough to the old culture to take it as a natural part of life. The result was a rank effervescence of burlesque in the popular media; one senses a parvenu desire to cut Literature down to size; a few generations earlier, this would have been repressed for reasons of taste; a few later, because the popular audience no longer was sufficiently acquainted with Literature to respond to burlesques. But now they swallowed entire plays. Shakespeare, in particular, was treated with the contempt bred by familiarity, as in *Othello Travestie,* which had a good run in 1834. Othello is a comic "darky":

> Potent, grave and rev'rend sir,
>> Very noble massa—
> When de maid a man prefer
> Den him no can pass her.

Or there is Hamlet's soliloquy, which was *sung:*

> To die is to sleep, nothing more,
>> And by sleeping to say we end sorrow
> And pain and ten thousand things more,
> O I wish it were *my* turn tomorrow!
> But perchance in that sleep we may dream,
>> For we dream in our beds very often—
> Now, however capricious 't may seem,
>> I've no notion of dreams in a coffin.
>> (*Ri tol de rol*)

Wretched stuff, far below the level of the burlesques of Racine and Corneille that the *Théâtre Italien* in Paris put on in the seventeenth century, or of Racine's own parody of Corneille's "rolling Alexandrines" in *Les Plaideurs*. But that was in another country and age.

The Shakespearean travesties were for lowbrows. They were succeeded by the more sophisticated burlesques of Gilbert and Sullivan, which were for the middlebrows, as were the parodies endlessly printed in *Punch* and such magazines. One gets a notion of their stupefying quantity from the six-volume collection that Walter Hamilton published between 1884 and 1889. Unreadable now, these tall, small-print, double-column volumes are interesting because they show that poetry was then common currency and not a peculiar diversion of the intelligentsia. Not very good poetry (though Volume V has 86 versions of Gray's *Elegy*). Some poems seem to have been written only to be burlesqued, as *The Raven* (60 versions), *The Charge of the Light Brigade* (21) and *Horatius at the Bridge* (36).* They have one thing in common: emphasis; both of rhythm and of emotion. These qualities are prominent in Ann Taylor's *My Mother,* which begins:

> Who fed me from her gentle breast,
> And hushed me in her arms to rest,
> And on my cheeks sweet kisses prest?
>> My mother.

And so on for eleven stanzas. Miss Taylor published her poem in 1803 and at once the burlesques began; Hamilton prints over a hundred of them. The rhythm and the sentiment were irresistible, so much so indeed that Miss Taylor herself was imitating Cowper's *To Mary,* doing a serious parody so to speak. Cowper was gloomier:

> The twentieth year is well-nigh past
> Since first our sky was overcast;
> Ah, would that this might be our last!
>> My Mary!

* Henry Wadsworth Longfellow falls repeatedly into this category, with his *Hiawatha, Village Blacksmith, Wreck of the Hesperus, Psalm of Life* ("Tell me not in mournful numbers / Life is but an empty dream") and above all his *Excelsior:* "The shades of night were falling fast / When through an Alpine village passed / A youth who bore mid snow and ice / A banner with this strange device: / Excelsior!" The situation is irretrievably comic, as is Longfellow's development of it, and folk burlesques sprouted immediately. I remember two from my childhood: one that wrecked the poem simply by introducing at the end of each line some variant of "Upidee-Upidah" and another that substituted for the all-too-dramatic "Excelsior" the name of a then much-advertised brand of soap, Sapolio.

The English still have a living parodic tradition; one might call it an upper-class folk art. It expresses itself in competitions in *The New Statesman* and, until lately, *The Spectator*, in which readers undertake such tasks as composing a Miltonic sonnet on photography with special reference to Princess Margaret's marriage, or a paragraph on Rock 'n Roll in the manner of (a) Dr. Johnson, (b) Carlyle, (c) St. Paul, or (d) Gertrude Stein. The best parody of Eliot, Henry Reed's *Chard Whitlow*, originated in a *New Statesman* competition; and Graham Greene is said to have won a prize (second) for his entry in one calling for parodies of Graham Greene. But what is impressive is the large number of entries, often in the hundreds, and the skill of those that are printed.

In the present century, with the important exception of Beerbohm's *A Christmas Garland*, the best parodies have come from writers associated with *The New Yorker*—Robert Benchley, Peter DeVries, Wolcott Gibbs, S. J. Perelman, Frank Sullivan, James Thurber, and E. B. White. A peculiar combination of sophistication and provinciality is needed for good parody, the former for obvious reasons, the latter because the audience must be homogeneous enough to get the point. The Oxford-Cambridge milieu of the last century was perfect—a compact cultural group that felt itself, with some reason, at the center of things and thus able to judge what was eccentric. A similar situation has obtained in New York City since the First World War. Before then the provinces made fun of the big city, from Artemus Ward and Mark Twain to the early Ring Lardner. But with *Main Street, Babbitt*, and the founding by Mencken and Nathan of *The American Mercury* in the early twenties, the balance of power shifted in favor of New York; the provinces were now the object of ridicule. The appearance of *The New Yorker*, with its defiant "Not Edited for the Old Lady from Dubuque"—a slogan long forgotten, since the magazine's readership has for two decades been as much outside New York as inside the city, a change that does not signify a victory of the provinces but just the reverse—crystallized this dominance of the urban wits. Furthermore, they had something on which to exercise their parodic conservatism —the rise of a literary avantgarde. Parody still appears in *The New Yorker* but not with the old vigor. Perhaps because the sense of fun has atrophied since the thirties. Or perhaps because the present avantgarde is too hermetic to be parodied. The real world has become so fantastic that satire, of which parody is a subdivision, is discouraged because reality outdistances it. What can a satirist add to the U2-Sum-mit-Meeting fiasco? Or to the dealings between the United Nations and Premier Lumumba of the Congo Republic—the latter a character right out of Evelyn Waugh's *Black Mischief*. Indeed, in the Congo tragi-comedy, history seems to be parodying itself.

Index

This index includes both the parodists and the authors parodied.
The names of parodists are italicized.